The Love of Many Things

Endpapers: Vincent van Gogh: Letter to John Russell, June 1888.

. . . I always think that the best way to know God is to love many things

[Letter from Vincent to his brother Theo, July 1880]

The Love of Many Things

A LIFE OF VINCENT VAN GOGH

David Sweetman

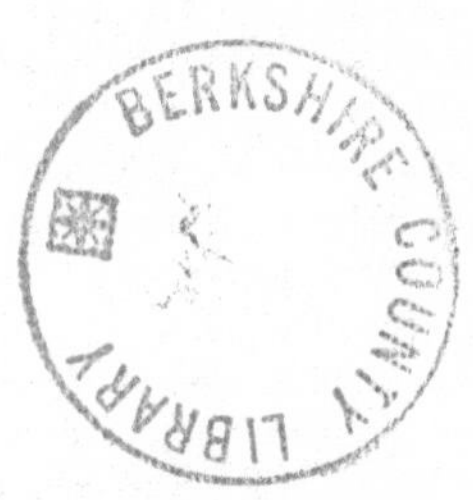

A John Curtis Book
Hodder & Stoughton
LONDON SYDNEY AUCKLAND TORONTO

British Library Cataloguing in Publication Data

Sweetman, David, *1943–*
The love of many things: a life of Vincent van Gogh.
1. Dutch paintings. Gogh, Vincent van, 1853–1890
I. Title
759.9492

ISBN 0-340-50371-6

First published in Great Britain 1990

Second impression 1990

The translation of Vincent van Gogh's letters is drawn from *The Complete Letters of Vincent van Gogh*, Thames and Hudson, London 1950.

Published by Hodder and Stoughton, a division of Hodder and Stoughton Limited, Mill Road, Dunton Green, Sevenoaks, Kent TN13 2YA. Editorial Office: 47 Bedford Square, London WC1E 7DP.

Designed by Cinamon and Kitzinger, London

Photoset by Rowland Phototypesetting Limited, Bury St Edmunds, Suffolk

Printed in Great Britain by Butler and Tanner Limited, Frome and London

For Vatcharin Bhumichitr

The sections in the text printed in Italic are quotations from Vincent van Gogh's letters to his brother Theo or, where indicated, to other members of his family and friends. A very few of the letters were written in English, the majority in Dutch or French. Most of these were translated into English in the early part of this century by Vincent's sister-in-law Johanna. No attempt has been made to correct the occasionally stilted phrases as they convey something of the oddities of Vincent's literary style.

Contents

	Preface	A Portrait	1
		Part One: 1853–1880	
1	[1853–69]	Funeral Procession through the Cornfields	7
2	[1869–74]	A Blank Canvas	24
3	[1874–76]	Breakdown	53
4	[1876–78]	Pray, my Soul	75
5	[1878–80]	Under a Sulphur Sun	95
		Part Two: 1880–1891	
6	[1880–83]	Theo	123
7	[1883–85]	The Potato Eaters	162
8	[1885–88]	Dark Green, with Black, with Fiery Red	196
9	[1888]	The Yellow House	250
10	[1888–91]	Accompanied like a Dangerous Beast	292
	Epilogue	Two Gravestones	349
		Acknowledgements	369
		Bibliography	371
		List of illustrations	377
		Index	381

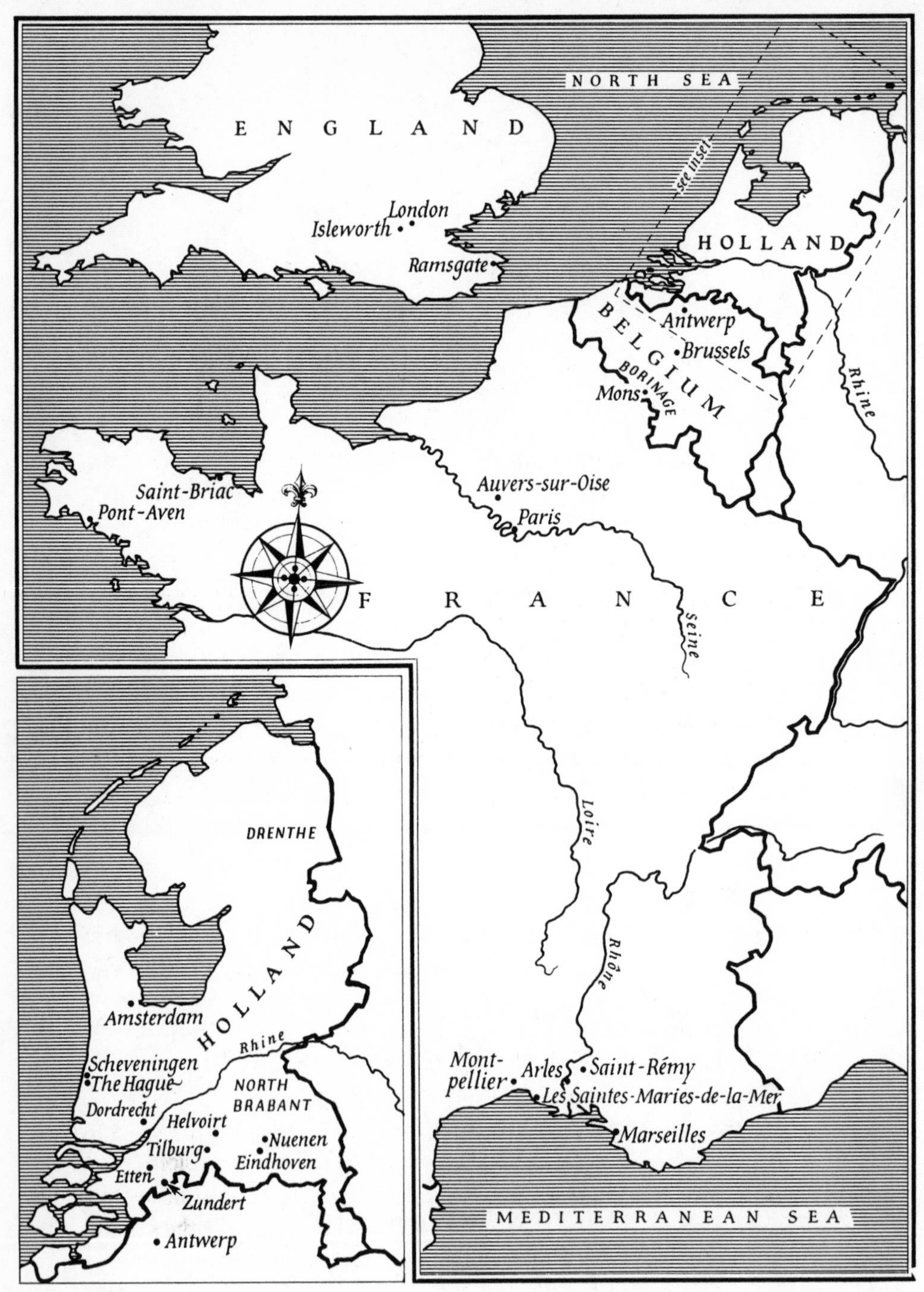

Map of places associated with Van Gogh

Preface

A Portrait

In the early evening of December 24th, 1888 Vincent van Gogh crept up on his friend Paul Gauguin, who was out taking an after-dinner stroll near their home, and attacked him with a cut-throat razor. At least that was what Gauguin – a notoriously unreliable source – was to claim some years later when there was no one left to contradict him. True or false, the story is now part of the myth that conditions our view of Van Gogh and which often distorts our judgement of his work. Whether matters got to that pitch of violence or not, the two artists had certainly quarrelled that cold, wet day in Arles. Yet only three months earlier Vincent had painted a self-portrait dedicated *to my friend Paul Gauguin* as part of a campaign to persuade him to leave Brittany and help create an artists' colony in the south of France. The portrait was intended to show Vincent in the guise of a novice monk awaiting the arrival of his spiritual master. A less arrogant man than Gauguin might have seen below the surface, for the shaven head and emaciated expression also revealed the punishing hours of work with too little to eat and too much to drink that had surely exacerbated the crushing and incurable mental illness threatening Van Gogh's sanity.

Gauguin had chosen to ignore the warning and even if that attack was a later embellishment, the evening certainly ended in bloodshed. The tragedy is well enough known: having, in Gauguin's version, failed to wound his friend, the demented Van Gogh rounded on himself in an act of bloody self-mutilation. Everyone is familiar with the story – much exaggerated – of how he hacked away part of his left ear. That violent act has also been absorbed into the myth that has made Van Gogh the archetypal artist of the modern age: ignored and rejected while sacrificing himself physically and mentally in the service of his art. He died two years later, aged only thirty-seven; a short life and an even briefer creative one, a mere eleven years as a painter with the most famous works crammed into the last four.

Only four years. It hardly seems possible. The name of a famous artist usually conjures up a small group of great works, yet with Van Gogh each of us has a wide selection of well-loved paintings: the Sunflowers and the Drawbridge at Arles, as recognisable as if they were near one's own home; those well-known faces: the Zouave in his bright red pantaloons, Roulin the postman, Dr Gachet. And there are scenes and objects as familiar as if they were memories from our own past: the café tables under a starry sky, the empty yellow chair, the turbulent cornfield with its lowering storm clouds, assailed by ominous black crows.

With such a list before us, it seems even more extraordinary that Van Gogh was a painter for so short a time. He went to considerable lengths to dedicate his life to other things, only surrendering to art when it had become the sole release from the misery and depression into which he had stumbled.

Those whom the world calls mad are usually shunned or mocked and Vincent experienced both reactions towards the end; yet today he is the most popular painter of the age, his Yellow Chair the most reproduced work of recent art. Astronomical prices are paid at auction for a simple bowl of flowers that he himself could not sell for a few francs. In the century since his suicide we have come to accept that his work, more than that of his contemporaries, speaks directly to us. He said of the portrait of his last doctor that he had given it *the sad expression of our time*, but whatever his own sufferings, gloom and depression are not the primary hallmarks of his work. Even that self-portrait painted for Gauguin rises above the initial mask of unhappiness as the spectator's reactions gradually yield to feelings akin to gratitude, a relief that someone suffering as Van Gogh clearly was should have had the courage to transform his misery into art. That self-portrait, far from showing the wreck of a life, is a triumph.

Indeed if one tries to look at the paintings with eye and mind uncluttered by the legends that have accrued about him in the hundred years since his death, one can see that the works themselves are gloriously, happily 'sane'. Even before his death Vincent van Gogh was being trumpeted as the isolated, rejected prophet of modern art. In his work – so the theory went – could be seen the swirling explosions, the mysterious unnerving colour of a mind obsessed. To support this, almost everything the artist said about his intentions had to be ignored or distorted and his own taste in art denigrated, for Van Gogh was a passionate lover of the art of his time, an art aggressively rejected by the founders of the modern movement. Only today, when Modernism is seen as just another school and no longer the historical goal to which all art had been inevitably developing, can we begin to take a fresh look at Van Gogh's life, unhampered by outdated theory. That is the intention of this book.

One must go back to his own words to discover the truth. He went to considerable trouble to explain his thinking in his extensive correspondence, and time spent with the paintings in tandem with a reading of his letters, mainly to his brother Theo, is one of the most illuminating pleasures the study of art has to offer. So rich is this material that THE life of Vincent van Gogh is clearly impossible. But there is always a place for A life as each generation tries to reach out to him as he tried so generously to reach out to us.

He himself longed to be understood and appreciated, and he reserved his greatest admiration for those artists who had won a wide popular following rather than those with mere cult appeal. He wanted to make art that would speak directly to ordinary folk. To help achieve this he signed his paintings simply 'Vincent' as if approaching the unknowable spectator with a friendly first name.

Part One: 1853–1880

Well, my own work, I am risking my life for it and my reason has half foundered.

[Letter from Vincent to Theo, July 1890]

I

1853 — 1869

Funeral Procession through the Cornfields

He preferred 'Vincent' to 'Van Gogh' because foreigners would insist on mispronouncing it – 'Van Gog' was one of the most irritating. A hundred years since his death he is most often called 'Van Go' or 'Van Goff' and neither would have pleased him any better. Simple, informal Vincent was easier and matched his character.

When he first learned to read, he could make out his name carved on a little tombstone beside the church where his father preached.

VINCENT VAN GOGH
1852

And below it:

Suffer little children
to come unto me
and forbid them not for such is
the KINGDOM
of GOD

The two words KONINGRIJK GODS were aggressively large, in deeply etched letters. And what a grim, possessive place that kingdom must have seemed to the young Vincent when he learned that the stone marked the grave of his still-born brother. When he asked about it, he was told a second mystery: the first Vincent had died on March 30th, 1852, while he, the second, had been born exactly a year to the day, on March 30th, 1853.

For the grieving parents the death of their first baby was made more tragic by the fact that they had married late and felt their chances of having a family slipping away. At thirty-three Anna van Gogh was three years older than her husband Theodorus and worried that time was against her. A tradition of large families added further pressure. Theodorus himself was one of twelve children of a Pastor Vincent van Gogh whose family was centred on The Hague. Having followed his father as a minister of religion, Pastor Theodorus was expected to set an example to his parishioners by producing a large Protestant brood, and there was understandable relief when the second child arrived so closely after the first. They were greatly concerned throughout the pregnancy but

---

Principal members of the Van Gogh family mentioned in the book

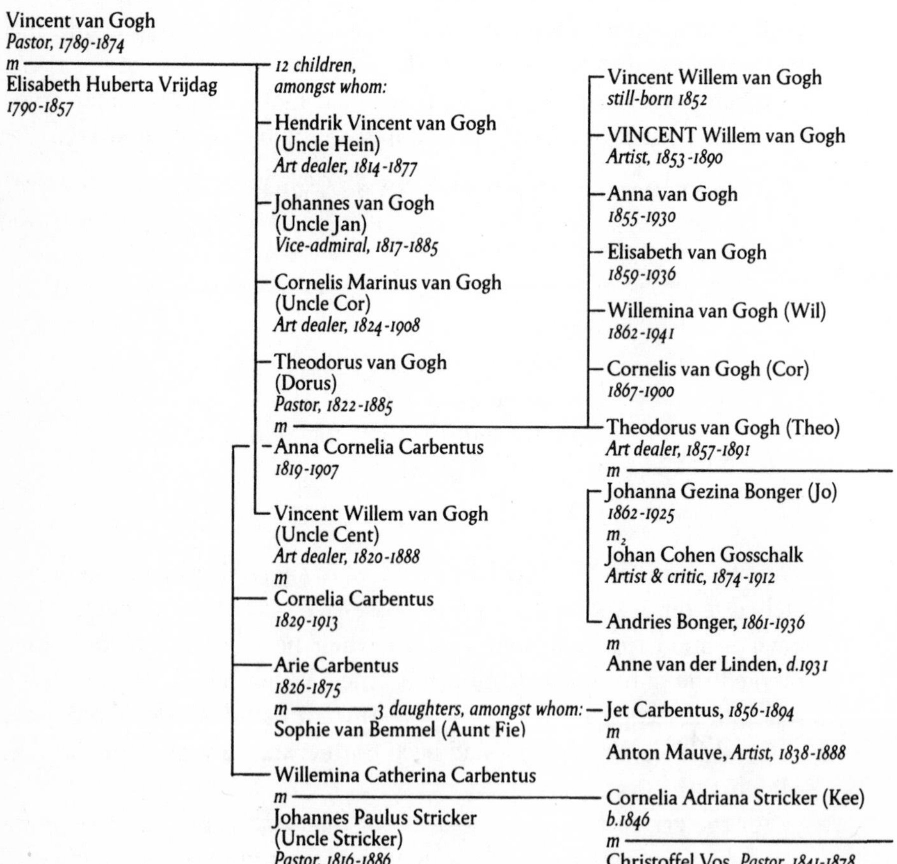

Anna was assisted in her labour by the local practitioner Cornelis van Ginneken who was thus the first of Vincent's many doctors and the only one to be entirely successful.

As bereavement was a protracted public affair in the mid-century the couple were still in mourning when the new baby arrived, though their all too evident happiness made this no more than an irrelevant formality. The living child had laid to rest the tragedy of the previous year and they named him Vincent Willem as a sign of a new beginning and in honour of his grandfather.

There was, however, another less sentimental reason for the choice of names. Pastor Theodorus' elder brother was also called Vincent Willem and he was the wealthiest man in the family. For a man like the pastor whose career had not prospered and who found himself saddled with a far-flung parish in a remote corner of Brabant with little prospect of advancement, the repetition of such brotherly attachment was clearly prudent. Uncle 'Cent' would be the new Vincent Willem's godfather and protector, and so it proved – for a time.

Throughout his life the second Vincent would sometimes refer to his stillborn namesake, but his parents were unlikely to have done or said anything to trouble him over the dead child. Both were goodhearted people: sin, guilt and death were not prominent in their religious beliefs and, although Theodorus was a minister in the notoriously strict Dutch Reformed Church, he was far from being a black-draped bigot. Indeed it was this relaxed approach to religion which had blighted his career.

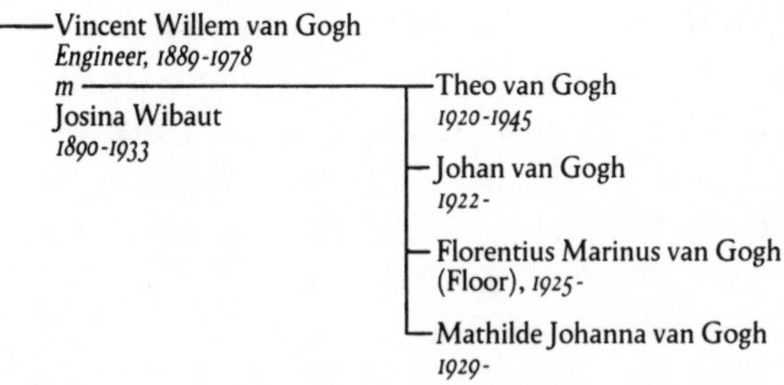

Johannes Vos
b. 1873

A student at a time when the church was divided between traditionalists and modernists, each group as uncompromising as the other, Theodorus had opted for a middle way and espoused the compromise faction. This was the 'nice' people's party and, as is the way with such unheroic groups, it found itself bereft of influence. Had he settled for one extreme or the other Theodorus might have gained advancement. His looks were in his favour – he was known as 'the handsome Dominie' – but he was an uninspiring preacher and it took all the influence of his pastor father to get him a place as unwanted as the little village of Zundert near the Belgian border. This was Catholic Brabant, which meant that 'Dorus', as his family called him, was left to minister to a scattered minority from a small church. It was the local Catholic priest who enjoyed status. But Dorus was determined to make the best of his first post in the flat Brabant farmland, with its settled peasant families, so unlike the bustling merchant cities of the north. Groot Zundert they called it, not because the village was in any historical sense 'great' but because the parish was so widespread. To walk across its level fields from boundary to boundary could take two hours, though as he loved walking this hardly bothered him. He soon learned that his parishioners got a little drunk and boisterous on feast days, but that too failed to irritate him. He was not the sort of man to rant from the pulpit and, later in life, if forced to advise his eldest son, his words would all be of tolerance and of choosing the middle path. When he quoted scripture it was usually the gentler New Testament sayings that sprang to his lips rather than the hell-fire of the Old.

Dorus was the only one of Pastor Vincent's children to follow him into the church. The three brothers closest to him, Vincent (Cent), Hendrik (Hein) and Cornelis (Cor), were art dealers. The exception was Johannes (Jan), who eventually rose to the rank of Rear-Admiral in the Dutch navy. Of these Cent was closest to Dorus – they even married sisters. When Cent was courting Cornelia Carbentus, daughter of another well-established Hague family, he was able to introduce his younger brother to her sister Anna. Although older, Anna had a lively, extrovert personality that complemented Theodorus' rather bookish mien. They were clearly well matched and were married in 1851, a year after Cent and Cornelia. Anna was to grow into a plump motherly figure, a voracious letter-writer, deeply concerned with the well-being of her family and friends. She was also an amateur artist of considerable talent. Dorus, as we can see in a later drawing by his eldest son, was to take on the appearance of a rather withdrawn antiquarian, with receding hair covered by a little indoor cap and a somewhat tired expression. They were evidently happy together and much loved by their parishioners, who wept for their lost child and rejoiced at their second.

When Dorus and Anna christened their second son with the names of the first – Vincent Willem – they can only have envisaged one destiny for the child: that he would grow up to become a member of their solid Dutch bourgeois family of clergymen, art-dealers and officers, all respectable and contented Dutch citizens of the kind who stare back at us from a canvas by Rembrandt. Indeed for the first twenty years of his life there were no grounds for thinking that Vincent was in any way different from those around him except in minor and at the time insignificant ways. Later such details would be pored over and blown up out of all proportion in an attempt to uncover incipient signs of both genius and madness. But at the time no one saw anything of the sort. Young Vincent van Gogh was a very ordinary child. His only remarkable feature was a shock of red hair, unusual in his family. From his podgy appearance he had clearly not inherited his father's good looks. That he was frequently naughty – ill-tempered is the phrase most often used – was a common criticism, though Anna van Gogh would have none of it and, when her mother-in-law, that famous progenitrix of twelve, attempted a little elementary discipline after one of baby Vincent's tantrums, relations were so severely strained it took all Dorus's tact and a sunset carriage ride to persuade the two disputants to kiss and make up. Far from such behaviour being a sign of artistic ferment welling up inside Vincent's tiny frame it was more likely the result of the child being thoroughly spoiled by his adoring parents. However, his position as an only child was not to last; a daughter, his sister Anna, was born in 1855. Eighteen years later they would travel abroad together and they occasionally exchanged letters, but he and Anna were never much more than acquaintances. It was the birth of Theo two years later in 1857 that brought Vincent a much needed companion. There were two more daughters, Elisabeth and Willemina, and another boy, Cornelis, but they were too remote to figure much in Vincent's life. It was in Theo that he found his lifelong friend. Far from resenting the new boy in the family, the four-year-old Vincent adored him from the first. They were more like twins, inseparable as soon as little Theo could toddle about. All their lives they would reminisce about their early years, recalling in detail things seen and done. Wherever they met they compared their immediate surroundings to the loved landscape of childhood. Towards the end of his life Vincent wrote to Theo:

> *During my illness I saw again every room in the house at Zundert, every path, every plant in the garden, the views of the fields outside, the neighbours, the graveyard, the church, our kitchen garden at the back – down to a magpie's nest in a tall acacia in the graveyard.*

Like their father the two boys loved long walks and spent hours studying the plants and animals they found, though in this Vincent was clearly the leader. Their sister Elisabeth remembered how Vincent knew the names of every beetle, how adroit he was at catching water insects and that he did not merely look but studied hard, turning things around in his hands, collecting and labelling them with the precision of a true scientist. Indeed, far from displaying any signs of an artistic vocation, it was easier to envisage him becoming a naturalist. His scientific approach was such that he tended to resent anyone treating his studies as if they were play. Elisabeth wrote later that he once modelled an elephant out of putty, but destroyed it when his parents made what he thought was too much fuss over it.

This love of nature was to remain an important strand throughout his life. It was deeply rooted in the Brabant countryside where he first chose to practise his career as a painter. We can see in his early canvases how untouched by nineteenth-century progress those farms and villages were: thatched cottages, where a peasant woman tends a goat and chickens scratch by the door; a farmer in wooden clogs following a bullock-drawn plough, a couple rooting in the earth for potatoes, a weaver working at the loom which fills the small room in his hovel. Mid-century Holland had consciously avoided the industrialisation of its more thrusting neighbours, and while the country was free of the worst excesses of *laissez-faire* capitalism that were so conspicuous in nearby Belgium, it also meant that rural poverty and backbreaking toil continued unchanged. Happily for the Van Goghs such misery was far worse in the villages in eastern Holland or in the squalid slums of Amsterdam, to which many desperate farming folk were sadly drawn. Brabant, while not rich, at least provided a living and it was possible to retain, as Vincent clearly did, a romantic view of agricultural life and to believe that in the toil of those who worked the land there was something noble, even holy.

That the good citizens of Zundert lived in ignorance of the greater events taking place beyond their borders was characteristic of the Dutch nation itself. After the secession of Belgium in 1830 the Kingdom of Holland had consciously chosen to stand aside from the manoeuvres of the great powers and to concentrate on resolving its own internal difficulties, most of which stemmed from the fact that while the majority of the population was Protestant there was nevertheless a very large Catholic minority. Pastor van Gogh was far more likely to be exercised over the funding of the local Protestant school than the growing power of Germany or the rise and fall of French governments. Not surprisingly, Vincent inherited something of this attitude. Although he would later become deeply concerned about social issues, his response was always at an immediate local level. The larger picture, the wider stage, held little interest for him and in all the more than six hundred and seventy surviving letters that he wrote there is barely any mention of the major political events of his day. War, *coups d'état*, assassinations, all passed him by, whereas a garden in flower, an intriguing novel or a brilliantly painted roofscape would each be lovingly described.

As a boy, all Vincent's knowledge of life beyond the fields of Brabant came from books. He was an insatiable reader. In subject matter he ranged far and wide, though he was equally capable of going into great depth if a topic truly gripped him. Religion and contemporary novels were his main passions and he was familiar with an astonishing range of poetry from all over Europe. For this he was surely indebted to his father rather than to the schools he attended. His first was the local day school for the Protestant community, though that did hardly anything to foster a love of literature, being essentially an overcrowded hall where farmers' children learned to read and write. Compared to their neighbours the Van Goghs were scholarly folk and, although the Dutch Reformed pastor did not have the pre-eminent position of his Catholic opposite number, he was still someone of standing in the community. His presbytery was a substantial two-storey house on the main street, in typical Dutch classical style with a scalloped upper storey reminiscent of canal-side buildings in Delft or Amsterdam. The roof sloped so sharply the bedrooms on the upper floor were quite narrow and as the family grew so the children had to be crammed into an ever-decreasing space. Little wonder that, as the eldest, Vincent grew to hate the sloping ceiling and to have a lifelong love of solitude. He was only really happy if he and Theo could find somewhere where none of the others could bother them.

The one who held the family together was naturally enough their mother. They all remembered that she could knit with 'terrifying speed' and was forever busy. Even when the children were grown up she continued to unite them by her indefatigable letter-writing. Most of her correspondence began with the disclaimer "I just send you a little word . . .", followed by a substantial letter filled with news about the others and advice for the recipient.

Although a pastor's income was modest, Anna had an indoor servant and, despite her growing family and her local duties as the pastor's wife, she was able to pursue her hobby: making pencil drawings of wildflowers for her album or a watercolour of a bouquet she had arranged. She wanted little Vincent to follow her and his surviving pencil sketches speak well of her encouragement: there is a startling sketch of a ferocious dog and a more than competent shaded drawing of a nearby bridge over a stream, both done when he was nine. But no one thought then that such things were extraordinary or in any way a pointer to some possible future career. There was nothing unusual in being able to draw well at a time when children were taught to be precocious at piano playing, water-colours, needlework and other homely arts. We may imagine a winter evening with the family gathered near a wood-fire in their living-room: the chairs of polished wood and leather, patterned tapestry covers on the side tables and large oil lamps of brass and

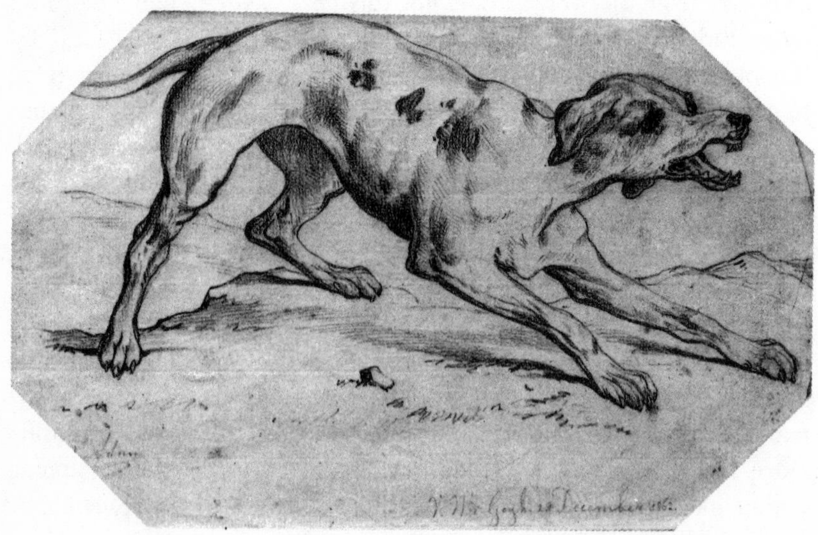

Drawing of a dog made when Vincent was nine.

cut-glass by whose light Pastor Theodorus is writing his notes for next Sunday's sermon and Anna is painting a spray of pink hyacinths. The scene embraces the two main strands in Vincent's life, religion and art. They were to tug at him for thirty years until the latter won. But first the young boy, as a son must, had to come to terms with his father, a man who, though far less narrow-minded and hard than many of his contemporaries, was still the embodiment of principle and discipline. Vincent was to spend most of his life wrestling with a longing to emulate his father and win his approval, which was matched by an even stronger yearning to break free from the world the pastor represented.

By and large Dorus left art to his wife. However, his study, probably a place not much loved by Vincent and his brothers, contained one significant picture, a tiny engraving of a funeral procession crossing a cornfield. This may have been the first professional work of art the young Vincent knew. It certainly had a profound and lasting effect on him. The black and white scene, about eight inches wide and four high, was signed by the artist Jacob van der Maaten, a popular engraver of local scenes in his day though now totally forgotten. In a sense it was hardly surprising the pastor should have wanted this picture. The artist's scenes of windmills and canals, and his re-creations of seventeenth-century Dutch life, were very popular with the middle classes of his day. There was, however, something very different about Van der Maaten's funeral procession. At a distance it appears to be a peculiarly morbid work: a line of black-caped, top-hatted mourners winds away from the spectator through a field of high ripe corn that looks rain-battered from the overhead storm clouds that lighten towards the horizon. The procession is moving towards the black silhouette of a village church. In the foreground is a recently cut clearing with what looks like the grim reaper, a hooded figure of death observing the passing scene. With its overcast sky and that emptiness peculiar to the landscape of the Low Countries the picture has a very unsettling effect and it is small wonder that years later Vincent could recall its every detail. Yet, when looked at close to, the whole scene changes: the grim reaper is merely a dozy old peasant doffing his cap to the mourners, who are themselves quite comic, chubby fellows waddling along like a line of penguins. With a sense of relief we see that this is nothing more than a work of bucolic humour. And yet, step back and there again all is death and gloom. Vincent would later acquire his own copy of Van der Maaten's engraving and the subject of the reaper would recur frequently in his work as would an echo of that ambiguity he sensed in the picture on his father's study wall. In the year before he died he wrote to Theo:

> *I am writing this letter little by little in the intervals when I am tired of painting. Work is going pretty well – I am struggling with a canvas begun some days before my indisposition, a Reaper, the study is all yellow, terribly thickly painted, but the subject was fine and simple. For I see in this reaper – a vague figure fighting like a devil in the midst of the heat to get to the end of his task – I see him the image of death, in the sense that humanity might be the wheat he is reaping. So it is – if you like – the opposite of that sower I tried to do before. But there's nothing sad in this death, it goes its way in broad daylight with a sun flooding everything with a light of pure gold . . .*

It would be wrong to see the tombstone bearing his name and the figure of the reaper as stark shadows lying over Vincent's childhood for, as with the engraving, look a little closer and there is ample laughter and childish fun. With Theo he was a typical carefree boy; with adults around he could be an equally typical moody little brat who liked to be left alone with a book or a sketch pad and did not wish to be interrupted. Years after his death, when his talents were already accepted, there was an attempt to record the recollections of those who had known him as a child. They proved wildly divergent: 'quiet and good-natured' said one neighbour, whereas a woman who had been the family's maid remembered thinking him the least agreeable of all the children. The only memory common to all was a vivid recollection of his red hair and freckles.

Whatever the differences, it is clear that he was hardly a popular child. All his interests – his love of books, of drawing and nature study – could hardly have endeared him to the boisterous farmers' sons who were his fellow pupils at the village day school. His parents were already worried about the influence of such boys on their son's behaviour, but when Pastor Theodorus learned that the schoolmaster was often the worse for drink they knew something had to be done about their eldest son's education. After little more than a year Vincent was removed from the school and was taught at home. This went on for two years until 1864 when he was eleven when it was realised that a broader education was needed. A pastor's income could not run to a grand city school. In any case his parents must have doubted whether he could be so abruptly separated from the countryside and brusquely introduced to city life. The solution lay in Zevenbergen, a village about twenty-five kilometres from Zundert, where there was a small boarding-school run by Jan Provily, a Protestant teacher known to the Van Goghs. Provily and his son Piet specialised in languages: French, English and German. However, it was not the curriculum but the nearness of the school and the fact that Vincent would be among boys who were thought of as his own sort that persuaded his parents to choose the Provilys' establishment. Whatever the reasons, the result was that from the age of eleven, when he was sent off to his new school, Vincent began to acquire so thorough a grounding in languages that he eventually became a fluent linguist able to speak and write French and English with almost the same facility as his native Dutch and with a good working knowledge of German.

Given his love of reading and learning it might be assumed that he would have enjoyed life at the Provilys' once he had got over the first shock of being away from home. Indeed, given his moodiness with adults and the fact that he made so much progress at the school, it must have seemed to his parents that theirs was a happy decision. It was only years later that Vincent told Theo how miserable he had felt as he watched his parents' little yellow carriage driving away from him down a road wet with rain. When his father returned a fortnight later to see how he was getting on, Vincent forgot his usual display of indifference and fell on the older man's neck. He told Theo how he had lived for that first Christmas when he would be allowed home. The stand-offishness, the tantrums if someone paid too much attention to him, the moodiness, had all been a façade. In truth he needed his family and was lonely and unhappy away from them. There is a photograph of him aged thirteen in 1866, now a thin, tousle-haired lad, whose fixed distant gaze and slightly pouting lower lip give the distinct impression that he is fighting back tears.

Of course the holidays were glorious. There was Theo again and even the rough-and-tumble of a large family must have seemed attractive after that first separation. Best of all were visits from Uncle Cent and Aunt Cornelia, a gentle-looking woman who made it her life's work to take care of her husband who was subject to frequent bouts of ill health. Having no children of their own, they were devoted to their nieces and nephews, who must have relished their visits not only for any gifts they might bring but also for the romantic aura of distant places that surrounded them. Uncle

Cent and Aunt Cornelia lived in Paris, and his business connections included Brussels, Berlin, London and even New York.

As Uncle Cent and Pastor Dorus watched Vincent and Theo playing together they must have smiled in recognition, for they too had shared a close, twin-like childhood. Cent had had to leave home as a teenager to start out on the career that made him a successful art dealer but he always remained in close touch with Dorus. Some years later, when Vincent had left home, Uncle Cent sold his house in France and bought a substantial property at Princenhage in order to be near his brother. He built a gallery on to the property to house his personal art collection. It was Uncle Cent who first introduced young Vincent and Theo to the world of art and of art dealing. He was the ideal mentor. As a teenager he had begun in The Hague working in a cousin's shop that sold artists' materials, but within two years he had taken over the business and transformed it into an art gallery. From the beginning he had realised that there was a market for new talent and he was soon displaying the work of younger painters in the windows of his new showroom in the Plaats, a fashionable square off the Binnenhof in the centre of town close by the Parliament buildings. When they discovered that Uncle Cent paid well, more artists flocked to his gallery.

The sort of art he was keen to attract was the new fashion for painting out of doors, direct from nature, a phenomenon then burgeoning all over Europe. The acknowledged leaders were a group of French artists based on the village of Barbizon in the forest of Fontainebleau near Paris. Uncle Cent collected Barbizon paintings and sold them in Holland, but his main aim was to nurture a home-grown version, a similar Dutch school based on The Hague and in this he was entirely successful.

What all the different groups of nature painters had in common was a rejection of the tired classical and religious subjects perpetuated by the academies and displayed in the various annual salons held in most European capitals. But in a way this revolution was caused as much by technical advances as by any deeply felt philosophy. The arrival from Britain of the new tin tubes of ready-mixed paint freed artists from the necessity to grind and mix their own colours and allowed them to work away from their studios. Until then the only way to record nature had been to make rapid water-colour sketches to be worked up indoors later. Now the whole work could be completed entirely in the open air, in direct contact with the subject. The other technical advance was quite simply the new railways which brought the countryside nearer. All over

Europe the results were similar – the effect of direct sunlight, of the artist's observing how it fell and how it affected the things on which it fell, led to a general lightening of the palette. The sombre tones of the studio classicists, varnished even darker, began to give way to lighter, airier paintings. And of course the old guard loathed it. To the academicians the nature painters seemed sloppy, their work unfinished. But Uncle Cent guessed, and correctly so, that wealthy townsfolk would happily pay for such colourful scenes of farms and seascapes. They would buy them to brighten up their new homes in the spreading suburbs around the old town centres, for while the methods might be new the appeal of the subjects was essentially nostalgic. For the last time in that century of rapid change, a major advance in art was matched by a comparable shift in public taste and Uncle Cent reaped the benefits.

If he had stopped there, Cent van Gogh would have proved himself The Hague's most successful dealer, but he went much further. He rightly believed that just as he had bought work by the Barbizon school and sold it in Holland so too he could find a market for his Dutch painters abroad. He knew that in France there was an aura attached to that vague concept 'the North', a heritage of the golden age of Dutch painting, of Rembrandt and Vermeer, which meant that the French still looked to Amsterdam (much as we today still look to Paris) long after it had ceased to be a major artistic centre. Playing his hunch Uncle Cent went to the French capital in 1861 and entered into association with the leading Parisian art dealer, Adolphe Goupil. As part of Goupil et Cie Uncle Cent had a wide market for his artists: there were two galleries in Paris and others in Berlin and London, and a 'correspondent' in New York. For a time another uncle, Hendrick (Hein), joined him in The Hague but eventually went on to open his own business in Brussels until he too merged with Goupil, reinforcing the family's interest. Goupil himself had made a fortune selling high-quality reproductions mainly following the taste of the annual official Salon, signing up each year's award winners like so many prize fighters. His main premises in the Rue Chaptal in Paris included printing presses, a gallery and a number of apartments for the use of the company's leading artists. At first Uncle Cent and Aunt Cornelia lived in one but as his hunch that the French would buy began to pay off he acquired a substantial mansion in Neuilly. His main contribution to the rapid growth of the Goupil chain was to reinforce the sale of original paintings and the passion for 'the North' meant that his own artists flourished and were exceptionally indebted to him. There was only one cloud over Uncle Cent's brilliant career, his health. He had always suffered from bouts of unspecified sickness and by the time he was introducing his young nephews to a knowledge of the art trade he was himself partially retired. Although he remained a leading shareholder and a director of the company, he had less and less to do with the day-to-day running of the galleries and preferred to spend the winter months in the more equable climate of Menton in the south of France. But whenever one of his visits coincided with Vincent's school holidays he would continue the young man's education in art and art dealing. To Vincent these were no more than pleasant afternoons, but to the older man they were an important part of an unspoken plan that his nephew might one day follow him into the business.

In 1866, at the age of thirteen, Vincent finished his elementary education at the Provilys' and was sent even further away from home, to the King Willem II State Secondary School in Tilburg. This would be his first real experience of town life as he was to board out with a family called Hannick, whose son Marinus had been a pupil at the school. As if all that was not strange enough for him, the school itself was far from ordinary – although only a small building, it had been the late King's palace and had been decorated like a fairy-tale castle with four turrets and a crenellated parapet. Fortunately its martial appearance belied its nature, for the school was extraordinarily liberal for its time. Its founder and first headmaster F. J. A. Fels had gathered round him a group of a dozen or so teachers of a remarkably high academic standard, many of whom went on to university professorships. Fels was good-natured and the school had an easy-going atmosphere. There is a class photograph taken on the main steps with Vincent in the front row, where everyone, staff and pupils, looks noticeably relaxed for what was generally a rigidly formal occasion. The curriculum, however, was a serious business with thirty-six hours a week devoted to academic subjects. But the extraordinary thing was that amongst mathematics and languages, four hours a week were set aside for art, a highly unusual subject at the time.

When Fels had been asked to set up the school he had brought in C. C. Huysmans, an artist, to create a course in drawing. Huysmans had been on the way to establishing a reputation in Paris when he was obliged to return home to take care of his blind father. Having been forced into teaching he decided to make the best of it and became an expert in art education and wrote a popular drawing manual. The Dutch Education Law of 1863 required schools to teach perspective, but at Tilburg Huysmans went way beyond this limited obligation by setting up a proper art room. He was certainly ahead of his time. Even his appearance was deceptive: square-jawed and unusually clean-shaven, he looked as if he might be a rather tough character when in fact he was deeply concerned for his pupils' well-being. Vincent and his fellows would troop into the art room dressed in loose-fitting dust-coats and sit at long benches set around a table on which Huysmans had arranged plaster casts and stuffed animals for them to draw. As they worked Huysmans would pass among them offering advice and encouragement. But as much as Vincent may have enjoyed this, the odd fact is that during his two years at Tilburg he never mastered the science of perspective, despite all Huysmans' efforts he just could not get the hang of it.

Fortunately, Huysmans was not content simply to fulfil the requirements of the education act and, when the weather permitted, he would troop his class outside to draw from nature. Huysmans had absorbed the new thinking about art and his methods happily complemented Uncle Cent's lectures. It was a unique opportunity. Fels had hopes that Tilburg could become a national centre for art education and the school had managed to obtain a grant of three hundred guilders to buy reproductions of the old masters which hung around the walls of the art room where the boys could study them.

Perspective aside, Vincent was good at his lessons and in the top stream. Although he had missed the usual preparatory year, he passed the first year's exams easily. But in his second year things changed. Mr Fels left and was replaced by Dr W. N. Fenger, a German who took pride in being a strict disciplinarian. Before long there were disputes with the staff and some of the pupils were expelled. Vincent never felt the force of Fenger's wrath, and none of the punishment records show that he was ever disciplined, but something did happen that radically changed his attitude to the school. In March 1868, half-way through his second year, he suddenly returned home and never went back. What happened remains one of the great mysteries of his life and is possibly the lost key to much of his subsequent behaviour. The reason was certainly not academic, for he had shone at Zevenbergen and handled the Tilburg exams easily. With his fluency in languages, a university scholarship ought to have been his for the taking. It has been suggested that the Van Goghs could no longer afford to continue paying his fees, but, if so, why send him back only to withdraw him half-way through the second term? In any case he was Uncle Cent's 'adopted' son and if money were needed it would surely have been readily available from that quarter. What we do know is that when he returned home that March his life came to a full stop – he had no work, nothing to occupy his time, no plans for his future – and this unexplained hiatus dragged on for fifteen months. In later years there would be similar fallow periods, but by then it was clear that he was suffering from a mental disorder which brought moments of manic obsession followed by a sickening plunge into deep melancholia. It is possible that this is what happened at Tilburg. If so, it would certainly have been misinterpreted as malingering or moodiness and, if it continued, his parents would have been asked to take him away. That there is no record of this does not necessarily rule it out. It was only when Vincent's mental disorder made him behave erratically and wrought alarming changes in his appearance that his family realised that something was seriously wrong with him. It is perfectly possible that he had an attack of some sort and that this went unrecognised or was misinterpreted.

Whatever happened, his life immediately after school must have been dreary. He was an intelligent fifteen-year old. Now that his only friend Theo was away at school all day, he had little to occupy the weary hours other than solitary walks in the neighbouring fields. In this way, a year passed. In a book she wrote in later life his sister Elisabeth described him at this time as "... broad as he was long, his back slightly bent, with the bad habit of letting his head hang; the red blond hair cropped close was hidden under a straw hat: a strange face, not young; the forehead already full of lines, the eyebrows on the large, noble brow drawn together in deepest thought. The eyes, small and deep-set, were now blue, now green, according to the impression of the moment."

Elisabeth also noted that under his 'ugly exterior' he seemed to be struggling with some sort of inner life. He certainly ignored his younger sisters and brother, after all little Cor was barely a year old and fifteen years his junior. But what was that inner struggle? We know from his later letters that he longed to dedicate his life to something, to be useful, to be committed to a cause. In the end that cause came to be painting, but at sixteen he had no such ambition and his longing to find a purpose in his life was without direction and can only have nagged away at him with the passing of each wasted day.

Throughout this trying time Vincent's mother and father were sure of only two things. Firstly, it was impossible for them to spend any more money on him, he had had his time at school and it was now the turn of the other children. Secondly, there was only one person who might help them resolve the problem – Uncle Cent. As Vincent had always been so fascinated by his uncle's descriptions of art dealing could this be a way out of the crisis? Given the Bohemian image of the artist today, it might be thought that Pastor Theodorus would never have considered such a career for his boy, but he knew that the sort of artists Uncle Cent dealt with were almost stultifyingly respectable. Art dealing in nineteenth-century Holland was a rather refined trade and Cent counted members of the Dutch court among his clients. The notion of the artist as an outsider, a 'pariah' as he would later be dubbed, was only just beginning to gain ground in avant-garde circles in Paris and it is not the least irony of Vincent's life that it would be he who would eventually come to exemplify such a description more than any other. But for the moment there was nothing in the world of Dutch art dealing that troubled the pastor or his wife.

Uncle Cent was delighted. He had always hoped to have his nephew in the business. He was already thinking of finally severing his relations with Goupil and moving back to Holland, so what could be better than if a member of the family were to take over? If the boy worked hard and showed promise then there was no reason why he should not become his uncle's heir.

Vincent agreed to the proposal. What else was he to do? After fifteen months of hanging about with time on his hands, he was now more than happy to be leaving his village again. The Hague, administrative capital of the country, must have sounded suitably adventurous. At sixteen it was surely time for a little excitement in his life.

It took a while for Uncle Cent to organise everything, but a place as an apprentice clerk at his old gallery was eventually created and by the early summer of 1869 everything had been arranged. Dressed in his Sunday best, his boots shined, his unruly hair slicked down, Vincent was ready to step out of the world of childhood. But as his parents' carriage took him off on the road to Breda, where he would catch the train to the coast, his excitement at this new adventure must have been tempered by an awareness that none of it was his own doing. Everything had been decided for him. He had merely acquiesced.

2

1869 — 1874

A Blank Canvas

Everything was arranged for him. He would stay with the Roos family, friends of his parents who lived in the Lange Beestenmarkt, an unexceptional street of fair-sized middle-class houses a ten-minute walk from the town centre where he was to work. While this was preferable to being a boarder in an anonymous guest-house, any other sixteen-year-old might have wanted more freedom. Not that Vincent complained: he was in some ways much younger than his age and had led a sheltered country existence. It was only during the coming four years in The Hague that an independent personality began to take shape. For the moment he went along with whatever was proposed, even letting the Roos family arrange his friendships – a nephew, Willem Valkes, was about the same age and automatically assumed the role of companion. The Hague was his family town so there was a ready-made community, especially at the crowded house of his mother's brother Arie Carbentus, his wife Sophie (Aunt 'Fie') and their three daughters. Vincent was content to drift into this circle and, although he claimed to find the conversation at the Roos dinner table a bit limited after the lively, informed talk at home, he soon came to like the family and would remain attached to them long after he left.

Even Willem turned out to be an acceptable companion. On their Sundays off they could take advantage of the fact that The Hague was only a small town whose streets soon merged into the surrounding woods and dunes. Apart from the old town centre with its fine seventeenth-century squares, most of the town was a garden suburb, more like an overgrown village. There were woods for walking in, lakes for boating on and – best of all – the nearby harbour of Scheveningen, still a tiny picturesque fishing village, behind which stretched the limitless dunes much painted by local artists. The dunes were a virtual wilderness, a rare moment of drama in the perpetual flat landscape, a desert of sandy hollows and high ridges that suddenly opened out to reveal the silvery-grey North Sea breakers pounding wide beaches, empty except for the occasional upturned boat or solitary fisherman spreading his nets.

It was this proximity of forest and sea to a convenient town and railway that made The Hague an artists' colony. At the heart of the city's artistic life was Goupil's gallery in the Plaats, the elegant little square opening on to the tree-lined lake across which stood The Mauritshuis, a former princely residence that now housed the royal art collections. The court patronised Goupil's and, when he began selling the new Dutch art, it was no doubt part of Uncle Cent's calculations that there would be a patriotic market for this home-grown product. When he was building up his reputation he made the King a gift of a collection of prints of the prize winners at the Paris Exhibition of 1867 and was rewarded with a knighthood. Suitably elevated, Uncle Cent's gallery could be patronised by Queen Sophie, who brought in her train social cachet and further custom.

There was, however, an odd twist to this success story: the so-called 'Hague' artists did not have much to do with the place. They arrived for painting holidays but always returned to livelier cities – some even lived in Paris. Uncle Cent's painters had been dubbed 'the Hague School' as much to differentiate them from the studio-based painters of Amsterdam as from any physical connection with the town. 'The Hague' was shorthand for the countryside, for nature and the new art of the outdoors. But as with most artificially created schools this definition did not bear close examination: they were not all painters of landscapes; interiors and street scenes were just as common. Yet so successful was Uncle Cent in creating a market for the school that the idea of The Hague became a self-fulfilling prophecy and gradually the artists associated with it began to visit the town more often and most eventually settled there. It was to be Vincent's good fortune that his four years at Goupil's coincided with this migration. He was to get to know each of the artists as they arrived and three at least were to prove very influential. Of course there had always been resident artists in The Hague, but they tended to be solitary individualists like Van der Maaten, who had spent two periods in the town before settling in Appeldoorn.

The first Hague School painter to make his home there was Joseph

Bosboom who, perversely enough, specialised in highly detailed church interiors, often peopled by tiny figures in seventeenth-century dress. At first sight this seemed to have absolutely nothing to do with the supposed love of nature that the name 'The Hague' was thought to represent, but in another way it pointed up the one thing that really did hold them together: all the Hague painters looked to the past, to the golden age of Dutch art, to Vermeer, the Van der Veldts, De Hooch and to the long list of artists who had also frequently used the farms, coast and towns of the Low Countries as subjects for their art. It was thought fitting that the newly independent kingdom of the Netherlands should have in its seat of government a school of artists that sought to restore what many felt was the broken line of national art. For, although the techniques were new and the practice of painting direct from nature made them part of recent movements in art which were spreading across Europe, in reality the Hague School was essentially traditional and nationalistic.

This conservatism was reflected in the imposing four-storey façade of the Goupil building, as solid and respectable as an undertaker's parlour. On public holidays and royal celebrations the entire frontage was festooned with bunting and a huge Dutch tricolour suspended from its centre, two floors down from the roof. Strollers emerging from the smart shopping area in the narrow streets behind the Plaats could admire the paintings on view in the three ground-floor windows. The interior displayed that precarious mid-century balance between opulence and respectability: bright, deep-flocked wallpaper was set against restrained dark wood surrounds; the extravagantly gilded frames in which the paintings were hung from floor to ceiling contrasted with the refined gentility of tapestry-covered banquettes. Entrances were swagged with heavy velvet drapes and anything that could be polished was. It was no place for youthful high spirits among the junior clerks – not that Vincent would have caught much more than a brief glimpse of that awesome outer world on his first day. As an apprentice clerk he had to learn the business in the back offices, mastering the extensive correspondence involved in ordering and despatching work between the various branches. A Goupil salesman was expected to know what was available in, say, Brussels or Berlin while at the same time having a shrewd idea of the sort of thing the other branches would like to have from any new work that had come into his own gallery. Later, when Vincent had progressed to the front salons and Theo had joined another branch of the firm, their letters often contained requests for certain works to be transferred.

Once the initial training period was over there was the business of handling clients to be learned. A carriage would draw up in the Plaats, the patrons – he formally besuited, she in full gown and bustle – would be ushered in. A senior figure would step forward to greet them while lesser employees like Vincent would hover respectfully in the background, ready to do any fetching and carrying that might be necessary. Given his occasionally tetchy character, all this might have proved too much for the young man, but oddly enough he seems to have thoroughly enjoyed acting out his role. This had much to do with the way the Hague branch was run. If it had been a long-established institution dominated by old men and set in its ways he might have found the atmosphere stifling. Fortunately it was a young company, still expanding and developing, and run by bright, ambitious people.

The manager, Hermanus Gijsbertus Tersteeg, was only a few years older than Vincent. He had already made a success importing foreign books when Uncle Cent, no doubt recognising his own youthful enthusiasm in the man, brought him into the firm. Tersteeg's elevated position must have surprised many of the clients for he looked even younger than his age. Given the rigid nature of most businesses at the time, Tersteeg was unusual in maintaining friendly relations with his employees. Naturally, as the nephew of one of the directors, Vincent was bound to be given some preferential treatment, but it was Tersteeg's way to invite all the juniors to visit him and his wife in the apartment above the gallery where they lived with their small daughter Betsy. Vincent often went, and became very close to the young family.

Despite this easy-going atmosphere it was quite difficult, as Vincent discovered, to define the role of a Goupil employee. While it was true the gallery sold artists' materials, this was a side-line, provided rather as a convenience for their artists than as an important source of income, and it would be wrong to think of the place as merely an art shop with Vincent and the others as shop assistants. But nor were they art experts loftily surveying the masterworks on display in the manner of the valuers in today's auction houses. The ideal Goupil man was expected to maintain a subtle blend of knowledge and self-effacement. If those imaginary clients knew what they wanted then they were congratulated on their taste and sold it; if it became clear that a little guidance were needed then it had to be gently proffered in such a way that the illusion was created that it was the clients and not the salesman who had first picked on the work in question. That Vincent slipped easily and uncomplainingly into so delicate a role is a minor miracle.

Of course there was much to make the work appealing, not least his first contact with real paintings after his uncle's monochrome prints – the thrill of colour, the unforgettable smell of oil paint and varnish. Most of all there was the desire to prove himself, the sheer will to succeed in his first job which made everything so important and interesting. Tersteeg certainly recognised all this in the younger man and quickly put him in charge of photographic reproductions, a new line for the company and one that proved very profitable – Vincent told Theo that he once sold a hundred in a single day. This may not have been art dealing in its highest sense, but it clearly gave the young man considerable personal satisfaction.

Absorbed as he now was by anything to do with art, Vincent soon made his first visit to the Mauritshuis, the royal art collection only a short walk from the gallery. More a large town house than a palace, the museum still retained the air of a private collection. Despite the building's moderate size, the works amassed by Prince Willem III and further augmented by public purchase were undoubtedly the finest single gathering of northern European art then available to the public. For the sixteen-year-old Vincent, suddenly to encounter great canvases like Rembrandt's *Anatomy Lesson*, the magnificent Rubens portraits and works by Jan Bruegel and Holbein ought to have made that visit one of the most memorable experiences of his life. But if it was, he remained untypically reticent about it. Only two works from the Mauritshuis were ever singled out for affectionate recollection: the *View of Haarlem with Bleaching Fields* by Jacob van Ruisdael and Vermeer's *View of Delft*, both the sort of Dutch landscape much admired by the Hague School and easily within the scope of the art that was already familiar to him. Not unexpectedly he liked what he knew, and was initially resistant to the commanding portraits and sensuous nudes of 'high' art. But it is also true that even when he had learned to understand and appreciate a wide range of styles and periods, he always remained faithful to his first love, the art of the Low Countries: domestic in scale, more concerned with faithfully setting down observations of the everyday world than with depicting an imaginary scene.

It was the same with the work stocked by the gallery. The leather-bound portfolios and polished cabinets stacked with engravings carefully interleaved with tissue paper offered almost every variety of contemporary work for Vincent to study. Adolphe Goupil had begun as a fine art printer, having abandoned the idea of becoming an artist himself, and the engraving and printing shop in the Rue Chaptal in Paris turned out an impressive range of work. Goupil's policy was to follow the taste set by the annual Salon, signing up the medal winners and quickly getting their award pieces engraved and printed. Selling original art was a fairly recent development; for the most part it was the wide selection of prints that drew customers to the galleries. Adolphe Goupil's daughter Marie had married Jean-Léon Gérôme, the hugely successful painter of episodes from antiquity like *The Death of Caesar* and of scenes of Arabian life, which were immensely popular at the time. With their carefully worked out design and high degree of finish Gérôme's canvases were the polar opposite of the more rough-hewn nature painting Vincent had learned to admire. But it was Gérôme who gave the elder Goupil his entrée into the studios of France's leading artists, the sort of men whose work tended to dominate the Salon and end up in the cabinets and portfolios of the gallery.

All this Vincent found easy to ignore. It was the other French art, the kind Uncle Cent promoted, the art of Barbizon, that he searched out. The problem was that as the works were only copies it was sometimes hard to capture the full flavour of the original. There was also the creeping doubt that the whole of this school of art was merely one vast, indivisible, underpopulated landscape: lift away one sheet and there was another almost identical, here a scene of cattle drinking by a pond, there a clearing on the edge of a wood. One man alone stood out from all this sameness: Jean-François Millet. As soon as Vincent discovered Goupil's copies of Millet's work he knew that this was the type of art to which his own inner vision could respond. As Millet's *The Gleaners* had been the sensation of the 1857 Salon Goupil's were perfectly happy to handle it and from the moment Vincent discovered a copy, it became an icon in his mental gallery of inspirational works. It was not so much the surface beauty of the work that impressed him, rather it was what he could interpret from it. Drawing on his own experience of country life, Vincent could see that Millet was offering far more than a charming vignette of women at work in the fields. The three women bending to pick the scraps of corn at their feet were no ordinary peasants

– those were the villagers in the background bringing in the main harvest – what Millet had concentrated on were, in effect, outcasts. As Vincent knew, gleaners were poor scavengers allowed on to the fields to pick a meagre living from the scraps left scattered after the harvesting was done. Vincent was by then accustomed to an art which celebrated the sanctity of labour, which proclaimed that peasant life was dignified and honourable, but *The Gleaners* went far beyond such elementary pieties. Millet seemed to be making a radical, political statement. It is important to keep in mind, however, that what Vincent had in front of him was a stark black-and-white print; had he seen the original painting the impact might have been, if not dampened, at least modified. With the added glow of colour and light, Millet's figures have many of the qualities of an altarpiece. In colour, his Gleaners are timeless and sanctified, their toil holy. But in the engraving they have all the force of a political cartoon, of an act of propaganda. And it was the engraving that Vincent knew.

The engravings Goupil handled were in differing degrees 'distant' from the originals and were made by professional engravers of varying ability. One of the best of the Millets was *Les Travaux des Champs* (*Field Work*), a single sheet with ten scenes of country labour – wood cutting, sheep shearing, spinning. But others, such as the print of *The Angelus* – the two peasants standing in their field, heads bowed in prayer – gave little more than a rough impression of the subtleties of Millet's masterpiece.

This distortion applied to other work Vincent discovered in those early years. The northern French artist Jules Breton had also had a success at the 1857 Salon with a large canvas, *Blessing the Cornfields in Artois*, which showed an open-air religious procession on the outskirts of a small village. Again, had he seen the original, Vincent would have realised that Breton was less forceful and even more sentimental than Millet, but, as before, he had only a stark monochrome image to go by. Even so it was clear that Breton in *Blessing the Cornfields* was more concerned about details of costume and ritual than the lives of the peasants who simply knelt, backs to the spectator, while the host was borne across their fields. There are no outcast gleaners in Breton's painting, presumably they will arrive later then the priest has passed by. Breton has been rather sharply disparaged as 'Millet's mild-mannered understudy', but Vincent never saw him as such. The simple faith portrayed in a work like *Blessing the Cornfields* was enough to earn him a place in Vincent's growing pantheon of admired artists, and there was always the obvious connection between Breton's line of figures and that other procession in his father's Van der Maaten engraving to enhance its virtues.

It was gradually becoming clear to Vincent that there was more to art than mere skill in setting down the observed world. Though he never strayed far from his early love for an art based on reality, he was to learn by degrees that much more could be done within the constraints imposed by the faithful observation of nature. His excitement at such discoveries was clear to his colleagues and, when his limited finances permitted, he would buy a print that particularly intrigued him. This was not yet the serious, professional collecting it was to become. It was rather the hobby of a passionate amateur struck by something unusual which he could use to brighten up his room.

For the moment Vincent knew little about French contemporary art other than the evidence of the prints. Only as time went by did he begin to learn something about the artists themselves. His experience of 'real' painters was confined to the local artists he met through the gallery. Goupil's was their main meeting-place: they called in to hand over work, discuss sales or just keep up with what the others were doing. To meet and talk with painters was a major incentive for the young employees, all of whom had been taken on because of their interest in art. The Hague artists were a dapper lot, smartly turned out in town suits, more like gentlemen on a sketching holiday than the rather self-consciously 'earthy' painters of Barbizon in their baggy peasant trousers and straw hats. The Hague School had a professional air: no French eccentricities and certainly no French morals: good husbands and family men. Vincent got to know each in turn as they settled in the town. He liked them and had no reason to think that their behaviour was anything other than apt for an artist.

The first to arrive, shortly after Vincent himself, was Jozef Israëls. He had recently married and, with two children to bring up, felt that his footloose days had come to an end. Although he would make painting expeditions when the children were a little older, he now made The Hague his permanent base. Although only forty-seven when Vincent first met him, his small frame, hunched shoulders and grizzled beard, along with his way of peering forward through tiny metal-framed spectacles, made him seem much older, more like the Talmudic scholar he had once wanted to be. Before he took up art, Israëls had considered becoming a rabbi, a route not unlike Vincent's own future path.

Israëls was already famous when they met. He had originally made his name as a history painter but a visit to Millet in Barbizon had converted him to the new art. After that experience he had lived in the Dutch fishing village of Zandvoort, where he painted simple incidents in the lives of the fisherfolk much as Millet had done with his peasants. What distinguished Israëls was the theatrical nature of his lighting, clearly derived from Rembrandt – a fisherman lights his pipe by the fireplace while his wife spoons food into their baby's mouth, a peasant woman makes pancakes for her watching children, both treated like scenes in a drama. Occasionally real drama intervened. After he saw the village turn out to try to save the victims of a shipwreck, Israëls' work took on the force of a Millet. Indeed, for Vincent he was a stand-in for the absent Frenchman – Israëls was Millet with colour. Sadly, Israëls' use of bitumen has meant that many of his works have darkened beyond redemption so that we can no longer share Vincent's pleasure in the evidence of the older man's skill.

To use the critical terms of the day, Israëls was a 'luminist' rather than a 'colourist'. He was also credited during his lifetime with founding the Hague School, though in retrospect we can see that his Old Testament qualities put him nearer to his mentor Millet than the more straightforward nature painting The Hague stood for. He was, however, the most successful of all the local artists Goupil handled, with a considerable foreign reputation and wealthy patrons. He bought a large French-style town house and a summer residence at Scheveningen. In town, his studio was a substantial carpeted and furnished drawing-room in which, somewhat incongruously, the master would sit in jacket and bow-tie dabbing at a canvas. But despite such worldly success there was much for Vincent to identify with: Israëls, too, was a somewhat awkward, nervous man who loved to take solitary walks at sunset along the sands near his beach house. He was in the habit of making rapid working sketches of details that he could use later – in no sense finished drawings, merely rough outlines or graphic notes – and this became a practice Vincent took up while in The Hague. There was no thought of creating art, they were simply *aide-mémoire* often scribbled in the margins of his letters. Vincent made a sketch of the path beside the lake near the gallery and drew a nearby canal; little more than doodles with far less 'finish' than the shaded drawings of his childhood. But surrounded by art and artists as he was, it is not surprising that he should have wanted to try his hand at drawing, though that was as far as it went. In nothing he said or wrote at the time was there any indication, however slight, that he considered becoming an artist himself.

At the end of summer 1870 Vincent was introduced to an attractive man whose upright bearing gave him something of a military air, at odds with his rather straggly beard. Vincent was impressed from the first and of all the new arrivals the 32-year-old Anton Mauve came closest to being an intimate friend. He already knew Mauve's work, which was nearest to the popular notion of Hague School art. Mauve spent most of his time painting the beaches near Scheveningen or working in the surrounding woods; there was a scene showing a group of peasants labouring in the fields near the dunes, that embodied all the elements the school was thought to stand for. While Mauve displayed few of the religious overtones of Millet and Israëls, he did approach that ideal of capturing the immediacy of nature, those momentary effects of changing light hastily set down with rapid, even rough, brushwork. In this Mauve was coming close to developments in painting that were even then superseding Barbizon in France, and for Vincent he was to act as a bridge between the sort of work he had grown up with in Holland and the new art he would later discover in Paris.

Unlike the diffident Israëls, Mauve was a strong-willed man and it was little wonder that Vincent was drawn to him as to an experienced elder brother. Where Vincent was gauche and awkward, Mauve appeared self-assured and worldly. But it was not always an easy relationship. Mauve's self-confidence bordered on arrogance, and there is a telling self-portrait in which disdainful eyes and a rather haughty tilt to the head bespeak a side to his character that brooked no disagreement. He was one of those people who pride themselves on never dissembling, who adopt a blunt plain-spokenness that often borders on insensitivity. But to the insecure Vincent this seemed yet another sign of Mauve's maturity.

Soon after his arrival Mauve was introduced to Aunt Fie and became a regular visitor. It quickly became apparent that he was much taken with one of her daughters, Vincent's cousin Jet, and she with him. Before long he and Vincent were going round to the house together. But as Vincent came to know Mauve better he learned that they had something else in common – Mauve too suffered acute and inexplicable bouts of melancholia. Mauve's first attack in The Hague was frightening; he was so crippled by it, his friends had to rally round to watch over him in case he did himself harm. So, if Mauve was sometimes sharp and irritable, Vincent could well understand and forgive. In any case, he had so much to learn from the older man. Mauve had travelled and his forthright ideas about art made many things far clearer.

It was about the time of Mauve's arrival that Vincent began to hear a great deal of nervous talk in The Hague's artistic circles about the disturbing news from France. As much of their business passed between the Goupil branches it was to be expected that anything likely to affect the French art trade would also affect the local artists. France and Germany were engaged in what seemed to most onlookers an incomprehensible quarrel supposedly over the succession to the Spanish throne. The better informed knew that in reality it was a power struggle in which the ultimately successful Bismarck sought to curb the impetuous French Emperor. The first word that the matter was serious came from one of the Goupil galleries in the Boulevard Montmartre. The Boulevard and the surrounding streets had been the scene of a huge, raucous demonstration in favour of war. So powerful was the image of France and of Napoleon III in the eyes of the Dutch that when war did break out the general feeling was that the French would win. There was stunned disbelief at the first reports that an inadequately prepared French army had suddenly surrendered at somewhere called Sedan. Worse followed when a few days into September word arrived that Napoleon III himself had been taken prisoner by the victorious Prussians. Even the relatively isolated artists' colony in The Hague shared in the dismay of all those who looked to Paris as the cultural capital of Europe. The world they had known seemed to have fallen apart in a matter of weeks and many had friends in what was now a beleaguered city.

As the year ended things grew worse. The citizens of Paris, disgusted with the peace terms and desperate to create some semblance of order in the midst of national collapse, set themselves up as an independent Commune on the lines of the Swiss cantons. Despite its subsequent glorification as the cradle of world socialism, the Commune had little clear idea of what it should do. It was riven with dissent from the beginning and, when it rather hot-headedly decided to hold out against the provisional government in nearby Versailles, it was, predictably, doomed. Not that this was at all clear to observers far away from the battle, dependent as they were on inadequate and infrequent despatches. That the citizens of Paris had continued to hold out and that they were reduced to near-starvation, eating rats and other vermin, filtered through, but it was only some time after the denouement that news arrived of the appalling events of 'Bloody Week' in the last days of May 1871, when Marshal Mac-Mahon's troops had apparently massacred the last of the Communards, some in the Père-Lachaise cemetery, others on the slopes of Montmartre. Whatever the truth behind these reports, they arrived with the glow of legend and, whatever they may have been in reality, the dead Communards were now slaughtered heroes.

For the young Vincent it was the most important political event of his life so far; he would later add to his personal collection an engraving of the women of Paris marching to the defence of the Commune. Until then he had known only the unruffled calm of Dutch political life,

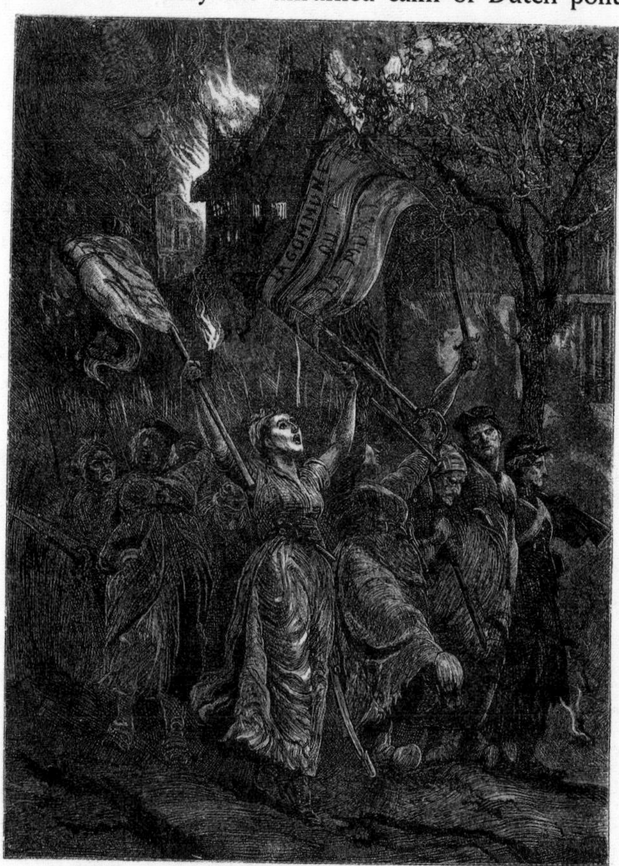

The Commune or Death: Women of Montmartre,
Boyd Houghton, *The Graphic*, 1871.

now for the first time he had caught a distant glimpse of violence and death.

Although the newly proclaimed Third Republic moved quickly to restore some semblance of normality to the French capital, the immediate aftermath of the collapse was that many foreigners fled the crippled city. The Dutch painter Jacob Maris would probably have stayed in France but for these recent events. With his comfortable, well-fed figure and long hair curling over his collar he resembled the popular image of a Parisian man of culture, a being fit to discourse on art and life at a boulevard café table. But clearly enough was enough. No one knew what might happen next and as everyone else seemed to be doing so, it was best to return home.

Jacob had two brothers, also painters, though each very different. Willem, the youngest, was the most 'Hague' in style. He painted the local landscape and had a passion for portraying the rather lugubrious Friesian cattle found on nearby farms. The middle brother Thijs was the most unusual and in many ways the most fascinating. From the start his work veered away from reality into a world of fantasy with haunted castles and mysterious veiled women. He eventually moved to London, where he drifted into obscurity, a rather sad, lonely figure, ahead of his time and not easy to place in any conventional category. Only very recently have there been some signs that he is beginning to achieve a new cult status.

It was the eldest brother Jacob who on his return had most direct contact with Vincent. His paintings showed the same commitment found in Israëls – studies of a tired fisherwoman resting in the dunes, a child begging from door to door – and not surprisingly the shadowy presence of Millet could again be discerned in the background. Jacob of course had up-to-date news of the master: despite the nearness of Barbizon to Paris, Millet had refused to lend his support to the Commune; he was never a man easy to categorise and had seen little reason to embroil himself in other people's politics. Then in his late fifties, he preferred to stay close to those he painted. Barbizon was barely a village, more a hamlet of whitewashed houses strung along a single road. Millet had rented one and a sympathetic landlord had built a studio near by. Although this was far from the city-dweller's ideal of genteel country living, it was hardly the life of extreme poverty that myth made it. Millet had a comfortable income and a housekeeper to look after him. With his stocky build and full beard he looked like a labourer, but if he chose to go out painting in wooden clogs and a high straw hat it was more because they were comfortable and made it easier to move unobtrusively among the workers he wanted to paint than from any necessity to live like a peasant. But in a world in search of heroes it was inevitable that Millet would find himself mythologised as a simple peasant painting his own kind, and that was the legend which found its way into Vincent's image of the great man. Millet became not only a painter to be admired but also a prophet to be followed.

Although he made no show of it at the time, we know from his later actions that Vincent had a deep and instinctive sympathy for the poor and the unfortunate. It might have been expected that after a profoundly religious upbringing he would have reacted against his father's faith. On the contrary, despite long hours at the gallery, he would go for private Bible lessons with a teacher called Hille in the Bagijnestraat not far from the Plaats. He struggled hard with these studies, which were entirely voluntary and which he believed to be very important to him. Little wonder that Millet's commitment and the stories of his simple, dedicated life had a profound effect on the young man's thinking. He was not discontented, he believed he had found an ideal career, the artists he had met liked him and invited him round to their studios, but he was in some ways distant, a naturally isolated person, studious and religious without making much outward show of it. His main love was still reading and for this The Hague was an ideal centre. As the base for the diplomatic corps it had bookshops which were well supplied with the latest works from London and Paris. Although Mr Tersteeg had left the book trade he was still devoted to literature and whenever Vincent visited the apartment above the gallery there was talk of this or that new work. Vincent was soon friendly with the Van Stockum family who were booksellers and was invited to literary gatherings and all this, along with his facility for languages, meant that he was soon embarked on a lifelong passion for French poetry and history and whatever new English novels he could find. As with painting, while his taste was broad it had clearly defined limits. From the start he showed a preference for books that dealt with ordinary life, but which drew from it a clear moral lesson; not surprisingly he would become devoted to Dickens and George Eliot. He also searched for any work that made reference to art: poems based on paintings, or an author who would draw a lesson from an old master. He read constantly and was forever recommending books and passing them on with enthusiastic comments to family and friends. A love of art and a love of books often go together, but seldom to the extent found in Vincent. Many artists consider themselves practical men rather than thinkers, but, as in much else, Vincent was utterly different and from the start he struggled to bring together his two loves, to find paintings that illuminated what he had read and books that explained what he had seen.

Admirable though this was, it made him an odd companion for less intellectual folk; poor Willem Valkes must have found him hard going at times. Vincent was very perceptive about things he read but less so about real situations. He would be at Aunt Fie's while Mauve courted his cousin yet he drew no lessons from it; he would happily read love poems and tales of youthful romance but he was happier with older people where the conversation was all about art or books, and seemed unwilling or unable to attempt the sort of small-talk at which Mauve was so fluent.

Not that he was unhappy. When he celebrated his eighteenth birthday in March 1871 he could look back on two full and expanding years of new people and new thoughts. Whatever else it might be, he had learned that art mattered, it was at the centre of things. After all, the artists he knew were social lions, they had no sooner settled in the town than they began to dominate the activities of the Pulchri Studio, The Hague's main cultural organisation. Founded in 1847, the Studio was partly an exhibition space and partly a social club. Most local artists joined. Van der Maaten had been a member in his Hague days and there is a rather stilted group photograph taken at the time in which many of the members sport black stove-pipe hats as if they were the originals for the comic mourners in the funeral procession. The studio was well funded and eventually built itself a large gallery in the Prinsegracht. By contrast the Hague Academy in the Prinsesgracht, with its classical portico and halls of antique casts, was thought to be out of touch. The new Pulchri Studio, in the fashionable arts-and-crafts style, combined the atmosphere of a Dutch farmhouse, a delft rack and craft pottery, with the air of a gentleman's club with its wood panelling and leather armchairs. Soon its annual secretary would be drawn from amongst the Hague School painters who gradually dominated its activities. The social nature of the club can be seen in the menus for its *soupers* – substantial banquets rambling through ten or so courses, sometimes in the gallery, sometimes in one of the better hotels. On the more serious side there were discussions and debates about issues in the arts, occasionally attended by Queen Sophie. At the grander openings medals would be worn.

That this was an odd way of behaving on the part of those dedicated to painting the hard toil of the peasantry must have been obvious to the young Vincent. But then there were many contradictions he was having to face. Despite his placid exterior, he was ultimately no different from any other teenager plagued with conflicting emotions and unsure where to look for answers. There is a last surviving portrait photograph of him taken at nineteen. He appears podgy and gauche. As a typical young clerk he is smartly turned out in a dark suit and tie, though as usual he has not been able to do much with his hair. Even allowing for the distortions of formal photography he looks distinctly uneasy, as if that other Vincent, the moody, ill-tempered youth of the Zundert days, had reappeared. One day, a friend found him sitting by the fire in Goupil's, rhythmically tearing the pages from a book and tossing them into the flames. He approached Vincent and saw that the book was a Christian tract. It emerged that it had been a present from Pastor Theodorus, but the rage that had caused Vincent to destroy it was never explained.

He certainly had not quarrelled with his father, at least not in any significant way. He went home whenever he could. Earlier that year the family had moved to Helvoirt, another minor parish not far from Zundert and certainly no more important, except that the stipend was slightly better. Dorus and Anna needed the extra money now that the other children were approaching school age. Anna, sixteen, was at boarding-school in Leeuwarden studying languages. Theo, fourteen, attended a day school in Oisterwijk a fair walk away, while Elisabeth, twelve, and Willemina, nine, were still being educated in the village. Little Cornelis, four, would not start his education for some time. There was also the impending problem of the three boys' military service. It was usual for middle-class families to buy their sons out but the cost was considerable. In the end all these expenses put too much strain on the pastor's income from Helvoirt and four years later he was obliged to move to yet another small parish which could offer slightly better remuneration. It was a far from satisfactory state of affairs though the couple were relieved that Vincent at least had settled down and were happy when they received glowing reports of his life and work from Aunt Fie and Mr Tersteeg.

What most pleased Tersteeg and his fellow directors was Vincent's personal commitment to art. It obviously meant much more to him than a mere job. He went of his own volition to Amsterdam to see the main national collections and, though it was no great distance and he had Uncle Cor or Uncle Jan to stay with, it nevertheless showed enthusiasm.

Today's Rijksmuseum was still at the planning stage and the national collection was kept in the Trippenhuis, a building dignified with an unusual classical façade which served to disguise the fact that it was only a large town house. Vincent's first reaction was anger at how crowded the works were. A painting of the gallery's interior by August Jernberg shows Rembrandt's *Night Watch* occupying an entire wall of a room dimly lit by a single window. In another drawing, Rembrandt's group portrait of *The Syndics of the Drapers' Guild* is almost lost under the clutter of surrounding portraits. Worse than the dismal hanging was the necessity to rotate the works on display so that at any time only a fraction of the collection was on view and in the end it was to take many visits over a number of years before Vincent had seen all the masterpieces he had heard about.

In July 1872, four months after his nineteenth birthday, he made his first foreign journey, to Belgium, again at his own instigation. Of course there was Uncle Hein to stay with, but it was still an adventure. The Belgian capital was very different from the unchanging cities of Holland; its centre was being transformed under the influence of the rebuilt Paris of the Second Empire though its outskirts were pockmarked with industrial suburbs and slums. The whole ethos of industrial Belgium was different from anything Vincent had encountered before, yet despite the bleak pockets of industry he passed on his journey, especially the ring of smoking factories and filthy dwellings as the train entered Brussels, he was immediately drawn to the country.

The main reason for his visit was the annual Belgian Salon. Although this could hardly compare with the much bigger Paris Salon, it still attracted a breathtaking body of work, room after room crammed with pictures from every conceivable school. Pompous history paintings of Romans, Greeks or medieval knights vied with society ladies portrayed in their silks and jewels. As a survey of official taste it was a fascinating experience but there were always worthwhile works amongst the acres of dross: Brussels was slightly more liberal than Paris and that year's show included three Manets and a Monet. The Hague was represented by a landscape by Jan Weissenbruch, another of Vincent's acquaintances, though he was probably more intrigued by that 'other' art, Henry Picou's *One Night of Cleopatra* or his *Greek Women Bathing*. It was the sort of thing Vincent had been shielded from till then and he was no doubt utterly bemused by its doubtful combination of simplistic morality and thinly veiled eroticism. Having been brought up on some of the best contemporary work it was fascinating to see the worst. He even crammed in a visit to the Museum of Contemporary Belgian Painters at the Palais Ducal, a collection of largely forgotten history paintings on local themes. Not that their secondary status would have disappointed him. He always found something worthwhile in even the most feeble work, picking out a detail worth remembering, a woman's pious expression, the colour of a doorway. He looked upon art as a cornucopia to be marvelled at and his attitude throughout his life remained catholic and celebratory rather than exclusive and judgemental.

Vincent's enthusiasm was not lost on his employers and Uncle Cent must have felt completely vindicated in having promoted his nephew. There seemed no reason why Vincent should not progress through the firm until he occupied a senior role, and already discussions had been opened as to how best his experience could be widened. The Hague could only be a first step; he would have to have first-hand experience of Goupil's other operations. At the same time there was Theo to consider. He was now fifteen and would finish school the following year. As he too had had the benefit of hearing Uncle Cent expound on art and art dealing he now wished to follow his elder brother into the business. Given Vincent's success, Goupil's were happy to concur and the family decided that it might be useful for him to visit Vincent in The Hague during the summer holidays. Though the two boys had always been close, that August of 1872 brought them together as never before; the age difference seemed completely immaterial now that they had the prospect of a joint career to talk over. There were differences of course – where Vincent had put on weight and was rather stocky like their father, Theo had taken on the same skeletal frame and narrow, pointed face as Uncle Cent. And while Theo tended to be calm and thoughtful, Vincent had his passions and enthusiasms followed by sudden plunges into moodiness and silence. But such things hardly bothered them and just as they had done so often at Zundert, the two young men spent much time on long walks and at some point they seem to have entered into a pact of mutual loyalty, vowing that no matter what might happen in the future they would always stand by each other. No doubt they both believed it would be Vincent the elder brother who would help and guide the younger. Indeed, as soon as Theo returned to Helvoirt, Vincent took the initiative. He wrote Theo a letter. It was only a short note but a crucial step, for it was through their letters to one another that this extraordinarily profound relationship would be fostered. At first their letters were short and few and far between, but gradually they grew, not only in frequency and length, but in the closeness of what they discussed – details of things seen and done, books read and analysed, paintings studied and explained. But more than that, there was to be an astonishing revelation of personal thoughts, doubts, beliefs, vividly put down just as Vincent experienced them, for sadly we only know what Vincent himself wrote, as Theo alone kept the letters he received. Some 670 have survived and, though some are lost, what we have amounts to one of the most telling records of an artist's working process in the whole history of Western culture. It has been well said that uniquely in the story of art we can know precisely where Vincent van Gogh was on a daily basis, almost from hour to hour, and what is even more astonishing is that we know exactly what he was thinking. Just occasionally Vincent falls silent or avoids certain experiences but in their own way these unrecorded moments are equally revealing.

Vincent's letters to Theo began in 1872. It was a slow start, consisting of little more than brief notes and good wishes. The following January, Theo went as an apprentice to the Brussels branch of Goupil, a major move from the home where he had been as cosseted as Vincent and obviously a cause for concern among the family. Although Uncle Hein was there, he too had periods of ill-health which meant that he could not play his full part as guardian of the young man's well-being. Vincent was very solicitous in those early letters, keen to cheer up his brother, all too aware of how lonely he must be now that he was away from home for the first time.

> *Don't lose heart if it is very difficult at times; everything will turn out all right. Nobody can do as he wishes at the beginning.*

It is all too easy to see Vincent as a rather moody and irritable person and to overlook the fact that this was often a mask. Those first letters to Theo reveal the other, sensitive Vincent acutely aware of his brother's need for affection and advice. The correspondence is soon full of their mutual business. Can Theo find the *Album Corot* for him? Has he seen a certain picture by Cluysenaar? Theo soon joined him as a collector of prints by Millet, Israëls and the others, his taste clearly led by his predecessor in the business. But more often the letters are simply the encouragement of an elder to a younger brother. Only as time goes by and they feel increasingly at ease with each other do more intimate revelations appear. Just before his twentieth birthday in March 1873, Vincent wrote to say that he was to be posted to the London branch of Goupil and although he was looking forward to the adventure he also made it clear that he was worried about the inevitable strangeness and loneliness he would experience. The letter ended with a touching postscript urging Theo to take up pipe smoking as a remedy for depression.

Vincent had just been to Amsterdam again, this time to see the exhibition of paintings that would later be displayed in the Dutch pavilion at that year's International Exhibition in Vienna. As a mammoth display of industry and technology the Vienna exhibition was one of the major events of the decade. All the European nations had displays of art and manufacture and there were other large-scale entries from Brazil, Japan and Egypt. Most were competing to offer their latest products and processes, but alongisde the heavy machinery and the household gadgets were the cultural showcases of the participating countries, intended to attract the ordinary visitor who might be less interested in water pumps and mining gear. The exhibition in Amsterdam, prior to its departure for Austria, was one of the largest assemblies of Dutch Old Masters ever attempted. The subsequent catalogue for the Vienna exhibition speaks of a Rembrandt Room, a Van Dyck Room, a Rubens Room, a Teniers Room. Between these celebrity salons were other works by Salomon van Ruysdael, Hobbema, Jordaens, and Jan Bruegel. Much of the work came from private collections and was accessible to the public for the first time in years, hence Vincent's keenness to see the exhibition before it left for the Austrian capital.

It was of course this enthusiasm which had convinced his employers to send him to England. The post in London meant promotion and though he was clearly worried about the strangeness of it all, he was also pleased with the compliment and excited at the prospect. If Brussels had been fascinating with its evidence of the new industrial Europe then how much more so must London be. Naturally he was sorry to leave The Hague. He had had four splendid years and had made good friends in Tersteeg and Mauve. He also felt part of the artistic community which had grown up during his time there. A few days before he left he went round to Jan Weissenbruch's studio to see his latest work and say goodbye. It was a mark of Vincent's closeness to the life of the Hague School that the 49-year-old Weissenbruch should have been happy to spend time showing the twenty-year-old art dealer his studies and sketches.

Vincent was sent to London via Paris so that he could see for himself the workings of the main Goupil branches. There were now three premises in Paris, all quite close to each other: the original gallery in the Boulevard Montmartre which showed newer work like Uncle Cent's group, the main gallery in the Place de L'Opéra and, a short walk away, the engraving and printing works, with apartments on the upper floors, in the Rue Chaptal. Adolphe Goupil, the founder, was still nominally in charge but effective control of the company was already passing into the hands of his long-time associate Léon Boussod, and Boussod's son-in-law René Valadon. Although this was only a brief visit, Vincent still saw evidence of the events that had so gripped The Hague, the ruined column in the Place Vendôme and the burned-out shell of the Tuileries, alarming reminders of the violence that had engulfed the French capital only two years earlier. Yet despite the violence of the last days of the Commune and the persecution that followed, Paris had quickly re-established its role as the cultural capital of Europe and Vincent spent hectic days cramming in visits to the Louvre, the Luxembourg (then with its own public collection) and the Salon which had opened earlier that month. Despite all the glories of the Louvre it was the collection in the Luxembourg which provoked his strongest reactions. The palace then housed a huge assemblage of contemporary art; in a few years' time it would be broken up and scattered among various national and provincial museums but Vincent had the good fortune to visit the collection when it was at its height. Much of the work was the kind of historical, classical and religious art favoured by the previous regime. Its *chef-d'oeuvre* was Thomas Couture's *The Romans of the Decadence*, a canvas on the scale of a mural which offered a flamboyant, though tasteful, orgy whose participants, in order to make a moral point, look distinctly bored. But for Vincent the most important thing was the chance to see original works by Breton. The Luxembourg had three major canvases: *Blessing the Cornfields in Artois*, *The Recall of the Gleaners* which showed a party of field workers carrying home their sheaves in a rich twilight glow and *Evening*, where a barefoot woman rests from her labours at the end of the day. Of course it was *Blessing the Cornfields in Artois* that he most wanted to see after years of studying it in black and white. He was not disappointed; the scale of the work, although less than Couture's orgy, was still impressive and the rich colour and the fine detail in the costumes surpassed what Vincent had imagined.

Breton was to dominate that first short stay in Paris, for when Vincent managed to get into the crowded Salon he discovered that his idol was that year's main prize winner. While the Louvre and the Luxembourg ought to have been enough to overwhelm him, the Palais des Champs-Elysées that housed the Salon was crammed with well over two thousand canvases, not counting an extra hall for that year's monuments. This was nearly double the Brussels entry but as before the majority of those singled out for awards were hardly memorable: Etienne-Berne Bellcour, Paul-Joseph Blanc, Jean-Paul Laurens, Jules Machard. Even Vincent with his limited knowledge of French art must have guessed that such works were not what truly mattered. Happily, the *Grande Médaille d'Honneur* had gone to Breton for a portrait of a girl wearing the traditional dress of Brittany. As Sunday was the free day Vincent could see how immensely popular the work was with the laughing, disrespectful Parisian mob who invested the galleries, turning the event into a fun-fair. Until then the artists he knew had been part of a closed circle, patronised by the elect of the upper strata of Dutch society, here for the first time in his experience was a man whose work spoke to thousands.

He left for London in mid-May, twenty years old, excited at the new life ahead and afraid of being homesick. He had much to think over on the long journey by boat and train, before his carriage rattled into the recently completed Victoria Station – confused ideas about life and art, an inchoate mix of religious beliefs and concerns about the poor. Only one thing was certain in all this, his life as an art dealer was now mapped out, for this new post in London was definitely a step up and when he returned to Paris it would surely be in a more senior position. But first there was the thrill of arriving in the industrial capital of the world. Paris breathed culture, but the sprawling metropolis that he could see from the carriage window stood for commerce, invention, that ill-named, ill-defined, self-propelling force called progress. Later he would see it through the eyes of Doré, whose engravings of the dark side of London were published that year, the best known of which shows a tightly packed terrace below a railway arch, its inhabitants little more than tiny insignificant ants trapped in a grimy fog-bound slum. This was the London of child labour and child prostitution, of homelessness and hunger, yet, at the moment that Doré recorded it, it was beginning to pass into history. Vincent arrived at a time when that dank, unplanned, festering sprawl was being transformed into an imperial capital. The evidence was everywhere apparent even on his walk from Victoria to Goupil's offices in Southampton Street. The recently opened Embankment had been built out into the Thames and along it stood bright new government buildings. Further on, mammoth construction work was carving out the Strand from the narrow streets that had formerly led up to the City. Ignoring the feats of engineering, the most extraordinary thing to Vincent was the unexpected taste for Gothic – the Houses of Parliament were his first spectacular encounter with what seemed to him a curious passion for the fantastical. Nor was it confined to grand public buildings, for when he arrived at the house Goupil's had arranged for him to lodge in, it too was Gothic. He omits to say where it was, but as he could walk to work it was probably the newly completed estate just north of Battersea Rise across the river from Chelsea. This was as far removed from the squalor of Doré's London as it was possible to get. Vincent happily recorded that his new home, along with its neighbours, had a garden with flowers and trees. He was much taken with the city's parks and open spaces. And whatever his fears may have been, they were soon dispersed when he learned that London was far more amusing than he had expected – his two landladies even kept a parrot. And he was not as lonely as he had anticipated, for he had three young Germans as fellow lodgers. At first he went about with them but they were better off than he was and he decided to forgo their company to save money. Goupil's were to pay him ninety pounds a year, not a bad salary but no fortune, and London was much more expensive than The Hague.

That aside, he was to pass one of the happiest years of his life. The work was satisfying; he had been sent to London as part of a planned expansion in the company's business. Until then, the London branch of Goupil's had merely acted as a wholesaler, supplying prints to other businesses. Now the idea was to open a gallery similar to the branches in France, Belgium, Holland and Germany. The manager, Mr Obach, was already looking for premises and within a month of Vincent's starting work the first batch of original paintings and drawings had arrived from France. As it was mainly clerical, the work was a little run-of-the-mill after the face-to-face contact with artists and public that Vincent had enjoyed in The Hague but at least he knew that it was only temporary. In any case he had first to improve his English and it was much easier to do that when working on letters and ledgers than while trying to handle clients. His progress was remarkable; within a month he wrote to Theo to say that he was reading Keats. Once confident in the language he was again put in charge of the *Galerie Photographique*, as at The Hague one of the biggest selling divisions. It was his first contact with the masters of English art, including Gainsborough, Reynolds and Turner, but they do not appear to have greatly impressed him. He was more taken with the occasional contemporary work handled by the gallery, such as John Everett Millais' *The Huguenot* and George Henry Boughton's *Puritans Going to Church*. He admired their religious sentiments. While he continued to have an insatiable appetite for all sorts of art his judgements still tended to be influenced by what might be called the 'Goupil Test': if his company dealt with it, then that was some sort of imprimatur. As the London branch specialised in the same French, Dutch and Belgian works as The Hague and Paris, it was still to those painters that he deferred.

A visit to the recently completed Burlington House in Piccadilly for the 1873 Royal Academy Summer Exhibition did nothing to predispose him to the English native talent. With only one and a half thousand entries this London 'salon' was a mere shadow of its European counterparts, as were most of the works. For someone so rarely critical Vincent was quite sharp in his description of what he saw. He singled out a work of historical fantasy, Poynter's *Fight between More of More Hall and the Dragon of Wantley* as being *awful*, one of the most damaging things he ever wrote about a painter's work.

During his stay in London he remained immured within the artistic confines of Goupil's, unaware of such as James McNeill Whistler and of the battles raging within the various artistic groups in England. He was untouched by the burgeoning interest in Japanese art, and did not become intimate, as he had in The Hague, with any of the artists the gallery handled. In retrospect it seems just as well. Had he discovered the 'impressionism' of Whistler's Thames nocturnes or learned about the Aesthetic Movement it could well have been a case of too much too soon. As it was, he hovered on the fringe of London's art world, unaware of its movements and conflicts. He continued to absorb whatever came his way, but only from the narrow range of Goupil's art. He visited the major collections but made little mention of them, and he studiously avoided the usual sights like Madame Tussaud's or the Tower of London. In any case, he had by then far more on his mind than English art. He had fallen in love.

It may seem unfair to summon up the faded photograph of Eugénie Loyer and to wonder how this painfully thin, sad-eyed creature with her indrawn lips and lank ringlets could have so bowled over the young Vincent. In reality she may have been a young flower, a delicate beauty. But even if one doubts it, it hardly matters. Vincent clearly found her so.

Eugénie was the daughter of his new landlady, Mrs Ursula Loyer. Concerned to keep down his expenses, he had moved to cheaper lodgings at 87 Hackford Road, Brixton, a short walk from the Oval. The street was one of the new rows of terraced houses running off the main roads leading south from the river Thames. Some were quite grand, like the four-storey houses along Brixton's Angell Road, built for well-off tradespeople. Humbler clerks could occupy the smaller houses in narrower streets like Hackford Road. Happily for Vincent, no. 87 was one of a group of survivors from a former age, square, white-painted, early Victorian houses in the late Georgian style a little larger than their newer neighbours. He described it enthusiastically to Theo, evoking memories of their cramped bedroom in Zundert:

> *I now have a room such as I always longed for, without a slanting ceiling and without blue paper with a green border. I live with a very amusing family now; they keep a school for little boys.*

The room contained the usual Victorian clutter; a heavy-oil lamp suspended from the admirably level ceiling, a large table with bentwood chairs taking up most of the floor-space, and a marble wash-stand with water-jug and bowl against the wall.

The landlady, Mrs Ursula Loyer, was the widow of a Frenchman, Jean-Baptiste Loyer, who had taught languages at Stockwell School. He retired in 1859 and when he died, left her to bring up their only child Eugénie. To make ends meet, Mrs Loyer took in lodgers and did some home teaching for local children. Vincent had his evening meals with the mother and daughter, and they were sometimes joined by a previous lodger, Samuel Plowman, a young engineer. Although mother and daughter were very close they had noticeably different characters: Mrs Loyer was a gentle, easy-going woman, while Eugénie was rather strict and school-ma'amish. She did in fact become a schoolmistress later in life and there is another rather prim photograph of her that does not suggest that she had softened with age. Despite this somewhat forbidding exterior, Vincent found in Eugénie the object of all the suppressed emotions that had been welling up inside him. She was nineteen, and there was no reason why he should not have tried to woo her. But that is the oddest part of the story: he said nothing. He did not ask her to walk out with him or try to speak to her of what he felt, and it is only with hindsight that one can make any sense of his cryptic comments to his family about Eugénie and her mother:

> *I never saw or dreamed of anything like the love between her and her mother. Love her for my sake.*

> *I have splendid lodgings. Oh fullness of rich life, your gift O God.*

Being in love, he loved everything, London especially. He bought a top hat so that he could appear more English and thus, rather quaintly garbed, he would set off every morning on the three-quarters of an hour walk to work. To the young Dutchman it was a journey through a place of mysteries, past the Oval where these strange English people played all their new sports of cricket, rugby and association football; on towards the great river, thronged with shipping. The new gasometers dominated the skyline wherever he looked, there was even a cluster just below St Paul's. London was aggressively modern, and once across Westminster Bridge he was plunged into the new city he had observed on his first day. Northumberland House was being demolished to make way for the Strand, the New Post Office was going up in Saint Martin's-le-Grand, and the final stages of the new Embankment were being completed. Once at Goupil's, however, work was monotonously regular. As there were no customers the place could close at six, early hours in those days, leaving him time for a gentle stroll home, his mind filled with the pleasant anticipation of seeing Eugénie. Even as the nights closed in, and the foggy gas-lit streets made the homeward journey less agreeable, there was still the thought of Eugénie to keep him happily trudging on.

Christmas with the Loyers was made perfect when they invited him to their party. Early in the New Year he received a pay rise. Everything was wonderful, with one glaring exception: despite what he felt for Eugénie, he still said absolutely nothing to her. Of course she must have found it delightful to have such a willing attendant, ever anxious to please and to do her small services. It is not as if Vincent was completely unaware of how a courtship should be handled; he had witnessed Mauve's interest in his cousin and presumably knew that when people felt attracted to each other they found ways of showing their feelings. And even if he had failed to see what went on in the lives of others he can hardly have ignored the evidence of great art. On that first visit to the Mauritshuis he must have seen that artists did not paint only landscapes. Rembrandt's *Susanna Bathing* or Rubens' portrait of his first wife *Isabella Brandt* can hardly have failed to excite some curiosity in the young man. Rembrandt invites the spectator to join the figure in the bushes in spying on Susanna's nakedness, while Rubens asks the observer to unite with him in savouring the woman he has married. Here were two deeply sensuous paintings which must at the very least have intrigued a boy from so sheltered a background.

But if we can only guess at the effects of art on Vincent's emotional development, we can be certain how this thinking was conditioned by the books he read. At some point, possibly before he left The Hague, but certainly by the time he was settled in Brixton, he had come across the work of the French historian Jules Michelet. As the author of the magisterial *History of the French Revolution*, Michelet was an obvious candidate for Vincent's huge appetite for scholarly books. But it was not Michelet's most serious studies which first engaged Vincent's interest; he had found an odd little book, a collection of Michelet's thoughts on love, called simply *L'Amour*. It was Michelet's strangest creation, most untypical, a loose collection of thoughts on women and how a man might deal with them. Vincent realised at once that this was just the guide he had been looking for. It was partly a philosophical treatise on the nature of women and partly a manual on how men could approach the challenge. From its pages Vincent discovered that a woman was weaker than a man and ought to work less; she was an ethereal dreamer; she was an earth-mother; you thought you knew her but she remained an enigma both soulful and delicate. The book was conveniently divided into chapters with headings such as 'Pregnancy and the State of Grace'. Unsurprisingly, it is often omitted from current lists of Michelet's work and few now bother with it. But to Vincent it was a godsend. One reason for its appeal was Michelet's use of art to reinforce his message – at one point he defines his idea of femininity by recalling a painting he had seen of a woman in black

> ... who took my heart, so candid, so honest, sufficiently intelligent, yet simple, without the cunning to extricate herself from the ruses of the world. This woman has remained in my mind for thirty years, persistently coming back to me, making me say: "But what was she called? What has happened to her? Has she known some happiness? And how has she overcome the difficulties of this world?"

The portrait Michelet described was an anonymous seventeenth-century work thought then to be by Philippe de Champaigne, which Vincent sought out on a later visit to the Louvre. The woman in black was a matronly lady, presumably in mourning. This was hardly an ideal of femininity for a young man, but he had no sooner read of Michelet's obsession than it became his own. The woman in black would reappear in various manifestations throughout his life, withdrawn, grieving, mysterious.

L'Amour had now become a path through the *terra incognita* of the emotions. Vincent often quoted it at length to Theo and genuinely believed that Michelet's opinions had the force of scientifically proven fact. Thus Vincent concluded that love was a mysterious coming together of two souls, a state which simply happened – you fell in love and the other person did too, it was all so easy.

That it should have happened in England away from the stable ties of home and family is not surprising. In any case Michelet had sanctioned it: *L'Amour* described Englishwomen as "... chaste solitary dreamers, home-loving, so loyal, so staunch, so tender, an ideal spouse". And there she was, just as he had known she would be, the ideal spouse, Eugénie Loyer. There was of course no need actually to do anything for according to *L'Amour* they would simply drift together in some undefined fashion. In such a state of mind, it was small wonder that any gesture on Eugénie's part, the merest thank-you, was enough to convince him that matters were proceeding exactly as the guide had predicted.

For about nine months he was happily in love, impatient to get home in the evenings to be near her, convinced of her love for him. This state of affairs might have gone on indefinitely had not Theo written to say that Anton Mauve was now engaged to Jet Carbentus. Suddenly the illusory and the real worlds collided. With few preliminaries Vincent told Eugénie that it was time for them to get married. In the ensuing silence Vincent needed no guide to tell him that she was utterly taken aback by his words. How could that be? Surely she too was in love with him, *L'Amour* was clear on that point? But there was worse to come. When Eugénie recovered her voice she not only told him she could not marry him but went on to reveal that she was secretly engaged to Samuel, the former lodger and constant visitor. Only someone as self-obsessed as Vincent could have failed to see any hint of what had been going on. His first reaction was to refuse to accept the situation; she would have to change her mind. But as he ought to have realised, Eugénie was far from being the wilting flower described by Michelet. She was a tough young woman with a mind of her own and she let him know it.

For Vincent this was the end of everything. The swing from euphoria to silence and dejection was sickeningly fast. He continued to go to work but could barely summon up the least interest in what was going on. People asked after his health but he only shook his head and said nothing. The evening meals were embarrassing, he had no appetite and nothing to say, and weeks drifted by in a cloud of depression. If he found Eugénie alone he would try again to persuade her but the answer was always a firm no.

As he was entitled to a summer holiday it seemed best to get away. Coping with the train and boat to Holland brought some relief, but when he arrived at the parsonage in Helvoirt he was so thin and dishevelled his parents were appalled. They kept on asking him what was wrong but all he could do was stare bleakly into space and say nothing.

3
1874 — 1876

Breakdown

If they had realised what had happened, his parents might have tried to keep him in Helvoirt. Away from Eugénie there was some chance of a slow recovery. But all anyone could prise out of him was garbled nonsense about there being 'secrets' at the Loyers' house. Had this simply been a case of his belatedly going through the misery of a failed love-affair, the sort of thing most young people have to cope with, then there would have been nothing to worry about. But his melancholy had gone beyond the business with Eugénie and he was now suffering a serious mental breakdown. That at least should have been obvious and any other family would have been far more concerned about his behaviour.

Unfortunately Vincent's state was by no means new to the Van Goghs. Two of Theodorus' brothers had such periods of unexplained sickness. Cent was forever disappearing to the South of France for the sunshine which helped lift him out of whatever it was that ailed him. And yet he lived to be sixty-eight, a fair age then, and was undoubtedly a highly able and successful man. It was the same with Hein in Brussels, a successful businessman, yet constantly ill. In fact the family had long accepted this sort of thing – Theodorus' own father, the elder Pastor Vincent, lived to eighty-five, fathered twelve children, was an able preacher and administrator, yet he was constantly having to be nursed by his long-suffering wife. And it was not only on Theodorus' side of the family that unexplained illnesses came and went. One of Anna's sisters suffered from epilepsy, and although there were as yet no signs that she had passed on the malady to her children there was always that threat hanging over them. Little wonder then that the two parents saw Vincent's behaviour as nothing more than another bout of the moodiness which had punctuated his childhood. As far as they could tell, he had gone through a bad patch in London, and no doubt he would get over it in good time.

In any case they had five other children to consider. Although Theo had taken Vincent's place at The Hague and so was less cause for concern than when he had been abroad, they were now preoccupied with the eighteen-year-old Anna who had just finished her language course and needed to find employment. In an attempt to resolve both problems they decided that she should go with Vincent to England where she could try to get a post as a teacher or governess, in order to improve her English. She would also be able to keep an eye on her brother, who showed no sign of emerging from his bleak mood.

Why should he? Away from the reality Vincent could think of little else except his idealised Eugénie. He drew the house in Hackford Road and sketched the view from his window there. If he could only get back and speak to her, then surely all would be well, Eugénie would see sense. He had only to give her love the chance to manifest itself and then she would be his. He had been wrong to take no for an answer. A new stubbornness was starting to build up.

He began to draw. Only a little, but it helped to pass the time and the activity seemed to keep at bay the endless cycle of unanswerable questions which plagued him. He made a brave attempt to pull himself

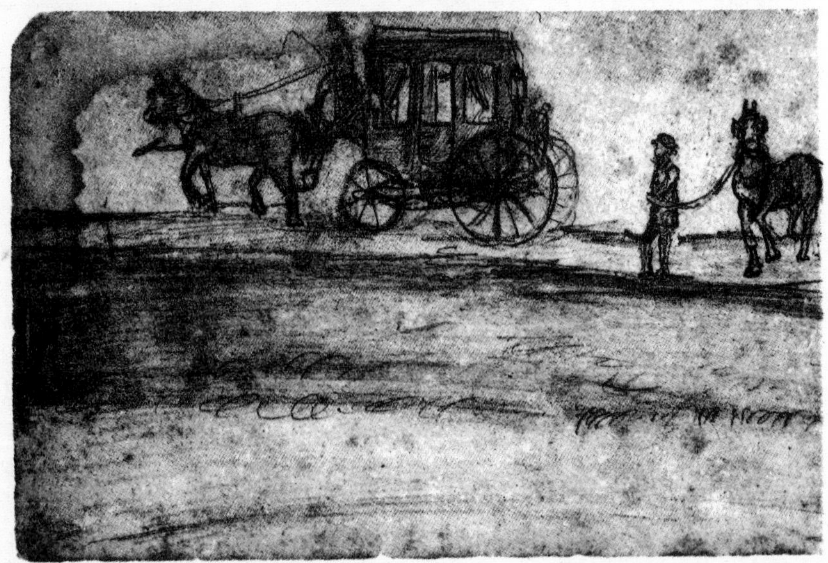

One of Vincent's drawings for Betsy Tersteeg.

together and find something positive to do. He suddenly remembered young Betsy Tersteeg in The Hague and decided to make her a present. He cut up some paper, folded it into three small books which he began to fill with drawings for her. In the end he made over forty sketches and it must have been a relief to everyone in the parsonage that he was suddenly so engrossed in something, no longer moping about doing nothing all day long. Most of the drawings are simple nature studies such as a wagtail sitting rather primly on its nest, the sort of thing he had loved to study as a child. Certain others seem to reflect some of his moods: a spider squats in the middle of a web surrounded by trapped bees and flies; a drawing of a coach and horses brings to mind the sad episode of his being left by his parents at the gate of his first boarding-school. Like the Hague drawings, Betsy's books show scant sign of talent, let alone genius, but the fact that he made them in the teeth of a strange and unnerving depressive attack shows courage. The three sketchbooks were later bound up with a fourth which was filled with writings and drawings by Betsy herself and the volume was in time passed on to her daughter. These sketchbooks mark the first stage in his discovery that the concentrated effort involved in creating something could help lift him out of himself and help him forget, if only for a short time, his inexplicable misery.

Seeing how much he had been helped by this means, his family were encouraging, especially his mother, who thought his simplest doodle showed great promise. Her inclination was to blame the Loyers for his unhappy state; she did not like this talk of 'secrets'. Surely it would be better if he moved elsewhere?

For their part, the Loyers can hardly have relished the thought of his return. His reaction to the news of Eugénie's engagement had been so exaggerated they had not known what to do. Their only hope was that his visit home would have shaken him out of it.

It was something of a relief, when he returned in July, that he had his sister with him. She provided a barrier against any further protestations of love. Not that anything had really changed. He read George Eliot's *Adam Bede* and was much taken with the hapless hero who remains ever faithful to his Hetty even when she becomes pregnant by the philandering squire. The novel's mix of hopeless love and unquestioning fidelity in a pervasive atmosphere of tragedy well suited his mood. Despite the restraining presence of Anna he still managed to cast a pall over the Loyers' household. It was awkward when Samuel called. The Loyers had no wish to be hurtful but it was intolerable that he should continue mooning around Eugénie hoping to wear down her resistance. A month after his return he accepted the inevitable. He left, moving to rooms in nearby Kennington New Road. The house was covered in ivy, increasingly his favourite plant, and he could still call round to see Eugénie now that the atmosphere would be less charged with emotion.

Unfortunately the new lodgings failed to restore his spirits. No meals were provided, so he and Anna had to eat in nearby cafés. Because she looked too young to be entrusted with children Anna found it difficult to obtain a position. Vincent was also finding things increasingly difficult at Goupil's where everyone was working towards the setting up of the gallery which would open as soon as premises could be found. In that enthusiastic atmosphere, Vincent's withdrawn moodiness seemed glaringly out of place. Mr Obach went to Paris to discuss whether the company should take over an existing business in nearby Bedford Street, but there was little doubt that he would also bring up the subject of Vincent's peculiar behaviour.

When Anna at last found a post, at a school in Welwyn, life was even more miserable for Vincent. There was meagre incentive to return to his lonely room after work. The fact that Goupil's closed so early now became a curse as the long hours stretched ahead of him. In his search for ways to pass the time he discovered the illustrated newspapers pinned up in display-cases outside their offices near Goupil's. He took to hanging about, studying the pictures outside the premises of the *Graphic* and the *Illustrated London News*, the two major publications that featured woodblock engravings on topical subjects. The 1870 Education Act had helped create a market among the newly literate for simple text and bold pictures, and Vincent quickly acquired a taste for the sharpness of this kind of work. Many of the illustrations were deliberately intended to jolt the conscience of the public, concerning themselves with the social iniquities of the day: *The Bitter Cry of Outcast London*; homeless children, filthy 'poorhouses', intolerable prisons, the back-street world of beggars and criminals, the whole squalid teeming underbelly of the industrial and imperial capital.

Vincent was not entirely unaware of the reality behind these images, for he had had a passing view of East End life when he visited the recently re-erected 'Brompton Boilers' Museum in Bethnal Green. This

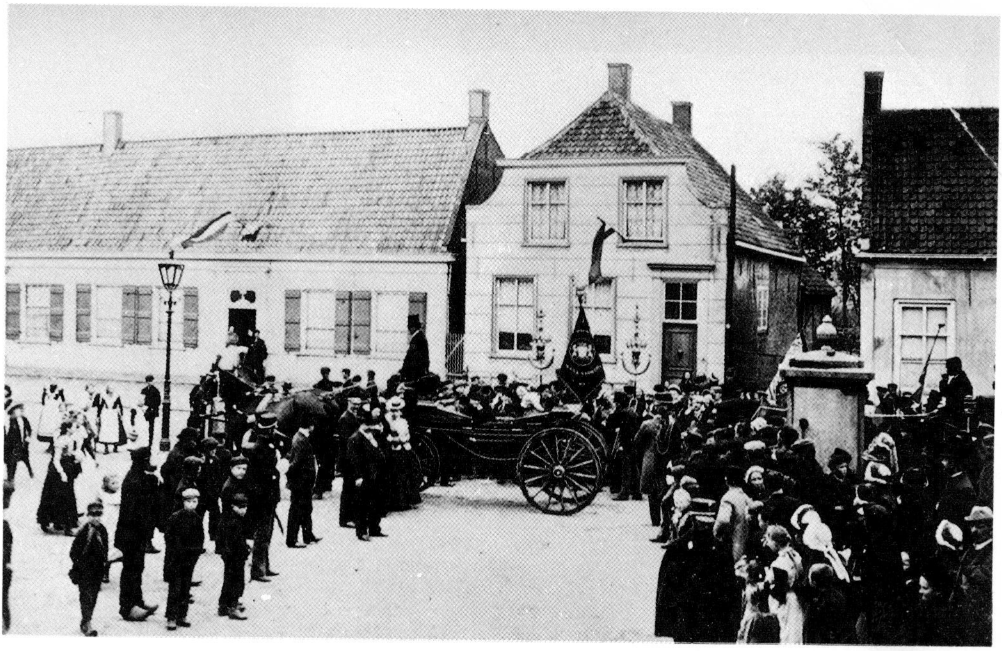

Vincent's birthplace: Zundert, Holland. His bedroom was on the top floor and he developed an intense dislike of the narrow room with its sharply sloping ceiling.

This *Funeral Procession through the Cornfields* by Van der Maaten was possibly the first professional work of art Vincent knew.

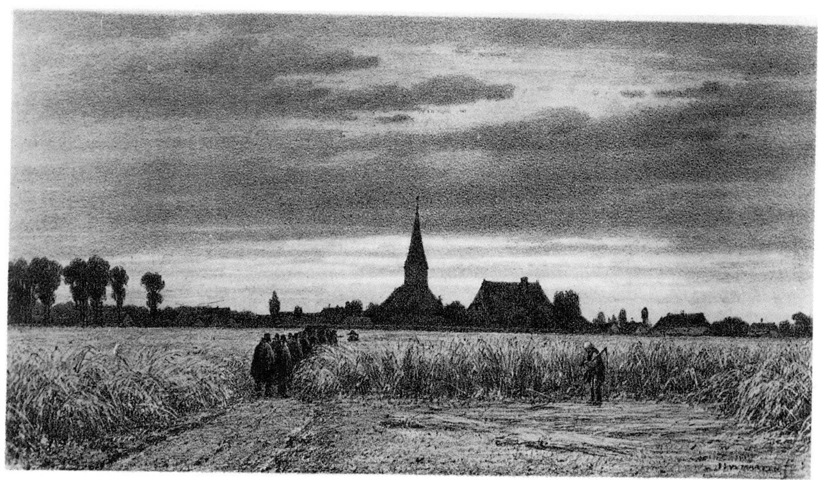

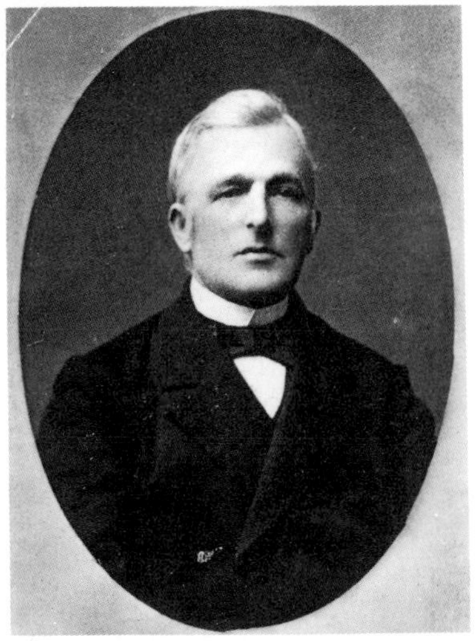

Father, Pastor Theodorus

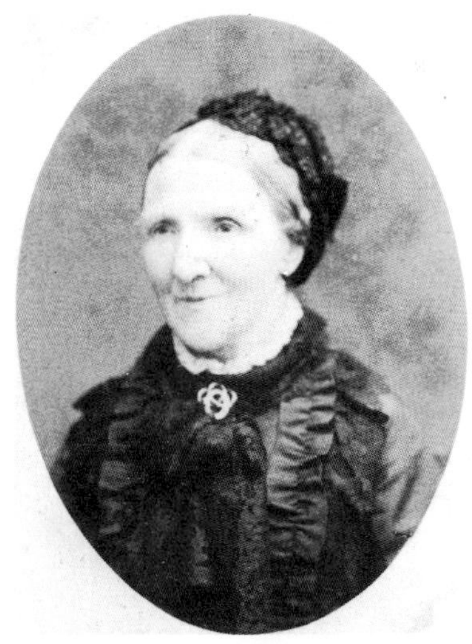

Mother, Anna Carbentus van Gogh

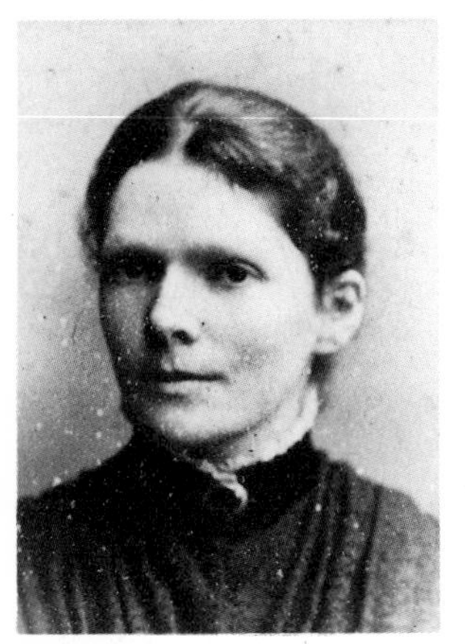

Elisabeth

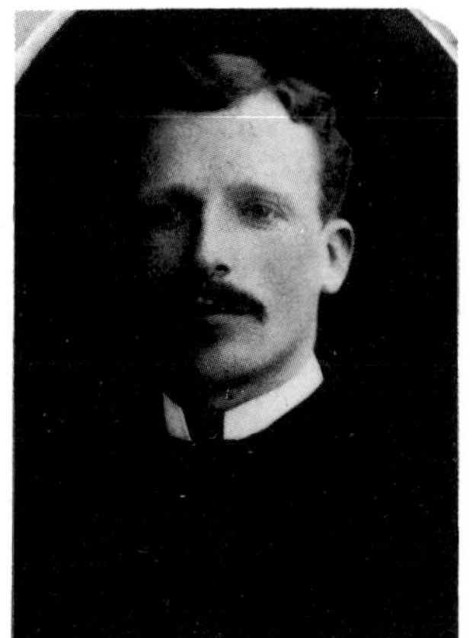

Theo

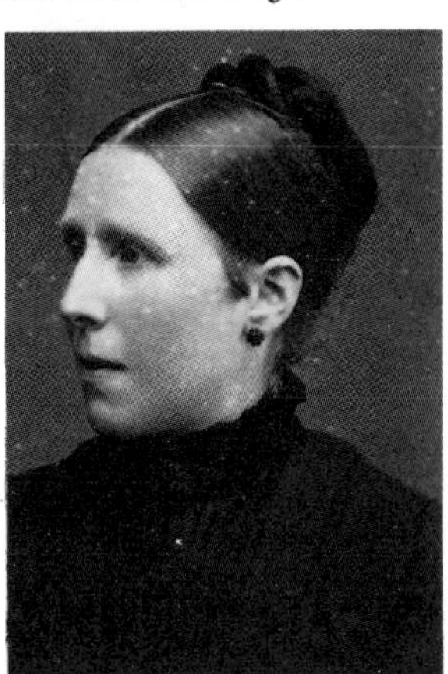

Anna

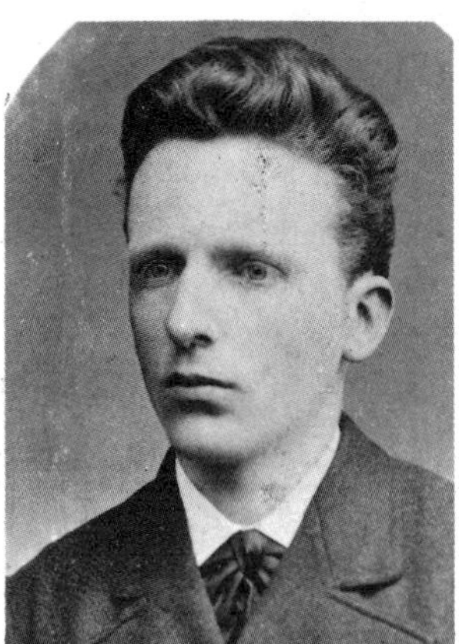

Cornelis

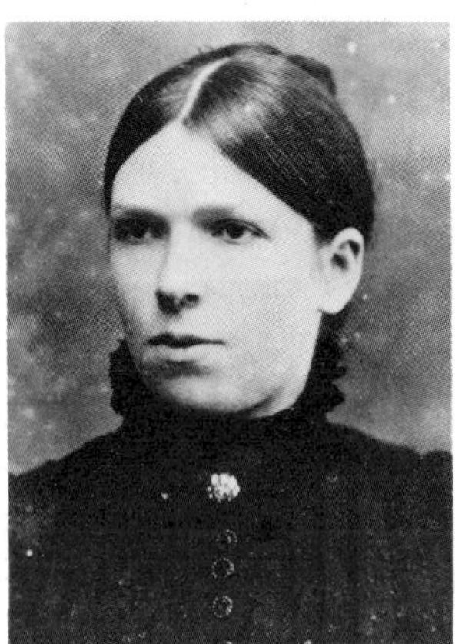

Willemina

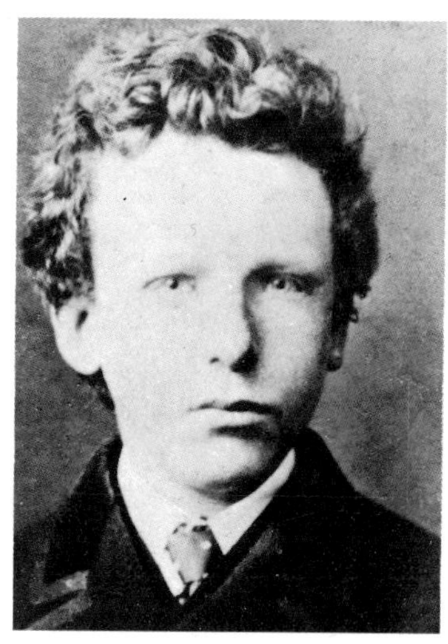

Vincent had an aversion to photography. These are the only two photographic portraits of him aged 13 and 19.

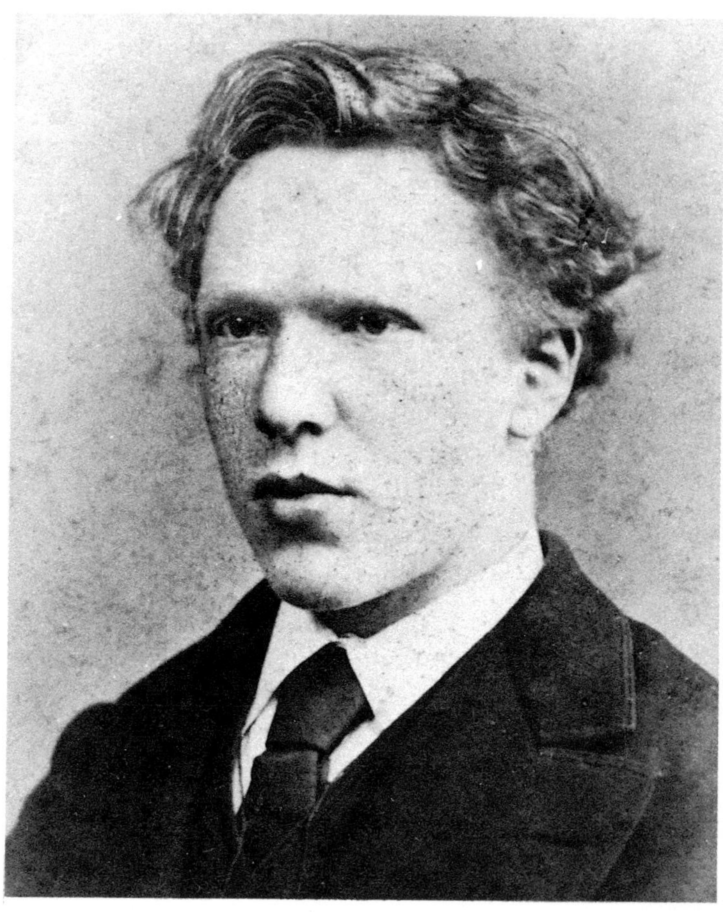

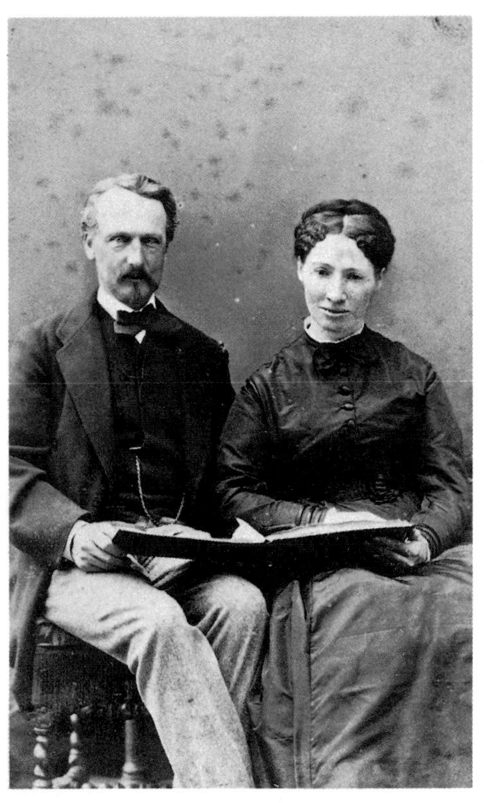

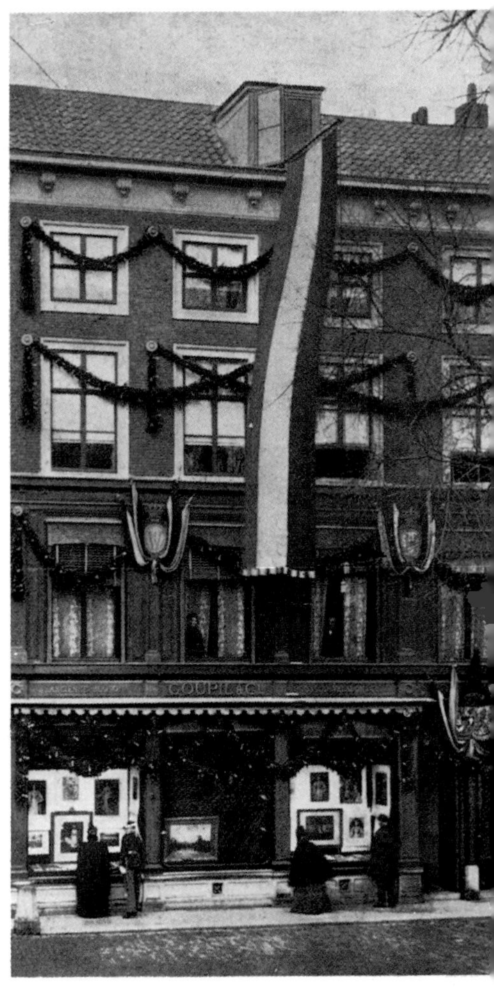

Vincent's rich Uncle Cent, the art dealer, and his wife, Vincent's Aunt Cornelia.

Goupil's art gallery, the Hague, where Vincent first worked as a junior art dealer.

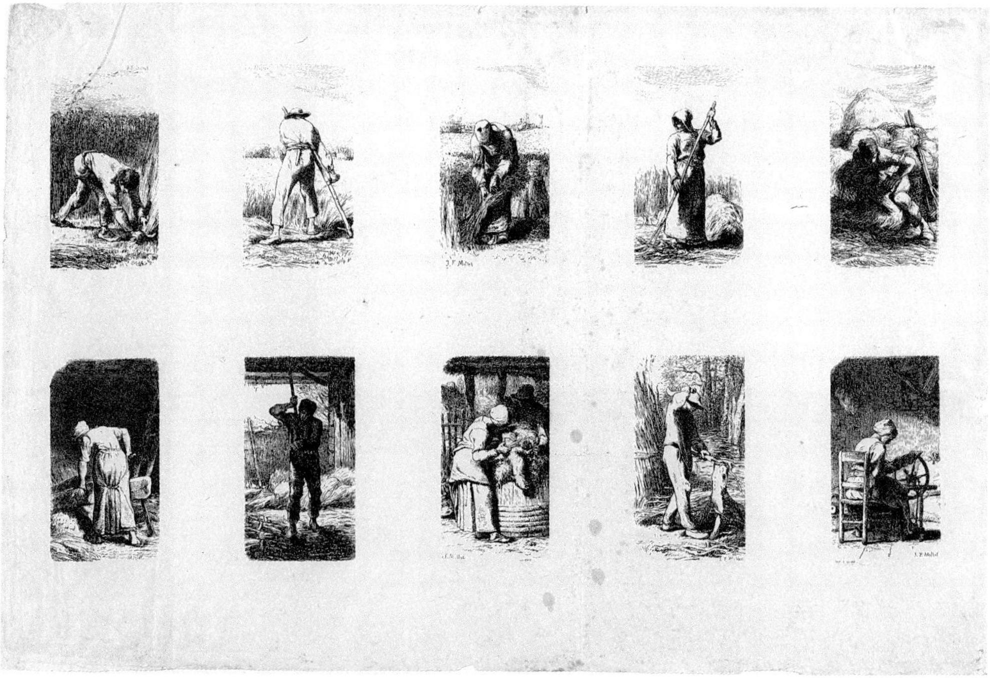

Two of the most powerful early influences on Vincent's taste: Laveille's engravings of Millet's *Field Work* and Jules Breton's *Blessing the Cornfields in Artois.*

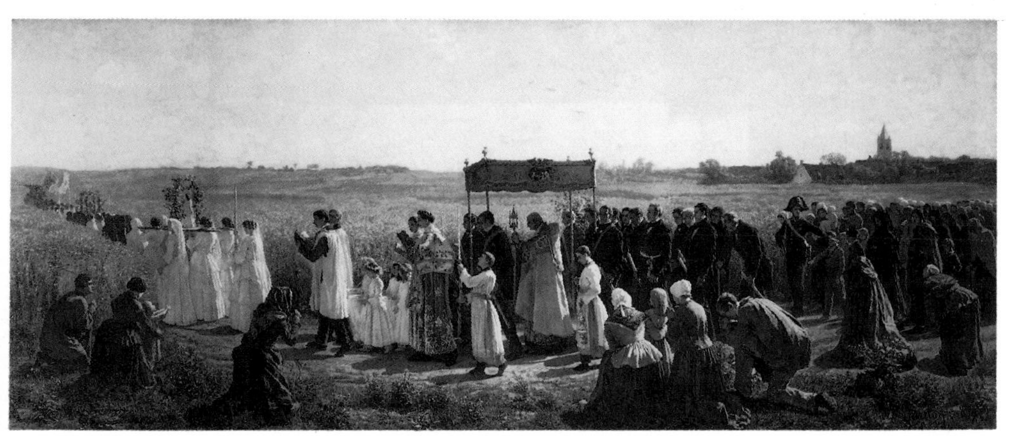

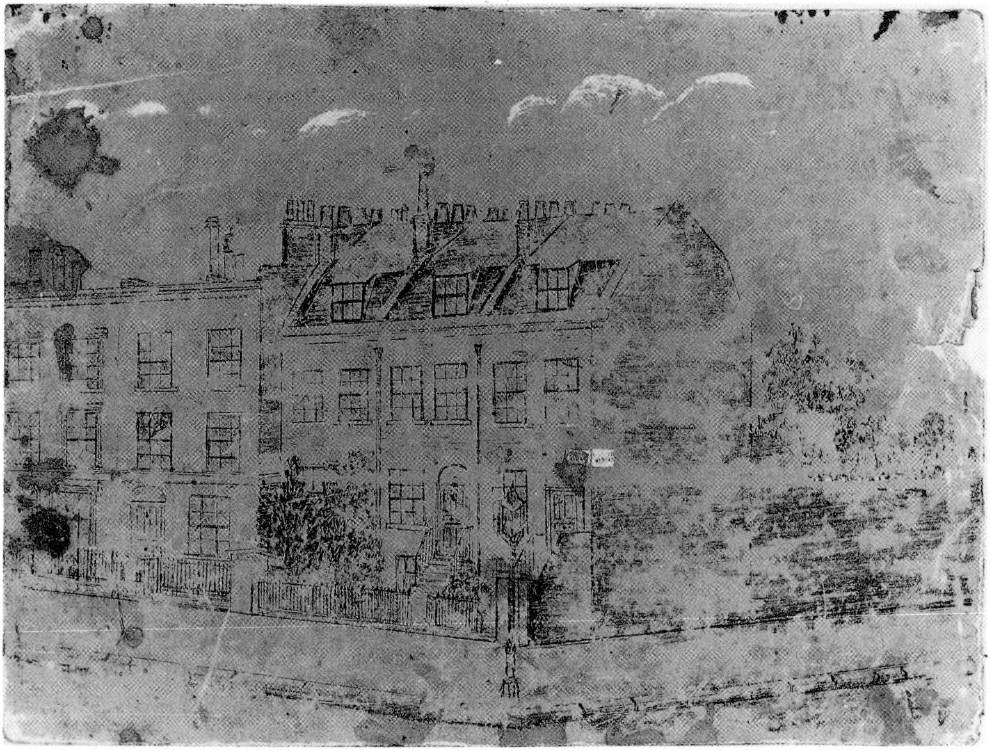

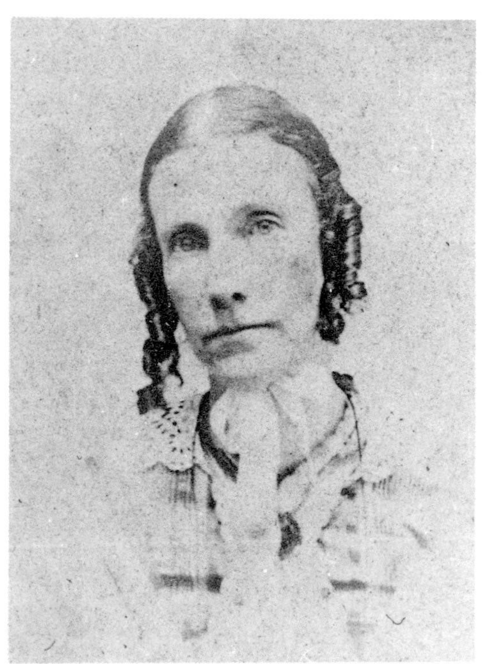

Discovered only a few years ago, Vincent's drawing of his lodgings in Hackford Road, Brixton, London, was his gift to Eugénie Loyer, his landlady's daughter with whom he had fallen in love.

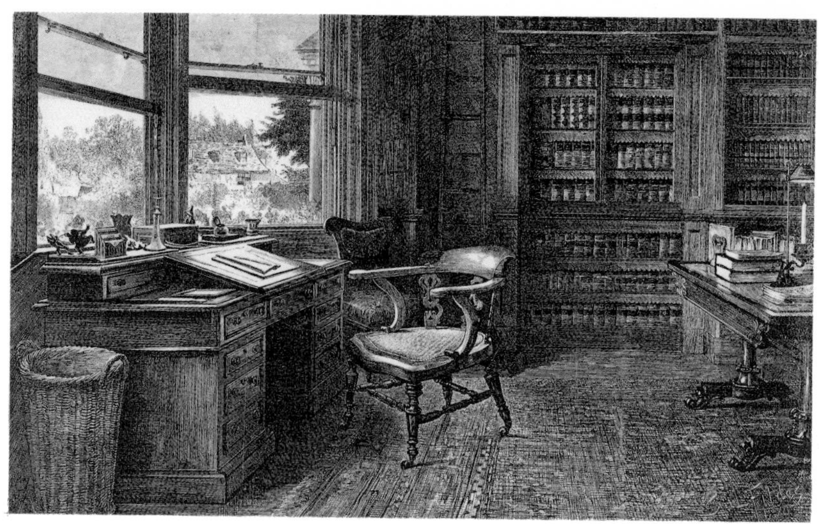

The Empty Chair, Gad's Hill, by Luke Fildes was a tribute to Charles Dickens, following the writer's death in 1870. The engraving had a powerful effect on Vincent's thinking.

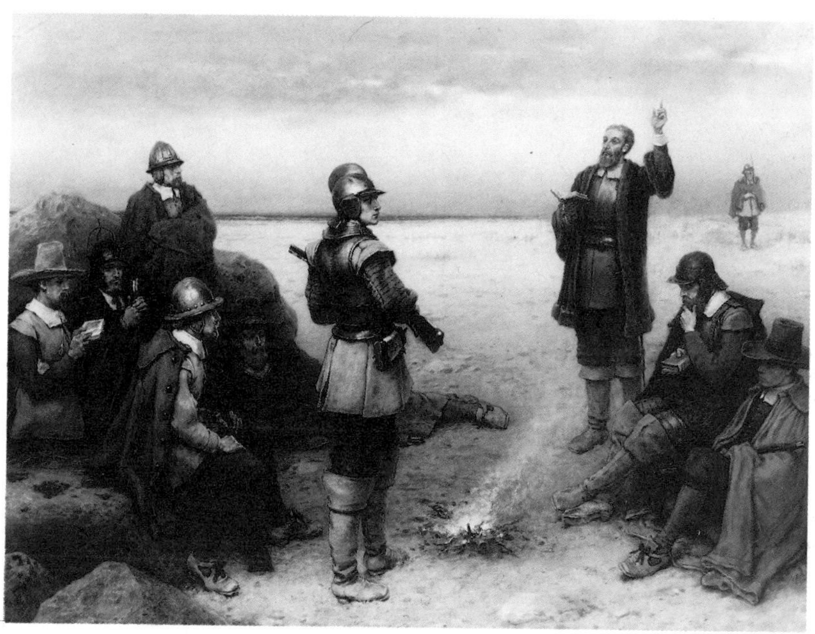

Vincent admired art on religious themes such as G. H. Boughton's *The Landing of the Pilgrim Fathers* – an admiration which has led some to criticise his taste.

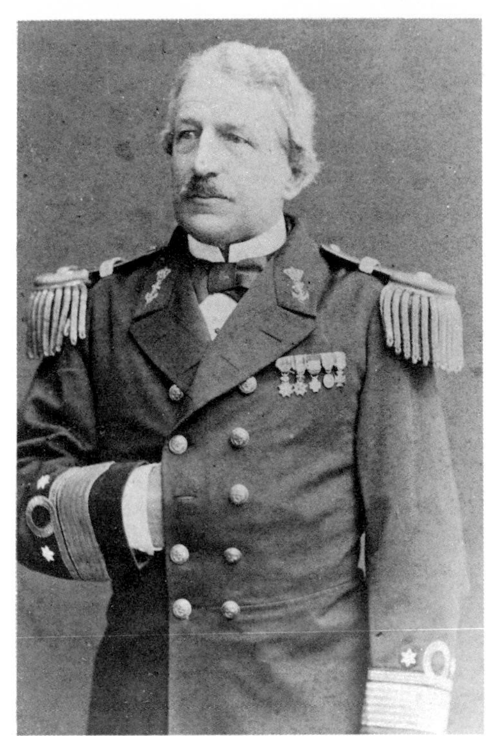

Right: Uncle Jan van Gogh
Below: Uncle Stricker
Below right: Mendes da Costa

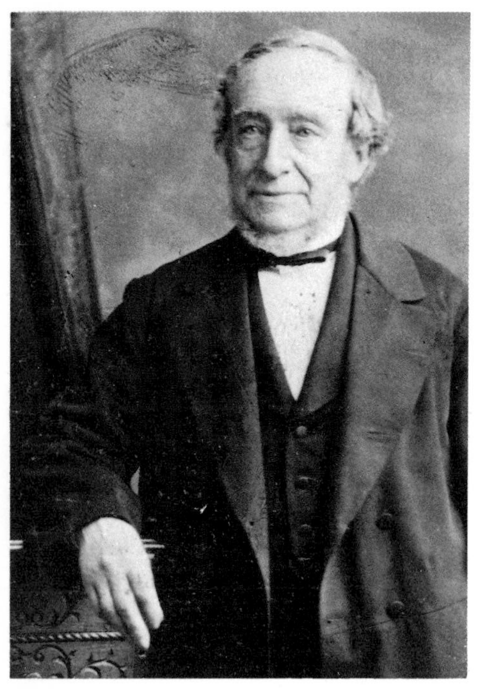

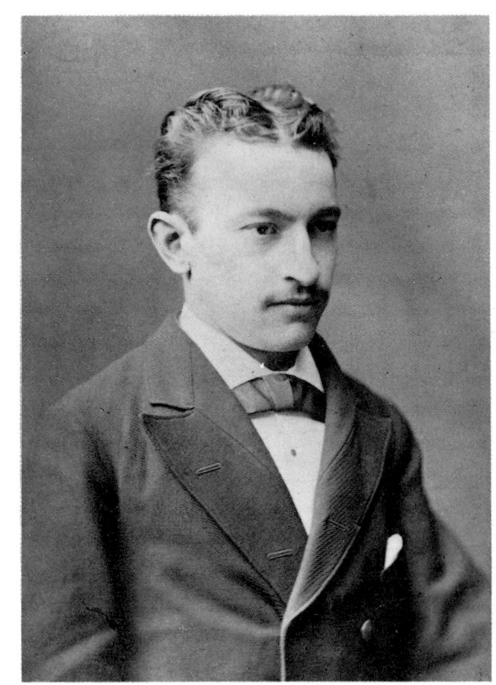

metal and glass hall had been dismantled to make way for the building of the Victoria and Albert Museum and re-erected on Bethnal Green as a temporary home for many of the exhibits from the Great Exhibition of 1851, the basis for the new museum's eventual collection. It was an eclectic display: the Raphael Cartoons had been brought from Hampton Court and around them were clustered an assortment of exotic artefacts from India, Arabia and China. But it was one thing to immerse oneself in this mysterious hoard inside the pretty iron and glass 'greenhouse', and quite another to pass through the world that surrounded it, for Bethnal Green was probably the most vile of all the East End slums. When he had been happily in love with Eugénie, his world safely bounded by middle-class South London and the smart commercial life of the Strand, Vincent had ignored such things; now he began to be obsessed by what he saw. Women in rags whose filthy children held out scrawny hands for coins, the brawling drunkenness of the public houses, and glimpses of another world of whores in ill-lit alleyways. Once he began to see such things they became overwhelming. He turned to his Bible for comfort, sitting up till late reading and re-reading it, finding it helped to shut out his own misery and the images of despair that lurked in filthy corners away from the brightly lit new London he had known. Then he began to see that there might be answers. Walking home late at night he could observe the young men and women dressed in strange uniforms, standing outside the drinking dens singing hymns and offering shelter to the destitute. The Salvation Army had just been formed and was beginning to make its presence felt in those parts of the city that every other agency of law and order had long abandoned. Not far from his lodgings was the Metropolitan Tabernacle at the Elephant and Castle where the first of the hugely popular revivalist preachers, Charles Haddon Spurgeon, had harangued thousands who desperately sought answers in a world where new riches were matched with seemingly hopeless poverty. Vincent bought Spurgeon's tract 'Little Jewels' and in the years ahead would often turn to it for inspiration. Massive evangelical crusades were being launched which offered clear solutions in the midst of all these teeming contradictions – the Bible, simply the Bible, offered the one significant answer. The *Graphic* and the *Illustrated London News* unveiled the purgatory that was life in London's slums while evangelists like Spurgeon and his disciples, the American missionaries Moody and Sankey, offered an immediate solution: the city of man might be Hell but anyone could enter at once into the city of God. Come forward and accept Christ into your life, they proclaimed, and the days of misery would be over.

Vincent was in a mood to respond to such a message. Why waste one's life peddling art to the well-off, when there was so much to be done for the poor and the wretched? Absorbed in this discovery and interested only in his study of the Bible, he could barely summon up the energy to get through his days at Goupil's. Even before Vincent had left for Holland Mr Obach had noticed that his once exemplary employee had been losing interest in the work, but he had hoped that it was only a temporary lapse and that a holiday would restore him. As it clearly had not done so, he was reluctantly obliged to take action. Paris would have to be told and the elder Vincent consulted. It was all very delicate. When the answer came it was that young Vincent should return to Paris. As it was clearly London which had caused this change of attitude, a move might put things right. Although Vincent had no option but to obey, he was far from happy to be taken away from Eugénie. But worse than this was his increasing fury at being manipulated by his family, obliged to follow a career mapped out for him, then moved about the chess-board of his uncles' business connections to suit their perception of his character and difficulties.

Once in Paris he sulked hugely. The letters to Theo ceased completely. This might, indeed perhaps ought to, have been the end of his career at Goupil's but, as before, those around him were too preoccupied with their own affairs to comprehend the full scale of his transformation. To reinforce the prescribed lesson in obedience, Monsieur Boussod put him in the main branch in the Place de l'Opéra away from the more liberated atmosphere of the Boulevard Montmartre, and that was the limit of his interest in the matter. The company was on the verge of massive restructuring and Boussod had more to worry about than a recalcitrant junior employee, albeit one who was related to a senior partner.

The company's main concern was who would succeed old Adolphe Goupil when he finally withdrew completely from the business. Of his four sons only one had taken any interest in art dealing but he had died in 1855 having, so it was maintained, exhausted himself working in the New York branch. Only one other son, Albert, had shown any love for art but as a collector, and even then, not of the art his father dealt in.

Albert Goupil had once thought of becoming an artist and even after he had abandoned that idea his main joy was travelling in North Africa with his brother-in-law the painter Gérôme when he made preparatory studies for his canvases of 'oriental' life, mosques, hammams, desert scenes. Eventually their long and for those days adventurous treks were used by Albert to acquire an extensive collection of Arabic art and craft. Albert was a colourful character. He never married and his apartment, also in the Rue Chaptal, had gradually taken on the air of a seraglio with prayer mats and carpeted divans, damascene brass lamps and hookahs, ivory boxes and inlaid calligraphy, Moorish fretwork. Only when he died in 1884 was it realised that he had built up one of the first major collections of Islamic art in France. At the time he was considered strange and he was certainly something of a disappointment to his father who was now obliged to dispose of the largest art dealing concern in Europe and thus, effectively, in the world. The ramifications of this empire were constantly expanding; Michel Knoedler, who had begun as a 'correspondent' for Adolphe in New York, eventually bought out the Goupil interest and ran his own gallery in close association with the original European network. In Paris, Léon Boussod was introducing his son Etienne into the business with Adolphe Goupil's blessing, for Etienne had married Gérôme's and Marie Goupil's daughter and would thus maintain a tenuous family link were he to take over the business. When this restructuring was complete the company was renamed Goupil–Boussod et Valadon Successeurs, though almost everyone continued to refer to it as Goupil's.

With all this being debated and argued over it is small wonder that Vincent's sulks were noted but left unchallenged. But in other, more important ways, a sea-change was taking place which would eventually transform the company and its world with far more effect than a mere juggling with the name, a transformation in which Vincent would one day play a major role. At the time, the Goupil galleries embodied a stultifying bourgeois respectability which had lain below the surface gaiety of the Second Empire and which now reasserted itself in the self-proclaimed 'Moral Order' of the Third Republic. The central hall in the main gallery was long and high, lit by overhead studio windows which were intended to reproduce the atmosphere of the Louvre or the rooms in the official Salon. Here, as in The Hague, the well-to-do strolled and admired the works and would turn to the salesmen to answer their questions and generally back their taste with gentle reassurance. The atmosphere was snobbish on one side, unctuous on the other. These were the last days of the mass art trade before colour reproduction burst on the scene. The middle classes were still buying original art or at least fine art prints even if these were limited to the narrow spectrum of taste ordained by the Salon prize winners. It was this which gave the official art world such power. Without its imprimatur the door to a fair income for an artist through establishments like Goupil's was closed. This was why the battles over who should and should not be accepted at the Salon were more than cultural wrangles: they were a matter of earning a living or, in some cases, going hungry. For over a decade attempts had been made to ameliorate the system – 1863 saw the first Salon des Refusés, but many of the works were so dreadful the official jury was almost vindicated. It was only in the late spring of 1874, just before Vincent's arrival in Paris, that something happened which ultimately transformed the entire artistic life of Europe. An exhibition was arranged in studios lent by the ever-adventurous Nadar (Félix Tournachon), sometime journalist, caricaturist and balloonist who had been the original for one of the characters in Murger's *Scènes de la vie de bohème*, but who was best known as the photographer whose camera had captured the major artists and writers of his day. Nadar's photographic studio on the corner of the Rue Daunou and the Boulevard des Capucines had long played host to such as Zola and Baudelaire but in 1874 it became the site of the single most important art exhibition of the day. The show had closed before Vincent moved to Paris but only his isolation from his colleagues can have kept him from a knowledge of what had happened, for the exhibition had been, depending on your point of view, either an attack on the very heart of French culture or a major artistic landmark. If nothing else the near-violence that most of the art world displayed towards what had been on show in Nadar's studios had already given the event mythic status.

The exhibition consisted of what we now accept as a roll-call of nineteenth-century genius: Monet, Renoir, Sisley, Pissarro, Cézanne, Degas, Guillaumin, Boudin and Berthe Morisot. There were over one hundred and sixty-five works of which Degas alone submitted ten. Renoir organised the hanging, choosing a background of reddish-brown wallpaper, while his brother Edmond organised the catalogue, doing his best to persuade participants to give their work appealing titles, especially Monet who, in the opinion of the others, rather boringly dubbed his pictures exactly what they were, a railway station or a street name. As it turned out it was just such an 'improved' title, *Impression: Sunrise*, Monet's hazy river view painted in 1872, that became the most famous work in the show. An irate critic seized on the invention and gave it to the entire group. They were, according to him, mere 'Impressionists', and the name stuck.

It is hard to convey the shock of that first Impressionist exhibition. We who have seen work striped in primary colours, pierced with vivid targets, glaring with day-glo and stippled with industrial enamel, can no longer experience the shock induced by the bright sunlit palette of the Impressionist painters. Earlier open-air painters, such as those of Barbizon and the Hague School, had certainly lightened their colour range but nowhere near as much as these painters did. Theirs was a scientific revolution in the way they chose to render the observed world. Many of the ideas they espoused had been current for some time. An earlier generation had read Chevreul and knew that an object of one colour casts a shadow tinged with its complementary. Delacroix had adopted this discovery but the Impressionists were the first to make it central to their working method, making a fetish of the way all the colours in a painting could be made to interact. It was the antithesis of the academic style, beloved of the salons, where each object was solid and individual, where a shadow was simply the darkening of the surface on which it fell. To the Impressionists everything had its own colour and that colour was a passing moment created by ever-changing light. They had to work quickly, in rapid dashes and strokes to capture it. In consequence these new works seemed formless unless looked at from just the right distance and in the right light. Then the kaleidoscope of stippled paint and swirling lines and blobs miraculously coalesced into a recognisable image. In retrospect it seems inevitable that painters would arrive at such a method. The daguerreotype and other forerunners of photography had relieved painting of many of its more humdrum tasks as the recorder of the visual world; what remained were those things the photograph could not attempt – painterliness, colour and brushwork. Inevitably also the subject of the work became less important than the way it was painted, and the one thing that most united the Impressionists was their depiction of quite ordinary scenes: Sunday outings by the river, a crowded street on a rainy day or a woman practising at a piano. If it had been a revolution to proclaim that peasants at work were a suitable subject for art, then how much more so was it to suggest that a couple seated at a café table were? That this combination of extraordinary technique and all-too-ordinary subject matter should have been too much for most people, whether dealers, critics or the average gallery goer, was only to be expected. But the fury of some of those who crowded into Nadar's studios went far beyond what the organisers had anticipated. Many of the reviews were cruelly mocking of what their authors took to be the amateurishness and incompetence of these 'unfinished' works. Underlying these barbs was a concern that an Impressionist work represented something dangerously radical, something beyond a mere revolution in style. In a typical Salon work each element was as solid as its subject was weighty, the high degree of polish showed that the painter had mastered his craft and had earned his wages like a good craftsman should. By contrast, the shifting, impermanent colours and light-hearted subjects of these newcomers seemed to be inviting the spectator to participate instead of imposing a single authoritarian view. They were subversively democratic. When the works from that first Impressionist exhibition were put up for sale, the auctioneer was forced to summon the police to restore order.

Only someone as isolated as Vincent could have failed to know what was going on. Had he bothered to talk with his colleagues he would surely have heard their shocked accounts of those incredible events. Had he done so he could readily have found out just what all the fuss was about. The dealer Durand-Ruel continued to show Impressionist works after the exhibition closed, despite the unwillingness of his customers to buy them. One might even imagine that Vincent was in a frame of mind to accept the new work; after all, he had been raised on the Hague School, admired Barbizon, worshipped Millet, all seen now as forerunners of Impressionism. Surely he would have made the short leap to the new? But this is the supposition of hindsight. At the time it was by no means a short leap. A wide chasm, both artistic and social, divided Uncle Cent's preferred artists from Monet, Degas, Renoir and the others. At the time there were those who regarded the lightened colours of the Barbizon as acceptably revolutionary but who could only view the Impressionists as children flinging paint around. Earlier artists like Courbet had shocked the public for all sorts of reasons – in his case an indifference to accepted canons of what was or ought to be beautiful – but the juries and the public had still acknowledged his skill, his craftsmanship. They may not have liked what he did but they could not doubt that he was a competent artist. But it was not so with the Impressionists. The whole notion of what was an artist had been called into question. If he had seen their work Vincent might have accepted *how* they painted, but he might well have been repulsed by *what* they painted. To him at that time, the basic requirement of art was that it should show simple sentiments such as love, charity and faith. He was not yet ready for the depiction of people enjoying themselves at a dance or simply strolling by the river. Perhaps it was a blessing that he remained ignorant of what had happened and perhaps it was equally fortuitous that the second Impressionist exhibition was not held until 1876, by which time he had left Paris.

That Christmas he was allowed to go home to Helvoirt, where he did everything possible to convince his parents that he must be allowed to return to London. Once again, if things had been normal, they could have asked Uncle Cent to look into what was wrong with Vincent, but he too was bound up with the changes in the company. As his old friend Goupil was leaving the business increasingly in the hands of Boussod and Valadon, it seemed a good time for Uncle Cent to follow suit. Being so devoted to his younger brother, he was setting up his retirement home in nearby Princenhage. The labour involved was considerable: a group of smaller houses had to be amalgamated into one and a large picture gallery built, to accommodate his by now substantial private collection. What with the transfer of the company's assets and the work on the house, there was little time to look too deeply into his nephew's condition. Uncle Cent took the easy way out: he contacted Boussod and bluntly asked him to let the boy go back to London. Equally preoccupied, Boussod agreed.

Predictably it came to nothing. Back in the same modest room in Kennington New Road Vincent sank into his old ways, obsessively studying the Bible and rarely bothering to go out except reluctantly to make the daily trek to Southampton Street. He made a half-hearted attempt to interest himself in what was going on there; another batch of pictures had just arrived for the new gallery with all the usual names: Maris, Israëls, Mauve and Breton. He even went to the Sixth Winter Exhibition at the Royal Academy and wrote to Theo about it. He only really liked the Constables because they reminded him of Barbizon. He might have appreciated Turner, but little was on display during his London years. He did see some that April when Christie's auctioned the Samuel Mendel Collection, but of the works he saw there he much preferred John Everett Millais' *Chill October*, the artist's first pure landscape. It had a haunted, empty feel, a chilliness emphasised by the silhouettes of distant migrating birds, an image that lodged in Vincent's memory.

Despite these occasional sorties into the world of art it was evident to his colleagues that his heart was no longer in his work. If Paris was too preoccupied to cope with him then maybe his old employers in The Hague would help? Mr Tersteeg suddenly arrived at Southampton Street, ostensibly to inspect the new premises, though as Vincent shrewdly observed, he spent little time on business and more on seeing the sights. He must have guessed that the real reason behind the visit was himself and that once Tersteeg had assessed Vincent's behaviour he was free to amuse himself.

Shortly after Tersteeg's return to Holland Vincent learned his employer's decision – he was to go back to Paris once more. They had concluded that something about London disagreed with him and would in future be deaf to his requests to be allowed to go on living there. He left only a few days before the new gallery was opened and was, perversely, bitterly disappointed to be missing it.

In Paris, Boussod was obliged to decide on his future. As Goupil's successor he was one of the most influential figures in European art. Over the coming years he would prove to be far more than just the administrator of the empire he had inherited; Boussod et Valadon changed and grew out of all recognition both in physical size and in the nature of the art it handled. But faced with Vincent at the début of his directorship, he may have felt that he still owed something to the old founders of the firm and should tread softly with Uncle Cent's nephew. Whatever his reasons, he decided not merely to indulge Vincent but to try to jolt him out of his mood by giving him new responsibilities. To the young man's surprise, far from being reprimanded, he was put in charge of the painting galleries in the Place de l'Opéra, which could be interpreted as promotion.

Two years earlier he might have relished the task, but by this time he no longer felt the least sympathy for what he was supposed to be selling. There he was, surrounded by the Salon art he had never much cared for and which he now felt to be irrelevant. It was an attitude that went beyond work; he even turned his back on the world outside. The recently rebuilt Paris with its thrilling new department stores, its streets so brightly lit that the centre seemed perpetually *en fête*, the new opera-house going up near by, were all ignored as he hurried home to his lodgings and the ever-present Bible. Someone like Degas rejoiced in the new pavement-side cafés where people of all classes were drawn to the free entertainment laid on by the proprietors. Singers and performers drew large crowds, so that there was a vibrant open-air theatre on every corner and square. The Impressionists seized on such scenes as subjects for their paintings, but the usually observant Vincent was blind to them. Small wonder that he had little contact with his fellow salesmen in the gallery. The newcomer to a religious experience seldom has the discretion to keep the discovery to himself. The convert's desire to share his new joy is overwhelming and deeply embarrassing to those invited to witness it. The understandable reaction is to keep well out of the convert's way or to indulge in elbow nudging, surreptitious winking and sniggering, which only serve to reinforce the outcast's sense of martyrdom and exaggerate his mania through loneliness and hurt. For Vincent there was nothing to do but hurry back to his rooms, impatient to assuage the miseries of the day with the balm of Holy Writ.

He had been told by Boussod that he would stay in Paris for six to eight weeks to see how things went, but any hopes that he might be allowed to return to London were quickly dashed when the directors finally decided that he must remain at the main branch in the Place de l'Opéra. He accepted the decision, as he did everything at that time, with indifference.

Realising that he was trapped in Paris he took a room in Montmartre, still a grassy knoll topped with windmills, just beyond the toll barriers that marked the boundaries of the city. It was one of the few areas untouched by Haussmann's rebuilding and was already a haunt of artists, though this meant little to Vincent other than, like them, he needed cheap lodgings.

It seems astonishing that he could have been utterly uninterested in so fascinating a place. On the slopes of the Butte, the Commune had ended in massacre. Some of those who survived and had not been hunted down in the persecution that followed the reimposition of Republican government continued to live a shadowy existence in the bars and dance halls that gave Montmartre its reputation as a haunt of criminals and bohemian riff-raff. The bitter-sweet world of rouged tarts and decadent bohemians that Toulouse-Lautrec would immortalise pulsed with life after the sun had set over the windmills and quarries which dotted the open ground beyond the Butte. Down its slopes, ramshackle hovels and open-air cafés began to twinkle with lights, and plaintive songs of love and betrayal could be heard from the crowded bars. But all Vincent cared about was the narrow world of his lodgings and his view over a garden hung with ivy and wild vines. He covered the grimy walls of his tenement with a selection of his prints, and the choice tells us much about his mood. He listed the selection to Theo and picked out Rembrandt's *Bible Reading*, describing it as:

> *A large old-Dutch room in the evening, a candle on the table, where a young mother is sitting reading the Bible beside her baby's cradle. An old woman sits, listening. It is a thing that reminds you of, "Again, I say unto you, where two or three are gathered together in my name, there am I in the midst of them."*

Near the Rembrandt was his own print of Van der Maaten's *Funeral Procession through the Cornfields*. Looking at it must have made him think of his father, for he got Theo to take a parcel of lithographs home as a present. To judge by the pictures he selected he was either trying to keep to what he knew his father liked or was sharing a joke with his brother. In one print, Anker's *The Huguenot*, an old man is shown propped on pillows being read to by his daughter, presumably a dig at their father's morbid taste.

Only on Sundays would Vincent allow himself a break from his rigid regime of work and Bible study. Then he would walk downhill to the centre of the city to visit one or more of the Protestant churches. Many foreign communities, like the English Methodists, maintained their own chapels and Vincent would visit each in turn sampling sermons and services like a taster intent on finding a blend to his liking. When the Sunday morning round was over he would make his way to the Louvre along with crowds of others taking advantage of the day when no admission was charged. It was usual for students and even seasoned practitioners to set up their easels in the galleries to copy the old masters, still considered the best method of learning how to paint. Stopping to watch them at work was as much a part of any visit as the contemplation of the masterpieces on the walls. For Vincent the two halves of the day had almost equal sanctity – the temples of God were followed by the temple of Art – for despite his lack of interest in Goupil's there was no diminution of his private obsession with paintings. On the contrary, it was an increasing sureness about his own taste that led him into difficulties with customers. He could no longer acquiesce when a client made what he saw as a wrong choice. If customers would insist on buying the historical tales that hung in the gallery and refused to consider the altogether better landscapes that he pointed out, then he no longer saw any reason to bow to their decision. They must be shown the folly of their choice and persuaded to buy the clearly superior piece chosen for them. Complaints about the young salesman multiplied, and before long Boussod had to be told. But despite what he heard, it did not quite add up. There was the day Jules Breton came to the gallery with his wife and daughters. When Boussod went out to welcome them, he found Vincent hanging about as excited as if the master's visit was the most important thing that had ever happened. What was he to make of such contradictions? The young man had to be introduced to Breton and was manifestly overjoyed to meet him. It was hardly the behaviour of someone who had lost interest in the business. Once again Boussod decided to do nothing.

In fact it was only the visit of one of his idols that could have shaken Vincent out of his torpor. He wrote to Theo to tell him about the encounter and to enthuse over Breton's salon entry *St John's Eve* with its peasant girls dancing round a St John's fire by moonlight. Theo must, he insisted, read Breton's poetry, every bit as good as his painting. But, Breton aside, what purpose was there in trying to sell art to the self-satisfied, well-to-do browsers who drifted round the gallery looking for something 'safe' to decorate their homes? It all seemed so pointless. Then, just as the last flicker of interest in art dealing was beginning to fade away, the *coup de grâce* came with the stunning news that Millet had died at his home in Barbizon. It was hardly possible – the old man had seemed eternal, as untouched by time as the peasants he painted. Millet stood for peasant certainties in the midst of metropolitan frippery. Vincent might be doomed to spend his days in a room filled with expiring Romans and bathing Egyptians but Millet at least was solid, out there in the fields and forests, his art above all real, something to believe in.

Not long after this news Vincent read about a sale of Millet's drawings that was to take place at the Hôtel Drouot. He went along clearly ready for a near-mystical experience:

> *I felt like saying, "Take off your shoes, for the place where you are standing is Holy Ground".*

It was from that moment he began to refer to the late painter as 'Father Millet'. At the sale of his effects, the Luxembourg bought some of the paintings and Vincent was among the first to see the new display. He told Theo he had studied a painting of *The Church at Gréville* with especial care. It was certainly an unusual subject for Millet, a single building rather than a scene of people at work. That it was a memory of childhood may explain why the artist recalled the church as being much larger than it really was: a tiny figure walking by, spade on shoulder, is dwarfed by it. Most of those who went to see the work were principally struck by the unusual way Millet had used bright dots and dashes to apply his colours. It was as if at the end of his life Millet too had been lapped by the spreading ripples of the new Impressionism. But Vincent had no eyes for 'Father Millet's' recent technique – it was that ominous, over-large church with the black silhouettes of birds flocking round its belfry that held him spellbound.

He had every reason to believe an era was ending; Millet's death was followed by that of another great nature painter, Camille Corot. Vincent joined the crowds at his memorial exhibition, as much a gesture of protest as an expression of love of the man's work, for Corot had suffered more than most from the stupidities of the art establishment. Despite his stature as one of the greatest landscapists of the age he had been humiliated the year before when the Salon jury had reluctantly offered him the medal of honour only to withdraw it at the last moment. For Vincent it made having to defend the type of Salon victors Goupil specialised in all the more unpalatable.

Uncle Cent had not yet left his mansion in Neuilly, so when Boussod warned him what was going on he took to dropping in on Vincent to see if he could sort out the problem. It did not take him long to conclude that religion was the source of all the trouble.

"Supernatural things I may not know," he said during one visit. "But I know everything about natural things."

But if he thought such *aperçus* would deflect his nephew he was deceiving himself. Reporting the conversation to Theo, Vincent tartly pointed out that one of Uncle Cent's favourite paintings was Gleyre's *Lost Illusions*. Vincent was clearly determined to hold fast to his.

There is no knowing just what Boussod and Uncle Cent said to each other after these encounters but they evidently put much of Vincent's trouble down to his increasing isolation. One result was that a new arrival at the gallery was sent to lodge at the house in Montmartre.

Harry Gladwell was an eighteen-year-old Englishman, the son of a London art dealer, who had been apprenticed to Goupil's to learn the business before joining his father's firm. It was a clever move on the part of whoever brought them together for Harry was almost as much an outcast as Vincent. With his gawky stick-limbed appearance, prominent red ears, protruding lips and close-cropped black hair, he had become the butt of the other apprentices' humour from the day he arrived. Sensing a fellow victim, Vincent took immediately to his junior though not without some private misgivings when he saw how much the young man ate. The ever-frugal Vincent disapproved of gluttony and the painfully thin Harry, still a growing boy, certainly enjoyed his food. Nothing daunted, Vincent soon had that failing, and much else, fully under control. For despite everything he could still attract friendship and Harry was soon hurrying home alongside him for a moderate supper followed by an evening of Bible study. They tried to read the Bible aloud to each other from beginning to end and there was that other faith to be shared: Harry was led to the shrine of Breton in the Luxembourg and encouraged to decorate his own room with prints acceptable to his new mentor.

Sadly, having a new friend and sharing his spiritual life with him did nothing to quieten Vincent's increasing religious fervour. On the contrary it intensified it; the letters to Theo are punctuated with quotations from sermons and passages from the Bible. He even sent his sister Anna the texts of certain English revivalist hymns including 'Nearer my God to Thee' and 'Oft in Danger, Oft in Woe'. In one thing at least he had changed, he had abandoned the search for temporal love. Even Michelet fell from grace:

> *Theo, I want to make a suggestion that may surprise you. Do not read Michelet any longer or any book (except the Bible), until we have seen each other at Christmas, . . .*

And a few weeks later:

> *I am going to destroy all my books by Michelet, etc. I wish you would do the same.*

Any hopes Vincent may have had that his religious fervour would please his father were misplaced. The older man had crippled his own career by his finely tuned moderation and was far from happy to discover that his eldest son had become a proselytising fanatic. He communicated his disfavour, conjuring up the image of Icarus flying too near the sun and countering Vincent's quotations from the Bible with more seemly ones of his own: ". . . above all let us have patience; those who believe hasten not."

For the moment that was all the older man could do for his son. Once again the family were being uprooted to another parish, not far away, in Etten. It paid a higher stipend and, superficially at least, was better in appearance; the church was much bigger with quite an impressive steeple and the house was larger with a fine drive and a big garden. Vincent was eager to see the new home and was soon writing to Theo to say how much he was looking forward to Christmas. What he omitted to tell him was the unpalatable truth that he was not due for leave that year. The holiday period was Goupil's busiest time with hundreds of customers buying presents for their families. Only a few members of staff were given permission to take their leave before January and that year Vincent was not among them. He decided to take it anyway and when he turned up at the new parsonage no one was aware of what he had done. As Theo worked near by in The Hague he could get across for the holiday itself but he too may have been ignorant of the fact that Vincent had simply slipped away from Paris without a word to anyone. After seven years with Goupil, during most of which he had been dedicated to his work, with the prospect of considerable advancement as his uncle's heir, Vincent had deliberately taken the one course of action that would ensure it all came crashing down around him. When his brother realised what he had done he could not understand, let alone justify it. Vincent still seemed interested in art and he had no other career in mind; it was totally irrational. Only Theo's loyalty to the vow they had made can explain his patience in the face of such behaviour. Though it must have been deeply embarrassing for him and hardly likely to help his own career, he never criticised Vincent nor uttered the least word of reproach.

Back in Paris, Boussod had no such vow to restrain him and as soon as Vincent returned to Goupil's he was told to go up to the director's office. The interview, however, did not progress quite as Boussod had planned. He began by pointing out that things had gone too far, but, instead of showing any remorse, Vincent merely expressed the hope that there were no serious complaints against him. Whether this was sarcasm or merely the revelation of his genuine belief that he had done no wrong mattered little. It sounded nothing less than impertinent and Boussod sharply told him that there were indeed serious complaints. Vincent heard him out, then calmly offered his resignation. There was nothing more to be said.

Only his family connections can have prevented him from being asked to leave at once. Instead, he was allowed to work out three months' notice until April 1st, 1876, a more than generous concession. But despite the civility of his treatment and despite his own evident desire to leave, it was still a terrible blow. So far all his difficulties in life had seemed to come from outside, even the disastrous 'affair' with Eugénie Loyer could be interpreted as an act of cruel fate. Now, for the first time, he alone had precipitated a crisis. He, whose path in life had been made so easy, had thrown it all away.

Only someone with a growing taste for martyrdom could have lived through those three months. Relations with his colleagues had been strained; now that they knew that he, the nephew of a senior director, had deliberately spurned an opportunity they could only dream of, their reactions were hardly favourable. To young men trying hard to build their careers without Vincent's enviable connections his gesture was more than perverse. They had thought him touched before; now they were sure he was mad.

Things were little better at his lodgings where he had to face Harry. The younger man had looked up to him, now what must he think? Near the end of the month Harry announced that he was going to move; he still liked Vincent, they would remain friends long after he had left Paris, but it was too difficult to handle his moodiness and increased obsession with religion. When he did come round Harry tried to take Vincent's mind off things by recommending books he should read. He tried George Eliot's *Felix Holt* and a little later her *Scenes of Clerical Life* but both the novel and the stories with their theme of noble suffering only served to reinforce his own perception of what had happened. Apart from Harry's rare visits, life was reduced to the Bible, the occasional novel and his pipe, though he did find one book that was to have a greater influence on his thinking than any other: Thomas à Kempis' *The Imitation of Christ*. It was not merely the book's clear rules on how the Christian life should be lived that intrigued him, but the whole background to the author's thinking. Thomas à Kempis' association with the Brethren of the Common Life and his belief that true contentment on earth would be found in lay communities pledged to moderation and simple living appealed to many in the mid-century who were appalled at the chaos, moral and physical, that rapid industrialisation had left in its wake. Alone in his Montmartre room, gripped by that forceful medieval tract, Vincent joined them in spirit. The book seemed to answer so many of the questions and confusions he had wrestled with since leaving home: 'How Sorrows are to be Borne Patiently', 'On Self-Denial', 'Renunciation of our Desires'. As with Michelet before, these were not vague suggestions, but clear-cut rules. Utterly alone, in communion with that holy guide, it was easy to see himself as the monk in his cell, the hermit in his cave. All evidence of any identification with the world around him now disappeared from his letters to Theo. Gone were any of those exact descriptions of things seen and done that had been one of the great joys of his writing. The fine balance between Art, Religion and Life had been lost.

As the three months' notice passed, the uncomfortable prospect of unemployment loomed, but whatever new work there might be for him would have to satisfy the new craving that Thomas à Kempis had inspired. The task would have to be 'useful', it would have to offer him the chance to lead a Christian life, preferably in England, of course – his thoughts never strayed far from London. This was partly the residue of his longing for Eugénie but mainly because it was the one place where his family's writ did not run. He discovered that the English newspapers on sale in Paris sometimes carried advertisements for foreign assistants to teach languages. They were only temporary posts and badly paid, if at all, but it was a solution of sorts. Teaching was a vocation and might lead to something even more dedicated, and at the least he would be in England. He began writing to various schools, though finding a post turned out to be surprisingly difficult. And there were other hurts to bear: Harry was given Vincent's position in the painting galleries. He knew he had no grounds for complaint and tried to put a brave face on it, but it hurt all the same and his letters to Theo kept absent-mindedly returning to the subject as if he could not get it out of his thoughts.

His first application, for a post at a school in Scarborough, was rejected. It was a blow, but he found some comfort in reading Bulwer Lytton's *Kenelm Chillingly* which he described to Theo as the adventures of a rich Englishman's son who only finds rest and peace away from his own kind and among the 'lower classes'; setbacks had to be seen as good for the soul.

He continued to honour his old heroes, buying three engravings by 'Father Millet' at an exhibition at Durand-Ruel's gallery, though if there were any of the new Impressionist works still on display he failed to register their existence. All in all, he was keeping on a remarkably even keel despite increasing worries over his failure to find anything to do. But it was unlikely that this state of equilibrium could go on if his applications continued to be rejected. It was to be a close-run thing. His twenty-third birthday dawned on March 30th, 1876, two days before his time with Goupil's was due to end, and he still had no prospect of employment. Happily for him, Harry called round at six-thirty that morning on his way to work and brought him a present of an autumn landscape to cheer him up. They talked for a moment together, but then he was alone again and the day stretched before him empty and hopeless. It was only the very next morning, as he was preparing to leave his room, that the postman brought the offer of an unpaid post at a school in Ramsgate. His relief was considerable.

He packed his prints and books and set off for Etten where he was to spend the fortnight leading up to Easter. As he travelled north he must have anticipated trouble; there would surely be an unpleasant encounter with his father now that he had thrown away his career and sunk to a job without pay and prospects in a seaside town across the Channel. To his surprise, Pastor Theodorus kept his feelings to himself and was once again unfailingly patient with his errant son. It may be that he had by then come to realise that all was not well in his family. During that holiday he went with Vincent to Brussels, where they saw Uncle Hein, who as so often before, was suffering from an unspecified illness, the same sort of thing that dogged Uncle Cent. If anything, Hein's condition was worse and when he died a few years later there was a quiet feeling of relief in the family that his sufferings were over.

On the return journey Theodorus and Vincent kept their talk firmly to art; religion was too sensitive a topic, the Rembrandts in the Louvre were safer. Back at the parsonage, Theo and Elisabeth arrived on the Sunday before Easter and though Vincent would have to leave on Good Friday to arrive in Ramsgate for the start of the new term, their holiday together would be remembered as one of the happiest.

So happy was Vincent and so miserable to be leaving them all that at each stage of the journey to Ramsgate – by train to Zevenbergen on the Friday, by the Saturday steamer overnight to Harwich and the Sunday trains to London, Canterbury and Ramsgate – he jotted down his succeeding impressions:

> *Before sunrise I had already heard the lark. When we were near the last station before London, the sun rose. The bank of grey clouds had disappeared and there was the sun, as simple and as grand as ever I saw it, a real Easter sun. The grass sparkled with dew and night frost. But I still prefer that grey hour when we parted.*

It was a remarkable swing in mood. After months of ignoring the world about him, of being blind to the excitement of Paris, here he was once more minutely aware of every detail in the changing scene, a sure sign that some interest in the world around him had been reawakened after those last dismal months at Goupil's. Surely this new life in Ramsgate offered some hope for the future? He was to be disillusioned almost as soon as he arrived.

4
1876 — 1878

Pray, my Soul

At first sight Ramsgate fulfilled all Vincent's expectations. The elegant cliff-front terraces of the upper town had pretty wrought-iron canopies and balconies. When he looked down to the harbour, the lower town seemed cosily familiar:

> *The houses near the sea are mostly built of yellow brick in the style of those in the Nassaulaan in The Hague, but they are higher and have gardens full of cedars and other dark evergreens. There is a harbour full of ships enclosed by some stone jetties on which one can walk.*

He made his way from the station to Spencer Square in the upper town, near the cliff edge, and there was nothing disappointing about his first sight of the school. Number 6 Royal Road was in a terrace of large houses that made up one side of the square. It overlooked the central garden with its lawn and surrounding lilac bushes enclosed by neat iron railings, the sort of English scene he had loved from his first days in London. But once he had been admitted to his new place of work doubt began to creep in.

As term had not yet started the owner and headmaster Mr Stokes was still away and Vincent could see immediately that the boys were bored. They lived above the school and evidently had little to occupy them. He was shown the nearby house where he would lodge with another assistant, but as soon as he returned to the main building he found disquieting evidence of the school's inadequacies. He wrote to Theo to tell him the bad news:

Another curious place is the room with the rotten floor. It has six washbasins in which they have to wash themselves; a dim light filters on to the washstand through a window with broken panes. It is a rather melancholy sight.

When Stokes eventually returned he was not as bad as Vincent feared. The boys seemed to like him, he even played marbles with them, but if he was displeased in any way they were sent to bed without supper. He was not a cruel man, he was simply capricious, hardly a quality to be recommended in someone with the care of children. What Vincent quickly realised was that Stokes' school was all too typical of countless small institutions which had sprung up all over the country to provide the sons of the new middle class with an inexpensive elementary education. Such schools existed as much to keep boys out of their parents' way as anything else and to describe them as Dickensian would be grossly to exaggerate their shortcomings. 'Dotheboys Hall' was a fictional example of the extremes of Victorian child abuse; Stokes' school was just a rather run-down money-making business. While it did little harm to its young clients, at the same time it did not do them much good. Worst of all, as Vincent noted, were the bugs, though he optimistically recorded that the sea-view from the upper windows made one forget them. He tried his best to cheer up the boys, telling them

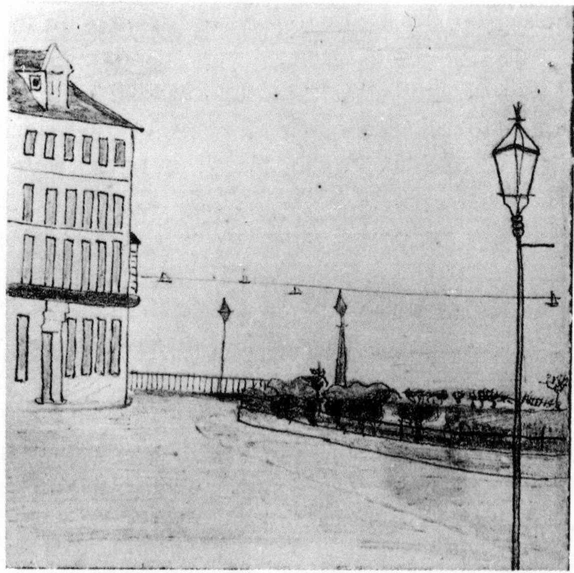

Vincent's sketch of the view from the upper window at 6 Royal Road, Ramsgate.

stories and taking them for walks. On one occasion they went on a hike to Pegwell Bay and on another witnessed a dramatic storm which caught Vincent's imagination:

> *The sea was yellowish, especially near the shore; on the horizon a strip of light, and above it immense dark grey clouds from which the rain poured down in slanting streaks. The wind blew the dust from the little white path on the rocks. To the right were fields of young green corn, and in the distance the town looked like the towns Albrecht Dürer used to etch. A town with its turrets, mills, slate roofs and houses built in Gothic style, and below, the harbour between the two jetties which project far into the sea.*

Such excitements were rare, however, and teaching aside there was not much to occupy him apart from church-going and a renewed interest in English hymns. Ramsgate was a pleasant enough place but he knew he would never find his vocation with Mr Stokes. Part of Mr Stokes' frustration may have arisen from a sense of failure, for he had originally wanted to be a painter but it had come to nothing. Had he told Vincent this, there might have been more sympathy between them, as it was Vincent simply wanted to get away. He sketched a bit to pass the time – a view from that same upper window showing the row of houses near the cliff edge – but time hung heavy and it was a relief when Stokes announced that he intended to move the school to London. He had found a house in Isleworth to the west of the city and intended to leave Ramsgate as soon as possible. Vincent was happy to go along with the move, especially when Stokes hinted at the possibility of a small salary, but he was also planning to see what other opportunities the capital might offer once he got there.

It all happened very quickly and after only two months in Ramsgate the day of the move arrived. Vincent decided to set off by himself on an astonishing hundred mile trek across southern England. He took in the sights of Canterbury before trekking to South London where he spent a night at the home of Harry Gladwell's parents. They were delighted to meet their son's friend and refused to let him leave the next day until a heavy storm had passed. Late that afternoon he was able to set off for Welwyn, where he spent the night at Ivy Cottage, where Anna was staying.

When he arrived at the Stokes' new home in Isleworth he soon learned that there was little chance of improvement; the promised salary was forgotten and Vincent started to look around for a less inconsistent employer. He had already tried to get a job as an assistant to a London clergyman but had been turned down. He began to travel into the City on his free days to see if any of the missions to the London poor might offer him a post. He had enough experience of conditions in the East End to know something of the sort of work they did but the minimum age for a trainee was twenty-five and, aside from youth, there was his shock of red hair, as well as the excitable accent to make the dour worthies that interviewed him doubt his suitability. He was just beginning to think that he would never break away from Mr Stokes and his depressing establishment when he was saved by a remarkable man.

The Reverend Thomas Slade-Jones was a local Congregationalist minister and from the moment Vincent was introduced to him he recognised the kind of dedicated Christian he admired. The Reverend Jones, as he was always called, looked like a kindly gnome with big features and a heavy beard, and he was indeed a good soul. He listened to Vincent's rambling ideas about his life and what he hoped to do but instead of turning away, as most did, he sympathised. If Vincent felt he had a vocation then Jones would try to help him. The minister had two congregational chapels in his care and preached at other churches, but he also ran a day school at his home in Isleworth and he told Vincent he could take him on as an assistant, and this time there would be a small salary. More important to Vincent was Jones' promise that if things went well he might be able to help out with some of the church duties. As this was just what he had been hoping for, he lost no time in saying goodbye to Stokes and moved into the handsome Queen Anne house on Twickenham Road that served as Slade-Jones' presbytery.

The house, Holme Court, was opposite the main church. Vincent had a room at the back overlooking a pretty garden with acacia trees and he soon hung a selection of his prints on the walls. Mrs Slade-Jones was a plump lady not unlike his mother and the fact that the church opposite looked uncannily like his father's first chapel in Zundert added to the feeling that he had in some ways come home. As his first duties included tutoring the Slade-Jones' elder children in German he soon felt part of the family.

At that time Isleworth and Twickenham, the two villages served by the minister, were well outside the London sprawl and so Vincent found himself back in the country again. Best of all, the school offered a genuine education to its pupils, and it was a relief to be doing something worthwhile at last. He was unusually happy, talking with the Slade-Jones' children, telling stories to the boarders or just strolling in the garden where he could smoke his beloved pipe away from the disapproving looks of Mrs Slade-Jones who loathed the smell of his cheap tobacco.

There was one sad, though moving, day when he took the train to south London to see Harry who had come home for the funeral of his seventeen-year-old sister. She had died as a result of a riding accident and the two young men felt a strong bond of friendship as they stood together in the church. They spent the rest of the day and most of the evening talking earnestly. Whatever had divided them in Paris was happily over and it felt like their first times together, when they would discuss the Kingdom of God and read the Bible. Harry walked him to the station and they strolled up and down the platform deep in conversation:

> *. . . I think I shall never forget those last moments before we said goodbye. We know each other so well: his work was my work; the people he knows there, I know also, his life was my life.*

After their farewells, the train took Vincent past St Paul's and on to Richmond. There he took the towpath along the banks of the Thames to Isleworth, the surrounding countryside still visible in the late light of August.

But despite the feelings of friendship with Harry and the Slade-Jones family, and even the new satisfactions brought by his work, the craving to serve was still gnawing away at him. He went again to one of the religious societies in the City because he had heard that clergymen in ports like Liverpool and Hull needed assistants with a knowledge of foreign languages to help with the missions to seamen. When that came to nothing he wondered whether he might obtain a post in one of the northern mining towns where there were evangelical missions to the miserable pit-head villages.

Sensing his young friend's frustration the Reverend Jones decided to reduce his teaching and let him help in the churches. Vincent was overjoyed. Apart from the Isleworth church there was the Turnham Green Congregational Church in Chiswick High Road which the Reverend Jones had founded in 1873. The original building had burned down and been replaced by what the locals called 'the tin tabernacle'. As well as these two congregational churches the Reverend Jones was also on the local Methodist circuit and preached at the Wesleyan Chapel in Richmond. This was good news to Vincent who felt increasingly drawn to Methodism with its emphasis on personal salvation, its crusading attitude and the fact that it chose to minister to the poorer sections of society. No doubt aware of his young friend's thinking, Jones arranged for him to begin his new role at the Monday prayer meeting at the Wesleyan Chapel. It was a good way to accustom the young man to public speaking before he tried to tackle a full sermon. Vincent spoke up as best he could and though it was evident he had inherited his father's weakness and would never find preaching easy, Jones was satisfied that he would learn to cope.

Despite his nervousness there were many things Vincent felt he wanted to say and he began making notes in a sort of 'sermon-book' so that he would be ready. He spent much of his free time re-reading Bunyan's *Pilgrim's Progress* which was beginning to assume an importance similar to *The Imitation of Christ*. The English Puritans seemed wholly admirable, their attempt to create the ideal Christian community in the New World fascinated him and one of his favourite English prints was Boughton's *The Landing of the Pilgrim Fathers* which conveyed a sense of the simple faith which had sustained them through their hazardous journey. He found similar themes in many different sources. The simple life and the shared community could both be seen in Thomas à Kempis, in the history of the Puritans, and even in his idealised view of Millet and the Barbizon painters turning their backs on the industrialised world.

Had these been merely the solitary musings of an obsessed young man they might not carry much weight for us, but in fact Vincent had arrived by his own route at ideas and solutions which preoccupied many at the time. John Ruskin, William Morris and the nascent Arts and Crafts movement all advocated the simple life based on creative labour and looked to the medieval craft guilds as a source of inspiration. The rapid industrialisation of the nineteenth century seemed to have offered equally unacceptable alternatives: gross consumerism for the successful, squalid poverty for the unsuccessful. Appalled by such a contrast and finding both ways of life demeaning, many were struggling to articulate a vision strong enough to beckon people towards an alternative way of life. Vincent has often been dismissed as a religious fanatic when in fact his thinking was in line with the major philosophical currents of his day. His tragedy was that he followed his path entirely alone. Because he had no one to share it with, he was utterly unable to express the nature and complexity of his thinking. To those around him he would either appear sullen and morose or he would rant and preach convoluted nonsense. He had, so it seemed to him, perceived great truths. Sadly they remained locked within him.

Only the Reverend Jones sensed that he had something to say and tried his best to help him. Early in November he arranged for Vincent to preach his first sermon at that same Wesleyan Chapel and the young man set out to write down a coherent statement of what he had come to believe. On the Sunday morning they arrived at the church together, the Reverend Jones led the service and when the moment came, called on Vincent to preach. It was one of the most terrifying yet most uplifting moments of his life:

> *When I was standing in the pulpit, I felt like somebody who, emerging from a dark cave underground, comes back to the friendly daylight. It is a delightful thought that in the future wherever I go, I shall preach the gospel; to do that well, one must have the gospel in one's heart. May the Lord give it to me.*

He copied out the sermon for Theo. Parts of it are not easy to understand but in some sections the tortured phrases drop away and the nobility of what he was trying to express becomes movingly lucid:

> *. . . Our life is a pilgrim's progress. I once saw a very beautiful picture: it was a landscape at evening. In the distance on the right-hand side a row of hills appeared blue in the evening mist. Above those hills the splendour of the sunset, the grey clouds with their silver linings of silver and gold and purple. The landscape is a plain or heath covered with grass and its yellow leaves, for it was in autumn. Through the landscape a road leads to a high mountain far, far away, on the top of that mountain is a city whereon the setting sun casts a glory. On the road walks a pilgrim, staff in hand. He has been walking for a good long while already and he is very tired. And now he meets a woman, a figure in black, that makes one think of St Paul's word: As being sorrowful yet always rejoicing. That Angel of God had been placed there to encourage the pilgrims and to answer their questions and the pilgrim asks her: Does the road go uphill then all the way?*
>
> *And the answer is: 'Yes to the very end.'*

> *And he asks again: 'And will the journey take all day long?'*
> *And the answer is: 'From morn till night my friend.'*
> *And the pilgrim goes on sorrowful yet always rejoicing – sorrowful because he is so far off and the road is long. Hopeful as he looks up to the eternal city far away, resplendent in the evening glow . . .*

Vincent had proclaimed the unity of all he held most dear: the pilgrim's progress of Bunyan's book and Boughton's painting. Art and literature brought together, for Pilgrim's lady in black is also the woman in Michelet's portrait. He had paraphrased Christina Rossetti's poem 'Uphill' and quoted the Bible. And throughout the sermon were references to his own love of the natural world. This was the Vincent who loved walking alone at nightfall, coming home, after the last train had left him at Richmond station, along the banks of the Thames watching the outline of the trees black against the darkening sky over Syon Park. Of course the pilgrim is himself and the journey his own.

The Reverend Jones was satisfied with this début and told him he would now be teaching Sunday School in the 'Tin Tabernacle' in Chiswick High Road. But first Vincent would have to go into London to collect school fees. While in town he suddenly decided to call on the Loyers. Eugénie was out but her mother gave him tea. Perhaps he felt that as things were going so well he could cope with such an encounter without provoking his former depression.

He spent the night at the Gladwells' in Lewisham and returned to Chiswick by underground the following morning. He had been asked to attend a meeting at the Turnham Green Church, where he was formally enrolled as a teacher and his name duly entered in the register as 'Mr van Gog'. That night he walked along the riverside to Petersham, where he preached his second sermon in the tiny Methodist chapel. He was much more at ease and jokingly warned his audience that they were in for some bad English. As he walked back to Holme Court there was nothing to cloud his contentment. He was doing exactly what he had prayed for and was looking forward to going home for Christmas. Surely now he could stop punishing himself and relax a little?

It was not to be. Just as all seemed to be going smoothly he experienced another violent change of mood, though this time it was not a descent into depression but its opposite. Like a rider whose mount suddenly bolts, his religious feelings gathered so dangerous a momentum he could only rein them in for brief intervals before a headlong rush carried him forward again. His condition only became clear towards the end of November when he wrote a letter to Theo that exposed just how erratic his thinking had become. The letter started calmly enough with a description of his first sermon, but, before he could post it, a letter from Theo arrived and he decided to add his reply. Between the two letters the change of mood is starkly apparent. The second opens with the melancholy lines:

Mine eye, oh weep no more, but hold your tears,
My soul, mourn no more, but pray, but pray, my soul.

Vincent went on to tell Theo there were hours and days when God seemed to hide his countenance. He recounted the story of his misery on that first day at school when he had watched his parents' carriage drive away, a secret he had kept locked within himself till then. With these recollections out of the way the letter takes on a breathless quality, religious thoughts, texts and parables tumble over one another, morsels of good advice are roughly scribbled up the margins:

Do you ever go to Communion? They that are whole need not a physician, but they that are sick.

It continued for page after page. He tried to bring it to a close late one evening after expressing a jumble of thoughts almost as if he were speaking in tongues. When he had calmed down somewhat he started again, slightly clearer at first as he recalled a carriage ride through the snow they had shared one Christmas. Soon, however, the ranting returned and quotations from scripture were confused with his own thoughts, finally ending on a note of near-hysteria:

"For I am with thee, saith the Lord, to save thee . . . All thy lovers have forgotten thee . . . I shall restore health unto thee, and take the plagues away from thee."

"The Lord hath appeared of old to me, saying, Yea, I have loved thee with an everlasting love." "As one whom his mother comforted, so will I comfort you, saith the Lord," "There is a friend that sticketh closer than a brother."

Whatever Theo made of that, one thing was clear: his brother was no longer rational and something would have to be done. As Vincent was about to travel home for Christmas the family must be warned.

His father had never approved of Vincent's return to England in the first place, and stories of his becoming an untrained 'curate' in London only increased his distress. It was time to accept what had been increasingly obvious for some time, that his eldest son had mental problems. Something was wrong and they would have to deal with it.

If they were expecting Vincent to act strangely when he arrived at the parsonage they had not banked on his ability to surprise, for the worst of his manic phase was already over by the time he began the journey to Etten. Indeed, at first sight there seemed to be nothing wrong with him and it took all of Pastor Theodorus' determination to press on with his plan. Vincent, he declared, must not return to England, there was no future for him there and it was evidently doing him no good whatsoever. He could not let his eldest son ruin himself as some sort of fanatical preacher in a foreign land.

The family must have feared that he would strongly object to this diktat, but to everyone's surprise he meekly agreed. It is more than likely that he too had been frightened by the mania which had gripped him and was only too willing to do anything which might help avoid another attack. Letting them take over his life again may have seemed the easiest solution.

He certainly had a happy enough Christmas, especially when Theo turned up, and, after the festivities were over, Vincent simply slipped back into his former existence, hanging about the parsonage, waiting for others to sort things out.

Just as they had done before, the family turned to Uncle Cent. It must have taken all Theodorus' powers of persuasion to convince his brother that he should continue to help. Uncle Cent had been deeply hurt by his nephew's departure from Goupil's and felt disinclined to do anything more for him. Still, Dorus was his favourite brother, he had just moved into the newly converted mansion in Princenhage to be near him, so better to yield. Vincent was summoned. If nothing else he would at last have the chance to see his uncle's fabled private collection on display, and no doubt Cent was more than ready to let his errant nephew reflect on what might have been his had he persevered in art dealing. But faced with the young man he had once thought of as his own son, he agreed to make one last effort – he would contact a Mr Braat who ran the booksellers Blussé & Van Braam in Dordrecht near Rotterdam to see if there might be a post in the shop for Vincent. When the message came it put Braat in an awkward position; his brother Frans worked in one of Goupil's Paris branches and, despite his retirement, Uncle Cent was still an influential force in the company. In truth there was no vacancy, but under the circumstances one would have to be created. Braat duly travelled to Princenhage to see the young man and it was agreed that he should have a week's trial in the New Year.

The family was delighted, it was surely the ideal situation for one who for days on end would be lost in a book. If he could recover only a degree of the enthusiasm he had once shown for art dealing he might yet make a career for himself.

Vincent travelled to Dordrecht in January 1877 and found lodgings in the Tolbrugstraatje in the house of a Mr Rijken, a corn and flour merchant. The old public weigh-house after which the street was named was just across the square from the bookshop, from where there was a superb view of the Voorstraat harbour and the pleasing jumble of picturesque houses rising from the water in traditional Dutch style. Indeed it was this proximity to the sea that was to give Vincent his place in the business, for not long after his arrival there was one of the sudden floods which periodically threatened the town. Lying awake, Vincent was the first to realise that the North Sea waters were lapping around the square and the surrounding streets. He flung on his clothes, ran over to the shop and roused the Braats, who lived on the upper floors. As soon as they had thrown open the doors Vincent raced down the stairs, struggling to carry the stock from the rapidly flooding basement to the apartment above. The family and anyone else they could raise were soon rallying to help, but it was Vincent who had raised the alarm and done most of the work. He was the hero of the hour.

Mr Braat was well pleased, and happy to confirm him in the post. This gave him the self-assurance at last to write to the Slade-Joneses to explain what had happened. The minister was sympathetic. He had no doubt witnessed some of the signs of Vincent's mania and realised that something was very wrong with him. Indeed, since that attack there was visible evidence of a plunge down the spiral of his mental instability: people noticed that he was either vague and lost in thought or suddenly talking and laughing too loudly. He knew this himself and wrote to Theo to say that one ought not to mind being thought eccentric. He was certainly aware of the reactions he provoked in others, his fellow lodgers at the Rijkens' could barely suppress their amusement at his odd behaviour. The one exception was a young schoolteacher, P. C. Gorlitz, with whom Vincent shared a room for a time and who became a good friend. Fortunately, despite his peculiarities, Vincent retained his ability to make loyal friends and Gorlitz has left a remarkably sympathetic portrait of Vincent at twenty-four:

> He was a singular man with a singular appearance into the bargain. He was well made, and had reddish hair which stood up on end; his face was homely and covered with freckles, but changed and brightened wonderfully when he warmed into enthusiasm, which happened often enough. Van Gogh provoked laughter repeatedly by his attitude and behaviour – for everything he did and thought and felt, and his way of living, was different from that of others of his age. At table he said lengthy prayers and ate like a penitent friar: for instance, he would not take meat, gravy, etc. And then his face had always an abstracted expression – pondering, deeply serious, melancholy. But when he laughed, he did so heartily and with gusto, and his whole face brightened.

Despite Gorlitz's evident sympathy his is still a somewhat alarming description of one so young; but if his fellow boarders found him comical, at the bookshop Mr Braat was less amused. He soon realised that the enthusiasm Vincent had displayed at the time of the flood had been a momentary aberration. Almost immediately afterwards any pretence of interest in the work of Blussé & Van Braam evaporated. His work was similar to that of a bookkeeper, checking stock in and out, and he had been given a high desk near the door, at which he stood waiting for deliveries. This was a gross error of judgement on Braat's part for Vincent soon took to wearing his English top hat again. If any clients were brave enough to seek help of this outlandish figure they found him distinctly unwilling to tear himself away from the private work which preoccupied him. When Braat succeeded in sneaking a look he found to his astonishment that Vincent was spending his days making a parallel translation of the Bible into French, German, English and Dutch, on sheets of paper he had ruled into four columns. After a while he set aside the Bible translation and took to sketching. But this seemed worse to Mr Braat who thought they were hopeless. Naturally, the older man was furious. He hadn't expected much from his young employee but this was intolerable. To cap it all, Vincent showed none of the respect due to a patron. He never troubled to formally 'call' on Mr Braat and his family, as he had done with Tersteeg in The Hague.

Though his parents were aware things could easily go wrong, they had no idea that the situation had deteriorated so rapidly. Vincent's letters revealed nothing of his feelings, rather they gave the impression that all was well. Even Theo, when he and Vincent made a journey to Amsterdam to visit the galleries, was denied the truth. Only Uncle Cent had some inkling of what was going on for Vincent had written to ask for his help in studying for the Church. Uncle Cent's response was brisk: as he could be of no assistance in this regard he saw no reason to continue the correspondence. It had happened at last, Vincent had finally alienated the one person who had ever been able to help him. He broke his silence and wrote to tell Theo what had happened but it was left to P. C. Gorlitz, who called on the Van Goghs while visiting their part of the country, to break the news that Vincent was determined to go into the ministry. He had been to see a Rev. van Hoorn in Dordrecht to ask for advice and it was clear, from everything Gorlitz said, that there was now no stopping him. After three months as a phantom bookseller the charade was over, and to Mr Braat's evident relief he announced that he was leaving.

Back home again it was perfectly clear that Vincent was no longer willing to go on doing as he was told. In any case there was not much left for anyone to tell him. When asked, all he would say was that he wanted to be a pastor like his father and grandfather before him, and, if anyone protested that he had left it too late or that he had not passed the necessary examinations, he doggedly repeated his wish. Eventually he wore them down and they reluctantly agreed. Yet his difficulties were hardly over. He was long past university age and in any case would have to pass the state examinations in classics and mathematics – a formidable curriculum in itself – before he could even hope to get into a theology faculty. But what could Theodorus do? If his son did have a vocation, how could he of all people stand in his way? The only solution was to again activate the extended family and see what resources could be mustered.

Vincent would have to live in Amsterdam and though there was not much money for him, one of the uncles could see that he had a roof over his head. Uncomfortably aware that the artistic side of the family had been alienated, they decided to approach Uncle Jan, the vice-admiral, who was then commandant of the Amsterdam naval dockyard.

As a widower whose children were grown up, he would have ample room in his official residence for Vincent. Better still, he was more robust and jollier than his rather pinched brothers with their endless illnesses. In his full dress-uniform resplendent with gold braid and medals Jan looked rather operatic and as a sailor and man of the world he was less likely to be over-critical of Vincent's ways than the distinctly stuffy art-dealing brothers.

The other key figure in this new scheme was a Pastor Johannes Stricker, Vincent's uncle by marriage, having married one of that seemingly unending line of Carbentus sisters. With a thick roll of beard beneath his chin and clean-shaven upper lip the Reverend Stricker looked a typical Dutch country pastor though he was in fact a theologian of repute and author of a much praised study entitled *Jesus of Nazareth, a sketch based on history*. Also a popular preacher, he had the metropolitan connections denied his isolated brother-in-law Theodorus. As the first task was to help Vincent cram for the state examinations, his contacts were essential and despite what he must have heard about his nephew, Pastor Stricker set about choosing the best teachers he knew. A young professor of classics, Dr M. B. Mendes da Costa, would deal with Greek and Latin, and Mendes' nephew Teixeira da Mattos, a teacher at the Jewish School, could handle the mathematics. Uncle Stricker warned Mendes that he would not have an easy task and described some of Vincent's odder traits, but Mendes was not discouraged. He was a clever choice because master and pupil would be near-contemporaries. With his stiff collar, high buttoned jacket, and neat centre parting, Mendes looked more like a fresh-faced young student than the increasingly scruffy Vincent. But such differences proved superficial; they were soon on first-name terms, and Mendes clearly enjoyed the hours they spent together in his rooms in the Jewish quarter, where Vincent came for his lessons. Although he too was struck by the red hair and freckles, Mendes found Vincent 'far from unattractive' and was intrigued by a face that expressed much 'and hid so much more'.

Vincent had only a year in which to cram for the examinations. He arrived in Amsterdam in May 1877, the season at which the old town with its canals and bridges, its flower market on the Singel, its imposing churches and narrow alleys, looked their best. He was to lead a curiously double life. On the one hand he was an impecunious student; on the other he was living in Uncle Jan's splendid town house at the entrance to the harbour, a building of some grandeur with two towers spiky with flag poles for official celebrations. It must have surprised passers-by to see the unkempt, shock-headed Vincent emerge from such a residence. If he felt the need of company he could always drop in on Uncle Cor's substantial premises on the Liesestraat, where he could observe the toing and froing on one of the city's more fashionable thoroughfares.

Not long after his arrival Vincent called on his Uncle Stricker and when he was shown into the pastor's sitting-room he found a young woman heavily swathed in the deepest black mourning. She was introduced to him as his cousin Cornelia ('Kee') Vos, the pastor's married daughter who was in mourning for the recent death of her infant son. It was a fateful encounter and it was not lost on Vincent that in her grief his cousin Kee had taken on the same rather stern look he had admired in Eugénie. The aura of tragedy which surrounded the young woman was further intensified when Vincent learned that her husband Christoffel was dying of an incurable lung disease. He had been a pastor himself, but ill-health had forced him to relinquish his post and he was now making a precarious living as a part-time journalist. They had an elder boy, Johannes, and Vincent was entranced by the sad picture of the grieving young mother with her surviving son clutching her arm. As she lived not far from the Strickers', Vincent became a regular attender at the Sunday morning services at the Oudezijds Chapel where his uncle preached so that he could call at the Vos house on his way home. He was thrilled when shortly after that first meeting Kee presented him with a copy of the original Latin version of *The Imitation of Christ*, undoubtedly the most perspicacious gift she could possibly have made.

With 'The Lady in Black' now an all-too-present reality, Vincent grew dangerously elated. Everything about the city seemed to feed his fantasy. Walking through the narrow, packed streets of the Jewish quarter he could study the engravings in the windows of the booksellers – he even found another copy of Van der Maaten's *Funeral Procession*. He then had the strange sensation of hearing a reference to the picture in a sermon about the parable of the sower at an early morning service for, aside from his lessons, he had embarked on a constant round of church-going with, as before, scant regard for denomination. His letters during his year in Amsterdam are largely a catalogue of sermons and texts, and are the least interesting part of his correspondence, leaving the reader with an impression of someone desperately trying to concentrate on a difficult task and wary lest his mind wander. The problem was evident to Mendes almost from the start. Good teacher that he was, he tried to encourage his pupil by giving him an easy Latin author to translate but this so fired Vincent that he immediately tried to make a translation of the original Latin version of *The Imitation of Christ* which his cousin Kee had given him. Inevitably, he stumbled and was soon complaining that Latin was a waste of time. Worse still, conjugating Greek verbs was beyond him and his complaints became more frequent:

> *Mendes, do you seriously believe that such horrors are indispensable to a man who wants to do what I want to do, give peace to poor creatures and reconcile them to their existence here on earth?*

Mendes did his best to defend his subject, though he was later to concede that he had secretly agreed with his pupil. But if Vincent was to fulfil a religious vocation and help those 'poor creatures' then Latin, Greek and all the rest of it had to be mastered. Despite his complaints, Vincent tried for a time to curb his wilfulness by bludgeoning the unwilling flesh. He would take a cudgel to his bedroom and belabour himself. Sometimes he deliberately stayed out so late he found the door locked and had to spend the night penitentially snatching his sleep on the floor of the outhouse. When the kindly Mendes found out what was going on, he was appalled, and Vincent had to use all his charm, arriving head bent, clutching a tiny bunch of snowdrops, to placate his teacher.

There are hints in the letters that his eccentricity was becoming more apparent. As well as visiting their churches he took to dropping in on those ministers he admired, some of whom chose to be out or otherwise engaged when he was announced. Between sermons there was still some art in the form of more visits to the Trippenhuis to ensure that he would see the full range of Rembrandt's oils and engravings.

As he despaired of Latin and Greek, art began to surface in his sessions with Mendes. Gradually the tables were turned and Vincent assumed the role of mentor, trying to introduce his teacher to the pleasures of painting. He even gave him one of his copies of the Van der Maaten engraving though Mendes was puzzled to see that Vincent had scribbled all over the margins. What Mendes did not realise was that these were by no means disjointed notes written at random. They were further evidence of the indivisibility of Vincent's thinking. Everything in those jottings related to the original inspiration of Van der Maaten's engraving: the Bible quotations spoke of sowing, reaping, and death, as did a poem by Longfellow which was copied out in the lower margin. Vincent had been drawn to the American poet by the paintings of Boughton, who had found inspiration in such poems as *The Courtship of Miles Standish*, the story of the Puritan captain. When Vincent read Longfellow's *Afternoon in February*, it recalled the Van der Maaten so vividly that he copied it onto the edges of the engraving:

Afternoon in February

The day is ending,
The night descending;
The Marsh is frozen,
   The river is dead.

Through clouds like ashes
The red sun flashes
On village windows
   That glimmer red.

The snow recommences;
The buried fences
Mark no longer
   The road o'er the plain;

While through the meadows,
Like fearful shadows,
Slowly passes
   A funeral train.

The bell is pealing,
And every feeling
Within me responds
   To the dismal knell;

Shadows are trailing;
My heart is bewailing
And toiling within
   Like a funeral bell.

But if Mendes was puzzled by what he thought was a rather crude disfiguring of a work of art, he was touched by what he saw of Vincent's kindness. Although the young man was short of money, relying on Theo for the stamps for his letters, he would give his last crust to someone in need, even to the point where he could no longer afford tobacco for his pipe. Mendes was moved by the way Vincent always spoke so kindly to the old aunt who opened the door for him when he arrived for lessons. She was slow-witted and deformed and usually the butt of jokes from passers-by, but Vincent was so good to her she would run up when she saw him coming, calling out: "Good morning, Mister Van Gort". And even that he forgave:

> *Mendes, however much that Aunt of yours may mutilate my name, she is a good soul, and I like her very much.*

What neither Mendes nor anyone else knew anything of was Vincent's obsession with Kee. Theo was surprised when his brother turned down the offer of a train fare to The Hague to see a Sunday exhibition of drawings. He had no way of knowing that Vincent could not leave Amsterdam on the one day when he was sure of seeing her. All Theo could tell from the letters was that, as before, his brother was frequently on the edge of melancholy:

> *. . . I breakfasted on a piece of dry bread and a glass of beer – that is what Dickens advises for those who are on the point of committing suicide, as being a good way to keep them, at least for some time, from their purpose. And even if one is not in such a good mood, it is right to do it occasionally, while thinking, for instance, of Rembrandt's picture, The Men of Emmaus.*

A fortnight later he describes walking through the Jewish quarter where he suddenly looked into:

> *. . . a big dark wine cellar and warehouse, with the doors standing open; for a moment I had an awful vision in my mind's eye – you know what I mean – men with lights were running back and forth in the dark vault. It is true you can see this daily, but there are moments when the common everyday things make an extraordinary impression and have a deep significance and a different aspect.*

Again the chance to undertake something practical took him out of himself. It was a requirement of the syllabus that he should be able to produce a map of the Holy Land. As can be imagined, this was the one task in all his studies that appealed to him. He went far beyond what was necessary and was soon turning out maps of anywhere that happened to interest him. Although this was solely for his own amusement, he occasionally offered them as gifts – one went to the Sunday School of a church he liked to visit.

Of course drawing maps was also a way of postponing what he ought to have been doing. Nine months had passed and even the ever hopeful Mendes had to concede that little short of a miracle would get him through the forthcoming examination papers. There was nothing to be done but tell Pastor Stricker the bad news so that he could warn the family, though for once that usually patient clan was in no mood for its problem child. Uncle Hein, Theodorus' ailing brother, died that December, an event which cast a pall over the Christmas celebrations. Nevertheless, despite his personal grief, Pastor Theodorus, prompted by Uncle Stricker, tried to give his son some gentle tutoring in the art of mastering Latin while they were together during the holidays. Vincent was by then devoted to his father who, as a pastor, seemed to embody everything he aspired to be. He told Theo how much better a person their father seemed than their uncles and how they should both try to be sons after his spirit. It was only from this paragon, sitting in his study beneath the familiar Van der Maaten, that Vincent could have accepted yet another lecture on Latin grammar. He vowed to work harder, and back in Amsterdam Uncle Stricker rallied round with some extra tutoring, though he must have realised that with only four months to go there was too much ground to make up.

It was only when Pastor Theodorus finally came to Amsterdam and had a meeting with Mendes that an end could be brought to any lingering hopes that Vincent might carry the day. It was incredible to the pastor that his son should be so bad at Latin and Greek when he was such an excellent linguist, fluent in French and English and with a sound knowledge of German. Why should he have fared so miserably? He was supposedly highly motivated; for just over two years he had talked of nothing but a religious vocation and knew well that this was the decisive point, his last chance to enter the ministry. Yet here he was, casting himself adrift again. It was more hurtful than all the earlier disappointments. Vincent had insisted to his father that his constant wish was to follow in his footsteps, yet he had wilfully thrown his chance away. Desperately trying to explain it to himself Pastor Theodorus blamed the English and French clergymen Vincent had met in Amsterdam whose ultra-orthodox views had no doubt corrupted him. It was all such a sorry contrast to Theo who had just been promoted to the Paris headquarters of Goupil's and was clearly destined to do all the things once expected of his elder brother. But to Pastor Theodorus the worst nightmare was when Vincent talked about becoming a catechist if he failed the exams. This was the lowest form of clerical life and the pastor found the idea deeply humiliating. The only ray of hope was his son's interest in missionary work. Determined to find an alternative to the catechist route, the pastor decided to contact organisations in Belgium to see if there was any hope of finding a role for Vincent in one of the evangelical groups working in the industrial regions. Disappointed and worried he returned to Etten, leaving Vincent to stumble on with his increasingly pointless lessons.

There may be no single explanation as to why Vincent behaved as he did. Had he succeeded at Latin and Greek he could certainly have entered the University where there was little to stop him qualifying for the ministry. But whatever the reasons, the result was clear to everyone including himself. There was no point in going on. He wrote to Theo:

> *Nothing less than the infinite and the miraculous is necessary, and man does well not to be contented with anything less, and not to feel at home as long as he has not acquired it.*

He wrote Theo a final letter from Amsterdam that May, then a long silence followed. He had gone home to Etten to think things over and to see what could be salvaged from the collapse of the only ambition he had ever fought for. He had insisted on being his own man, on making his own choices and like everything else it had come to nothing.

5

1878 — 1880

Under a Sulphur Sun

Vincent left his father to cope with the crisis. Pastor Theodorus was good-natured but it was unusual for him to exert himself so much. He was in many ways a rather complacent man, a tendency not improved by years of being shuffled around out-of-the-way parishes, but he now knew that something was wrong with his son, something that would in all probability never be put right, and that only he could handle the immediate situation. He was used to waiting for what he referred to as Vincent's 'blows' to fall and his main spur to action was probably the understandable desire to get Vincent off his hands. However, even the Belgian missions were not proving easy; the various controlling bodies were desperately under-funded and took few risks with the people they enlisted. The one glimmer of hope was a recently formed group in Brussels which ran a training school in the suburb of Laeken before sending successful candidates to the Borinage, the coal-mining region in the south of the country on the French border. The Borinage was one of the worst industrial areas in Europe. Its poverty-stricken miners led lives of near-slavery in conditions of unimaginable squalor and Theodorus may have reckoned that there would hardly be a surfeit of candidates for such grim work. But how to proceed?

The answer came with the Reverend Jones, who travelled over from Isleworth as soon as he heard what had happened to his one-time assistant. The two ministers got on famously and it was Jones who insisted that they should press on with trying to get Vincent a missionary post. He proposed that the three of them go to Brussels to see if they could sort out the situation face to face. Theodorus wrote and was told they would be welcome to visit and could be lodged in the home of one of the parishioners of the mission church. At first sight the school seemed a small-scale affair in a few rooms over the church hall in Kathelijne Square but when they spoke with Master Bokma, the headmaster, they realised that the course itself was just what they were seeking. It was both shorter – three years as opposed to six – than the university theology school and, although there was some Latin and Greek, it was in most essentials practical rather than academic. The two pastors were then introduced to the Reverend de Jong, the founder, and a fellow director, the Reverend Pietersen. The two men were like night and day: de Jong the strict superior, Pietersen the friendly confidant. Indeed Pietersen was keen to give Vincent a chance but the situation hung in the balance until the presence of Jones tipped the scales. As Jones spoke no French they all had to struggle along in English, and it soon became apparent that Vincent was a fluent linguist. While there would be no call for him to speak English in any work he might do with the mission society, the very fact that he had so thoroughly mastered a foreign language considerably impressed them. Setting aside their reservations they decided he should attend the school for a trial period.

He was set an exercise to write before his arrival and his choice was typical: he wrote an essay based on Rembrandt's *The House of the Carpenter* and spent much of his last days in Etten working on this and amusing himself making sketches. As he passed through Brussels on his way to the school he made a drawing of an inn called, prophetically, 'Au Charbonnage' – 'The Coalfields', which he sent to Theo with an accompanying description of the miners he had seen, for even in advance of his arrival at the Mission School his thoughts were already running ahead to the Borinage and the work he might do there. The result was an impatience that made it impossible for him to settle down to the course of studies before him and from the outset his attitude to the school was provocative. He had clearly taken another turn down the descending spiral of eccentric behaviour, refusing to sit at a desk, choosing to perch uncomfortably on a chair, balancing a book on his knees. This self-induced discomfort hardly impressed his teachers and when Bokma, during a classics lesson, asked him: "Is this dative or accusative?", and he replied: *I really don't care, sir*, it was obvious that there was not much they could do with him.

That Vincent was undergoing a considerable internal struggle was immediately clear to Bokma and the others. Not long after his arrival he learned that Christoffel Vos had at last died of his lung disease leaving his widow Kee to mourn a second time. The image of the woman in black, her child Johannes beside her, must have been deeply unsettling. That the struggle within him was anguished and painful was not in doubt. It could also become violent as was shown by a curious incident following a language lesson. Asked to explain the word *falaise* (cliff) Vincent asked if he could draw one on the blackboard. This was refused, but when the lesson was over he strode wilfully to the front of the class and began to do just that. A fellow student sneaked up and tugged at his jacket to tease him whereupon Vincent whirled round and lashed out at him with his fists. The young man fled. Everyone there recalled the incident long afterwards, so appalled were they. We may suppose that Vincent was too, for this was the first occasion when his rage had descended to violence.

One can hardly blame the school authorities for deciding after the three months' trial that there was no point in his continuing, though they chose to cite his inadequacy as a preacher as their reason. Whenever called upon to speak he had laboriously read out one of his prepared sermons. But these missionaries were evangelists, expected to win over the hearts of simple people brutalised by grinding labour. The ability to speak extempore and from the heart was a major part of the task ahead and it was easy to fault Vincent there.

Even then he refused to abandon all hope of a vocation, and for its part the mission committee was reluctant to reject completely someone who was, after all, the son of a fellow minister. Vincent suspected that it was Pietersen who was most sympathetic, for when Theodorus wrote asking them to give his son one last chance the committee was swayed in his favour. They would allow him to go to the coalfields for a probationary period as an unpaid assistant; if he showed signs that he was settling down, he would be considered for a temporary post in the New Year.

It was effectively the lowest form of Christian vocation, no better than being the catechist his father dreaded, but Vincent was pathetically grateful for it. This was what he had long desired, the chance to prove himself through dedicated, humble service. From Brussels he travelled by train to the elegant medieval city of Mons, a haven of culture in the industrial south, and thence into a blasted wasteland of mines and slag-heaps, the dust-begrimed coalfields of the Borinage, perpetually overcast with dank, sulphurous clouds. It was beyond anything he had ever known before, as if he had left behind him the ideal of unspoiled nature that so preoccupied the artists of his day and was seeing its mirror opposite, a Mephistophelian inversion. Yet he, whose sympathy for the poor had always been fed by the pastoral and picturesque, a poverty eminently suitable as a subject for art, was at first unable to absorb the abject ugliness of what he saw from his carriage window. It was as if art refused to release him so easily. It was just before Christmas 1878 and the scene was softened by new-fallen snow, the slag-heaps like mountains, the miner's hovels merely white hillocks, so that he was reminded of the Bruegels he had seen in the Brussels museums. It was 'Peasant Bruegel', the sort of scene where hunters make their way home over a white expanse against which everything – bare-branched trees, blackbirds in flight, the distant mountains and cottages – is picked out with the precision of an etching. In his enthusiasm for this new venture Vincent's first impressions of the coalfields were far from the usual catalogue of filthy dwellings, muddy countryside and polluted fields and rivers that most observers described. He told Theo it was *very picturesque* and as he began to explore the place he was struck by the way the roadside shrubs stood out against the snow drifts as in Dürer's engraving *Death and the Knight*, with its spiky roots and thorns, stark against the white background:

> *. . . here blackthorn hedges surround the gardens, fields and meadows. Now, with the snow, the effect is like black characters on white paper – like pages of the gospel.*

Above all he was reminded of Thijs Maris, the most romantic of the three painter brothers. Only an optimist like Vincent could have compared Maris' misty landscapes, his dappled light at the edge of a wood, the haunted castle glimpsed through a tangled forest, with Belgium's Black Earth country, but that was just what he did.

Vincent could take this romantic view because he had no real experience of what conditions were like close to the pit-heads. He had rented a room in the house of a pedlar called Van der Haegen in the Rue de L'Eglise in Pâturages. The house stood on a culvert below the church of St Michel on a slight ridge above a cluster of cottages which, although not much more than small peasant dwellings, were nevertheless incomparably better than the wretched hovels clustered round the entrances to the mines. Van der Haegen charged him thirty francs a month, a considerable amount when the daily rate for an adult miner was then under three francs. Vincent began work almost at once, walking the half-hour journey to Wasmes where he was to preach. En route he passed the collieries with their high wheel-towers and enormous stacks of pit-props used to support the sinuous tunnels over two thousand feet below the surface. The coal workings in Belgium and northern France were as yet barely mechanised and the pits were notoriously dangerous, a fact made clear when he visited the churchyards with their monuments to the ten killed in one disaster, the twenty killed in another. Shortly before his arrival the Agrappe mine at Frameries had suffered an appalling firedamp explosion, further proof that human life was expendable in the Borinage.

Wasmes, Vincent's destination, stood on the edge of the Colfontaine woods. In the Rue Dubois, the Salon du Bébé acted as a community centre and prayer house for the local Protestants in what had once been a minuscule dance hall. Its tiny main room could accommodate about a hundred people and Vincent's task was to preach to the miners and their families. For his first sermon he chose three parables: the mustard seed, the barren fig-tree, and the man born blind. There is no record of whether he addressed each of them separately or if he tried to find a message common to all three. Each is in some way about things which are wrongly assessed at first and only later seen for what they truly are. The mustard seed is the Kingdom of God, which begins as a near-invisible thing, but grows, at first secretly, until it is all-encompassing. The barren fig-tree symbolises the elders of the Jews who failed to see Jesus for what he was; and in healing the man born blind Jesus shows that he is there to open the eyes of the people.

These are not the easiest of Biblical texts to speak on and it was either courageous or foolhardy of Vincent, no doubt nervous on his first day, to open with them. He was more comfortable conducting Bible readings in the miners' homes, even though some of his illusions were lost as he began to experience first hand just how wretched the lives of the Borains truly were. Far from living in cottages like his landlord's, most of the underground workers occupied wooden shacks clustered near the colliery gates. These were dark, cave-like shelters, often roofed only with moss, and filthy from the coal dust that lay over everything close to the slag-heaps. In the valley below Wasmes was the Marcasse pit and around it a cluster of hovels. These were the homes of those Vincent was to teach. Many of them were descendants of the Huguenots who fled France after the revocation of the Edict of Nantes in the seventeenth century, beginning the long tradition of nonconformism that was so notable a feature of the Borinage. At that time there were about thirty thousand miners but there were also about two thousand girls and two and a half thousand boys under the age of fourteen working below ground. Most started at the age of eight and the presence of young women working alongside men in such gruelling conditions was one of the prime reasons the good citizens of Brussels thought the region needed missionaries. Zola, one of the authors who most influenced Vincent, was at that time writing his Rougon-Macquart novels of which the thirteenth, *Germinal*, gives an extraordinary picture of life below ground in the mines of Northern France, in every respect identical to that in the Borinage. In *Germinal*, the eighteen-year-old haulage girl Mouquette spends her life among the miners in that semi-dark underworld, flimsily clad, foul-mouthed and promiscuous. Tales of these 'immoral' encounters both horrified and fascinated the Christian gentlefolk who lived a safe distance from the mines that were the source of their industrial fortunes.

But as yet Vincent knew little more than they did about the realities of that other world below ground. During his first month in the Borinage he was fascinated by the Borains and their simple life, intrigued by the shacks *scattered along the country roads* where *in the evening, light shines kindly through the small-paned windows*. His continuing illusions were evident in his Christmas sermon in the Salon du Bébé which was centred on the humble stable in Bethlehem and the hope for peace on earth.

He described all this in his first letter to Theo written the day after Christmas, presumably his first chance to relax. This is the period in his life when he wrote least to Theo, always a sign that there was something he could not express, and the few letters he did write show signs of that increasing inner struggle first seen at the mission school. As we read his thoughts and follow his actions it is like witnessing someone battling with God, someone saying: 'I will go to the absolute limits to follow Your commands so that I can know if this is what You want of me.' In the Borinage Vincent set out to test himself, but in a way it was also a challenge to God, a subconscious way of breaking free from Him by going to the uttermost limits of religious self-mortification. It was already clear from his behaviour at Laeken that a crisis was approaching. Since that violent explosion in the classroom the last vestiges of self-control had been slipping away. As the abject poverty of the miners gradually became clear to him it could only be a matter of time before he would try to insinuate himself into their outcast world.

The pedlar's house was too isolated from the miner's colony and soon after Christmas he left Pâturages and moved to the house of a baker, Jean-Baptiste Denis, first in the Rue du Petit Wasmes and, when the family moved a short while later, in the Rue Wilson on the outskirts of the town. This house stood on a ridge that backed on to the bleak fields on the other side of which were the hovels grouped at the gates of the Marcasse pit. He was coming closer but was still an outsider.

He was welcomed by Pastor Bonte, one of the three ordained ministers in the region whom Vincent was there to assist. There were a number of small Protestant churches scattered about the mining communities but often services were held in makeshift meeting halls like the Salon du Bébé. Not long after his arrival, Vincent assisted one of the ministers at a religious gathering held in a stable or a shed, he was not sure which, but it is clear from his comments that such simplicity appealed to him and that he was increasingly dissatisfied with any luxuries he felt he had. The Denis house was as comfortable as the pedlar's had been and kept him apart from the shuffling figures he saw each morning and evening making their way across the frozen fields to the black mine shaft. As if to offset this, he started to give away what little he had, a crust of bread, some items of clothing. He had been his usual dishevelled self when he arrived, but Jean-Baptiste and his wife soon noticed that he was becoming scruffier and his clothes were unchanged. Also he was not eating properly, preferring to take away what he was given and pass it on to the miners when he visited them.

His hosts also realised that this went beyond charity or mere eccentricity. Vincent's behaviour was too extreme to be so easily dismissed. When Madame Denis discovered that he had found a room in one of the shacks near the mine and he announced that he wanted to move into it, she realised that something would have to be done. It was not just that he wanted a room of his own; he clearly intended to share the lives of the miners. But the hovels were merely crude shelters not unlike the outbuildings on a farm, and for him to move from her snug brick-built house to one of those wooden sheds was to enter an almost animal-like existence. She realised then that Vincent must be protected from himself, and wrote to Pastor Theodorus to warn him of his son's intentions.

It was no easy journey from Brabant to the Borinage and Pastor Theodorus had neither the spare money nor much inclination for such a venture, but he had seen enough of Vincent's manic ways to know that he was needed. Vincent may have hoped that his father would approve of what he was doing. Might he not see his son as a latter-day St Francis of Assisi giving all he had to the poor and living as they did? He soon learned otherwise. Having undergone the rigorous training for the ministry Pastor Theodorus had seen plenty of young theological students suddenly plunge themselves into excessive self-mortification. Such people were usually eased out of seminaries and training colleges or sent away until they calmed down. But, as the Pastor knew, they were difficult to argue with, for they knew they were doing precisely what Christ commanded and would not see reason.

Initially, his father's arrival seemed to calm Vincent, and he made a genuine attempt to show him what he could do. They visited the three Protestant ministers in the area and the pastor accompanied his son to two home Bible classes. In the end Theodorus' approach to his son's situation was entirely practical: if Vincent agreed to go on living with the Denises and give up the idea of moving in amongst the miners, he would intercede on his behalf with the missionary authorities to try to get his position confirmed. As this was what Vincent longed for most, he accepted, saying that the room he had rented would only be used as a studio if he felt like doing some sketching. To encourage this, Theodorus commissioned some of his large maps of the Holy Land at ten guilders each, a useful supplement to the small allowance he already made.

But once the restraining presence of his father was removed it was not long before Vincent felt his resolve weakening. After Pastor Theodorus had written to Brussels the mission authorities confirmed Vincent's post, and decided to defer an inspection till later in the year, thus removing the last restraint on his behaviour. No doubt he meant to keep his promise to his father, but soon events overtook him. Not long after the pastor's departure one of the miners asked him if he would like to go down a pit. How could he refuse an opportunity to see at first hand what the true lives of the poor wretches were like? One cold morning he joined the queue of shuffling figures in their rough, filthy work clothes, waiting his turn to pass the imposing brick portals of the Marcasse entrance. He was taken down the shining white-tiled corridors to the wheel shaft and the open cage that would send them hurtling more than two thousand feet to the shadow-world below ground. The Marcasse was one of the oldest mines in the region with an appalling safety record. Vincent's account of that visit is one of the most gripping in all his correspondence. It is astonishing how accurately it echoes the novel Zola was writing at almost exactly the same time. Although Zola had no knowledge of Vincent's letters (and Vincent would only read *Germinal* years later) the two descriptions could almost be by the same hand:

> ZOLA: He wondered at times whether he was going down or up. There were moments when there was a sort of stillness – that was when the cage dropped sheer, without touching the guides. Then there would be sudden tremors as it bobbed about between the beams, and he was terrified of a disaster. In any case, he could not see the walls of the shaft although his face was glued to the netting. At his feet the huddled bodies were hardly visible, so dim were the lamps, but the open lamp of the deputy in the next tub shone out like a solitary beacon.

> VAN GOGH: *Imagine a row of cells in a rather narrow, low passage, shored up with rough timber. In each of those cells a miner in a coarse linen suit, filthy and black as a chimney sweep, is busy hewing coal by the pale light of a small lamp. The miner can stand erect in some cells; in others, he lies on the ground. The arrangement is more or less like the cells in a beehive, or like a dark, gloomy passage in an underground prison, or a row of small weaving looms, or rather like a row of baking ovens as the peasants have, or like the partitions in a crypt.*

Zola describes the misery of finding water pouring through the cage roof, the intense cold, the wet blackness with a sudden flash of light where men were working. Vincent also writes of the ever-present water, the curious effects created by the miners' lamps as they worked in the *maintenages* – the small cells carved out from the main tunnels. There were sights to pierce the heart: stables two thousand feet underground where ponies broken with toil spent their wretched lives; worse still, children, girls as well as boys, some only eight years old, filthy and in rags, pulled sledges of coal through tunnels too small for the animals. And hanging over all this was the constant fear of accidents, the collapsing passageways propped up with flimsy wooden props, the chilling fear of a firedamp explosion. He had already seen the effects of the explosion at the Agrappe mine:

Did I tell you at the time about the miner who was so badly hurt by a firedamp explosion? Thank God, he has recovered and is going out again and is beginning to walk some distance just for exercise; his hands are still weak and it will be some time before he can use them for his work, but he is out of danger. Since that time there have been many cases of typhoid and malignant fever, of what they call la sotte fièvre, *which gives them bad dreams like nightmares and makes them delirious. So again there are many sickly and bedridden people – emaciated, weak, and miserable.*

In one house they are all ill with fever and have little or no help, so that the patients have to nurse the patients. "Ici c'est les malades qui soignent les malades" *(here the sick tend the sick), said a woman like,* "Le pauvre est l'ami du pauvre" *(the poor man is the poor man's friend).*

Small wonder the Borinage was the cradle of socialism in Belgium. Most mine owners knew little of conditions in their mines and cared less. Cowed by poverty, disorganised and lacking leaders the miners had been impotent to change their wretched conditions, but during his year among them Vincent witnessed some of the first stirrings of protest. His experience down the Marcasse pit and his subsequent identification with the miners' cause were to be two of the most powerful influences on his thinking in the years ahead. To call Vincent a socialist is probably to go too far as he was incapable of projecting himself into a wider political situation, but everything that the word is taken to imply in terms of supporting the poor, the labourers, the unfortunate, as opposed to the educated and successful, he himself would readily have acknowledged. Before Marcasse he had viewed a painting by someone like Israëls as a scene from a rural idyll; now he saw in it the underlying pain and hopelessness of so many working lives. For Vincent, unstable as he was, it was an unbearable revelation.

The only way to assuage his anguish was to take action, to punish himself with excesses of labour so that there was no time to dwell on the suffering he now saw all about him. He would go from hovel to hovel acting as a nurse to families where everyone of working age had been laid low by the illnesses of the pits: old men coughing up their lungs after years of inhaling coal dust, children and young men crippled in accidents or afflicted with mysterious diseases no one could identify. He would tear up his own linen for bandages and give what meagre food he had to hungry children. When he had no more to give, he would lie on the floor of his filthy shack and weep with frustration at what he saw as his own failure. If he could not preach, at least he could give, but if he could not give, then what was he there for? Though he might himself despair, the mining folk were grateful for his kindness. He had noted in a letter that despite the brutalising effects of the mines, those who worked them were sensitive, independent people with a strong distrust of anyone who was domineering. His humility won their confidence.

Madame Denis continued to be concerned about Vincent. She asked him why he had to mortify himself so much, to which he replied, *Esther, one should do like the good God; from time to time one should go and live among His own.* Years later Pastor Bonte of Warquignies remembered Vincent in his old soldier's tunic and shabby cap. As the miners were perpetually stained with coal dust, he too had given up washing. When Madame Denis remonstrated with him his reply was as before: *Oh, Esther, don't worry about such details, they don't matter in heaven!*

The only thing that eased his mind was the selection of prints he had arranged around the walls of his room. He continued to ask Theo for news of Israëls, Maris and Mauve even though the genteel life of the Pulchri Studio was by then a world away from what he had experienced in those terrifying underground chambers. Having tried to describe the shock of that visit, he told his brother he would try to sketch it, to give him a better picture of what he had glimpsed in the flickering light of the miners' lamps. It was an idea that grew on him, a subject never fully realised in art, that half-lit subterranean world. The problem was that the subject was so fresh in his mind, so powerful and frightening, he did not yet have the courage to tackle it. All he could attempt were some sketches of the miners' life above ground. One that has miracuously survived shows a coal-heaver staggering up the slope of what must be a slag-heap, a shovel across his shoulder, his head half-covered in a sacking hood to protect his back and shoulders when he hauls away his load of foraged coal. It was roughly done, a first try in a mix of black chalk, pencil and ink applied with pen and brush. But despite the crude workmanship he did attempt to round out the figure with touches of white highlighting. Even though the subject was original it seems familiar, for he had consciously set out to emulate his idol 'Father Millet' in the solid outline and bulk of the figure. Although he had drawn a miner on his way to pick coal there are echoes of Millet's field labourers bending to their toil, of the washerwoman shouldering her linen on the river bank, the peasant and his wife planting potatoes.

Very much a first effort, Vincent's coal-heaver still has remarkable force, clearly displaying the artist's feelings for the miners and their plight; and for all its crudeness that sketch is a giant stride from the modest topographical outlines of places where he lived which had formerly decorated his letters.

Such images of miners at work were to haunt him long after he left the Borinage. He had already seen pictures of coalworkers and, more tellingly, engravings of mining accidents in the illustrated newspapers he had admired in England. Later, when he was building up his collection of black and white prints he would bemoan the difficulty of finding more examples of work such as Mathew White Ridley's *The Miner* or the anonymous engraving from *L'Univers Illustré* of a group of rescue-workers being lowered down a mine shaft after a firedamp explosion. Both reminded him forcefully of his time in the Borinage, too forcefully in the latter case, for in the spring of 1879 the Belgian coalfields were to see one of the worst series of catastrophes for years and Vincent was to live through some of the most horrendous moments of his life.

The word 'firedamp' may seem self-contradictory but it well sums up the unholy coalition of methane gas and air that used to cause sudden, violent explosions deep within the mines. No one could understand it, but every spring the underground workings would be seared with flames and shaken by pressure that caused tunnels and shafts to collapse. Only recently was the discovery made that the deadly gas built up during the cold winter months so that with the advent of warmer weather it burst into the fireball explosions so dreaded by the miners. Above ground the leaves were coming into bud; below, an inexplicable carnage was taking place. The hamlets of the Borinage are marked with monuments to those subterranean massacres. One of the worst occurred in Pâturages in 1934 when forty-one miners were killed in a single explosion, a disaster on such a scale that the Belgian flag was lowered to half-mast over the Royal Palace in Brussels. The next day an explosion at a neighbouring pit brought the death toll to fifty-three men plus innumerable ponies trapped in the workings. The bodies that could be raised were barely recognisable, stripped naked by the burning force of the blast. Most could not be recovered and were sealed below ground. By the thirties such events shocked the public and led to an outcry over safety in the mines, but in Vincent's time these disasters often passed unnoticed by the outside world, and even in the Borinage they were looked upon as just another curse the poor had to bear. To Vincent, however, his first experience of an explosion was a terrible revelation.

As ever it was in the spring that the firedamp explosions began. The first was on April 16th at Frameries. Although Vincent had seen people in the villages crippled from previous accidents this was his first encounter with the wounded and the dying. The explosion was recorded in two contemporary newspaper illustrations which show that this was no mere underground flash fire but a blast so powerful it broke through to the surface, engulfing one of the wheel-towers in flames and causing the surrounding buildings to implode. The effect on those below ground is unthinkable. The only ray of hope amid the devastation was that the Agrappe pit with its second wheel-tower offered another source of access to the devastated subterranean chambers and an escape for any who had been far enough away from the blast to have survived. Immediately following such a catastrophe everyone in the locality rushed to the pit-head to help haul up the survivors and treat their wounds, and, of course, Vincent was among them. It was a tragic business and one with which he was to become all too familiar: the blast in the Agrappe was followed by firedamp accidents at the Boule and Quaregnon pits. Below ground hundreds lay dead. Such survivors as there were had to be hauled by hand to the surface, most in a pitiful condition. There was no system of health care for the miners and most nursing was done by the people themselves. Vincent was everywhere, tearing such linen as he had left into bandages, which were dipped in olive oil and wax to cover the burns. On April 26th 1879 *Le Monde Illustré* published an engraving by Daniel Vierge which became part of Vincent's treasured collection. The picture shows the burned and naked body of a victim at the Agrappe being hauled to the surface in a wooden box while his fellow miners and their families anxiously look on. In a much later letter to Theo he would compare the drawings of Vierge to the writings of Victor Hugo, a great compliment from him.

A figure that stands out in the newspaper engraving is a uniformed and armed policeman overseeing the rescue, hardly surprising when one considers the resentment that was gradually beginning to replace the miners' earlier fatalism about the annual firedamp carnage. Those first stirrings of protest would culminate in the 1880s with the series of desperate and often violent strikes which formed the basis of the working-class movement in the coalfields. In his next letter to Theo in

June Vincent mentions making the acquaintance of a mine foreman who had been involved with early strike activity. One of the sons of his landlord Denis was about to become engaged to the foreman's daughter, so the man was often at the house when Vincent visited. He was clearly impressed by the man's good sense and sympathetic to what he was doing. In the same letter he writes of rereading *Uncle Tom's Cabin*:

> *There is still so much slavery in the world, and in this remarkably wonderful book that important question is treated with so much wisdom, so much love, and such zeal and interest in the true welfare of the poor oppressed that one comes back to it again and again, always finding something new.*

Curiously, this letter makes no reference to the pit disasters. In fact it was Vincent's first letter for three months and although he expresses the hope that Theo will visit him en route to take up his permanent post at Goupil's in Paris, the brothers at that time appear to be less close than usual. Rather like a soldier who discovers he cannot communicate, even to his closest family, the terrible things he has experienced, so Vincent seems to be estranged from Theo by the horrors of that terrible spring.

Another reason for his reticence was a further worsening of his mental state. Where the miners had initially overlooked his eccentricities and shown some gratitude for the humble way he tried to help them, reactions now polarised; there were those who thought him mad and those, more sympathetic, who treated him like some kind of Holy Fool. We know from the wife of Pastor Bonte that he was sometimes taunted by children in the street.

It was at the point when he was most distraught that his fate overtook him. That July, a Reverend Emile Rochedieu arrived from Brussels to inspect the novice missionary on behalf of the committee. What he found was a shambling, dishevelled, unwashed penitent, crippled with self doubt yet unshakeably convinced of his own destiny. To a man like Rochedieu, a clergyman, even a mere assistant like Vincent had to have a certain social standing. One could only bring people to God by representing the pattern of bourgeois values to which they could aspire. Vincent with his newly acquired loathing of the rich, his total identification with the impoverished miners, his uncontrollable urge to live in imitation of Christ, was repugnant to such a man. To Vincent the arrival of that dark-suited, disapproving figure must have reawakened all his neuroses over his father.

It was a clash of opposites. The all-too-appropriately named Rochedieu (roughly 'God's Rock') observed Vincent's duties, noted his good works and no doubt admired his sympathy for the condition of the miners, but he decided to fight his ground over Vincent's role as an evangelist. Having attended a meeting at which Vincent preached, Rochedieu had no difficulty in deciding he was a failure. His task was not to tear up his linen for bandages but to preach the word of God and convert the miners to Christianity. Helping them materially did not necessarily advance that cause. Rochedieu returned to Brussels to submit his report. Shortly afterwards Vincent was dismissed. He was utterly cast down. Of course he could have predicted it. Of course he had done nothing to satisfy a man like Rochedieu whom he had known would one day appear. Yes, it is possible he was once again trying to break down the bars that caged him. But to know this cannot diminish the intensity of his anguish when the message was brought to him. Down and down he had sunk with each passing year; now it was all over; he had done everything for God and God had surely rejected him.

When he had recovered from his initial stunned reaction he cast about frantically for some way to reverse the situation. To whom could he turn? He had effectively disobeyed his father; the Reverend Jones was too far away to be of any help. The one person who might be able to get the committee's decision rescinded was the kindly Reverend Pietersen in Brussels, who he believed had been his supporter when he was first allowed to go to the Borinage. He decided to beg Pietersen to intercede for him. He was too impatient to write; it was better to go in person. With the pittance he had received from the Mission authorities now cut off he was almost penniless and could think of no other solution than to set off on another of his extraordinary hikes, this time to Brussels. For some reason he decided to take with him the drawings of miners he'd been working on; he may have known that Pietersen was an amateur artist and hoped that they would enlarge the older man's sympathies towards him. There was certainly some ill-formed plan rattling around in his troubled mind.

He did not head straight for Brussels, and although his exact movements are not known he appears to have walked to an army base on the outskirts of Mons where he knew that one of his fellow students from the mission school, J. Chrispeels, was doing his military service.

How Vincent knew this, and why he should have gone there when he had not been friendly with any of his classmates remains a mystery. What we do know is that for Chrispeels every young recruit's nightmare came true when he was called from the parade ground to meet a visitor only to see the bizarre figure of Vincent clutching his bundle of drawings, and pathetically eager to talk to him. What Chrispeels saw must have appalled him. Although Vincent had been scruffy when he last knew him, he was now a scarecrow scantily clad in the few rags that remained to him, unwashed and filthy. His self-imposed regime of near-starvation had given his features a gaunt, emaciated look and hollow, pointed face akin to Uncle Cent's and Theo's but with the disturbingly penetrating eyes that were to remain with him from then on and which are familiar to us from his self-portraits. The privations of the Borinage had finally created the Vincent the world knows. To the young soldier called over to see him it was a nasty shock.

Vincent unfastened his portfolio and spread out the drawings. Chrispeels wondered what he was supposed to say. He thought the figures looked stiff and 'queer', he had no especial affinity with art and

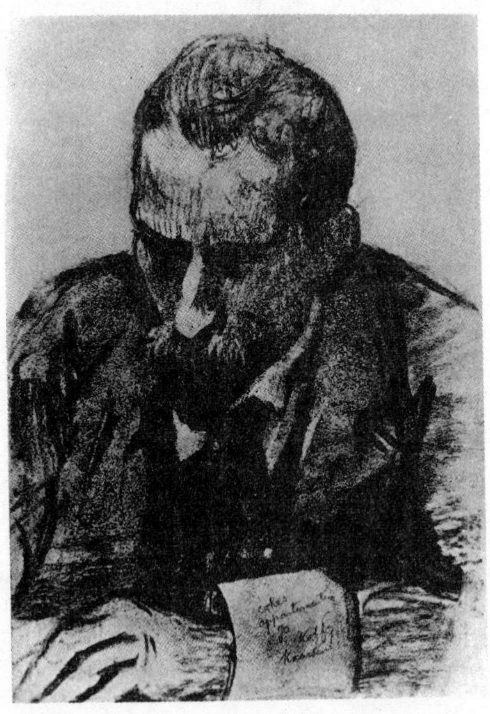

Portrait of Theo van Gogh by Meyer de Haan, 1889.

could not imagine why he had been chosen for this demonstration, though he realised that something was clearly wrong with the artist himself. Chrispeels offered the usual conventional words of congratulation which appeared to satisfy his strange visitor, who promptly gathered up his work and set off again on his journey. But Vincent's effect on people was never quite straightforward. Odd he certainly was, even disturbing, but other, more sympathetic feelings were often generated by the powerful concentration people saw in his eyes. Years later Chrispeels recalled that Vincent's bizarre visit had somehow done him good.

It was a Sunday evening and still light when Vincent arrived in Brussels. He went straight to the Reverend Pietersen's home and rang the bell. The door was opened by the clergyman's daughter who took one look at the vagrant on her doorstep, screamed and ran inside. When he hurried to see what the trouble was Pietersen was more sanguine. The committee had been left in no doubt by Rochedieu about Vincent's peculiarities, though the reality after days of tramping along dusty roads and sleeping in hedgerows must have been hard to stomach. Nevertheless, Pietersen, who was indeed the kindly soul Vincent took him for, led this shuffling penitent into his study and tried to make him welcome.

Although Vincent had originally made the journey in order to ask the clergyman to get him reinstated, this had given way to the desire to show him the portfolio he had brought. Pietersen leafed through the sketches and came to an extraordinarily perceptive conclusion: the young man's crisis was less one of religion than of art. He studied the drawings carefully, questioned Vincent on his intentions and, happily, praised the results. Aside from that curious interlude at the army barracks, Pietersen was effectively Vincent's earliest 'public', the first person invited to look at his work not as a sketched illustration to a message but as a thing in itself, a work of art. The world has cause to be grateful to the kindly pastor for his foresight in giving the young man encouragement and thus starting that process of acceptance of himself as an artist which had been so long delayed. That moment when Vincent nervously pulled open the portfolio can be seen as the instant when his life as an artist began.

There was, however, a great deal of the old life to be cleared away first. Pietersen realised Vincent had not yet surrendered his belief that he had a vocation within the church and it was pointless to tell him baldly that he did not. He saw that Vincent would have to come to this conclusion for himself in his own good time. The pastor's advice, eminently sensible, was that Vincent should return to the Borinage and continue his missionary work unpaid, as he had done initially. No doubt the young man imagined this might gain a renewed acceptance by the Synod, but it is clear that Pietersen realised that in time this craving to abase himself would gradually subside. He said goodbye to the much restored Vincent and then wrote to his parents to reassure them. "Vincent strikes me," he wrote, "as someone who stands in his own light."

The next day, before he left Brussels for the long hike back to the coalfields, Vincent used some of the money he had left to buy a sketchbook of 'old Dutch paper'. Thus far he had made his drawings on whatever scraps of paper he could lay his hands on; such an expensive outlay marked another, albeit tiny, step in the new direction his life was taking. So too, did his decision to rent a room in the home of Monsieur and Madame Decrucq in the village of Cuesmes. The Decrucqs both worked in the nearby Agrappe pit. One of Vincent's reasons may have been that the adjacent house was occupied by a Reverend Frank who might be a useful witness to his self-appointed missionary work. But there was also the fact that the Decrucqs' room, although small, would provide a slightly better work space than a dark pit-head hovel. Though close to the mines, their rather bleak cottage was built on a stretch of open ground which had some feel of the country about it and less of the oppressive, looming presence of the slag-heaps and winching towers than Wasmes had had.

He now made a brief visit to his parents in Etten where his mother noticed he read Dickens all day. He had discovered *Hard Times* and was soon identifying himself with the hero Stephen Blackpool, one of the victims of the dehumanised textile mills in the fictitious 'Coketown' who stands at odds with a world that fails to recognise his personal vision. This idea of standing alone, shunned by the world, was to assume a larger role in Vincent's perception of himself as time went by and back in Cuesmes this attitude was reinforced by Theo's visit *en route* for Paris when for the first time the two brothers failed to see eye to eye. On the surface their brief time together was much the same as ever – they went for a stroll by an abandoned water-logged quarry which reminded them of a canal they knew as children. But instead of continuing this pleasant reminiscence Theo suddenly told Vincent he had changed, "You are not the same any longer." No doubt upset by Vincent's appearance and irritated by his wasting his life as a failed missionary, Theo rashly suggested he should leave the Borinage and take up some trade or other. Although they parted amicably enough, Vincent was furious and a subsequent rambling letter mockingly referred to the possibility of his becoming a baker. There was bitterness in the humour and although the letter struggled to show some gratitude for Theo's concern the overall message was one of irritation at what he saw as his brother's lack of understanding. The letters ceased abruptly; for the first time there was a serious rupture in relations.

Vincent's last letter was dated October 15th, 1879 and he closed it with the words: *I have drawn another portrait.* As this would be the only piece of news from him that Theo would have for ten months it was an appropriate image to be left with, for despite Vincent's renewed attempts at charitable work, it was the increasing time spent drawing that was the most important part of his life during the long silence. True, Decrucq took him on a second visit down a mine but this seemed to stimulate his social conscience rather than his religious fervour. Shortly afterwards there was agitation at a neighbouring pit and Vincent went to see the owners to speak on the miners' behalf. Decrucq later recorded: "He wanted a juster share for us, but they only insulted him. They said: 'We'll have you shut up in the madhouse, M. Vincent, if you don't leave us in peace.'" But Decrucq was also clear that when a subsequent strike became violent, it was Vincent who persuaded the men not to set fire to the pit, telling them: *... not to be unworthy men, for brutality destroys everything that is good in man.*

It was his identification with the miners' condition that pulled him most strongly towards art, and the few examples of those first tentative drawings that survive would have been dubbed social realism in a later age. We know he drew a portrait of Madame Decrucq returning home from her work in the mines but that is lost. Those that survive include a group of miners bearing coalsacks strapped across their foreheads and another of a group of male and female miners going to work across a wintry field heading towards what appears to be the Marcasse pit at Wasmes. As before, these are rather roughly done, the shading crudely scumbled in, the hands and feet ill-proportioned. But he was not unaware of these faults and was now trying out Bargue's drawing exercises – earlier he had simply pinned some of its examples to the wall so that he could admire them. A popular primer at the time,

Bargue's course offered clear black-and-white studies of faces, with anatomical outlines that the learner was encouraged to copy as faithfully as possible. It was a working practice as old as Western art, though in our own day it has been much frowned upon for discouraging free expression. Vincent did not find it so, and indeed seems to have enjoyed the discipline. But we should not imagine that he had progressed to some kind of artistic idyll, calmly spending his days working on his pictures. On the contrary, despite the onset of winter, he continued to visit the miners and to give away whatever wretched clothing he had left and to pass on any food he could afford from the pittance his parents were occasionally able to send him. As with everyone else who watched this self-mortifying behaviour the Decrucqs pitied him but felt powerless to stop him. They were grateful for the way he nursed their young son through typhoid fever. (Later the boy was to die in a firedamp explosion at the Marcasse pit aged only eight.) The worst thing for his hosts was that they could hear Vincent weeping to himself at night as he tried to sleep without cover in the bitter cold of a bad winter. What they could not know was that his anguish came not so much from the physical suffering, though that was acute enough, but from the spiritual battle which was pulling him this way and that. Although he had begun to draw seriously, he was far from surrendering his Christian vocation. The pendulum moved tentatively and painfully as he struggled with his conscience and his fear of the spiritual void which might open up were he to admit that the religious life was not for him. As the winter progressed he found it increasingly difficult to go on drawing and suddenly stopped making sketches of the miners. With the advantage of hindsight it is clear that what was needed was some sort of jolt, something akin to the Eugénie Loyer episode which had provoked his religious fervour in the first place. He needed something that would dislodge his striving after God and leave him free to accept his new vocation.

He must have had an inkling of this himself for at some point that winter, we do not know when, he decided he had to get away. His first thought was to go to Barbizon to join the community of artists which remained there but it was so far away that the idea defeated him. Then he conceived an extraordinary plan: he would go to see the painter Jules Breton. Of course he had always admired Breton and he had heard, presumably from Theo (it was the sort of detail an art dealer would know), that Breton had recently moved back to his native province, Artois, which lay just across the French border from the Borinage.

Breton had built himself a new home and studio in his birthplace Courrières just outside Lens, so if Vincent wanted to seek the advice of someone he admired then Breton was certainly the nearest to hand. But proximity aside, what had Vincent done worth showing him? Although he could excuse his visit on the grounds that he had once fleetingly met the great man when he and his family had visited Goupil's, what more was he going to say to him and what could Breton then say that could possibly help? The idea seems to have been to make some sort of gesture, a pilgrimage for art, a way of breaking free from the mines and from his obsessive identification with the suffering of the miners.

Whatever his reasons it was not the time of year to be trudging across the open fields of Hainaut. Of all his Herculean walks this was incomparably the worst. Although only a distance of some seventy kilometres, most of it was spent in freezing rain and as he had only ten francs with him he was obliged to sleep in haystacks and woodpiles, waking each morning rimed with frost. He should have turned back after the first night, but he was determined to drive himself to the limit of endurance, to punish himself. Most of the time he was aware of little except extreme physical discomfort, though this would briefly give way to euphoria as he looked over the stark beauty of the endless flat landscape, unmarked by even the smallest rise. He was fascinated by the people he passed and sketched some of them, peasants in the fields and weavers in their hovels. Prophetically he watched a flock of crows wheeling above him; they reminded him of a Millet or a Daubigny. Then the dark gloom descended again and he forced his sore feet to walk on. It took him a week to reach Courrières.

What was he hoping to achieve? He said later that he wanted to find work, so he may have thought Breton would take him on as an assistant, though when one considers the exact realism of Breton's highly worked oils beside Vincent's almost childlike sketches the idea seems preposterous. As he approached Courrières his spirits lightened: the foggy wastelands of the Borinage were behind him and although there were still mine-shafts dotted about the region there was much more a sense of countryside and village life than in Belgium. When one sees the depressing modern suburb that Courrières has become it is almost impossible to understand why a poet and painter like Breton chose to return there and it takes an effort of will to realise that in the 1880s it was largely open country reminiscent of Holland with its low landscape and vast skies.

Breton, despite his huge fame at the time, was a sympathetic person and might well have handled his strange visitor delicately had they met, but it was not to be. When Vincent found the place and saw the forbidding brick wall surrounding it with what he described as 'Methodist' regularity, his courage failed him. He stared at the wall and could not bring himself to knock at the door. Though now largely forgotten, Breton was one of the most eminent artistic figures of his time. Only five years after Vincent's 'visit' his *Song of the Lark* was one of the most famous prize winners of the nineteenth-century Salons. While it is easy to comprehend Vincent's attachment to Millet, many have difficulty in understanding his life-long admiration for Breton's more romantic view of peasant life. Vincent's attachment has been seen by critics as a distinct lapse of taste, but what such critics failed to realise was that Vincent had the putative craftsman's intense admiration for the more skilled practitioner. Whatever he may have lacked in interpretation, Breton was a master of detail: of the evening sky, the fold of a dress, the grouping of figures. But more than technique, Vincent admired the fact that Breton had an immense popular following, that he spoke to people beyond the limited world of galleries, salons, dealers and critics, an ability which the isolated and rejected Vincent was always to admire.

Unable to disturb the calm of Breton's home, Vincent went into the village and cast about for some sign of the master. He looked in cafés to see if any of his paintings were hanging there; they were not. All he could find was a picture of the artist in the window of a photographer's shop. He went into the church near the studio, a rather gaunt northern edifice, in which he found a copy of Titian's *Burial of Christ* which he thought very beautiful. Perhaps Breton had made it? There was no way of telling. And that was it. He had made his pilgrimage and there was nothing for it but to turn round and go back.

If anything the return was worse than the going. The ten francs had been spent, though he managed to exchange some of his drawings for food and a few coins, his first sales and an encouraging sign. But that aside, was this peculiar pilgrimage worth the terrible suffering he had gone through? He always believed it was and when he eventually reopened contact with Theo he said that on leaving Courrières he had suddenly realised that he would

> *... rise again: I will take up my pencil, which I have forsaken in my great discouragement, and I will go on drawing.*

For someone who wrote so naturally, it was an unusually pompous way of saying that he was about to dedicate himself to art; it reads like a holy vow or an oath of allegiance and in a way it was both. But the journey had done more than foster in him a commitment to art; it had given him a deep yearning to create an art about and for ordinary people, the miners he had seen coming away from the pits near Courrières, the bent figures of men and women digging in the fields of Artois.

> *I should be happy if some day I could draw them, so that these unknown types would be brought before the eyes of the people.*

Back in Cuesmes he worked hard at his exercises and read a great deal – Hugo's *Les Misérables* exactly suited his mood – but he was still unsure how best to set about his new life. With the coming of fair spring weather, he travelled home to Etten but he quarrelled with his father who had despaired of ever seeing his son settle to anything. Vincent's only idea for the future was a vague notion that he might go back to London. No doubt at his wits' end the pastor agreed to help but the subject was dropped and the suggestion abandoned. It was an unhappy visit and the only positive result was a gift of fifty francs from Theo which his father had been keeping for him. Once more in the Borinage he felt obliged to write and thank his brother and this letter, written in July, turned into another of his long rambling confessions as he attempted to clear his mind and set out the change of heart he had undergone. Stripped of its inessentials the letter revealed that Vincent had finally reconciled the duality which had dogged his life: art and religion were no longer opposites tearing him apart but one and the same thing. The two sides of his nature – his father working on his sermon, his mother at her water-colours – had merged.

> *I think that everything which is really good and beautiful – of inner moral, spiritual and sublime beauty in men and their works – comes from God, and that all which is bad and wrong in men and their works is not of God, and God does not approve of it.*
>
> *To give you an example: someone loves Rembrandt, but seriously – that man will know there is a God, he will surely believe it.*

> *To try to understand the real significance of what the great artists, the serious masters, tell us in their masterpieces, that leads to God; one man wrote or told it in a book; another, in a picture.*

The letter also heralded the final shift in his relationship with Theo; the fifty-franc gift symbolised a reversal of roles by which Theo would become the elder brother forever supporting his 'younger' brother financially and morally. However, that ten-month silence was not the last time Vincent would quarrel with him, for despite his infinite kindness Theo was no more spared the violent changes of mood than anyone else, but the vow made in The Hague was never broken by the younger man.

As if to establish this change, requests for help followed immediately upon the re-establishment of relations, though these were initially confined to artistic aid. At first Vincent could think no further than learning how to draw; painting seemed far beyond him as yet and his plan was to become an illustrator like the English engravers he had so admired in the illustrated newspapers. He was still obsessed with the idea of creating art from the life around him and his first solution was to try to make himself a sort of Millet of the Borinage. In a letter that August he asked Theo to send him his copy of Millet's *Field Work* so he could try to copy it. He asked Tersteeg to get him Bargue's *Charcoal Exercises* and told Theo he would like to make a study of Breton's *The Recall of the Gleaners*. Now that he had started to make pictures there seemed so little time. He had not even learned perspective at school; his hands and feet came out too big and awkward; he was twenty-seven and had the drawing skills of a child, but if he could learn to do what Millet had done all would be well. He sent Theo a hasty copy of his drawing of the miners going to work, but it was not easy, for soon the nights would be drawing in and his room in the Decrucqs' was ill-lit and cramped. Worse, he felt lonely. It was hard to make art, even something as basic as those first studies, without someone to share the experience. He longed for the company of those with the same ambitions as himself, he even resurrected his old dream of a community of like-minded souls, though now it would be an artistic rather than a religious group. But where to find such people? Millet was dead and Barbizon far away, he knew no one approachable in Paris, only nearby Brussels seemed at all possible.

He left Cuesmes for the Belgian capital quite suddenly in October

1880. But despite the hardship he had experienced, despite the gloom and suffering of the Borinage, the thought of leaving depressed him and on the eve of his departure he went to see Pastor and Madame Bonte in Warquignies to say goodbye and pour out his unhappiness.

> *Nobody has understood me. They think I'm a madman because I wanted to be a true Christian. They turned me out like a dog, saying that I was causing a scandal, because I tried to relieve the misery of the wretched. I don't know what I'm going to do. Perhaps you are right, and I am idle and useless on this earth.*

He left them, barefooted even in the autumn chill, his bundle on his shoulder. A group of urchins ran after him shouting "He's mad! He's mad!" He never returned though he often thought of doing so. Years later when his friend, the Belgian poet Eugène Boch, told him he was going to the Borinage, Vincent was full of encouragement and described it, with all the lyricism of hindsight, as:

> *The country of the oleanders and the sulphur sun.*

So his first illusions returned at last, and the Black Earth Country was once more a scene out of Bruegel or Dürer.

"He's mad! He's mad!" the children shouted as he left, but as he watched him go Pastor Bonte said to his wife: "We have taken him for a madman and perhaps he is a saint."

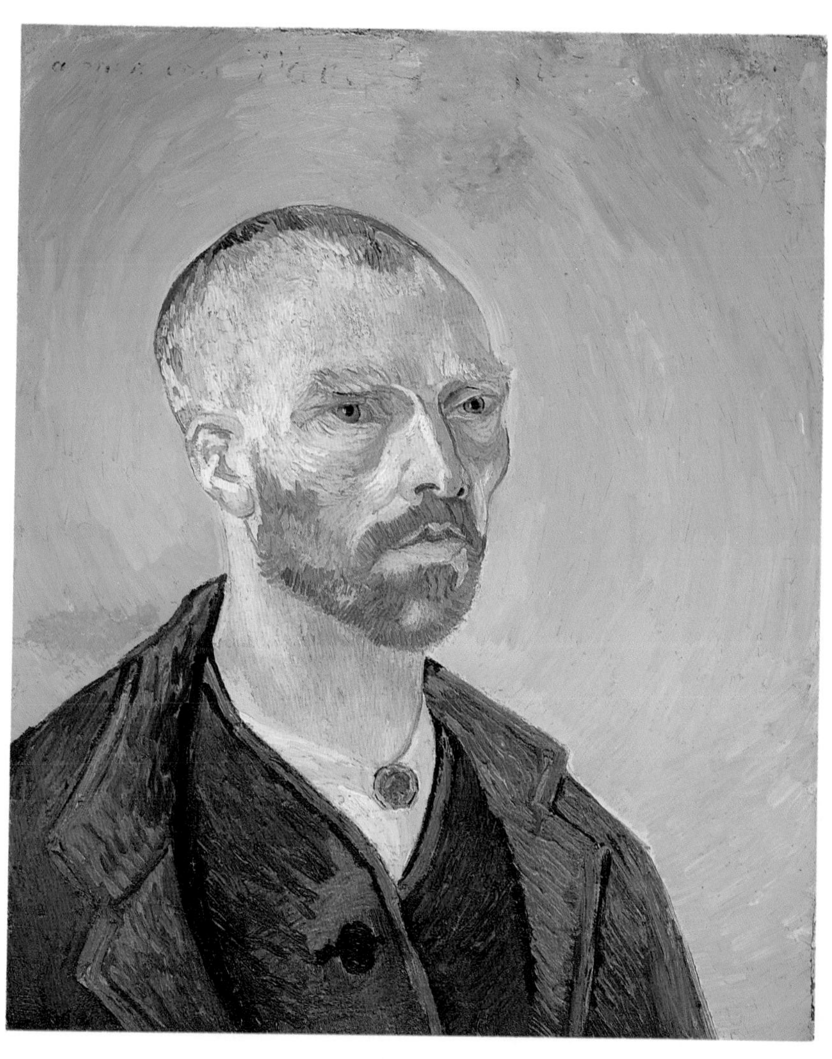

Although dedicated 'to my friend Paul Gauguin', this, the most famous of Van Gogh's self-portraits, was painted only a short time before he is said to have attacked Gauguin with a cut-throat razor.

I

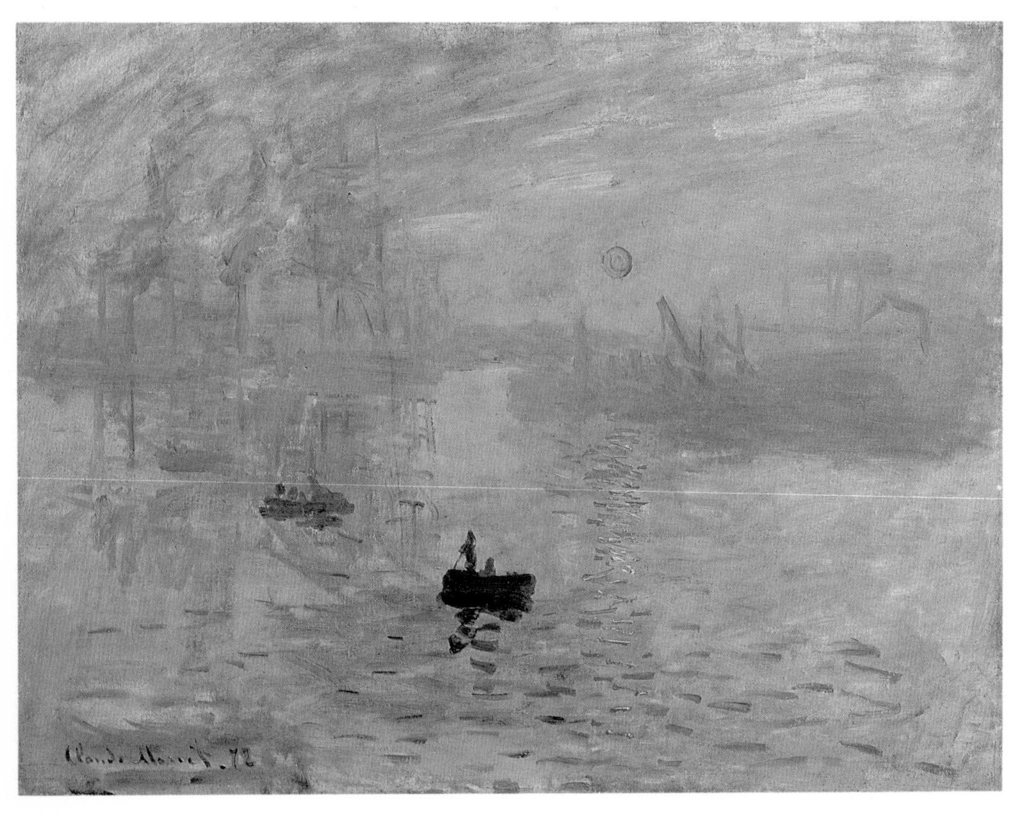

An unsympathetic critic took the title of Claude Monet's *Impression: Sunrise, 1872*, and gave a name to the new movement in art: Impressionism.

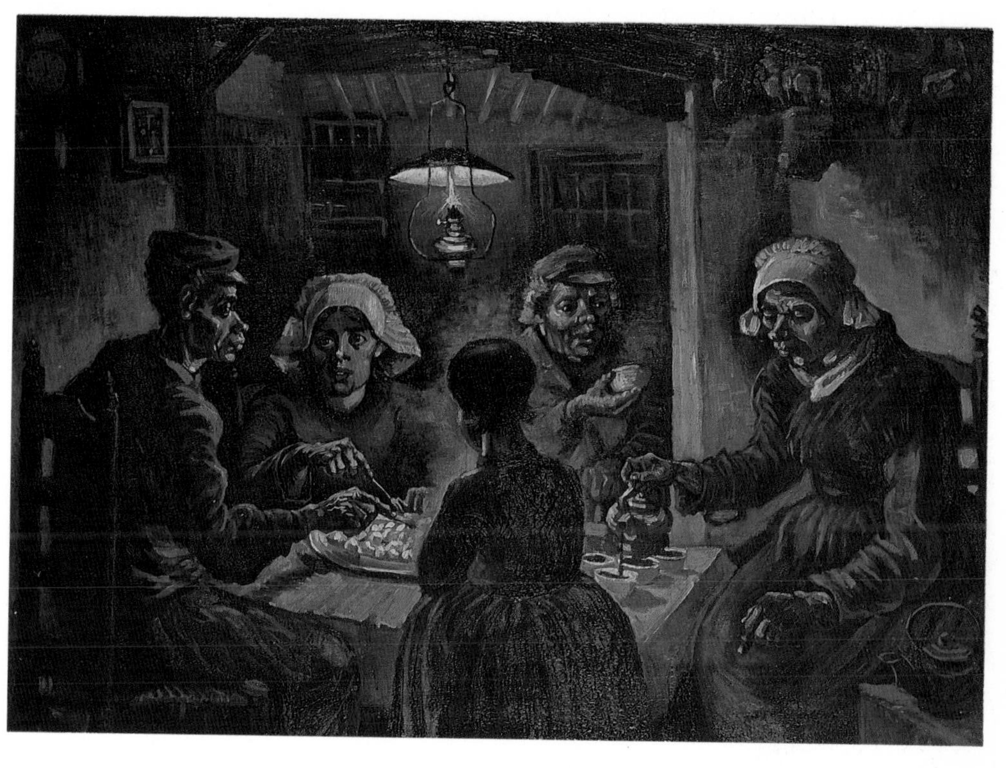

The finest single work of his Dutch period, Van Gogh's *The Potato Eaters* is in fact a group portrait of a peasant family he knew.

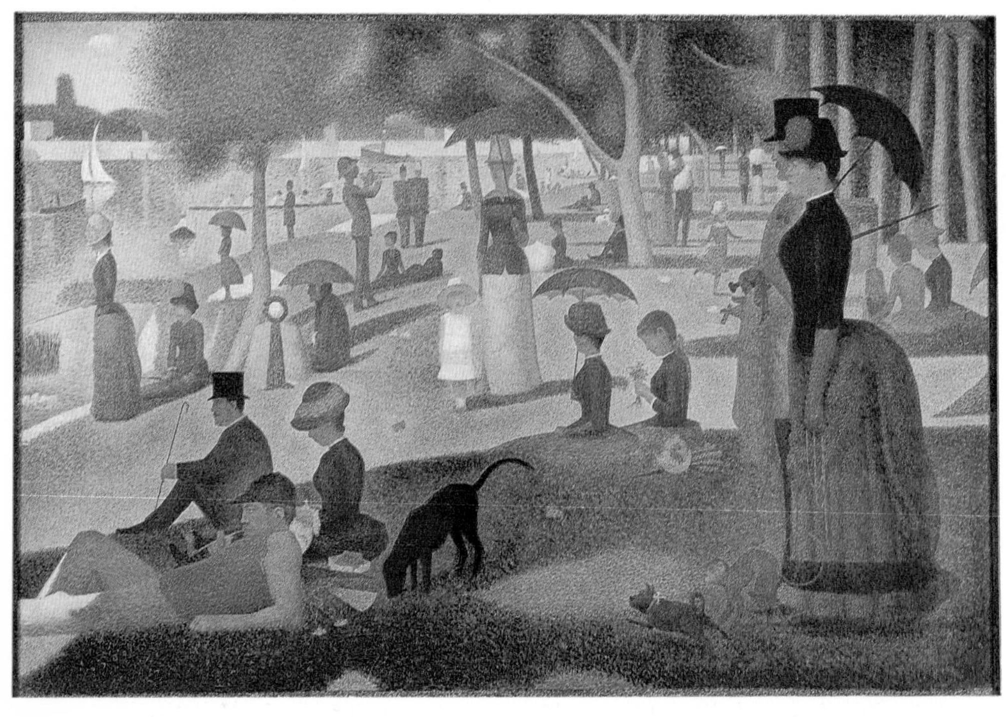

First exhibited in 1880, Georges Seurat's *Sunday Afternoon on the Island of the Grande Jatte* was the single most influential painting of the decade and marked the beginning of the new art that followed Impressionism.

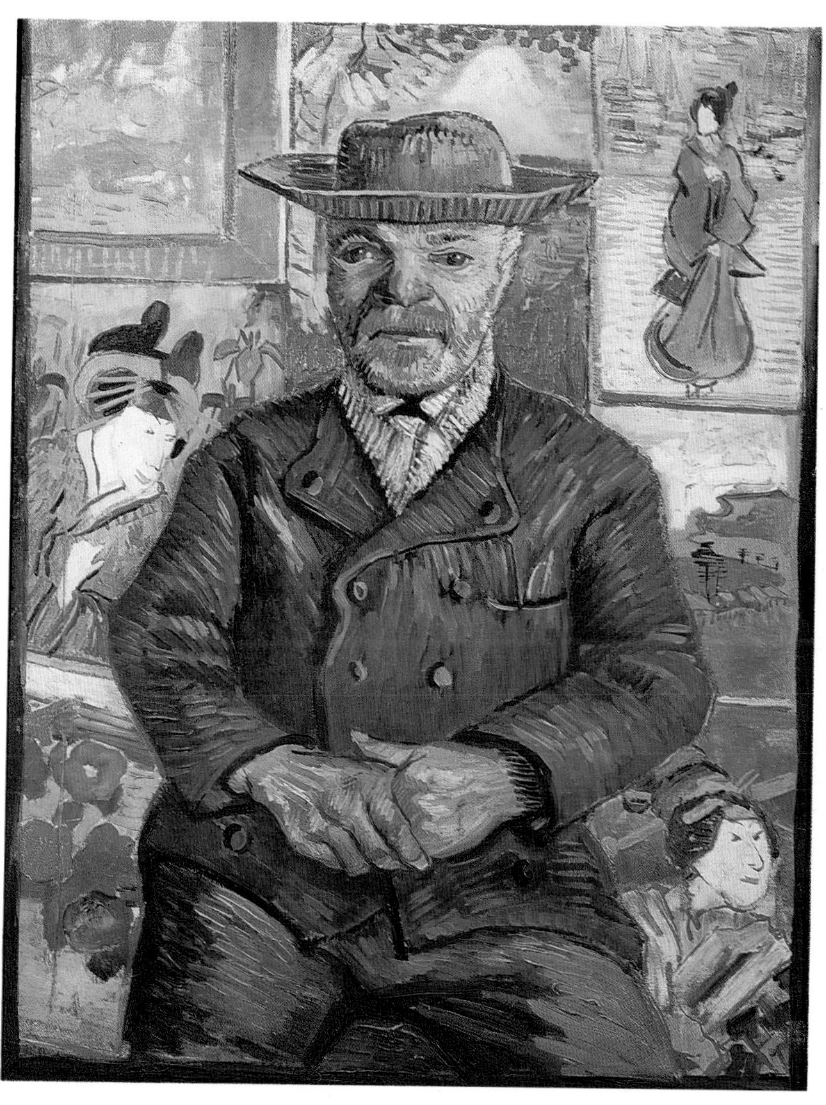

For his portrait of *Père Tanguy*, the one-time revolutionary and political prisoner who became his second father, Vincent surrounded the old man with a selection of the Japanese prints kept in Theo's apartment.

V

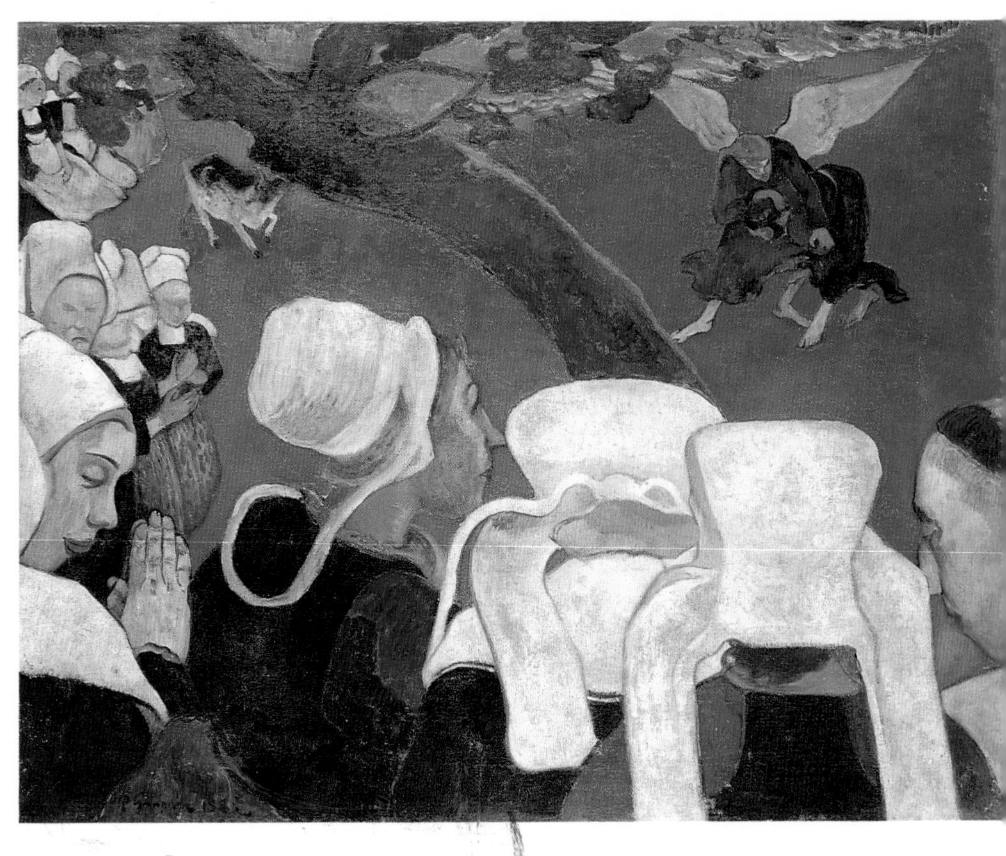

As with Seurat's *Grande Jatte*, Paul Gauguin's *Vision after the Sermon, Jacob Wrestling with the Angel* marked a further break with Impressionism and the beginning of Gauguin's mature period.

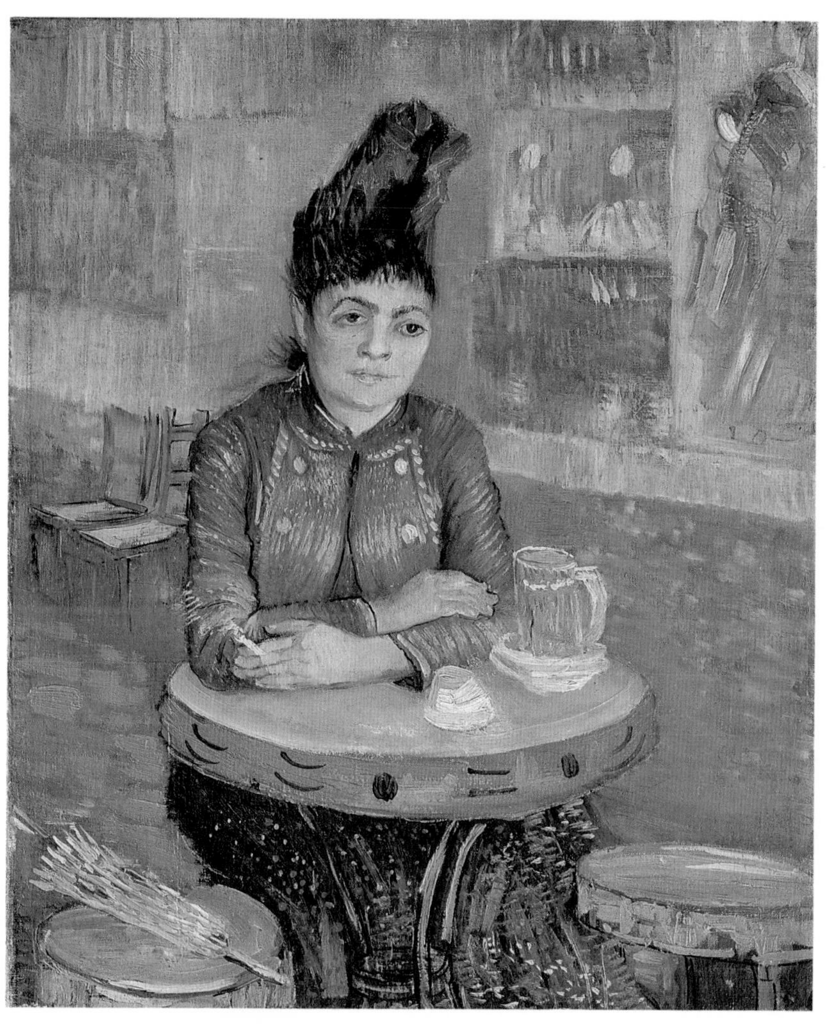

Whether or not she was his mistress, Vincent's portrait of *Agostina Segatori at the Café du Tambourin* shows a remarkable tenderness towards someone who was usually seen as a hard-headed business woman.

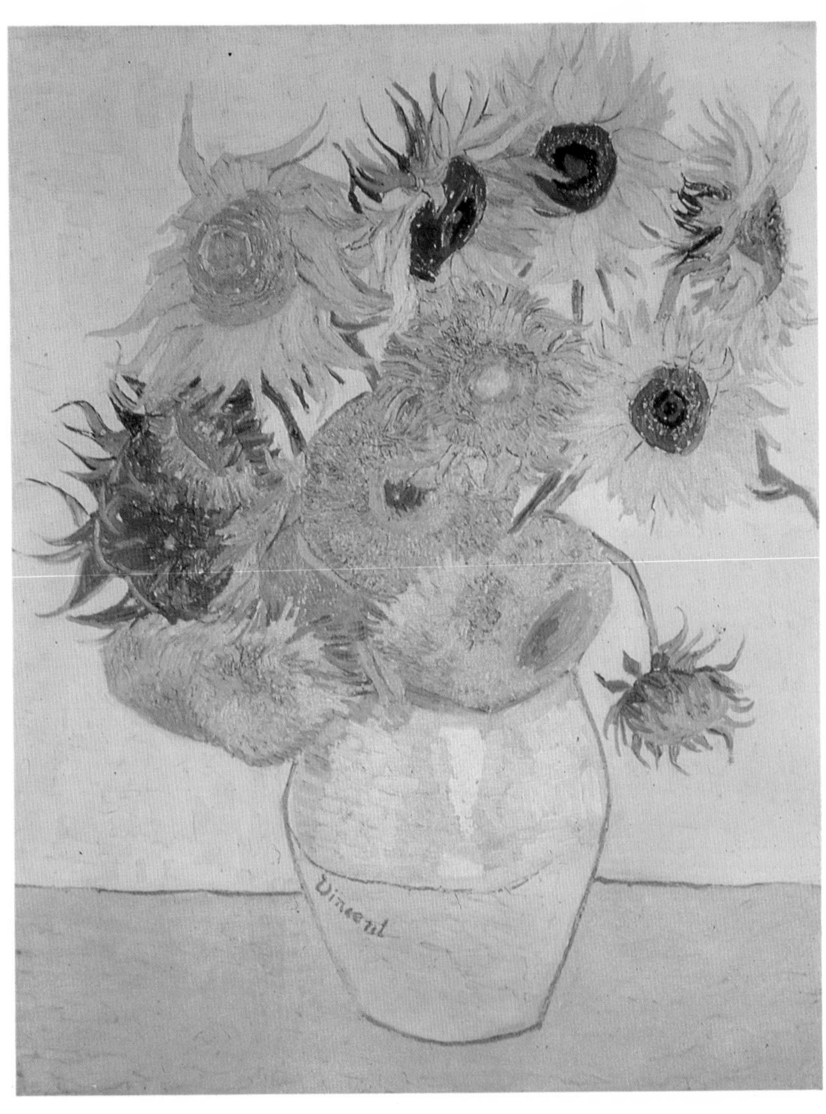

Vase with Twelve Sunflowers combines a burning image of the life-giving sun with the 'devil mistral'.

Part Two: 1880–1891

Later on they are bound to recognize my work, and they will surely write about me when I am dead. I will make sure of that if life grants me the time.

[Vincent in conversation with Anton Kerssemakers, 1885]

6

1880 — 1883

Theo

The first Theo knew of Vincent's sudden move was a letter from Brussels dated October 15th, 1880, written in French as if to drive home the fact that a new life was under way. It made no reference to the old life and all the usual religious obsessions had vanished. Of course there were new difficulties to be wrestled with and Theo's help was urgently solicited. Alone and uncertain which way to turn, Vincent had gravitated towards Goupil's Brussels branch and its manager Monsieur Schmidt, hoping to get advice on how to improve his skills. Unfortunately, his reception had been inexplicably cool, though Vincent put this down to his having been dismissed from the company. What he did not know was that Schmidt was currently locked into a complex legal battle with the Van Gogh family and had been amazed to find himself confronted by one of its members asking for help and advice. Despite this bizarre situation, Schmidt had not been unpleasant and, although far from warm in his welcome, had at least given the young man the best advice he knew. He told Vincent that he should register for entry to the Brussels Academy, where he could receive the basic training he so manifestly lacked.

When he read all this, Theo's reactions must have been very mixed. Here was his brother wildly launching himself on yet another new life without much evidence of any aptitude for it. It was too similar to his plunge into religion, an excess of enthusiasm with little inclination to undertake the necessary training, for, as his letter made clear, Vincent was not disposed to accept Schmidt's advice and preferred to train himself from his copy-books. It appeared to be a repeat performance of his inexplicable resistance to learning the classics in Amsterdam.

By this time Theo had become part of the French art world in a way

Vincent never had. He saw the difficulties of an artist's life at first hand and his brother's naïveté must have appalled him. Having observed the complex interaction of studios and famous artists, of art schools and salons, Theo had learned how they moulded styles and forged reputations, and knew that no one could succeed without such help. Indeed, the sheer scope of things seen and done by Theo in his first two or three years in the French capital was extraordinary, but it went well beyond being merely the pastime of an intelligent young man in search of artistic stimulation. While Vincent was in Brussels learning to be an artist, Theo was learning what the implications of such a step might be for his brother. It was as if they were two halves of a single creative personality, and though it would be seven years before they came together, Theo was making sure that when they did so his half would be ready for the union. From the moment when Vincent decided to be an artist and first turned to his brother for help, Theo's life was to be inextricably linked to his. Although it was never planned, Theo's experience of the Paris art world was radically to affect his brother's new career. Eventually, Vincent realised this and would forcefully proclaim that Theo was the joint creator of the paintings he produced.

Initially, they appeared to have little in common. Having been immured in the Borinage over the past two years Vincent had no idea how meteoric his younger brother's progress had been in the firm he himself had abandoned. Theo had arrived in Paris in 1878, just twenty-one, and with only modest prospects. His uncle's influence had waned and his own rather mild manner made it unlikely he would attract the notice of his superiors. But although he appeared quiet and withdrawn, Theo was also a thorough student of his subject and it was soon clear that he knew more about art than most of his colleagues. However, it was to be a chance meeting that changed his fortunes dramatically. In 1878 the somewhat shaky government of President Mac-Mahon, the man who had so brutally suppressed the Commune, determined to show the world that the 'horrors' of the German defeat and the resulting siege of the capital were over and that Paris was herself again. A major international exhibition was ordained. The site chosen was the open ground before Les Invalides and the rising slope on the opposite bank of the Seine. A huge rotunda was built in a vaguely Moorish style that might have pleased Albert Goupil but few others. Called the Palais du Trocadéro it stood on the site of today's Palais de Chaillot, which replaced it for the 1937 World's Fair. The Trocadéro was the main exhibition hall for art and culture – industry and commerce were relegated to another pavilion on the Champ-de-Mars across the Seine. Typical of the cultural confusion of the times, the Trocadéro was a gaudy brick temple composed of irreconcilable details; from round Roman arches to medieval lancet windows. Inside, Goupil's set up a stand to display its favourite artists and young Theo was left in charge. That there was some surprise when he managed to sell a picture indicates that Goupil's saw their presence there more as a publicity exercise than a business opportunity. But suddenly, while Theo was alone on the stand, the crowds parted and in the sepulchral hush that usually surrounds the great and famous, he found himself face to face with none other than the Comte Marie-Edmé-Patrice-Maurice de MacMahon, Duke of Magenta and second President of the Third Republic and man of the moment on his official tour of the Exhibition. Although a kindly-looking old badger, with his silver hair and whiskers, MacMahon was in reality a devious conspirator, currently contemplating an internal *coup d'état* to ensure that only the most right-wing and basically unreconstructed monarchists ran the new republic. Within a year he would be ousted, but for the moment he was the centre of attention and there was this unknown young Dutchman, unfazed by the encounter,

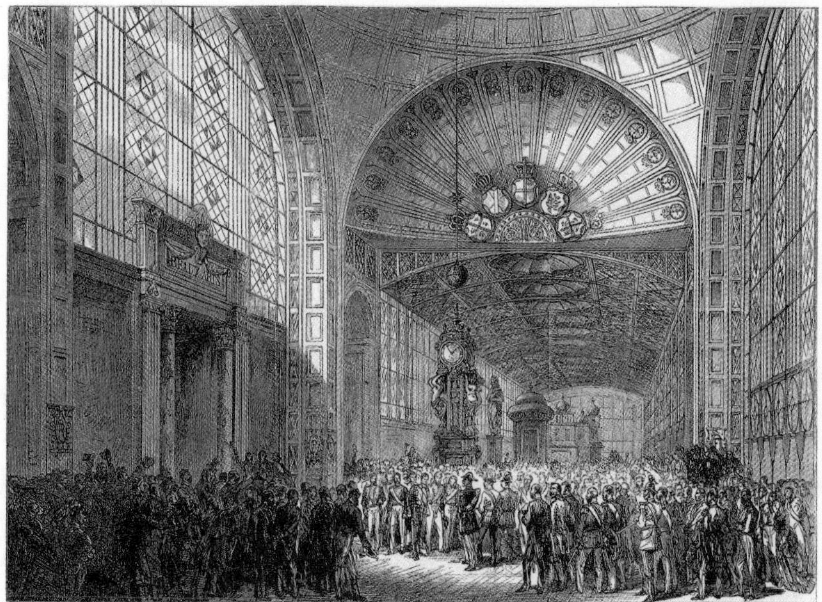

The World's Fair, Paris 1878, *The Illustrated London News.*

answering what he was asked as best he could. By the time the old man moved on, Theo was made.

To the partners, Boussod and Valadon, it was obvious they had someone of value on their staff and a series of rapid promotions elevated Theo to the directorship of the smaller gallery in the Boulevard Montmartre. It was a heady success for one so young, and would have far reaching effects for his brother as well as many other new artists in Paris, for Theo had quickly realised that there was more to art than the work currently favoured by the gallery in the Place de l'Opéra.

Initially Theo's contacts had been within the world that Goupil's cultivated. Its most eminent artist remained old Goupil's son-in-law, Jean-Léon Gérôme. A decade earlier Gérôme would have been less in evidence but by the late Seventies a bad bout of dysentery in Algeria had forced him to limit his travels. He had now settled into a life of some glory in the Parisian art world with a substantial house and studio on the Boulevard de Clichy, daily rides in the Bois de Boulogne, where his military bearing often had him taken for a cavalry officer, and large numbers of young hopefuls from all over the world clamouring to be his pupils. To Theo, Gérôme stood for everything necessary for advancement in the world of dealers and buyers: he was a member of the Institute, sat on the Salon jury and taught at the Ecole des Beaux-Arts; he had received all the highest national honours; and his work was bought by those two touchstones of artistic success in the mid-nineteenth century, the French State and nouveau riche American millionaires.

Despite the man's awesome standing, Theo was far from overwhelmed. He was quick to see that Boussod and Valadon were no longer keeping ahead of taste as they had in the days when Goupil and Uncle Cent had been willing to risk patronising the Barbizon and Hague School painters. Though it barely seemed possible at the time, Theo dared to believe that despite his high honours and huge fees, Gérôme's reputation might not last. So justified has that assessment been that it is almost impossible now to take a balanced view of Gérôme's life and work. History has imprisoned him as the enemy of the new, the arch-opponent of the heroically struggling Impressionists whose art he did everything to thwart. Undoubtedly he behaved badly in trying to frustrate attempts to hold a memorial exhibition for Manet in the year following the artist's death, but that was untypical of the man and Gérôme in his lifetime was better known as a rather more sympathetic teacher than some of the narrow-minded academicists who opened their studios to the young. If one can stop seeing Gérôme's work as the polar opposite of Impressionism and accept that both were part of the realist movement which dominated the mid-century, the fog of prejudice begins to lift. When Theo was first introduced to him, Gérôme was working on closely observed studies of animals and they, along with his earlier studies of Arab architecture and dress, were attempts to render the visible world with a truthfulness which the Impressionists also sought in their own way.

That each was blind to the other's approach was perhaps inevitable, and indeed sad for Gérôme who lost the battle and was relegated to obscurity. Today, when he might have expected a degree of 'forgiveness' and rehabilitation, his work has come under renewed attack by opponents of Orientalism who view him as part of a subtly racist attempt to reduce non-European peoples to the sub-status of amusing exotics. In Theo's day the assaults on his lofty eminence were just beginning. Zola, who had taken up art criticism, attacked him for being a mere copier of photographs. It was true that Albert Goupil's main task had been to carry the camera equipment on their journeys, but this hardly seems a devastating criticism. It was what Gérôme stood for in terms of the establishment which irritated his opponents and made their judgement of him biased; he may have been a bit sharp and haughty but that was due as much to his rough peasant origins as to any snobbery on his part. Certainly, his pupils adored him and he was increasingly open-minded as the years passed, even taking on the young Fernand Léger at the turn of the century. A photograph of him in old age shows a kindly face; he is wearing the full regalia of a Grand Officer of the Légion d'honneur complete with cockaded hat, yet he looks curiously bedraggled as if he had dressed in this finery then taken a walk in the rain.

The significant point for Theo, and thus for Vincent, was that Goupil's manager in Brussels, M. Schmidt, had been quite right in recommending a would-be painter to attach himself to someone like Gérôme. The career of an artist, at the time, was a matter of apprenticeship and the hoped-for patronage of the master. Young painters moved from school to academy to studio, hoping to perfect various techniques and attract the support of a powerful teacher, Gérôme being one of the most influential, though he was notoriously unwilling to use undue influence to help his apprentices.

Theo found a classic example of this system when he was introduced to a young fellow Dutchman, Anton van Rappard, who visited the gallery in October 1879. Currently a student of Gérôme, Van Rappard was the son of a family of the minor nobility who were willing and able to pay for his artistic education. Thus far this had meant studying in Holland, Germany, Brussels and Paris. When Theo first met him, Van Rappard was twenty-one and it says much about Theo that the student painter felt very nervous at the encounter and was considerably overawed by Theo's erudition. Although they were much of an age, it was clear to Van Rappard that Theo was already a man to be reckoned with.

Despite the young painter's nervousness, the encounter was friendly enough, perhaps because Theo sensed that he and Van Rappard shared an interest in new ideas. His stay with Gérôme was only a stage on his itinerary, and he was still looking around to see which of the current schools best suited him. When Theo compared Van Rappard with Vincent, the conclusion was obvious: whereas Van Rappard had youth and family money to back up his search, Vincent had now reached an age when a long apprenticeship would be impossible. In any case, there was not the money to pay for it. It was clear that whatever Vincent's new life might involve, it would fall to Theo to support him. Why, from the start, Theo was willing to do so is puzzling, given that Vincent had shown no especial talent for art and was already demonstrating his unwillingness to follow any of the conventional ways to acquire the necessary skills. But support him Theo did, partially out of a deep belief in art which, like Vincent's, bordered on the religious, but mainly because of his unwavering love for his older brother. They were even coming to resemble each other; as Vincent starved and bludgeoned himself his face took on the same spare, narrow look as that of his younger brother. Of course Vincent looked merely haggard, while Theo, if not handsome, managed to look fairly distinguished, sometimes clean-shaven, sometimes with a close-cropped beard similar to Uncle Cent's, though as friends noted, Theo too could occasionally look gaunt and unwell. Vincent was basically tough, whereas Theo had inherited something of the family frailty. Their enthusiasm was similar, their temperament different. Where Vincent plunged into anything new with an overpowering nervous intensity, Theo sought balance, as if aware of his weaknesses. He made sure that he had a life outside the narrow world of Goupil and its artists by joining the Dutch Club, a social group for lonely young Dutchmen living in the French capital. The conversation may not have been sparkling but it offered a wider circle of acquaintance. It was at this club that Theo first met a young man called Andries Bonger, a commercial clerk, and while his was hardly the world Theo moved in, Andries would gradually become his closest friend and an essential ally in his dealings with the ever more difficult Vincent.

In one other and very important way, Theo differed from his brother – women were not impossibly idealised creatures to him. He had not long been in Paris before he acquired a mistress. This is not to suggest that he did not have difficulties with his relationships, but at least they were played out at the level of actual human contact rather than the abstract dramas in which his brother participated so miserably.

All in all, Theo succeeded where Vincent failed, he led a real Parisian life. His salary was small but he was able to supplement it with commissions on his sales. He found an apartment in the Rue Laval on the edge of Montmartre and was soon patronising the neighbouring Chat Noir café first in the Boulevard Rochechouart, later in the Rue Laval itself. The Chat Noir had a notoriously louche cabaret where poets and pimps rubbed shoulders, and jaded aesthetes sipped absinthe. Progressive in their art, anarchic in their politics, varied in their sexuality, the patrons of the Chat Noir were at another pole from the world occupied by Jean-Léon Gérôme. At the Chat Noir a saucy egalitarianism reigned. If Gérôme had ever passed the Swiss Guard with halberd, on duty at the café entrance, he would probably have had apoplexy. The waiters were kitted out in the green, braided uniform of the Académie française and the whole place with its bric-à-brac décor was visibly against every element of good taste the establishment held most dear.

Theo was soon an accepted member of the élite, not too strenuously insulted by Salis, the proprietor, and generally assured of one of the better seats. This was heady stuff for the young Dutchman and it signified an emancipation from the narrow world of Goupil's that his brother had never achieved. Whereas Vincent had managed completely to ignore the Impressionist revolution which incensed so much of the Parisian art world, Theo wholeheartedly embraced the new art. In 1879 he went to the Fourth Impressionist Exhibition, an event that was to change not only his own perception of art but also ultimately that of his brother. Intriguingly, the fourth exhibition was the turning-point in the evolution of the movement, the point where it became apparent that the period of 'High' Impressionism was ending and that a second stage was about to declare itself. For the brothers – and one must now begin to think of them in unison – it was incredibly fortunate that Theo's interest began just at that crucial moment. Of the artists represented at the Fourth Exhibition, Theo was most attracted to the work of Camille Pissarro and that fact, too, was to have far-reaching consequences for Vincent. Although Pissarro was older than even the first group of Impressionists, his support for Cézanne and later Gauguin and Seurat, and his own involvement with their experiments, made him the bridge between the first and second stages of the movement. That Pissarro and Theo became friends was Vincent's great good fortune.

Because Theo was not simply an art lover but also a dealer, it was obvious to him as he strolled round the gallery that the initial furious reactions of public and critics were by then somewhat muted, for here was the *beau monde* of fashionable ladies and men-about-town come to see and be seen. They might scoff but they were there. A few even bought, only a handful, but it was a fact not lost on the young gallery manager, and it was not long before Theo began to learn something of the history and the group politics of this new art. It was significant that Renoir did not exhibit at the Fourth Exhibition and that it was Monet's last group show. They had been the twin pillars of the movement. Already the image of the two artists, hungry and dejected, working side by side on the banks of the Seine, creating those sparkling scenes of picnics and swimming parties, had taken on an heroic status. That moment of experiment had given way to a decade of fulfilment between 1870 and 1880, the decade of High Impressionism, so splendid it left younger artists with little room for manoeuvre.

When Theo came to know him better, he realised that Pissarro was the bridge between the original Impressionists and a second wave of younger artists struggling to find new forms of expression. As Theo quickly learned, everything in Pissarro's background disposed him to resist the settled view. Born in 1831 on the island of St Thomas in the Danish Antilles, of a Creole mother and a Portuguese Jewish father, he had further compounded this heady mix by running off to Venezuela with the Danish artist 'Fritz' Melbye who became his mentor. By the age of twenty-three he had made his way to Paris and discovered the work of Corot. But the other great destabilising factor in Pissarro's life was a deep-rooted uncertainty about his own talents, which left him constantly open to new influences. When he first discovered the fledgling Impressionists he was completely bowled over by Monet's experiments and surrendered so totally to the other man's style that he almost submerged his own personality. This was all the more strange as Pissarro even looked much older than the others. A Santa Claus beard and tiny glasses gave him the air of a benign elderly uncle. Other reactions to him were mixed: the somewhat right-wing Renoir distrusted his anarchist politics but it was hard to dislike someone with a touching faith in homoeopathic medicine and a childlike passion for anything new. It was the latter which ultimately caused a breach between him and his associates, for while the newer adherents of Impressionism were grateful for his support, most of the original group thought he was undermining their achievements by bringing in those who wanted to go further down the path of experiment.

Much of Pissarro's open-mindedness came from a natural gentleness allied to strong radicalism. He had to flee to London during the 1870 war and he painted some of his best Impressionist work among the mists and snows of the city's newer suburbs.

It was his return to France that stimulated a change of direction. He moved his family to Pontoise in the countryside north-west of Paris where, despite crippling poverty – he rarely sold a painting – he generously invited the 33-year-old Paul Cézanne to come and join him. Despite his age Cézanne was still struggling to find his place as an artist. He was troubled by parental interference and still working with a dark-toned palette heavily influenced by Manet. It was Pissarro who introduced him to the liberating effects of open-air painting which gave him the release he needed. Pissarro saw to it that his protégé was represented in the First Impressionist exhibition even though it was obvious from the start that he was far from accepting all the tenets of the 'movement', loose as they were. Pissarro introduced Cézanne to his collector friend Dr Gachet in nearby Auvers, and in general acted as a father figure. As Pissarro was the Impressionist most concerned with solid form, as opposed to the flickering effects of light, he had far more in common with what Cézanne was struggling to achieve than the others of the group.

Pissarro's support of Cézanne was a simple act of kindness, but his links with the much younger Paul Gauguin were a great deal closer. Although born in Paris, Gauguin's journalist father had found it prudent to seek temporary refuge in his wife's native Peru after Napoleon III's *coup d'état* of 1851. As he was only three years of age at the time the family fled, this enabled Gauguin to refer to himself later as 'a savage from Peru'. He was sent back to France to be educated but as soon as he was old enough he became a seaman in the French merchant marine and for the six years up to 1871, sailed from the arctic fringes of Norway to the coasts of South America, a fact that must have endeared him to Pissarro. Back in Paris once more he attempted to settle into the manifestly unsuitable life of a stockbroker, helped by his guardian who was a collector of modern art, including the work of Pissarro. Gauguin married a Danish woman, Mette Sophie Gad, two years later but was soon chafing at the restraints of his settled life. At first he sublimated his yearnings for adventure by dabbling in collecting himself, but being a mere spectator was not enough and gradually he started to paint. What had begun as Sunday painting came to dominate his life. In 1876 he had a painting accepted by the Salon and met Pissarro whose form of Impressionism he soon absorbed. Eight years later he finally threw up his job on the stock exchange and began working full time with the older man.

At its simplest, Impressionism was concerned with the act of seeing and the struggle to record what one was seeing; what that something was mattered less. The Impressionists were content to represent the life of the new urban population without comment or judgement, hence the boating parties, street scenes and railway stations. But Pissarro, mainly in his drawings and lithographs, showed an interest beyond surface gaiety with pictures of peasant life which harked back to Millet. True, he often produced such rural scenes in order to earn badly needed cash to feed his family but they also revealed a side to him that was not fully at one with the practice of Monet and Renoir. And although Gauguin would spend almost a decade under the influence of Pissarro's Impressionist style he too was to show increasing signs of impatience with what he came to feel was a dead end, with the way the once experimental side of Impressionism had now been codified into an agreed style. Indeed it was Pissarro's insistence that Gauguin should be admitted into the Fourth Exhibition which more than anything else broke the unity of the group. As Theo quickly noted, from then on Impressionism would move gradually but surely to its apotheosis as one of the major artistic movements of the century. It would be others, often supported by Pissarro, who would become the new experimenters.

Having acknowledged and understood these personalities and factions, it remained for Theo to decide how to respond. He was soon aware of the role of men like Paul Durand-Ruel, the first promoter of the Impressionists, who had nearly ruined himself exhibiting their work when no one would buy it. Then there was Durand-Ruel's rival Georges

Petit, who soon latched on to the rising school and tried to corner their work. Was there a place for Theo in all this? It was unclear whether Boussod and Valadon would welcome moves to promote such uncommercial stuff. But in his own quiet way Theo was just as single-minded and determined as his brother and from that visit to the Fourth Impressionist exhibition his mind began to turn on schemes which would enable him to be more than a mere spectator.

Theo's tactic was patiently to wear down the resistance of the senior partners until he was allowed to use an upstairs room in the Boulevard Montmartre gallery as a showcase for the new art. Not that he was given a completely free hand. If any significant purchases were to be made, both Boussod and Valadon insisted on accompanying him, even though they had little appreciation of the work in question. Only the fact that Theo was so good at maintaining the profits from the main gallery stopped them from stifling this new venture at the start. Indeed the few works that were sold were usually acquired by Theo himself who was building up a significant collection of the new art. But occasionally the partners' criticisms stung. Theo's confidence could be seriously undermined by this insensitive lack of support and if this came at a time of private stress, then Theo would sometimes despair. Why not emigrate to America where, as Durand-Ruel discovered, there was more sympathy among the rich collectors for avant-garde art? At such low moments, the one thing which ultimately restrained him was the halter of his brother's dependence.

Theo must also have been aware that alone among the dealers he fully understood the changes which were slowly taking place in the 1880s. Even a progressive dealer like Durand-Ruel could not see beyond the high Impressionism of the previous decade. Theo's greatest strength was that, like Pissarro, he was capable of appreciating often opposing styles. Because of the 'victory' of Impressionism in this century, we tend to judge all other forms of late nineteenth-century art in relationship to it, either as the lesser or 'defeated' art such as Gérôme's, or as art that grew out of or reacted against Impressionism. Yet the truth is that the Impressionism of Monet and Renoir overlapped with what came to be called Post-Impressionism. Theo was there at that moment and was at the same time aware of other forces at work. One of his companions at the Chat Noir was an impecunious young artist named Henri Rivière, who made a precarious living designing shadow plays, which were rapidly becoming the cabaret's greatest attraction. These were no small scale cut-outs flickering behind a cloth screen. The scenes were large, anticipating the cinema, and Rivière's figures, sometimes in card, sometimes in zinc, were projected at differing distances creating marvellous illusions of depth. Later, coloured cut-outs would be used in an attempt to imitate the bold effects of the then fashionable Japanese prints. Accompanied by avant-garde music or the wilder excesses of contemporary poetry, the plays held audiences spellbound in the magical glow of an oxyhydrogen lamp. The Chat Noir's greatest triumph was in 1887 with a version of Flaubert's *La Tentation de Saint-Antoine* in which Rivière first introduced his coloured figures. These stunning images drew an impressive group of literary and musical admirers including Verlaine and Rimbaud, Zola, Debussy and Satie. But Rivière's greatest enthusiasts were the younger artists and illustrators who recognised in his bold flat shapes and solid colours something that they were themselves striving to achieve. Where Impressionism had attempted to capture the fleeting moments of reality – the red and green in dappled sunlight, the blueness of fog – others were now looking elsewhere. Realism, Naturalism, even Positivism, all different ways of defining the same phenomenon, had grown out of the nineteenth-century belief in man's capacity to transform his environment, to define it and thus control it. Radical and progressive, the reader of Zola learned of the poverty of the miners and the hardships of the city dweller, but it was inevitable that there would be a reaction once the shock of revelations about the underclass of prostitutes and petty criminals had abated. Between 1870 and 1890 the reaction set in. Exotic far-away places such as Tahiti and Tonkin were added to France's overseas territories and a burgeoning interest in obscure faiths merged with a return of interest in the occult and the irrational, while the ideas of British and German philosophers from Herbert Spencer to Schopenhauer helped break down the earlier certainties of scientific progress. Inevitably new forms of art slowly reflected these interests and in Theo's time they were just beginning to emerge. The names we now know them by – Symbolism, Cloisonism, Les Nabis – came later; at first the various groups were as shifting and as inchoate as the background figures in Rivière's shadow plays. Indeed for many in the audience it was exactly those flat cut-out figures in their vivid colours that best represented the route they were beginning to take. Perhaps the sensations created by colour could and should be divorced from the subject represented? Perhaps it was not the people in the street or the boat on the water, or the train steaming into the Gare St Lazare which made you feel happy, sad, pensive or violent; perhaps it was simply the colour green or a particular shade of yellow? In some way as yet undefined, colours might evoke certain basic emotions. The effects created by Rivière on his screen at the Chat Noir called into question the relevance of chiaroscuro and perspective, which underpinned the whole idea of re-creating reality. But if the time-honoured language of the painter's art was losing its meaning, where was meaning to be found?

Theo noted these reactions and kept an open mind. There was so much to see and absorb, it was worth getting away from the major galleries and looking into the shops which sold artists' materials, where it was often possible to find extraordinary work by poverty-stricken artists left there in exchange for oils and canvas. One of his more exciting discoveries was at Joseph Delarebeyrette's, a shop which he found stuffed with utterly original flower paintings by an obscure Provençal artist named Adolphe Monticelli.

These bouquets of flowers were worked up in a thickly encrusted impasto of rich raw colours. They were like nothing Theo had ever seen before, completely different from the Impressionists, who seemed positively restrained beside the violence with which Monticelli handled paint. Sadly, Delarebeyrette could not enlighten Theo about the author of the works except to say that he believed he had been one of the countless unknowns who had disappeared during the final days of the Commune. Monticelli had lived on the outskirts of the city and had been in the habit of calling at the shop when he walked into town. Some time in 1871 his visits had ceased, and that was all Delarebeyrette knew.

Theo attempted to introduce Vincent to some of his discoveries, though trying to explain the new ideas of art by letter proved a frustrating exercise. For some years the two brothers travelled along parallel tracks not yet fully in unison, but Theo persevered, helping where he could, watching from a distance as his brother struggled to master the skills he needed.

Alone in Brussels, Vincent had three main concerns, foremost among which was basic survival. The city was expensive and his father could only send him sixty Belgian francs a month. A close second came his doubts about whether he would succeed in his new career. Third, would he find someone to share the journey? He had begun with a room in a lodging house but soon moved to a small hotel above a café on the Boulevard du Midi. Even that tiny space set him back fifty francs a month with nothing more than coffee and bread provided. Part poverty, part instinct had guided him to the fringe of what was even then the nearest thing to Brussels' Bohemian quarter. The nearby Academy of Fine Arts meant that there were shops selling artist's materials and the possibility of meeting other struggling painters. It was an isolated niche in the rapidly expanding metropolis. Across the city, on the old military parade ground, Brussels was celebrating the nation's fiftieth birthday with the construction of a grandiose monument to the country's economic success, though it was not without significance that the new Arc de Triomphe was so behind schedule that it had to be temporarily completed in papier mâché to be ready for the great day. Vincent well knew the hard industrial reality hidden behind this paper façade, an all too appropriate symbol for the burst of construction and invention that was transforming western Europe. Characteristically, Vincent remained completely indifferent to it. Wherever he was, just around the corner, just beyond the next horizon, some great feat of engineering, some magnificent example of the new urbanism, was being unveiled, while he remained insulated from all contact with it. Between 1880 and 1890, Europe was transformed from a culture which still had its roots in the countryside to one largely industrial and urban. Every move Vincent made was in a sense a flight from this new reality.

He had every reason to resent the city. With the few francs that remained after his rent had been paid he could barely afford paper on which to draw, let alone an occasional hot meal. These bouts of prolonged hunger were serious assaults on a health already weakened by the privations in the Borinage. But far worse were his fears that he might fail. Anything was bearable if the end was justified. But who could tell? He still said that all he wanted was to be an illustrator, but this was probably to cushion himself against failure. Had he desired nothing more than to be a graphic artist as he sometimes claimed, then he could have tried to apprentice himself as a jobbing illustrator on one of the newspapers. As it was he haunted the artists' quarter, desperate for contact with other painters. He did meet one or two young men, as poor and as keen to become artists as he was, but they could offer him little except the knowledge that he was not completely isolated in his struggle.

Alone in his hotel room, Vincent worked away at the exercises in his copy-books, as yet not fully aware of the irony implicit in his choice of Bargue as his exemplar. Although Charles Bargue, an accomplished but minor painter, had given his name to the course, the later sections of the exercises had been produced by no less a figure than Gérôme. As Vincent knew, old Goupil had brought Bargue and Gérôme together and published the results in 1868. Bargue had contributed a series of isolated studies of arms, ears and parts of the body which gradually led up to the full torso, while Gérôme had created a number of figure ensembles. So beautifully precise were these simple engravings that the books were often split up and framed as individual prints, as Vincent had originally done with his copy, which is why it is virtually impossible to find a complete *Bargue* today. Each part of the body would often have an accompanying, much simplified outline to help the student rough out the shape before attempting to complete the fully rounded drawing. This method inevitably emphasised line at the expense of shading or tone, so that two elements, angularity and black outline, were soon established as Vincent's basic working method. Gérôme, in agreeing to participate in the course, had intended just such a result. The student who adopted the technique would be placed firmly in tune with his own thinking and, by extension, would find himself at odds with methods like Impressionism which rejected hard outline in favour of the softening, diffusing effects of light. The advantage of the Bargue exercises was that they offered progress by easy-to-follow stages, essential to someone as naturally inept as Vincent. The rare examples of his early exercises which have survived are witness to the discrepancy between the myths about the word 'genius' and the altogether cruder reality of someone who began with scant evidence of natural ability, yet struggled to dominate his craft to the point where the word might have some genuine meaning. Simply to master the elementary proportions of the human figure and to achieve some semblance of perspective were the first tasks he set himself, and in this Bargue was a good master for the time being. Vincent's main resources were singlemindedness and an insatiable capacity for hard work. He was not a natural artist, he made himself into one there in the minuscule hotel room above a dingy Brussels café, day and night turning out innumerable rough, bad, hopeless sketches but gradually mastering control of eye and hand until he was able to subject both to his will. If 'genius' is perhaps the wrong word, then 'courage' must replace it, for he never took the easy path.

Having decided that a knowledge of anatomy would improve his figure drawing he boldly glued together five sheets of 'Ingres' paper and drew a full-size skeleton. Then he went to the School of Veterinary Science where he begged a teacher to let him have some animal skeletons to draw.

To go on working in such total isolation was impossible, however. He needed someone who would look at his efforts, who would criticise and not reject him out of hand. This was why he had called on Schmidt at Goupil, though he rejected the older man's suggestions. His first letter to Theo had asked him for any contacts in Brussels who might be sympathetic, and in his reply Theo suggested William Roelofs, one of the Hague School painters still living outside Holland but whose work, so Theo imagined, would appeal to Vincent. Sadly, Roelofs was not only in his sixties but also artistically old before his time. He had the same rigidly classical view of the artist's apprenticeship as Schmidt, but as a *plein-air* painter himself found any suggestion of Gérôme's influence anathema. The sight of the Bargue exercises was not pleasing. He advised Vincent to give them up and to work direct from nature, though only on a limited basis at first. Plaster casts were the recommended interim stage. And, like Schmidt, he also strongly advised the young man to enter the Academy and get some formal training. Perhaps the only positive thing to come out of the encounter was the news that Roelofs spent part of the year working direct from nature in some of the remotest corners of their native land such as Drenthe and the Frisian Islands. The thought was appealing to Vincent, already weighed down as he was by the problems of survival in the big city.

His situation was slightly eased when his father began to send him 100 francs a month and he could at last afford the occasional hot meal. It was not his financial straits that kept him away from the Academy, where entry was free to anyone with a letter of recommendation from the Town Hall. Rather it was Vincent's acute analysis of the singularity of his position – at twenty-seven he was beyond the age when most young people entered the drawing classes at the art schools. Having come late to art, he was driven by an almost overwhelming sense of urgency. He had to make up for lost time. It was also the case that he was no longer as open-minded as most students of art. They know only that they want to be artists and are willing to accept long periods of study before they discover just what sort of artists they will be. But Vincent knew exactly what he wanted to do. His was to be an art of and for the poor. The Millet of the coalfields was not yet dead, and, when not copying Bargue and other exemplars, he still drew scenes from the Borinage, heavily outlined figures wending their way to and from the pits or field workers copied from Millet. Nevertheless it was hard to ignore two forceful characters like Schmidt and Roelofs when both gave the same advice. Reluctantly he went through the procedure of applying to the Academy, though whether he would actually go once his entry had been processed remained to be seen.

Casting about for further contacts, Theo heard that the young Anton van Rappard was planning to leave Gérôme's studio to enrol at the Academy in Brussels. It must have puzzled Theo why someone should choose to leave the very Mecca of European art and the studio of one of its leading practitioners to lose himself in a provincial art school when most movement was in exactly the opposite direction. Such questions aside, what mattered now was that he might agree to meet Vincent. The proposal reveals a certain desperation on Theo's part. He well knew Van Rappard's nervousness, and the thought of an encounter between one so easily upset and the volcanic force that was Vincent must have given him pause. Worse still was the unavoidable fact that Van Rappard was upper class: his father was a *Ridder* or hereditary knight, a member of Holland's minor nobility who enjoyed a comfortable post as a municipal functionary. In every way the young Van Rappard had been cushioned against life's hardships and had found nothing but encouragement in his desire to become an artist. Vincent's basic antipathy to the well-off, and his own near desperate financial state, hardly augured well for the encounter. Still, as there was no one else, Theo took the risk.

They met at nine o'clock in the morning in Van Rappard's rooms in the Rue Traversière in the palpably respectable St Joost-ten-Noode district, a setting which must have put Vincent immediately on edge. The younger man's shyness was written all over him: he looked youthful and withdrawn, his hair close-cropped and beard trimmed to stubble with slightly crossed eyes which gave him a dreamy, vaguely bemused air. Confronted by Vincent's wild-eyed, red-headed bluster, he must have felt singularly ill at ease. It was clear from the start that they had little in common. To some extent Van Rappard looked on art as an extension of the superior social world into which he had been born, a milieu of dining clubs and members' societies, all anathema to Vincent. But somehow they survived this first meeting and agreed to see each other again. Vincent wrote to Theo to say he had found Van Rappard to be: *one who takes things seriously*. On subsequent visits Vincent examined the younger man's drawings and was impressed – they were very accomplished, albeit in the formal style of the academies. This was just what Vincent needed, someone slightly in advance of himself, not so far as to assume the unwelcome role of a teacher, but just far enough to nudge him onward.

They could see each other infrequently that winter, for Van Rappard had to begin his classes at the Academy. Whether Vincent finally gave in and went with him is not known, for he lapsed into another of his inexplicable silences. It is true that Theo was also very preoccupied with his own work and the increasing difficulties with his mistress, and found it hard to write, but there is always the possibility that Vincent suffered another bout of depression. The weather was persistently gloomy, cold and wet and he was existing on a near starvation diet. A sudden attack of paranoia may explain the letter in which he accuses Theo of deliberately ignoring him because he was afraid to compromise himself with someone who had broken with Goupil's. As soon as his wits returned, he hastened to apologise, offering the explanation that his drawing had been going badly. The only hopeful sign was that he had managed to work from real models at last, having persuaded his neighbours, an old porter, a young boy and a working man, to sit for him.

Early in 1881, both brothers had a bad shock: news came that Pastor Theodorus had suffered a collapse. Though he seemed to recover quickly enough it was clear that he was no longer the man he had been and the brothers' confidence in his durability was shattered. Vincent wrote home trying to reassure his father that all was going well with his new life: he was making progress, he explained, and had managed to borrow a skeleton from a painter who had subsequently praised the drawings he had made of it. The skeleton probably belonged to the Dutch artist Adrien-Jean Madiol who had settled in Brussels and who may also have been asked for advice. With Van Rappard still preoccupied with his classes, Vincent had again been on the look-out for a mentor and at some point came across Madiol. In a letter to his parents in February Vincent mentions receiving the occasional lesson and at thirty-five Madiol was certainly of the right age to be of help, even though his rather sugary seventeenth-century Dutch interiors, with titles such as *The Coffee Break, The Old Uncle*, or his most praised piece, *The Card Game*, had little to say to Vincent who would no doubt have noted his ample technique and left it at that. Of all the painters who crossed Vincent's path, Madiol was the least likely to survive the storm of change then brewing in Paris, and it was probably a mercy that he died suddenly twelve years later, before he could be overwhelmed by events. At the time, however, he cut a rather dashing figure with a full mane of swept-back hair and jauntily curled whiskers and it may have been this which prompted Vincent to abandon the ragged look he had assumed in the Borinage and to try to do something about his appearance. Whatever the reason, he bought some second-hand clothes, which must have been a relief to Van Rappard who was now seeing quite a lot of him.

With the coming of spring and the winding down of the Academy's winter courses they had begun to work together. Vincent's lodgings were unsuitable as a studio, the light was bad and the owners ill-disposed to his habits. They even objected when he tried to pin up his usual selection of prints and Van Rappard suggested that Vincent might care to come and work in his new apartment in the Rue des Eglises not far from his former home. They made a strange couple: Van Rappard careful and precise, patiently blocking out his drawing; Vincent nervous and impatient, stabbing with pencil or chalk, aggressively erasing his mistakes. More often than not the results displeased him and the crumpled drawing was thrown aside as he started at once on another. It did not matter, he knew that this was only practice. Time and hard work would train hand and eye. But he was equally sure perfection had its limits and he would try to persuade Van Rappard that technique was no substitute for the emotional force a drawing should seek to convey. The younger man listened, but clearly was doubtful. His days with such as Gérôme had left him with the belief that there were fixed standards of perfection to which everyone should aspire. Vincent seemed to rely on some personal standard of acceptability which he himself would recognise once he had achieved it. This was why he was afraid to put himself in a position where someone else would try to mould him. He was prepared to observe Van Rappard tackle a particular detail, if that was what he felt he needed to know, but that was as far as it went.

Although still cautious after his illness, Pastor Theodorus decided to visit Brussels to see for himself what this new life meant. It cannot have been an easy encounter. Vincent's last visit from the Borinage had been decidedly disagreeable and it was hard for Dorus to disguise his disappointment at his son's decision to abandon the ministry after he and the rest of the family had done so much to promote his avowed ambition. Then again, to deal in art was acceptable, even the life of a Hague School painter, like his nephew by marriage Anton Mauve, was within standards he could comprehend. But this Bohemian life in Brussels was another thing entirely. As he had shown time and time again, the pastor was by no means narrow-minded but it must have been difficult for him to resist a sense of personal failure when he saw that emaciated face and listened to the torrent of excitable talk as Vincent explained his new life. At least there was his new friend Van Rappard who was evidently respectable and manifestly in the Mauve tradition. But what would become of his own son? Had he real talent? Was this a further wild enthusiasm that would end with another collapse?

Most depressing for the older man was the unavoidable fact that Vincent was at an age when he ought to have been earning enough to help the family instead of continuing to accept their aid, with no prospect of ever being independent. True, he did talk of getting work as an illustrator eventually and there were vague plans to sell his drawings, but such hopes receded when Theodorus looked at the sketches themselves. There was so much more to be done before anyone would consider buying them. Before he left he told Vincent that Theo had been secretly sending him the extra forty francs a month. This gave Vincent a further cause for regret over his recent outburst and was a sharp reminder of just how dependent he was on others.

As he boarded the train that would take him back to Holland, the older man must have felt ambivalent about what he had seen. Clearly Vincent was absolutely determined, but so he had been before. Vincent's chances of achieving anything worthwhile were slender. That also was clear – and depressing. There was no conclusion, only the certainty that they would have to continue to support him as they might an invalid or other family dependant. It was an unhappy situation for someone no longer in full health.

For Vincent the only true reality was what was happening on the sheet of paper before him, all else was merely irritation. For the moment life was bearable, he had just enough money to eat moderately and to pay for materials. Van Rappard's rooms gave him a studio though how long this could last was a looming problem. Neither of them cared for the life of a big city. In Van Rappard's case this was primarily because his artistic interests were in the countryside and he was keen to leave now that the good weather had come. Vincent's feelings were as ever more complex. True, he also saw country people as his subjects, but he could just as well have found the underclass he yearned to unveil in his art among the struggling workers of the industrial zone that fringed Brussels. Every day he passed factory hands, porters, seamstresses, child labourers, all the bent, silent folk who shuffled to and from the gaunt brick manufactories, engine sheds, and mills, whose economic success the nation was currently celebrating, and yet Vincent could only think of peasants labouring in the fields or the miners below ground as suitable subjects for art. To him the city was something to be suffered while he learned the skills with which he could carry out his plans. When the city had surrendered its secrets then he could return to the coalfields and begin to make the art he believed in. Other than that, nothing. The city dragged him down, made him ill. Whenever they could, he and Van Rappard would escape into the countryside, to work in the fields which lay beyond the last fringe of houses and factories. Once they were walking near a quarry where they watched the diggers at work, and saw a woman plucking dandelion leaves and a farmer sowing. The vision had been too much for Vincent. Would he, he asked himself miserably, ever be able to paint such things?

Van Rappard's studies would come to an end that May and he told Vincent he was planning to leave. Vincent too longed to make a complete break, to head off to such wild untouched places as painters like Roelofs would visit in the summer months. But how could he afford to get there? Then he heard that Theo was planning to be at home for Easter and the situation resolved itself.

At the quiet country parsonage reactions were understandably mixed at the arrival of the errant first son. True, in his 'new' clothes he was more presentable than expected but what did he plan to do? Vincent aside, the Van Gogh family were reasonably happy. Anna had given them their first granddaughter, Sara, the year before and, although Elisabeth was having difficulties with her language studies, there was always the exemplary Theo to convince them that all was well – his mother had been so thrilled when she heard of the encounter with President Mac-Mahon. But Vincent was a disappointment in every way. It must have been hard to make him really welcome and once Theo had returned to Paris there was no one to watch over him. It was awkward having him at the parsonage and difficult to explain his eccentricities to the simple farming folk whose moral exemplars the Van Goghs were supposed to be. It was not as if he were a 'real' artist when all he could show were crude copies from exercise-books.

Vincent himself was increasingly aware that such drawings had taken him as far as they could. He had learned a great deal from Bargue and other course books on anatomy and perspective, but they did produce a rather stilted effect. He hoped this would change now that he could work direct from nature as everyone seemed to think advisable.

Such talk only added to his parents' fears. While he occasionally spoke about eventually returning to Brussels it was soon clear that he was settling down to a steady routine. He had begun, inevitably, by making a copy after Millet's *The Sower*. It was so exact he even used pen-strokes to imitate the scratching of the etching needle. This homage to the master was his way of settling in; that done, he was out in the fields and lanes whenever the weather was good enough for him to draw outside – a cottage on the heath, the trees around the churchyard, woodcutters in the nearby pines. But whatever he did was still imbued with that air of sanctity that Millet gave his peasants so that Vincent's country scenes often show the distant steeple of his father's church and the labourers he drew have a sturdy dignity. But he was still having difficulty with the human figure. Bargue taught how to draw bodies in isolation, but his method lacked any emphasis on modelling, the building up of figures by shading and volume, and this deficiency made it hard to 'settle' them into a composition. As solitary studies they might be satisfactory, but it was awkward fitting them into a landscape or an interior. He drew a peasant standing by his door holding a sieve, but it turned out rigid and unconvincing. He knew where the fault lay and tried to remedy it by drawing real people. He recruited Willemina to pose by their mother's sewing machine, though he wished it had been a spinning wheel. He visited workplaces in the village in order to practise perspective by drawing the craft implements in the blacksmith's forge or the carpenter's shop. But 'real' people were difficult. A peasant called Schuitemaker was drawn sitting by his hearth, his head bowed in his hands with weariness; Vincent managed to make a touching study of age and exhaustion but it was technically crude, like a cartoon and indeed it had been inspired by a figure in one of the illustrations in the *Graphic* which showed a weary girl in a similar pose. Acknowledging its origins, Vincent scrawled *WORN OUT* in English above his signature. It was a frustrating point to be at: on one hand he had passionate feelings and had found the sort of subject that could embody them, on the other his skills were still not up to the task.

A month after his return to Etten, Van Rappard came to stay for twelve days. It was a happy time, the two friends going out together on sketching tours. Van Rappard drew the vicarage and gave his sketch to Willemina. They both drew the nearby marshland and, while Van Rappard's was more accomplished technically, using only a few well-placed lines to create the overall effect of distance and water, Vincent's cruder version embraces exact details of reeds and water-lilies with all the fascination of a born naturalist.

They even made a visit to Princenhage in an attempt to see Uncle Cent. Perhaps Vincent hoped his well-born friend might effect a reconciliation, but the older man's indisposition prevented him from receiving them, or so they were told.

Vincent urgently needed advice on how to improve his figure drawing but Van Rappard could not help. They were friends and it had been good to have someone with whom to share the lonely days, but he was only a bit more experienced than Vincent and after he left, Vincent decided that his best hope was his cousin Mauve in The Hague. As a new-found member of the family he could hardly refuse a request for advice. Vincent set off at once and everyone proved very encouraging, Tersteeg was welcoming and Mauve pored over the drawings, commenting freely on the problems as he saw them. To Mauve, Vincent was working in the wrong medium, which in turn was frustrating his technique. He should abandon pen-and-ink and take up brush, crayon and chalk which would help him mould his figures more readily. Dramatically, Mauve insisted that he start painting at once. Vincent was nervous, he still thought of himself as an illustrator and the idea of tackling the complexities of colour was daunting. Still, he was greatly encouraged by what Mauve had said and felt he could overcome the impasse the copying books had become.

In Etten that October he drew his father's young gardener Piet Kauffmann. The difference is startling. Although the lad's pose, kneeling with a small hand-sickle, was probably inspired by Millet, the overall effect in black chalk and water colour is suddenly successful, the figure settles comfortably into its background. It seems that hard work was at last beginning to pay off and that if he persisted he might surely achieve something. But that was to reckon without the intervention of the outside world. As long as he was isolated within the confines of the parish, alone with his studies, all might have been well, but as summer appeared his parents announced they were expecting a visit from their niece, the recently widowed Kee Vos and her son Johannes. If Vincent had shown any sign of what this news meant to him, they might have had the foresight to cancel the invitation. As it was, her arrival that August loomed like an impending catastrophe.

If anything, the black of her mourning seemed more intense and her face harder and more profoundly sad. Vincent was overwhelmed. In the Borinage he had been able to shut out the image of the woman in black. Now she was here, her child at her side, the strict swept-back hair, the rustle of black silk. He was enthralled, and as ever said nothing. He played the doting uncle, taking Johannes for walks. He had always loved children and everyone remembered the drawings for Betsy Tersteeg. If he seemed to stare at Kee rather a lot, well he was an artist and was working on her portrait, perhaps his first. Mother and son spent August at the presbytery and might have stayed longer had Vincent been able to contain his feelings. Suddenly they came pouring out in a garbled, passionate torrent. Her reaction was as brusque as Eugénie's had been seven years before: "No, no, never." The phrase haunted him. He repeated it in his letters to Theo over and over again, letters that at first set out to show how the phrase did not mean what it seemed and how he still hoped to win her over. It was the London disaster all over again and yet clearly he had learned nothing. What was new was the violence of his reaction. This time there was to be no passive acceptance of failure, no deep unspeaking moodiness to mask his misery. This time he let everyone know of his love and his intention to persist. Kee left as soon as she could and Vincent bombarded Theo with pathetic requests for money to enable him to follow her to Amsterdam. The family was appalled, though oddly enough Uncle Cent seemed to think his nephew's determination was, if not admirable, at least a sign that there was some spirit in him.

For two months Theo held out. Vincent wrote to Kee's father Pastor Stricker but he too was furious. He went on drawing but had developed the notion that his work would only improve if it were touched by *her* gentleness. Van Rappard came back in October but stayed only a day or two, finding Vincent in no state to enjoy their outings. He spent most of the time badgering Van Rappard not to return to Brussels and the life drawing classes at the Academy. When Van Rappard had gone Vincent once again bombarded Theo with requests for help with Kee.

By November, Theo had weakened and agreed to send the fare, not realising the drama that would ensue.

As soon as the money arrived, Vincent hastened to Amsterdam and went straight to Uncle Stricker's house on the Keizersgracht and was reluctantly allowed into the familiar dining-room. She was not there but his suspicions were aroused: the table was set only for two, clearly they had removed the third setting in order to disguise the fact that they had hidden her from him. He insisted on seeing her. The Pastor said she had left. Without hesitating Vincent stretched out his right hand and held it above the funnel of an oil lamp, over the scorching heat.

> *Let me see her for as long as I can keep my hand in the flame.*

This was not so much drama as low comedy. The Strickers were more angered by the unseemliness of Vincent's behaviour than panicked by his recklessness. Calmly, the pastor stepped across and blew out the lamp. Vincent was burned but not seriously. Bathos descended. He left.

In a dangerous frame of mind he travelled from Amsterdam to The Hague to see Mauve. His cousin remarked on the burn on his hand, but Vincent concocted a story to satisfy him and began to ask for further advice about painting. Happy to play the teacher, Mauve set up a still-life and gave him some first lessons in the use of the palette and other tips about colour, unaware that his pupil's mind was elsewhere.

As soon as the lesson was over Vincent stalked off into the town. What happened next was perhaps inevitable. It would be presumptuous to try to describe it better than he did himself when he felt able to confide in Theo:

> *. . . I hadn't far to look. I found a woman, not young, not beautiful, nothing remarkable, if you like, but perhaps you are somewhat curious. She was rather tall and strongly built; she did not have a lady's hands like Kee, but the hands of one who works much; but she was not coarse or common, and had nothing very womanly about her. She reminded me of some figure by Chardin or Frere, or perhaps Jan Steen. Well, what the French call une ouvrière. She had had many cares, one could see that, and life had been hard for her, oh, she was not distinguished, nothing extraordinary, nothing unusual . . . . . . That woman was very good to*

> *me, very good, very kind – in what way I shall not tell my brother Theo, because I suspect my brother Theo of having had some such experience. So much the better for him. Did we spend much money together? No, for I did not have much, and I said to her, Listen you and I don't need to make ourselves drunk to feel something for each other; just put what I can spare in your pocket. And I wish I could have spent more, for she was worth it.*

So in the end he had paid for – love? No, he was not so naïve as to believe that. But he did believe that he had purchased more than her body:

> *And we talked about everything, about her life, about her cares, about her misery, about her health, and with her I had a more interesting conversation than, for instance, with my very learned, professorial cousin.*

He returned to Etten less tolerant than his experience might have made him. In fact he was in a distinctly belligerent mood and was genuinely aggrieved when his parents showed how furious they were over his behaviour at Uncle Stricker's. The whole episode seemed to him so distant he could hardly believe it mattered any more. Theodorus more than Anna had passed from concern and fear at his son's increasingly uncontrollable actions to a state of cold fury. At one point he even swore at him, an event which, with a fine disregard for reality, Vincent thought deplorable in a minister. If anything, Vincent blamed God and religion for his parents' reactions. He had hero-worshipped his father and now that patriarchal figure had let him down. Where could he turn but to the one person who seemed to offer him help towards the only thing that now mattered, his new religion, his art? Mauve could take on the role his father had so unforgivably abandoned. Early in December he went to The Hague again and was relieved to find that Mauve was willing to consider giving him lessons on a more permanent basis. There seemed no reason to stay in Etten any longer. He returned for Christmas but his behaviour was deplorable; he refused to attend church on Christmas Day. He may have wanted to make a point about his despair at religion and to punish his father for what he saw as his lack of compassion but in a close community like Etten, where the Protestant minority felt the need for solidarity in the face of their vastly superior Catholic neighbours, Vincent's gesture went too far, and on Christmas Day of all days. He was clearly trying to cause trouble and he did.

Pushed to the limit, the kindly pastor told his son he had better go. He left for The Hague that day, utterly unrepentant, convinced that right was on his side and that his father was completely unreasonable. For once Theo refused to humour him and sent a stinging rebuke accusing him of being childish and impudent, but such criticisms were useless against the impregnable armour of Vincent's self-righteousness. Religion was not merely abandoned; in its organised form it was now the enemy. So far his life had been structured within the moral framework of the Dutch Reformed Church, anything remotely identifiable with sin had been rigorously avoided. Theo in Paris had more quietly liberated himself from such restraints. With no confrontation with his parents he had managed to adapt to a world of night life and love, a world where absinthe and 'the hour of the flesh' were there to be enjoyed. Vincent as ever could have no such balance. From then on prostitutes were to be his most frequent female companions, often his only companions.

At first Mauve knew nothing of this new side to his cousin's life and welcomed him as both a member of the family and a pupil. His help was entirely practical: he lent Vincent money so that he could find somewhere to work. Though the sum was modest, it was a generous act and Vincent was able to look for a place, albeit some way out of town. As The Hague was rapidly expanding into the surrounding dunes and woods, Vincent was able to find a half-finished building near the Schenweg, a neutral characterless strip that clung to the outer edge of the spreading suburbs. It had a space which could be called a studio, and Vincent never objected to long walks. Vincent's drawings record this curious no-man's-land, neither town nor country, with vistas of gasometers, factory out-houses, views across the scattered roofs to the surviving farmland. They are a unique record of that moment in the history of most European towns when industrialisation and urban growth finally divorced town from country with an unappealing band of suburban sprawl. There is something ineffably sad about the people who drift into these drawings, they are always distant and impersonal. Birds wheel ominously over the wasteland more like miniature vultures than seabirds. Gratifyingly, he found that his technique had developed sufficiently for him to make a success of the subject; he used perspective with a sense of drama, leaving a large part of the picture space empty, creating a feeling of underpopulated wasteland whose characterless buildings cluster at the horizon.

That much of his new confidence came from contact with Mauve, Vincent always admitted. So fulsome was his praise for his cousin that one might imagine they must have had a master-pupil relationship for at least two or three years. It comes as a surprise, therefore, to realise that they worked together for only a matter of months. Nor is it easy to identify precisely what it was that Vincent learned from Mauve. In terms of subjects and emotion he owed more to Israëls whose peasant characters were used by Vincent as direct models for his own work. What Mauve gave him was the courage to use colour, urging him to paint when he was still convinced that all he could hope to acquire were the skills of a black-and-white illustrator. Just before he left Etten, Mauve had sent Vincent a painting kit and once in The Hague he gave him lessons in the use of water-colours:

> *Yesterday I had a lesson from Mauve on drawing hands and faces so as to keep the colour transparent. Mauve knows things so thoroughly, and when he tells you something, he exerts himself and doesn't just say it to hear himself talk; and I exert myself to listen carefully and put it into practice. Yesterday I told Mauve again that it was so necessary for me to earn something, but I will not ask him for money, as he gives me something that is much better than money; and besides, he has already helped me with my furniture, and that is more than enough.*

Money was of course a constant preoccupation but he had high hopes that Tersteeg would buy some of his work and initially his old employer was encouraging. He was, however, no longer the young high-flyer Vincent had known when he first lived in The Hague but a settled family man, whose hair was beginning to recede along with his more liberated attitudes, a fact that escaped Vincent's notice. He simply assumed that the family were still as before and took the children, Betsy and her brother Johan, for walks in the dunes and dreamt of the day when his new water-colours would be on display in the window of his old gallery in the Plaats. It is curious that Vincent so utterly forgot the whole ethos of Hague life. Even after Mauve had put him up for membership of the Pulchri Studio, he failed to see precisely how middle-brow and respectable the local artists were. With hindsight it is clear that, if nothing else, there was bound to be a clash of morals.

Since that first encounter with a prostitute his life had changed utterly. Some time early in the new year he formed a relationship with one of the women he had encountered. He called her Sien, though her full name was Christine Clasina Maria Hoornik. She was three years older than him, though she looked even older. Unmarried, she had a five-year-old daughter, Maria Willemina, but had already lost two previous children and was pregnant again when Vincent took up with her. That it was her wretched condition and pain-hardened features which attracted him, rather than any charm she may have had, needs no arguing. That his feelings for her were confused by his lingering memories of Kee is shown by a drawing he made of her in which she is clearly wearing an identical black silk dress, even down to the last ruche and tassle, to the one Kee had worn. Was Sien the original prostitute from the previous November? It is not unreasonable to see him falling in love with the first woman with whom he had sex. Was it his child she was carrying as some have insisted? Unfortunately for those in search of the descendants of 'genius', the dates are wrong. In any case he never acknowledged the child as his and, if it had been, he would uncharacteristically have acted out a lie for the rest of his life. No, Sien was already pregnant when ever he met her, and the father of the future child was unknown. This did not matter to Vincent. Every gram of feeling he had for the oppressed and downtrodden was now projected into this frail figure. Not that her background entirely merited such an excess of feeling. Far from being the tragic product of some desperate broken home, Sien seems to have had a reasonable upbringing, albeit as one of eleven children. Her mother had been widowed only recently and there does not appear to have been any pressing reason, other than an inability to pull herself together, why Sien adopted her particular life. Basically, she was lazy and prostitution was the easiest way out of her problems; though it was true that by the time Vincent met her, the advent of another baby had made her situation difficult while at the same time she was trying to take care of one of her younger sisters. She also had a younger brother who was causing trouble. Vincent visited her from time to time but as the months passed he gradually assumed the role of her sole protector, though at first this side of his life was kept strictly apart from that other world of the Pulchri Studio.

While Vincent bent over backwards to give Mauve due credit for his help, his cousin was not the easiest of men. If he found something to praise in Vincent's work he went wild with enthusiasm, but if something displeased him his fury was bafflingly intense. Such extreme responses were potentially dangerous when inflicted on one as unstable as Vincent. Predictably, Vincent's own reactions made matters worse. On one occasion Mauve gave him some plaster casts of hands and feet, standard objects of study for an art-student then, and told him to practise drawing them. Vincent took this as a personal affront and after carrying them home, his anger fuelled by thoughts of how badly Mauve was treating him, he flung the casts in the coal bin and smashed them. Mauve's reactions were hardly more rational: he began to mimic Vincent's admittedly peculiar mannerisms and to make fun of his appearance by drawing clever but cruel caricatures.

At least Vincent had found a measure of contentment with Sien, but it could only be a matter of time before he and Mauve would reach a crisis and at the end of January, not more than a few weeks after their lessons had begun, Mauve suffered a debilitating depressive attack. When Vincent appeared at the studio he was told that his cousin was too busy to see him, that he was working on a large painting for that year's Paris Salon and could not be disturbed. At first Vincent accepted the excuse, although it hurt him that Mauve had not chosen to explain things to him face to face. After a few days, Vincent began to suspect that this was Mauve's way of telling him that he was no good and that he could not help him anymore. Walking to and from his cousin's house he was assailed by doubts about his abilities. Desperate for reassurance he contacted the painter Jan Weissenbruch who had so kindly befriended him as a young dealer all those years ago. Weissenbruch came round to see him and took it on himself to examine the drawings of the sparse scrubland near the studio and water-colours of nearby Scheveningen. Fortunately, Weissenbruch was an extrovert, the polar opposite of the manic-depressive Mauve. He was a stylish dresser whose sunny disposition was reflected in his landscapes which avoided the sombre ochres and deep browns of his confrères. He jokingly told Vincent he was known as 'the merciless sword' because of the honesty of his criticism and then went on lavishly to praise the younger man's efforts, especially his ink drawings. He counselled Vincent to pay no attention to Mauve's change of mood as it had nothing to do with the quality of his work.

This was precisely what Vincent needed to hear for he was also having trouble with Tersteeg. At first the dealer had bought a small drawing for ten guilders but now he was showing a mysterious reluctance to consider any of the other works Vincent brought to him and had even suggested that he might do better to give up the idea of becoming an artist. It is probable that something of Vincent's other life had already begun to filter through to the elegant world of the Plaats and that the newly respectable Tersteeg was outraged at these intimations of louche behaviour.

Alternately puzzled and angry at these changes in attitude, Vincent struggled on with his work, waiting for Mauve to relent. He was able to draw from the life two evenings a week at the Pulchri Studio, and he found an old woman willing to sit for him, though his condition appeared to her so wretched she occasionally brought him a share of her own meagre food. His best model of all was Sien, for with her he was not merely studying an anonymous physique but was able to express his most complex feelings. Some time that April he drew her, naked, seated in the open air, her head resting on her crossed arms, her pendulous breasts hanging over the pregnant swell of her belly. In the bottom right-hand corner he wrote the English word 'Sorrow'. As soon as he finished he knew that it was good and wrote at once to Theo saying that it was the best figure he had yet made.

That he should continue to give his work English titles is not surprising as he spent much time reliving his English life, trying to digest the cacophony of images and words he had encountered there. He reread Dickens and George Eliot, and began to collect the newspaper engravings he had admired in London, buying bound sets of the *Graphic* and assembling back copies of the *Illustrated London News*. He would carefully remove the illustrations which pleased him and mount them neatly on stiff paper. The peak of his collecting came early in his second year in The Hague when he acquired the 212 volumes of the *Graphic* from 1870 to 1880. They were to form a valuable resource which he would use as models. A drawing he made of men digging peat near the town echoes a number of illustrations on similar subjects: *Undergraduates making a road near Oxford*, *Diamond Diggings in South Africa*. One engraving to which he often returned was S. L. Fildes' *The Empty Chair*, a highly charged image of Dickens' study with his empty chair by his desk, made to commemorate the author's death in 1870. That an everyday piece of furniture could be endowed with so much meaning and emotion was very appealing to Vincent who came to look on Fildes' picture as an almost perfect example of what art ought to be and do.

Given the strong attraction of these engravings he might well have slipped back into his pose as an illustrator and abandoned his first attempts at painting. Fortunately Mauve recovered from his depressive mood and told him to come to the studio again. As if to make up for lost time he made Vincent take up oil-painting, brushing aside his nervousness about the complexities of the medium. As before, Mauve was good on the basic techniques involved and Vincent was soon attacking canvases with his usual gusto.

And there was more good news, this time from Uncle Cor, the other art dealer in Amsterdam, who commissioned him to make twelve views of The Hague. It was a wonderful opportunity, his first chance to earn a living from his work, and he set to with a will, sketching in the Jewish quarter, working on a busy street scene near a bakery. He finished the work quickly and despatched it to Amsterdam. Back came a commission for six more. Soon he would be independent at last but just as he was about to start on the second series he was blown off course by another twist in his relations with his cousin. From the start of their lessons in oil-painting Vincent had proved far too independent for the highly dictatorial Mauve. To Mauve's horror, Vincent insisted on using his fingers to manipulate the paint; it seemed obvious to him that something so tactile should be felt and closely worked onto the canvas. To Mauve this was childish. Again they began to argue and once more it was difficult for Vincent to get in to see him.

While he was still trying to finish the second commission, Van Rappard came to visit and expressed great enthusiasm for Vincent's work. He lent him some money to repair one of the drawings which was slightly torn. But that was one of the few happy interludes in an increasingly depressing time. Vincent was becoming aware of a growing hostility among the people he knew in The Hague. To his distress Uncle Cor sent no word that he was satisfied with the second batch of drawings and no further commissions arrived. It was puzzling, as if he too had been touched by the new malign spirit that Vincent felt all around him. Matters might have continued like that, with Vincent being quietly ostracised and nothing being said openly, had not Vincent and Mauve met while walking in the dunes. It was a surprise to both of them that they should cross in this wild place but Vincent seized the opportunity to ask if Mauve would come to see his work and talk things over. Mauve was furious: "I will not come and see you, that's all over." There was a painful silence then Mauve blurted out: "You have a vicious character." At this, Vincent turned and walked away.

Much distressed and longing to explain himself he at last wrote to Theo to tell him about Sien. What was he supposed to do? How, he argued, could he abandon someone in need? No sooner was the letter sent than he suffered agonies of indecision. What if Theo were angry at his taking up with a street walker? What if his brother turned against him? It was an immense relief when Theo replied in sympathetic terms though he counselled against any notion of matrimony. He well knew that Vincent's sentimentality could seriously cloud his judgement and while he was not censorious about his brother's sexual behaviour he also recognised that Vincent was incapable of making rational long-term decisions in such a situation. What Theo did not know was that there was another problem – Vincent was now suffering from venereal disease, no small matter given the state of treatment then. Sien's time was also approaching and just as she had to leave for the hospital in Leyden Vincent was forced to go into the City Hospital in The Hague for urgent treatment. It was a double torture: to such agonies as the insertion of a catheter into his penis was added his distress at being apart from Sien at this crucial moment. The treatment dragged on for three weeks. His father came to visit, though there are no reports of what must have been a grim encounter. Vincent merely recorded his wish that they had met under other circumstances. It is probable that the attack of gonorrhoea had passed and that he was being treated for the after-effects, the tightening of the urinary passage. Such treatment was essentially primitive, with the 'bougies' on the catheter being gradually increased in size so as to widen the narrow channel. He seems to have taken it calmly enough, perhaps accepting it as a judgement; the worst thing was not being allowed to smoke his pipe.

When he was released he went with Sien's mother and sister to Leyden where they found that she had given birth during the night to a boy, though only after much pain and difficulty. Vincent was overwhelmed by the baby who despite a forceps delivery was in good form. When mother and child were eventually released and Vincent's course of treatment ended, he decided he had to make a home for them. They moved to a larger house near by with Vincent full of hope about their future. It is clear from his letters that despite his father's disapproval and his isolation from the other artists in The Hague, Vincent was truly happy with this new domestic life. He drew little baby Willem in his cot and in his mother's arms; all his love of children poured into his work. That he was completely in love there need be no doubt. He called

Sien *A star in a dark night*. And it is a sure, if worrying, sign that on the drawing he made of her, he not only inscribed the word 'Sorrow' but also put a quotation from Michelet: "How can it be that there is in the world one woman alone – deserted?"

Sien was no great beauty. Even in his portraits, her expression is rather grim, though they seem to have settled into a reasonably contented existence together. The problem was that the world refused to share their contentment. Tersteeg especially was driven to extraordinary lengths of spiteful behaviour when he discovered what was taking place. On first seeing the ménage with the little baby he furiously accused Vincent of being mad and he may have been the one who warned Uncle Cor of what was going on and thus put an end to the commissions. He even threatened to get Theo to cut off the allowance. Tersteeg's over-reaction was puzzling. Could there have been something in his own life that made the idea of a prostitute so repellent? Certainly the once liberal young manager had become a posturing moralist of the most shrewish kind. He may have written to inform Pastor Theodorus of the situation. From whatever source the news came it certainly shattered Dorus' and Anna's final hopes that anything might be salvaged of Vincent's life. The pastor's reaction was extreme and in its own way unhinged – he started making enquiries about how he could go about having his son certified insane and went so far as to try to find a place for him in a mental home in Gheel in Belgium. Somehow word of these schemes filtered back to Vincent who was understandably outraged – there are howls of fury in his letters to Theo and in a way he never forgave his father for it. Happily, Pastor Theodorus abandoned his enquiries. He was once again preoccupied with another move to a new parish in the village of Nuenen near Eindhoven and had no further time for his eldest son.

It was a curious fact that once his parents had moved the only home Vincent knew was the one he was trying to create himself. Not without difficulty. Sien was no home-body and Vincent was soon forced into the unnatural role of having to set a good example around the house, encouraging her to tidy up and do the housework. Despite his apparently Bohemian ways, he had a suppressed craving for the normality of family life which, having surfaced, drove him on. In any case he had always loved children and was absolutely besotted with Willem:

> *... the little one is a miracle of vitality, already he seems to oppose himself to all social institutions and conventions. As far as I know, all babies are brought up on a kind of bread porridge. But he has refused this most energetically; though he has no teeth yet, he bites resolutely at a piece of bread, and swallows all kinds of eatables with much laughing and cooing and all kinds of noises: but he absolutely keeps his mouth shut for porridge. He often sits with me in the studio on the floor in a corner, on a few sacks; he crows at the drawings and is always quiet in the studio, because he looks at the things on the wall. Oh, he is such a sociable little fellow!*

The combination of Willem and a determination to convince himself that Sien was improving kept him going. In any case he could not be too hard on her at first as she was still very weak. He explained to Theo that her nervous system remained sensitive, which could indicate that she was suffering from post-natal depression rather than the purely physical ailments he assumed she had. In either case she would probably have been unable to pull herself together, her natural inclination being to let things drift. She would lounge about listlessly waiting for something to happen. His drawing of her in a nightgown, hunched by the stove smoking a cigar, shows her typically indolent, content to do nothing. Now her condition meant that she could even be excused the minimum labour of posing for him as she had before. That, and possibly the desire to get away from the sickroom atmosphere, drove him back to open-air painting, this time working in the newly discovered oils.

With no Mauve to restrain him, he simply invented his own way of doing things. There are forest glades thick with paint applied directly from the tube, an unheard of method but one he found rich with possibilities. There is a picture of a cow lying in a field that is almost a bas-relief so heavily moulded are the white contours of its muzzle. Working in isolation he was beginning to form an approach to painting that was uniquely his own. He still kept to the old distinction between a study and a completed picture. The Impressionists and the Hague School painters had disregarded such a division, the finished work was the one made there and then in the open air from the experience of the moment but Vincent could not yet accept this. He made studies in the open but still believed that a truly finished painting was more than just a straightforward record of nature. The artist must reorganise this basic material, using invention and imagination, before he could consider it finished. His woodland scenes at this time often contain the solitary figure of a woman among the trees. His original inspiration came from one of the English engravings, *Reflections* by Percy Macquoid, which showed a woman in white leaning against a tree, staring at reflections in a lake. Vincent's *Girl in White in the Woods* draws directly on Macquoid in order to go beyond the simple representation of nature by evoking an emotional response to the figure mysteriously alone in that deserted place. Vincent's intentions were not symbolic, the figure does not represent some other hidden meaning, his intention was to imbue the scene with his own reactions and emotions. If he felt loneliness then the grass is sodden and crows wheel hungrily over icy hard fields; happiness, and the sun blazes in the sky and flowers are delirious with fire.

He was working entirely from instinct and was unaware that this emotive use of colour came close to the ideas Theo was hearing about in Paris. By contrast his reading remained firmly entrenched in French Naturalism in the form of Zola and more Zola, the de Goncourts, Hugo and English reforming novelists such as Dickens. In a sense these new landscapes stand outside his theoretical view of what art ought to be, whereas his drawings continued to follow his earlier belief in social concern. There are scenes of people gathered at the public soup kitchen which exactly mirror similar subjects in the *Graphic*. He had also come across one of the pitiful 'orphan men', Adrianus Jacobus Zuyderland, who lived on charity in the Protestant Old Men's and Women's Home. Vincent made a number of portraits of him with his number, 199, prominently on his sleeve.

His life with Sien had many parallels with his response to the poverty and distress of the coalfields. She had fallen and he would save her, though, as the drawing of her smoking a cigar showed, her capacity for self-absorption and indifference must have made it hard to retain the illusion that she was anything other than a slut. They might have been able to work out their differences if they had not fallen into a trap so classic it is usually the butt of cheap jokes: her mother came to stay. The model for her daughter's fecklessness, the older woman was almost destitute when Vincent took pity on her and let her move in for Christmas. Far from being grateful the wretched creature seems to have begun at once to undermine all Vincent's attempts to pull Sien out of her slovenly inertia. By bizarre coincidence, Theo's mistress was in hospital and her mother was making trouble. For once the two brothers had problems to share other than Vincent's usual monologue about his lack of money. The worst thing about Sien's mother was her total distrust of everyone, an attitude she appears to have communicated to her daughter. The result was that Sien's relationship with Vincent was thoroughly poisoned. It was a miserable state of affairs and it seems to have spread to the others. Vincent made a telling drawing of the younger sister, posed sideways, her hair roughly cropped for fear of lice, warily looking back at him out of the corner of her eye with an expression that bespeaks a deep mistrust of what he may be doing. He was dealing with people too suspicious and sunk in their ways to be so easily redeemed by his facsimile of a bourgeois home.

His yearning for stability was easily outmatched by Sien's waywardness. As Theo's allowance was now stretched between six of them it was difficult to counter the effects of her younger brother's secret whisperings that she should go back to her old way of earning money. They barely had enough to eat and Vincent was increasingly weak with hunger: one day he had to tell a disgruntled tradesman that he couldn't settle his bill for repairing a lamp, whereupon the man knocked him effortlessly to the ground. With his life full of such humiliations it is small wonder the letters to Theo became a litany of begging and pleading.

In the end the situation resolved itself. Early in the new year of 1883 there were clear signs that the affair was ending badly. Although Sien was most often morose and silent, there were times when she flared up and threatened to end it all, warning him she would drown herself if whatever displeased her was not remedied. She could hardly be expected to understand his commitment to his work and his need to spend most of the money Theo sent on paints and canvases, but no one knows what really passed between them in the slow decline of tolerance that is the death of love.

Theo at least understood. With a difficult mistress on his hands he was in no position to moralise even if he had wished to. In mid-May Van Rappard came on a second visit and he and Vincent went to Utrecht together, a welcome break from the squabbling. Van Rappard had been painting in the remote northern area of Drenthe, where Roelofs had spent a summer, and the idea of so barren and underpopulated a place inevitably appealed to Vincent who now saw the city as claustrophobic and destructive. Especially after his return when Sien's behaviour worsened. He adored the baby and desperately wanted to create a family, but as soon as things seemed to be going well she would flare up again and threaten to drown herself if she didn't get her way.

Van Rappard returned in August and the sense of freedom he brought with him was overpowering. He was about to set off for Drenthe again. Vincent was tempted but he wavered. How could he abandon her and the children when he knew full well what she would do the minute he left? Yet it was as if the city itself was destroying him and only the countryside, the true, wild, unspoilt country, could give him release.

Thankfully, Theo came and saw at once how far things had deteriorated. Vincent was obliged to take some hard words from him, for Theo was determined to see changes made. He had pointedly brought him a suit, a gesture which provoked some tart remarks from Vincent about those who would insist on criticising his Bohemian ways. But Theo made no attempt to hide his disapproval of the whole set-up and told Vincent he had to leave her. At first Vincent absolutely refused to accept this and when Theo returned to Paris his letters made it clear that he would not follow his advice but this was only the last vestige of resistance fighting on. Deep down he knew that Theo was right and that he must have it out with 'the woman' as he now referred to her.

> *I talked it over with her seriously, explaining fully what my situation is, that I must go away for my work, and must have a year of few expenses and some earnings, in order to make up for a past that has been rather too much for me. That I foresaw that if I stayed with her, I should very soon be unable to help her any more, and should get into debt again here, where everything is so expensive, and that there would be no way out. So that, in short, she and I must be wise and separate as friends. That she must get her people to take the children, and that she must look for a job.*

Doubtless he realised such advice was wasted. His other plan was that she should try to make a marriage of convenience with someone who would take care of the children but he guessed that she would do no more than take the easy way out once he was no longer there to guide her. She did make some show of trying to find work but always came home with the same sorry tale. The house grew oppressive but even the lengthy walks that he took no longer brought release. It was impossible to get far enough away from the ever burgeoning city and the *horrible green toy summerhouses and all the absurdities the heavy fancy of retired Dutchmen can invent in the form of flower plots, arbors and porches.*

The only possible solution was to follow Van Rappard, Mauve, Roelofs and all the others who had escaped to the wild north-west, the only part of the country where the creeping tentacles of Holland's belated industrialisation had not yet spread. Drenthe alone remained a haven for artists longing to escape the urbanised world.

He kept trying to persuade them both that it was over:

> *She is unhappy about it, as I am, but she is not disheartened and keeps busy. I had just bought a piece of material to make study linen of, and have now given it to her to make underwear for the kids, and some of my things can be altered for them too, so that she will not leave me empty-handed. So she is very busy sewing these things.*
>
> *When I say we part as friends, it is true – but the parting is final . . .*

Word that the affair was ending did much to convince Theo in Paris of his brother's commitment. Theo knew too well that to succeed Vincent would have to reject anything that might deflect him from his work. He had clearly made rapid progress; the childish sketching, the ill-proportioned figures had been disciplined into something already well beyond competence. Painting had begun and there was every reason to think that there too he would master the skills he needed. But Theo was also aware of the other Vincent, moody and changeable, ever capable of finding someone else to blame for his abandoned plans. Determined to stiffen his resolve, Theo wrote to him with the uncompromising injunction that "Perhaps your *duty* will make you act differently." The word lodged in Vincent's mind for he knew Theo was right. He told Sien it was over, he was leaving for Drenthe. If nothing else, Theo had made it clear that he was not merely the paymaster of their joint fraternal enterprise, he was also its conscience.

7

1883 — 1885

The Potato Eaters

On September 11th, 1883 Vincent left by train for Hoogeveen in the fenlands of southern Drenthe. Sien and the two children came to the station to see him off. He was wearing the same brown 'peat-carrier's' suit he had always worn when he went to the countryside to paint for the day, but this time they knew he would not be coming back. It was a miserable parting and, to add to his distress, Willem was passed into the compartment to sit on his lap until it was time to leave. As the train finally pulled away, he could no longer delude himself that Sien would have anything other than hard times ahead. He was thirty and his one attempt at a stable relationship had fallen apart, now there was a long, slow journey to be made, with time enough to turn these unpleasant things over in his mind.

His only hope was to look ahead to the work he would do in Drenthe. He had studied a map of the region and had been delighted to see that not only were there no cities, there were also no towns of any substance. The centre of the area was empty, crossed by a solitary canal which meandered through what were marked as peat fields and this promise of solitude was highly appealing after the clutter of The Hague and its relentless sprawl.

It was already dark when the train pulled into the tiny station in Hoogeveen and he could barely make out his new surroundings as he walked to the house of Albertus Hartsuiker where he was to lodge. The Drenthe, he would discover, was so empty the government had begun resettling paupers from the overcrowded southern cities on its barren fenland. The few signs of human activity displayed an almost exaggerated Dutchness as, half-hidden in the sunken waterways, peat-barges seemed to drift across the flat heath. Traditional drawbridges were all that broke the monotonous landscape and almost nothing had touched the simple existence of the peasants, whose lives were spent cutting turf or scrabbling in the soft black soil for potatoes.

As soon as there was a fine day Vincent began to explore this curious world, working on a series of large empty landscapes as if to celebrate his liberation from the stranglehold of the suburbs. The people seemed to live in the earth for the moss roofs of their cottages ran right down to the ground making them look more like burrows than buildings. He was painting one when he noticed two sheep and a goat browsing on its roof. The goat got so far up it was peering down the chimney before a woman ran out and shooed it away.

But such comic moments were rare. If he passed a mother and child on the heath he found himself weeping helplessly. He received no word from Sien and could only assume that she and her mother had returned to their old home and she, presumably, to her old trade. The dank landscape matched such gloomy thoughts. He painted two dark silhouettes bent to their back-breaking toil in fields which are little more than layers of deepening blue. The only bright spot was a partial reconciliation with his father. Now that he had left Sien and the possibility of his marrying a prostitute had receded, letters could be exchanged. There was no doubt a desire on his family's part to encourage him to stay where he was; they were in no mood to have him home again.

Although it paid slightly better, the parish of Nuenen was Pastor Theodorus' smallest yet. The church was even tinier than his original chapel in Zundert and the presbytery, a short distance away on the main street, was something of a comedown after their substantial house in Helvoirt. It had been built in 1764 and was visibly dilapidated. The advantages of Nuenen were that Cor, the last of the children still at home, could travel easily by train to his secondary school in Helmond, while a smaller place was easier to manage now that the Pastor and his wife were no longer young. This would not be the case, however, if they had to suffer the disruptive presence of their eldest son; thus, they can only have been pleased when they learned in early October that Vincent had travelled even deeper into Drenthe's remote other world.

He went by peat-barge to Nieuw-Amsterdam hoping to meet some of the artists he knew to have worked in that far-away place. At first, the local innkeeper, Hendrick Scholte, was wary of admitting such an odd-looking traveller. He eventually relented, though his daughters were scared at having the farouche stranger in their gloomy house. Vincent did his best to win them over, playing at trains and horseback riding with the youngest daughter who was only four. It was harder with the slightly elder daughter, Zowina-Clasina, but eventually she was pacified. Her father explained that the stranger was an artist, though this cannot have meant much to her at the time.

The Scholtes' hotel faced the canal, with a drawbridge which Vincent painted. Every morning he would search the sky and, if the weather seemed promising, would set off in search of subjects, such as a cottage on the open heath or figures at work in the peat fields. He was painting more than drawing, though in a way there was little distinction, as he was effectively drawing with paint. Had he stayed longer with Mauve he might have more quickly understood what it was to be a colourist, for although he was hardly an Impressionist, Mauve also created his effects through the interplay of light and colour rather than heavy outline. On his own, Vincent was forced to reinvent the wheel, trying to solve for himself all the problems that artists had encountered since painting began. Perhaps, without fully realising it, he was fighting the old battle between the rigid use of outline favoured by the classical painters of the eighteenth century and the more expressive use of paint favoured by their romantic counterparts. At first he tried a combination of both in the way he had done in The Hague when he had used thick layers of pigment to mould shapes, as if the paint itself were a drawing material. But working alone out on the heaths and fens he quickly resurrected another method: by darkening his palette, then using slightly lighter colours as highlights, he found he could make objects solid and round. It was a technique which echoed Rembrandt and the other Dutch masters, as if that curious stretch of untouched Holland had led him back to the heart of Dutch painting with its rich dark colours and glowing edges of light. To some extent it worked, for his solid lumpen cottages acquire a looming presence on the fringes of the dank peat bogs. If nothing else, they matched his depressed spirits and, though he quickly realised it was a method with only limited possibilities, he was content to exorcise his misery in this way. Yet even those dark lonesome hamlets failed to satisfy his craving for absolute wildness, somewhere completely apart from civilisation. That November he persuaded Scholte to take him to Zweeloo, the site of what was thought to have been the oldest human settlement, a truly lost world. They set off before dawn, riding in an open cart. When Scholte left him Vincent began to explore but all he found was a cluster of dwellings and a stark church with what he described as *an old stumpy tower* which reminded him of Millet's Gréville. He sketched it and walked about hoping vainly to find some evidence of the other artists who had passed that way. It was an impossible dilemma: on the one hand he wanted isolation in a desolate wilderness, on the other he still longed for that artists' colony of his imagination. He walked back alone in the failing light.

Once more out in the fields around Nieuw-Amsterdam he struggled to make paint work, increasingly aware that it might take years to find the solutions others had already tackled; he needed help, and this longing grew in tandem with his increasing loneliness. The desire for extreme solitude had been misplaced and just as he was beginning to accept this he was stunned by news from Theo that all was not well at Goupil's. Something had provoked a breach between him and the senior partners, presumably their reluctance to let the young man have his way with the upstairs gallery. Theo's thoughts were now turning to America, a fresh start in New York might be a way out. He could presumably count on the help of Goupil's correspondent Roland Knoedler, successor to the founder Michel, in setting up on his own. Vincent was aghast. Without Theo what would become of him?

For once he tried tact, writing to say he did not want to be a burden on his brother who must do what he thought best. But Theo was so preoccupied he failed to reply immediately and his silence plunged Vincent into depths of despair. Was he abandoned at last? He cast about for any hope of support he could think of. His father had sent him some money, so perhaps the solution was to go home to Nuenen, where he would be taken care of, if Theo decided to leave.

While he agonised over the alternatives, he tried to continue working, sometimes with haunting results: there is a *Sunrise on the Plain* which exactly recreated the world of the masters of the Dutch Golden Age. Using Indian ink and wash he evoked those feelings of emptiness, the open foreground, the vast sky, characteristic of so much of the art of Holland. A tiny sail and a distant dark cottage point up the insignificance of human effort in so desolate a place. All the attempted lightness of the Hague School has been extinguished in those eerie half-lit peat fields. Vincent's Drenthe has none of the picturesque qualities valued by Mauve and the others. His Drenthe is harsh and hostile and for once his art is an exact reflection of his emotions, of his mood of numb sorrow, much exaggerated by the grim winter weather.

The depressing mists of November had deepened into the long darkness of December. It was increasingly hard to work. He could not shake off a cold that pulled him down even further. When Theo eventually wrote it was clear he was still thinking of leaving for America. In his depression Vincent finally accepted that the wilderness was no solution when loneliness and sadness were things he carried around within him. Once more he would move on.

He gave the Scholtes no warning, insisting he would be back. He set off, leaving most of his things in his room. It was a six-hour walk across the heath to the station in Hoogeveen with rain turning to snow. Bedraggled and sick, he spent much of the walk muttering to himself about the injustices he had suffered, grumbling about Theo; but gradually, as so often before, contact with rawest nature began to calm him.

Next came the long train journey to Eindhoven in the south of the country, then a further journey to nearby Nuenen. By the time all this had been accomplished his appearance was everything his family dreaded. They could barely disguise their displeasure at his unheralded arrival. Little more than a long main street with the tiny octagonal Dutch Reformed church at one end and the recently built Catholic church of St Clement at the other, Nuenen was too small a community to disguise someone so eccentric. The overwhelming proportion of the population was Catholic though some of the more prominent inhabitants were members of Pastor Theodorus' congregation. His neighbour and an elder of his church, Jacobus Begemann, had managed to open one of the few successful textile factories in a place where a third of the men, and many of the children, were home weavers. Begemann was himself the son of a minister and hardly the type to be sympathetic to the discovery of someone like Vincent in the house next door. The diminishing Protestant community already had enough problems. Most of Pastor Theodorus' time was taken up with charitable work on behalf of his meagre band of parishioners and the last thing he needed was this aggressive, unkempt vagabond around his home. Vincent realised his family's feelings at once:

> *They feel the same dread about taking me into the house as they would about taking a big rough dog. He would run into the room with wet paws – and he is so rough. He will be in everyone's way. And he barks so loud. In short, he is a foul beast.*

The situation was not improved by Vincent's new tendency to be irrationally critical of his father; having virtually worshipped him during his religious period, he now turned against everything the man stood for. He even indulged in wild rantings about the hypocrisy of the Church and its supporters. Faced with a run-down parish and increasing rural poverty this was hardly what Pastor Theodorus merited. The Dutch Poor Relief Act of 1865 had thrown responsibility for charity on to religious organisations while pressure on land had reduced agricultural workers to penury. Men like Dorus were barely able to cope and it was his post as District Governor for the Society for the Promotion of Welfare that occupied most of his efforts. None of this affected the harsh judgements of his eldest son, who now saw all forms of organised religion as a personal affront.

For the first three weeks or so after his arrival life in the parsonage was intolerable but then Theodorus drew him aside and they had a long heart-searching talk at the end of which a modus vivendi was agreed. "At the least", Theodorus told Theo, "we undertake this experiment with real confidence and we intend to leave him perfectly free in his peculiarities of dress etc." As ever it was the family which was having to adapt to him, though at first he still insisted this was only a short stay and that as soon as he felt able he would return to Drenthe. It was a visit to Van Rappard in Utrecht just before Christmas which changed his mind.

Van Rappard had already written to advise him to remain in Nuenen and now repeated the advice more firmly. Still feeling abandoned by Theo, Vincent found Van Rappard *less dry* than before and told him that he valued his opinions about his work more highly than those of his brother. This was quite a change, since the two men had virtually fallen out over Van Rappard's finicky attention to technique, about which Vincent could be stingingly dismissive. Van Rappard was aware that he was one of the few prepared to tolerate such "fanatical vehemence". Only rarely had Van Rappard risked a tentative criticism of the work Vincent sent him, and then only by letter. This Vincent had tolerated, and had on occasions responded quite warmly to his friend's comments. But it was some studies of weavers that Van Rappard had been doing that more than anything that was said, convinced Vincent it might be worthwhile staying in Nuenen. That part of Brabant had seen a move away from farming into cottage industries and he could see at once how the weavers in their tiny hovels with their great looms filling the single room could be a powerful image of human toil.

> *When the monstrous thing of grimed oak with all those sticks is seen in such sharp contrast to the grayish atmosphere in which it stands, then there in the centre of it sits a black ape or goblin or spook that clatters with those sticks from early morning to late at night...*

So he decided to remain, and his family must make the best of it. Happily, they had noticed some progress in his work and were becoming convinced that at last he was serious in what he was doing. Despite his father's doubts about its suitability, Vincent was allowed to use the outhouse which jutted into the garden behind the parsonage as a studio. He was soon getting the place organised. An old mangle was moved away, a stove was installed and a wooden stool was ordered so that he would have somewhere to sit while he worked. The view across the garden was beautiful even in winter, and at least he was warm and there was good food available if he wanted it.

Back in Drenthe, the Scholtes awaited his return. A vast quantity of paintings and drawings were stacked in his room. When it became clear that they had seen the last of their peculiar visitor they locked the room he had called his studio. Few other visitors ever came and they did not know what to do with the strange works the strange man had left behind. As time went by they fell into the habit of giving them away as birthday and Christmas presents with the result that about forty have survived. For the rest, one day they found they did need the space, so Zowina-Clasina, the elder daughter, stuffed them one by one into the stove and burned them.

Vincent was to spend almost exactly two years at Nuenen. He would produce over 280 drawings and water-colours and, significantly, almost the same number of paintings. One of the first, a view of the octagonal church where his father preached, shows the worshippers gathered outside after the service, one of them apparently in mourning. From the start he began a slow move back from the darkness of the Drenthe to that lighter look he had learned from Mauve, though he may have reworked this particular painting later when his palette was even lighter. At all events it is much less solid and block-like, the brushstrokes shorter and sharper, adding a variety of colour missing in the sombre expanses of the Drenthe works.

Despite this fresh start, his fears about Theo and the future were still with him. He drew the parsonage, and his sister Elisabeth noticed how the old-fashioned building had been turned "into a haunted house surrounded by wild grasses, like the tree swept to one side by the wind, with a few small figures, one cannot see who they are, nor what they are actually doing".

While his family believed that they were living in a home, Vincent saw himself trapped in a ghostly ruin. It took an accident to bring about a rapprochement. On January 17th, his mother was returning from Helmond when she lost her footing as she stepped from the train and fell to the platform. She broke her thigh bone and as she was a heavily built lady it was a serious matter. Vincent was out painting on a nearby farm when the news was brought to him. He hurried back to the presbytery in time to watch the doctor go through the tricky and painful process of setting the fracture. The shock made him realise just how much he cared about his mother and he promptly made himself her nurse, fetching and carrying whatever she needed. Of course there was only so much he could do but he was helped by the Begemann sisters from next door and when the weather improved and the hip had set, he helped her out into the garden where she could sit in a comfortable cane chair and take the sun. Every day, Margot, the youngest of the Begemann sisters, came round to talk with them. She was ten years older than Vincent, a plain but kindly woman and more than willing to help in this crisis.

To amuse his mother, Vincent brought her what he called trifles – sketches and paintings such as the one of the church he had made earlier which he thought would please her. It was as if he had transferred his love and admiration to the other half of his inheritance: where once it had been religion and his father that had attracted him, now it was his mother and the world of drawing and painting she represented. As her health began to improve he felt able to leave her for a time while he went off on painting expeditions around the village where he could study the men digging and sowing, a woman feeding chickens at her cottage door, or the edge of a wood. There is an odd feature which recurs in many of these studies; sometimes it is in plain view at the centre of the composition, more often just visible beyond the trees – a strange isolated tower. When he drew the pretty garden he could see from his bedroom window at the back of the house, the tower is there in the distance across the open fields beyond the village. It was all that remained of the original Catholic church, abandoned when the new St Clement's opened the year before. The surviving tower would soon be demolished but for the moment its squat turret and sharp steeple standing forlorn in the abandoned graveyard drew his eye wherever he placed his easel.

Whatever he may have thought of his son's appearance, Pastor Theodorus was pleased to see him working so industriously and was more than delighted by his thoughtfulness towards his mother. There was a true reconciliation at last, though there was a disturbing consequence of the accident, the ever more frequent presence of Margot Begemann. Of course it was kind of her to help; with only three men in the parsonage apart from the maid, a woman was certainly needed. But Margot was a forty-one-year-old spinster and her delight in talking with Vincent was becoming alarmingly clear. The family had had enough experience of Vincent and women to be wary of this development. There had been fears when he went to The Hague to collect some of the work he had left behind, but, while the visit had been extremely painful for him, nothing untoward had happened. Sien's children had been boarded out with other members of her family, while Sien herself had so far resisted the easy life she had led before and was working as a washerwoman. Although Vincent knew they could not return to their former relationship, this effort on her part only added to his remorse at having abandoned her. He blamed Theo, whom he increasingly held responsible for having separated them.

Theo patiently endured Vincent's irrational recriminations. Each post seemed to bring a fresh demand for money and if he tried to suggest that he was unable to comply, his brother's letters would become increasingly petulant. At one point Theo, trying to be firm, resolutely refused to reply, but this provoked a thinly veiled threat from Vincent that he would kill himself, at which Theo succumbed and answered his entreaties. In a sense Theo knew he was trapped. He could never break free from Goupil's so long as he was chained to Vincent. Fortunately, whatever the details of the quarrel between him and Boussod and Valadon had been, they had somehow been resolved by the spring and he was now allowed a measure of freedom in the work he could display in the upstairs room. In March he made his first sale of an Impressionist work, a picture by Pissarro which went to a dealer called Guyotin for

150 francs, a profit of twenty-five francs to Goupil. While this was hardly earth-shattering it was a sign that he had begun to break new ground; and it was a windfall for the ever-needy Pissarro who had just moved into a new house at Eragny-sur-Epte, then about two hours from Paris, and whose wife Julie was expecting another addition to a family already too large to feed on the meagre proceeds from his rare sales. In spite of such difficulties, Pissarro remained determined to try out new ideas and was still optimistic in the face of Julie's frequent sharp comments on his shortcomings as a bread-winner.

By then most of the original Impressionists were living away from Paris and, although the society founded to exhibit their work would not be disbanded for another two years, any sense of a working group, meeting in cafés, going on painting outings by the Seine and so on, had clearly gone. Others were now challenging the art establishment and 1884 saw the first of the Salons des Indépendants, yet another attempt to escape the stranglehold of the official Salon jury. Among the first to exhibit with this new outlet was Georges Seurat, a young artist in his mid-twenties. Seurat had had all his entries for the official salon rejected, but it was his large canvas *Bathing at Asnières* which attracted most attention when the 'Indépendants' opened on May 15th. Although few had any idea who this newcomer was, it was clear that a leader had emerged from all the disputation about the new art that would some day succeed Impressionism. At least so it seemed to an even younger exhibitor, Paul Signac, who recognised in Seurat's formal arrangement of stiffly posed figures on a riverbank an advance on what he was tentatively reaching towards himself. But it was the way Seurat had used short strokes of pure colour, set down side by side leaving the eye to mix them, that most struck the younger man. It was a technique the Impressionists had occasionally used, though only on an instinctive basis. Here was a painter altogether more rigid, more 'scientific' in his approach. The two young men met and decided to exchange ideas.

For the older Pissarro and other visitors like Theo, a major change was clearly under way and as if to signpost the transition there was the drama of the 'Manet Affair'. Manet had died the previous year, and when his friend Antonin Proust, the Minister of Education, had tried to organise a memorial exhibition at the Ecole des Beaux Arts he aroused the fanatical opposition of Gérôme who argued both that Manet had no formal connection with the Beaux-Arts and that his works were nothing but '*cochonneries*'. Indeed Gérôme was unwise enough to circulate an open letter that he had written, but never actually posted, to the new Minister of Education, Jules Ferry, proposing that the exhibition be put on at the Folies Bergère. This mean-spiritedness towards a dead colleague would eventually do great harm to Gérôme's reputation, though at the time it was Manet's exhibition which attracted almost universal obloquy. Only his fellow Impressionists and a few supporters like Theo were at all aware of his outstanding role as the great precursor of the new art.

Theo wrote to Vincent in praise of the paintings in the exhibition but it was not easy to explain what was happening in Paris. Try as he might, Theo found it impossible to penetrate the miasma of self-righteousness and recrimination that emanated from Nuenen. Worse than the requests for money were Vincent's frequent suggestions that Theo should throw up his job and become an artist himself. More galling was his rather impertinent description of the painter's life as that of *a man amongst men*. Apart from the illogicality of proposing that Theo give up their joint source of income, on which he made constant demands, there was his total lack of understanding of Theo's vocation. The artistic life in Paris, with its gripping battles and political tribulations, was only a distant whisper to Vincent out in the fields of Brabant struggling with an ox-plough, a sower scattering seed, a watermill by a river. In his good-hearted way, Theo knew he had to accept the one-sidedness of their relationship. Vincent even proposed that Theo should stop giving him an allowance and instead 'buy' his work on a regular basis, in other words pay him a salary in exchange for the parcels of drawings and paintings that would be despatched to Paris. Theo as ever agreed. Anything to keep the peace.

That May, Pastor Theodorus' increasing ill-health forced him to resign his post as District Governor of the welfare charity. This was a bad sign and Theo was soon aware that his father's condition was not helped by the serious relationship developing between Vincent and Margot Begemann.

Even allowing for the improvement brought about by the way he had helped nurse his mother, Vincent was all too aware that his constant presence in the house still upset his father. With his new 'salary' from Theo, a way to ease this friction presented itself. He would find a studio somewhere in the village where he could be out of the way for most of the day. Yet in the end, even this seemingly intelligent solution was muddied when he chose to rent two rooms from Johannes Schafrat, the sacristan of the Catholic church at the other end of the village, which meant he would be spending much of his day effectively under the roof of Father Thomas van Luijtelaar, the local priest. Although that part of Brabant was notable for the lack of friction between the two religious communities, it was one more irritation for the poor pastor who was only too aware of the ridicule his bizarrely dressed son had brought on his family. Nevertheless, they tried to be encouraging, for at least Vincent was away much of the time and his mother even allowed him to push her recently acquired wheelchair round to the sacristan's house so that she could see for herself how his work was progressing.

As his parents had decided to give him free board, he had, with Theo's 'salary', a reasonable amount of money for once. Although there were debts from the past to be settled, he could afford the materials he needed and with his new preoccupation with colour this was obviously crucial. Obtaining materials meant going to nearby Eindhoven and the proximity of the town allowed a balance between city and country where before he had lurched from one to the other. If Nuenen bored him, he could slip into town for the day. Not that Eindhoven was any great metropolis, its rapid growth into a major industrial city was a decade away. Nor was it one of Holland's great ancient centres. Eindhoven was a backwater of minor interest to the visitor. Its main edifice, the church of St Catherine, fashionably Gothic, had been built only twenty-five years before. But here he could meet people beyond his family circle. The main aim of most visits was Jan Baijens' hardware store where decorators' products, household paints and brushes could be bought. Baijens also dealt in a limited range of artists' materials. He made up his own oils, though their consistency was unreliable, as Vincent discovered when he painted the 'old' station in Eindhoven, a long low building depicted in winter, where the white he used for the snow has clearly run uncontrollably. But as these colours were all there was to be had, it was useless to complain.

The unique status of Baijens' store had made it a meeting-place for the amateur artists of the town and, inevitably, Vincent became a figure of considerable interest to them. His appearance alone marked him out as a true 'professional' Bohemian and before long he had been approached by a fellow customer, Antoon Hermans, to see if he would give him some lessons. Hermans was a retired goldsmith who had made a fortune three times over, buying and selling important collections of antiques. In retirement, he amused himself as a painter and was eager to learn more.

Vincent himself approached another customer, Vandersanden, the organist at the church of St Catherine, to enquire about music lessons. He had been reading theories about the affinity between music and colour, and wanted to see if they were true. Vandersanden, an elderly man, no doubt intrigued by so eccentric a figure in a place like Eindhoven, agreed to give him piano lessons but they were not a success. One dreads to think what odd sounds so impetuous a person as Vincent could unleash on a musical instrument but more worrying to his teacher was his habit of suddenly stopping in order to point out the connections between a certain tone and Prussian blue or dark green. The old man grew afraid that he had taken in a madman and the sessions ended.

In Nuenen, the sexton Schafrat must also have been having second thoughts about letting his two rooms when he saw how the jumble Vincent always accumulated had quickly filled every corner. Although he had made some shelves and cupboards himself and had had others run up cheaply by a local carpenter, these were now piled high with things collected on his walks – moss, plants, stuffed birds, a bobbin, a spinning wheel. Two village lads, Piet van Hoorn and Leonardus Kuyten, would sometimes explore the wooded areas near the village collecting bird's nests for him. These Vincent kept in one of the cupboards to use for still-life paintings when he could not work outside. There was an old stove with a great pile of ashes beside it and a couple of chairs whose cane seats were starting to unravel. The carpenter had made him a box for his paints and cut him out a palette as well as a perspective frame strung with diagonal wires through which he could observe the receding scene as he drew it. But the clutter of objects was nothing beside the stacks of drawings and paintings that quickly mounted up.

His output was astonishing, most of it still done out of doors. If he was looking for a site in the village, he would stalk the spot, turning this way and that, before making a mark with his shoe where he planned to set up his easel. The youngster Piet van Hoorn recalled that the usual reaction of passers-by was: "There is that fool again." But if children came too near while he was painting they swiftly tasted his anger.

Life was much easier when he followed his plan to paint the weavers in their cottages. He would set off in the morning to the isolated hovels outside the village in search of willing subjects. He took some bread and cheese with him, for despite the wholesome food provided by his mother he still insisted on eating frugally, often rejecting meat or any other 'luxury', though he would take a nip of cognac, his one indulgence. His appearance on these outings was everything his father dreaded; if the weather was inclement, he wore a shaggy overcoat and a fur hat that was described as making him look like a drowned tomcat in the rain. This was unlikely to bother the weavers who slaved at their machines from sun up to sun down and probably welcomed any distraction. Vincent had first been intrigued by weavers as a subject when he had seen them at work on his epic walk to Courrières three years before – an interest re-awoken by Van Rappard's sketches – now he had an abundant supply of models. The most astonishing thing about their lives was the way the huge loom entirely filled the main room in their cottages, often leaving only enough space for a high chair in which a baby could be left to amuse itself watching the rapid to and fro of the shuttle while the weaver's wife was occupied elsewhere, usually preparing fresh shuttles in the doorway. In such a confined space man and machine became one, and in his earliest drawings Vincent concentrated more on the mechanical details of the apparatus, leaving the human operator as what he called *the spook in the machine*, no more than a dark outline. He much preferred the older and larger two-shaft looms dating back to the previous century, but because of the way they totally filled the small space it was hard for him to step back far enough to judge their proportions properly, so that the resulting distortion adds a further power to those awe-inspiring, clattering and whirring monsters. During the six months between January and June 1884 he moved from drawing to painting them. Man and machine, barely differentiated, take on a sombre presence in the residue of the dark tones he had adopted in Drenthe; there is a *Weaver Seen from the Front* which gives the impression that the silhouetted figure is driving a futuristic engine of war, a Jules Verne creation, straight at the spectator.

That May, Van Rappard came for ten days and again they worked together. Vincent was so convinced about his darker colours that he bullied the ever pliable Rappard into using the same range. Indeed they both worked on a woman spinning yarn, presumably at the same time, with the result that they can only be attributed because of Van Rappard's continuing technical superiority when it came to 'finish', the face of his woman is more academically 'correct' though as ever there is a crude power to Vincent's that makes the younger man's look somewhat insipid by comparison. Despite that, Vincent was full of enthusiasm and encouragement for his friend's work and was much cheered by his visit. These were the good times, for he felt that with the weavers he had found a unique subject largely untouched by any other 'painters of peasants' and one that he ought to be able to sell.

Theo arrived for a short visit just after Van Rappard's departure and was bundled round to the studio to see them, but his reaction was deeply disappointing. By then involved with Pissarro and the others, Theo had no time for these apparently retrograde essays in dark tones. He had written to Vincent about Manet but it was clearly impossible to explain something so visual by the written word alone and even when they talked it was still obvious that Vincent had only the vaguest notion how far-reaching the artistic revolution in Paris had been. It was impossible to deflect him from his absolute conviction that the real revolution in colour had been achieved by Israëls. Worse, he had already formed a few inaccurate notions about Impressionism. Before Theo arrived he had discussed the subject with Van Rappard whose work, they concluded, might be classified as belonging to the new school, so little did they understand it.

If Theo was not much taken with Vincent's new style he must also have been profoundly worried by what he heard of his brother's private life. It was clear to the family that the Margot Begemann affair was by no means dying down. They were seeing more of each other, going for walks and taking gifts to the poorer members of the parish. As it was evidently Margot who craved his company, they could hardly blame Vincent this time. In a reversal of his previous relationships it was she who was obviously obsessed with him and it was all Vincent could do to calm her down. He might have handled the situation better if her family had not behaved so badly. Of course they had reason to be worried. Being so close to the Van Goghs they were well aware of Vincent's past, a sorry tale hardly likely to recommend him as a future son-in-law, but individually their behaviour seems to have been motivated more by selfishness than out of concern for Margot. Her two sisters were clearly jealous: the scope for a Protestant marriage within their own class was restricted and the prospect of spinsterhood loomed before all the Begemann girls, so that the sight of Margot walking out with a man, even one as unprepossessing as the bedraggled Vincent, was gall to the housebound creatures. Worse was the father's implacable insistence that it was her duty to help him with his business. He saw no reason for her to leave home for the useless painter and said so.

Indeed they all said so, and often, so that the poor woman, already unstable and neurotic, was unhinged by their constant nagging. She appealed to Vincent who did his best to reassure her, but as the summer progressed the situation worsened. Vincent asked her brother Louis, the only one at all sympathetic to her, to try to persuade the family to treat her more gently. Vincent then consulted the local doctor to see if there was any way to calm her down. Margot was now talking obsessively about marriage, though she well knew her family would not countenance Vincent as a son-in-law. She also let Vincent know that her family's attitude was no barrier to their making love if he so wished; but he chose to ignore the suggestion, either because he was unsure how she would react emotionally or because he had some sense of what would happen to her if rumour of an affair got about.

His assessment of her mental condition proved all too exact. They were out walking one day in July when she suddenly fell to the ground in a convulsive fit. His first startled reaction was that she was having some sort of nervous attack, but her incoherent speech and the sheer violence of the spasms quickly showed him that it was something far worse. He begged her to tell him what the matter was and she mumbled something about promising to keep it to himself. When he had sworn that he would keep her secret, she confessed to swallowing poison. She had managed to get her hands on strychnine, used at the time as an ingredient in homemade tonics. A large dose of strychnine would have blocked all inhibitory signals to her brain, hence the uncontrolled muscle contractions. Because her entire system had gone rigid, including the involuntary breathing muscles, the result should have been death by suffocation; but as she admitted later, she had taken 'something' she believed would ease the pain. As it was probably one of those other household stand-bys, laudanum or chloroform, that 'something' must have relaxed the muscles sufficiently to keep her alive until Vincent carried her back to the house where her brother administered a strong emetic which brought up most of the poison. At any event she did not die, though she was very sick indeed and had to be sent to a doctor, a family friend, in Utrecht, to recover. She was away for six months, which was undoubtedly the best thing for all concerned, though with considerable injustice Vincent's family held him largely responsible for the scandal which rocked the village and became the sole topic of conversation for weeks.

It was probably the desire to escape this ill-feeling which drove him to spend more time outside Nuenen. He made a number of drawings in Eindhoven of the church and the weigh-house, and tried to find something to do that would keep him away from his father's disapproving looks. He hoped to obtain a commission from old Hermans, the goldsmith, who was full of plans for the new house he had just built and who wanted to have a series of six painted panels in his dining-room. From what Vincent heard at Baijens' store, Hermans was proposing to paint the panels himself and tended to favour the Saints as a subject. Vincent quickly set about dissuading him, arguing that peasant life was what his fellow diners would most appreciate. The scenes could also reflect the four seasons. This idea probably came from his reading Sensier's biography of Millet which described a commission to decorate the salon of the industrialist Frederic Hartmann with paintings representing Spring, Summer, Autumn and Winter. Hermans was sufficiently taken with the idea to visit Vincent's studio where it was agreed that he would make some preliminary sketches. These were full size so that Hermans could see the final effect. They drew heavily on Millet's figures, especially the sower who was to represent Spring. The problem was that the walls of Hermans' rectangular dining-room, being of unequal length, meant that the four seasons had to be stretched to six pictures. Several permutations were discussed before a solution was agreed: two for Spring, *Planting Potatoes* and *Ox-team with Women Planting Potatoes*; one for Summer, *The Wheat Harvest*; two for Autumn, *The Sower* and *The Shepherd*; and one for Winter, *Wood-gatherers in the Snow*. It was arranged so that Summer and Winter would face each other on the two short walls. Hermans liked the full-scale sketches and proposed that Vincent paint the scenes as finished canvases which he, Hermans, would then copy onto the panels. It seemed an ideal arrangement, by which Vincent would not only be reimbursed for the work but also given money to pay local people to pose for him. In the end the original concept was spoiled when Hermans insisted on cramming too many figures of his own into the potato planting scene, while Vincent's four wood-gatherers in the snow came out like his first disconnected figure studies rather than a balanced composition in a landscape. It was a great disappointment and, for whatever reason, Hermans never paid him.

However, there was a brief cause for hope that September when he received an anonymous commission for a drawing, until he realised that Margot was behind it. Although recuperating in Utrecht she was still concerned about him and hoped to help him in this roundabout way.

Having guessed the truth, he simply sent her a sketch and refused to accept any money. But the incident made him realise that she would be coming home soon and, as his father's health had suffered enough over the last incident, it was perhaps time to be thinking of leaving before her return. That, and his new desire to unravel the mysteries of colour, made him far less resistant to the idea of some sort of formal training than he had been. Perhaps he should go to Paris where he could stay with Theo and work in one of the ateliers. He had heard the name Fernand Cormon from some of his Dutch friends who had used his studio in Montmartre. On the other hand, the easiest solution was to go to the nearby academy in 's-Hertogenbosch where he would be able to work from models and get technical advice when he needed it. He put these ideas to Van Rappard on his next visit that October but the younger man was all for going further and suggested he should enrol in a school with a good reputation, say the famous academy in Antwerp which was accepted throughout Europe as a first-rate starting-point for budding painters. As so often before, Vincent seized on the idea with surprising single-mindedness. He must immediately create a portfolio of work to show to the authorities in Antwerp. Van Rappard had been working on a series of portrait heads – very well, that was what Vincent would do. He could use the local people as models. He would make thirty – no, fifty – he could even do them on commission. It would solve everything, he would earn money and prepare his application studies all at the same time. Of course he would need a modest amount of capital to get started and wrote to Theo asking for some extra cash to pay the peasants to sit for him, though Theo must understand that this was only for a short time as he would soon be earning enough to pay his own way . . .

Discounting his over-enthusiasm, there was some sense in the idea. With the completion of the harvest and the onset of winter, the local people had time on their hands and would be happy to work for money or gifts of food. He had occasionally worked on portraits before, though his fishermen in The Hague had really been copies of figures from his collection of English illustrated journals. Sien and the children, however, had been drawn from life and had been among his first successes. Now he began to study the local physiognomy with the exactness of an ethnologist, as if he were outlining a species. At the same time he exaggerated what he found almost to the verge of caricature. There was certainly nothing idealised about his peasants. They are seldom beautiful and are clearly individuals, though they are moulded until they represent more than themselves, until they show something of the hard work that had shaped their lives and thus their faces. When he turned to painting them, he made them stare out from black backgrounds like so many Spanish saints, icons of the poor.

Much of the winter of '84–'85 was spent working with his peasants, who were repaid with gifts of coffee, a great luxury then. He began with isolated heads then progressed to full figures – a man in a cap seated at a table, a woman shelling beans, another making pancakes. Some are identifiable. The man in the cap is Francis van Rooy and a woman spooling thread is probably Cornelia de Groot, his married sister. They all lived together in a small grey house, beyond the village along the Berg from the parsonage, opposite the local windmill. Vincent often passed the de Groots' home on his excursions and would call in to ask the family to pose for him. As he worked on these figures, the idea began to form that he might do a group composition; though just what it would be was not yet clear.

Despite his disappointing experience with the commission for Hermans' dining-room, Vincent was still willing to help those in search of guidance. One of the villagers, Dimmen Gestel, was allowed to come to the studio to have his sketches criticised, though he admitted later that he had found Vincent's own work so strange he had not fully benefited from what he had to say. His second pupil, Willem van de Wakker, had left some paintings to be framed at Baijens' where Vincent saw them and was impressed enough to ask the store-keeper to send the young man to the Nuenen studio. Van de Wakker lived in Eindhoven but worked in the Nuenen telegraph office so the two often passed each other on the road and soon became friends, though it was often hard-going, as Vincent was merciless in his criticism of the young man's work. Van de Wakker was most impressed by the speed at which Vincent worked and the amount he could produce in a day's painting excursion and so keen was he to develop their friendship, he got his mother to invite Vincent home for a meal. The good woman provided a spread of her best dishes only to be faced with a horrified Vincent who insisted on being given some plain cheese with any crusts of bread they might have. It was the same at home where he refused to sit at table and, in imitation of his practice at the Brussels mission school, ate his frugal meal at a chair apart. Propped on another chair in front of him would be whatever painting he was working on, which he studied intently as he struggled to chew his crusts with his remaining good teeth. Such behaviour did nothing to improve his relations with his father who was still smarting over the Begemann incident. Their neighbours no longer visited for fear of meeting Vincent. Even Pastor Theodorus' decision not to concern himself with his son's appearance was sorely tried when Vincent returned from Eindhoven one day wearing a suit he'd had made out of some lilac cloth with yellow spots. To look like a wild man had been bad enough but to look like a clown!

It was not as if the two men could simply agree to avoid each other. The pastor had only to see one of Zola's novels lying about to be provoked into an endless argument that could keep them both up far into the night. Zola and the other French realists were dangerous godless radicals to the country parson and he blamed them volubly for his son's behaviour. Vincent for his part could never desist from trying to show someone the error of his ways. A stand-off was impossible, and the arguments dragged on interminably.

With such an atmosphere at home, and still feeling estranged from Theo, it was hardly surprising that Vincent should have tried to find a close friend upon whom he felt he could rely. Van Rappard might have been first choice but he was seldom there. In the event he settled on Anton Kerssemakers who worked as a tanner in Eindhoven. Fortunately, Kerssemakers' calm good sense was a steady counterbalance to Vincent's wilder enthusiasms. An amateur artist of some promise, Kerssemakers was decorating his office with some landscapes when Baijens told him about Vincent and offered to put them in touch. Again a visit to the Nuenen studio was proposed, an outing that almost put an end to the budding relationship when the visitor tried to take in both the amazing clutter and the 'raw and unfinished' work that he saw lying around. After that visit Kerssemakers decided to let the matter drop but when he found that some of the images haunted him, he decided to persevere with his new teacher. Vincent would come to his apartment opposite the Old Station – it was from a window there that he painted the 'melting' snow scene – and occasionally Kerssemakers would come to Nuenen and go out painting with him. Vincent's teaching methods were rigorous. At first Kerssemakers was made to work solely on still-lifes and was encouraged to study Vincent's collection of illustrated journals. As the pupil was eight years older than the teacher he sometimes despaired that he was starting too late but Vincent, although he never tempered his criticism, was always enthusiastic and ultimately encouraging.

It was Kerssemakers who first noticed how the abandoned church tower in the old graveyard was a magnet to Vincent. They frequently headed that way when they painted out of doors. Once they went out to one of the old water mills which Vincent liked to paint and as these were some way from town Kerssemakers tried to persuade him to take a decent meal in a wayside inn. To his amazement, he too was confronted with the same rather offended, puritan Vincent who refused sugar for his coffee or butter for his bread and ended up eating nothing more than cheese and crusts as usual. That his 'pupils' put up with this difficult, sometimes petulant, master says much about Vincent's underlying charm, but the fact that he was willing to assume the role of teacher also shows how confident he had grown. Everyone noticed the assurance with which he tackled a blank canvas, the confidence with which the paint-loaded brush jabbed forward with no hesitation and the economy with which a few quick strokes could outline a bending figure or a line of trees. But the one thing that puzzled Kerssemakers was the way Vincent rarely bothered to sign his work or, if he did, never with his full name. It was only when tackled about it that Vincent revealed his dislike of having his name mispronounced by foreigners. He was certain they would 'butcher' it if they saw it on a painting: *while the whole world can pronounce the name Vincent correctly.*

Although it was good to have friends like Kerssemakers to talk to, it is clear from their later reminiscences that the group had little idea of what he was striving for, while some could barely disguise their dislike of much of his work. Given their reactions it is not surprising that he was still lonely – he told Theo he had *never begun a year with a gloomier aspect, in a gloomier mood, nor do I expect any future of success, but a future of strife.*

The decision, taken that February, by the Nuenen municipal council finally to demolish the old tower only served to increase this mood. For Vincent, that strange isolated stump had come to mean so much more than a mere ruined building; he saw in it the collapsing church his father so stubbornly adhered to: *those ruins tell me how a faith and a religion moldered away – strongly founded though they were.* This attitude must have greatly pained Pastor Theodorus, afflicting him with a sense of failure. He had laboured all his life to hold together tiny congregations in the remote parishes to which he had been assigned, congregations which were being almost daily eroded by migration from the land to the cities. There may have been economic reasons, but it was hard not to have a sense of personal failure. Now here was his eldest son, once a candidate for the ministry, affecting to despise everything he believed in. In the past he had referred to Vincent's bizarre acts as falling on him like blows. So close at hand, they fell heavier and heavier.

Vincent was not entirely unaware of the decline in his father's health and spirits but there was so much else to think about, long hours of trying to decide on the subject of his grand composition, something suitable to act as a summation of all that he had been doing since Drenthe. One evening in March, when he was coming home from painting in the fields, he passed the modest grey house of the de Groot family and decided to call in. As he went through the open door he saw the family gathered round their table, lit by an overhanging oil-lamp, each dipping into the common dish of potatoes which was their usual evening meal. He knew at once that this was the scene he must paint. As usual it recalled other works he admired – a peasant feast on Christmas Eve by Léon Lhermitte and Charles de Groux's *Saying Grace* – but more important than any prior inspiration was his own immediate and personal interpretation of the scene:

> *. . . those people, eating their potatoes in the lamp-light, have dug the earth with those very hands they put in the dish, and so it speaks of manual labour, and how they have honestly earned their food.*

Seated round the table that evening were Cornelia de Groot and her daughter Sien de Groot, both in the bulky black peasant costume and elaborate white head-dress of north Brabant. With them were Cornelia's two Van Rooy brothers including Francis in the cap he had worn when Vincent had painted him before. When Vincent first attempted to re-create their meal, he posed them as he had seen them in the glow of the oil-lamp hung above the table. But as he quickly discovered, working in half-light produces far from satisfactory results, thus for his next attempt he persuaded them to re-create the scene during the day so that he could work in a clearer light. His main problem was how to balance the picture. Simply putting two large figures in the foreground with the two smaller in the background left an unnatural open space, but if he moved the foreground figures closer together they blocked those behind. He was not discouraged by these failures; he knew he had found a subject that would enable him to say much and was happy to go on until he got it right. He even returned to make studies of individual hands and faces in order to prepare himself for the final work.

Then tragedy struck. On March 26th his father, returning to the presbytery, arrived at the front door where he collapsed unconscious on the threshold. When Anna and the maid tried to lift him they knew at once he was dead. As before, Vincent was out working on one of his peasant heads, and had to be sent for.

One can only guess at the complexity of his reactions on being shown the dead body of his father. Sorrow? Guilt? There was the book-lined study with his father's empty chair and the engraving by Van der Maaten, a confusion of images and memories impossible to digest at once. His letters immediately following the death are strangely empty of reference to it, suggesting either total indifference or a grief too deep for words. All he was able to express was an immediate concern for his mother. The following days were terrible for him. The Uncles arrived for the funeral, disapproving figures whom he had alienated one by one – Uncle Cent, Uncle Stricker, Uncle Cor. He was grateful when Theo arrived, for their sister Anna, who could no longer disguise her condemnation of his behaviour, had now joined their ranks. The interment was only made bearable by the demonstrations of affection on the part of the pastor's loyal congregation who had overlooked his poor preaching in favour of such manifest good works. The once handsome Dorus was laid to rest in the old Protestant churchyard within sight of the abandoned tower now awaiting the demolition men who would finally reduce it to rubble.

After the burial Vincent took Theo round to his studio and showed him his latest work. Whether he had grown accustomed to Vincent's darker style or out of pity for what he must have been going through, Theo was more encouraging, especially over the sketches for *The Potato Eaters* and he agreed to take some of the painted peasant studies back with him. When everyone had left, however, Vincent found it impossible to return to what he had been doing. For days his usual restless energy found no outlet. Then, as if to follow the advice he had given his pupils, he forced himself to draw a still-life: he set up a bowl of flowers and put beside it his father's pipe and tobacco pouch. The symbolism of the flowers depends on language: 'Honesty' in English; 'Pope's Pennies' in

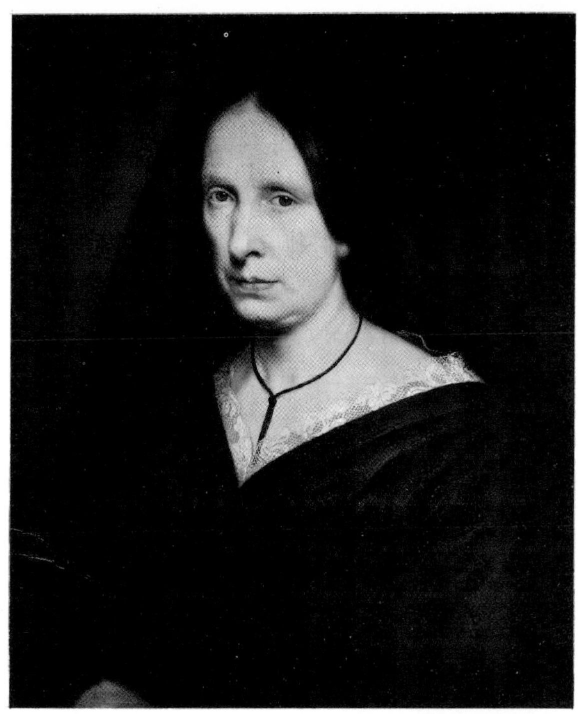

It was his attachment to this anonymous seventeenth-century French painting *Woman in Mourning* that led Vincent into a miserable fixation with his recently widowed cousin, Kee Vos, seen here with her son.

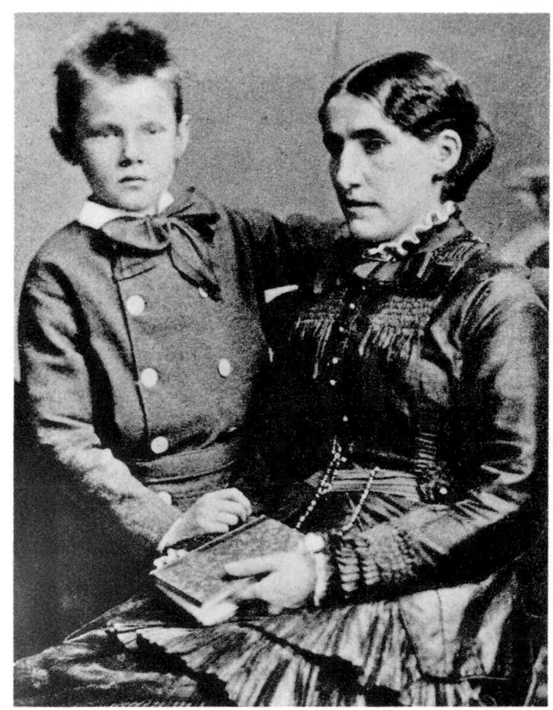

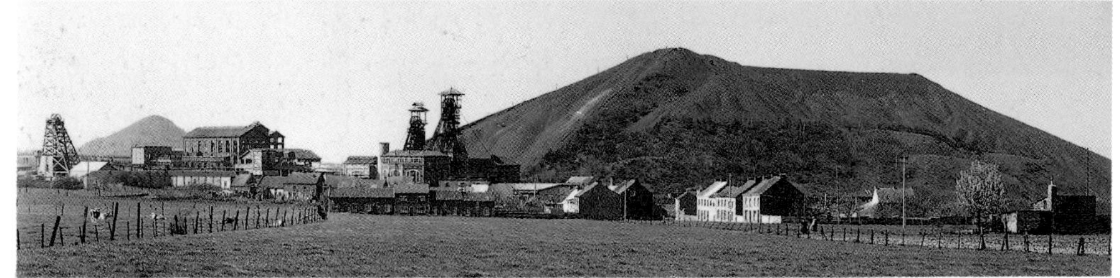

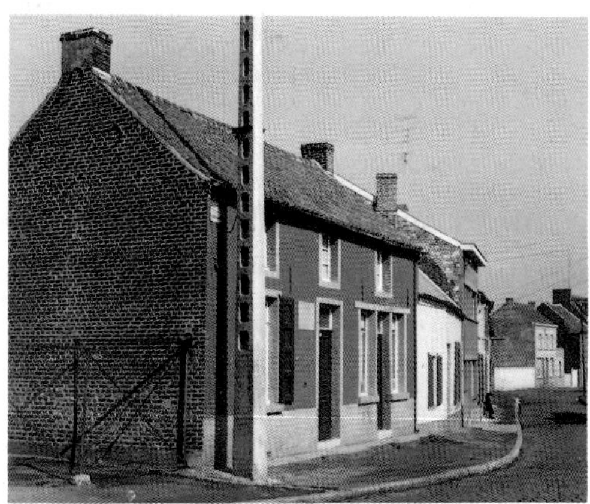

The Marcasse pit in the Borinage, now abandoned, and the nearby Denis house where Vincent lodged.

One of Vincent's earliest adult drawings, *The Miner's Return*.

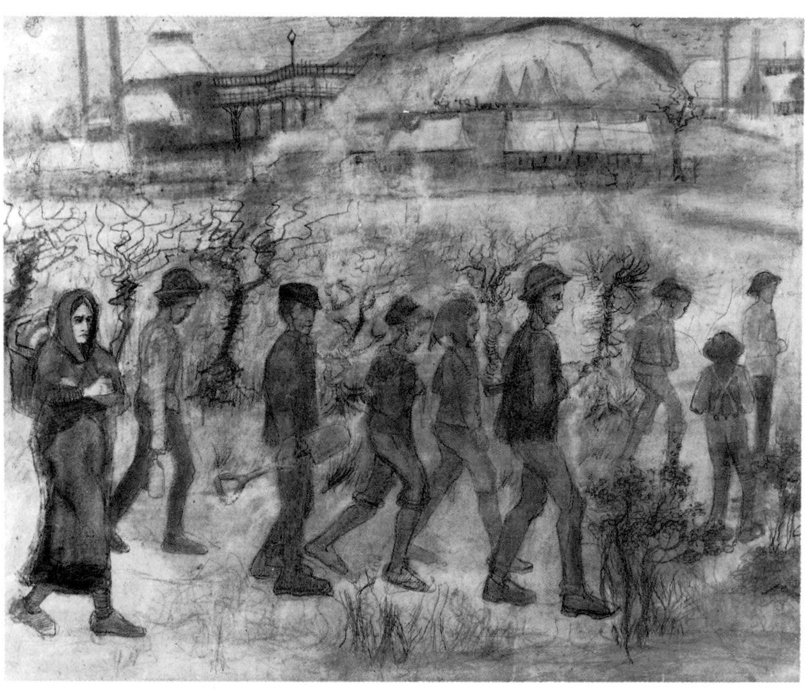

Camille Pissarro and Paul Cézanne

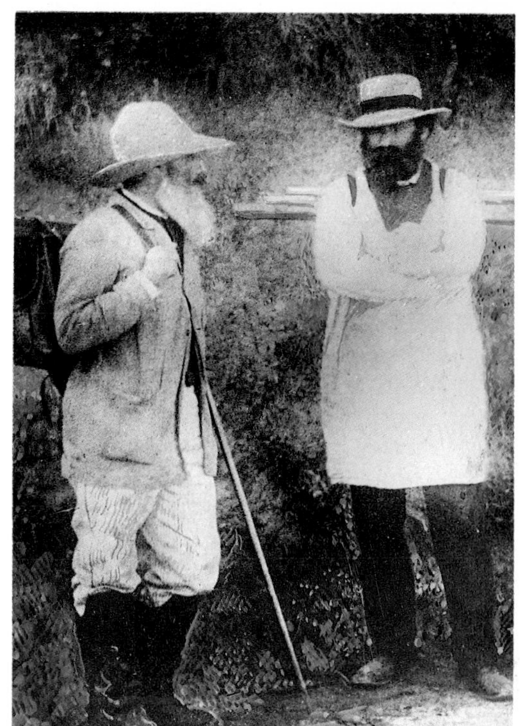

The most famous artistic cabaret of the 1880s, the Shadow Theatre at the Chat Noir Café drew patrons as different as the Prince of Wales and Emile Zola.

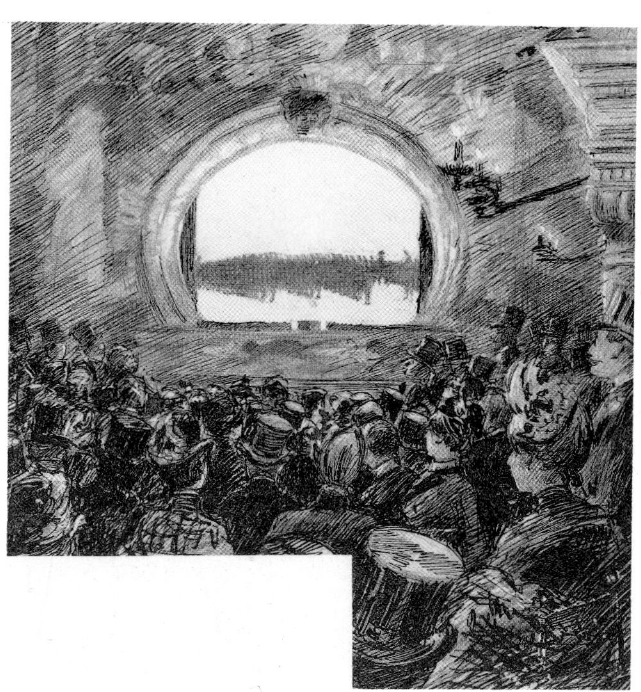

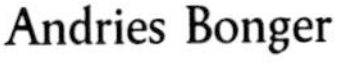

Andries Bonger

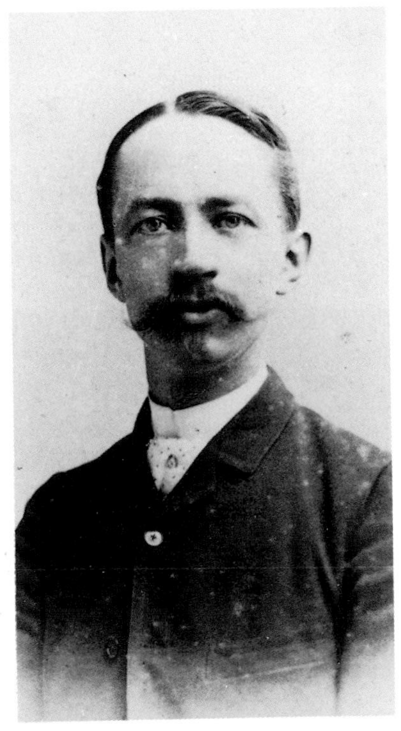

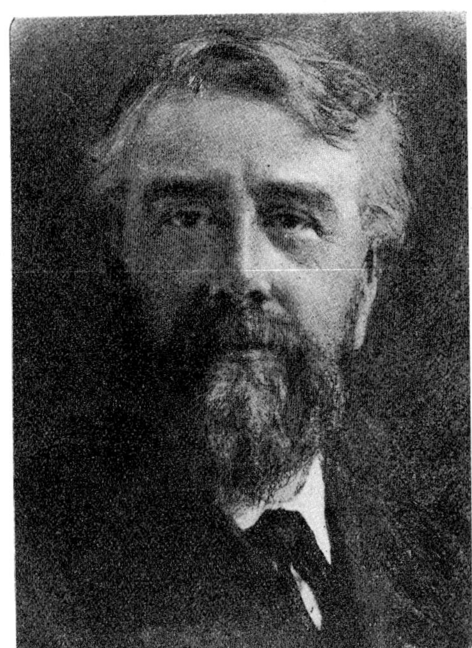

Anton Mauve

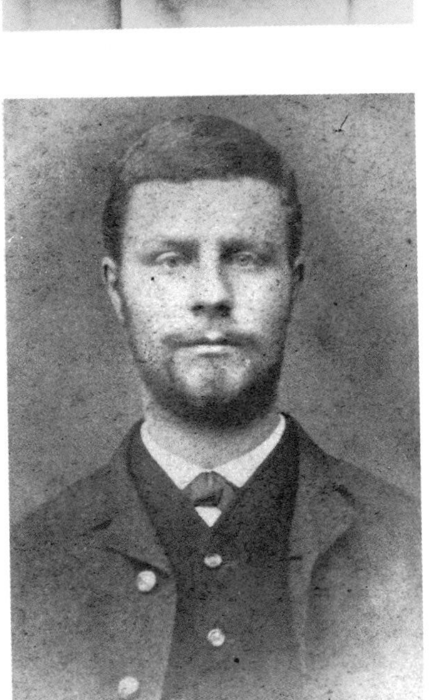

Anton van Rappard

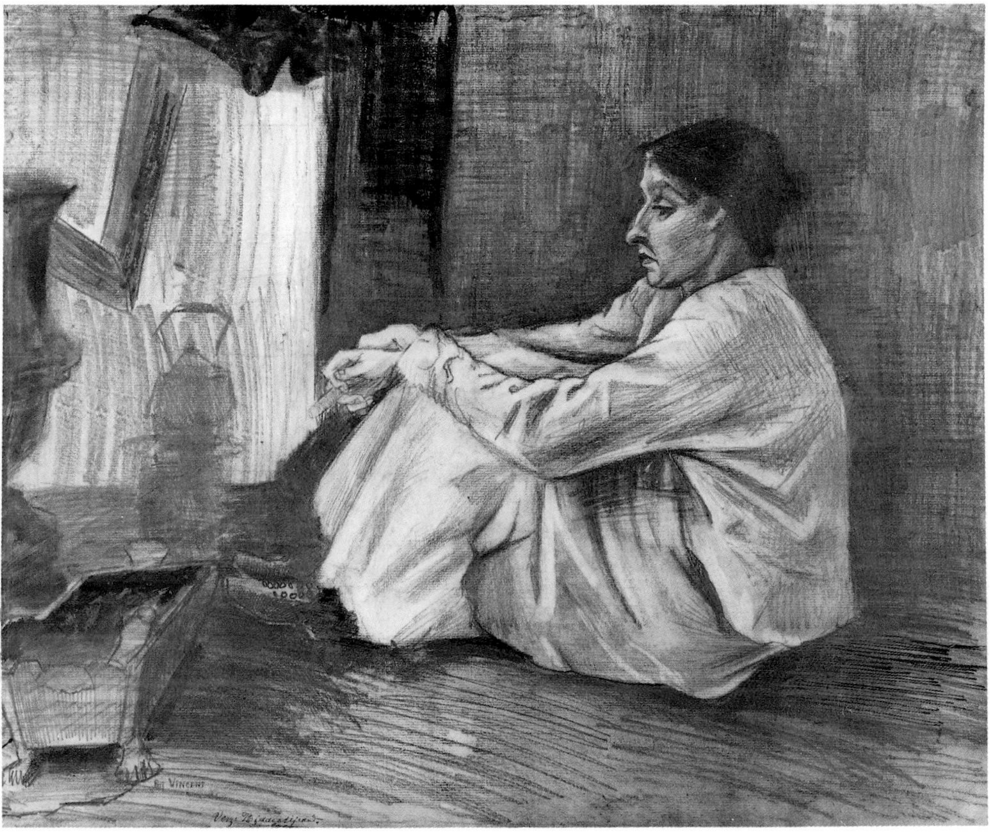

Indolent, unattractive, the prostitute *Sien Hoornik* was, nevertheless, the subject of one of Vincent's strongest passions.

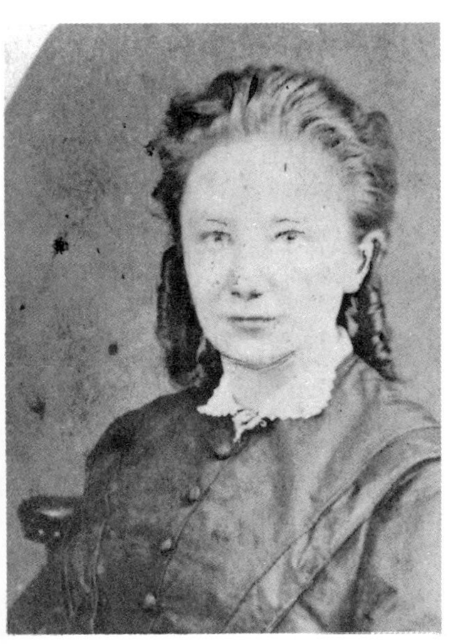

Margot Begemann,
the only woman to fall
in love with Vincent.

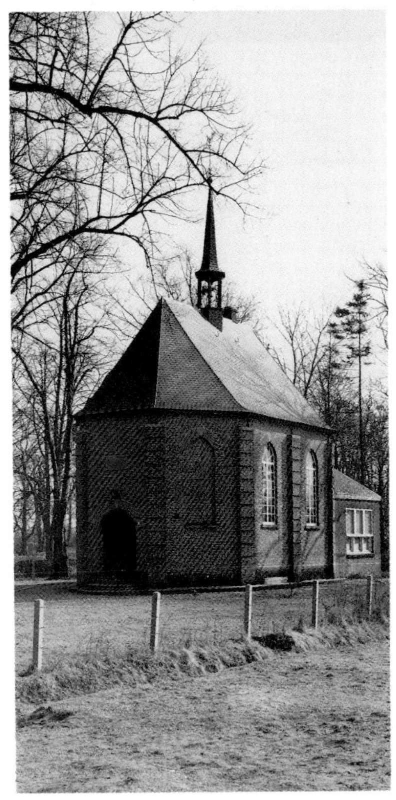

Pastor Theodorus' chapel in Nuenen, the Brabant village where Vincent worked on scenes of weavers in their hovels.

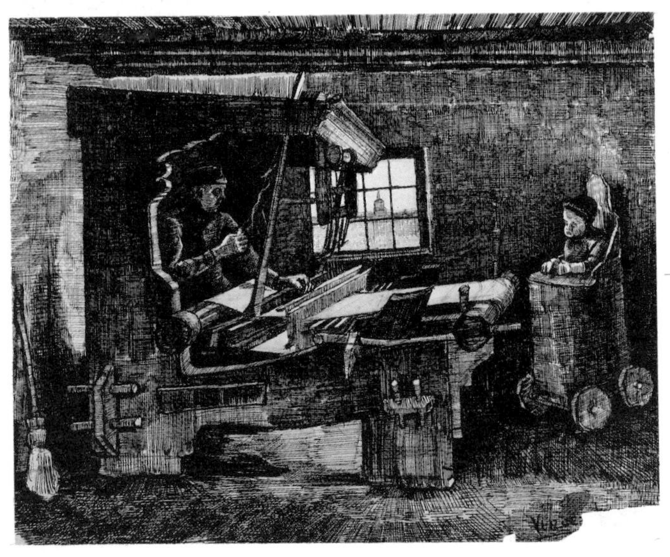

Through the window of the cottage can be glimpsed the abandoned tower of the old catholic church, an image that came to obsess Vincent during his time at Nuenen.

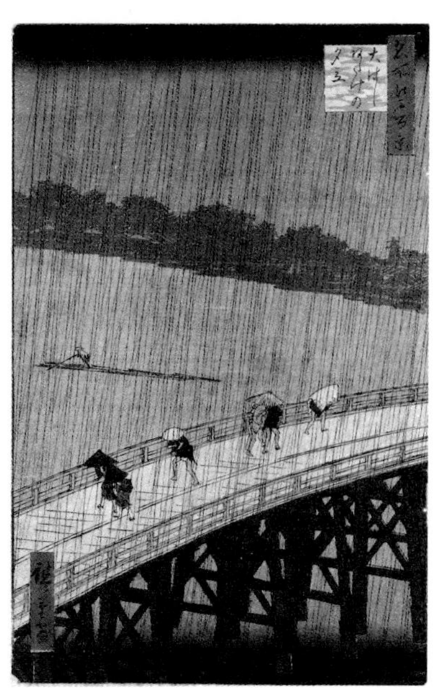

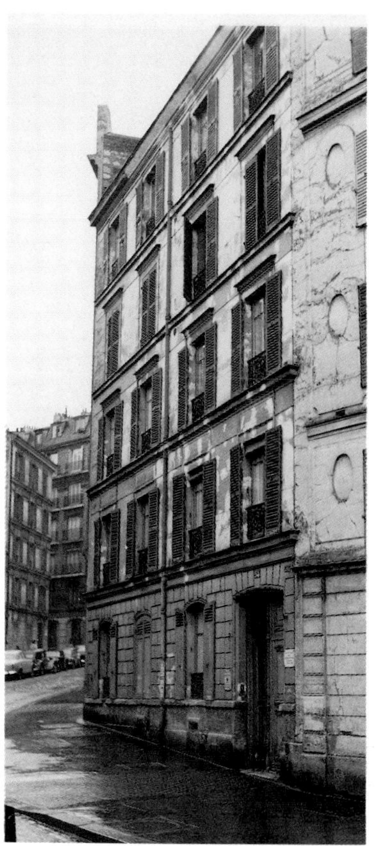

One of Vincent's Japanese prints, *Ohashi in the Rain*.
Right: Vincent and Theo's lodgings, 54 rue Lepic, Paris.
Below: Vincent's painting of windmills on the Butte Montmartre.

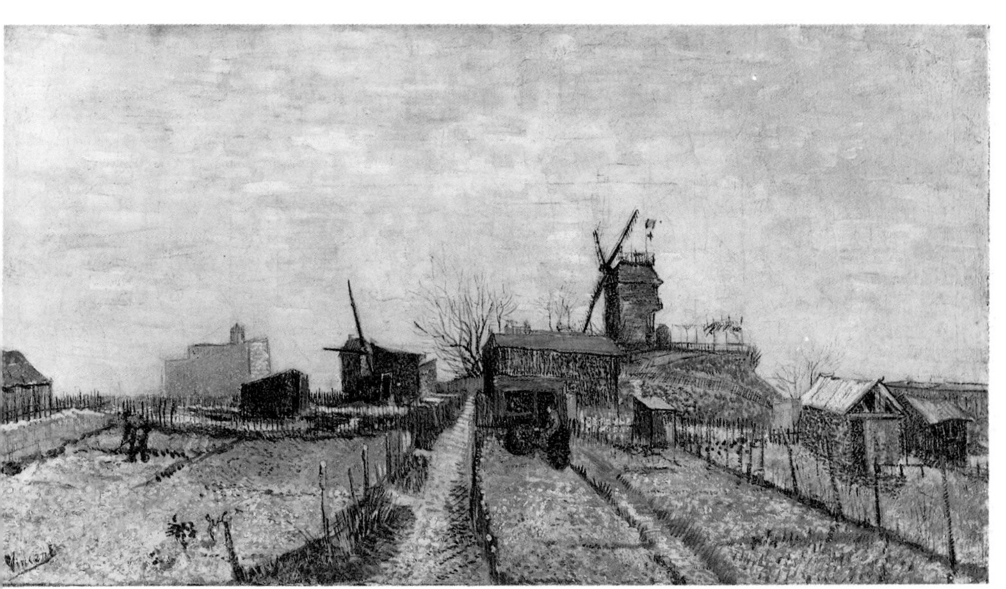

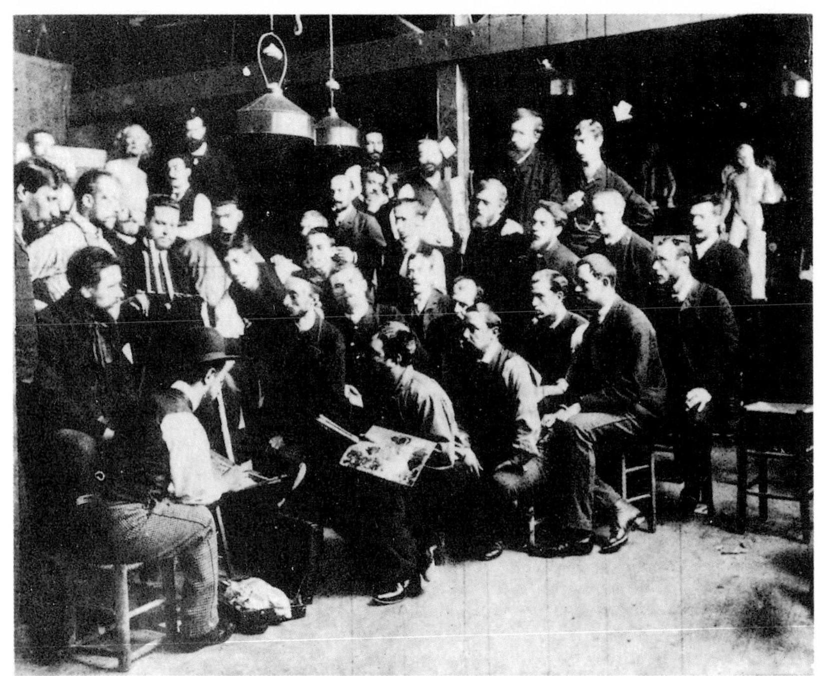

Cormon in his studio surrounded by a group of his pupils. Toulouse-Lautrec is in the foreground; Emile Bernard at the back, arrowed.

A few doors from Cormon's studio, the gardens of the Moulin Rouge, with the famous elephant.

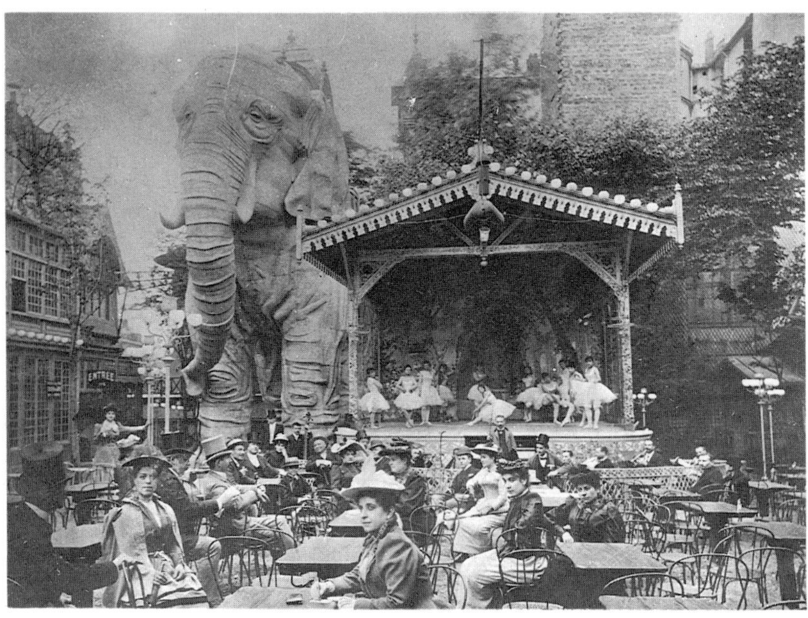

French; 'Judas Pennies' in Dutch, though as he used all three languages all these interpretations are possible and he may have been thinking a little of each of them at that confused moment. He sent the sketch to Theo, as he did a painting made later in the year which more clearly set out his testing relationship with their father – another still-life, though this one consisted of a candle, an open Bible and a novel by Zola. The Bible is massive and doom-laden but its words are mere paint blurs on the canvas, illegible smears. The novel, by contrast, is light yellow, with its title clear and legible: *La Joie de Vivre*. His father's death had done nothing to modify his judgements.

He was no less hard on himself. Apart from the first still-life, he was unable to resume the pattern of work that had formerly filled his days. Any sort of inactivity was a form of torture to him. Work was a way of sealing off his mind from the endless debilitating questioning and doubt that threatened to overwhelm him; it helped fight off the demons. By going without sleep or food, by working until he dropped from exhaustion, he could bludgeon his mind into a stupefied silence. Not to work was terrifying.

He tried to distract himself by reading. He had already discovered theoretical works which explained something of the way Delacroix had used colour. Now he studied them to see if there was anything relevant to his own painting. Why did Delacroix's canvases look so much more vivid than those of his contemporaries? Was there a secret formula that others could acquire? Again, it was a case of his finding his own way down a much-travelled route. Long before the Impressionists, Delacroix had been fascinated by the writings of Eugène Chevreul, the optical scientist who had formulated what had been previously only an instinctive knowledge of how colours affect each other. From time immemorial, artists had accepted that there was no such thing as a unique colour, that each colour was affected by those next to it. But it was Chevreul who went some way towards explaining the phenomenon. In the 1820s Chevreul had been consulted by the Gobelin tapestry manufactory to discover why certain yarns seemed drab. He found that there was nothing wrong with the dyeing process, only that a curious optical effect was at work which he eventually identified as the simultaneous contrast of colours. He demonstrated that if you took the three primary colours, red, blue and yellow, mixed any two together, say red and yellow to make orange, and put the orange beside the unused primary blue, the result was startling. Side by side the two colours orange and blue had an electric effect on each other. Chevreul's explanation was that blue must be the complementary of orange. Any combination would do. Mix blue and yellow to make green, put that beside its complementary, the unused primary red, and the result was a vivid interaction between the two. But, as Chevreul told his patrons, if they wove too many complementary threads together, say orange/blue, green/red, violet/yellow, they would have the equally curious effect of cancelling each other out as the eye would see only an overall greyish tint. On reading Chevreul, it had been obvious to Delacroix that what would work for thin strands of thread would also be applicable to brush strokes. Not that he thought of filling a picture with violent complementaries, but there had been uses in moderation, a touch of green next to a reddish skin tone made the flesh more alive. But when Vincent tried to recall such details from the paintings by Delacroix he had seen in Paris, he failed. It was too long ago and so, frustratingly, the things he was reading had to remain in the realm of theory. The one positive result was that he at last began to accept that Israëls might not be the final word on colour though as yet it was impossible to connect such thinking to his own work.

He returned to the unfinished *Potato Eaters* but his palette was no different from before, if anything it was darkened by constant overpainting as he struggled to get the composition right. It was by then late spring 1885 and with longer hours of daylight in the studio he could work and work, scraping away what did not satisfy him, building up layers of pigment till the figures were moulded on the canvas. He eventually accepted that four figures would never balance. Lhermitte in his engraving had put a small child in the foreground to fill the otherwise empty space. He seized on the idea and pushed two of the adults to either side of the table, making a rough circle of five figures. A sense of activity was created by having the child and the two left-hand figures dip into the bowl of potatoes while the woman on the right pours coffee, which the man beside her drinks. He knew it was good, though not yet perfect. He sent a sketch to Theo and wrote to say he intended to make a lithograph of it, wondering whether the new magazine *Le Chat Noir*, an offshoot of Theo's favourite café-cabaret, might publish it.

The idea of the lithograph came from his pupil Dimmen Gestel, who was the son of a printer. The father's main work was printing cigar-bands by lithography and Vincent knew he would be able to bully Dimmen into persuading the older man to co-operate. He only wanted to make a small print, but being unsure about 'art' the elder Gestel presented him with a lithographic stone so large he had to get help to carry it to the station. He drew *The Potato Eaters* on to the stone as he had painted them so that the prints inked in reverse. But the real difference was that as he was now drawing and not painting, his handling of the figures was far more detailed and with the exception of the silhouetted child in the foreground, the four adults are recognisably the Van Rooys and the De Groots. When he returned to Gestel's and pulled off twenty prints it was clear at once that this was a great improvement. Although the lithographs were too bland and had none of the atmospheric effects of the painting, there were new qualities there which satisfied him, and he gave each of his pupils a copy. Some of the trial prints were only on flimsy tissue paper and the one he gave to Kerssemakers eventually disintegrated, but Theo was sent a good print on fine paper in the earnest hope that he would place it, so sure was Vincent that he had at last achieved something worthwhile. What he knew he must do next was to reconcile the best qualities of the painted version with those of the lithograph. He began at the end of April, though in difficult circumstances; his quarrel with Anna had not subsided and the atmosphere at the presbytery was deadly. Although the church authorities had given his mother permission to stay in the house for another year while she sorted out her affairs, there was already an air of change and impermanence. In any case, it was impossible for Vincent, who could be riled by the merest glance, to tolerate the open hostility of the eldest of his sisters. He decided to move into the studio at Schafrat's house. There were two good rooms where he could have been very comfortable, but with his usual taste for martyrdom he chose to sleep under the eaves where he would be both uncomfortable and cold.

That aside, the final version of *The Potato Eaters* fulfilled all his hopes. To have portrayed real people proved the necessary counterbalance to the artificial dolls-house setting in which he had crammed them. The figures sit at a table that spreads backwards into the picture in reverse perspective. There was nothing inept or accidental about this: he wanted to create a disturbing claustrophobic closeness which would exaggerate the roughness of the features, the twisted faces and gnarled hands. Each figure looks away at a different angle, each one staring into his or her own space as if to say: "We are here together but we are each one of us alone, caught for a moment in the glow of this oil-lamp". Despite all the layers of paint, the lamp-light fell on his humble diners with a deeper richness of colour than he had achieved so far, a resonance which lifts the figures out of the surrounding darkness. The canvas is thick with paint, more like clay than pigment. It matched his favourite quotation from Sensier's book about Millet: "His peasant seems to be painted with the earth he is sowing."

A few weeks later Theo sent him a copy of Zola's *Germinal*, the novel of life in the coalfields of Northern France. The first fifty pages brought it all back to him: the hissing terrifying descent in the cage, the damp low tunnels and the sudden glimpses of the huddled figures seen in the flash of a miner's lamp in the *maintenages*. And then he knew what he had seen when he had bent low to step into the De Groots' house on that distant evening and realised exactly what it was he had painted. *The Potato Eaters* was not only a testimony to peasant life in Brabant, it was also his hymn to the subterranean world of the Borinage which he had longed to portray, but had not had the skill even to attempt. Now he had done so, and was satisfied.

Cautiously he accepted from the first that his own assessment of his achievement would not be reciprocated by others. He sent a lithograph to Van Rappard, no doubt expecting the usual to and fro of gentle criticism that marked their relationship. Vincent, so sure he had created a masterpiece, would probably have resented unfavourable comment even from his friend but might have swallowed it if it had been moderately expressed. He was not prepared for what did arrive. For once the timid Van Rappard was seized with a tigerish vehemence. His strident comments were so uncomprehending of the work, that they hold a mirror up to its merits:

> You will agree with me that such work is not meant seriously. Fortunately you can do better than that, but why then did you see and treat everything so superficially? Why didn't you study the movements? Now they are only posing. How far from true that coquettish little hand of the woman in the background is – and what connection is there between the coffee kettle, the table and that hand that is lying on top of the handle? What on earth is that kettle doing? – it isn't standing, it isn't being lifted up – so what then? And why isn't that man on the right allowed to have a knee, a belly and lungs? Or are they located in his back? And why must his arm be a metre too short? And why must he do without half his nose? And why must

> that woman on the right have some sort of tobacco pipe stem with a little cube on the end for a nose. And after that, while working in such a manner you dare to invoke the names of Millet and Breton. Come on! In my opinion art is too sublime a thing to be treated so nonchalantly.

Of course, if one was talking in terms of Millet and Breton, Van Rappard was quite right: *The Potato Eaters* traduced every canon of their art. Here was none of the holiness nor the sentimentality that made their paintings of peasants 'high' art. By distorting the perspective, by creating the crudest features for his subjects, by making them stare into the void in so disturbing a way, Vincent had deliberately undermined any possibility of associating this meal with a form of peasant Mass; these figures are not holy, they are deprived, nor are they to be admired nor pitied, their dignity is their own not ours to grant them.

Vincent simply folded up Van Rappard's letter and sent it back to him.

Vincent's mind was now on other things. Preparations for the final demolition of the old tower had begun and he could not resist being there at each stage of its slow transformation. First he painted the auction, held at the gateway, when anything movable was sold. Prosaic things like the slates from the steeple were stacked beside more emotive items such as the wooden crosses from the former church. His painting of the auction avoids any overt comment on what he felt, the activities speak for themselves, only the two birds wheeling in the sky suggest carrion crows. But it was those birds that finally came to dominate his finished view of the tower. He painted it when the steeple had been torn down and only the stump of the building was left. It looks like a squat military fortification set among the old graves. Above it the crows circle, indicating death. They evoke memories of Millet's *Church at Gréville*, and Millais' *Chill October*. The two remaining windows and the doorway of that stump are the three sockets of a skull and this painting, more than the still-life, could be his father's *memento mori*. One can see Vincent standing in the dead man's study staring at the Van der Maaten on the wall, its churchtower black against the horizon. Now his father and the tower were gone. It was doubly the death of religion. The abandoned graves moved him most, the anonymous peasants lying in the very soil that once they had dug.

This intense concentration on death must have worked some catharsis in him, for he had no sooner finished the last painting of the tower than he returned to the living with a new assurance. He began his most fully realised drawings of peasants thus far, drawing them at their labours, their full figures, usually bent double, often seen back or side view as they get as near to the earth as possible. He had conquered Bargue, for although the heavy outline is still there, he now showed a painter's rounded use of light and shade that makes them rock-like.

He had sent *The Potato Eaters* to Paris but all his hopes of recognition remained unfulfilled. He bombarded Theo with suggestions about how to approach his dealer contacts and the way he advised Theo to avoid the anticipated criticisms gives a fascinating insight into his own perception of what he was trying to do:

> *Tell Serret that I should be desperate if my figures were correct, tell him that I do not want to be academically correct, tell him that I mean: If one photographs a digger, he certainly would not be digging then. Tell him that I adore the figures of Michelangelo, though the legs are undoubtedly too long, the hips and the backside too large. Tell him that, for me, Millet and Lhermitte are the real artists for the very reason that they do not paint things as they are, traced in a dry analytical way, but as they – Millet, Lhermitte, Michelangelo – feel them. Tell him that my great longing is to learn to make those very incorrectnesses, those deviations, remodelings, changes in reality, so that they may become, yes, lies if you like – but truer to the literal truth.*

It was all to no avail. Despite the occasional flicker of interest, faithfully reported by Theo, no one was serious enough to buy. How could it be otherwise, when even the more established Impressionists, who at the very least had had a *succès de scandale*, still found it impossible to earn a decent living from their work? Since his first sale of a Pissarro the previous year, Theo had made considerable efforts to sell other Impressionist work, yet in 1885 he was only able to sell one Sisley, a landscape by Monet and a garden by Renoir. Europe was in the grip of a recession, as Durand-Ruel discovered when his exhibitions in London, Rotterdam and Berlin reaped meagre financial rewards. In such an economic climate Durand-Ruel can hardly have been best pleased to find a young Dutch puppy snapping at his heels. Although Theo's sales were no better than his, the Boulevard Montmartre gallery was an increasing threat to Durand-Ruel's pre-eminence as the leading promoter of the avant-garde. The space Theo had been allowed was on the mezzanine floor where there were two quite small rooms whose size and low ceilings made them unsuitable for the heavyweight historical pieces that filled the walls of the main gallery downstairs. As time went on Theo made the rooms a meeting-place for artists and friends, who would use the gallery as a club between five and eight. It was a pleasant port of call for the well-to-do on their way home from their offices in the nearby business district so that Theo was able to attract the curious who would otherwise never even have glanced at new art. Although sales remained rare Theo's personal salon had an atmosphere which Durand-Ruel's often empty showroom could not match.

That summer Theo decided to visit Nuenen and to bring along his friend Andries Bonger. The two young Dutchmen had only taken up with each other the previous December of 1884. After they first met at their expatriate club back in '81, Andries had been too preoccupied with being young in Paris to be bothered with more serious friends. At first he worked seven days a week in a Franco-Dutch commercial agency where not only were his wages derisory but he was also obliged to sleep on a makeshift bed under one of the counters. If he was ill the situation was intolerable, all he could do was walk the streets until he shook off whatever was wrong with him. Coming from a musical family, he had a natural artistic bent and had rapturously visited the Louvre when he first arrived, but he had chosen to ignore that side of Paris in favour of its more notorious entertainments. That was until a combination of long hours, too little to eat and too much night-life had eventually taken their toll. Fortunately for Andries he was introduced to Dr David Gruby, a Hungarian Jew with a heavy accent who had once treated Heine. Gruby's eccentric ways had made him something of a cult figure among the city's artistic set. His cures were notoriously unusual but he does seem to have had advanced ideas about healthy living, as when he told Alexandre Dumas the younger to take a daily walk to the local fruit stall, buy three fresh apples and eat them unpeeled while strolling under the arcades of the Rue de Rivoli. It was perfectly sound advice, though oddly put, and such prescriptions had led to Gruby being threatened with expulsion by the medical authorities. Despite such unconventional ways it was Gruby who instituted the strict regime of rest, diet and exercise which put Andries on his feet again, whereupon the young man became a devoted admirer, ever ready to recommend the seventy-year-old doctor to his friends.

It was in this reformed frame of mind that he had sought out Theo when he saw him again at the Dutch club. They went to the theatre that December and Theo set about introducing his friend to his own enthusiasm for the new art. He found a willing pupil, so much so that Andries would eventually become a serious promoter and collector of contemporary painting, but their friendship was sealed when Andries came to comfort Theo the day he received word of Pastor Theodorus' death. Both men had much in common and it was obviously good for Theo to have someone to counterbalance the eternally demanding Vincent.

When the two men arrived in Nuenen they found the family situation far from tranquil. Although Vincent was living at the studio, there had been considerable ill-feeling over the inheritance since Vincent had walked out of the official inventory of his father's property, a fact duly recorded by the local notary. Pointedly, the visitors received a written invitation to 'call' on Vincent at his lodgings: *before dinner, let us say the afternoon between three and five.*

With any family other than his own, Theo might have found such childish behaviour comic. As it was he knew only too well how Vincent could magnify any imagined slight. He must have felt some trepidation in making the call for he had had no success in selling *The Potato Eaters* and this would undoubtedly be held against him. Happily Vincent and Andries got on well. Vincent was pleased to encounter another enthusiast for modern novels. The three of them talked about art, though it was clear that Vincent had still not fully understood all the things that had been happening in France. His view of Impressionism was thoroughly muddled; he assumed that anything that was not 'academic' in spirit was automatically 'impressionistic'. For the moment their only real point of contact was over the perpetual problems of money; Vincent had overspent on his allowance and Theo was in no mood to raise it. When they parted the younger brother must have been glad the encounter had passed with so little acrimony and that Andries had escaped, as it were, unhurt. One could never predict the outcome of such encounters.

Other visitors were not so fortunate. The distraught Van Rappard, desperate to repair the breach between them, had despatched an artist friend, Willem Wenkebach, as an emissary of peace. His meeting with

Vincent was hilarious. Passionate conversations about art would switch without warning to furious tantrums on Vincent's part whenever he took umbrage at some innocent remark made by the visitor. His head reeling, Wenkebach went with Vincent to Kerssemakers' house in Eindhoven for dinner where a casual remark made Vincent fling his fork down on the table and storm out. Thinking he had seen the last of this odd fellow, Wenkebach was amazed when Vincent turned up at the station the next morning as if nothing had happened and saw him off saying politely: *I hope you'll come again soon.*

In the end, Vincent did make some effort to respond to Van Rappard's overtures but things could never be as before. He wrote to him that September but the letter was formal and stilted and it was the last contact between them. Vincent seldom returned to the past and was so absorbed in what he was doing he had scant time for regrets.

So all in all, Andries Bonger had had a more than reasonable reception and there was no hint that Vincent felt slighted or nervous at his brother having a close friend. Andries left to join his sister Johanna in Amsterdam where Theo would join them a few days later.

Alone again, Vincent was faced with another of his periodic crises, though as with the Begemann incident he was once again entirely innocent. Not long after he completed *The Potato Eaters* one of the sitters, the unmarried De Groot daughter Sien became pregnant. Apart from the curious coincidence of her first name and the obvious fact that he had seen a great deal of her as he worked, there was nothing else to link them. But to the peasants of Nuenen it was all too obvious that it was the weird *schildermenneke*, the little painter fellow, who was guilty. At this point Father van Luijtelaar stepped in and warned his Catholic parishioners not to pose for the Protestant painter. If they needed the money or the gifts he offered then the priest would pay them instead. At a stroke Vincent's main source of models was withdrawn and his home threatened as Schafrat was forced to tell him that he would have to leave as soon as possible.

With no human figures available, he doggedly accepted his own advice to his pupils and took up still-life again: fruit, bottles, a hat, things lying round the cluttered studio he would soon have to vacate. There were the birds' nests from the cupboard, dense bowls of knotted twigs set on branches, the paint again thickly built up as he worked to achieve the effect of tangled foliage. The significance of his painting such things when his own 'nest' was about to disappear cannot be ignored, but it is perhaps more telling that he was eking out the best of the autumn days as a recluse in his studio.

Clearly his time in Nuenen was coming to an end and one sure sign that things were about to change was his renewed interest in city life. He and Kerssemakers spent a day in the gallery in Antwerp where Vincent enthused over the visible brushstrokes in a Frans Hals and that October he and Kerssemakers decided to visit the newly finished Rijksmuseum in Amsterdam. Vincent went ahead, as his friend had family problems, and they met up the following day in the waiting room in the Central Railway Station. When Kerssemakers arrived he found Vincent in his furry outfit sitting near the window sketching city-views impervious to the jostling crowd of mocking people gathered round him. Once in the new museum Vincent positioned himself in front of Rembrandt's *The Jewish Bride* telling Kerssemakers to return at the end of the day as he would certainly find him right there.

And he did indeed spend the entire day staring at that one painting, though as he recorded later, his thoughts were not just on Rembrandt but also Rubens, Velasquez, Delacroix – on colour, colour, colour. From the theories he had been reading and from what he had understood of Theo's reports, there was so much more to the use of colour than he had formerly believed. Just what it was still eluded him, but he knew it was there in the Rembrandt before him.

Back in Nuenen for a final month, he tried subtly but steadily to lighten his palette with a series of autumn landscapes. He even painted the family parsonage as a pleasant home, no longer a haunted house. Perhaps it was a way of saying farewell. His mother would have to leave in the new year, having decided to move to Breda, and there was no longer any reason for him to hang on. He would go to Antwerp and enter the Academy. But as usual he was unable to make a clean break and behaved as if he was going only for a short time. He left all his work and the rest of the clutter of objects at Schafrat's, so that his mother was obliged to clear it all out when she was packing up the presbytery. Years afterwards she was asked what had become of it all and though she wasn't sure, she thought the man who had assisted her with the move might be able to help. One story had a pedlar pushing round a barrow-load of paintings which he sold off for a few coins each; another told of nude life drawings being destroyed at the command of an irate housewife, of canvases used to repair an outhouse or glued to a broken door. Many were lost, though given such treatment a miraculous number were eventually tracked down.

Before Vincent left he had called on Kerssemakers in Eindhoven to give him one of the autumn studies, still wet. Not for the first time, Kerssemakers pointed out that Vincent had forgotten to sign the painting. Vincent said he would probably do so when he came back. He never did, but as he also told Kerssemakers:

> *. . . It is not really necessary. Later on they are bound to recognize my work, and they will surely write about me when I am dead. I will make sure of that if life grants me the time.*

8

1885 — 1888

Dark Green, with Black, with Fiery Red

Antwerp. It was the docks on the banks of the Schelde that caught Vincent's imagination. Of course he saw the sights: the Grote Markt, the Cathedral, the Town Hall, the winding streets of the old town – he drew some of them – but it was the harbour that gripped him most:

> *Flemish sailors, with almost exaggeratedly healthy faces, with broad shoulders, strong and plump, and thoroughly Antwerp folk, eating mussels, or drinking beer, and all this will happen with a lot of noise and bustle – by way of contrast, a tiny figure in black with her little hands pressed against her body comes stealing noiselessly along the grey walls. Framed by raven-black hair – a small oval face, brown? orange yellow? I don't know. For a moment she lifts her eyelids, and looks with a slanting glance out of a pair of jet black eyes. It is a Chinese girl, mysterious, quiet like a mouse – small, bedbug-like in character. What a contrast to that group of Flemish mussel eaters.*

It was over two years since he had been with Sien and despite the Catholic priest's accusations, Nuenen had kept him chaste. There may have been *maisons de tolérance* in Eindhoven, though if there were he made no mention of them in his letters. But the docks in Antwerp were notorious for the pleasures of the flesh and Vincent seized the opportunities offered in the winding lanes and alleyways. It was to be a season of the flesh – the street-walkers took him for a sailor so for once his odd appearance did not count against him. And there was flesh in the art he sought out. Antwerp was Rubens' city and it was not hard to find what he was looking for: *The Assumption of the Holy Virgin* above the high altar in the Gothic splendour of the cathedral of Our Lady had been completed *in situ* by the master. In what was then the Musée de l'Art Ancien there were *The Adoration of the Kings* and *The Triptych of the Merchant Jan Michielsen.* Earthier than Rubens' later nudes, in one a lance pierces Christ's side which gushes blood and in another the Saviour's nose dribbles blood, both grotesquely human and sublime. What was the secret of Rubens' flesh, the pink glow, the roundness of it? Walking to his lodgings in the cold winter rain Vincent pondered the problem and nurtured a growing dissatisfaction with his own work, too grey, too sombre. He was staying in what was then the Rue des Images, a winding nondescript commercial thoroughfare, a good way from the harbour. The room was above a colour-shop which was all there was to recommend it. He tried painting the view across the roofs from the back window but the rather dingy result is as depressing as the reality must have been. Better to hang around the more colourful streets and be taken for a sailor.

While Rubens was the patron saint of Antwerp's cultural past, the doyen of its cultural present was the recently deceased Baron Leys, a painter best known for large-scale episodes from Flemish history, an influence still dominant in the local artistic milieu. Vincent went to see the frescoes on the theme of Christmas in the sixteenth century that Leys had made in 1857, to decorate the dining-room in his house. After Leys' death they were moved to a small room in the Flemish Town Hall leading off the larger chamber Leys had covered with major moments from the city's history. The murals were incomplete at the time he died in 1869 aged only fifty-four, but those he had finished exemplify a lifetime's commitment to the fastidious re-creation of a frozen literary/historical world: *The Duchess of Palma, in troubled times, hands the keys of the city to the Magistrate* being typical of subjects whose every well-pleated robe and precisely embroidered flower were hallmarks of Leys' attention to detail. Although the dining-room frescoes had already noticeably faded, Vincent still found much to admire. Despite Leys' rather plodding patriotism – he had been created a Baron in 1862 – the work was not without a certain sensitivity to problems that currently preoccupied the scruffily dressed Dutchman. Surprisingly, Leys too had admired Rembrandt and Delacroix and had tried, within self-imposed limits, to bring dramatic lighting to his somewhat static compositions. The worst that could be said of the late Baron was that his artistic heritage now lay like a dead weight on the city's cultural life and that his followers lacked even the hint of adventurousness of the original. Sadly, as it turned out for Vincent, some of these 'Leysians' currently held posts at the Academy.

The new term would begin in January. For the moment he puzzled over Rubens and tried to find a blonde model to help work out how the master had done it. He did get girls to sit for him that December and tried to weave threads of unadulterated red into the skin tones as he believed Rubens had done. Coloured outlines could also create sudden movements in a way a black one never could, so he hung around a cheap dance hall and used quick strokes of red in an attempt to capture the fleeting passage of the women, dancing together in a reckless polka. Then one day, not long after his arrival, came a stunning revelation which changed everything. He discovered shops that sold the most entrancing, exotic prints with bold, uncompromising outlines and vivid blocks of pure primary colour; Vincent had belatedly tumbled into the 'Floating World': he had discovered Japan. How he had avoided this revelation for so long is another mystery. When he lived in London the art world there was already gripped by the passion for japonaiserie and Paris had quickly followed. In neither place does he seem to have noticed what other artists had already seized on in their search for fresh ways to approach colour and form. It took the grey, rain-washed alleys of the old port to open his eyes to the mysterious figures in richly patterned kimonos, their raven hair piled high. Originally used as cheap packaging for exports of porcelain, the prints had soon found admirers and imitators from Whistler to Manet. The graphic artist Félix Bracquemond accidentally discovered a volume of Hokusai's work when visiting his printer and he was soon among the first to discriminate between these 'anonymous' wrapping papers and the great works of art some clearly were. From harbour-front stores to grand city-centre galleries, Japanese prints had become an art for all. And in the same fashion, artists took from the prints whatever they were seeking, so that it becomes impossible to speak of their influence as if it were a single definable quality. Some artists admired the unusual pose, the way the grouping of figures ignored the rigid limits of the print, allowing figures to 'bleed' off the edges as if the scene had been 'chopped' out of reality. Some were struck by the cartoon-like simplicity of the prints, others were drawn to a way of life they depicted, the calm meditative world of the tea ceremony, where a correct gesture or a single perfect flower could be contemplated in ethereal silence. Later, Vincent would find many reasons for his admiration, but at first it was the liberating power of colour that made him stop and look. The prints were cheap; he bought some; then he bought more, decorating his dismal room with these curious glimpses of another life – Mount Fuji capped with snow, a geisha preparing tea at a charcoal stove. He returned to the shops often, beginning to appreciate the range of the work. He bought more and suffered for it; although they were cheap he had scarcely any money. Working in colour was cripplingly expensive and with rent to pay he no longer had the whole of Theo's allowance to use for materials. He stopped eating. He would go without food for days on end. Again he dreamt up a plan to sell his work: perhaps a dealer would take a drawing of The Steen, the old citadel, or maybe he could sell some portraits. They were pipe-dreams, of course, though he did try to smarten himself up a bit before he hawked sketches around the galleries. As ever it was Theo who would have to save him:

> *. . . I beg you most kindly but urgently – let one of your creditors wait, i.e. at least 50 fr (they can stand it, do not be afraid), but please do not let it be me . . .*

He was kept going by the hope that attendance at the Academy would in some undefined way solve his problems. He had left a selection of his work for Charles Verlat, the director, to see and was awaiting news of his decision. In the meantime he read an extract from Zola's latest novel *L'Oeuvre* in a magazine and was intrigued by the descriptions of Impressionism, about which he was still considerably confused. Indeed, judging from his comments to Theo after he had read the piece, he seems to have thought that all would be made clear once he had entered the Academy and begun to study under Verlat. He was to be quickly disabused.

The Academy's pretty white studios, in a former Franciscan monastery, were set among trees in a quiet residential area not far from the Town Hall. Vincent was summoned to see the director that January. He arrived on the appointed morning still wearing his fur hat but dressed now in a cattle merchant's blue smock. There was a class of about sixty students, some of them from England, and he found himself an easel and set to work. He had not been able to afford a palette so he had torn a piece of wood from a packing-case. The students were painting two decorously draped male models posed as wrestlers and Vincent joined them, working in his usual rapid-fire manner, dabbing at the canvas he had brought with the inevitably over-loaded brush. Before long the floor about him was covered with blobs of paint. Verlat entered.

Nobody could have been less likely to understand Vincent than Charles Verlat, Director of the Antwerp Academy. At sixty-two he was well set in ways that had never been more than moderately adventurous. As a young man he had gone to Paris and studied under the Couture of *The Romans of the Decadence*, learning to master a dead classicism. It was a joke among the students that he had disgraced himself by painting thirteen spokes on a chariot wheel. Perhaps in reaction to this heinous error and the ridicule it provoked, Verlat had espoused the new realism of Courbet and was thought in Antwerp art circles to be the French master's most fervent disciple. That this was already very old hat was probably of small moment in such a provincial backwater; indeed Verlat had long abandoned any hint of true realism and had taken to producing monumental scenes of stylised peasant life, jolly fellows all, as far removed from Courbet as it was possible to get. For relaxation he produced small humorous works in which monkeys played human roles, his 'monkey business' as he so drolly dubbed them. Not that there was anything especially humorous about Verlat. It was commonly agreed that he was pompous and his rather irritated expression did not belie the judgement. He was the archetypal cultural bureaucrat. In 1879 he had devised the 'General Plan' for instruction at the Academy, one of whose tenets was a moral objection to the study of the female nude – hence the tactfully draped male wrestlers – despite the fact that the naked female form had been at the core of Western art education since the Renaissance. The 'General Plan' decreed that nude plaster casts were acceptable. All of which suggests that Verlat was unlikely to take kindly to anyone questioning his orders.

Verlat glared at Vincent's effort, demanded to know who he was, then ordered him to go to the drawing class. Flushed with embarrassment and anger, Vincent gathered up his brushes and makeshift palette and disappeared behind the wooden partition which divided the two schools. His sudden dishevelled appearance in the crowded drawing school caused a commotion greater than usual as he knelt and began to unroll his drawings to show them to Eugeen Siberdt, the drawing master. So bizarre was his appearance and so strange the work, that there was soon an unruly milling crowd gathered about him, laughing and joking. The students, always too many for the space available, were frequently boisterous, which was why Piet van Havermaet, a retired policeman, was on hand to keep order. This time he failed completely.

Siberdt the drawing master was no better than Verlat. Although he had visited The Hague and was still only thirty-five, he had remained immured against the art of the open air. A period of making historical studies under Leys had gradually given way to portrait painting and on top of his salary at the Academy he made a comfortable living as an official portraitist. He too was stuffy, but worse was the fact that Van Havermaet, the ex-policeman, often stood in as an instructor when Siberdt was otherwise occupied. The verdict, that Vincent should not paint, was unanimous. In their view, he was unprepared for the task. Drawing from antique casts was what he needed. Despite the fact that he had resisted such advice from Mauve, whom he admired, Vincent made the best of it, though as he was desperate to learn to master the human figure in colour it was a curiously punishing regime to have accepted. It was also painful to find himself the butt of his fellow students' savage humour and he withdrew into himself, hoping to be left alone to attack his drawings with all his usual intensity. Fortunately, one or two of the members of the drawing class were less childish. Horace Livens, a young Englishman who had come from Croydon Art College, had London in common with him and seemed to find Vincent fascinating. Livens, or Levens as his name is sometimes spelled, even painted Vincent's portrait, though he reveals a distinctly haggard old man for someone who was only thirty-two. Not that Vincent had found another rebellious spirit. All his life Livens acknowledged a debt of gratitude to Verlat's instruction and admitted without regret that his work continued to show traces of the influence of Baron Leys. Vincent advised the young man to go to Paris, which indicates the way his own thoughts were turning, and Livens eventually followed his advice before returning to London to assume a rather nondescript career as a painter of moderately impressionistic street scenes and harbours, which had a slight success in Edwardian England. Like Verlat, he had a side-line in animal paintings though he preferred farmyard fowl to dressed-up monkeys.

Of the Belgian students, Victor Hageman was the most sympathetic. In later years he went on to be a painter and engraver of pictures which captured the life of the docks with their traditional nautical handicrafts. As he often featured poor immigrants and characters from the nearby Jewish quarter, one imagines Vincent would have thoroughly approved of his efforts. Like Livens, Hageman too enjoyed a brief period of success when his work appeared in major exhibitions after the turn of the century. Before he died in 1928 he wrote down his impressions of the fiery creature who had suddenly burst into that sleepy backwater.

The heart of the problem was that Vincent knew he had passed beyond what Verlat and the others had to offer. Verlat's plan was inevitably based on acceptable French lines and these had been effectively set out by Gérôme and Bargue in their drawing course. But Vincent was by then in the process of growing out of a system of drawing which placed total emphasis on outline. The drawing classes, with students seated around the antique casts, were expected to approach the creation of volume by breaking the object down into geometric shapes which were then rounded out. It was the last triumph of the method of the followers of Ingres, the ultimate classicism that saw colour as the mere in-fill to line. Yet Vincent was now gripped by its opposite as exemplified by Rubens and Delacroix, painters who seemed to him to round out the flesh of their figures by working from the inside outwards. He did not object to drawing casts, indeed he was beginning to see great potential in this method of study. It was how he was asked to do it that galled him, especially when he saw the results in the painting classes where any attempt at flesh appeared *painfully flat*.

It was all so different from what he had imagined. He did see some point in the casts, yet he still longed to try painting the human body, something forbidden by Verlat. Then he learned that some students got round the interdiction by forming their own drawing clubs where they joined together to hire a model and share the cost of a few beers. He joined two of these clubs for evening sessions, some of which were held in the old 'Degulden Winkal' (the Shop of the Gold Merchant's), in the beautiful setting of the Grote Markt. One of the clubs had managed to hire a tutor, Frans Vinck, though he was little better than the teachers at the Academy. He was barely a few years younger than Verlat and was a fanatical imitator of Baron Leys without any of the sensibility of the master. Vinck's best-known work, *The Confederates Before Margaret of Palma*, testifies to hours of mind-numbing toil reproducing details of embroidery and wall decoration with a pernickety verisimilitude rendered pointless by the overall dullness of the scene. Nevertheless the clubs had live models and Vincent's sketchbook of the time reveals his ability to master traditional figure-drawing, which testifies to a degree of willingness to do as he was told when he believed it worthwhile.

At the Academy, however, he found it hard to conform. His teachers were becoming increasingly irritated with his way of attacking the paper with crayon or chalk, intent on rounding out the figure before him. Worse still, another student was beginning to imitate his method. Vincent tried putting on a show of false humility in order to ease the growing tension, for he was in no fit state to do battle with his teachers. He was simply too weak and was beginning to pay the price for having pushed himself to the limits of physical endurance. Still starving himself to buy materials, he often felt faint, a symptom of his stomach's reaction to such reckless treatment. But there were other, more worrying problems. His teeth hurt badly and when he decided he had to deal with them, the dentist was merciless. About ten were rotten and out they came, at a crippling cost of fifty francs. But it was when he turned to a doctor that he discovered just what toll his season of the flesh had taken. He had syphilis and was sent to a new hospital near his lodgings to be given the limited treatment available at the time. The disease was incurable but the symptoms could be diminished with chemical baths. He looked ten years older than his age and a morbid fascination with this transformation led him to paint a self-portrait, the cheeks more sunken, the red beard fuller to hide the effects of the missing front teeth.

Much of his behaviour, his increasing bad temper and grumpiness, can obviously be attributed to his physical condition and it could only be a matter of time before something pushed him over the edge. The crisis came when the class at the Academy was asked to draw a plaster cast of the Vénus de Milo. Vincent complied after his own fashion, creating an earthy wide-hipped mother-figure, more a naked Flemish housewife than a classical goddess. The drawing was too much for Siberdt who peered at the offending item through his pince-nez, seized it from the easel and tore it up. Vincent exploded, shouting that Siberdt did not know what a woman was, that she *must have hips, buttocks, a pelvis in which she can carry a baby.*

According to Hageman's recollection of the encounter, that was the end of Vincent at the Academy. But this must have been his later dramatisation of an admittedly theatrical moment, the perfect end to an act with Vincent storming off stage. The truth was not so tidy. Vincent seems to have avoided his teachers from then on, but contrived to slip into the cast-room from time to time to work on his own. Either way, that moment of crisis marked the end of his hopes for any real help from the Academy; and it was very nearly the end of his determination to be an artist, for at the same time there was for him a sudden resurrection of the past. The Belgian newspapers were full of the appalling events in the south, where the miners of the Borinage were in revolt at last. Early in 1886 political agitation spread to the coalfields. The Socialists were demanding an increase in salaries along with the abolition of the much abused privilege, inevitably confined to the well-off, of buying boys out of military service. They also wanted universal suffrage. The Government responded with force. In March a general strike spread through the Borinage and this time there was violence, the Government armed the police and called up the civil guard. The hated blacklegs were ordered down the pits and miners were sent to prison for begging for food and drink for their families. The right-wing Catholic Press demanded that a law forbidding the display of the red flag be enforced. At the end of the year a commission was set up to investigate the wages paid to the miners, its findings contested at every step by the mine owners. The conclusion, that wages had actually been decreasing in recent years, led nowhere. There were one hundred and twenty deaths down the mines in 1886 alone.

As he read the newspapers, Vincent could see clearly the suffering that lay behind the statistics; according to one report a man had been condemned to prison for begging a butcher to give him meat for his family. Surely something could be done? He considered returning to throw in his lot with the miners, sacrificing himself, serving them again. At such odds with the Academy he was tempted by a clear aim in life, something unequivocally positive. It was his weakest moment, yet he must have known in his heart it could never be. That stage in his life was over; without a belief in God to sustain him what could he hope to achieve there?

At first tentatively, then with increasing persistence, he began to suggest to Theo that he might come to Paris. He was ill, coughing up grey phlegm, hungry and disillusioned. Paris was the only solution. He knew he would have a hard task persuading his brother to pay for his fare and tried to convince him that Paris was essential for his studies. Clutching at any straw he recalled the name of Cormon whose atelier he had heard about from other Dutch painters. He began to tell Theo how much he wanted, needed to get to Cormon's, the one place where he would find the sort of sympathetic advice so sadly lacking in Antwerp.

For once Theo adamantly refused to be cajoled or bullied. He was in no mood to contemplate the arrival of his difficult sibling. He may resolutely have stood by Vincent and encouraged him but he did have his doubts. He once told a friend, the Dutch painter Just Havelaar: "I should not be surprised if my brother were one of the great geniuses and will one day be compared to someone like Beethoven." But on another occasion he let it be known that he thought Vincent's was only a moderate talent. It is easy to see why he swung between the two opinions when one considers how wildly Vincent's work varied at the time. Even his comments on what he was doing must have seemed ridiculously provincial to the metropolitan Theo. His inability to come to a basic comprehension of what Impressionism meant when it was already being supplanted by newer schools must have irritated his brother.

But any opinions Theo may have held of Vincent's talent were not the primary reason why he tried to deflect him from coming to Paris. Theo knew only too well what the close proximity of that unpredictable character would mean to him. He had enough problems as it was. His apartment in the Rue Laval was tiny, and his mistress, known to posterity as 'S', was becoming increasingly difficult. To introduce Vincent into this already claustrophobic ménage was to invite trouble. He continued to resist.

Unfortunately, as Theo realised, his case was weakened by his inability to sell Vincent's work. It was the cause of considerable rancour on the artist's part and Theo knew that if he could only sell one or two pictures, he could more easily persuade Vincent that all was going well, and that there was no need for him to leave Belgium. Swallowing his pride, Theo contacted a friend and rival dealer Alphonse Portier to see whether he might be able to help.

Portier lived not far away, higher up the slopes of Montmartre. He was a retired cloth importer who had made a small fortune in the Peruvian boom of the late fifties and had then indulged his passion for art by buying into a colour and artists' materials business. When this had achieved the aim of bringing him into contact with several painters, he decided to retire and become a part-time agent-cum-dealer. Like Theo, his taste was for the new, and poor old Durand-Ruel, who was still suffering for having been the first to support the Impressionists, found himself with yet another rival.

Portier was a kindly soul and agreed to take some of Vincent's work including a lithograph of *The Potato Eaters*, about which he was enthusiastic, as Theo instantly reported back to Vincent. But Portier too got nowhere. It was hard enough to sell the infinitely more accessible Pissarro. Portier's method was to take round a selection of his stock to the homes of the small circle of collectors he cultivated but in Vincent's case, no persuasion on the dealer's part could induce them to hand over even quite small sums of money for what they saw as mere gaucheries. Posterity has been vouchsafed awesome photographs in which dealers like Portier and Durand-Ruel can be seen, seated in their living-rooms, surrounded from floor to ceiling with what are now priceless canvases which they found impossible to off-load for the equivalent of a week's lodging in a moderate hotel.

There was nothing more that Theo could do. He took comfort from Vincent's latest letter which seemed to suggest that he intended to spend the summer in Brabant before returning to Antwerp and the Academy again. Theo could relax, it was early March and the weather was improving; the danger had receded. Then one morning he arrived at work to find a messenger with a note for him. The man had been paid to bring it from the nearby Gare du Nord. As soon as Theo saw the scribbled black crayon he knew that what he had dreaded had happened.

> *My dear Theo,*
> *Do not be cross with me for having come all at once like this; I have thought about it so much, and I believe that in this way we shall save time. Shall be at the Louvre from midday on or sooner if you like.*
>
> *Please let me know at what time you could come to the Salle Carrée. As for the expenses, I tell you again, this comes to the same thing. I have some money left, of course, and I want to speak to you before I spend any of it. We'll fix things up, you'll see.*
>
> *So, come as soon as possible.*
>
> *I shake your hand.*
>
> *Ever yours, Vincent*

Theo obeyed the summons.

It was no mere whim that led Vincent to propose what he called the 'Salle' Carrée as the rendezvous for this, to Theo, unwelcome encounter. The Salon Carré, a large cubic space, with an overbearing Baroque ceiling, was at the core of the relatively small cluster of galleries, courts and rooms which then housed the museum's collection of old masters.

Work by favoured living artists were displayed in the Luxembourg. The Salon Carré had at one time housed the annual Salon and on study days it was almost a national studio, with visitors obliged to negotiate the complex mobile platforms which supported the vast canvases needed for the copying of Veronese's *Marriage of Cana* or one of the other outsize tableaux which challenged each other across the cluttered room. For Vincent the fact that Delacroix hung in the neighbouring Gallery was the ultimate magnet, enabling him at last to test the theories he had been studying against the reality. It was something to distract him as he nervously awaited his brother's appearance. At least he could soothe his nerves with the thought that this canny choice of meeting place made it unlikely Theo would express his feelings other than gently.

There is no record of what passed between them. Indeed after Vincent's note from the station all correspondence inevitably dries up, with the frustrating result that Vincent's time in Paris is the least documented section of his career as an artist. Fortunately, other sources of information, mainly from the astonishing range of people he met over the following two years, go some way towards filling the gap.

Whatever was or was not whispered in the sepulchral confines of the 'Salle' Carrée, there was no escaping the fact that Vincent had come and would have to be taken care of, at least for the immediate future.

Their arrival at Theo's bachelor flat at 25 rue Laval, a narrow side-street below the Boulevard de Clichy, must have gone some way to explain to Vincent his younger brother's reluctance to have him to stay. It was simply too small. He was certainly not going to be able to work there without considerable inconvenience to both of them. Confronted with this harsh reality, he hesitated, for once deprived of his usual single-minded energy.

When he did begin to paint some weeks later, his efforts were tentative. A self-portrait, with a less than confident stare, shows him wearing a rather pompous black hat and overcoat as if to proclaim that the rustic had now become a city-dweller. Bowls of flowers were about all that could be tackled within the confines of the tiny apartment but Vincent set to with a resurgent enthusiasm. He produced over thirty different vases of flowers in that year alone and there were even some studies of sunflowers, despite their awkward size. A cursory glance at these richly layered and coloured bouquets shows that he and Theo must have been to Joseph Delarebeyrette's shop in the Rue de Provence, by then a veritable museum dedicated to Adolphe Monticelli.

Only three years before, Delarebeyrette had learned that far from dying in the Commune Monticelli had escaped the carnage and made his way back to his native Marseilles where he now lived and worked. The dealer immediately set off to see him and had been delighted to find that his style was if anything more flamboyant than ever. Soon new works were on their way to Paris, though they were still hard to sell. French collectors preferred Monticelli's style of the 1860s, when he'd painted Fêtes Champêtres in an almost parody Rococo manner, that had supported him in his exile's life in Paris. There was, however, an unexplained market for Monticelli across the Channel, where the occasional British collector would take a chance on the later works.

The effect of Vincent's visits to the Rue de Provence was immediate: a painting like *Flowers and Sunflowers* is almost a pastiche of a Monticelli, with the same centrally placed vase made solid by thick layers of pigment and the same vibrantly coloured flowers whose petals are 'sculpted' with paint. Whatever Delarebeyrette could tell him about the painter only quickened Vincent's interest, creating an image of a lusty, devil-may-care peasant with a passion for gypsy music, who would stay up all night painting by candle-light and go into ecstasies over the play of light on a flower. Not only did Vincent imitate Monticelli's art, he also seized upon any details of the man's life he could discover and began to consider heading south to join him. What he and Theo did not know was that a somewhat dissolute existence had led to Monticelli's second stroke in 1884 so that the irascible old man had to be shadowed by members of his family lest he suffer a sudden collapse during his daily walk. Then, almost at the same moment that Vincent was delving into the treasure-house of his work, Monticelli died at the age of sixty-one. The local obituaries rather tartly chose to praise the early works and subsequent history has done little to bring his later art to a wider public. Monticelli's absolute individuality and his abstention from any school or promotional system has meant his exclusion from the potted summaries of 'contemporary' art, though he has always had his staunch defenders. Towards the end of 1886 a Scottish dealer, Alexander Reid, arrived for a short stint at Goupil's, intending to buy works by Monticelli for his family's gallery in Glasgow. He shared a room with Vincent and gave him a Monticelli while Vincent repaid him by twice painting his portrait. Eventually they fell out, supposedly over Reid's having a love affair, but the rift was more likely due to the fact that Theo and Vincent had by then started to collect Monticelli's work and were irritated to find they were harbouring a rival.

For Vincent, Monticelli's rich colour, his lack of any restraint other than that of his own inner vision, allied to Vincent's growing belief that each of them was isolated and misunderstood, conspired to make him one of the key ingredients in the rich mix of those Paris years. As time went by Vincent's feelings about him increased. He widened his knowledge of the man's range, for as well as the flowers there were Provençal landscapes and marine paintings of the coast near Les Saintes-Maries-de-la-Mer in the Camargue. When he eventually saw Monticelli's portrait Vincent rather fancied himself stepping out *with an enormous yellow hat, a black velvet jacket, white trousers, yellow gloves, a bamboo cane and with a grand southern air.*

But while Vincent fantasised, Theo worried. The apartment was too small even for flower painting. What was particularly irritating was that despite his pressing demands from Antwerp, when he had claimed that he urgently needed to study at Cormon's atelier, Vincent now showed no inclination to do so. Evidently it was Paris he had wanted and having come was content to wait and see what new sensations the city would offer.

His arrival virtually coincided with the final publication of Zola's *L'Oeuvre*. Those in the know saw the novel as a sign that Impressionism in its purest form had run its course. There was evidence to support this view in May when the eighth and final Impressionist exhibition turned out to be largely the work of Pissarro and the second wave of younger artists to whom he was now committed. Pissarro had tracked down Georges Seurat a year after that first Salon des Indépendants and had been as overwhelmed by Seurat's new work as he had originally been by Monet's Impressionism. It was Pissarro who insisted that Seurat and Signac exhibit with the Impressionists even though it meant that most of the older members would decline to participate. When he had begun organising the exhibition two years earlier, the old guard were not best pleased at the admission of such youngsters to their ranks. As Pissarro wrote to his son Lucien:

> Yesterday I had a violent run-in with M. Eugène Manet on the subject of Seurat and Signac. The latter was present, as was Guillaumin. You may be sure I rated Manet roundly. – Which will not please Renoir. – But anyhow, this is the point, I explained to M. Manet, who

> probably didn't understand anything I said, that Seurat has something new to contribute which these gentlemen, despite their talent, are unable to appreciate, that I am personally convinced of the progressive character of his art and certain that in time it will yield extraordinary results . . .

Pissarro's justification came when Seurat dominated the Eighth Exhibition with his overwhelming canvas *Sunday Afternoon on the Island of the Grande Jatte*, a work so clearly different from anything the Impressionists had attempted that it at once became the *cause célèbre* of the Paris art season. Gauguin had nineteen paintings on show, but as these were still firmly within the Impressionist camp they failed to attract the same attention as the lone Seurat, whose method was uncompromisingly revolutionary. Whereas Monet and Renoir had attempted to capture the flickering impermanence of the moment, that hazy imprecision which is the sudden fall of light on the changing world, Seurat had approached the problem by an almost diametrically opposite route. His figures, calmly, classically posed on their Sunday outing beside the Seine are not caught by thick flickering brushstrokes but by the patient building up of tiny dots of colour: the moment no longer fleeting and ephemeral but made permanent, eternal. However, it was in his choice of colours that Seurat's triumph lay, for he had indeed succeeded in creating the still, luminous quality of a limpid sunny afternoon, despite the plodding nature of his method.

Such contradictions were all of a piece with the young man himself. The son of a suburban functionary, he had worked his way methodically through the education system from local *Lycée* to municipal art school then on to the Beaux-Arts, quietly plotting out his route. He was a difficult character, hard to get on with and dedicated. He saw what the Impressionists had done with colour but decided it was too sloppy for him. Monet had said: "We paint just as birds sing", but this was too intuitive for Seurat who felt that with time and application one ought to be able to define the rules which underpin the making of a painting. His stance was hardly surprising when the nineteenth-century faith in scientific progress was yet to be compromised by technological failure; and if new inventions could make the world a better place, why should this approach not apply to the arts?

Given his desire to formalise the making of a painting it was inevitable that Seurat would immerse himself in the study of colour to an ever greater degree than his immediate forebears. Like them he began with Chevreul, then, just as Vincent had done, he followed the route from Delacroix to the Impressionists. But where they had looked to colour theory to help render nature more vividly, Seurat began to discern other messages in the many studies he applied himself to. At the Beaux Arts he had attended lectures by David Sutter who introduced the young man to the connection between painting and music. As Sutter put it, "There are colourists' eyes as there are tenor voices." It seemed to relate to what Chevreul had called 'abstractions' as opposed to 'the image of the concrete'. The American artist James McNeill Whistler had already proposed the idea that a painting could be thought of not as a landscape or a portrait but as a nocturne or a symphony and it is interesting to recall that Vincent had tried, albeit without success, to discover the connections between colour and music with his piano lessons in Eindhoven. Significantly, the 1880s in France saw a burgeoning interest in the once despised Wagner as writers and artists moved further from the realism of the previous generation and came to admire what they saw as the marriage of the mythological and the abstract in Wagner's music.

Seurat found more evidence of these ideas in 1885, when Charles Henry published *A Scientific Aesthetic* which proposed a connection between colour and the evocation of mood or emotion. According to Henry, vivid colours such as red or yellow produce feelings of happiness where the more sombre colours such as blue lead towards sorrow or gloom. From then on Seurat's course was set, his aim, the use of scientific colour theory, especially the optical mixing of pure colour applied direct to the canvas, to create an art which would be a 'synthesis' – a word much in evidence from then on – of nature and the artist's remaking of it as he attempted to induce sensations or emotions through the eye of the beholder.

It was Seurat's willingness to concern himself with scientific and mathematical research into colour and optics, as well as the relatively new study of aesthetics, that makes him so crucial an influence on the work of his contemporaries, especially Vincent. While others may not have had the inclination for such detailed investigations, they would nevertheless acquire a second-hand awareness of them from Seurat's art. Any artist who stood spellbound before the *Grande Jatte* and who subsequently returned to his studio to use some of the techniques would unwittingly find that he was in effect joining a movement in artistic thinking that had been growing over the fifty or so years since Chevreul began publishing.

In the simplest terms, and it must be emphasised that it was only in the most elementary ways that many artists recognised these developments, the various theorists had been proposing an art in which the abstract qualities of a work were seen as more important than the motifs depicted.

When they met at the time of the first Indépendants, Seurat and Signac had recognised that they were both heading along roughly the same route. Seurat was inevitably the theorist and the younger Signac chose to defer to him but it would be wrong to assume a master/pupil relationship. Signac had a better awareness of how colour could create effects of light, which he had learned from studying the works of Pissarro, and Seurat owed much to his advice, as witness the limpid, light-dappled effects in the *Grande Jatte*.

Work aside they could not have been more different. While both were children of the city's outer limits, Seurat's bourgeois suburban upbringing had little in common with Signac's childhood in Pigalle. Signac's father was a draughtsman, so the boy had grown up on the fringes of the artistic community with a free run of the neighbourhood studios where the solid, reliable history painters were known by their 'period' with characters like Roybet 'the Musketeer' and Luminais 'the Merovingian'. As a student at the local Collège Rolin, Signac had hung around the nearby cafés and galleries, looking incongruous in his high-collared, brass-buttoned, military-style tunic. Despite this school outfit and his evident youth he would listen in to the conversations in the artists' supply shops and even as a teenager had already discovered the Impressionists and understood what it was they were trying to do. As a young man he got to know Henri Rivière of the Chat Noir which ultimately brought him into contact with Theo. Signac's appearance said it all: he looked like a cheeky urchin, clean-shaven with a flat hat pushed to the back of his head. When he met Seurat in 1884 the contrast was striking, for his new friend hid tall good looks behind a straggly beard and sober dress which made him look preternaturally old. Signac was open and outgoing, Seurat so secretive it was only a week before his death at the age of thirty-one that his mother learned that he had a mistress and a one-year-old son. At least Signac talked to people about things other than work. For Seurat there was nothing else worth opening one's mouth about.

When the two young men first began to compare ideas it was inevitable that Seurat would insist they take a thoroughly methodical approach to the task ahead. Impossible as it was to believe, Chevreul was still alive, and Signac was duly dispatched to question the 98-year-old scientist on some of the implications of his writings. Could M. Chevreul explain what he meant by the division of light? Signac was obliged to repeat the question several times but in the end all the old man could suggest was that he should go and talk to his old friend Ingres. As Ingres had been dead for twenty years and had not been particularly interested in colour theory anyway, it was clear to the two young men that they would have to work out their own solutions.

Seurat's own method as used in the *Grande Jatte* was a rigid emphasis on the optical mixing of colour, the essentially simple principle that, instead of mixing a colour on the palette before applying it, two or more pure colours could be juxtaposed on the canvas so that at a certain distance the eye of the spectator would mix them. Of course many had tried a partial application of this technique, but even the Impressionists had fought shy of doing more than highlighting certain passages in a work in this way. Seurat, with all the conviction of a convert, applied it rigorously. His *Sunday Afternoon on the Island of the Grande Jatte* was the faithful result of that conviction. Seen close to, there were myriad dots of pure colour, a kaleidoscope; stand back and there was a pellucid harmonious scene. Such a studio-based work may seem far removed from the old war-horses' naturalism and realism with their insistence on *plein-air* painting and yet nothing could better capture the feeling of static heat, the windless stillness of a hot summer's afternoon, than the *Grande Jatte*. If that seeming contradiction is still intriguing today, one must imagine its effect on those like Vincent who wandered into the exhibition in the upstairs rooms of the famous Maison Dorée restaurant in the Rue Lafitte to experience it for the first time. Inevitably the critics were lavish in their abuse, though one, Félix Fénéon, did try to counter the savagery with a brochure called *The Impressionists* which became in effect a rejection of the old guard and a defence of what he was already referring to as 'Divisionism'. Fénéon clearly explained Seurat's technique: "Take the grass: most of the brushstrokes give the local value of the grass; others, orange in tone, are scattered here and there to stand for the almost imperceptible action of the sun . . ." And he concluded: "This is a kind of painting where cheating is impossible and 'stylish handling' quite pointless. There is no room in it for the bravura piece. The hand may go numb, but the eye must remain agile, learned and perspicacious."

Seurat's fanatical dedication to the application of his scientific principles – while working on the *Grande Jatte* he had refused to talk to other artists painting by the river – gave him a dangerously appealing quality for those lacking similar strong convictions. Pissarro had fallen under his spell almost as soon as he discovered the young man's work and Lucien, his son, had followed suit. Seurat and Signac were flattered to have the older, more experienced painter on their side and Camille Pissarro was at least able to help them with his knowledge of how paints faded and changed after drying. That aside, the help was largely one-sided and Pissarro, although still turning out his gentle ethereal landscapes, now did so in the dotted Divisionist manner. The older Impressionists despised his change of heart and when he found it impossible to sell anything in the new technique his long-suffering, though far from silent, wife Julie decided that he had done it just to spite her. So fraught had the once harmonious world of the Impressionists become that when Julie trudged out to Zola's house at Médan, her one-year-old daughter in tow, to beg for financial help, she was humiliatingly refused entry or as much as a glass of water before being sent on her way.

For Vincent, there was no conflict. Impressionism and Divisionism had arrived as one, albeit initially confusing, package in the person of Pissarro. In the two months since he had been in Paris Vincent had at last seen for himself what Impressionism really was and had simultaneously witnessed an altogether different approach. It was a fortunate coincidence, for he was made aware from the beginning that there was no single, unique solution to be found.

That June, Theo managed to find an apartment in the block at 54 rue Lepic where Portier lived. The street was far from being one of the narrow twisting alleys that characterised 'village' Montmartre; it had been driven through the old shambles at the express command of the first Napoleon as part of a plan to sweep away the insanitary slums. The scheme foundered, and after his fall the Rue L'Empereur became the altogether humbler Lepic. It was broad, however, and as such hosted the local market. Where it first climbed away from the Place Blanche and the nearby Moulin Rouge on the Boulevard de Clichy, Lepic was lined with open-fronted butchers', greengrocers' and bakers' shops, often overhung by heavy baroque awnings which gave them a theatrical appearance appropriate to a *quartier* dedicated to drama and fantasy. Higher up, it was crossed by the Rue des Abbesses, a memory of Montmartre's past as a place of pilgrimage, after which Lepic began to turn and narrow and generally quieten down as it rose in an inverted question mark below the summit of the Butte. Number 54, on the right, was just where the curve grew steeper. The block looked over Paris though Vincent preferred the view from his room at the back, where he could see through a gap in the houses opposite to the fast disappearing countryside of Clichy and St Ouen. In his first months he had made some attempt to come to terms with the great city, walking down to the centre and painting a view of the Louvre and an avenue of trees in the Luxembourg gardens, but now he abandoned such efforts and literally turned his back on it. He became a true denizen of the 'hill of martyrs' with his world limited to the south by the streets just below the Boulevard de Clichy where the colour merchants were situated and to the north by the stretch of riverbank where the Seine unexpectedly twists back on itself to create those large islands, among which was the Grande Jatte, so beloved of Sunday trippers and *plein-air* artists.

Fiacres and horse-buses clattered up the ever-steeper Rue Lepic heading for the summit of the Butte, past the surviving windmills and shuttered drinking dens, on to the vast building site where the aggressively white outer walls of the new basilica of the Sacré-Coeur were starting to be all too visible above the jumble of houses, much to the disgust of the local inhabitants who well knew that the building was intended as an act of atonement for the sins of the godless Commune in which many of them had participated. How they had laughed when Abadie, the nonentity picked as architect, nearly despaired on discovering that the foundations were riddled with old mine-workings. Unfortunately, so the locals reckoned, he had been prevailed upon to persist so that now, rising on piles driven forty metres deep, the main walls were almost finished. To the artists and poets of the Butte it was clearly going to be a mediocre affair and the best thing to do was to ignore it. Though as the scaffolding grew ever higher, it became clear that this would be difficult, and that the peculiar nipple-like domes of the basilica would eventually loom over the remotest corners where haunts like the one-time Cabaret des Assassins, now the Lapin Agile, had formerly retained an air of furtive isolation.

A Montmartrois was essentially anarchic in his politics and general outlook, an attitude shared by most of the immigrant artists fleeing the bourgeois respectability of Haussmann's grand boulevards. The Rue Lepic straddled the two worlds and number 54 was typical of the new apartment blocks of the period: five storeys with a recessed attic floor, the first four with tall windows, their shutters fastened back against the white-washed walls. Such blocks provided the staple features of city life, not least of which were the fearsome concierges, true heirs to the harridans who had rushed down from Montmartre to set fire to the Tuileries and the Hôtel de Ville in the last hours of the Commune – each one encumbered with a pug-faced emaciated daughter longing to get into the *corps de ballet* and be immortalised by Degas.

All that concerned the two brothers was that the apartment was bigger, they had their own rooms and there was a place for Vincent to work. Portier was a sympathetic neighbour and was willing to help Vincent meet his contacts in the art world. He introduced him to Pissarro's son Lucien, who, although ten years younger, was also starting out as a painter. Lucien, like his father, was fascinated by Impressionism while at the same time being drawn to the newer ideas of Seurat. For Vincent it was time to apply some of these discoveries and where better than the surrounding neighbourhood which offered a choice of either city or countryside. He had only to leave the apartment block and climb further round the Rue Lepic to come to one of the three surviving windmills, the Moulin Debray, sometimes called Le Blute-Fin, which was topped by a platform or belvedere from which visitors could look down on all sides of the hill. One of the great spectacles was to watch the layers of morning mist lift away to unveil Haussmann's new city below. The following year it was possible to follow the progress of the building work on the site facing the Trocadéro Palace where Theo had made his name and where preparations for the 1889 Universal Exhibition were moving apace. Remorselessly, the steel cat's-cradle of the four great legs of a strange tower would rise beyond the height of the surrounding blocks – yet another brainchild of Gustave Eiffel, fresh from his triumphant realisation of the Statue of Liberty which had gripped Parisians for a brief season as it too towered above their houses before being taken down and shipped in sections to New York. Although Eiffel's new tower would be the tallest construction in Europe, Vincent continued to prefer the opposite view from the belvedere, north-west to where the light industrial areas of Asnières and Clichy could still be construed as open country.

Immediately below the windmill, allotments and market gardens clung tenaciously to the descending slopes, again bringing some feel of the countryside. Once more, Vincent found himself in that curious hinterland between urban sprawl and imperilled nature. The Impressionists had taken the Paris of Baron Haussmann with its wide boulevards and more recent great railway termini as subjects for their art. Now Vincent extended this urban vision into scenes of the fringe world near his new home, where scrubland and small-holdings were threatened by factory chimneys and railway shunting yards.

Initially, the ochres, browns and blacks of Holland are still apparent. This was not inappropriate, for he had not yet fully absorbed the life his new home offered and seems to have looked on this hill of windmills as if it had been transplanted from Holland. There is something rather sanitised about his Montmartre. He ignored the '*maquis*', the shanty town on the southern slope of the Butte. A squalid slum of planks and sheet iron, much of it pilfered, it was home to a motley crew of the desperately poor, failed bohemians, drunks and petty criminals who had fallen outside the final limits of society. There was nothing romantic about the *maquis*: it was a fetid dump where rag-clad urchins played among the refuse and wild brambles. In all his paintings of the Butte, Vincent neatly tidies up crude reality, as if he had enough to do to master the problems of colour without embracing his earlier social concerns.

It was when he was returning from one of his painting sorties that he first met the older Pissarro, who was walking down the Rue Lepic with his son Lucien. Vincent was still wearing his blue cattle-merchant's smock, though his bedraggled appearance would hardly have mattered to the elderly Pissarro, himself a devotee of the bohemian floppy hat and baggy clothing. Vincent was overjoyed at the opportunity to meet the artist of whom his brother had spoken so highly, some of whose works he had studied in the apartment. Ignoring the laughter of the other passers-by Vincent hastened to arrange his canvases along a wall and began to show his studies to the bearded old man who was as ever delighted to give advice and encouragement.

Vincent was extremely fortunate in the critics he approached; had he consulted any of the 'grander' Impressionists such as Degas, they might have destroyed his confidence or at least forcefully pointed him in directions that might have blunted his powers. As it was, those members of the group with whom he was able to talk freely were sympathetic to his fumbling attempts to absorb the confusing tendencies and ideas which made up the Paris art world of 1886. In that first year there was Pissarro, who was despite everything a disciple of Father Millet, and in the following year there would be Armand Guillaumin, whose robust version of Impressionism had much in common with what Vincent was aiming for himself.

During the summer of 1886, Vincent was still finding his way through the maze; he dedicated a still-life with apples to Lucien and was given a collection of wood engravings in exchange. To Horace Livens at the Academy in Antwerp he wrote about how he was settling in and how he hoped to be able to make more exchanges with other artists. He told Livens about his flower painting and of his attempts to

> *. . . render intense colour and not a grey harmony . . . I lately did two heads which I dare say are better in light and colour than those I did before.*
>
> *So as we said at the time: in colour seeking life the true drawing is modelling with colour.*
>
> *I did a dozen landscapes too, frankly green, frankly blue. And so I am struggling for life and progress in art.*

He makes it clear that what he is doing is not exactly like the Impressionists, which indicates his continuing struggle with the habits of the past. One problem, he told Livens, was again the lack of money to pay for models and the only solution to that was to enter the atelier of an established artist where, for a relatively small fee, he would be able to draw from the nude and also have his efforts criticised by a master. This thought led him back to his first plan to go to Cormon's studio in the nearby Boulevard de Clichy. In addition there was now another, more pressing reason why Vincent needed to work away from the apartment: as Theo's friend Andries Bonger was quick to notice, the younger brother was beginning to show signs of strain. A troublesome mistress was one thing, but a brother who never tidied his things, who was perpetually argumentative and who veered between intransigent demands and wheedling dependence made the tension unbearable. It was all too much. Andries wrote to his parents in Holland: "Theo is looking frightfully ill; he literally has no face left at all. The poor fellow has many cares. Moreover his brother is making life rather a burden for him, and reproaches him with all kinds of things of which he is quite innocent."

While Vincent's way of life was punishing to himself, his robust constitution was a powerful ally, a weaker man would have collapsed long ago. But Theo had inherited the same feeble health which undermined his uncles and the strain of Vincent's presence was taking its toll. He fled to Holland for a summer break and Andries moved in to keep Vincent company.

Despite some misgivings, Andries liked the older brother and, newly introduced to art by Theo, was capable of understanding something of the struggle that Vincent was engaged in. But with Theo away the two young men had their hands full coping with 'S', who was once more causing trouble. Theo was in Holland as much to see Andries' sister Johanna again as to visit his family and Andries himself was courting from afar another Amsterdam girl, Anne van der Linden. Neither saw anything out of place in keeping a mistress, except when, as now, she turned awkward. 'S' seems, from their oblique comments on the problem, to have been highly strung and to be in the habit of coming round and making scenes. With Theo away she suddenly moved into the apartment to the great consternation of Andries and Vincent who wrote to Holland to say that one or other of them would have to go as: *sometimes we are really frightened by her* . . . Vincent's ruse for getting her out was that they should find someone else to take her on, though Andries expressed grave doubts about whether such a vague scheme could work, despite Vincent's willingness to volunteer for the role as her new lover.

None of this can have been much reassurance to poor Theo who was not only trying to win Johanna but also attempting to persuade his uncles to back him in setting up a gallery on his own. Those wily old birds seemed to have sensed, even at a distance, that the new art favoured by their nephew was not the sort that had brought them large houses and fine carriages. They declined and Theo returned to Paris, though time away from his brother had at least eased his mind considerably and the fact that 'S' is never mentioned again would indicate that the domestic problem had somehow resolved itself. But no sooner was he back in the Rue Lepic than Theo could see that nothing else had changed. Theo had, as Andries records, considerable taste and had decorated the apartment beautifully as a showcase for what was rapidly becoming a major collection of contemporary art. Every room was designed as a focus for the paintings so that it was depressing to find the place strewn with Vincent's belongings, wet canvases propped against the walls along with the odd bits and pieces he had found on his excursions, for all the world as if he were back in the studio in Nuenen. There were even balls of different coloured wools, the results of Vincent's attempts to imitate Chevreul's studies of tapestry threads. This disorder was more than Theo could stand. In the circumstances, Cormon's atelier was the only solution.

The studio was only a short way down the steep slope of the Rue Lepic, where it ran into the Boulevard de Clichy at the Place Blanche. Clichy, along with the other 'Petits Boulevards', formed part of the plan to push the city northwards. The buildings along its length were still an uneasy mix of the old tumbledown two-storey houses and new apartment blocks, most standing in aggressive isolation from their huddled neighbours. This combination of new and run-down made the neighbourhood a useful source of accommodation for artists of all kinds. Even the altogether grander Gérôme had his studio, in a new building of course, at number 65. Cormon at 104 was nearer the scruffy heart of things, where the artistic life of the boulevard rubbed shoulders with the cafés and cabarets that had until recently stood outside the city toll gates and thus sold wine far cheaper than bars 'inside' Paris. A few doors from the Moulin Rouge, the entrance to Cormon's building led into a sequence of wide courtyards, in one of which stood his wooden studio.

The appellation '*atelier libre*' for Cormon's studio gives a false impression. Some ateliers were virtually open to anyone who turned up and indeed milling crowds of sometimes quite rowdy young men would gather around the nude models, the main reason for their needing such places. At one time the studios had been a necessary preliminary to entry to the Beaux-Arts, though by the eighties they had become finishing schools in their own right with students coming on to them after a period in one of the academies; Antwerp for all the dimness of its teaching was an accepted route. In the ateliers there were almost as many foreign students as French and the whole business was a lucrative source of income for the grand masters who ran them, hence Gérôme's large intake. But Cormon was more selective and it was usual for him to demand some form of recommendation before opening his portals to an unknown.

Cormon, with his lank strand of hair across a broad forehead, was known as the 'thinnest and ugliest man in Paris'. A curious mix of opposites, he had changed his name from Fernand-Anne Piestre – his father had written scripts for the music-hall – and had become a member of the art establishment par excellence, working on large-scale official commissions such as the ceilings of the Petit Palais, and holding all the usual senior posts including a place on the Salon jury, a Beaux-Arts professorship and membership of the Institut. But he was no dour worthy; his students reckoned he had three mistresses on the go at the same time and he let the management of the nearby Moulin Rouge hang some of his paintings in their garden café, which was hardly the gesture of someone concerned only with his social standing. Every year the main studios took part in the Arts Ball at the Moulin Rouge, a wild affair sealed off from the outside world, in which each participating atelier built a float and its students appeared in flamboyant fancy dress hoping to win the first prize of fifty bottles of champagne. The description of one such effort by the Atelier Cormon is most revealing: his students, at his direction, were all dressed up as fur-clad prehistoric brutes surrounded by extinct mammals, giant tropical plants and crude stone tools, in other words a Neanderthal dream-world. In effect this was no joke, it was Cormon's preferred environment. Quite at odds with all the prevailing movements, Cormon, in his own work, chose to depict remote prehistoric scenes. *The Flight of Cain*, his most popular work, had, by its huge size alone, held the public spellbound at the 1880 Salon and in '84 his *Return from the Bear Hunt* had reaffirmed his reputation as a crowd pleaser. He had started out in the familiar Orientalist vein after his travels in the Near East but these hairy Neanderthals were uniquely his own. It must be said that Cormon's creatures look remarkably like the popular image of blond Gauls, all shaggy hair and pelts, despite the fact he was literally standing on top of the new researches into prehistory: it was the sheer weight of bones found in the mines which honeycombed the Butte that had led Cuvier to reconstruct the first extinct mammals half a century earlier. But paleontology, prehistory or whatever mattered scarcely a jot, for in truth Fernand-Anne was living in a world of his own and could not have cared less about reality. Certainly, the modern world did not attract him and his tragedy was, like Gérôme, that he lived way beyond the period of his glory. He recorded as much in a diary kept during the First World War. In January 1918 he remarked on how sad it was to look back over one's life; he rather envied Gérôme who had died before the conflict began and grumbled somewhat about the women in his life, a burden for a man of seventy-two. But Cormon lived on until 1924, when the modern world finally caught up with him. He stepped out of his studio, then in the Rue de Rome, and was run over by one of the new-fangled petrol taxis. It took some time to disentangle him from the back wheels. His funeral was feebly attended for by that time he was quite forgotten.

So it is hard to realise that young men once longed to work in his atelier and not merely because of his eminent position. He was much admired as a colourist, someone who had absorbed the lessons of Delacroix, and indeed he was far more open-minded than many of his fellow teachers, a state perhaps forced on him by events which took place earlier in 1886.

The trouble began with a young student called Emile Bernard, son of a cloth-merchant from Lille, whom Cormon had agreed to take on at the exceptionally young age of sixteen. Everyone was entranced by Bernard's cocky self-assurance; but that someone so young would soon be at odds with the rather fusty atmosphere of the atelier was probably foreseeable. The place was nothing if not gloomy. Old palette scrapings covered the grey walls and a notice with a quotation from Robert Kant set the tone: "The new must wait their turn to speak, and their turn never comes." Such reticence did not appeal to the young Bernard who quickly developed an interest in the new colour theories and to Cormon's annoyance began covering parts of his paintings with dots of pure colour. Not only did he persist in this, he even tried to cheer up the studio by painting red and green stripes on the filthy old brown backcloth that was draped behind the model. Cormon was furious and told Bernard senior to take his son away. Despite the ensuing row with his father, the young man had no intention of surrendering his determination to be an artist and promptly set off on foot to Brittany where it was fashionable for artists to enjoy the cheap inns and the quaint customs of the region, with its beautiful scenery, during the summer months. Bernard had sown the seeds of rebellion, however, and Cormon was soon obliged to close the studio throughout the summer until other troublemakers had left.

Cormon was also unfortunate in his choice of '*massier*' or head student who was supposed to help supervise the others. He had picked a twenty-year-old southerner, Henri Marie Raymond de Toulouse-Lautrec Montfa for the role and had even selected him to assist with the illustrations he was preparing for an edition of Hugo's *La Légende des Siècles*. Lautrec had been chosen despite the Impressionist influences that could be clearly discerned in his work. Furthermore, his appearance was disquieting. He appeared to suffer from dwarfism, which had stunted his legs – in fact the results of childhood accidents. Although not exactly a midget, he walked awkwardly and exaggerated his oddity by seeking the company of only the tallest people. On the other hand, he was the scion of an extraordinarily grand aristocratic family and it must have seemed doubly unfair to Cormon that having been honoured with the role of '*massier*' Toulouse-Lautrec hardly bothered to turn up at all.

Cormon was in a way partly responsible for the problem, having, rather progressively, encouraged his students to work out of doors – imagining that they would venture beyond Montmartre into the countryside on the far side of the river. That Henri Marie Raymond got no further than the bars and brothels of the Butte is part of today's popular image of the period.

So why, when he reopened his studio, with these recent troubles fresh in his mind, did Cormon succumb to the clearly odd-looking Vincent? Perhaps he thought that someone older than the other students would moderate their regrettable tendency to high spirits. Certainly his appearance and surly manner spared Vincent the childish initiation ceremonies that were usually visited on newcomers, and from the start he was left to himself. Only Toulouse-Lautrec on his rare visits seems willingly to have talked to the newcomer. Perhaps to him Vincent was just another 'character' to add to the collection of bizarre types he was building up on his daily round of the local bars. As if the reality of Vincent wasn't odd enough, there was soon a largely fictitious character to bolster Lautrec's interest – one story had Vincent turning up one day with a gun, intending to shoot Cormon. Such tales seem to have stemmed from one of the few Englishmen Cormon allowed into the atelier. And Archibald Standish Hartrick was nothing if not English. He had started out at Julian's, a similar establishment, but a friend, the Australian painter John Peter Russell, had managed to persuade Cormon to take him on. Hartrick eventually became a book illustrator well thought of by the English artistic establishment between the wars. He survived until 1950, and the chapter in his biography dealing with those heady days in Paris shows that over the years they had taken on a distinctly mythic quality. His account of student life in Paris reads like the high jinks of a minor English public school and it was hardly surprising that he gravitated to the Australian Russell, a big man, whose main activity outside art was amateur boxing. These two must have looked on Vincent as something from another planet. But despite the story of the gun, most of Hartrick's observations ring true. He noted that the Dutchman insisted on being called by his first name and that he was:

> a rather weedy little man, with pinched features, red hair and beard, and a light blue eye. He had an extraordinary way of pouring out sentences, if he got started, in Dutch, English, French, then glancing back at you over his shoulder, and hissing through his teeth. In fact, when thus excited, he looked more than a little mad; at other times he was apt to be morose, as if suspicious. To tell the truth, I fancy the French were civil to him largely because his brother Theodore was employed by Goupil and company and so bought pictures.

With someone as tart as Hartrick hovering about the studio is it any wonder Vincent took to hissing through his teeth? It certainly worked, for Hartrick never really knew Vincent while they were both at Cormon's and only met him in the new year at Russell's studio in the nearby Impasse Hélène where Vincent sat for his portrait. Not surprisingly, Vincent found the 28-year-old Australian far more sympathetic than the gossipy Englishman. Russell had quarrelled with his well-to-do family in Sydney and was now living with his Italian mistress and dabbling with the new Impressionism. More to the point, he admired Millet. Despite favouring the new, Russell consistently praised Cormon for his draughtsmanship, though he could see why Lautrec found the idea of 'classical poses' with the models wearing what they all disparagingly called 'firemen's helmets' more than a little foolish. Russell was struggling to break free from the High Victorian version of classicism he had learned in London and both he and Lautrec saw talent in Vincent's efforts and understood his attempts to work his way through the confusions of the different schools emerging at the time. While Hartrick himself remained immune to such struggles, he could still describe Vincent's work with reasonable accuracy and understanding:

> At this time, Van Gogh was making his first pictures with the division of tones, painting still-life, flowers and landscapes of Montmartre. There is no doubt that this plunge into pure colour stimulated him violently, and he piled the oil paint on in a way that was astonishing and decidedly shocking to the innocent eye as well as to that of the more sophisticated.

One is left wondering whether Hartrick considered himself an 'innocent eye' or 'more sophisticated'? Either way it is hard to avoid the conclusion that Archibald had been snapped at by Vincent at some point and was still nursing a grievance when he wrote up his memoirs. That aside, his description of the work is tolerably fair and is borne out by another student, François Gauzi, who later recalled a particular incident that illustrates Vincent's thinking. Gauzi remembered Vincent ignoring Cormon's express instructions that they should discipline themselves by drawing only the posed models without trying to improve the setting. This meant in particular the sensitive issue of the backdrop, restored to a fustian brown after the Bernard incident. Inevitably, Vincent changed this ruling, covering the dais with a vivid blue drape on which he posed the fair-skinned model as if on a couch. The golden hue of her skin stood out almost violently against the blue and Vincent began work on his canvas with all his usual fury, even working on when the model was resting. Later in the day Cormon arrived to offer the normal round of criticism, but the old bird had learnt wisdom and was not about to provoke another student rebellion. He chose instead to ignore the rearrangement or indeed anything to do with colour at all and when he arrived at Vincent's easel, he limited his remarks to some comments on his drawing skills. By an extraordinary coincidence, the young Bernard had just returned from Brittany and, cockily disregarding his banishment, had come to the studio to see old friends. What should he find but someone successfully carrying out his own revolution. Bernard saw that the others were laughing at Vincent behind his back but that he simply took no notice. Bernard returned that evening and found Vincent alone, patiently copying one of the antique sculptures, going over and over his drawings. Later still, he found him again at Tanguy's, an artists' materials shop that was a meeting place for local artists and so they were able to speak at last.

It is hard to imagine the Montmartre of the 1880s without Tanguy's shop and 'Père' Tanguy, its jovial proprietor. As he stares out at us from the portraits by 'his' artists, Julien François Tanguy with his squat shape, moon face, close cropped hair and benign expression has become an icon of the period. Vincent remarked on his Buddha-like qualities, and his cluttered shop in the Rue Clauzel was referred to as 'a tiny chapel of art'. Certainly his customers found him near saintly for he not only made his premises their unofficial club but let them exchange paintings for paint, which in most cases was tantamount to charity as he could rarely, if ever, sell them. He was a sturdy Breton, over sixty when Vincent first met him, who had drifted into the colour grinding business before the Commune. As a passionate revolutionary he had of course joined in the conflict and had served two years in prison after the siege. Despite his new role as a small tradesman he remained a committed socialist and clearly equated the new art with his political stance. To Tanguy, the Impressionists were painters of the people despised by the 'system' and in opposition to those establishment figures who exhibited in the fancy galleries and salons of the *Grands Boulevards*. So much was the new art a matter of faith to him that he was liable to order out of his shop anyone who asked for a tube of black paint, though he usually relented soon afterwards. He had recognised in Cézanne an artist whose convictions matched his own in intensity and had made himself his most fervent supporter, supplying him with materials in exchange for almost his entire output. Many a student would enter the small dark interior of the shop to study the Cézannes ranged about the walls and to hear a lecture on the work by someone who had started out in life as a plasterer. In all senses, Tanguy was a marvel. By late 1886 Vincent almost vied with the departed Cézanne as the old man's most frequent visitor, indulged to the point where he was allowed to rummage in the paint drawers to find the colours he sought. Far more than Cormon's studio the shop was Vincent's school, for there at last he was able to satisfy his craving to meet and talk with other artists.

When Bernard's father had tried to deflect him from a career in art by withdrawing financial support, it was 'Père' Tanguy who made sure the young man had what he needed. When he met Vincent, Bernard had come into the shop to hand over the work he had been doing in Tanguy's native Brittany. Bernard had been staying in Pont-Aven, a village that became an artists' colony during the summer months, and at some time during his stay had come across Gauguin; this was no more than a passing encounter, however, as both were still unsure where their work was leading and they had little to say to each other as yet. It was a frustrating time for Gauguin who had sensed that there was something beyond Impressionism but had so far failed to grasp what it was. Archibald Standish Hartrick was another of that summer's visitors and although they never properly met, he had stayed at the same auberge as Gauguin and was able to note that he was still painting under the influence of Pissarro while tentatively trying out some of the ideas of Seurat and Signac – the ubiquitous dots in other words.

What Gauguin and Bernard did have in common was the attraction both felt for this part of Brittany, then still a remote, almost primitive place. Hartrick described it as:

> a country of gigantic sand dunes, like the mountainous waves of a solid sea, between which appeared glimpses of the Bay of Biscay and the Atlantic rollers. All this, peopled by a savage-looking race, who seemed to do nothing but search for driftwood, or to collect seaweed, with strange sledges drawn by shaggy ponies; and with women in black dresses, who wore the great black 'coif' (like a huge black sun bonnet).

The many crosses by the roadside were just one sign of the lingering simple faith of the Bretons and it was this air of otherworldliness, of mystery and superstition which appealed to both Gauguin and Bernard. Such things were completely different from the bright, everyday world of the Impressionists with their street scenes and boating parties.

When he returned to Paris in the autumn of '86, Gauguin was taken to hospital for a month suffering from angina, but once he recovered he began working furiously on strange ceramics, many influenced by the pre-Columbian art he had seen on his journeys as a merchant seaman. A large number of the pots were self-portraits and as he was unable to sell these distinctly impractical vessels his financial situation grew desperate and he began to dream of wild places where he would find both mystery and cheap living.

When Bernard returned to Paris that same autumn he went to see the recently opened Salon des Indépendants where Seurat again exhibited the *Ile de la Grande Jatte*. The young Bernard was so overwhelmed he went home to rework his Pont-Aven pictures with the new 'dots'. It was these retouched works that Vincent now saw at Tanguy's. As were most people, Vincent was greatly taken by the young man's enthusiastic manner and determined to know him better.

For the moment Vincent had most contact with the diminutive Henri de Toulouse-Lautrec. He alone seemed to ride out the artistic shock-waves of that disturbing year. With a bravura Vincent could only envy, Lautrec had quickly found the direction that suited him. Far from struggling against total indifference as most of the younger painters did, Lautrec had his supporters from the first. A personal and highly original blend of aspects of Impressionism with a dash of mordant caricature, presented with a bold graphic simplicity drawn from Japanese prints, his art had an instant popular appeal. The two men had not much to offer each other in the way of art but Lautrec seems to have found Vincent's gaucheries and wearisome habit of alienating everyone appealing, for he too had suffered from public aversion to his appearance. The stumpy, black clad aristocrat with his fleshy face and bulbous eyes peering through his pince-nez, and the emaciated Dutchman in his workman's blue, with his hunched shoulders and suspicious looks, were soon familiar partners in the bars and cabarets of the Butte. That December Lautrec took Vincent to the Mirliton to hear his friend Aristide Bruant, the most foul-mouthed and outrageous of the *balladiers*, whose risqué songs unveiled the realities of life among the outcasts of the Butte and the Maquis. His cutting satire found a counterpart in Lautrec's drawings of the people of that café world. He always seemed to depict them, not as they were or as they wished to be, but as they surely would be one day: the faces a little too sunken, the mouth a little too pulled down, the lines on the neck . . .

So there was Vincent, the man who only six years earlier had wept because he could not punish himself further in the service of God and the poor, now sitting in the louchest bar in Europe, listening to a godless satirist cruelly mocking the foibles of his listeners and everything Vincent had once believed in. Bruant served only weak beer at his cabarets but there were plenty of other bars to go to afterwards. Lautrec was famous for never sleeping or at least only dozing in a cab as dawn was about to reveal the all-too-seamy side of the *quartier*. One painting by Vincent sums it all up: in the foreground is the edge of a café table, through the window the backview of a distant figure and the trunk of a tree set in a pavement, all irrelevant details, for on the table stands the true subject, a carafe of water and a sturdy glass of cloudy yellowish liquid – *absinthe*.

Until it was banned in 1915, absinthe was the drug of the day; a myriad half-crazed poets hymned its hallucinogenic properties. After water was added to the colourless spirit its yellowy, slightly emerald tinge gave it its haunting name, La Fée Verte, the Green Fairy. The trick was to sip it slowly all day so that a perpetual dream-state could be maintained. The danger was that the body's tolerance grew so that stronger doses were needed; Lautrec eventually perfected a devastating concoction dubbed the Earthquake for the dancer Yvette Guilbert which combined absinthe and cognac. Lautrec's only portrait of Vincent shows him staring blankly into the distance, a glass of the Green Fairy in front of him. Clearly it was not his first that day.

For someone beset by Vincent's nagging cares, such release must have seemed the answer to his every prayer. And his trailing around the cafés and bars in the wake of the indefatigable Lautrec must have been a relief to Theo, who was being driven witless by Vincent's endless capacity for argument. That December Theo had an attack of some kind and a worried Andries noted that it left him stiff, as if he had suffered a bad fall. It was the first of what were to be increasingly regular seizures. Vincent may not have been fully aware of his brother's condition but he tried to make amends in the only way he knew, through his art. He embarked on a series of still-lifes, or perhaps one should say portraits, of boots. The classic of the series has two boots side by side which on close examination turn out to be both for the left foot. One stands up straight; the other flops down with its lace rather touchingly draped across its sturdier companion as if tentatively embracing it.

Despite such displays of affection, Theo can only have been relieved that Vincent was spending so much time away from the apartment; though he cannot have been pleased to discover that one of the reasons was absinthe. Sober, Vincent would argue about anything, drunk he would sit by Theo's bed and continue the debate far into the night. The Green Fairy was notoriously perverse in how it affected people and Theo would have been well aware that it was popularly held responsible for many of the murders and other violent crimes gruesomely recorded in the gutter press. Indeed the drink was a popular obsession. Following the Pernod family's conversion of a pleasantly liquorice-flavoured health cordial into an industrially produced spirit, the government had issued it to troops on service in difficult colonial climes. They had returned with a taste for it which had blossomed when a thoughtless tax on wine led the poor to look for a cheaper alternative. The Green Fairy spread rapidly and by the last quarter of the century it had a romantic aura for intellectuals and artists slumming it in the bars and dives of the seedier parts of Europe's capitals. There was much ritual as to how the drink was served. Water might be added through a strainer containing sugar and the miraculous swirling opacity this produced seemed to pre-figure the trance-like state the drinker might eventually achieve. The first concerted moves to have it abolished were soon under way, with the church taking the lead; the principal ingredient of absinthe was after all wormwood, a plant that many believed to have sprung up in the wake of the serpent as it fled the garden of Eden. More rational abolitionists emphasised absinthe's potency and its danger to health, though its true properties were never fully understood until long after it was banned. In most cases the real effect of the drink was no more than any other strong dose of alcohol: it made the drinker very drunk indeed and was to some tragically addictive. How the drinker behaved was more a matter of his own physical and mental state than any inherent qualities of the Green Fairy. Lautrec, who kept his hollow cane filled with an emergency supply of the stuff, eventually succumbed and had to be forcibly locked away to dry out. Even in those early days when Vincent's drinking was a new thing, it must have worried Theo that someone so unstable was flirting with so notorious a substance. By an unnerving coincidence the abolitionist newspaper *L'Etoile Bleue* ran a cartoon showing a demented addict making a ranting speech to no one in particular – the character is the image of the emaciated Vincent.

Lautrec's portrait of Vincent was painted at their recent regular haunt, Le Tambourin in the Boulevard de Clichy, a cabaret and restaurant famous for its superb Italian food. The décor was inspired by its name – tables and stools were tambourine-shaped and the theme was echoed on the elaborately decorated menus and fittings. The owner, Agostina Segatori, a faded beauty probably in her late forties, was one of the characters of the *quartier*. Originally from the region of Naples, she and her waitresses wore their native folk costume and were a familiar part of the colourful life of the neighbourhood. There had been a wave of such southern Italian beauties in the 1860s, drawn to Paris by the prospect of the riches to be earned from modelling for the city's artists. How they knew this and why they risked so much in order to get there is a mystery, but come they did. The self-regarding Charles Dubosc, who for nearly half a century had modelled for most of the salon stars, recorded his displeasure at this invasion. He decided to abandon posing for a living because of the influx of Neapolitan girls and his memoirs record how these 'bread-snatchers' were really only on the look-out for a husband, preferably a painter; a sculptor was second best. However, the 62-year-old Dubosc, who insisted that he had kept his elegant form, was able to retire comfortably on the proceeds of his rented properties. As Vincent well knew, hiring models in Paris was prohibitively expensive, which was why young artists used the ateliers. The rapacious Neapolitans had found a strong market and 'La Segatori', as she was often called, had done very well indeed. She had posed for Gérôme, her dark looks being eminently suitable for harems and slave markets. When Corot, in his sixties, had been prevented by severe gout from walking out to paint landscapes, he had posed her in front of an imaginary Italian hill-town, similar to the places he had sketched on his visits to her native land. He looked on painting southern beauties like Agostina as a form of relaxation, though it is unlikely that Vincent or anyone else knew of such work as the master virtually suppressed his figure paintings during his lifetime. They became widely known only after an exhibition at the Salon d'Automne in 1909. If it was money she was after, then La Segatori would certainly have been well rewarded by Corot, for the old man was famously generous. On one occasion he bought Daumier's house from his landlord and presented it to the artist just as he was about to be evicted. He was even in the habit of signing forgeries of his own work out of pity for the forger's poverty, hence the common joke that 'Corot has painted 3,000 paintings, of which 10,000 are in America'.

Money she did make, but if Agostina had also been after a husband, painter or sculptor, she was less fortunate. She seems to have let love get in the way and allowed herself to succumb to the charms of a Swedish painter in his late twenties. This man, August Hagborgs – he dropped the final 'S' when he decided to settle permanently in Paris – was one of the horde of minor realists who would later be succeeded by a horde of minor impressionists. He eventually settled for marine subjects with such titles as *High Tide in the Channel* and *Normandy Fishermen*; his peasants were 'jolly' rather than 'suffering', while his fisherfolk were noticeably hale. He excelled himself when he painted Agostina's portrait, managing to capture her irresistible combination of sultry childishness and stiff-backed resilience. She would need the latter, for the young Hagborg eventually left her. She had looked after her savings, however, and as her looks faded and modelling jobs grew scarce she opened her restaurant and prospered.

Ten years earlier Vincent would probably have found her striking looks forbidding. Now that time had etched character and grit into her features, she was very much within his preferred canon of female beauty. Such things were certainly on his mind, for he had been producing a series of extraordinary nudes, whorish figures provocatively exposed, naked except for seductive white silk stockings but with hideous, simian faces. Were these realistic portraits of some urchin-like street walker or the product of drunken fantasies? Perhaps both. Although he kept these paintings largely to himself he did not disown them. The Paris works, with the exception of the still-life for Lucien Pissarro, are usually unsigned, but a painting of one of these whorish creatures sports a rampant 'Vincent', far bolder than his normal signature.

Whatever lay behind these secret pictures, Vincent was evidently ready for someone like La Segatori, with her worldly air and her reputation among the artists. As he had no money Vincent had come to an arrangement whereby he could exchange paintings for the lavish meals the restaurant served at its tambourine-shaped tables. Not that Agostina would take too many risks – she only wanted the flower paintings which she thought might sell. The young Ambroise Vollard, about to begin his career as a picture dealer, happened to visit the restaurant just as the pictures were being hung and overheard someone asking Agostina if 'Vincent' had been in.

"He's this minute gone out," she is supposed to have said. "He came in to hang up those sunflowers, and went off again at once."

It was only years later that Vollard realised who it was that he had just missed, though the recollection, especially the reference to 'sunflowers' is rather too pat and was probably a later embroidery.

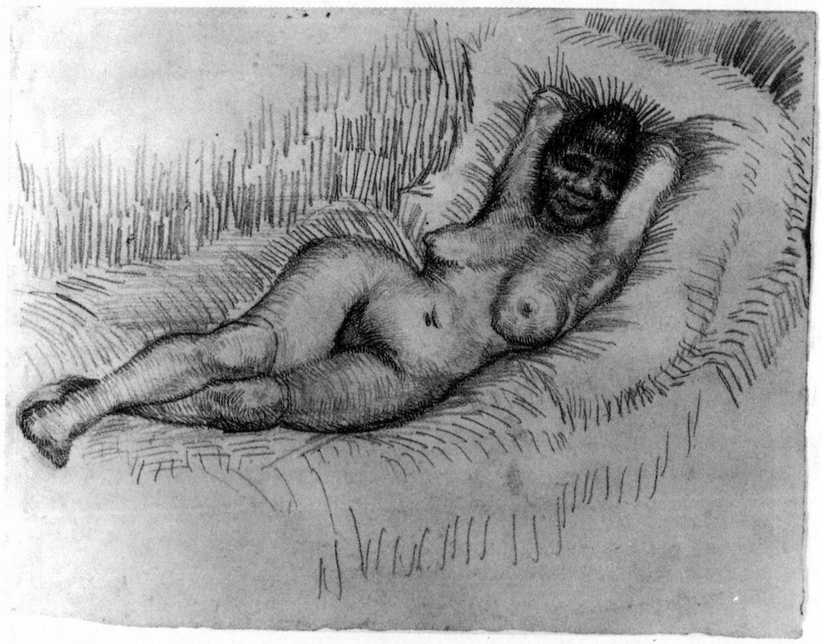

Reclining nude by Vincent.

Nevertheless, he also noted with more accuracy that La Segatori's attachment to art and artists was somewhat at odds with her business sense and if she did let Vincent eat free there must have been a good reason.

Indeed the wags of Montmartre had no doubt that Vincent was expected to render payment in other ways. Whatever the truth of the rumours the two of them certainly had a stormy relationship that bore all the signs of a love affair. Yet, despite the rows, his portrait of her, seated at one of her tambourines, a cigarette in hand, an empty beer mug before her, shows a tenderness towards one whose life must have been pretty tough that is very touching. Vincent soon persuaded Père Tanguy to accompany him to the restaurant, much to the chagrin of his wife who was far from happy to have the old man staggering home at all hours befuddled with absinthe. Vincent got the rough edge of her tongue and he began to refer to her as Xanthippe, the shrewish wife of Socrates, which was unfair, as she was normally as open-hearted as her husband.

The alternative to drinking sessions at the Tambourin was Lautrec's gatherings at his studio on the corner of the Rue Tourlaque and the Rue Caulaincourt, where he, Bernard, Anquetin and others would passionately debate the art of tomorrow. Suzanne Valadon, one-time model and future painter, has left a poignant description of Vincent's presence at these gatherings: "He would arrive carrying a heavy canvas under his arm, which he would place in a well-lighted corner, and wait for someone to notice him. No one was in the least concerned. He would sit down opposite his work, surveying the others' glances and sharing little of the conversation. Finally wearying, he would depart carrying his latest example of his work. Nevertheless, the following week he would return and commence the same stratagem again."

Surrounded by such indifference Vincent began to grow impatient with his rate of progress. He had learned nothing from Cormon and like Lautrec stopped going to the Studio. Bernard was too preoccupied with his own search for a new means of expression to have anything to teach him. Louis Anquetin alone had a brilliantly original way with composition – the unusual angle of a café awning, the way he placed a reaper in the distance leaving the foreground of his cornfield dramatically empty – devices that one day Vincent would use as he had Millet's figures. But he needed more than vague admiration, he needed a leader. Had he met Seurat he would no doubt have been bowled over as Pissarro had been, but without the older man's experience to counterbalance the effect. Had that happened, the story of Vincent's art might have been considerably different. By evading the seductive power of Impressionism for so long he had avoided the fate of many who became mere minor exponents of the style. There seems no end to the ranks of *fin de siècle* Impressionists, dutifully applying the discoveries of Monet, Renoir and Degas to their own corner of the world. In the same way, had Vincent encountered Seurat in person he might have been a disciple, a second-level Divisionist. Fortunately he came across the altogether more friendly though less charismatic Signac, as usual in the 'tiny chapel of art' that was Père Tanguy's shop.

In a way Vincent simply attached himself to the younger man. They had passed the time of day a few times at Tanguy's before they saw each other, again by chance, painting in the neighbouring countryside. Whenever they met in this way, Vincent took to following the younger man. He would set up his easel near Signac's on the banks of the Seine and they would work through the day side by side. It is to Signac's credit that he accepted his new companion without complaint. Perhaps because he was a child of Montmartre and had been familiar with its bohemian fringe since he could walk, Signac was more tolerant of the eccentricities of those involved in the creative life. In many ways, of all the artists who stumbled into Vincent's story, Paul Signac stands out as one of the least judgemental and most consistently tolerant of his peculiar behaviour.

It was also fortunate for Vincent that Signac had, despite the force of Seurat's personality, remained very much his own man. Where Seurat had arrived at his 'dots' as an intellectual solution to a theoretical problem – the optical mixture of colours – Signac had simply been entranced by the little commas of pure colour he had seen in the work of Monet and Guillaumin and had adopted them as his own. Despite their shared studies, Seurat and Signac had quickly diverged in method. Seurat's art by its classical, patient 'science' was from the start a return to the studio painting of an earlier generation. His later painting *Les Poseuses* not only offered a view of the model from three different angles, it also showed *La Grande Jatte* propped against a wall of the studio, a pointed reminder of where it had been painted – as laboriously as any academic history painting. Indeed, there were those who saw in Seurat not a dangerous revolutionary but a secret agent for the Beaux-Arts system out of which he had grown. It was true that he had not so much extended Impressionism as utterly rejected everything it stood for, spontaneity, direct contact with nature, obedience to the shifting dictates of light. Signac, by contrast, never stopped working from nature, probably because the painter Gustave Caillebotte had introduced him to the pleasures of yachting, so that boats, harbours and rivers became a lifelong passion. Clearly the meticulous working up of tiny dots of paint was impossible in the open air and Signac quickly adapted 'Pointillism' as it also came to be called, by using larger squares of colour.

It was Signac's love of the river which led him out to Asnières and Clichy and his encounters with Vincent. The Boulevard de Clichy led into the Avenue de Clichy, which stretched beyond the old city fortifications out to the Commune de Clichy on the southern bank of the Seine. Further west was Asnières and the Grande Jatte. Unspoiled grassy banks or gasworks, you only had to turn through a few degrees and you could change from pastoralist to a painter of industrial life. Vincent hovered between them.

Vincent himself could not have said precisely what their working side by side meant. Signac would certainly have explained Divisionist technique, though Vincent had seen enough of Seurat's *Grande Jatte* to know that such studio work was not for him and would have seen no point in adopting the new method wholesale. Signac himself was nearer in spirit, witness his *Quai de Clichy* done that April or May, brilliantly poised between the immediacy of open-air painting and the timelessness of a studio piece. Vincent, however, was more drawn to the earlier Signac of 'Monet's commas' whose work he knew from Theo, because he could use such a technique in his own imprecise, intuitive way. He began a series of wonderfully light and airy views in and around Clichy and Asnières that are his first major works since *The Potato Eaters* had triumphantly concluded his Dutch period. He depicted the river with its railway bridge, the park at Asnières, quiet suburban back lanes, light greens and yellows, pale blue skies, a little red on the suggested outlines of a distant figure. Black has been abolished, the north has receded. The new 'dots' were useful for foliage and grass, but he felt free to take as he needed which cannot always have pleased Signac, fervently employed on his missionary task. However, it is clear from his recollections that Vincent's sheer force fascinated him:

> We painted together on the river banks, we lunched at roadside cafés and we returned by foot to Paris via the Avenues of Saint-Ouen and

> Clichy. Van Gogh wearing the blue overalls of a zinc-worker, would have little dots of colour painted on his shirt sleeves. Sticking quite close to me, he would be yelling, gesticulating and brandishing a large, size thirty, freshly painted canvas; in this fashion he would manage to polychrome both himself and the passers-by.

When Vincent painted the interior of one of the restaurants where they lunched he was at his most out-and-out 'Divisionist'. Everything was ordered, not only the glasses and plates neatly laid on the lined-up tables but also the way it was executed – the careful build-up of the dots of colour came close to Seurat's sleepy afternoon feel. There are no customers, the atmosphere is very sedate and one has to force oneself to remember that the last time Vincent painted a setting for a meal it was that dark, earthy peasant dinner. What had happened to the burning desire to make art of and for the people? How was it he could carefully recreate the genteel atmosphere of a suburban restaurant from which all signs of life had been expunged? It is true that in some of the scenes near Asnières there is the occasional figure walking down the otherwise empty lanes. Such figures do bear some resemblance to Millet's field workers trudging home, but only vaguely: each one is really no more than a balancing element in the overall composition, a device rather than a person. At least the new technique forced him to exercise patience, to observe carefully and to work up his colours slowly by the laborious Divisionist method, but where was the real Vincent van Gogh in all this? Occasionally he could not resist throwing caution to the winds and letting his heart rule his head, as in a painting of the vegetable gardens on the slope of the Butte where instead of dots he applied the colour in short sharp lines that seemed to be sucked into an invisible vortex just off the centre of the canvas. All that Seurat calm is swirled away, and in its place is the emotional Vincent, imposing his own impetuous intensity on the landscape before him.

That swirling, vertiginous method was surely closer to his real self, for as the year progressed so did his drinking and his unruly behaviour. Theo wrote to their youngest sister Willemina:

> My home life is almost unbearable. No one wants to come and see me any more because it always ends in quarrels, and besides he is so untidy that the room looks far from attractive. I wish he would go and live by himself. He sometimes mentions it, but if I were to tell him to go away, it would just give him a reason to stay; and it seems

> I do him no good. I ask only one thing of him, to do me no harm; yet by his staying he does so, for I can hardly bear it. It is as if he were two persons: one marvellously gifted, tender and refined, the other egoistic and hard-hearted. They present themselves in turns, so that one hears him talk first in one way, then in the other, and always with arguments on both sides. It is a pity he is his own enemy, for he makes life hard not only for others but also for himself.

But Theo knew he could never abandon Vincent; to do so would be to destroy his art and by now that was unthinkable. Leaving aside the drunken quarrelling, Vincent had widened Theo's artistic contacts in the year and a half he had been in Paris. There were also hopeful signs of a distinct personal style emerging despite the force of the new ideas which threatened to engulf him. He had something to give back as well – his enthusiasm for the art of Japan. This may seem surprising for the prints were by then well known and the Impressionists had already adopted the strange high angles of the Japanese street scenes for their paintings of the new boulevards. The bold colours of the prints had encouraged them in their own experiments and the Japanese love of water and bridges had entered their vocabulary. Some, like Monet, collected japonaiserie – he had painted his wife Camille dressed in a kimono and holding a decorated fan – and the habit of collecting the cheaper prints was common among a wide variety of artists. The Australian John Peter Russell had been a collector ever since a visit to Japan when he was nineteen, and Vincent knew of Henri Rivière's interest since Theo had started taking him to the cabarets at the Chat Noir. It is strange to reflect on how many people in the last century became absorbed by this 'floating world' of actors and courtesans, theatres and entertainments, by those inexplicable 'incidents' along the Tokaido Road, at once so accessible yet so unfathomable, a world about which they knew so little.

Vincent's role in the general enthusiasm for Japan was as a rejuvenator of interest and as a mentor to some who had not previously imagined that Japanese art had any particular message for them. Vincent was a frequent visitor to Samuel Bing's emporium in the Rue de Provence not far from Delarebeyrette's shop. Bing was a collector of japonaiserie as well as a merchant, and was driven by a mission to convert people to all things Eastern. The ground floor room was almost a museum, with Japanese objects stylishly displayed in glass cases. As many manufacturers as artists came to study his ceramics and fabrics, and the Goncourts would later blame the decline of French art on the rise of an industry which, under Japanese influence, had created the widely popular art-nouveau objects the brothers despised. At Bing's, prints were stacked on every floor even up to the attics where Vincent, much approved of by the proprietor, was allowed to rummage and even on one occasion take Bernard and Anquetin. The two men were readily converted by the work they saw and by Vincent's enthusiasm for it. To Bernard, the curious scenes were even more mysterious and inexplicable than the ancient culture he had glimpsed in Brittany. As with most people, he found in the prints exactly what he wanted to see. Of course knowledge of Japanese art had improved considerably since Bracquemond first discovered Hokusai. The original belief that all the prints were works of high art meant to be seen in the cool, refined setting of the tea ceremony had given way to a realisation that most were nothing more than a cheap popular art form meant for mass consumption by the unrefined. They had after all been used as wrapping paper. It was only when Western appreciation of the prints filtered back to Japan that they began to achieve any status in their home territory. Vincent had got hold of the notion that they had been produced by a guild of artists dedicated to creating a readily accessible art for all. He had heard how Japanese poets exchanged verses, creating poems together, and transferred the idea to painting. He was forever trying to persuade the artists he met to exchange work with him, occasionally with success. Part of this was his desire to help swell Theo's collection, but a greater stimulus was his continuing desire that some form of artistic community might evolve.

With such ideas in mind he persuaded Agostina to let him put on an exhibition of Japanese prints in the Tambourin. It opened in March 1887 and drew in all the painters he had so far met. The portrait he painted of La Segatori was probably done during the exhibition as there is a print of a woman in a kimono on the wall behind her and on the stool beside her is a brightly coloured parasol which may have come from Bing's.

The effects of the exhibition were far reaching, especially on Bernard. He had visited the apartment in the Rue Lepic and seen the brothers' collection, and when he returned to Pont-Aven that spring, Japan was very much on his mind. Gauguin on the other hand was off in search of real exotica of his own. Having had enough of Paris and poverty he left with his friend Charles Laval, bound for Panama where he hoped his brother-in-law would help him on his way to some unspecified tropical paradise. As far as he was concerned it was goodbye Paris. He had no intention of coming back.

For Vincent, there were various ways the prints entered his own artistic vocabulary. Not least was how they challenged Western orthodoxies about perspective. Hiroshige's bridges span his rivers at impossible angles but the effect is doubly dramatic; Vincent tried it out in some of the paintings of the railway bridges at Asnières and was pleased with the results. In Antwerp he had hesitated before the Japanese use of bold colour but in Paris his resistance was overcome and it helped nudge forward the process of lightening his palette. By the spring of 1887 his work sparkled with light dots of colour, somewhere between Impressionism and Pointillism. For once he seemed carefree and lighthearted as if he had stepped outside himself, and left his usual nagging worries behind. In such a state of mind one wonders how he must have felt when he visited the Millet exhibition at the Beaux-Arts in May 1887. It can only have seemed treacherous to contemplate those humble peasants, the originals of all the prints he had admired, now that he no longer attempted to follow Millet's concern for the human condition. True, there were peasants in many of the Japanese prints, bent figures scurrying along on bandy legs, shielded from the arrow fall of rain by their wide straw hats, but they were almost embarrassingly comic when set beside Father Millet's noble souls.

If Vincent's work had taken on a lighter touch, there was little echo of it in his personal behaviour. The atmosphere in the apartment was increasingly tense and Theo was glad to be able to make the occasional trip to Giverny to see Monet whose work he had started to handle. Monet had only recently moved to his country retreat and was just beginning the laying out of the wonderful gardens that would be immortalised in his final paintings. There also, the influence of Japan could be sensed in the organisation of the lily ponds with a tiny round-backed bridge in the Japanese manner. Even in its embryonic state this peaceful haven provided Theo with a few moments of calm before his return to the inevitable arguments.

The early summer was especially difficult. Signac left for the south and Vincent was forced to work on his own. He continued to walk out to Clichy and his colours continued to lighten, but as so often before something was beginning to eat away at him. The arguments with

Agostina were growing worse. At some point he made a similar arrangement to exchange paintings for meals with the nearby Restaurant du Chalet which indicates that La Segatori had already stopped feeding him. In July they 'formally' parted, though there was a continuing acrimonious dispute about the paintings he had left at the Tambourin. He was in a bad state. Most of his new friends were away. He had lost his niche at the Tambourin and the drinking only exacerbated his moods.

Then the worst thing possible happened: Theo again went home for the summer and this time Vincent learned that he was seriously courting Andries' sister Johanna. His letter to Theo after he heard the news was a depressing mix of false good wishes for the marriage and a wheedling account of his own miseries. He even revealed that Agostina was unwell and that he suspected she had had an abortion, though he said he did not blame her. With thinly veiled sarcasm he told Theo that should he get married he could end up with a country house like many other picture dealers, meaning of course their Uncle Cent. He ended with another vague threat: *It's better to have a gay life of it than commit suicide.*

How seriously Theo treated these words is not known though they can hardly have made his courting any easier. One line in the letter gave some clue as to what lay behind Vincent's state of mind: *. . . I will take myself off somewhere down south, to get away from the sight of so many painters that disgust me as men.*

When Theo returned to Paris it was not difficult to discover what lay behind that cryptic remark – his brother was no longer as thrilled to find himself part of the Paris art world as he had been six months earlier. There were too many factions pulling him this way and that. Too many cliques and certainly too many quarrels.

Whereas most artists enjoyed denigrating each other's ideas – Gauguin was particularly adept at it – Vincent loathed the café bitchiness he heard all around him. The artistic community, far from being a medieval guild, was fractious and sarcastic, a loose collection of super-egos, each, like Seurat, jealous of his discoveries and furious if someone else received the credit for them. Despite their own persecutions, the original Impressionists had not hesitated to try to prevent any newcomers from exhibiting at their shows and only the good-hearted Pissarro had challenged their exclusivity.

One quarrel in October 1886 had neatly illuminated the growing split in the new Post-Impressionism. As Signac was going away for a time he told the temporarily homeless Gauguin that he could move into his studio. He omitted to warn Seurat of the arrangement and he, fastidious as ever, refused to hand over the keys. Gauguin, not the most patient of men, took offence on an epic scale and even stalked out of a café when the newly returned Signac entered. It was all very silly, but as the Seurat/Signac school was soon to be seen in opposition to that of Gauguin/Bernard, there was a degree of prophetic rightness about the incident.

For someone like Vincent, normally so generous about another's work, watching the painters manoeuvre or, worse still, listening to them fight their corner, was a deeply depressing experience. The atmosphere around the cafés of Montmartre was beginning to destroy him and on top of everything there was the renewed possibility that Theo's support might be less than certain. One of the reasons he was arguing with Agostina over the paintings was that he believed they were partially Theo's and that he had no right to leave them with her. He decided to go round to the restaurant to try to sort the matter out, only to find himself rudely ignored by the staff. Next he picked a quarrel with Tanguy's wife when she tried to refuse him any more credit.

Fortunately for Theo, Emile Bernard was back from Pont-Aven and was willing to take on Signac's role of painting companion. Bernard's parents had recently bought a house in Asnières and when his grandmother came from Lille to live with them she paid for a wooden 'atelier' to be built in the garden for her grandson to work in. He invited Vincent to join him, and using the place as a base the two set off for the same sites he had once painted with Signac. There is a photograph of them sitting at a café table which has been set up on the riverbank. Unfortunately (as it is the last ever taken of him) Vincent is backview. The railway bridges that feature in all their work can just be seen in the far distance.

It is revealing to contrast Signac's light, Divisionist realisation of that scene with the new-look Bernard. While in Brittany he had abandoned the use of dots and was now in favour of flat patches of colour with clear dark outlines – the Japanese prints had made their strongest conquest. Bernard's painting of the railway bridges is so completely different from Signac's it is difficult to remember that they had stood on almost exactly the same spot. But in one important regard the two young men were following a similar approach. Like Signac, Bernard was not trying to fix a moment of reality but was attempting to use colour to stimulate an emotional response in the spectator. That autumn, Louis Anquetin joined them on their outings and he and Bernard began moving further towards abstraction. It was impossible that Vincent should resist two such forthright and convincing personalities and he too edged away from the light Pointillist techniques derived from Signac towards the 'flatter' colours his new partners favoured.

Vincent and Bernard both made portraits of Père Tanguy and Vincent's shows how much he straddled the two systems. In the two portraits of him Vincent made that autumn, Tanguy is posed in front of a backdrop of Japanese prints, itself a fascinating insight into Vincent's collection. While the old man looks solid, Buddha-like, reliable, the paint is applied in short strokes laid over solid patches of colour giving the effect of agitated movement. Along with the pure colour in the backdrop of Japanese prints, this is less a portrait of Tanguy than a celebration of the electric sensations unfettered colour can unleash. The two portraits of Tanguy strike a tension between the calm of the subject and the emotion of the method. They are the first works to reveal the Vincent most people recognise – the unrestrained colourist with a richness of hue bordering on the violent.

For Vincent, working alongside Bernard and Anquetin went some way towards easing the loneliness which plagued him and he began to talk about organising a joint exhibition. They would be the painters of the 'Petits Boulevards', those unrecognised artists who lived and worked around the Boulevard de Clichy as opposed to the 'Grands Boulevards' like the Boulevard Montmartre or one of its neighbours where galleries like Goupil's were situated.

That October, Alphonse Portier brought Armand Guillaumin up to meet the two brothers. As one of the original Impressionists, Guillaumin obviously fascinated Vincent who had so far had direct contact only with Pissarro. Guillaumin had already seen some of Vincent's paintings and liked them and on that visit he saw a new still-life of scattered books – *The Parisian Novels*. Vincent was celebrating his love of French literature by a joyous explosion of colour, playing on the bright yellows of the book jackets themselves and heightening the mood even further by limiting the range to yellow, orange and red, then intensifying the effect with small touches of green. There could have been no better way for Guillaumin to see how Vincent was discarding literal realism; there were no legible titles on the books, all sensations were created through colour alone. For his part Vincent felt drawn to Guillaumin in much the same way he had with Pissarro. The two were very similar in outlook, being alone among the original Impressionsts to remain open to newer ideas.

After Pissarro left for the countryside, it was at Guillaumin's studio at the Quai d'Anjou that the younger crowd congregated. Vincent now joined them. Part of Guillaumin's charm was his lack of pretension. Poverty kept him working for the Department of Roads and Bridges earning him the sobriquet 'a republican and a ditch-digger' from the ever snobbish Degas. Whatever else his ditch-digging had done, it had kept him fit and younger-looking than his forty-five years. Only the year before he had married a woman of twenty-seven. As she was a brilliant schoolteacher at the Lycée Fénelon, considered the best girls' school in the capital, there was clearly a more sophisticated side to him than his rather rough appearance suggested. He was in fact as keen a reader as Vincent, though he was no theorist like some of the younger painters and his work sprang from the realities of his working life rather than any particular intellectual scheme. He had recently been promoted from ditch-digging to inspector on night duty and these odd working hours led him to paint in the early morning or late evening, thus transforming his use of colour from the light midday look of the Impressionists to an altogether deeper, more vigorous range that immediately appealed to Vincent. It was also reassuring to find someone content to work in his own quiet way, after all the noise and chatter of café society. To Vincent, Guillaumin was *more sure of his ideas than the others*, and was a useful stabilising force in a time of conflicting influences. The older man helped reinforce Vincent's rejection of Seurat's classicism and helped him accept his own emotional responses to the world.

Both men had violently passionate personalities. Guillaumin had had to swear to his new wife that he would always control his temper in her presence, an undertaking which often maddened him to the point where the only solution was to refuse to speak at all, sometimes for as long as a week. With Vincent, however, he found the roles reversed. On one occasion Vincent no sooner arrived at the studio than he became wildly overexcited about one of Guillaumin's drawings of a labourer unloading a barge which, to him, looked incorrect. Vincent stripped to the waist and started wielding an imaginary shovel to show how the figure ought to look. Understandably, Guillaumin came to rather dread these visits, though for Vincent they were highly enjoyable and an oasis of calm good sense after the in-fighting of the others:

> *. . . if all were like him they would produce more good things, and would have less time and inclination to fight each other so furiously.*

Despite his growing irritation with them, Vincent pressed on with his plan for an exhibition of the artists of the 'Petits Boulevards'. The obvious place for it was his new haunt, the rather pompously named Grand Bouillon, Restaurant du Chalet, at 43 avenue de Clichy, which boasted a room as large and high as any gallery and which was even lit from above by a skylight. Why the owner eventually went along with the plan is a mystery, for his customers were not exactly enthusiastic when they found brilliant but inexplicable bursts of colour all over the walls of their regular eating place. Bernard, Anquetin and a young Dutch painter, Hans Koning, were included and the show opened that November. It was a financial flop but at least it drew their fellow artists and showed the neighbourhood what its inhabitants were up to. Seurat attended, though Vincent was not there that day, and of course Pissarro and Guillaumin were supportive, but it was another stray visitor who was most to affect Vincent's future. Despite his determination never to return, Paul Gauguin was back in Paris once more and, despite the lingering after-effects of dysentery, determined to catch up with what had been going on in his absence.

It is not hard to imagine why Gauguin's arrival at the Restaurant du Chalet should have had such a lasting effect on Vincent. Forceful and, to outward appearances, self-confident, the older Gauguin must have exuded mature good sense in the midst of all those squabbling youngsters. That this was a carefully cultivated and inherently superficial image was to prove to be Vincent's ultimate downfall, but for the moment he was overawed.

Despite a slight difference in their ages (Vincent was thirty-four and Gauguin thirty-nine), and considerable differences in build, Gauguin normally robust, Vincent hunched and emaciated, they now looked almost alike. The ordeal of his wanderings had left Gauguin gaunt and unwell and bereft of his normal, rough-hewn physique. Along with Laval he had arrived in Panama only to discover that his brother-in-law was far from willing to help them. Gauguin had found work with the company that was digging the Panama Canal, Gustave Eiffel's other great project, but was discharged after two weeks. Laval had gone down with yellow fever and tried to commit suicide and it took all Gauguin's considerable will-power and the homoeopathic remedies he had learned from Pissarro to keep them both going. They managed to make their way to the island of Martinique where they found an abandoned hut up-river from a village in the tropical haven they had been dreaming about. For a few weeks the painting was marvellous; what Bernard had tentatively begun in Pont-Aven, Gauguin, surrounded by vibrant colours and sensuous forms, undertook to excess. The island women in their bright cloths were geishas from the Japanese prints; Mount Pelée was their own Fujiyama; and, as with Bernard in Brittany, the fractured brushstrokes of the Impressionists were abandoned to admit simpler, stronger, flatter areas of colour. The landscapes in the hills, the women picking mangoes, the coconut palms along the seashore were all imbued with a feeling of indolence and sun-drenched lassitude.

Then sickness struck again, this time at Gauguin who went down with anaemia, malaria, dysentery and hepatitis. He was desperate. His wife Mette, whom he had abandoned in her native Denmark with their five children, showed no sign of being willing to come out and share this new life. The local doctor advised him to leave for his own good and in the end he was forced to forsake Laval and find a ship on which he could work his passage home. But as he watched his tropical heaven disappearing beyond the ship's wake, Gauguin knew that the canvases he was bringing back were his own and that he was no longer a mere follower of Pissarro. He had never lacked self-confidence, even when he had little reason for it, but now he was absolutely convinced he had found the one true path.

When Vincent saw the Martinique paintings he knew they were extraordinary and as soon as he heard Gauguin's liberally expressed and forthright opinions he was enthralled. There was no one now to counter such a force, Guillaumin had left Paris for a winter holiday with his wife on the Côte d'Azur and it was difficult to see Bernard since Vincent had quarrelled with his father. The elder Bernard had expressed doubts about his son wasting his life as a painter. As art was a sacred calling to Vincent the father had felt the full force of the Dutchman's wrath. The wooden studio in Asnières was therefore closed to him and the two could only meet occasionally in the Rue Lepic apartment.

To the impressionable Vincent, Gauguin's traveller's tales only added to a growing feeling that he had never really lived. It was almost a sense of loss, as if his life had been sacrificed to the various obsessions that had gripped him, whereas here was Gauguin, showing his amazingly colourful canvases, with stories of bare-breasted nymphets offering themselves to strangers. Even without such comparisons, Vincent felt low, absinthe and the creeping effects of syphilis were causing an acute deterioration of his mental and physical health. It was a bitter winter and his behaviour was becoming increasingly volatile. Models refused to pose for him and if people irritated him while he was painting out of doors there would be unpleasant scenes. It was now obvious that such behaviour was a symptom of illness rather than merely eccentric behaviour.

Theo sent him to his doctor Louis Rivet who had his surgery in the Faubourg Montmartre not far from the gallery, but Andries insisted that Vincent should also see the man who had saved him, Dr David Gruby, who lived in the Rue Lepic itself. Gruby had built an observatory on top of the block at number 100, where he studied the stars. He was also a naturalist with original ideas on parasites and his study was so filled with the debris of his field trips that it made Vincent's rooms seem tidy. More bizarre than ever, Gruby had taken to calling on his patients in the middle of the night if it suited him, and was not averse to letting some know that they bored him. His cures were ever more peculiar: one woman was told to perch on her piano in a white dress, another to get her maid to sit on her. He was in many ways the ideal doctor for someone like Vincent, and his memorable advice, 'no women', undoubtedly came from an accurate diagnosis that most of Vincent's problems were the result of drinking and whoring and that if he rested and took care of himself much would change. For the time being at least, Vincent did as Gruby ordered and stayed quietly at home.

When his strength began to return he passed the time making his own versions of Japanese prints. A courtesan in a kimono is set in a wide painted border which completely turns the genre on its head, being composed of a welter of thick brushstrokes rather than flat areas of pure colour. Vincent was clearly trying to cheer himself up, for the cranes (*grues*) and frogs (*grenouilles*) in the border are Parisian slang for prostitutes and relate to the woman's supposed profession.

As his convalescence dragged on he turned again to painting his own face. He had often done so during his two years in Paris as if he needed to examine himself from time to time though what these self-portraits reveal is far from straightforward. The series is not a simple progression. It did not begin with that first image of himself in his sombre black city outfit, then move through his remorseless decline, until it reached a final portrait which shows a haggard bewildered wreck. Rather he moved restlessly back and forth between those two extreme states. Only when seen together do the self-portraits show how buffeted he had been by city life. In the first half of '86 he stares out at the spectator like a lost child asking for help; in the summer of '87, in his bright yellow straw hat, he seems to have found peace; yet a few weeks later the expression is unhinged, his hair spiky, as if an electric charge had just passed through him.

He had recovered enough in the new year of 1888 to resume his café life accompanied by Theo. Occasionally they would meet Camille and Lucien Pissarro, Bernard and Gauguin, not that their conversation was especially stimulating. It is rare for artists and poets to talk about their art; more often they display an obsession with money, or rather the lack of it, and these sessions in the cafés of the Petits Boulevards were no different. The iniquities of the gallery system and the fact that artists earned such paltry amounts from it was the usual cry, though the only solution anyone came up with was Vincent's highly unrealistic idea that Theo should somehow support them all. The one unfortunate result of this fanciful suggestion seems to have been to raise the hopes of Gauguin that the Van Goghs might prove a solution to his current destitution. On the way back to France he had again deluded himself with the idea of selling his pottery, only to find that the manufacturer he had worked with was no longer in business. As Gauguin was still ill and found it almost impossible to paint, his thoughts turned increasingly to leaving for Brittany once more. At Vincent's prompting Theo had already included Gauguin in one of his exhibitions in the upstairs gallery and he now bought one of the Martinique paintings for his own collection.

Vincent was disturbed by the way Gauguin and Bernard clashed on those occasions when the conversation drifted from money to painting itself. They were too close in what they were doing to be able to relax in each other's company and having been so long in the shadow of Pissarro, Gauguin was no longer prepared to tolerate being anything other than leader. Despite the obvious fact that Bernard had made his own discoveries, Gauguin was determined to have his position as the principal innovator of what he termed 'synthetism' recognised. They argued away, driving Vincent into ever deeper depression. Then suddenly, at the beginning of February 1888, Gauguin left for Pont-Aven and Vincent found his absence harder to bear than the quarrelling. Why was he staying in Paris when it made him feel so ill? He painted a final self-portrait: stoical, unemotional, as if he has been drained of all enthusiasm and can only wait passively for whatever fate will offer next. There had been too much to absorb, the shifting crowd of people struggling to establish themselves, battering at his consciousness with their ideas, their enthusiasms, their intemperate struggle to convince the world of their rightness. One of his last paintings in Paris is a portrait which encapsulates much of those two years. The Italian costume suggests that the sitter is in some ways a memory of Agostina, though her mask-like face has echoes of the secret nudes. The background is simply a coloured surface, her chair is two striped lengths of colour. The woman and her costume are made up of formal patterns of colour, a natural outcome of his copies of Japanese prints that winter. The colours glow with an inner fire. The woman's face is hard and from her hand two flowers droop, as if wilted by the warmth of the pigment. The result is intense yet uninvolved.

He needed to get away, needed to have room to absorb the plethora of ideas which had almost submerged him. Toulouse-Lautrec had described the Provence of his childhood in ways that made it sound like heaven on earth. Why not go south, away from another winter in Paris?

Theo was understandably delighted to support such a move. Vincent's first idea was to go to Marseilles, the home town of Monticelli, where he assumed something of the admired artist's colour had originated. Then John Peter Russell told him about Arles and its surrounding countryside where an American friend of his, Dodge MacKnight, was painting. It sounded a likely spot to spend some time before going on to Marseilles; after all Monticelli had painted his seascapes at the nearby town of Les Saintes-Maries-de-la-Mer.

Vincent went to say goodbye to Bernard who was shocked to see how much he had deteriorated since they last met. He was leaving not a moment too soon. In a sense the city had had its revenge; he had thought he could live in it while ignoring it, yet the pressures and strains had proved too much for him. As before in Brussels, Nuenen, The Hague, Drenthe and Antwerp, the desire to leave had no sooner arisen than he was off, leaving everything behind and closing his mind to the past. How wonderful the south would be, the sun of Provence, the warm colours. Better still, living would be cheap and other artists would surely come and join him once he had set up his studio – perhaps even Gauguin might be persuaded? As ever, he travelled hopefully . . .

When he stepped off the train at Arles, Vincent discovered the town under a blanket of snow; Lautrec had lied about the perpetually sunny climate. No matter, it was the Borinage once more, only this time it was not Bruegel but a winter scene from a Japanese print. As soon as he had found a room in an inn, he dashed off a note to Theo to tell him about it. Not that Theo had any need to be reminded of his brother's existence. The night before his departure Vincent had persuaded Bernard to come round and help cover the walls of the apartment with his paintings so that Theo would still feel his presence after he was gone. Surrounded by the self-portraits in all their manic moods poor Theo can only have marvelled at the pain of it all. But if he had expected to feel relieved once his brother had gone, it was not to be. Instead he could only admit to a sense of emptiness and loss.

9

1888

The Yellow House

The railway station was a short distance from Arles. When he left it, Vincent turned right down a short street that led into a broad square, the Place Lamartine, just outside the medieval walls. To his right he could see the Rhône; to his left the main road curved around the stone fortifications and headed to Marseilles; ahead of him were the two squat turrets of the Cavalry Gate, main entrance to the old town. He walked through them and up the Rue de la Cavalerie. On his right was a charcuterie and opposite, a small bistro, the Restaurant Carrel, which had upper rooms to let. This was Vincent's first home in Arles.

Because our image of the place has been so heavily conditioned by Vincent's re-creation of it and because he rigorously excluded much that displeased him, it is easy to think of the town as a tiny ancient citadel surrounded by the unspoiled fields and farms of Provence. It was not quite like that, as Vincent quickly learned.

True, the surrounding countryside was not merely untouched, it was in many respects virtually wild. The town bordered the Grand Rhône just below the point where the Petit Rhône split away, placing Arles at the apex of the triangle which was then the wilderness of the Camargue, a flat low-lying area of salty lagoons and marshes still home to herds of wild horses and untamed bulls, with sudden startling flights of flamingo. The immediate countryside, the Crau, was marshland with rocky outcrops though the creation of canals had transformed much of this into good farming land. In the distance to the north-east ran a chain of hills, the Alpilles. To the south of the town was the Arles–Bouc Canal, a major waterway which, to Vincent's evident fascination, had been spanned with a number of drawbridges in the style of the Low Countries and which would have been perfectly at home in Drenthe. The town was bounded by the Rhône to the west and the straight sweep of the main Paris–Marseilles railway line to the east. Laid in the mid-century, this track had transformed a once sleepy backwater.

Inside the near-intact city walls little seemed to have changed. The large Roman arena and the Church of St Trophime with its impressive Romanesque portico were the principal sights, together with the cluster of picturesque narrow streets paved with the 'villainous sharp stones' that had so irritated Henry James. Apart from such eminent visitors, Arles was not then a popular centre for tourists. Its inns were notoriously ill-appointed. The women of the town, the Arlésiennes made famous by Alphonse Daudet, were, however, well known for their beauty and for the gracious way they still wore their lace-trimmed long black costume with a tiny cap topped with a prominent black bow.

The rare visitor who did brave the inadequate hostelries could marvel at a grandiose town hall, seemingly far too imposing for a place with a population of a mere twenty-three thousand. Stranger still was the surprising number of inmates in the madhouse within the old Hôtel-Dieu, the town's main hospital, a fact locally attributed to excessive smoking and drinking in the bars around the Place Lamartine. This was the new Arles, for it was the railway which had dragged the old town into the modern world.

There was nothing haphazard about this. It was the precise result wished on the town by the poet/politician Alphonse de Lamartine, who had recognised the stagnation and decline of Provence and was determined to see that Arles received some share of the new industrial progress. Lamartine was the hero of the 1848 revolution, the man who proclaimed the Second Republic from the steps of the Hôtel de Ville and whose courage prevented another reign of terror, "Yes, start with me, if you are looking for a victim. Butchers! do you think you represent France?" Lamartine, in the brief interlude before Napoleon III's *coup d'état*, was one of the most influential men of the new dispensation. Arles got its rail-head and more, it became the locomotive centre for the south, with a cluster of factories where rolling stock was built and repaired and which, with 1000 craftsmen, was the town's largest single employer. By the time of Vincent's arrival, smoking factory chimneys were as much a part of the roofscape around Arles as the medieval church towers. Gasometers and a two-level metal bridge across the Rhône linking the town to the suburbs of Trinquetaille, completed the picture.

So powerful was the railway interest and the promise of prosperity which came with it that the track had been allowed to desecrate the most ancient of all the town sites, the Alyscamps or 'Champs Elysées', a pagan and early Christian burial ground where imposing sarcophagi lined what had once been a long shady path of great antiquity. Since the railway line heading south to Marseilles cut right across it, the remaining severed path had been reduced to a small public garden beyond which were more factories and chimneys. Old and new sat uneasily together, a fact reinforced by the presence of between five and eight hundred Italian immigrant workers drawn by the new jobs and looked down on by the locals as 'Savoyard monkeys'. When Vincent arrived, there was also a regiment of light infantry, the notorious Zouaves, stationed at the local barracks. These men had a well deserved reputation for trouble. To 'act the Zouave' had entered the language as a description of a swaggering, devil-may-care boyo, an impression undoubtedly exaggerated by the exotic Zouave outfit of bright red baggy pantaloons, blue and gold embroidered waistcoat and floppy fez which harked back to the original Algerian recruits, though many were by then southern French. It was the Third Zouave regiment which was resting at the Calvin Barracks having only recently returned from the battle of Tonkin. They were soon to be posted to North Africa, but for the time being were largely free to wander about and enjoy themselves in a place famous for its 'Grecian' beauties; a number of *Maisons de Tolérance* just inside the city walls catered for the expectations so roused.

At first Vincent chose the old Arles, though only just, the Restaurant Carrel being only a short walk inside the Cavalry Gate. It was a modest bistro but to Vincent's consternation it turned out to be no cheaper than Paris. Worse, the weather continued to be exceptionally bad. For a place which usually benefited from the mild Provençal winters, with only the occasional freezing mistral to vary the calm, the winter of 1887–88 was memorably bitter. None the less, he endeavoured to keep up his spirits and to carry on with the various tasks he had set himself. He tried to track down any Monticellis which might be on sale locally and he quickly found an antique dealer who claimed to know of one. He pursued his usual routine of settling into a place by painting its most obvious features. In this case he made three studies: one of the famous Arlésiennes, another of a landscape in the snow, and a third of a view from the front window of the Carrel across the road to the local charcuterie, in all a fair summary of his first impressions of the town. Having in this rather cat-like manner marked his boundaries, he let the place take over. He found he could purchase paints and canvas either from a nearby grocer or from one of the bookshops, though not everything he needed. There was the same trouble he had found in Eindhoven, the quality was variable with white the main nuisance, it just would not dry and paintings had to be left spread about for days on end. Given the limited space available to him this became a major concern. He still felt weak after his last months in Paris. His stomach and teeth bothered him, but he was confident things would improve. He felt that it was poor circulation which lay at the root of his condition but that now he was in the south his blood was beginning to *think* of circulating again. He was increasingly certain that whatever was wrong with him was hereditary but told Theo he hoped that there would be fewer breakdowns than before. He certainly made an effort to put things right. He was drinking less – he admitted to being a virtual alcoholic at the end of the Paris period – and while his diet was still haphazard and dependent on how much he had to spend on materials, he tried to eat more sensibly, even down to taking two eggs for breakfast and ordering a better quality wine with his meals until his stomach improved.

Despite having chosen to live in the town he gave the place only a cursory and rather critical appraisal, he disliked the Musée Réattu but was better disposed to the Museum of Antiquities. He came to admire the Romanesque portico on the church of St Trophime though it disturbed him as he felt there was something *cruel* about it *like a Chinese nightmare*. The overall impression is of someone standing apart and observing things in which he feels no especial involvement:

> *Must I tell the truth and add that the Zouaves, the brothels, the adorable little Arlésiennes going to their first Communion, the priest in his surplice, who looks like a dangerous rhinoceros, the people drinking absinthe, all seem to me like creatures from another world.*

Reality intruded quite early on when he happened to stumble on a gathering outside one of the brothels where the police were holding an enquiry into the double murder of two Zouaves by two Italians. Vincent seized the opportunity to slip inside the establishment and thus began his principal connection with the old town, a regular round of the local 'houses'.

> *I saw a brothel here last Sunday – not counting the other days – a large room, the walls covered with blued whitewash – like a village school. Fifty or more military men in red and civilians in black, their faces a magnificent yellow or orange (what hues there are in the faces here), the women in sky blue, in vermilion, as unqualified and garish as possible. The whole in a yellow light. A good deal less lugubrious than the same kind of offices in Paris.*

The *Maisons de Tolérance* were in the *quartier reservé* a short walk from his lodgings but he soon settled on the Maison de Tolérance No 1 run by a Madame Virginie. He referred to these sessions as his 'hygienic practices', so much had his contacts with the opposite sex been reduced to the status of mere bodily function. Only his unhappy past experiences of trying to form a true relationship with a woman can offer an excuse, though he did have continuing contact with one of Madame Virginie's girls called Rachel whose rather shy, withdrawn manner made her easier for him to get on with. Nevertheless, there is something ineffably sad about the thought of him shuffling along the dark backstreets of Arles when the few coins in his pockets made a visit to Madame Virginie's possible, the more so, when one thinks how deeply emotional and indeed loving a man he undoubtedly was and how much he longed to express his true feelings.

When he came out after that first visit a full-scale riot was under way. All the submerged resentment against the 'Savoyard monkeys' had boiled up and a lynch-mob was charging about attacking any Italians they could find, with the result that the immigrants were forced to flee their homes. Vincent was gripped by the image of the excited crowd rushing along the narrow streets and when he eventually discovered the bullfights in the Roman Arena it was the great sweep of people covering the steep terraces which fascinated him rather than the ritual slaughter in the ring below. He made a note to paint such a press of people at some point in the future.

After the first few days, when he had finished his three first pictures, most of his time was spent outside the town, beyond the railway sheds and the factory fringe, in the snow-covered fields. Within three weeks of his arrival, and despite the freezing conditions, he came across an almond tree already in blossom. It was a matchless promise of spring to come and a reminder of everything he had travelled south to find. He broke off a couple of branches, took them back, set them in a glass and painted two studies of them. The effort was liberating; away from all the pressures of Paris he was free to use whatever he wished of all the methods and techniques that had formerly swamped him. He could if he so wished 'draw' with paint, a first outline in dark blue, say, making a contour which he could then fill in with colour. On the other hand he could use dots and sharp lines of pigment to create a burst of foliage or a sudden swirl of movement. Theories no longer seemed important, these techniques were there for him to use as he wanted.

Although it was still bitterly cold, the weather was imperceptibly improving when he experienced his first mistral, the sudden, sometimes violent wind which depressed the spirits as much as it rattled the tiles on the roofs and caused the shutters to crash against the buildings. As the wind swirled so did the branches of the cypresses and the tufts of clouds in the sky, but when it had passed there was the burning sun at midday, and the desire to walk was once more irresistible. To the north, out on the road towards the Alpilles range of hills, he found the abandoned monastery of Montmajour, an extraordinary complex of buildings of different periods including a medieval church, cathedral-like in its spaciousness, and a later tall, gaunt fortress which loomed over the surrounding plain, built to defend the monks against the bands of mercenaries that plagued Provence in the fourteenth century. Closed after the revolution and partially dismantled by Vincent's time, the impressive ruins were a classified national monument and restoration had already begun. It was the reverse of his tower in Nuenen though the eerily empty buildings still spoke of religious decline.

To the south of Arles where the Arles–Bouc Canal ran inland from the Rhône, he discovered the first of the drawbridges. He made several paintings and drawings of it, first testimony to his newly liberated colour with the blues in the water in sharp contrast to the oranges of the bridge and the riverbank. Japan is there in the idea of the bridge itself and the solid, almost abstract effect created by strong outlines and clear areas of colour. Again he used whatever brushstrokes suited the picture: rapid movement for water, sharp gestures for the grass. The result is entirely his; he had found a method that allowed him to do what he wanted or rather what he felt.

Looking at these sunny, happy works the observer is left with the sensation that there are two Vincents, for despite trying hard to begin afresh in Arles, all his old problems continued to plague him. We see nothing in these joyful paintings of the suffering of the man who painted them. He was intensely lonely, though he rarely allowed himself to admit it and tried hard to pretend otherwise, but he seized on Gauguin's first letter from Brittany. It turned out to be a piece of special pleading: Gauguin was worried about annoying Theo by writing directly to him about sales and preferred to unburden his difficulties over his health and debts to Vincent in the knowledge that he would intercede. Despite his miseries, Gauguin retained a canny sense of business and suggested that he could, if need be, reduce his prices. Ignoring his own problems, Vincent did as Gauguin knew he would and wrote to Theo and to John Peter Russell whom he hoped might buy one of Gauguin's paintings.

In Pont-Aven, Gauguin waited on events. If the Van Gogh brothers wanted to help him, then as far as he was concerned, that was fine. In fact the only hopeful sign, in what had proved a rather dismal period, was the news from Arles that Vincent was encouraging his brother to sell more of the Martinique works. In his lodgings at the Auberge Gloanec, Gauguin was inclined to become morose. "You complain about being alone," he wrote to his wife Mette in Copenhagen. "What about me? I'm alone in a room of an inn from morning till night. I have absolute silence. Nobody to exchange ideas with." Or one should perhaps read, nobody to harangue with his latest theories. To be fair, he was still suffering from the after-effects of the dysentery he had contracted in Martinique, but on the other hand he had the support of Marie-Jeanne Gloanec, mistress of the auberge, who let him use an upstairs room as a studio and allowed him virtually unlimited credit. Without that he would not have been able to survive. He had temporarily alienated his previous saviour, his ex-stockbroker colleague Emile Schuffenecker, who had taken him in when he had returned to Paris in such a run-down state the year before. Himself an amateur painter, 'good old Schuff', as Gauguin patronisingly called him, had been in considerable awe of his guest. In the group portrait he painted of the Schuffeneckers, Gauguin depicted him slightly stooped, rubbing his hands together like a subservient tradesman while his wife Louise sits rather regally in the foreground. In the end, however, even 'good old Schuff' had started to suspect that something was going on between his wife and his guest, hence the real reason behind Gauguin's hasty departure for Brittany.

Pont-Aven, outside the summer painting season when it was overrun by artists, was rather bleak. A cluster of small slate-roofed houses in a sheltered valley, the place offered few distractions, especially in bad weather when there was no incentive to climb the surrounding hills or to visit the farms which spread down to where the Aven flowed into the Atlantic. When Gauguin tried to paint, all the fire of his Martinique works seemed extinguished by the February mists. It was as if he was being dragged backwards.

Not the least contradiction in Gauguin's character was the unexpected quirk that while he was able to play fast and loose with other men's wives without the least qualm, he was scrupulous about settling his debts, and deeply concerned until he had done so. It irked him to have to run up credit with the doctor as he struggled to regain his health. Even after Easter when he felt much improved and the weather changed for the better, there was still loneliness to contend with. The first painters who began to drift in were all the type of dullards found at Cormon's and the other ateliers. He had nothing in common with them and as they spent a lot of their time making rude remarks about Impressionism, the antipathy was mutual. The days hung heavy. He was forty on June 7th but he felt much older. He even suggested to Mette that she might join him but she was not to be persuaded. Though his feelings about this were ambiguous, he genuinely missed their five children and started painting pictures of local youngsters at play, boys bathing and girls dancing in their peasant costume.

It was soon after this birthday that Vincent first suggested he join him in Arles and, feeling so low, Gauguin was tempted. It had been evident since they met in Paris and from the tone of his letters from Arles that Vincent was another 'good old Schuff' ever ready to bolster Gauguin's own opinion of himself, something he sorely needed right now. He wrote to the Van Goghs to express his interest in their plan but for the moment that was as far as he would go.

While he awaited Gauguin's decision, Vincent in Arles did his best to create some sort of artistic community with anyone he found locally. His first contacts were two amateur painters, a grocer and a magistrate, who called on the new artist in their midst. As we hear no more of them it would be safe to assume that they took one look at the astonishingly brightly coloured works in his room and never returned. Then, to add to his isolation, word came of the sudden death of Anton Mauve while on a journey to Arnhem. Although they had quarrelled and Mauve's behaviour had been small-minded, even cruel, Vincent understood what lay behind it and had never ceased to be grateful for the way Mauve had introduced him to, indeed bullied him into using paints and had thus had some part in everything he was now doing. His death must have seemed yet another example of the miserable condition of the artists he knew, men like Gauguin and indeed himself, often hungry and sick, frequently mocked or at best ignored. Why should their lives be so grim? Could not something be done about it? He had already written to Theo suggesting ways to improve conditions; perhaps they could persuade Tersteeg to act as an agent for the new art in Holland and England. To his fury his old boss had not bothered to reply. Now Vincent revived the idea of an association of artists, though he accepted that Theo could not afford to be its paymaster. Rather, the richer artists, by whom he meant the original Impressionists, would somehow support the poorer, the 'Petit Boulevard'. These were pipe-dreams but they helped fend off his loneliness. He wrote to Emile Bernard proposing that he too should come to Arles to join the group he desperately wanted to set up. Further complaints from Gauguin in Pont-Aven merely fuelled the illusion that he too was about to leave and join him. He even wrote to Toulouse-Lautrec, though the idea of that most Parisian of artists settling into a life in the countryside around Arles was preposterous. Not surprisingly, he never replied and Vincent dropped him from his schemes.

While the plans for a 'Studio of the South' took up one side of his life, Vincent pressed on with his work. He had come across a mixed orchard and, presumably with the permission of its owner, set about painting the various trees as they came into blossom. It was the first major sequence of work in his new home. He began in late March and finished in late April, fourteen wonderful canvases: apricot, cherry, apple, peach, plum, pear, always a single type of blossom to each canvas as if they were living bouquets. In Paris there had been city flowers, cut and posed; these were the living spring colours of Provence. Only the rare appearance of a ladder or a scythe indicates that human beings might be involved in this natural process. Once again he used whatever technique he thought appropriate at the time: thin washes of colour, thick impasto, a near Divisionist use of dots, blocks of colour. Though he may have been painting several different orchards, the overall impression is of one particular place seen from many angles, as if he were trying to establish artistic control over a defined segment of the world, just as the orchard itself was bordered with neat cane fences and rows of cypresses which shielded the delicate trees from the sudden destructive winds of the mistral.

He felt bound to give credit where he believed it was due and took a canvas of a pink peachtree in blossom with a similar tree sheltering behind and wrote on it:

SOUVENIR DE MAUVE

VINCENT THEO

Though today, only the single name Vincent remains.

He wrote to Theo to explain that he wanted to make three studies of each fruit tree: a tall upright picture with a horizontal one on either side, in other words a triptych and evidence of his new religion, nature, a harkening back to his childhood obsession with the plants and insects in the gardens and fields of Zundert.

At last he had some company. He had got to know the other foreign artist in the town, a young Danish painter, Christian Mourier-Petersen, who was in the middle of a three year 'tour' through France and Holland. At thirty-one, Petersen had, like Vincent, come late to painting. He had begun studying medicine but the strain of examinations had brought on a nervous disorder and a recent visit to Paris had probably done nothing to improve matters. Coming from a small town in his native Denmark he was no doubt happy to settle back into the quiet life of a place like Arles and in many ways his attitudes were distinctly parochial. He had seen the last Impressionist exhibition in the Rue Lafitte, but made clear to Vincent that he was more drawn to the northern realist painters like Heyerdahl and Kroyer, familiar to him from his youth. Vincent chose to ignore his prejudices; at least he had read Zola and the Goncourts, and could talk about books. They started spending their evenings together, though they had little in common, for Petersen produced work which Vincent thought *dry but very conscientious*. Timid and unsure of himself, the young man wanted to go to Paris to see the Salon and thence to Holland to complete his education before returning home. He was hardly a suitable candidate for Vincent's 'Studio of the South' but for the time being there was no one else.

John Peter Russell's friend, the American Dodge MacKnight, who was staying in the nearby village of Fontvieille beyond the abandoned monastery of Montmajour, occasionally called when he was in Arles. The 27-year-old MacKnight was in Vincent's words a *Yankee*, which evidently meant he found him irritating, though not having seen the man's work, he withheld any final judgement and for the time being MacKnight was disinclined to give him a sight of what he was doing. Between visits, Vincent fantasised that MacKnight might at least be a wealthy Yankee who could help set up his artists' co-operative. MacKnight had worked at Cormon's and knew Anquetin, surely a good sign. But when Vincent eventually tramped out to Fontvieille and saw MacKnight's watercolours, they showed how much the young man was floundering amid the conflicting theories of the time. Vincent could only acknowledge that his 'strength' was a façade and that at heart MacKnight was indecisive. Some measure of the man can be gained from his later claim to have discovered Vincent, "a completely mad guy but a good fellow".

Better to spend the evenings talking with Mourier-Petersen, despite his often impenetrable Danish accent. When irritated, Vincent called him *Dr. Ox*, but Petersen had some family money which was always useful and could afford to drink cognac and water rather than the poor man's absinthe. Despite his longings for home, he showed some predilection for change and Vincent did his best to persuade him to stay longer in the south and try out some of the new ideas.

There was better news from Paris. Theo had entered a number of his works for the forthcoming Salon des Indépendants. Vincent wrote back to say that he wanted to be listed as 'Vincent' in the catalogue, on the usual grounds that his full name would only be mispronounced. And Tersteeg at last replied to Theo, reluctantly agreeing to take a consignment of new art: "Send me some Impressionists, but only those that you yourself think best."

Despite such caution, the news was encouraging. Vincent longed to send the first batch of orchards to Theo but was restrained by the zinc white which refused to dry. The whole question of materials was beginning to irritate him, the town's supply was virtually exhausted and he sent Tasset & Lhote, the Paris suppliers, a mammoth order for paint and canvas which was clearly going to be very expensive. Then he heard that there was renewed sniping between Boussod, Valadon and Theo over the upstairs exhibitions and began to worry about his only source of income. He determined to economise by using less paint and canvas and was further nudged back towards drawing by the discovery of clumps of reeds along the banks of the canals, which could be sharpened into first-class implements. Their suppleness meant they could give a sharp pen-like mark or, with less pressure, give some of the qualities of the brushstroke. If he used a sketchbook at this time it has not survived and all the evidence is that these drawings were not seen as preparations for painting but as works in their own right, although the subjects do follow the pattern of the paintings. First he marked out his territory with a view from the upper floor of the Carrel, then he took in surrounding landmarks like the drawbridge and a view of the town from the bank of the Rhône. But the most haunting were simply views of open countryside around the town, empty of human activity, often with the same open foreground he had used in The Hague, any houses and trees clustered at the horizon. Nothing could be more assured than these scenes; and while the precision of drawing may seem inappropriate to the evocative concerns of a colourist, Vincent transcended such apparent limitations, using dots and short strokes as he did in the paintings to suggest foliage or grass or the movement of a path. Despite the economy of means he created some exceptionally subtle effects: a trampled patch in a cornfield, the precise shapes of irises at the edge of a meadow, all set down with an awesome self-assurance for one so plagued by insecurity.

Comparing such work with what he wrote about himself it is clear that anyone attempting a direct connection between the man and the art should tread cautiously. The Vincent with a reed pen firmly in his hand, his eye fixed on the skyline of Arles or the washerwoman by the King's Canal is not the moody, difficult creature sharing a drink with Mourier-Petersen in one of the night cafés when the day's work is done.

Sometimes his work did not go well. In one letter to Theo he explained how he had spoiled a large painting of a cherry tree, in another he made a mess of a painting of the bridge, but this was inevitable and did not depress him. It was the 'real' world that lowered his spirits, the way the local people seemed unfriendly, or his continuing suspicions that he was being cheated. Of course, much of this isolation may simply have been the townsfolks' not unnatural aversion to his odd appearance and manner. The people of Arles were a close-knit community sealed off within their culture and able to escape into their own Provençal dialect, effectively a separate language. The railway had brought work but had failed to open up that hermetic society. Inside the walled town, strangers were strangers and their only value was as a source of income. From the start Vincent was convinced they were overcharging him. He had managed to get his rate for the room at the Hotel-Restaurant Carrel reduced from five to four francs a day but this only led to a distinct ill-feeling on the part of the owners which did not soften even when he was clearly unwell.

> *You know, if I could only get really strong soup, it would do me good immediately: it's preposterous, but I never can get what I ask for, even the simplest things, from these people here. And it's the same everywhere in these little restaurants.*
>
> *But is it so hard to bake potatoes?*
>
> *Impossible.*
>
> *Then rice, or macaroni? None left, or else it is all messed up in grease, or else they aren't cooking it today, and they'll explain that it's tomorrow's dish, there's no room on the stove, and so on. It's absurd, but that is the real reason why my health is low.*

It is likely that his bad teeth and peculiar eating habits had produced a stomach ulcer which would have been exacerbated by his bouts of nervous anger. He was convinced that the owners of the Carrel were still overcharging him and at the beginning of May he took the huge step of renting a small derelict house, one half of a double-fronted, yellow-painted building right on the edge of the Place Lamartine facing the city gate. Where it bordered on the river, the 'Place' was a quiet public garden, at its centre it was a busy crossing where the road over the old stone bridge from Trinquetaille merged with the main route from the north, then divided once more to pass into or around the town. This was the heart of that other Arles brought by the railway. Behind the 'Place' was the station itself, and around it were the cafés and night haunts of the town's underclass. It was in many ways a significant gesture on Vincent's part, though at first it was no more than that for the house was uninhabitable – the nearest lavatory was in the hotel at the back which belonged to the same landlord. He intended to go on staying at the Carrel while he fixed it up. But the significance of the gesture was clear in his own mind. In this yellow-painted house he would have a place to bring his fellow artists. The fifteen francs a month it cost was a great improvement on the four francs a day at the Carrel and with others sharing there would be considerable financial inducement to set up a colony of some kind. He began to make plans for furnishing it, starting with a bed and a mattress. If nothing else, it meant he would have to stay put; until recently he had continued to believe he would move to Marseilles and had even invested in some new clothes suitable for the city. He still planned to go there one day but for the moment there was too much to occupy his mind – Mourier-Petersen was leaving for Paris and could take the first consignment of work for Theo. Then there was an out-and-out quarrel with the owners of the Carrel over his bill. He reckoned they had gone on charging him for the more expensive wine he had taken when he was ill even though he had long ago gone back to the regular stuff. They wanted sixty-seven francs; he insisted it was only forty. The argument was heated. He left, moving into the Café de la Gare a few doors down from the Yellow House. The owners of the Carrel seized his trunk and refused to release it until he settled. Vincent paid in order to retrieve his belongings but stormed off to the local court to bring a case against them, even though he was petrified he might lose and have to pay both the bill and the legal fees.

While he awaited the magistrate's verdict he settled into his new lodgings run by Joseph Ginoux and his wife Marie. The Café de la Gare was an easy-going meeting place and all-night drinking den whose location meant Vincent had once more returned to his usual position on the fringes of local society. The Café played host to railway workers, stray Zouaves, the odd local '*voyou*'. They could stay up all night if there was nowhere else to go, drinking absinthe, sleeping at the tables. Despite their somewhat louche establishment, Joseph and Marie Ginoux were a good-hearted couple and from the start they liked him; Marie suffered from some form of nervous or depressive condition so they had much to sympathise over.

Nearby, on the corner of the street leading to the station was a house with pink and green shutters where Madame Vénissac ran the restaurant where he now took his meals. He could eat for a franc, or 1 franc 50 if he wanted something really special, and as Madame Vénissac was better disposed to his needs than the owners of the Carrel, his health rapidly improved. He was further cheered by the magistrate's decision obliging his former hosts to repay twelve francs.

Vincent was no sooner feeling better, however, than Theo wrote to say he was consulting Dr Gruby who had diagnosed heart trouble. Vincent suggested that Mourier-Petersen might stay with him for a while and the young man left with two paintings and two drawings. Theo then wrote proposing that Vincent enter drawings for a Dutch exhibition, and, thus prompted, he began work on some studies around the old monastery at Montmajour. His real desire, though, was to travel across the wild Carmargue to the fishing village of Les Saintes-Maries-de-la-Mer where Monticelli had worked. Late May was the time of year for pilgrimages to the village, where it was believed the three Marys, the sister of the Virgin, the mother of the apostles James and John, and Mary Magdalene, had landed in AD45 and converted Provence to Christianity. There was also a separate gypsy pilgrimage to the shrine of their servant Sarah. Vincent seems to have been less interested in the sacred nature of the occasion than in the practical fact that the fare, by diligence across the marshy plain, was much reduced during the festivities. Another reason he was attracted to the place was because Uncle Jan, the seafaring member of the family, had once voyaged along that stretch of coast and of all his uncles, Jan, who had died three years earlier, had always been the least critical of his behaviour.

Before leaving there was the problem of Gauguin. More letters outlining his debts had been passing between Pont-Aven, Paris, and Arles and it was now proposed that if he joined Vincent a way might be found to settle his bills and provide him with an allowance. For Vincent the problem was how to furnish the Yellow House. He could not obtain credit for the beds but managed to purchase some crockery and a coffee pot, which he arranged as a still-life and painted with the simple clarity of a poster as if advertising his new domesticity. The result was so bright and clear he told Theo that it *absolutely kills all the others*.

It was this home-making that delayed his trip to Les Saintes-Maries. The house had to be redecorated and his share of the cost temporarily crippled his finances so that it was not until May 30th that he was able to catch the early morning diligence for the fishing village. The main religious celebrations were over but it was a sufficiently jolly outing to overcome his distaste for travel, which, in his telling phrase *beats you up*. There was also the chance to see the Carmargue with its *grass plains where there are herds of fighting bulls and also herds of little white horses, half wild and very beautiful*.

Les Saintes-Maries was appropriately dominated by a stone church, the only other structure of note being an ancient fortress used as a barracks. For the rest, there were clusters of fishermen's hovels, some with long, low thatched roofs, which reminded him of Drenthe. But there the comparison with the North ended for this was the Mediterranean at last, his first sight of it, and its impact was stunning. He had intended to concentrate on drawing, which he wanted to be *more spontaneous, more exaggerated*, and had brought only three canvases. But once he saw the place he knew immediately that here was the vision of colour he had been longing for. His description of it is a brave attempt to capture the ephemeral: *The Mediterranean has the colours of mackerel, changeable I mean. You don't always know if it's green or violet, you can't even say it's blue, because the next moment the changing light has taken on a tinge of pink or gray.*

He had managed to find board and lodging for four francs (having knocked them down from six), though he quickly learned that if there was an exceptionally good catch, the local fishing fleet headed off to Marseilles, leaving the village virtually without food; he compared the local butcher to one of the Arab meat merchants in a Gérôme painting. No matter, he only stayed four nights, having such a limited amount of materials, but the effect on his work was astonishing. It was not the canvases he painted – in any case, they had to be left behind to dry – the crucial work was in the carefully annotated drawings and water-colours meant to be worked up into paintings on his return. In the end the preliminary sketches themselves turned out to be the most important work, especially a water-colour study of fishing boats on the beach which precipitated a radical new use of colour. The sinuous shapes of the boats, with masts like spiky bamboo were distinctly exotic but it was the almost violent contrast of blue and orange which ultimately created a barbaric effect. Everything about the work was liberating – he made the first drawing for it in only an hour on the Sunday morning he was due to leave. He proudly informed Theo that he had not used his perspective frame, having done it free-hand with the spontaneity he craved. His letter to Theo from Les Saintes-Maries is eloquent:

> *Now that I have seen the sea here, I am absolutely convinced of the importance of staying in the Midi, and of positively piling it on, exaggerating the colour – Africa not so far away.*

Back in Arles there was a slight loss of nerve and the oil version of the fishing boats had slightly muted colours, but that was a temporary reversion, the effects of this vision of Africa could not be restrained. Just before the trip he had begun a second series of seasonal paintings of the harvesting then taking place all round the town. Now the colours take on a new intensity: yellow haystacks in a yellow field with yellow houses; a sower (somewhat out of season) after Millet, the man and his field in jabbed strokes of violet, contrasted with yellow ochre and carmine, while the wheat on the horizon, the sky and a great burning sun are once more a gilded yellow. Far from finding the harvest colours more muted than the season of spring blossom he seems to have felt himself surrounded by something altogether richer and more intense:

> *It has become very different from what it was in spring, and yet I certainly have no less love for this countryside, scorched as it begins to be from now on. Everywhere now there is old gold, bronze, copper, one might say, and this with the green azure of the sky blanched with heat: a delicious colour, extraordinarily harmonious, with the blended tones of Delacroix.*

A sudden downpour, four days of unseasonal heavy rain from July 20th to 23rd further intensified these reactions. Unable, like the farmers, to work in the fields, he decided to return to portrait painting. But how to get a model given the stand-offishness of most of the locals? Here his new life outside the city walls came in useful. As he was now one of the outsiders, drinking in the late-night cafés, meeting other 'foreigners' in the brothels, he was beginning to make friends at last. Apart from Joseph and Marie Ginoux he had a drinking companion, one of the postal employees from the station, a Joseph Roulin, and just before he left for Les Saintes-Maries Vincent had also made friends with a second lieutenant in the third regiment of Zouaves. This young officer, Paul-Eugène Milliet, was still recovering from an illness contracted during the Tonkin campaign. He wore the yellow-and-blue-striped campaign medal on his jacket with the regiment's number three prominent on his high collar and the headband of his red kepi. With a Second Empire goatee he was a dashing fellow but unlike most of his fellow officers he had interests outside soldiering and whoring, the usual preoccupations of the local Zouaves. Milliet was an enthusiastic amateur artist and Vincent did what he could to help, asking Theo to send a copy of Cassagne's *ABCD du Dessin* and taking him on sketching trips. They went to Montmajour in early July. With Milliet in his dark-blue and red uniform and Vincent in his rough working clothes and tattered straw hat, how odd they must have looked walking out of the town, past haymakers and gleaners finishing the short harvest before the burning heat of high summer. Not that the young officer was above joining the painter in a raid on a garden where they stole *some excellent figs*. But despite that temporary aberration Milliet was nothing if not a soldier, his whole life had been bound up with service discipline. As the son of a military policeman he had been raised entirely in barracks and knew no other life. He had only been promoted to the rank of junior officer during the recent campaign so no doubt he felt his career was going well. The regiment was about to be sent to North Africa, which offered all sorts of opportunities for advancement. The stumbling-block ahead was a written examination which he was obliged to pass and he knew he would have to set aside his artistic hobby in order to do some serious swotting before travelling to Paris to sit the papers. While he liked him as a friend, Vincent was less impressed with the soldier's artistic abilities, an opinion matched by Milliet's view of Vincent's talents. "A canvas should be 'stroked'," Milliet recorded later. "Vincent attacked it. Sometimes he was a real savage." With the reckless courage of a decorated warrior, he even told Vincent what he thought and was duly rewarded with a furious riposte. They were soon reconciled as Vincent haughtily maintained that Milliet was not to be blamed for his gauche opinions. In every way the relationship between the bohemian Vincent and the ramrod Milliet was the strangest of all his passing friendships. The second lieutenant's view of Vincent from a soldier's stand-point was of course unique:

> His face was a bit sun-burnt, as if he had been serving up-country in Africa. But of course he hadn't; he had none of the makings of a soldier, not one. An artist? Of course he was an artist, he drew very well indeed. He was a charming companion when he wanted to be – which didn't happen every day. We often went on good walks around Arles, and in the country we would make no end of sketches. Sometimes he would set up his canvas and start daubing straight away. After that there was no budging him. The fellow had talent in his drawing, but he became quite different when he picked up his brushes. As soon as he started painting I would leave him alone, otherwise I should have to refuse to tell him what I thought, or we would start arguing. He hadn't got an easy nature and when he lost his temper you'd think he'd gone mad.

Of course Vincent was no less biased in his reactions and not without a certain wry humour in his perception of his subject. As he wrote to Theo: *Milliet today was pleased with what I had done – the 'Ploughed Field'; generally he does not like what I do, but because the colour of the lumps of earth is as soft as a pair of sabots, it did not offend him, with the forget-me-not blue sky flecked with white clouds.*

But if Vincent could just about swallow his friend's criticism of his painting, he was unable to stomach the young man's taste in popular literature which he constantly attempted to improve. Despite their obvious differences, the two seem to have tolerated each other to a remarkable extent and when Vincent needed a model that rainy July, it was Milliet who came to his aid, bringing along a young soldier from the regiment to sit for his portrait in the full dress uniform of the Zouaves: baggy red pantaloons, embroidered dark-blue waistcoat, sky blue cummerbund and tassled red fez. Apart from the still-life of coffee cups it was the first time the Yellow House had been used as a studio, and with his dark, North African face and gaudy outfit there could have been no more powerful image than that of the young Zouave with which to inaugurate the place. Outside in the fields there were always the obligations of nature pulling him back from the brink of abstraction, imposing its own disciplines; but sealed off in the house, with so exotic an apparition before him, Vincent could become as 'Japanese' as he wished:

> *I have a model at last – a Zouave! a boy with a small face, a bull neck, and the eye of a tiger, and I began with one portrait, and began again with another; the half-length I did of him was horribly harsh, in a blue uniform, the blue of enamel saucepans, with braids of a faded reddish orange, and two citron yellow stars on his breast, an ordinary blue, and very hard to do, that bronzed feline head of his with the reddish cap, against a green door and the orange bricks of a wall. So it's a savage combination of incongruous tones, not easy to manage. The study I made of it seems to me very harsh, but all the same I'd like always to be working on vulgar, even loud portraits like this. It teaches me something, and above all that is what I want from my work. The second portrait will be full length, seated against a white wall.*

It is that well-known, second portrait which shows Vincent at his most extreme. The blunt triangle of the soldier's red pantaloons dominates the centre of the canvas, the tiled floor slides down out of the picture leaving the figure isolated, like a cut-out, divorced from any sense of place, not unlike the robed geisha in the print he had copied in Paris. He knew exactly what he was striving for and expressed it bluntly, *In a way all my work is founded on Japanese art...*

What he was now doing was beyond the comprehension of those around him. MacKnight came with a friend but both refrained from making any comment on what they saw. This companion, who was staying out at Fontvieille with him, was a 33-year-old Belgian, Eugène Boch, a poet and painter. There were immediate similarities with Van Rappard, for Boch's industrialist father was well able to support his son's whims and had already done so with the elder daughter Anna who was studying art in Brussels when the young Eugène decided to follow her example. He had done a spell at Cormon's where he had met Lautrec, though he always felt himself to be an open-air painter and in '84 had travelled to North Africa, more for the unusual landscape than the scenes of oriental life so beloved of Gérôme. With Vincent's current preoccupations, Boch's contact with the dreamland across the Mediterranean must have been fascinating and as he gradually came to know Boch, Vincent grew to like him, certainly more than the bumptious MacKnight. He was intrigued by the young poet's strange equine face, *rather like a Flemish gentleman of the time of the Compromise of the Nobles, William the Silent's time and Marnix's. I shouldn't wonder if he's a decent fellow.* When he visited them both at Fontvieille he found Boch's work acceptable, despite his as yet unsuccessful attempt to come to terms with Impressionism. But the most appealing thing about him was the amazing fact that Boch had been born in La Louvière near to the Borinage. Why did his new friend not go back home? Surely there was more to be done in the land of the oleanders and the sulphur sun than here in Provence? Who but Vincent could have convinced someone born beneath those sickly yellow skies and grey smoking slag-heaps that it was an artistic Mecca? For in the end, Vincent prevailed and Boch did indeed return home, much to his advantage, for the coalfields stimulated his best work, ethereal images of smoking mine-heads and bleak cottages nestling beside dark pit-heaps.

Behind this encouragement was Vincent's still unsuppressed desire to return to the coalfields himself. Africa or the Borinage – only Vincent could have been torn between such opposites.

That summer Theo had sent some of Vincent's work to Holland as planned but none were sold. Vincent had to be content with the pleasure of knowing that his work was at last on show in his native land, though Tersteeg manifested his continuing opposition to the new art by claiming that a landscape by Sisley must have been painted when the artist was slightly drunk. It was increasingly difficult for Theo to brush aside such comments. He was beginning to be rattled by the impossibility of selling the work he loved and had reached the point where he was actually angry when he succeeded in selling a Meissonier or a Bouguereau, the two fashionable painters whose work he found most distasteful.

Equally disagreeable was a message from Tanguy with a bill for materials which Vincent had failed to settle before he left Paris. Vincent denied the claim, admitting only that he owed money to Bing for some Japanese prints and ascribing the whole unpleasantness to Tanguy's shrew of a wife. Given that Theo eventually settled both accounts one can assume that Vincent had muddled the whole thing. Unlike Gauguin, he seems to have had a distinctly cavalier attitude towards debts. As he seldom profited from the money which came his way, he looked on the claims of others as a form of aggression. Indeed he was much more concerned to sort out Gauguin's finances than his own and the customary requests for fifty or a hundred francs which punctuate his letters to Theo were now joined by an endless toing and froing over Gauguin's intentions about Arles. There is something humiliating about Vincent's supplications and something at the same time coquettish and bullish about the way Gauguin toyed with the idea.

There were failures of a kind with work too: he tried unsuccessfully to create an overtly religious painting, though why he should have wanted to do so at this juncture is not clear.

> *I have scraped off a big painted study, an olive garden, with a figure of Christ in blue and orange, and an angel in yellow. Red earth, hills green and blue, olive trees with violet and carmine trunks, and green grey and blue foliage. A citron yellow sky. I scraped it off because I tell myself that I must not do figures of that importance without models.*

Happily more models were available, including a young girl of about sixteen whom he called La Mousmé after the character in Pierre Loti's *Madame Chrysanthème*, which he had just read. The Oriental fragility of the girl was pointed up by a spray of blossoms in her hand and was further emphasised by having the thin bentwood chair on which she sits depicted twice as large as life thus highlighting her tiny wasp-waisted frame. The same chair can be seen in the portrait done a few weeks later of his drinking companion Joseph Roulin, but now the seat is reduced in size to bring out the man's height and strength. Roulin was the new Tanguy in Vincent's life, the blunt man of the people, the reliable old rogue always there when needed. The various portraits of him bring out what Vincent called Roulin's *silent gravity and a tenderness for me such as an old soldier might have for a young one.*

Although only ten years older than Vincent, Roulin's full beard and calm manner gave him a fatherly air, though as they spent much of their time hanging round the bars and brothels he had little else in common with the late Theodorus. Much has been made of their drinking, so that Roulin is often portrayed as an incurable alcoholic. The responsibilities of his job make such a thing doubtful. Although Vincent always referred to him as the 'Postman Roulin' he had long since given up the role of the jolly country *facteur* and was by then postal agent at the station, where he was responsible for overseeing the unloading of the mail sacks and their security until transferred either to the post office in Arles or onward to Marseilles or Paris. Given that many ordinary folk sent cash by post – Theo always put the fifty and one hundred franc notes for Vincent straight into the envelopes with his letters – Roulin's dependability was *de rigueur*. Later in life he received first the postal service's bronze medal of honour and later its silver. So he was unlikely to have been an alcoholic, though certainly a man who liked his drink and who knew how to enjoy himself.

Joseph Roulin had been born in the nearby village of Lambesc where he had married his wife Augustine. After an unhappy spell in Nice he had managed to engineer a transfer to Arles where they now lived in the Rue de la Cavalerie, not far from the restaurant Carrel, with their two sons Armand, seventeen, and Camille, twelve. When Vincent first met the family, Madame Roulin was again pregnant. Although ten years younger than her husband, childbearing had left her with a rather plump motherly figure. Unlike Madame Ginoux, Augustine Roulin was somewhat frightened of Vincent, though unlike Tanguy's wife she does not seem to have resented him drinking with her husband who, as she well knew, would have done so anyway. For his part, Vincent thought their marriage as *exemplary* as that of his parents, though there the resemblance ended for, unlike Pastor Theodorus, Roulin was a passionate Republican, despite having been obliged to swear an oath of allegiance to Napoleon III when he joined the postal service twenty odd years earlier. He was highly likely to break into a stirring rendition of the Marseillaise which transported Vincent back in imagination to the revolution whose centenary the nation was about to celebrate. Politically, the passionate Roulin was not a man to argue with. As befitted someone obliged to hump sacks of letters and then be responsible for guarding them, he was just over six feet tall and cut a resplendent figure in his blue uniform trimmed with gold. As the son of a peasant farmer he cannot have had much formal education, but he had a love of learning typical of a politically conscious worker and would happily read whatever was recommended to him. Above all he was one of the rare people truly to appreciate Vincent's work, despite its radical nature and, when asked to pose, vehemently refused any suggestion of payment, though his salary of 135 francs a month left just enough for his absinthe. It was a kind gesture that did not quite work out as Vincent agreed to give him his meals and the cost of feeding someone so big quickly made a dent in his resources.

From all that Vincent wrote to Theo about him and from the portraits themselves, 'the postman' appears a kindly soul. He already had a Russian look which in old age made him resemble Tolstoy with broad white beard and black skull-cap. In Roulin Vincent had at last found a model who fulfilled all his earlier intentions of painting ordinary folk, for in every sense 'the postman' was a man of the people. More even than the De Groots and the Van Rooys of Nuenen, the entire Roulin family came to represent an ideal. He painted them all: Armand the sad-eyed young man about to go into the army, Camille the child, always in a jaunty cap of some sort, and then the baby Marcelline born on the last day of July while Vincent was working on his first studies of the father. Ever taken with children, Vincent was entranced by the way his friend doted on the new arrival and he painted the child being held up for inspection by her mother and made a number of portraits of the plump Augustine, comfortably seated in her chair, watching over the child.

No doubt stimulated by these images of loving simplicity he searched out similar subjects. There was a local gardener, Patience Escalier, who had once been a cow-herd in the Camargue. He was an ideal subject with his lined, kindly face and his peasant's smock and straw hat and Vincent longed to send his portrait to Paris where he wanted it hung beside one of Lautrec's paintings so that the *sun-steeped, sun-burned quality, tanned and airswept, would show up still more effectively beside all that face powder and elegance.*

In the middle of August Second Lieutenant Milliet left for Paris, taking with him a consignment of canvases for Theo, and it was as if another stage in Vincent's life in Arles had ended. He had thought vaguely of joining Gauguin in Pont-Aven but now he set his mind firmly on the idea that Gauguin should indeed come south, and like a bride preparing the marriage chamber, he embarked on a series of paintings of sunflowers with which to decorate the Yellow House.

Despite the improved summer weather, Gauguin felt no better than before. He was still lonely, his stomach and his debts still irked him and it seemed easier to agree to Vincent's wheedling suggestions that he move south than to go on by himself. Then all of a sudden, to his immense relief, the situation changed. First his friend Charles Laval managed to get back from Martinique and came to join him. With his rather timid look, peering through his pince-nez, Laval was just the sort of rabbit who could provide all the adulation Gauguin craved. They were soon out painting together, and Laval, as before, hung on his every word. Vincent would have to wait. Then in the middle of August Emile Bernard arrived, bursting with theories, plans and new ideas. He too had been pursued by letter from Arles but had also decided not to join the extended community Vincent was apparently trying to set up. In an act of curious self-abnegation Vincent had suddenly changed tack and started to encourage Bernard to leave Saint-Briac where he was painting and move to Pont-Aven so that he could be with Gauguin. To Vincent any community, even one in which he had no part, was better than none.

The encounter between Bernard and Gauguin threatened a repeat of their former tetchiness. Ominously, the younger man had made further strides with the simplification of line and colour, while Gauguin had been treading water. Fortunately for good relations, Bernard had decided to play the role of disciple, so that peace could break out between them. To crown this unexpected cordiality, all was suddenly made perfect by the arrival of Bernard's eighteen-year-old sister Madeleine, chaperoned by their mother. They all painted her that summer but no one made her look as pretty as Gauguin did, her hair piled high, an electric blue dress echoed in the hint of shadow about her almond eyes and the pair of embroidered slippers on the floor beside her. The edge of a Degas drawing of ballet dancers on the wall behind her was meant as a tribute, as, in every sense, was the whole picture. Gauguin was in love with her and could not resist showing by her quizzical sideways glance that she knew full well what was on his mind.

The portrait is a family tribute in another way, too, for Gauguin had found himself regenerated by what he saw of Emile Bernard's work. Younger and far less inhibited, Bernard had been making drawings in Saint-Briac with the simplicity of stained glass and the abandon of caricature. That May the critic Edouard Dujardin had given such work the name 'Cloisonism' after medieval enamel work whose bold colours were separated by metal cloisons. In the game of leap-frog the rivals were engaged in, Bernard was clearly ahead for the moment. He also had an intense relationship with Catholicism which attracted him to the obscure medieval practices still common among the Bretons and his work in Pont-Aven began to combine the vivid 'Japanese' look they both sought, with the mysticism and strangeness much prized by the patrons of the Chat Noir. That September Bernard painted a group of Breton women wearing their traditional full dresses, pinafores and elaborate coifs after one of the '*pardons*', the religious gatherings whose Celtic ceremonial, inexplicable to outsiders, harked back to a druidical past. It is a work that goes much further than either he or Gauguin had yet attempted. The background is a flat area of colour while the figures have the simplified appearance of a child's cut-outs.

Not to be outdone, Gauguin immediately followed with a scene in which the same Breton women are gathered outside their church when they suddenly see a vision of the sermon they have just been listening to, Jacob wrestling with the angel. It was flatter, brighter and bolder than the Martinique paintings and he knew at once it was the unexpressed, ill-defined 'something' he had been struggling to find.

Of course, Gauguin hated being reminded of his debt to the younger man and the two would waste a considerable amount of energy in the coming years claiming credit for the new development, each denigrating the other's role in inventing it. For the moment, however, things were calm because Bernard called him 'le Maître' while Gauguin referred to him as 'le petit Bernard', and, of course, there was Madeleine. They took their meals at their own table, apart from what Gauguin called 'the band of simpletons' from Paris. It was usual for the entire Auberge to celebrate Marie-Jeanne's birthday and, when one of the 'simpletons' objected to Gauguin adding a bright new still-life to the decorations, he signed it Madeleine B. and left the objector pacified by the delusion that it was an amateur effort by Bernard's sister.

Gauguin was essentially an intuitive painter; it was Bernard who had the ideas and who articulated what he did with a supporting theory. The older man was happy to draw on the younger man's flow of thoughts for the one thing he admired in Vincent's letters was the fulsome explanations of what he was doing and he was glad to be able to reply in kind, offering the Dutchman his own philosophy of art, generally culled from Bernard's dinner-time talk. Sadly, Theo was not having quite the success in selling his work that he had hoped for. Still, the fact that the Van Goghs took such an interest in him was a crucial prop in the support structure Gauguin desperately needed. But money remained his biggest worry; not all the debts had been repaid.

Thanks to Vincent's constant harping on the subject, Theo was now in the position of having two painters to maintain. His salary of 7000 francs a year plus commissions was more than adequate for someone in his position but hardly enough for him to adopt the role of a major patron of the arts. Yet even at a distance Theo found it hard to gainsay his brother. Despite having been in a state of collapse when Vincent left, Theo still adored him and now he was gone felt something valuable had been taken away.

That April, Andries Bonger married his fiancée Anne van der Linden and moved to Passy. Although they often visited it was not the same as when he and Andries had taken their meals together every day. In March, Theo took in a lodger, the Dutch painter Arnold Koning. He too had been ill and been treated by Dr Rivet, and his concern for healthy living entailed the introduction of breakfast to the Rue Lepic apartment. But as soon as Koning was fully recovered he left for Holland and although there would be other lodgers like Mourier-Petersen from time to time, Theo was most often on his own. To add to this there was the renewal of his old problem with Boussod and Valadon. It was hard to defend his upstairs gallery when all he could get for a Renoir was 150 francs, while the main gallery at the Place de L'Opéra paid 27,000 francs for a portrait from Cabanel's studio and sold it the same day for 30,000 francs. The difference was too vast to ignore. It was possible to make a profit of 30,000 francs – say 6000 American dollars, at the time – on a single painting by Gérôme. No wonder Boussod and Valadon thought him foolish to bother with works which frequently remained unsold and only occasionally brought in a few hundred francs at most. So tricky were relations, that Theo studiously avoided displaying Vincent's work lest the partners found an excuse to criticise him for nepotism. And yet he remained as determined as his brother, a courage curiously at odds with his withdrawn appearance. The symbolist poet Gustave Kahn described him timorously showing a client a Renoir. "He was," Kahn recorded, "white, blond and so melancholy he seemed to hold out the canvases as if they were begging bowls." But Kahn went on to say that despite this reserve, Theo still showed such an iron certitude about the value of the new paintings that he occasionally had his successes and, while he might not have the salesman's patter, he was nevertheless an excellent critic who could talk with painters and writers as a "certified amateur".

Theo certainly deserved better than the self-centred Gauguin as a dependent. The latter could not even be bothered to get Theo's name right and mostly wrote 'van Gog' on his notes and letters. With a fine disregard for reality he even resurrected the idea that Theo should fund an artists' co-operative which he, Gauguin, would graciously administer. Under normal circumstances such a proposal was impossible. Theo already gave Vincent 150 francs a month, effectively a quarter of his basic income, not counting any commissions. But that July Theo's situation changed with the death of Uncle Cent, who left him an inheritance. Vincent was bitterly hurt to be ignored at the last, but it was no more than he ought to have expected. In any case Theo made it instantly clear that he had no intention of using the money himself but would devote it to their joint 'plan'. He consequently wrote to Gauguin telling him he too could expect 150 francs a month as a 'salary' in advance for the work to be sent him for sale, and pointedly reiterated Vincent's wish that Gauguin should join him in Arles, where they could share expenses and make the best use of the money. Gauguin's reaction to all this was to write to 'good old Schuff' voicing his deep suspicions that the Dutchman was secretly speculating in his works and was trying to corner the market in them. Knowing nothing of this ingratitude Theo kept up the pressure to get Gauguin to carry out his promise and leave for Arles, where Vincent was becoming increasingly excited at the prospect of his arrival. Gauguin wavered. He was not unfamiliar with the south; in 1883 he had visited the Musée Fabre in Montpellier near Arles, where he made a copy of Delacroix's *Portrait of the Mulatto girl Aline*, the precedent for his *négresses* in Martinique. But what were the attractions of Provence compared to the mysteries of Brittany and the presence of Madeleine?

Vincent could think of little other than his preparations for Gauguin's arrival. Even the subjects he painted were picked because they would make suitable decorations for the guest bedroom which was why he began making flower studies once more.

He had, of course, painted sunflowers in Paris but never the twisting, sun-searching southern blossoms he now depicted. They scream yellow. Some are set in a yellow vase on a yellow table, some are violently alive, burning with sunshine, others are dead, limp, exhausted, but not with the tranquil death of a real sunflower when it passes into a dry-brown state before scattering its polished seeds; this was death by self-immolation, a yellow suicide. At one and the same time there is the wondrous life-giving sunshine of Provence and the *devil mistral*, life and death together. Before he started painting he would drink innumerable cups of strong black coffee, deliberately over-stimulating himself so that he could *reach that high note of yellow*. It was a dangerous game. Sometimes he would work all day in the orchards and fields, then spend his evenings pouring out his schemes in letters to Theo, plans for selling his work, for creating an artists' colony or whatever was uppermost in his mind that night. All too often he would stay out all day in the blazing sun with nothing but his battered straw hat to shield him from the intense heat as he forced himself to complete painting after painting. He had delayed so long, was there enough time left? When the light failed he would make his way back into the town to sit on a café terrace downing absinthes and brandies, one after the other, till his thoughts were anaesthetised and he could stagger off to sleep or find a moment of human contact at Madame Virginie's 'house'. The contrasts were everywhere apparent: alone and away from the artistic denizens of Paris he had achieved great things, yet he longed for Gauguin, notoriously the most demanding of them all, to come and transform his life. Then sometimes he had doubts, perhaps it would be better if Gauguin did not come, he might not like the place. No, he must come, Theo must see to it. The letters flew back and forth between Arles, Paris and Pont-Aven. If Gauguin was preoccupied, he simply failed to reply. Weeks passed, then debts and doubts returned and Vincent would write again and raise the hope that Paul would indeed travel south. Once more, furniture would be bought, gas-lighting installed, further paintings made to decorate his room.

The contradictions were apparent in his work. He painted old Patience Escalier again, but then wrote to Theo to say:

> *I should like to paint the portrait of an artist friend, a man who dreams great dreams, who works as the nightingale sings, because it is in his nature. He'll be a blond man. I want to put my appreciation, the love I have for him, into the picture. So I paint him as he is, as faithfully as I can, to begin with.*
>
> *But the picture is not yet finished. To finish it I am now going to be the arbitrary colourist. I exaggerate the fairness of the hair, I even get to orange tones, chromes and pale citron-yellow.*
>
> *Behind the head, instead of painting the ordinary wall of the mean room, I paint infinity, a plain background of the richest, intensest blue that I can contrive, and by this simple combination of the bright head against the rich blue background, I get a mysterious effect, like a star in the depths of an azure sky.*

There could be no better description of his belief in the symbolic properties of colour. There was nothing haphazard or naif about his methods; he went on to paint a portrait exactly according to that outline, for he had been referring to the poet Eugène Boch. Much to everyone's relief, MacKnight left for Paris at the end of August and Vincent and Boch could see more of each other. Unfortunately, he too would be leaving soon, acting on Vincent's advice to return to the Borinage, leaving only Roulin as an occasional drinking companion. Little wonder Vincent's old feelings of isolation began to return. He didn't speak Provençal and felt shut out. Roulin was fair company over a glass of absinthe but he needed someone with whom he could discuss art. With Boch gone there was only the prospect of Gauguin's arrival to look forward to.

Vincent barely ate and was now drinking too much coffee, cup after cup, making himself ill. He began staying up at night, taking that starry background from the portrait of the poet and magnifying its sense of infinity: a night view across the Rhône from just near the house, or the brightly-lit exterior of the café in the Place du Forum. He stuck candles around the brim of his hat so that he could see the effects of his colours, re-enacting the stories he had heard about Monticelli working by candle-light. If the locals had had their doubts before, they were confirmed now that they saw him so oddly festooned and painting, of all things, the moon.

Again, there were sharp contrasts in his work: out of doors he found empty star-washed spaces, but when he painted the night-time interior of the Café de l'Alcazar on the eastern side of the Place Lamartine, he revealed a gas-lit underworld in violent red and green where what he called 'night-prowlers' took refuge. An unused billiard table fills the centre of the room, the clock on the wall reads one o'clock, a waiter stares blankly in the direction of the artist and figures are sprawled across marble tables lost in uneasy sleep. The conflict between jangling colours and exhausted people is unnerving.

Then suddenly, news arrived from Pont-Aven: Gauguin was coming and so too were Bernard and Laval.

Theo must send more money for the following:

Dressing table and chest of drawers 40fr
4 sheets 40fr
3 Drawing boards 12fr
Kitchen range 60fr
Paints and canvas 200fr
Frames and stretchers 50fr

Hopes were running dangerously high:

> *Well, yes, I am ashamed of it, but I am vain enough to want to make an impression on Gauguin with my work, so I cannot help wanting to do as much work as possible before he comes. His coming will alter my manner of painting and I shall gain by it, I believe, but all the same I am rather keen on my decorations, which are like French painted porcelain.*

That was written on one of the good, the *magnificent* days. Up went the paintings, in came the sticks of furniture. By mid-September the place was nearly ready. He moved in, overjoyed to have his own place at last, to be free of hoteliers. The weather was appropriately beneficent, a rare moment in what had been an exaggeratedly unstable year when deadening heat had alternated with the depressing mistral. But as before, such good days could not last. There were unseasonable storms. Trapped inside once more, he painted the newly returned Milliet in his dress uniform, kepi at a rakish angle, 'colonial' style, posed in front of the simple emerald flag of the Zouaves with its golden crescent moon and star. But the second lieutenant fidgeted and was a bad sitter.

As he awaited Gauguin's arrival he wrote to him, describing his feelings in terms of cringing servility:

> *I have expressly made a decoration for the room you will be staying in, a poet's garden . . .*
>
> *. . . And what I wanted was to paint the garden in such a way that one would think of the old poet living here (or rather from Avignon), Petrarch, and at the same time of the new poet living here – Paul Gauguin . . .*
>
> *However clumsy this attempt may be, yet it is possible you will see in it that I was thinking of you with a very strong emotion while preparing your studio.*

Gauguin sent the letter on to 'good old Schuff' presumably to show the original devotee that now he had a rival.

Next Vincent wrote to Pont-Aven proposing that they should exchange portraits and immediately bought a small mirror so that he could start on his own while he waited for Gauguin's response. At the Auberge in Brittany the table discussed the idea. Gauguin did in fact begin to paint Bernard, but could not get to grips with it and so they all decided to make self-portraits. When Gauguin had finished his he sent Vincent an explanation of the symbolism of the work – the glow of the flesh, he explained, was the fire of creativity, the flat yellow background stood for the purity of the Impressionist artist and the fact that the work was signed 'les Misérables' indicated that such an artist had the status of Hugo's hero Jean-Valjean, that solitary figure hounded by the world. When the Van Goghs read this they both guessed what Gauguin was really saying and wrote at once to make it clear that should he agree to go to Arles he would be well taken care of. In reply Vincent sent Gauguin a description of the portrait he had painted of himself – *all ash-coloured. The ashen-gray colour that is the result of mixing malachite green with an orange hue, on pale malachite ground, all in harmony with the reddish-brown clothes. But as I also exaggerate my personality, I have in the first place aimed at the character of a simple bonze worshipping the Eternal Buddha.*

The underlying impression of Vincent as a 'bonze', a Japanese monk, humbly awaiting the arrival of his monastic superior, was no doubt very flattering to the recipient. Though when the pictures were eventually

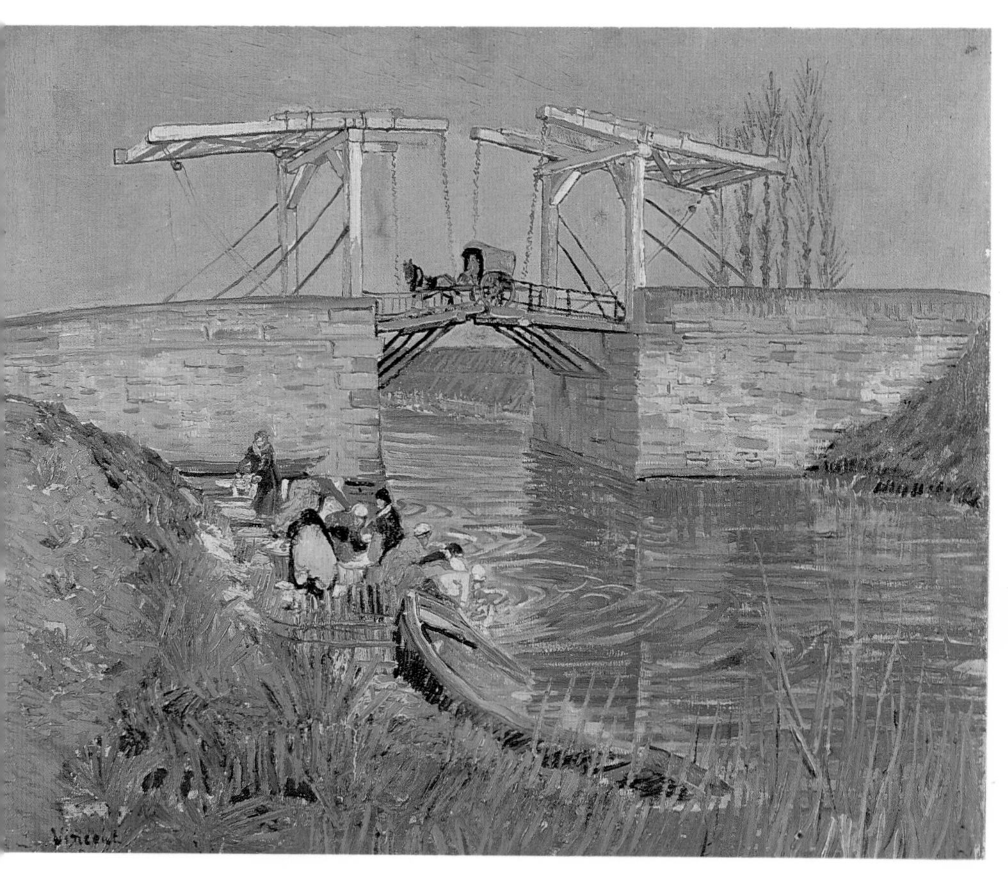

Although among the first of the works created in Provence, *The Bridge at Langlois* is a curious echo of Vincent's childhood.

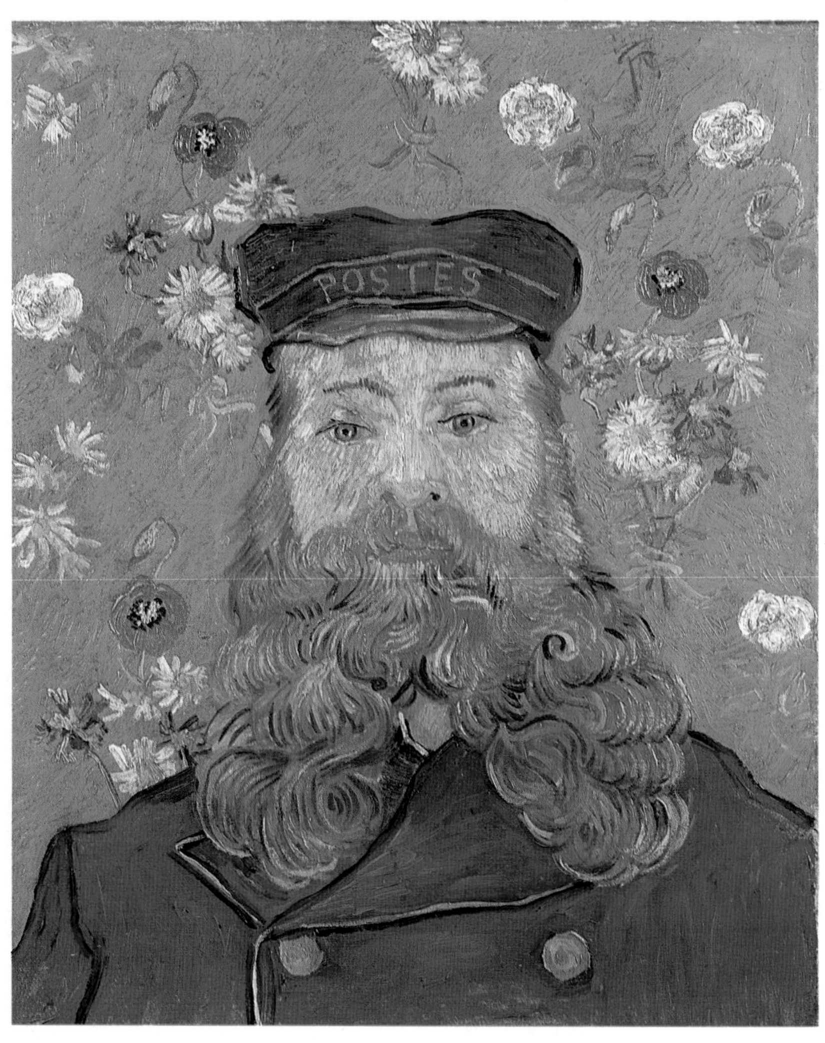

The Postman Roulin, solid and reliable, was one of the few citizens of Arles who stood by Vincent after the first of his violent seizures.

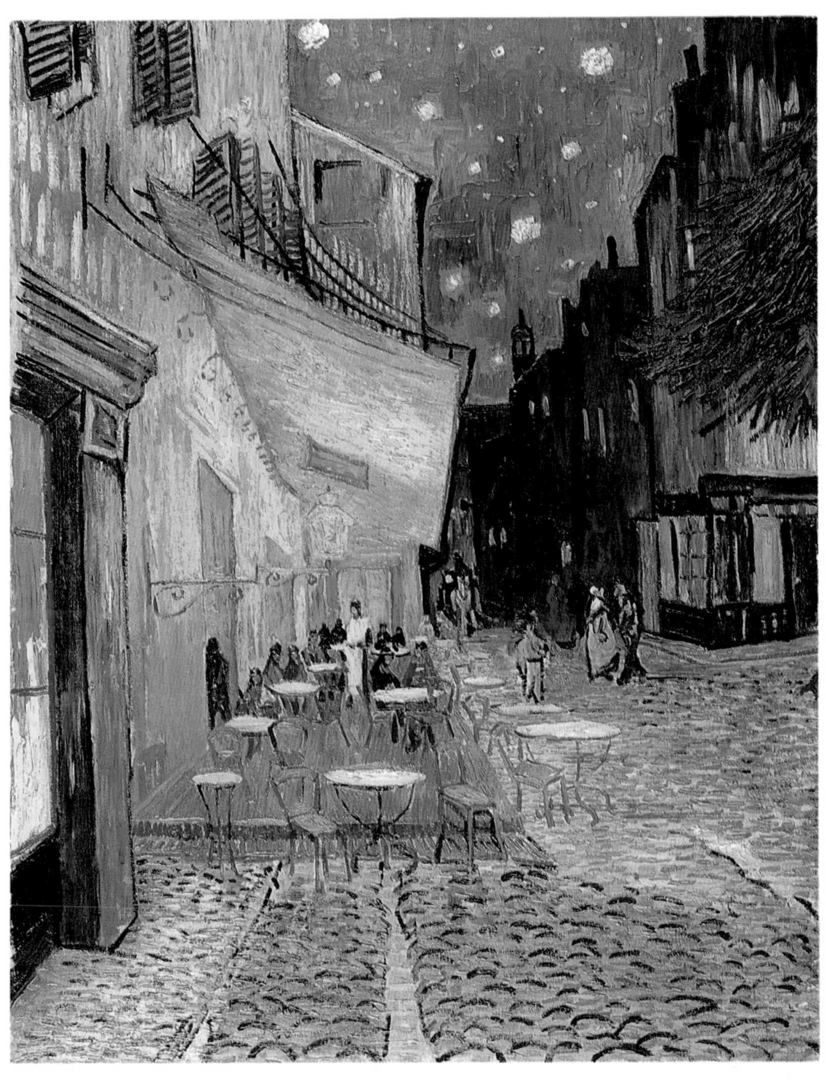

Depicted as a night scene of tranquil beauty, *The Café Terrace on the Place du Forum* was in reality one of the bars where Vincent drank himself into a state of nervous exhaustion.

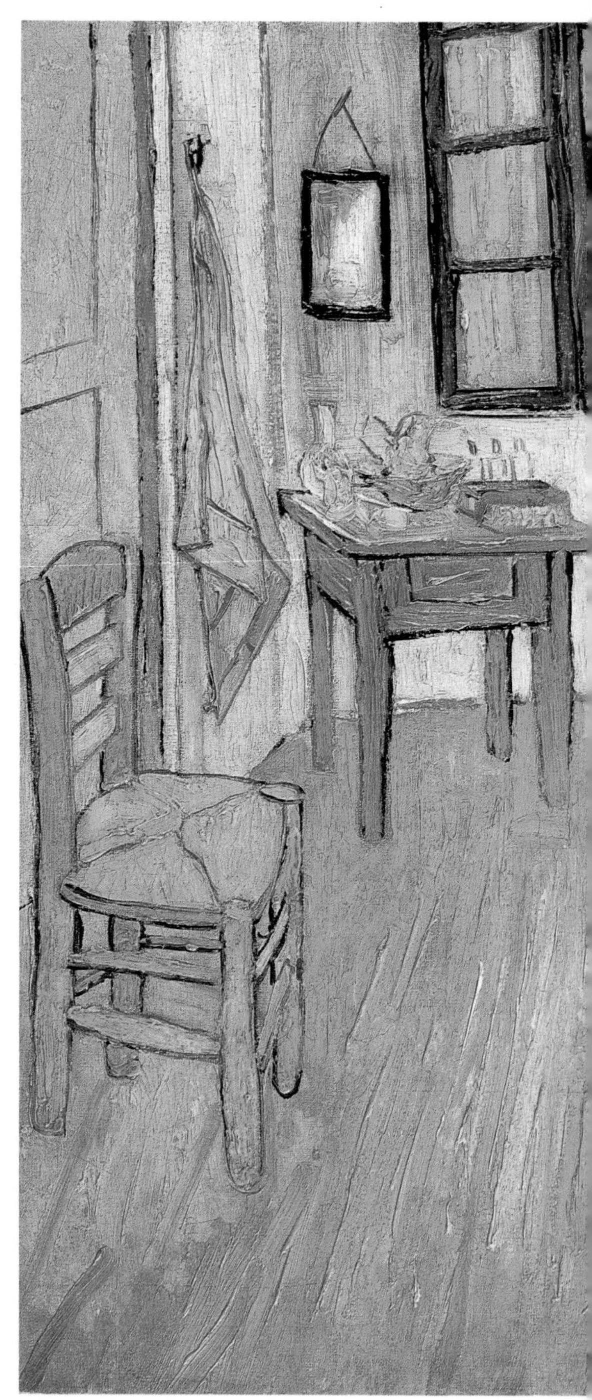

In an attempt to convince himself that all was well Vincent painted this pleasing image of domestic peace, his own bedroom. A few weeks later he was found on the same bed covered in blood.

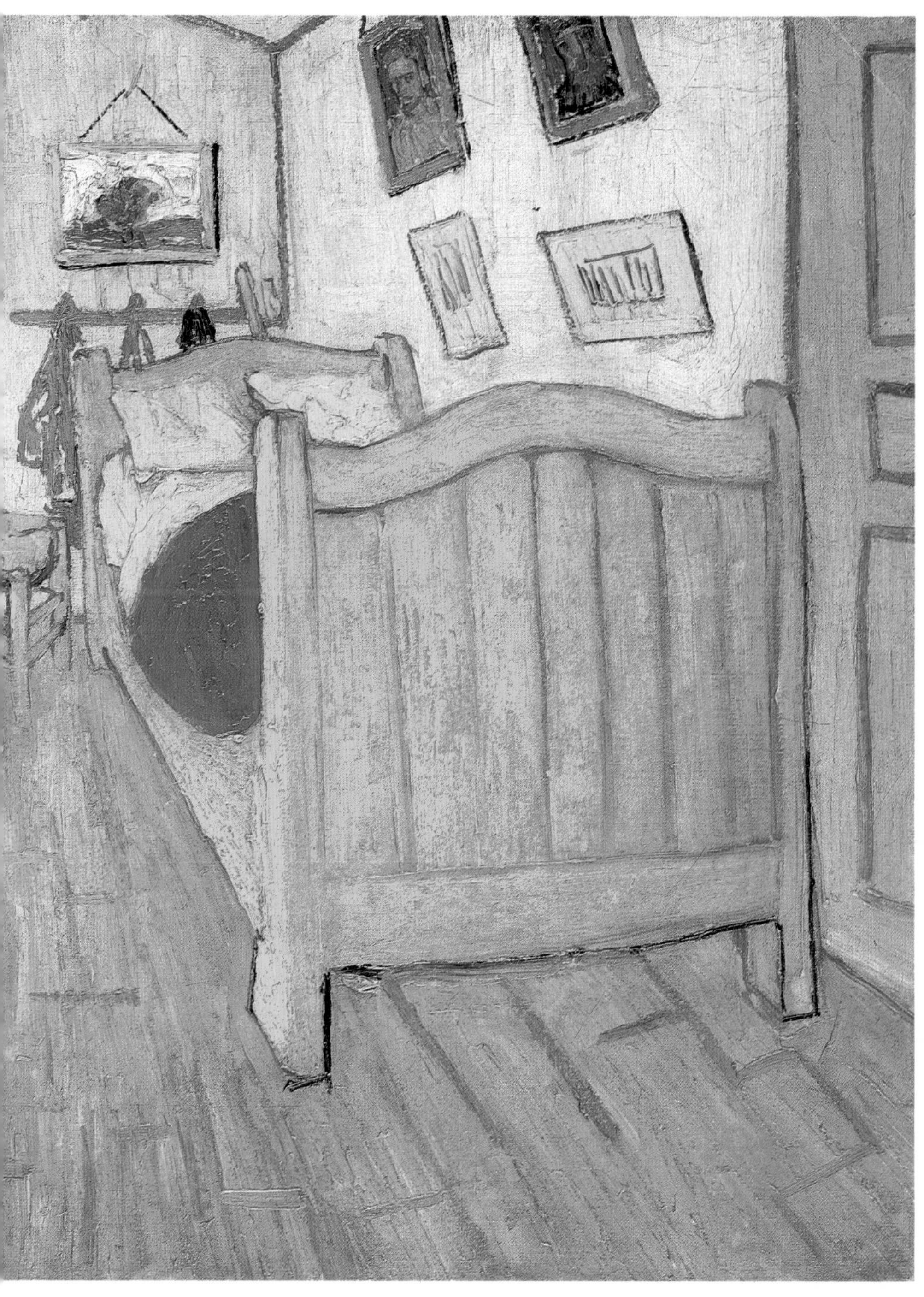

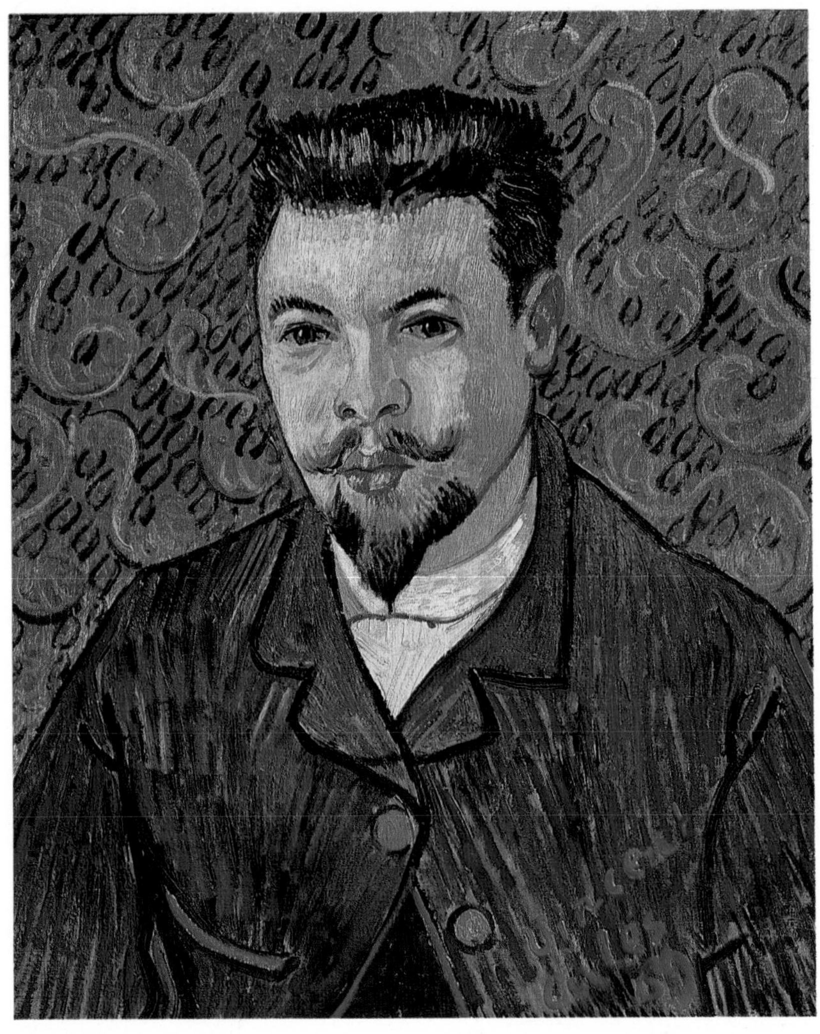

The Portrait of Doctor Félix Rey was a tribute to the most sympathetic of his doctors, though the painting never pleased its subject and was eventually used to repair a chicken coop.

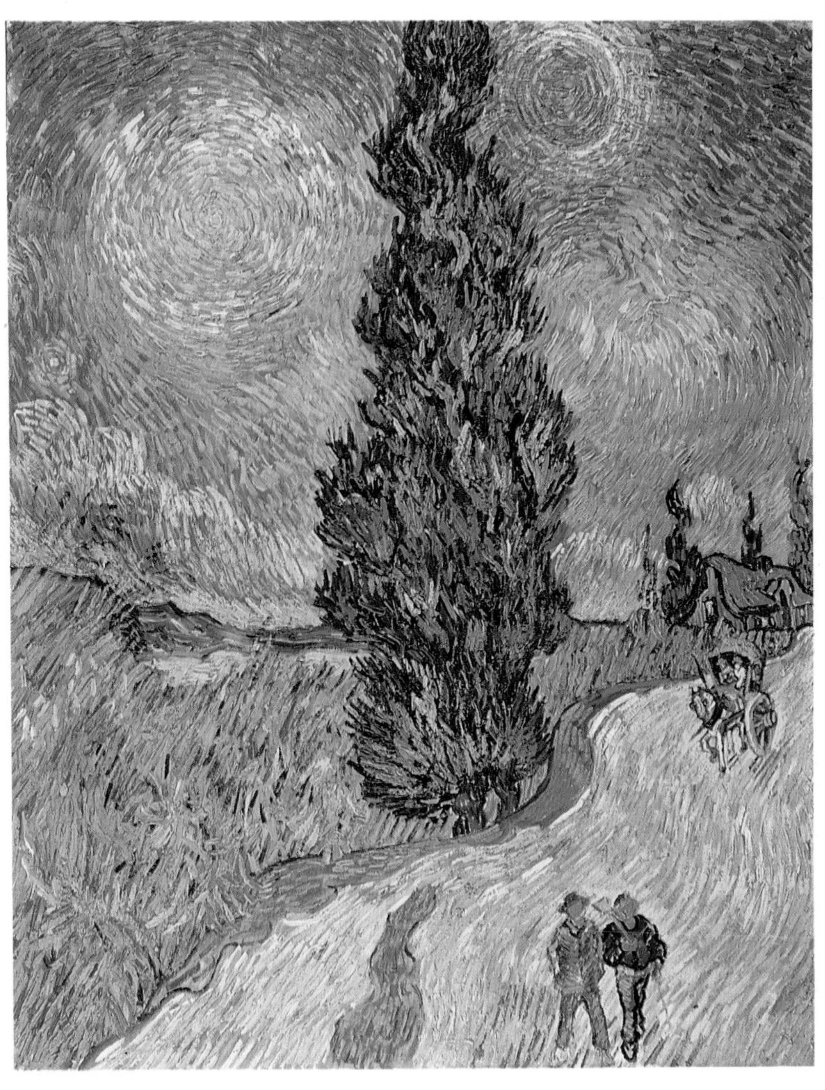

Long thought to be one of the most poignant images of southern France, Vincent's *Road with Cypresses and Star* contains tiny, almost secret references to his northern childhood.

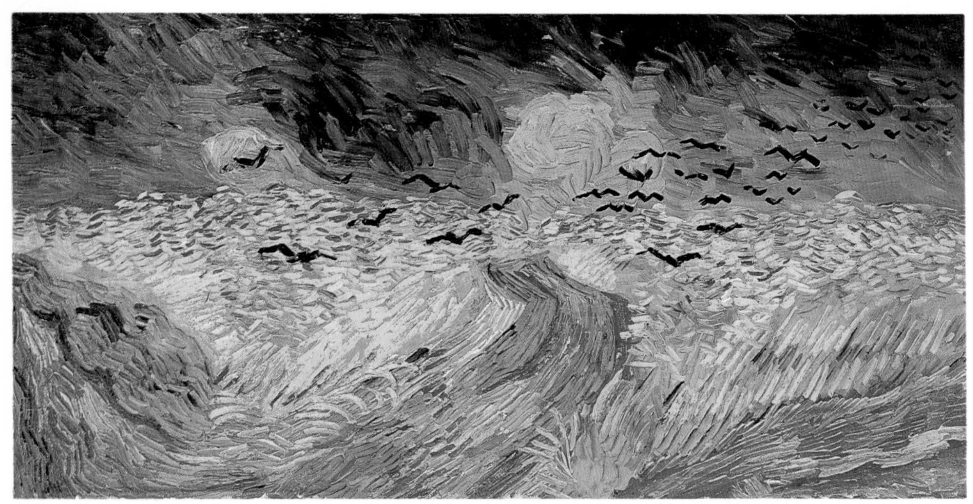

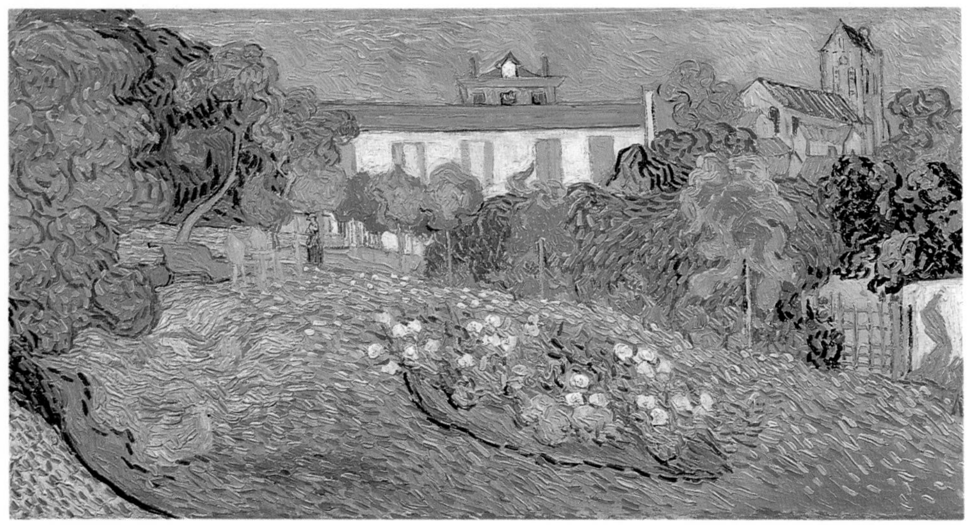

Whether *Crows over the Wheat Field*, a scene of delirium and fear, or *Daubigny's Garden*, one of his most balanced pictures, was the final painting he ever made has long been disputed by those wishing to show that his life was or was not a tragedy.

exchanged, Gauguin ought to have paused for thought. Far from appearing totally serene and Buddha-like, Vincent has the look of a shaven-headed criminal, wary-eyed and haggard, yet still potentially dangerous. As a gift for Gauguin, it was an astonishing act of premonition, almost a warning. But by then Gauguin had decided to go and nothing was likely to deflect him.

Theo finally forced his hand by agreeing to take on a parcel of his work in order to settle his debts and to advance him his fare on the promise of future work. It was becoming impossible to delay any longer.

His impending arrival threw Vincent into a state of nervous collapse, less food, more coffee, absinthe with Roulin. Maybe Gauguin should not come. What if Arles displeased him? What if the weather were bad? What if . . . ?

In a desperate attempt at domesticity he painted a picture of his upstairs bedroom with its yellow bed, two yellow chairs, a yellow towel and a yellow light at the single window. Beside the window is the sand-coloured table on which he kept his wash things, a water jug and bowl, his cut-throat razor, a carafe for drinking water. On the wall above hangs the mirror he had bought to work on his self-portrait. The portraits of Milliet and Boch hang above the bed, the red cover of which provides the one vibrant note in this golden symphony. The far wall does appear to slope away at an odd angle, a fact which has been interpreted as a sign of his mental instability. The truth is much simpler, the room was not a perfect rectangle and Vincent had recorded its odd shape just as it was. Indeed, he told Theo that everything in the painting was to be suggestive of sleep or rest and with its golden haze, nothing could better evoke the silent hot siesta of a Provençal summer afternoon.

It was a fantasy of course. The truth was that, as with Theo's flat in Paris, the Yellow House was a shambles. He paid a local woman a franc a time to come in twice a week and clean, but nothing could stop the rising tide of debris he scattered everywhere. His working areas were a mess of paint-droppings and half-squeezed tubes, oozing paint as their caps were never replaced. Yet the painting of the bedroom showed there was a longing for order, the longing that had manifested itself when he had tried to live with Sien. But with Gauguin's arrival imminent hysteria gripped him and for once he even admitted to Theo that it was akin to madness. Just as he had begun to find himself, just as he was mastering all the contradictions that had unsettled him in Paris, he was once more reduced to the insecure novice waiting for – what? He hardly knew himself. All certainty was gone, and with it the money for his food, spent on furniture and expensive frames for the 'decorations'. What if Gauguin arrived and could not find the house? He took Gauguin's self-portrait round to Joseph Ginoux and asked him to watch out for the visitor. He had no idea when he would arrive but on the night of October 22nd his raw nerves must have temporarily ceased to plague him for he slept well and long, that is until a banging at the door brought him awake with a jolt.

Gauguin might never have left Brittany except that things had turned sour at the Gloanec. He owed Marie-Jeanne an appalling amount of money for his board and lodging; two parish priests had refused his offer of *The Vision after the Sermon, Jacob Wrestling with the Angel*, to hang in their churches; and then he learned that Madeleine Bernard favoured Charles Laval, who turned out to be not quite so unassuming and subservient as he had thought; they were even talking about getting married. In any case, with Emile Bernard about to leave for compulsory military service, she and her mother would soon return to Paris.

Having decided to leave he then found Vincent showering him with doubts about whether everything would be to his liking in the south. Gauguin ignored them, sent a trist farewell note to Madeleine and boarded the slow train to Provence. The journey lasted two days and two nights. He arrived, utterly exhausted at five in the morning of October 23rd. The train was early, there was no one to meet him and it was cold. He had no idea where to go and doubted whether anyone around at that hour would be able to tell him. There were two cafés, lit up and evidently open, the Café de la Gare, just down from the station, and the Alcazar further round on the same square. The former being nearer, he went in. The proprietor was no doubt keeping a wary eye on the handful of all-night customers but to Gauguin's surprise, he suddenly looked up, peered at him and announced with some satisfaction – "You're his pal."

Having thus encountered Monsieur Ginoux, Gauguin was given the instructions he needed. His guide directed him along the Place Lamartine to the yellow building with two pediments. Because it was still so early, Gauguin waited a while but as soon as it was light he went to announce his arrival.

Vincent's nervous excitement on being dragged out of bed by the long-awaited master can be imagined. He was pathetically eager that Gauguin should like everything – the house, his work, Arles. For the moment the newcomer said nothing. The place was a mess. Then there were the lovingly hung 'decorations'. Gauguin glanced at the violent complementaries and bit his tongue. Vincent insisted on showing his friend the delights of Arles and lavishly praised the beauty of the Arlésiennes though Gauguin was clearly unimpressed. A 'hygienic' visit to one of the favoured brothels went down better, and more were planned. The following morning they started work and Vincent's studio in the south was under way.

Much of what is known about their life together comes from Gauguin's memoir *Avant et Après* written fifteen years later when he was over-anxious to justify his own part in the subsequent tragedy, at a time when it was commonly accepted that he had behaved badly. Unfortunately for him his rather pompous insistence that everything good had come from him while everything that went wrong had been Vincent's fault only succeeded in convincing his opponents of the contrary. His account of their life together is so biased and in places silly – he even claimed that Vincent had forgotten how to write Dutch – that the reaction of many has been to discount everything he wrote. By extension, Gauguin's artistic influence on Vincent is often seen as a disaster. Some have even gone so far as to suggest that it was because Gauguin had interfered with his art that events unfolded in the way they did and that it was Gauguin's malign dominion over the younger Vincent which provoked the horrors that are so well known. None of these conclusions, however, are borne out by the facts and while it is true that one must tread carefully with his account of their time in Arles, much of what he wrote is confirmed by other sources. The biggest mistake has been to assume that because the events were so crucial to both their lives they must have taken up a great deal of time. As with Mauve, so lasting was the effect that one assumes they must have been together for many months. In reality Gauguin was in Arles for only a matter of weeks; he arrived on October 23rd and left almost to the day two months later.

This was the very issue which most disturbed their relationship: Gauguin thought this would be a brief visit, perhaps six months at the most, before he set off for the tropics again, while Vincent was obsessed with the idea that his friend should stay at least a year so that others would be encouraged to join them. Any suggestion that Gauguin planned to leave was deeply disturbing to him, so right from the start there was a built-in time bomb ticking away, ever ready to explode. This fear led Vincent to be excessively subservient to his friend's whims, fawningly accepting his judgements and adjusting his own ways to accommodate whatever Gauguin proposed, though Gauguin's self-regarding assertion that he had completely taken command of Vincent's working method is not borne out by the facts. Vincent had been working towards abstraction before Gauguin arrived and if he was nudged further down that line by the strong-minded view of his new 'master' it was as much because the will was already there as because of any control on Gauguin's part.

It is all too easy to dislike Gauguin because of the bad light which he himself often sheds on his behaviour and it is essential to remember that he too was lonely, and under considerable pressure, working so far outside the accepted artistic canons of his day, that he could have scant reassurance that what he was doing had any value. Vincent endured it by retreating into fantasy with his unrealistic schemes for an ideal artistic future based on a shared community. That this should seem far more humane and attractive than Gauguin's mask of arrogance and self-assurance, should not hide the fact that both were survival mechanisms in an impossibly isolated situation. Arrogant and difficult Gauguin may have been but there were many who saw behind the mask. Years later his son Emile, who had every reason to feel abandoned by his wandering father, could only recall him with deep affection and until the end of his days Vincent thought of him as the best of friends.

Despite his somewhat unnerving silence, Gauguin went to considerable lengths to get their joint existence off to a working start. As the main advantage of their sharing the Yellow House had always been Vincent's contention that two could live as well as one on the money Theo sent, Gauguin set about putting some order into their affairs. It was clear from the moment he arrived that not only was Vincent chronically untidy, his sloppiness meant that much money was simply wasted, but at the same time he ate badly if at all. Gauguin instituted a few elementary reforms: all monies were kept in a box and certain sums were earmarked for essential purposes, though significantly 'hygienic' ones headed the list, followed by tobacco, leading on down to the rent, the final item. On top of the box was a piece of paper and a pencil so that each could note down any withdrawals. Another box contained money for food divided into four amounts for their shopping days. At Gauguin's suggestion they gave up the nearby restaurant and he did the cooking. One can easily see why: "Once ... Vincent wanted to make a soup. How he mixed it I don't know; as he mixed his colours in his pictures, I dare say. At any rate, we couldn't eat it."

That comment tells us as much about Gauguin's attitude to the work Vincent had been doing as to his culinary skills for the older man found all this interest in Monticelli and his thick impasto unacceptable. Vincent's methods seemed 'messy' and uncontrolled, though Gauguin admitted to liking the Sunflowers more than he liked Monet's version of the same subject. Vincent was touchingly pleased though determined not to have his head turned by such flattery.

The fact is that in the first three or so weeks of their time together, Gauguin was distinctly ambiguous in his approach to what Vincent had been doing; he even began work on a portrait of Madame Ginoux which was nothing less than a homage to his host's recent work. Not only did he put the Zouave soldier and old Roulin in the background of the picture but also he used red and green complementaries in a way which echoes Vincent's original *Night Café*. Uncharacteristically, Gauguin even wrote to Bernard to admit as much, though he went on to complain that the result displeased him and that such a use of colour, while it was all right for others, always made him apprehensive. That aside, there was a great deal of shared experience during those first weeks; they took walks together and painted the same subjects. If there were differences at this stage they surfaced in their long discussions about art rather than in the actual work they were doing, though as Vincent still appeared to accept whatever Gauguin chose to say, friction was minimal. He was genuinely entranced by Gauguin's traveller's tales of his childhood in Peru, his youth as a sailor and the hardships of the journey to Martinique. If they met up with the newly returned Milliet in one of the bars the two travellers could swap stories. The Third Regiment of Zouaves had at last received its orders and on the first of November the Second Lieutenant and his men would leave for Marseilles and transhipment to North Africa. Worryingly to Vincent, this seemed to arouse all Gauguin's desires to return to the tropics but for the moment he tried to share the fantasy; he too would eventually emigrate, to North Africa or wherever, and the Yellow House could become a way-station for artists from the North heading for the sun. Gauguin listened to Milliet's stories about the campaign in Tonkin and pondered the idea of heading East. When they were alone in the Yellow House he polished his stories, gratified by Vincent's attention. Ironically, it did much to establish his own conviction that he was indeed the 'savage' adventurer of his own legend and increased his determination to resume his travels.

But so far life with the two Van Goghs was working out fine for him. Theo had put on a show of his work at the gallery and wrote to say how Degas had admired it. There were even some sales. Domesticity reigned supreme; Gauguin bought a chest of drawers and some kitchen equipment. Vincent was amazed at how good a cook his friend was and both might have begun to feel better except there was still too much drinking. This was the flaw in Gauguin's well-laid regime: having established a sound domestic economy, he would suddenly throw caution to the winds and go on a rip-roaring binge. No doubt this amused old Roulin who enjoyed a good drinking session but it unnerved Vincent who needed discipline and order, not wild nights in the Alcazar followed by penny-pinching economies.

Things were quieter after Milliet left, bearing a picture from each of them, though there was still much use of the 'hygiene' part of their finances. Nevertheless, Gauguin tried to make savings on materials by buying a cheap length of strong burlap for them to paint on.

By mid-November Gauguin felt more sure of himself and less inclined to muzzle his own, ever stronger views. The onset of yet another dreadful winter made them give up their painting trips and as there could be no more working from nature, Gauguin began to nudge Vincent towards using memory and imagination. According to Gauguin they should tame inadequate reality with a synthetist approach; nature was all right as a starting point, for sketching, but the next stage was the manipulation of these elements into poetry. It was not so far from what Vincent had been doing himself but he had always continued to do it in direct contact with nature, out in the fields. Memory and studio-based work involved a much greater leap into the abstract, but that was what the 'master' insisted upon and their second three-week period saw Vincent trying to imitate his friend's approach.

At some point they had visited the Hôtel-Dieu, the hospital in the centre of town. Its buildings were set round a square courtyard laid out as a formal garden with a rigid pattern of flower-beds. The nursing nuns, their convalescent patients and the unfortunate occupants of the ward for the mentally ill, strolled in this calm setting and enjoyed whatever break there might be in the almost consistently bad weather. Gauguin seems to have liked the formal pattern of the garden and began a painting of it, which quickly developed into a place of the imagination. The Arlésiennes who walk in Gauguin's garden are strangely veiled creatures, not unlike Arab women, perhaps a reference to the dream of North Africa. Some elements in the picture, while they look strange, can be explained – the trees wrapped in cones of protective yellow straw were a commonplace during the southern winter, though in Gauguin's hands they assume an almost otherworldly look. But some things are not so simple, the way a bush in the foreground looks like the snout of a monster or a spindly garden seat at the top of the picture transforms itself into a poisonous insect trying to clamber out of the frame. One must assume that Gauguin was exaggerating in order to wean his friend away from reality. Vincent duly obeyed by painting his own version of the hospital grounds which he turned into a memory of the garden at his parents' home in Etten. He tried hard to fill it with equally symbolic and unexplained mysteries. At first enthusiastic, he wrote to Theo: *Gauguin gives me the courage to imagine things, and certainly things from the imagination take on a more mysterious character.* At the same time he wrote to his sister Willemina to say that the two figures in the foreground of his picture could be her and their mother out for a walk. Whether they really were he does not say, and the younger woman could equally be their cousin Kee. But no matter how hard he tried to be mysterious, it did not seem to work and after a while he wrote to Theo to say he had spoiled the picture. He continued praising Gauguin and trying to reassure his brother that they were getting on famously but he very quickly gave up trying to follow his friend's dictates and returned to his own way of doing things with a series of portraits of the Roulin family, a clear indication that he remained faithful to nature.

Far from Gauguin having driven him to despair by distorting his way of working, Vincent seems to have taken what he wanted from amongst the older man's ideas and adapted them to his own vision, as he always did. He painted a highly stylised dance hall and a panorama of the crowd at a bullfight, both reconstructed from memory but in each case he slotted in portraits of the Roulins as if to keep himself firmly rooted in observable reality. Rather than any tension over their work provoking a crisis, it was more the clash of two such unique personalities trapped in a confined space by day after day of rain that caused the trouble. Vincent portrayed the problem quite openly with his own blend of reality and symbolism in two paintings now called *Van Gogh's Chair* and *Gauguin's Chair*. They can be interpreted as day and night: on Vincent's chair, yellow and sunlit, his friendly old pipe and some rubbed tobacco await him; while Gauguin's chair is dark green, brown, blue, with a lit candle and two books ready for the reader as the evening draws in. Vincent's is a 'living' chair; Gauguin's recalls that of the dead Dickens, and hints at departure. Not that they sat reading much; after working in this claustrophobic way they would go to one of the cafés and drink all evening.

Vincent was getting suspicious – was Gauguin really planning to leave? Things had not worked out. He was unable to follow the other man's lead and it was obvious Arles had limited attractions for his visitor: the place bored him, the women weren't as beautiful as he'd been led to believe. Unlike Brittany, with its roadside crosses and its ancient ceremonies, the South evoked little mystery. Vincent's drinking was worrying, he could be rowdy then silent by turns. Sometimes Gauguin would wake up in the night and find him standing by the bed, staring down, immobile. For the moment he could control the situation "... it was enough for me to say to him, quite sternly, 'What's the matter with you, Vincent?' for him to go back to bed without a word and fall into a heavy sleep."

In his befuddled state, Vincent was probably checking to see that Gauguin was still there, though such behaviour could only bring nearer the day when the other would be driven out. Still trapped by the weather they worked on side by side, Gauguin on a portrait of Vincent as he painted a bunch of sunflowers, significantly not from memory but from a bunch in a bowl beside him. Gauguin stood over Vincent, looking down on him, and Vincent had no idea what the work was like until it was finished. When Gauguin invited him to see it Vincent was appalled: *It is certainly I, but it's I gone mad.* It was clear what Gauguin was thinking and Vincent was deeply hurt. In the past any suggestion, from Tersteeg or his father, that he was mentally unstable had produced howls of outrage in his letters to Theo. This was surely the crisis point. That night they went to the café as usual and Vincent ordered a weak absinthe, presumably all too aware of the mood he was in. No matter, according to Gauguin's account, Vincent suddenly picked up the glass and hurled it at him. Gauguin ducked, then grabbing him by the arm, frogmarched Vincent home where he immediately fell asleep. When he woke the next morning he had a vague memory of the event and tried to apologise.

"I forgive you gladly," Gauguin claimed to have replied, "and with all my heart, but yesterday's scene might occur again and if I were struck I might lose control of myself and give you a choking. So permit me to write to your brother and tell him I am coming back."

The letter was duly sent and Vincent passed the next few days in hell as his dreams of a studio in the South crumbled around him. To his credit Gauguin was concerned and tried his best to keep him from despair. He proposed that they should go to Montpellier for the day, to visit the museum where he had once copied Delacroix's mulatto girl; such an outing might break the dark mood that had engulfed him. The Musée Fabre had re-opened ten years earlier, rebuilt to house the magnificent bequest of a local art dealer and collector, Alfred Bruyas, who had left the city over a hundred works, many of them seminal paintings of the mid-century. Their trip, by train, ought to have been just the restorative Gauguin wished, there was enough variety in the collection to please them both. Gauguin could see himself in the role of Courbet saluting the sea or being respectfully greeted by Bruyas himself in that self-regarding masterpiece *The Meeting* and for Vincent, there was Delacroix's *Femmes d'Alger* to call up the dream of North Africa. But sadly, the visit only provoked another wave of disagreement which went on long after they got back to the Yellow House that night.

Gauguin wrote to Bernard bemoaning Vincent's lack of appreciation of Ingres, Raphael and Degas, "all the people I admire"; he found Vincent's persistent adherence to romantics and realists like Daumier and Théodore Rousseau intolerable. For his part Vincent at last revealed to Theo how *electric* and exhausting their arguments had become.

Despite it all, Gauguin took pity on Vincent and tried to convince him he would stay. His explanation to Schuffenecker shows he was hardly the uncaring monster so often portrayed: "My situation here is very awkward; I owe a great deal to (Theo) van Gogh and to Vincent and, in spite of some discord, I cannot be angry with an excellent fellow who is sick, who suffers, and who asks for me. Remember the life of Edgar Poe who became an alcoholic as the result of grief and a nervous condition. Some day I shall explain all this to you. In any event I shall stay here, but my departure will always be a possibility."

Of course, that was just what Vincent still suspected and what drove him to the limits of despair. Nothing Gauguin said could convince him that the end was not near. And still it rained and still they remained shut in in the Yellow House. December 23rd was the worst day of all, the tension was palpable. Vincent was working on a portrait of Madame Roulin holding the cord with which she rocked an unseen cradle even though any thought of a mother and child could always upset him, bringing as it did painful memories of Sien and baby Willem. It was an unwise subject for someone in his condition. The day dragged on but after they had eaten their evening meal Gauguin could stand it no longer and went for a solitary stroll in the nearby public garden. Gauguin's memoir is the only authority for what happened next:

> I had almost crossed the Place Victor Hugo when I heard behind me a well-known step, short, quick, irregular. I turned about the instant as Vincent rushed towards me, an open razor in his hand. My look at that moment must have had great power in it, for he stopped and, lowering his head, set off running towards home.

Gauguin decided that this was more than he could handle and he too headed off. He found a hotel and went straight to bed, though he was too agitated to sleep until three in the morning. He awoke at seven. It was the day before Christmas, though he was hardly looking forward to the feast as he set off back to the Yellow House to sort things out. He had no sooner entered the Place Lamartine than he saw a great crowd milling round the building with a number of policemen near the door. When he pushed his way through he found himself confronted by a short man in a bowler hat who turned out to be a superintendent of police. The man's tone was far from pleasant: "What have you done to your comrade, Monsieur?" was the unnerving question and while he began to stammer his total ignorance of what was going on, it gradually dawned on him that he was being accused of murder. They went inside where to Gauguin's horror there were bloodstained towels scattered on the tiles in the downstairs room. A trail of blood led upstairs to Vincent's room where the apparently dead body lay, as Gauguin put it, curled up like a gundog under sheets pink with blood. Gauguin nervously went over and reached out his hand. To his profound relief he could feel the warmth emanating from his friend's body.

Gauguin turned to the superintendent and in a low voice said: "Be kind enough, Monsieur, to awaken this man with great care, and if he asks for me tell him I have left for Paris; the sight of me might prove fatal to him."

And having satisfied his interrogators, he fled.

10

1888 — 1891

Accompanied like a Dangerous Beast

LOCAL NEWS

> Last Sunday at 11.30 pm, one Vincent Vaugogh [sic] painter of Dutch origin, presented himself at the *Maison de Tolérance*, No 1, asked for one Rachel, and gave her . . . his ear, saying "Guard this object carefully". Then he disappeared. When informed of this act, which could only be that of a poor lunatic, the police went next morning to this person's house, and found him lying in bed giving no sign of life. The unfortunate man was admitted to hospital at once.

Forum Républicain, Arles, December 30, 1888.

In fact the police had been involved almost from the start. Alphonse Robert, whose beat was the *quartier réservé*, was passing Madame Virginie's when he heard an uproar and rushed in to find Rachel in a faint amidst general commotion. The cause, a roll of newspaper, was unwrapped so that Robert could see the grisly object it contained. According to Robert, it was a whole human ear. He confiscated it and proceeded to take down the story of its delivery.

Robert was not unused to bloodshed on his particular beat: he was the officer who had arrested the Italian responsible for the murder of a Zouave outside the same brothel, only to find himself defending the man against a lynch mob. But this story of a mad artist, head swathed in bloody cloths, handing over one of his ears into a harlot's safe-keeping, was nothing if not original. Having got the details he returned to the Gendarmerie and reported to his superior, Superintendent d'Ornano, who took charge of the evidence, still wrapped in newspaper.

It was d'Ornano who led the band of policemen that descended on the Yellow House and who subsequently decided to release Gauguin, once he saw that the swaddled figure on the bed was still alive. D'Ornano then sent for a carriage to take the mutilated Van Gogh to the Hôtel-Dieu. Gauguin went straight to the telegraph office and wired Theo what had happened, urging him to come at once. At the same time Vincent was handed over to Dr Félix Rey, a hospital intern and assistant to Dr Urpar the senior physician. The ear was also handed over but as too much time had passed for a suture to be considered the limp flap of flesh was put into a jar of alcohol in case it might be needed as evidence. Some months later it was thrown out.

The wound was dressed; no sign of infection was found, but the patient's mental state was judged to be critical. Theo arrived late that same day, having dashed straight to the station on receipt of Gauguin's telegram. When he saw his brother he was convinced there was nothing anyone could do. Vincent was catatonic and dangerously enfeebled by loss of blood. He had not sliced off his entire ear but had made a good attempt at it. Holding the open razor in his right hand, he had sliced through his left ear; starting high at the back and hacking downwards so that all the lower part of the ear had been chopped off. This had left part of the upper ear still attached as a hideous flap of flesh. He had sliced through at least one of the auricular arteries and the loss of blood was dramatic, accounting for the terrifying display of spattered towels and sheets that had confronted Gauguin that morning. Whether Vincent had run straight back to the Yellow House and done the deed immediately following his confrontation with Gauguin or whether he had got drunk and done it later in the evening no one could say and, from the first, he himself had only the haziest recollection of what had occurred. Fortunately, old Roulin had also been at the brothel that night and had dragged Vincent away before Robert arrived.

Inevitably, there has been prodigious speculation as to the reasons behind his self-mutilation and the subsequent donation of the result to the unfortunate Rachel. A classic schizophrenic act? – having failed to harm Gauguin had he then turned his violence on himself? Or was he simply filled with self-loathing at the way he had precipitated the thing he most feared, the alienation of his much needed companion? The explanations multiply. It was later discovered that he was tormented by voices; had these hallucinations begun that night, and had he attempted to silence them by cutting away the offending organ? He always said it was poor circulation which lay at the root of his physical weaknesses; had he sought blood-letting as some sort of remedy? The Rachel incident likewise brought forth ingenious suggestions. Was he imitating the climax of the bullfight when the matador is offered the bull's ear as a sign of his victory, a theory which ignored the obvious fact that the bull does not slice off its own ear.

Whatever the cause, it was clear to Theo, who had experienced Vincent's earlier bouts of depression, that this was something far far worse. Later explanations, long after the event, must be suspect, for without a patient there can be no diagnosis. All we know for certain is what those who were charged with treating him thought at the time. In that regard Vincent was initially very fortunate. While the worst days of Bedlam and Charenton were undoubtedly past, the treatment of the mentally ill was still capriciously uneven throughout Europe, and while progressive medical opinion was leaning towards a more enlightened view of mental breakdown the chances of anything resembling intelligent treatment, especially at a public hospital, were rare indeed. Vincent was lucky: while Dr Rey, the young intern who had taken charge of him, was no expert in the care of the mentally ill, he was nevertheless reasonably *au fait* with recent ideas which had taught him that the patient should not suffer. Rey was only twenty-three and was still working on his doctoral thesis, 'Antisepsis in the Urinary Passages', through the nearby University of Montpellier and was soon to go to the Faculty of Medicine in Paris for the final viva voce. He was to become something of an expert on tuberculosis and had already made a name locally for his work during a recent cholera epidemic, for which he had been awarded the silver medal of the Ministry of the Interior. His parents lived in Arles and his photograph shows him very much the favoured son, slightly podgy from his mother's Provençal cooking; one who, with his stylish goatee and hair *coupé en brosse*, seems destined to be a bon viveur, comfortably established and at ease with life. He was certainly the ideal man to minister to the poor emaciated figure brought to him by Superintendent d'Ornano. Where another might have done only the minimum to succour a lunatic outsider, evidently no more than a vagabond, Félix Rey did everything possible for his strange patient.

On Christmas Day a distraught Theo went to call on the local pastor of the Reformed Protestant church, the Reverend Frédéric Salles, who lived quite near the Hôtel-Dieu. It was clearly impossible for Theo to stay on in Arles when there was no way of knowing precisely how long this situation might last, but Salles offered to visit the patient and report on his condition. The next day Theo took the train back to Paris, accompanied by Gauguin, who was no doubt already rehearsing his reasons for having failed to disarm the clearly demented Vincent three nights before. Despite his later bluster, Gauguin had been deeply disturbed by the sight of his friend swaddled in bloody sheets. It seemed to affect him in peculiar ways. Not long after the return to Paris, he went to a prison to witness a public guillotining; and a short time later he made another of his portrait pots, though this time the ears have been sliced away and a lurid red glaze runs over the surface like a torrent of blood.

After Theo had left, the ever-loyal Roulin called at the hospital and was equally shattered both by what he saw and by his brief and pathetic talk with his once lively companion. When he returned home he secured the help of Armand or Camille to write down his reactions in his simple yet formal manner which were duly sent to Theo.

> Arles, 26 December 1888
>
> Monsieur Gogh,
>
> I have been to see your brother Vincent. I have promised to tell you my opinion about him. I am sorry to say that I think he is lost. Not only is his mind affected, but he is very weak and downhearted. He recognized me but did not show any pleasure at seeing me and did not inquire about any member of my family or anyone he knows. When I left him I told him that (I) would come back to see him; he replied that we would meet again in heaven, and from his manner I realized that he was praying. From what the concierge told me, I think that they are taking the necessary steps to have him placed in a mental hospital. Please accept, Monsieur, the greetings of him who calls himself the friend of your beloved brother.

The next day Madame Roulin visited the hospital but after she left, Vincent had a violent attack and had to be put in an isolation room. Although no expert, Dr Rey began to see a possible diagnosis: it could be that his patient was suffering from a form of epilepsy presumably provoked by a combination of bad diet and absinthe, and aggravated by overwork and excessive amounts of coffee. When Roulin called the next day it was thought better that Vincent should not be disturbed by any visitors and he left without seeing him. Rey considered transferring him to a mental hospital in Aix-en-Provence, but then he started to improve. It became clear that he was not permanently affected but had had some sort of attack which seemed to confirm the epilepsy diagnosis. Vincent made mumbled requests for them to fetch Gauguin, a sign that he was beginning to be more aware of the world around him. On December 31st the Reverend Salles was able to tell Theo the greatest worry now was that Vincent's indignation at being locked up might provoke another collapse. But by then progress was continuous and the humble Roulin felt obliged to write to Theo apologising for his initially despondent view of his friend's situation. Sensibly, Dr Rey allowed Vincent to attempt a return to his former life. He encouraged him to walk a while in the hospital garden, the same that he and Gauguin had painted. A short time later Roulin was allowed to escort him to the Yellow House, where the sight of his paintings cheered him up enormously.

All went so well he was permitted to leave the hospital as early as January 7th, though a report on his actions and their possible causes still had to be sent to the mayor who would decide what, if any, action should be taken. Concerned to ease his patient's rehabilitation, Dr Rey and two of his colleagues were among his first visitors back at the Yellow House. Vincent attempted to overcome their all-too-evident mystification at their first sight of his paintings by giving them a talk on complementary colour theory, which he told Theo they were *uncommonly quick at understanding*.

He resumed painting almost at once and persuaded the doctor, whom he saw on his daily visits to the hospital when his ear was dressed, to sit for him. Despite Vincent's conviction that Rey had understood his work, the resulting portrait never meant much to the good doctor who submitted to Vincent's attentions willingly enough but had little time for the result. Rey's parents were actually scandalised by the red beard and green hair given to their beloved son, not to mention the gaudy arabesques which whirled about his inexplicably thin head. They assumed that this was simply the pastime of one of their son's crazed patients and the picture soon found its way into their loft. Despite what Rey thought of the work, his loyalty to Vincent was unwavering and the young doctor now joined the tiny group of Arles friends, the Roulins and the Ginoux families, and now the Reverend Salles, who had alone stood by Vincent through his terrible crisis.

For nearly a month Vincent's precarious state of health hung in the balance, always with the risk of another attack. He returned to the dangerous subject of Madame Roulin seated by her daughter's cradle, which he had been working on when he collapsed, but there were no apparent after-effects. Then he painted himself, staring into his little mirror as before so that it appears to be the right ear that is bandaged. The self-image he reflected was undoubtedly raw; in his high buttoned great coat and rather dotty fur cap he has the air of a simpleton, and his painfully apprehensive expression speaks of the terror of madness which now gripped him. There is no self-pity; rather, there is self-analysis, and he even displays a determination to conquer his fears by using the most uncompromising complementaries yet: the green coat against a background of red, the blue fur hat against orange. And as before there was a clear division between art and life – resolute on canvas but all too feeble in reality.

It may also be wrong to seek too rigid a connection between events in his life and his sudden attacks. Nevertheless, two things may have unnerved him. On January 9th he received his first letter from Andries' sister Johanna Bonger in which she delicately broached the news of her engagement to Theo. Given his usual reactions to any hint that Theo might waver in his support for him, this announcement, though not entirely unexpected, must have worried him. Later in the month there was a disruption nearer home: Roulin was offered a slightly better-paid post at the railway station in Marseilles. While he had no desire to leave Arles, especially as he would be separated from his family for some time, he felt that with a new baby he could hardly afford to refuse. His leave-taking from the infant Marcelline at the end of the month particularly affected Vincent, no doubt bringing back memories of Willem seated on his lap at the station in The Hague on that dismal day only five winters earlier.

On the second of February he returned to the *Maison de Tolérance* to apologise to Rachel, the only sign that he was aware of what he had done on that extraordinary night. Despite having fainted at the sight of his severed ear, Rachel evidently had considerable sang-froid, for she waved away the whole incident saying that such things were not out of the ordinary round there.

In a way the visit was an indication that he was coming to terms with the crisis, recognising what had happened and trying to deal with the consequences of his actions. To outward appearances he was bearing up well. He was finishing Madame Roulin's portrait and making copies of some of his sunflower paintings. In fact, he was far from well. He was, so he firmly believed, being poisoned – there were poisoners everywhere. He knew it for certain and was sure there were other victims too. Over a period of three days the conviction grew and with it his appearance again took on an unnerving demented look. His cleaning woman came and was appalled. She could see that he had not been eating and his mumbled nonsense about the food being poisoned terrified the simple woman, who felt that the only thing to do was report his crazed behaviour to the police. Once more d'Ornano took up the case and had the house watched. It was soon clear to him that the woman was right, Vincent was mad, and on February 7th he was arrested and taken back to the Hôtel-Dieu where he was incarcerated in an isolation cell. When Salles hurried round to the hospital to find out what had happened he discovered Vincent hiding under the bedclothes refusing to say a word. At a loss what else to do, the kindly Salles asked for a fire to be lit in the cold room and left to ask Theo what arrangements he wanted made.

As before, Vincent quickly recovered from the attack, though one of Rey's colleagues, a Dr Albert Delon, confirmed in the official report to the police that Vincent was hearing accusing voices and did indeed believe he was being poisoned. He was kept in the Hôtel-Dieu for ten days after which he was allowed to visit the Yellow House during the day time; though it was agreed that he would take his meals and sleep in the hospital.

It was a reasonable compromise and one which might have done him much good. Whatever the nature of his ailments might be, the hospital kept him away from alcohol and the other excesses that resulted from his loneliness in the Yellow House. At the Hôtel-Dieu he had company after a fashion and less need to spend hours drinking himself into moody oblivion. This protection, which left him free to work during the day, was the ideal regime. Sadly, the citizens of Arles were determined that it should not be.

Some of Vincent's neighbours had been alarmed by the original incident with the razor; now stories about his belief that he was being poisoned began to unite opinion against him. His landlord in the nearby hotel had already tried to evict him, but now there was a concerted group unanimously determined to get him out. That he was only at liberty during the daytime did nothing to calm the increasingly inflamed conviction of those who saw him as a dangerous lunatic. Parents turned a blind eye to the way their children tormented the madman, chasing after him whenever he appeared in the street. A man called Jullian, who in later life went on to be the municipal librarian, recalled with shame how as a youth he had taken part in the baiting: "I remember – and I am bitterly ashamed of it now – how I threw cabbage-stalks at him! What do you expect? We were young, and he was odd, going out to paint in the country, his pipe between his teeth, his big body a bit hunched, a mad look in his eye. He always looked as if he were running away, without daring to look at anyone. Perhaps that is why we used to pursue him with our insults."

Not content with allowing the children to pester him, thirty citizens got up a petition to the mayor accusing Vincent of drinking too much and of being a threat to women and children. This was duly passed on to d'Ornano who decided, despite having just made a perfectly pleasant visit to Vincent, that popular opinion was not to be thwarted. He ordered Vincent to stay at the hospital while he interviewed a delegation of the petitioners. Each of the five petitioners he spoke to had their complaints recorded. They make sorry reading. That of a middle-aged seamstress who lived not far from the Yellow House is typical:

> The man van Goghe [sic], who lives in the same sector as I do, has, during the last few days, become increasingly mad; consequently everyone in the neighbourhood is frightened. The women especially no longer feel secure because he indulges in touching them and also makes obscene remarks in their presence. As a matter of fact, this individual has taken me by the waist in front of the shop of the second witness and has lifted me into the air, on Monday, day before yesterday. This madman is becoming a public danger, and everybody clamours for his internment in a special institution.

Small wonder Vincent thereafter referred to the citizens of Arles as *cannibals*. In the end, d'Ornano gave in to their pressure and reported in their favour. The Yellow House was sealed up and Vincent was obliged to remain at the Hôtel-Dieu. The Reverend Salles was appalled at this involuntary commitment believing that it should have been a medical rather than a police decision to have Vincent incarcerated.

Worse still, on d'Ornano's orders he had been put back in the isolation cell and forbidden books, paints and even his precious pipe. The bed in the special room was a fearsome thing, high sided and fitted with restraints. Fortunately Dr Rey and the other hospital administrators refused to accept this injustice and these restrictions were soon eased. Someone from the hospital went with him to the Yellow House to collect some of his belongings so that he could go on working, and Dr Rey let him use his office if he wanted to write to Theo and accompanied him on short walks into town. Rey agreed with Salles that the best thing might be for Vincent to give up the Yellow House and move to another part of town where he was less well known and where there would be less antagonism. Rey's mother had a modest apartment that was empty and, setting aside her doubts about Vincent's talents, agreed to go along with her son's suggestion that she should rent it to his patient.

Vincent's difficulty now was that fear of a relapse was weakening his ability to cope with the outside world – it seemed so much easier simply to stay where he was, surrounded by sympathetic people like Rey. Theo, deeply distressed and powerless to do more than send money, wrote to say that Paul Signac would shortly be travelling south and would come to Arles to see what could be done.

Signac arrived on Saturday March 23rd. He had last seen his old painting companion well over a year ago and now found him huddled up and bandaged, locked away in a madhouse. The authorities noted the concern of the younger man and exceptionally allowed him to take Vincent on a visit to the Yellow House to see the paintings. The police had smashed the locks and then sealed up the front door and when Signac went to obtain permission to break in it was at first refused. Not to be outdone, Signac insisted that they had no legal right to prevent his friend from entering his own home. The police backed down, and Vincent and Signac forced their way in.

When they entered the shuttered rooms, they found Vincent's paintings waiting like forgotten treasures in a half-lit cave – the *Night Café, Madame Roulin,* the *Fishing Boats at Les Saintes-Maries*, the *Starlit Night*, the various paintings of sunflowers and harvests. Stacked in these cluttered chambers was one of the greatest achievements of nineteenth-century art, produced in less than a year, and looking at them once more was the man who had started out a mere eight years before virtually unable to hold a pencil and who had done all this in so short a time. Signac can only have looked at his hunched, wounded friend in amazement.

They sat at their ease talking about literature, painting, socialism, whatever occurred to them. Signac found it very pleasant and seems not to have realised how tiring the excursion must have been to his companion who had not been away from the hospital for some time. As dusk fell, a mistral blew up, and this may have intensified Vincent's agitated state for he suddenly grabbed a bottle of turpentine and was only prevented from drinking it by Signac's rapid intervention. Realising how bad things really were, the younger man hurried his friend back to the Hôtel-Dieu and the watchful eyes of his warders.

The next morning, Signac returned and took him for another walk before leaving for Cassis near Marseilles. The two friends said goodbye, not thinking it was the last time they would see each other. Signac would send an encouraging letter from his new address and also wrote to Theo to report what he had seen and done with Vincent. That aside, it was clear to Signac that there was nothing practical he could do though, as he told Theo, he remained hopeful that all would be well.

Saturday March 30th was Vincent's thirty-sixth birthday. The same day, Theo left for Amsterdam to prepare for his wedding. A few days later Roulin returned from Marseilles for a last visit; his family had now joined him there and he no longer needed to come to Arles. After he had left, all that remained for Vincent was the life of the hospital. He painted the gardens in the courtyard, sunny and joyful. Soon he was allowed to work in the surrounding countryside, even though no one really liked what he did. One day Dr Rey was walking down a dimly lit corridor when he made out Vincent carrying one of his canvases. It was a painting of the long fever ward occupied by the victims of the endemic cholera and typhoid which were to become Dr Rey's specialities. Rey studied the picture with the double line of curtained beds and the usual group of dispirited inmates huddled round a single old-fashioned stove. It was not a particularly flattering image of the place and not surprisingly Rey declined Vincent's offer of it as a gift. He knew what his family's reactions would be if he came home with such an object. As they were talking Rousseau the pharmacist came by, but despite Rey's encouragement he too said he had no time for such nonsense. It was only when Monsieur Neuvière, the hospital's bursar, appeared that they could find a taker for the gift. Vincent was pathetically pleased when the man accepted it. Neuvière thought it "curious" but he held on to it and years later gained a small fortune from his passing fancy.

By then it was clear that Vincent was becoming increasingly institutionalised. With the Yellow House closed and his furniture stored with the Ginoux at the Café de la Gare, there was nowhere else for him to go. The paintings were despatched to Theo, who had by this time returned to Paris with his bride, and was clearly in no position to take his brother in. The question of Rey's mother's apartment was brought up once more. She was only asking a paltry six to eight francs a month for a place with running water; but Vincent could not face the move. Life in the hospital was not unpleasant, for he was allowed to call on Rey in his private rooms at the hospital if he needed company, though there were times when the doctor must have regretted his generosity. On one occasion Vincent came in while Rey was shaving:

What are you doing, doctor?

"You can see well enough, I'm shaving."

Ah – if you wish, I could shave you myself.

Whereupon Vincent, his expression suddenly dangerous, tried to seize the razor. Only Rey's stern command that he ". . . Clear out at once . . ." put an end to the incident. Vincent scuttled off, back to his room.

On April 19th, the Reverend Salles wrote to Theo outlining the options open to them:

> He is entirely conscious of his condition and talks to me of what he has been through and which he fears may return, with a candour and simplicity which is touching. 'I am unable,' he told me the day before yesterday, 'to look after myself and control myself; I feel quite different from what I used to be.' In view of this there was no reason to look for an apartment and we have given up all attempts in this direction. He has, therefore, requested me to obtain the necessary particulars, in order that he may be admitted somewhere and also to write to you in this sense. Considering this decision, taken after mature deliberation, I thought that, before turning to you, I would obtain some information regarding a private institution near Arles, at St Rémy, where it appears that the inmates are very well treated. I send you the reply which I have received and the prospectus that came with it.
>
> I am, as always, at your entire service and you may freely make use of me. I add that those who know your brother and particularly the doctors, approve the decision and regard it as very wise, in view

of the state of isolation in which your brother will find himself after leaving hospital.

The institution proposed by Salles was the asylum of St Paul-de-Mausole, near the small town of St Rémy-de-Provence. This was north of Arles in the direction of Avignon. Vincent accepted the suggestion willingly. He had recently suffered three fainting fits after which he remembered nothing of what had happened. He was sure he was not mad but equally afraid that madness might at any time strike him down and that only a prolonged period of recuperation could stave off this horror. He was sorry to be leaving Rey and the others but not downcast at the prospect of surrendering himself to an institution for the insane. The Reverend Salles went with him on May 8th and two days later, the pastor again wrote to Theo to reassure him that all was well:

> Our journey to St Rémy took place under ideal circumstances. M. Vincent was perfectly calm and explained his case himself to the director, like a man who is fully conscious of his position. He has stayed with me until I left and when I said goodbye to him, he warmly thanked me and appeared somewhat moved by the thought of the radically new life in that house. Let us hope that his stay will be truly beneficial for him and that soon he will be regarded as capable to resume his complete freedom of movement. M. Peyron assured me that he will receive all the kindness and care which his condition demands.
>
> Yours ever,
>
> Salles

The man into whose care Salles handed Vincent was Dr Théophile Peyron, who since 1874 had been Director of what was called the Asylum for the Alienated. He was fifty and had been a naval doctor before settling first in Marseilles where he began to specialise in nervous diseases and mental illness. He was thus the first 'expert' to confront Vincent's condition. Vincent described him as *a little gouty man – several years a widower, with very black spectacles. As the institution is rather dull, the man seems to get no great amusement out of his job, and besides he has enough to live on.*

Unlike the Hôtel-Dieu, which was a public institution, the asylum took private patients. Presumably concerned with profits, Peyron was rather stingy, a fact quickly noted by Vincent, who compared St Paul's to the rather run-down establishment of someone rich but ruined and now dead. But it is noteworthy that Vincent chose to comment on the faded curtains and scratched furniture rather than the bars covering the windows and the bottoms of the staircases, sealing off the upper and lower floors. Despite the fact that his bedroom on the second floor was a cell with a heavy metal door, Vincent seems not to have shared the impressions of later writers who were shocked at the bleakness of the place. It is probable that the atmosphere of isolation and dullness was deliberately cultivated as most of the inmates were thought to be in need of calm and seclusion. With that as its aim, the asylum was the ideal place, situated two miles from a small, rather sleepy town famous only as the birthplace of Nostradamus, with none of the distractions of Arles.

The year before Vincent's arrival the Provençal poet Frédéric Mistral, in the company of other poet friends, had been to St Rémy to visit the Roman ruins, a triumphal arch and tomb, on the nearby Plateau des Antiques. As these poets walked about drinking in the atmosphere of an ancient Provençal past and scenting the wild flowers which grew in profusion on the lower slopes of the Alpilles, the sound of a bell drew them to the adjacent cloister. One of them thought it resembled an Italian monastery, slumbering in its old park, "hiding, so near to all that luminous poetry, such misery and such obscurity".

Vincent's perception of the place was a good deal more prosaic, but the asylum did retain much of the atmosphere of the monastery it had been until the French Revolution. It was divided physically into men's and women's sections, the latter being run by nursing nuns of the Order of Saint-Joseph d'Aubenas with their Sister Superior, Sister Epiphanie, being responsible to the director Dr Peyron. The nuns also prepared the food and handled the laundry for the men's section, which was run by male attendants under a chief guardian, always known as the Major, Charles-Elzéard Trabuc.

At the time of Vincent's arrival at the asylum its monastic calm was enhanced by the fact that only a quarter of the available rooms were occupied. He was one of just ten male patients undergoing treatment though despite such small numbers, there was still a goodly round of nocturnal screams and cries which made Vincent think of beasts in a menagerie. Far from this upsetting him, he seems to have found comfort in the realisation that he was not as badly off as some of the poor creatures amongst whom he was now living. There was a 25-year-old epileptic with whom Vincent became quite friendly, though the young man's attacks were a constant feature of life in the asylum. Another 23-year-old was noted in the register as an 'idiot' because he could only make inarticulate noises, while a third suffered from the delusion that he was being followed by the secret police. A few days after Vincent's arrival what was described as a 'maniac' was brought to the asylum whereupon the poor creature proceeded to wreck his room, breaking the bed and tearing up the sheets. Vincent noted that whilst it was sad to watch, the man was handled with great patience.

As a voluntary inmate whose brother paid the fees, Vincent was guaranteed special care. He was given the same mouldy-tasting food as the others but Theo managed to arrange for him to have his own bedroom so that he was distanced from the worst noise of the public ward. He was also allowed another of the empty rooms to use as a studio. As for treatment, Dr Peyron had quickly concurred with the substance of Dr Rey's diagnosis. His entry in the register of the voluntarily interned described the patient as:

> . . . suffering from acute mania with hallucinations of sight and hearing which have caused him to mutilate himself by cutting off his right [sic] ear. At present he seems to have recovered his reason, but does not feel that he possesses the strength and the courage to live independently and had voluntarily asked to be admitted to this institution. As a result of the preceding it is my opinion that M. Van Gogh is subject to epileptic fits at very infrequent intervals, and that it is advisable to keep him under prolonged observation in this establishment.

Thus Vincent could be reassured that he was not in the strictest sense mad, merely subject to temporary attacks. Peyron soon learned of the incidence of epilepsy in the Carbentus family and as drink, syphilis, bad diet and overwork may each in their different ways have contributed to the crisis it was not unreasonable to prescribe rest and calm. As with Rey, Peyron's diagnosis has often been challenged subsequently as the 'attacks' were unlike classic epileptic convulsions with violent spasms and tongue biting. The strongest alternative diagnosis, schizophrenia, relies on the way he attacked someone else (Gauguin) and, having failed, turned upon himself. But the difficulty is that the only witness to that attack was Gauguin, whose account is highly unreliable and self-justifying. Gauguin himself only recalled the episode years later; on first returning to Paris he did not include the attack in his description of the evening's events to Emile Bernard. In any case, had there been an alternative explanation, it would have made no difference given the treatments available. Rest and calm formed the main part of any regime, though St Paul's also specialised in hydrotherapy and had a ward with a long line of deep baths in which patients lay for hours. The only other 'cure' at Peyron's disposal was the administration of heavy doses of bromide used as a primitive sedation and a remedy for sleeplessness, and which, over long periods, could be effective in controlling epileptic fits. Combined with opiates it was thought to be useful in coping with violent patients, the drawback being that prolonged use could induce the very symptoms the chemical was meant to suppress. Vincent was prescribed baths twice a week, but it was the tranquillity of the place that was considered best for him and, as he rather ruefully noted, it was a cure which would be easy to follow even while travelling *as they do absolutely nothing*.

Whatever the treatment, Vincent's problem was one which faces anyone plunged into sudden mental breakdown: to reverse what has probably been building up over a lifetime. Whatever the illness might be it was not going to disappear overnight, it would take time, and Peyron's first concern was to dissuade Vincent from discharging himself when he began to feel rested.

At first this hardly arose as Vincent showed no desire even to leave his room and was only with difficulty persuaded to explore the grounds of the asylum. Peyron arranged for Vincent's studio room to overlook the garden and was happy that the patient should occupy himself with painting, provided he did not exert himself too much.

Like a wounded animal cautiously emerging from the security of a cave and proceeding to sniff out the surrounding countryside, Vincent slowly absorbed the asylum; he painted the irises in the garden, close to so that the plants cover the canvas, as if to block out the view. His next picture begins to reveal a corner of the asylum garden with a stone bench under a tree. Then there is an arched cloister inside the asylum and a view of his studio which shows he had begun to pin up some pictures. From the window he painted the enclosed field at the side of the asylum, where the outside world, the farms and the distant hill, were safely kept at bay by the boundary wall. Sometimes the other inmates would shuffle up to see what he was doing, though he found their bemused attentions less troublesome than those of the people of Arles who had laughed and goaded him as he tried to work.

Slowly his fear of the outside world receded and by June things were going so well that Peyron said he could paint beyond the walls provided he was accompanied by an attendant. The warder usually chosen for the task, Jean-François Poulet, was a young man of twenty-seven, familiar with the surrounding countryside and able to act as guide as Vincent set off in search of suitable places to paint. Not that everything always went smoothly. On one occasion they had just returned and were going upstairs when Vincent turned and kicked Poulet in the stomach. The attendant let the matter pass but was amused by Vincent's explanation the next day that he had been compelled to do it because the Arles police were after him. On another occasion a walk into nearby St Rémy had to be cut short when the sudden nearness of so many strangers in the streets began to upset him. But against these small reverses could be set the triumph of a potentially unsettling visit to Arles, accompanied by Monsieur Trabuc the head attendant, when he went to collect some of his belongings. Better still, he appeared to show no adverse reactions when his sister-in-law Jo wrote to say she was expecting a baby, the surest indication of how unreliable it can be to attempt to link outside events to his breakdown. For him this was, in fact, a period of extraordinary calm, yet this was also the time when he painted what have often been interpreted as his most 'disturbed' paintings: convoluted olive trees, swirling cypresses against spiralling clouds, stars that explode in serpentine arabesques. While he was creating such 'tortured' images he was also making nearly exact copies of some of the canvases he had done in Arles, including Madame Roulin by the cradle and the sunflowers. They barely differ from the originals and show no sign of swirling, exploding madness, which would surely have broken through had his dementia controlled his art. If anything, his St Rémy paintings demonstrate a return to his earlier ways of painting. The blatant use of complementaries has begun to give way to colours that are closer in the spectrum – blues and greens together – and more muted, more 'northern' as he now began to refer to anything different from the bright world of the 'South' he had experienced in Arles. He had begun to have longings for 'home' and was starting to equate the 'South' with the misery that had befallen him and blame the burning yellow sun, the bright southern colours and the sheer 'electricity' he had experienced in Provence for most of his problems.

Then, just when everything seemed to be going so well, disaster struck. He was out painting in the fields. The day was very windy and he was concentrating on some swirling, agitated trees surrounding the entrance to a quarry when he became aware that he was on the verge of another attack. He refused to let it master him and stoically went on painting until the scene was finished, but by the time he got back to the asylum he was clearly no longer in control of himself. At first Peyron withheld the news from Theo, presumably hoping the attack would pass quickly. But it dragged on for five days, and with Vincent unable to write his habitual letters, an anxious Theo had to be informed. It was the longest period of collapse thus far, with his mind wandering and any periods of sleep troubled by nightmares. Weakened and demented he somehow made his way to the studio and, in a re-run of the incident with Signac, tried to kill himself by squeezing out the tubes of poisonous paint and forcing himself to swallow the oily mess. Poulet found him and restrained him just in time, but the incident convinced Peyron that it was his extreme addiction to painting which had driven him to choose a symbolic means of suicide. The solution was obvious: he should paint no more, the studio must be closed.

As Vincent gradually recovered his senses and his stomach eased from the emetic which had brought up the pigments, he felt he would now go mad from the boredom of that already dull place. When he recovered enough to write, he begged Theo to intercede to have the injunction lifted, but two further weeks were to pass before Peyron was satisfied that the disturbing dreams had diminished and the patient was sufficiently master of himself to be trusted to return to the studio. Even so, it was two months before he felt able to step outside the asylum again.

His condition was the same as when he had first arrived, he found it impossible to leave the building, even to walk in the walled garden. At the same time he was determined to prove to Peyron that he could be relied on not to try to poison himself if he were left alone with his paints. As his abhorrence of the outside world meant that he was effectively confined to the studio, his only solution was again to use himself as a model. Since his arrival at St Rémy he had ignored portraiture; now he could do nothing else. He may also have wanted to 'examine' himself, for his self-portraits were often a way of assessing his condition. At any event, his first effort was a clear message to Peyron: full of information of a literal kind. He painted himself in what could be called his 'professional' outfit, wearing a blue artist's smock and pointedly holding his palette and brushes. The expression on the green-hued face – even the eyes were green – appearing out of a dark background, is less easy to interpret than those where he is clearly haggard or apprehensive; though it may be that he was trying to present a neutral 'healed' look which would reassure his guardians. As the portrait was a mirror-image his left ear was actually his right and thus appeared whole, though this too could have been another attempt to show how much he had recovered. Despite such obvious manipulation it is clear from his letters that he believed the only means of telling the truth about a person was the painted portrait; he detested photography, which is presumably why we have no late photographs of him. Given this key from the artist himself it is tempting to ascribe all manner of apocalyptic meanings to his self-portraits but unless his own letters support them, such interpretations are bound to vary wildly. In his second St Rémy portrait, for example, the canvas was almost entirely blue: blue background, blue jacket and waistcoat, blue tints in the face. He wore an ordinary jacket with a collarless shirt which could be interpreted as a sign that he had now accepted his place as just another shabbily dressed patient. The swirling blue of the background, and the forceful lines in the blue clothing left his staring eyes as two fixed points in a maelstrom, as if he were trying with all his force to resist the chaos gathering momentum about him. But such a reading is subjective; he may have intended no such thing. We are on surer ground with his first painting of the outside world since his suicide attempt. This is clearly a view from the security of his bedroom window, surely a reflection of his nervous state. This interpretation is reinforced when one learns from his letters that he did not paint it from the window itself but re-created the image in his studio as if even to gaze on the actuality of the outside world were too much for him. Equally significant are the more sombre, less resonant colours he chose; although it was still high summer the picture suggests that autumn has already come, another small sign of his turning back towards the North, an urge which was coming to dominate his thoughts.

He grew increasingly dissatisfied with the asylum. The nuns irritated him, he was wary of the other patients who might be dangerous, the food was bad and the hours of boredom long. He would like to leave, perhaps for another asylum near Avignon or better still away from the South. He asked Theo if there might be any chance that Pissarro would take him in, as he had Cézanne and Gauguin. Yet his portrait of the 'Major', the head guardian Trabuc, and another of his wife show how grateful he was for their solicitude. Trabuc had taken on the role of father figure and man-of-the-people from Roulin, who had in turn inherited it from old Tanguy.

In Paris, Theo and the pregnant Jo had moved to a larger apartment and Theo had stored most of Vincent's work at Tanguy's, so relations had clearly been restored. Once again Vincent had his work on show. Theo had entered the *Irises* and *Starry Night over the Rhône* for that year's Indépendants and had had an enquiry from 'Les XX' in Brussels about whether Vincent might participate in their next show.

Les XX (les Vingt) was an avant-garde group with much the same aims as the Indépendants, in their case to by-pass the official Brussels Salon. Since the arrival of French intellectual exiles in the last years of the Second Empire and throughout the Commune, Belgium had become finely attuned to cultural developments in France and had experienced a literary and artistic renaissance of its own. What Les XX organised every year went beyond a mere alternative salon; it had grown into a fully fledged arts festival with concerts, poetry readings and lectures being given concurrently with the core display of paintings. The exhibition comprised work by the Belgian members of the group together with invited entries from other countries, mainly France. So prestigious had the event become that it was not uncommon for the otherwise ignored avant-garde of Paris to solicit invitations, indeed Gauguin may have done so only the year before. Thus the fact that the founding secretary of Les XX, Octave Maus, had himself approached Theo was something of an honour, though no doubt Maus had been encouraged by his cousin Eugène Boch, who was by then following Vincent's advice and painting in the Borinage. The great advantage of the Brussels system was that once an artist was selected he was not only allowed to choose the works he wished to show but also to dictate how they should be hung. This accorded exactly with Vincent's express desire to have his paintings seen in certain groups and colour arrangements; when he replied to Maus, Vincent asked for slightly more space than normal so that he could create just such a grouping for the first time.

This was only one of several signs that Vincent's period of total obscurity was beginning to end. Theo was able to report the enthusiasm of those he invited to the apartment to see his work and there were even the first stirrings of interest from writers about art, albeit only the most avant-garde, who were themselves struggling to be recognised.

Not surprisingly, Vincent viewed Theo's reports with some concern. Isolation had not induced a willingness to accept recognition at any price, on the contrary his ideas of how his works should be exhibited were precise and even went as far as the style of the framing and the background colour against which each canvas ought to be hung. He was equally determined that from the start he and his ideas should not be misrepresented by someone who had failed to grasp what he was trying to do. It is all too easy to slip into the notion that Vincent was a poor innocent, a Holy Fool, utterly at odds with an artistic world that had rejected him. It must not be forgotten that he himself had been an art dealer employed for years by Europe's leading international gallery, and that he had an acute awareness of how the system worked and of how he might relate to it. While he longed to create art for the people, he set his sights on a small élite which he believed could come to appreciate what he was doing. His main concern was that such a group should at least understand and like the paintings for the right reasons. By contrast, he was forever giving away paintings to ordinary folk, usually with disastrous results. The 'Major' and his wife were both presented with the originals of their portraits which they subsequently lost. Fortunately, Vincent was now in the habit of making copies of his work and it is usually these second thoughts, presumably less overworked and more polished than the first attempts, which have come down to us.

One crucial and unique original has survived: the self-portrait he made as a belated gift for his mother's seventieth birthday. He had rather lost touch with her, but a letter from her that July of 1889 had impressed him with *how firm and regular* her handwriting was for a woman of her age. He knew that she must be upset by the impending departure of her youngest son Cor who, like many young Dutchmen, was about to emigrate to the Boer Republics in South Africa. But he was also sure that Theo's recent marriage and the imminent arrival of a grandchild must have brought her considerable contentment. The birthday self-portrait he painted that September was his attempt to please her and as such it shows little of her son as he then was. Rather it was an attempt to re-create his appearance twenty years earlier when he was clean-shaven with good strong features, with no hint of the ravages that time and mental illness had brought. It harks back to that last photograph of him as an insecure, tousle-haired boy of nineteen poised to begin his career with Goupil's. He meant to cheer his mother with a memory of her eldest son in happier days, but in truth the portrait is suffused with an air of infinite sadness and loss. He never again painted his own portrait – with one small exception. When he next made a copy of the painting of his bedroom in the Yellow House in Arles, one of the pictures he put on the wall above his bed is a tiny replica of his birthday portrait. The other picture in the room is probably his sister Wil and that *Bedroom* too was sent to his mother, presumably as a further way of convincing her how simple and wholesome his life was despite all the depressing news of him she must have heard over the years since they had last met.

Thoughts of his family and such gestures towards his mother must have merged with his longing for the North, and can only have compounded his sense of failure over his mission to establish a studio of the South. Gauguin and the others were once more in Brittany and there was only the occasional letter to give Vincent any sense of what was being achieved there. So it was partially to create a community of his own, and partially to re-examine the things he most associated with his northern life, that prompted him to embark on a series of paintings derived from some of the black and white prints he had collected. These bore no relation to the student copies he had made earlier when he was learning to draw. The prints were now starting points from which he developed his own work – he compared such activity to that of a musician reinterpreting a composition. But in choosing Millet as his first subject he was also signalling a return to other values. He again asked Theo to send him Millet's *Field Work* and he made his own version of *The Drinkers* by Daumier. It was as if he saw these dead artists as members of his own metaphysical studio. He rejected any suggestion that in making these 'copies' he was no longer working from nature and made it clear he looked on the prints as being as real as living things, as if he were painting a tree or a flower. Yet he was deeply upset when Bernard sent him a set of photographs of religious paintings he had been doing in Brittany including one he called *Christ in the Garden of Olives*, a subject Gauguin had also tackled. Vincent's reactions ignored his own 'copies' and insisted on the role of the real, as opposed to the abstract or imagined, as the sole basis for art:

... that nightmare of a 'Christ in the Garden of Olives', good lord, I mourn over it, and so with the present letter I ask you again, roaring my loudest, and calling you all kinds of names with the full power of my lungs – to be so kind as to become your own self again a little.

The 'Christ Carrying his Cross' is appalling. Are those patches of colour in it harmonious? I won't forgive you the spuriousness – yes, certainly, spuriousness – in the composition.

As you know, once or twice, while Gauguin was in Arles, I gave myself free rein with abstractions, for instance in the 'Woman Rocking' [The portrait of Madame Roulin] *in the 'Woman Reading a Novel', black in a yellow library; and at the same time abstraction seemed a charming path. But it is enchanted ground, old man, and one soon finds oneself up against a stone wall.*

So incensed was Vincent that he stepped outside and painted an olive grove direct from nature with no imagined Christ to render the work 'spurious'. And by applying his colours in thin short strokes as if he were re-establishing his own version of Divisionism, he further distanced himself from what he now believed was the false route being taken in Brittany.

Of course his response to Bernard's photographs was unnecessarily harsh towards someone younger than himself, someone who had remained a staunch friend when others had fallen away. Given Vincent's own reaction to criticism, as in the Van Rappard affair, he should have phrased his letter more gently. But if nothing else, the force of his response indicates that he was emerging from the state of drifting inertia which usually followed an attack. It even stimulated an entire series of olive groves, noticeably darker in colour, and he felt certain this more sombre palette was a reflection of his new peace of mind. In the middle of December he wrote to tell Theo how discreet his colours were becoming:

I think that probably I shall hardly do any more things in impasto; it is the result of the quiet, secluded life that I am leading, and I am all the better for it. Fundamentally I am not so violent as all that, and at last I myself feel calmer.

He told Theo that although he was resigned to spending another year in the South, he felt that his paintings of Provence would *somehow be linked, I hope, with our distant memories of our youth in Holland.* But he still worried that he was a continuing drain on the family's finances and even began to question whether he should have stayed with Goupil's.

Of course Theo wrote back to reassure him. What matter that he had never sold anything? Look at Pissarro and Gauguin, whose "recent paintings are less saleable than those of last year. Last week he wrote to tell me that one of his children (in Copenhagen) fell out of a window, and was picked up nearly dead. And yet they hope to save him. He would do anything to get a little money, but I am unable to procure it."

To reassure his brother further that his work was gradually being accepted Theo described the framing of the pictures which would go to Brussels and told him how two of the *Sunflowers* were now on show at Père Tanguy's.

Theo's letter was dated Sunday December 22nd, 1889. The very next day Vincent wrote to his mother, enclosing a note to his sister Willemina, in which he reminded them that it was exactly a year since he had suffered his first major attack and described the work he was now doing. Having finished the letters he went out to paint and then it happened: without warning or explanation another attack began. Once again he tried to swallow his paints. Once more they got him back to the asylum and forced up the poison. The attack lasted a week and Peyron acknowledged that it was a bad one. At some point during his convalescence Vincent saw one of the serving boys filling the lamps with kerosene and with suicidal determination managed to gulp down some of the fuel before he could be stopped.

The attack did not seem to follow the pattern of previous crises, however. Peyron's diagnosis, that there was a link between Vincent's journeys outside the asylum and his breakdowns, had been challenged only a month before when Vincent had visited the Ginoux's in Arles with no immediate after-effects. Now the doctor persuaded himself that his earlier diagnosis, that it was painting which had caused the attack, was the correct one. It explained why Vincent had swallowed his paints. There was, after all, a certain logic to it and once again the conclusion was that he must be forbidden to paint for the time being. There was nothing punitive about Peyron's decisions. He allowed Vincent to draw to help pass the time, but he was not to paint.

Yet as soon as the Reverend Salles came to see him it was clear that recovery was again almost immediate. Salles found him full of complaints about the asylum and clearly alert once more. As if to re-establish contact with the outside world Vincent sent the Roulins a gift of two paintings. Now, more than ever, he needed the support of someone like old Roulin, but in the asylum there were only poor lost souls wandering about the corridors or staring into infinity. Between attacks he was effectively sane and thus the unending hours in that dreary place brought ever-increasing torture. Not to be able to paint made such confinement intolerable.

Just as he was struggling to prove to Peyron that it was safe to let him use his materials, he had his first major exhibition. On January 17th 1890 the annual Les XX exhibition had its vernissage in Brussels. Among the members exhibiting that year were Anna Boch, the sister of Eugène; Henry de Groux, the son of the Belgian history painter Charles de Groux, much admired by Vincent; and Theo van Rysselberghe, the main proponent of Belgian Neo-Impressionism, who had caused an uproar among the critics the year before. The critics had dubbed painters like Van Rysselberghe *Les Bubonnistes*, thus vilifying their work as a plague upon the national culture. But the previous year's brouhaha was a mild prelude to the storm of protest which was about to be unleashed upon the current exhibition. Among the year's invited artists were Eugène Boch, Cézanne, Lucien Pissarro, Odilon Redon, Signac, Toulouse-Lautrec and Vincent. The organisers seem to have assumed that Cézanne would be the critics' principal target, but the night before the vernissage Henry de Groux refused to have his work exhibited next to "the execrable vase of sunflowers of Monsieur Vincent or of any other agent provocateur". It was suddenly evident that it was the unknown Dutchman who would be this year's notoriety. De Groux withdrew his entries, but turned up at the banquet the following night spoiling for a fight. He was so rude to Signac and Lautrec, who had travelled from Paris for the celebration, that there was a terrific row which ended with de Groux being obliged to resign his membership of Les XX. One account speaks of a duel being threatened and seconds nominated but as de Groux was almost as short as Lautrec, some sense of how ridiculous it all looked may have helped calm them down.

While the usual programme of poetry readings and literary talks unfolded and the concerts of contemporary music with Fauré and Franck prominent were under way it was the battle over Vincent's work which excited most interest. Given that the critics had loathed the gentle tones of the Pointillists it was hardly surprising that they should react savagely to Vincent's uncompromising colours.

One article alone stood out against the trend. Although not directly related to the exhibition, an appreciation of Vincent by a young writer called Albert Aurier was published in the Brussels journal *L'Art Moderne* on the day of the infamous banquet. *L'Art Moderne* was socialist in temper and consistently advocated a link between art and social progress in defiance of the increasingly popular doctrine of art for art's sake. Aurier's article was a reprint of a piece first published earlier in January in the first issue of *Le Mercure de France*, and was to be the only major study of Vincent's work to appear during his lifetime. It was almost excessively fulsome in its praise of his art, but it also contained many assumptions about Vincent's intentions which prefigured later distortions that would gradually overwhelm the public image of his life and work.

Aurier was actually a law student struggling to make his name as a writer. He was a friend of Bernard, who had told him about Vincent and he had briefly met Theo in November 1888 when he had visited the Rue Lepic to see Vincent's work. That and a perusal of the paintings stored at Père Tanguy's had given the young man a fair insight into the range of Vincent's art, including some of the most recent St Rémy canvases. Aurier had already described some of the earlier work in the edition of April 8th, 1899 of a short-lived journal he had founded called *Le Moderniste* – one of the first uses of a word that was soon to replace Impressionism as the catch-all for the new art. *Le Moderniste* did not last long, but Aurier's attachment to its principles lived on and his profile of Vincent was a bold attempt to place the painter firmly among the new moderns.

The title of his article, "Les Isolés" (The Isolated Ones) sets the tone. Vincent is portrayed as a loner, a terrible maddened genius, often sublime, sometimes grotesque, whose life is indistinguishable from his art. To Aurier, Vincent was a visionary who by his very nature was doomed to be misunderstood; in other words the modern artist par excellence, one who would "never be understood except by his brother artists, those who are truly artists . . . and by those of the common people, those totally insignificant people, fortunate enough to have escaped by chance from the benevolent teachings of public education". Aurier saw the new art in terms of battle and put Vincent in the vanguard of his attack upon the despised traditionalists identified as Gérôme and the history painter Meissonier. Aurier was obviously ignorant of Vincent's long devotion to the latter artist. In fact the supreme irony was that, just as Vincent's thoughts were turning back to Millet and to his roots in the North, he was suddenly being extolled as a foremost representative of the new symbolism and the struggling avant-garde.

Whatever the distortions of the article, it did lift Vincent from utter obscurity and brought him to the attention of the growing circle of artists and writers involved in the new art. There is a touching account of his mother and Willemina, who were visiting Paris to assist Jo during her confinement, sitting together with Theo at midnight reading Aurier's article in *Le Mercure* and discussing its importance long into the night. For Theo at least, it was some recompense for the blind faith with which he had supported his brother over the years.

As yet Vincent knew nothing of the critical storm in Brussels, nor that a lone voice had praised his work. He had been more concerned about Marie Ginoux who was suffering another bout of depression. Peyron allowed him to visit her in Arles but two days later he had another attack which seemed to confirm the doctor's other diagnosis that it was the world outside the asylum that provoked his crises. There was, therefore, no longer any reason to stop him painting. He was ill for a week and Peyron waited until he had recovered a little before letting him see the letter announcing that Jo had given birth to a son and was going to name it Vincent Willem in his honour. The supposedly shattering effect of this revelation, with its echoes of the faraway graveyard in Zundert, has preoccupied many of those who have written about Vincent, but in truth he showed no immediate reaction at all. He seemed to accept the birth quite calmly and wrote expressing his joy and his intention to paint a picture for his namesake. It was when Peyron gave him Aurier's article that he showed most concern and he proceeded to devote much of the time when he was not painting to drafting a careful response. His first concern was to thank Aurier for his kind remarks but he was determined also to challenge the reference to Meissonier whom he was at pains to defend.

Having been allowed to paint again, one of his first canvases was the work that for many people best represents his stay at St Rémy: his reworking of Gustave Doré's *Prisoners' Round*, a piercing black and white image of a circle of prisoners dolefully undergoing their exercise period in an enclosed prison yard whose stark walls shut out all hint of the sky above. Many have assumed that this was Vincent's way of showing the reality of his experience at St Rémy. True, he found the asylum numbingly boring, but he was hardly a prisoner and his reworking of Doré's picture was probably more a gesture of defiance and an expression of his increasing desire to get away than a literal representation of life in those rather shabby cloisters.

Another sign of his return to the past was the revival of his voracious appetite for books; he was reading Shakespeare's historical dramas to help fill the empty hours. It was at this point too that he began to contemplate the possibility of reworking some of his own originals. He wrote to Theo and to his mother asking them to send any of the early drawings they might still have so that he could work on their subjects again now that his skills were so much improved. Thus he came to make a painted version of one of the earliest drawings from Etten, the old man by the fire with his head in his hands, which he called *At Eternity's Gate*. He had worked on versions of this both in Etten and in The Hague; that he should return to it once more was a clear indication of the direction he was seeking – a way to escape from the road to abstraction which he now saw as inherent in all the new movements in art. By trying to reawaken his interest in the 'committed' art he had originally intended to make he hoped to maintain that close contact with the 'real', the natural world, he now believed to be essential to the true artist.

Despite the severity of his last attack and the depressing realisation that each time they seemed to get worse, he was still much concerned about Marie Ginoux. As he could no longer visit her, his only way to express his feelings was to paint her portrait. Gauguin had left behind his version of her, wearing traditional Arlésienne dress, and Vincent decided to use that as the basis for a portrait of his own. He wanted to make her smile again, and indeed he does show her with a smile playing on her lips, but her pose, head slightly to one side, resting on her hand, conveys a prevailing sense of melancholy and speaks of the effects of her depression. He made several versions, in one of which he placed two books beside her, Beecher Stowe's *Uncle Tom's Cabin* and Dickens' *Christmas Stories*, symbols of caring and sympathy, and further proof that he was rereading some of the novels which had so influenced him in the past. This preoccupation with earlier modes of thought is also shown in his letters, where there is an increasing certainty that since Millet's time art had somehow taken a wrong turn. As he wrote to his sister Wil:

> *Oh Millet! Millet! how he painted humanity and that Something on High which is familiar and yet solemn. And then to think in our time that that man wept when he started painting, that Giotto and Angelico painted on their knees – Delacroix so full of grief and feeling . . . nearly smiling. What are we impressionists to be acting like them already? Soiled in the struggle for life . . . "Who will give back to the soul what the breath of revolutions has taken away" – this is the cry of distress uttered by the poet of another generation, who seemed to have a presentiment of our weaknesses, diseases, wanderings.*
>
> *Millet set the example by living in a hovel, and holding intercourse only with people who did not know the bounds of pride and eccentricity.*
>
> *So rather a little wisdom than a lot of energetic zeal. And the rest – like all the rest –*

On February 22nd Vincent set off for Arles bearing a version of her portrait as a gift for Marie Ginoux. He never reached the Café de la Gare and when he failed to return to the Asylum that evening, it was at first assumed that he had found somewhere to stay overnight. But the next day, a Sunday, word was brought to Dr Peyron that he had reappeared and had suffered another attack. A carriage was dispatched to Arles to bring him back but when he was lucid enough to answer questions it transpired that he had no recollection of where he had spent Saturday night. The portrait had vanished and could not be found.

In his letter to Theo, Peyron assumed the effects of the attack would pass as quickly as before, but in this he was mistaken. It was two months before anything resembling normality returned. From the end of February until the end of April Vincent drifted in and out of deepening moods of despondency. Just when he appeared to be calm and lucid he would retreat into mumbling suspicion and recrimination. His thirty-seventh birthday, on March 30th, was just another day lost in this void. Theo tried to raise his spirits in a letter describing how well his paintings had been received at the 1890 Indépendants, where even Gauguin had said that Vincent's work was the chief attraction. But no amount of cajoling could pull him out of his misery and all he felt capable of doing was a series of tiny drawings called *Memories of the North* which showed a thatched cottage and a couple in a carriage not unlike the first drawings he had done for Betsy Tersteeg a lifetime ago.

When he eventually felt able to send a note to Theo on April 24th, he tells of his distress in a postscript:

> *I take up this letter again to try to write, it will come little by little, the thing is that my head is so bad, without pain it is true, but altogether stupefied. I must tell you that there are, as far as I can judge, others who have the same thing wrong with them that I have, and who, after having worked part of their life, are reduced to helplessness now. It isn't easy to learn much good between four walls, that's natural, but all the same it is true that there are people who can no longer be left at liberty as though there were nothing wrong with them. And that means that I am pretty well or altogether in despair about myself. Perhaps I might really recover if I were in the country for a time.*

He certainly meant the North, which for him had become 'the country' whereas the South was imbued with those ills which he had formerly associated with city life. He had fled from The Hague to Drenthe and later from Paris to Provence, from city to country; now he was convinced that only a return to the land of his childhood would effect the cure he craved.

Theo had already written to Pissarro telling him of Vincent's hope that he might be able to stay with him for a time. Perhaps wisely, the old man bowed to his wife's insistence that he do no such thing. Instead he wrote to tell Theo about his collector friend Dr Gachet, a long-time supporter of the Impressionists, who lived in the village of Auvers-sur-Oise, an hour by train from Paris.

Dr Gachet had already treated a number of artists with great sympathy and understanding. Theo had first met him at his Paris consulting rooms in March and was surprised when the doctor, having listened to his recital of Vincent's symptoms, insisted that this was not madness and that whatever it was could be cured. Since Vincent insisted on leaving St Rémy at once, Theo wrote to Auvers to ask for the doctor's help. The solution Gachet offered was that Vincent should lodge in a nearby inn so that he would be able to visit the doctor's home whenever he wished. As the asylum had clearly made no progress towards a cure, Theo accepted that this might be the wisest course.

Peyron offered no objections. Vincent can only have been an embarrassment to him as it was now apparent that, if anything, he was getting worse. Vincent's determination to leave as soon as possible was prompted by his conviction that there was always a period of remission between attacks and that he should travel north while there was still time. The plan was that Vincent should travel first to Paris where Dr Gachet could examine him before finally deciding on their next moves. But who would accompany him on the train? While correspondence passed between Gachet, Theo and Peyron, Vincent threw himself into another orgy of painting. One of his last works in St Rémy, the *Road with Cypresses and Star*, is probably his most famous canvas of the period. Countless people accept it as the quintessential vision of Provence, yet the hidden irony is that the cottage in the background and the horse and cart on the road are the same as the ones he had drawn in his *Memories of the North*. How would poor Bernard, whom Vincent had so strongly upbraided for departing from nature, have reacted had he known that his purist friend had incorporated such 'unreal' memories in his key painting of the South?

In the end Vincent was allowed to travel alone. He wrote to Joseph and Marie Ginoux to say how sorry he was he had not been able to see them again. He asked them to send on some of his belongings especially his little mirror, instructing them to paste strips of paper across the glass so that it would not be damaged. It was the only possession about which he seemed seriously concerned. He travelled first to Tarascon whence he telegraphed to Theo to say he would be arriving at the Gare de Lyon at 10 a.m. the following day. He seems, judging by his appearance on arrival, to have boarded the train without a qualm and to have passed a restful night. By contrast Theo, alarmed at the thought of his travelling alone, had been unable to sleep. Back at the asylum Dr Peyron completed his final report on his departed patient, writing in the column marked 'Observations' the single word "Cured".

This is the word that must have crossed Jo's mind when she first saw her brother-in-law. Having expected someone ill and troubled, she was astonished to find a healthy, broad-shouldered man who looked in far better health than her own husband. Since their wedding Theo had had frequent bouts of ill health, and before her son's birth there had been much family concern that he too might inherit the family weaknesses.

Happily, that fear had passed but Theo still gave cause for concern. When he left for the station to collect Vincent and failed to reappear, for what seemed to Jo an eternity, she grew worried. It was with considerable relief that she finally saw an open fiacre drive into the courtyard of the block and thus caught her first glimpse of the man who had so dominated her husband's life and, since their marriage, her own.

Johanna Gezina van Gogh was pretty in a rather boyish way. Her fresh, clear complexion, short cut hair and slightly too prominent nose, made her look much younger than her twenty-eight years. That and the fact she had married into a somewhat flamboyant family make it all too easy to think of her as a shy, retiring girl who dutifully followed where her new husband might lead. But it would be quite wrong to interpret her adoption of Theo's enthusiasms as slavish marital obedience. Jo had a mind of her own. She had been a top level student of English and had worked for a time in London at the British Museum. She had written a dissertation on Shelley and, until her marriage, had taught English at a high school for girls in Utrecht.

Theo had introduced her to art for which she turned out to have a natural enthusiasm. There was nothing contrived or merely dutiful about her love of her brother-in-law's work, it was completely genuine. After their marriage she and Theo had moved to the apartment in the nearby Cité Pigalle and she and Theo had spent their first days hanging and rehanging Vincent's paintings to achieve the display Theo felt each merited. There had then been much coming and going of artists and others as Theo tried to create an awareness of what his brother was doing. In all this, Jo was his willing helper and it is small wonder that she was excited at the prospect of her first meeting with someone so central to her new life.

The Vincent she discovered, that first morning, was in sparkling good form. The fact that he had finally managed to leave the asylum and was about to embark on a new adventure had clearly stimulated him enormously. He was transparently happy.

The two brothers went in to see the sleeping baby Vincent, and Jo saw that both had tears in their eyes. They spent the rest of the day together and the next morning the new Uncle Vincent got up very early so he could spend a while alone looking at his pictures hung on every wall and at the unframed canvases spread out on the floor of the dining-room. Later that morning the two brothers went round to Père

Tanguy's to see the attic room which Theo had rented to store the rest of the work, as well as their joint collection of paintings by other artists.

Tanguy was one of the few members of the old group whom Theo let Vincent meet on that visit, presumably so as not to overexcite him. Vincent had hoped to see as many exhibitions as they could manage during his stay, but the ever-watchful Theo restricted their activities to the Salon du Champ-de-Mars. This was yet another group which had been set up in opposition to the official Salon and this was its first exhibition. One of the group's leaders was that same Meissonier whom Vincent had recently defended to Albert Aurier.

Given Meissonier's participation and that of the sculptor Rodin, it was clear this venture was no gathering of young radicals. It was not only the Impressionists and the 'Indépendants' who had taken a stand against the official art world for, as the Champ-de-Mars exhibition showed, even those working within what might have been thought of as the accepted canons of both subject and style, could fall foul of the official jury and be provoked into action. One such was Puvis de Chavannes who at sixty-six was already a senior figure in the art world and yet, like Meissonier, still at odds with the inner group of men like Gérôme and Cormon who dominated the art establishment. Vincent had admired the occasional example of Puvis's work that he had seen when he lived in Paris, but now he was gripped by his painting entitled *Inter Artes et Naturam*, a canvas which was the centre of attention at the exhibition.

The painting was probably a smaller version of Puvis's mural on the same subject in the Musée des Beaux-Arts in Rouen, and at first glance such a stiff composition consisting of groups of figures in modern dress arranged around a formal garden in imitation of classical poses seems hardly the sort of subject to have inspired the new artists. Yet Pierre Puvis de Chavannes, despite his solitary, even wayward vision, was one of the rare figures admired by nearly all the different Paris factions, and the influence of *Inter Artes et Naturam* can be traced in the work of such diverse artists as Aubrey Beardsley and Pablo Picasso.

To the casual observer Puvis could be seen as the official artist par excellence; his murals decorate the Panthéon in Paris and other official buildings from Boston in America to town halls all over his native land. Yet in his own stubborn way Puvis had been just as revolutionary as the Impressionists. He too had rejected the formal classicism of the establishment. He had enrolled in Couture's atelier but as he put it: "I slept in his studio for three months and when I woke up I left it." Puvis had also chosen Courbet and Manet as starting points for his art, but unlike the Impressionists he had continued to adapt the classical traditions, absorbing much of the lighter palette of his contemporaries while remaining loyal to allegorical subjects such as War, Peace, Work, Rest. Despite this allegiance he had known rejection by the official salon and much of his time was spent executing large-scale public commissions for provincial centres such as Amiens, whose governing officials proved surprisingly sympathetic to his unique blend of old and new. More surprisingly, so too did his fellow artists. Today, his reputation has been obscured by the overwhelming victory of Impressionism as the dominant style of the end of the century, but at the time he was seen as a valid alternative, a living link with the past. He had neither descended to dead pastiche as had most Salon artists, nor was he an advocate of a rupture with the mainstream Western tradition, a path it seemed the Symbolists were taking. Indeed, when some of those who had earlier backed the new art began to have doubts about how far such experiment should go, it was Puvis who could offer a way back to a more balanced view. In that sense *Inter Artes et Naturam* was in itself a form of manifesto, a call for harmony between art and nature, between the past and the present. It is therefore less surprising, given his own return to earlier art, that Vincent was profoundly moved by the painting when he first saw it with Theo.

The brothers returned to the apartment where they found Theo's brother-in-law Andries who had been invited to join them. As before, his relations with Vincent were excellent. Andries was now something of an art expert in his own right, with a burgeoning interest in the Symbolist painters. But so relaxed an evening could not prevent Vincent from feeling overwhelmed by his sudden return to the city. The following day, Monday, it was decided that he should not stay on until Friday when he was due to visit Dr Gachet's clinic in the Faubourg Saint-Denis. He would leave the next day for Auvers where he could see him at his home.

Vincent travelled by train as planned and on arrival walked the short distance up the slope from the station, past the house built by the painter Daubigny, along the winding Rue des Vessenots to the substantial square-built house of his new protector.

Gachet had chosen Auvers-sur-Oise not only because of its nearness to Paris, where he had opened a clinic for nervous diseases, but also because of its artistic connections. The nature painter Charles Daubigny, much admired by Vincent, had first come to Auvers, then a pretty village in a valley surrounded by a sea of cornfields, in 1857. Three years later Daubigny built himself the substantial house Vincent had just seen and Daubigny's presence had attracted friends like Corot and Daumier to the village along with their followers and pupils. Auvers grew, like Barbizon, into an artistic community and its surrounding forests and fields became recognisable motifs of French nineteenth-century landscape painting. Daubigny was still active when Gachet first arrived, and when Pissarro promptly settled in nearby Pontoise to be joined by Cézanne and later Gauguin a line of artistic continuity was maintained. Gachet bought a large two-storey residence, formerly a girls' hostel, on the slope above the town where, by then a widower, he lived with his son Paul and daughter Marguerite.

There was a great deal to suggest that Gachet and Vincent would like each other. Gachet was a man of the north; he had been born in Lille not far from the Borinage and had spent much of his childhood in Belgium where he had learned to speak Flemish. He used the Flemish words for 'of Lille' ['van Ryssel'] to sign his etchings. And that too was an indication that he and Vincent might get along, for Gachet was not merely a collector of art but also a passionate amateur who often exhibited alongside his professional friends. As a young man, he had wanted to be an artist and had decided on medicine very much as a second choice. Even as a student at the Faculty in Paris he had accompanied a childhood friend Armand Gautier, a student at the Beaux-Arts, on his excursions among the artistic community and thus came to know Courbet and other painters. In Paris he worked in the Salpêtrière and Bicêtre Hospitals that specialised in coping with the mad. In 1856 he took his friend Gautier into the exercise yard in the women's section, where he painted the depressing sight of mad women arguing in groups or wandering aimlessly about; one stands facing the wall, shutting out any contact with the world. By a curious coincidence Gachet chose the same university, Montpellier, at which to present his thesis as Rey would so some twenty years later. Fascinated by the subject of mental health Gachet chose 'A study of Melancholy' as his title, though there was also another, more personal reason: he too was an occasional sufferer from those inexplicable black moods that drive some to utter despair.

As a doctor, Gachet was distinctly unusual. In his student days he had so dreaded dissecting the human cadaver he began smoking a pipe to take his mind off the experience. Studying the mind was clearly less upsetting. While in Montpellier he had met Bruyas whose collection would one day so stimulate Vincent and Gauguin. He had visited Courbet and travelled to Marseilles to find Monticelli whose work he had bought. On the way back he had met the young Cézanne for the first time. In Paris he became a friend and collector of the struggling Impressionists. It would be hard to imagine contacts more appropriate for one about to take charge of Vincent.

Gachet was sixty-one when Vincent came to his village and he was delighted to welcome him and willing to help, as he had Cézanne when he spent time in Auvers. However, as the rather hasty diagnosis he had given to Theo makes clear, he seems to have assumed from the start that there was little wrong with Vincent and that all he needed was rest and the occasional chat with a sympathetic listener. Their first encounter must have reinforced such an impression, for despite three exhausting days in Paris, Vincent was in good shape. As long as he held up there might be no need for any help other than the occasional friendly meeting. The potential danger was that if Vincent suffered another attack there would be no one immediately to hand to help him. Should he get violent or try once more to poison himself, he was effectively on his own.

Later, Vincent's time in Auvers seemed to expand in the memories of those who knew him. To Dr Gachet, his friendship with the painter and his role as his doctor and adviser grew to mythic proportions. In fact, Vincent was in Auvers for no more than sixty-nine days and was only an occasional visitor to the doctor's house. Indeed, from the start, Vincent seems to have guessed that Gachet would not be much use to him, and with the uncanny prescience of one who recognises his own weakness in another, he summed him up with considerable acerbity:

> *I have seen Dr Gachet, who gives me the impression of being rather eccentric, but his experience as a doctor must keep him balanced enough to combat the nervous trouble from which he certainly seems to be suffering at least as seriously as I.*

Unlike Cézanne and other earlier visitors, Vincent was unimpressed by Gachet's house with its antique tables crowded with pots of plants, vases of flowers, statuettes and other curiosities so that visiting artists could always find a ready made still-life to hand. To Vincent it was all *black, black, black* . . . except for the stunning collection of Impressionist paintings which included a winter scene by Pissarro, flower studies by Cézanne and an early nude by Guillaumin.

Despite initial misgivings about Gachet's own state of mind, Vincent determined to let things take their course. Later that first day, he was led down the hill to the Auberge St Aubin, but when he discovered it charged six francs a day, nothing the doctor could say would persuade him to remain in the place. In the end, Vincent went off on his own to find somewhere cheaper. He settled on a café with some upstairs rooms next to the modest town hall that looked uncannily like the one he had known as a child in Groot Zundert, perfectly square with a pointed central tower.

The inn was owned by Arthur-Gustave Ravoux and his wife. They only charged three francs fifty a day with board, though the cramped room with narrow metal bed at the end of a narrow dark corridor facing the stairs was far from inviting. As it was rapidly filled with paintings, almost one for each day he spent in Auvers, that hardly mattered. Perhaps what appealed to him was the downstairs café, where a stove and billiard table gave it a passing resemblance to the night café in Arles. Whatever his reasons for choosing the place, the odd thing was that he had stumbled on one of the few families in the village who didn't much care for Dr Gachet. A Dr Mazery was the local practitioner, but Gachet was generally much admired for his willingness to treat the needy free of charge. Something about Gachet, however, had irritated the Ravouxs, as their later recollections make clear, though they always omitted to reveal what it had been that had upset them. This aside, they seem to have liked Vincent and let him use a downstairs room as a studio when he could not paint out of doors.

Having found a room, Vincent began work the very next day, much attracted to the winding streets of thatched cottages. Many of the gateways, like the one before Dr Gachet's house, were covered in ivy, always Vincent's favourite plant and a sure symbol of the North. After the intense heat and colour of Provence the cooler climate, the late spring flowers and the more subdued tones were just what he had wanted. He wrote to Theo to send him Bargue's exercises again so that he could undertake a refresher course in drawing. But this initial happiness was not to last. The excitement of meeting Jo and seeing the baby Vincent for the first time, as well as the move to Auvers, produced a delayed reaction. He went to see Gachet, but it was one of his Paris days and Vincent became irrationally upset about the incident. No one was spared. He wrote a letter to Theo to ask why he had not written, and why he had omitted to make proper financial arrangements for him when he was in Paris. He went on to say that he did not think they could count on Gachet at all as *he is sicker than I am or shall we say just as much.* He also complained about the *bed-bug-infested hole* at Tanguy's where Theo had stored his paintings. The letter was a litany of complaint.

Theo's first letter to Auvers contained good and bad news in equal measure. Vincent had sold a painting in Brussels to Anna Boch, Eugène's sister, and for the not unreasonable figure of 400 Belgian francs. It was the first true sale outside the family, leaving aside exchanges made with other artists. But this uplifting event was marred by Theo's revelation that instead of coming to Auvers for their summer holiday as they had hoped, he and Jo would have to take the 'little one' to their parents in Holland. Vincent was not best pleased and their decision, more than anything, was to become a point of obsession in the coming weeks. In a way, Vincent's ill-temper seems much closer to his former depressive state than the violent seizures he had experienced in Provence. If that were so, then it could be interpreted as a hopeful step back from the brink, a move away from the violence of Arles and St Rémy. Unfortunately, there was no one now to monitor and help direct such improvement, though it was perhaps fortunate he did not see Dr Gachet until the following Sunday, by which time his intense irritability had somewhat abated.

Gachet had invited him to Sunday lunch. Believing Vincent would benefit from good food and sympathetic company, he intended that Vincent should lunch with him once or twice a week. True, Vincent no longer insisted on bread and cheese as his only diet, he had become southern enough to prefer a plate of olives, but that was as far as it went. At the Auberge Ravoux he would join the other boarders and eat the simple fare put before them, but the prospect of a formal meal of several courses was still intolerable to him. Nor was it really suitable for Gachet himself who suffered from weak digestion and could only persevere with such a repast out of a sense of duty. The first meal ought to have been the last but against all the evidence Gachet continued to believe this was the best way to help his visitor. In a sense it worked. Vincent needed someone to lean on, and Gachet was all there was. Despite the uncomfortable lunches, when he chafed to get back to his painting, he gradually stopped grumbling and complaining and began to see the doctor as a possible help. After a fortnight he could write to his sister Willemina that Gachet was *a true friend ... something like another brother.*

The doctor was less successful in getting Vincent to share his enthusiasm for etching. Some years before he had installed a press in one of the third floor attics and while Guillaumin and Cézanne had shown only a passing interest, Gachet must be given some of the credit for the large body of prints which form so important a part of Pissarro's oeuvre.

The attic studio was an interesting phenomenon in its own right, being decorated with the death masks of guillotined murderers. A passionate interest in anthropology and history had helped Gachet overcome his aversion to cutting up people and so embark on this gruesome collection. The masks aside, the room was a jumble of weird and wonderful objects that gave it the look of an alchemist's laboratory. Gachet's own work was clearly influenced by the earlier paintings and drawings of Pissarro and thus unlikely to interest Vincent but prompted

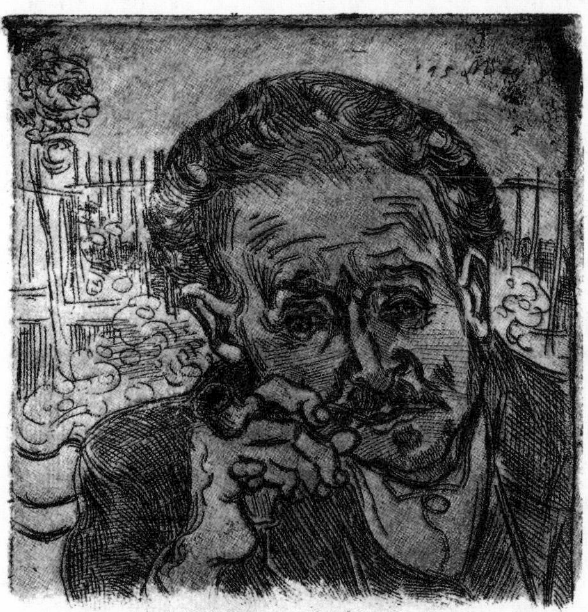

Vincent's etching of Dr Gachet.

by his host he agreed to try his hand at etching. He decided to etch a portrait of Gachet himself, smoking his pipe out in the courtyard at the back of his home, where they ate their midday meals.

In a sense posing was to be Gachet's principal contribution to Vincent's life in Auvers; the two portraits he went on to paint of the doctor are among his best. As a subject Gachet was clearly fascinating. He was short with intense blue eyes, a full moustache with a tuft of whiskers under the lower lip and a mane of red hair – reputedly dyed – which he kept brushed back from his forehead and frequently covered with a sort of white naval cap with a fawn brim. His normal garb was an alpaca frock-coat, though on occasion he wore a blue ambulance worker's smock he had acquired when he worked in a Paris hospital during the Siege of 1871. Indoors, during the winter months, he would wear a rather flamboyant dark red dressing-gown with a fur collar and cap.

The two portraits are almost identical, though in one there are two books on the table, the Goncourt brothers' *Germinie Lacerteux* and *Manette Salomon*, symbolising two of the doctor's interests: one a tale of neurosis, the other the artistic world of Paris. In both paintings Gachet is depicted in the mood of sad-eyed melancholy which Vincent described to Gauguin as *the heartbroken expression of our time*. In both versions, Gachet, like Madame Ginoux before, rests his head on his hand, a pose Vincent evidently identified with depression. In the first portrait there is a stem of foxglove in a glass, in the second Gachet is holding it in his left hand. The foxglove or digitalis was the homoeopathic treatment for heart disease; it was also one of the principal ingredients of absinthe, though whether Vincent knew that is not known. (Later medical investigators pin-pointed a form of digitalis poisoning, from excessive absinthe drinking, as a possible cause of his attacks, though he is unlikely himself to have been aware of such things.) As for etching, despite Gachet's prompting and Vincent's childlike pleasure in pulling different coloured impressions off the plate, his first attempt remained his last. More were planned but never executed, which is sad when one remembers his wish to create an art for all and his usual practice of making several versions of the same painting, especially the portraits.

He returned to the Gachets' house on Tuesday and painted in the garden before the inevitable lunch, after which Gachet went with him to see the small selection of work he had brought with him to Auvers. These included his self-portrait in artist's smock done in St Rémy and a version of the portrait of Madame Ginoux, *L'Arlésienne*. Gachet was, by his own account, immediately entranced by Vincent's work, by no means an inevitable reaction, even on the part of someone with advanced tastes. But, despite such interest, at no point does the doctor seem to have considered buying a picture.

For the remainder of that week Vincent was on his own. On Mondays, Wednesdays and Fridays, Gachet took the train to Paris and his clinic in the Faubourg St Denis. Over the years his dislike of surgery had developed into something akin to revulsion which led to an interest in alternative medicine from homoeopathy, an enthusiasm he passed on to Pissarro, to the more *outré* fields of electrical treatment, including a form of electrolysis for combating the narrowing of the urethra (presumably related to venereal disease), much of which now seems cranky. There were two sides to Dr Gachet. On the positive side he was an early advocate of preventive medicine with an advanced interest in hygiene and antisepsis; he had once visited London where he met Lister. On the other hand, in an age when great strides were being made in surgery his total opposition to it was odd. In 1883, when Manet was suffering from gangrene, Gachet did his utmost to advise his friend to discount his own doctor's advice that his foot should be amputated. When Manet submitted to the operation and subsequently died, Gachet's rather strange explanation was that a dandy like Manet could not survive the shock of losing a part of himself.

As Vincent was not to return to Gachet's house until lunchtime the following Sunday he slipped into a pattern of life maintained throughout his brief stay in the town. He would get up at five and go out painting if the weather was fine, return briefly for lunch at the Ravouxs' auberge, take a short rest and then go off to paint again until it was time for supper. He was in bed by nine.

His letters are far less detailed about his work at this time and subsequent memoirs by those who knew him inevitably concentrate on his doings rather than his paintings. Most accounts are contradictory, self-serving, or downright fanciful and must be read with caution. The Ravouxs' twelve-year-old daughter Adeline recounted her memories of the strange guest in her father's auberge when she was in mid-life and was determined to show that her father had been closest to Vincent and not the Gachets, about whom she was distinctly sniffy. Despite these reservations some things ring true, for instance her description of Vincent's inevitably shabby appearance in a short blue jacket and peasant's straw hat, as well as the way he spoke French correctly but slowly, searching out his words. Despite her attempt to build up the importance of her family's relationship with the painter she inadvertently reveals that they barely spoke and that they always addressed him as *Monsieur* Vincent. The one exception was the Ravouxs' baby Germaine, with whom Vincent played each evening before she was put to bed and he had his supper. Adeline was certain that Vincent never drank while he was with them, her father had always insisted on that fact. He took his meals with two of the other painters who formed part of the loose colony of artists drawn to the picturesque beauty of Auvers. One, a fellow resident at the auberge, was a Dutch painter, Anton (Tom) Hirschig, who had arrived soon after Vincent. In his early twenties, he spoke rather laughable French and must have been delighted to find a fellow Dutchman with whom he could talk. Conversation had to be divided, however, as their fellow diner, Martinez de Valdivielse, spoke only Spanish or French. Martinez lived in the village but took his meals at the inn. He was a Cuban-born painter, a friend of Pissarro, though the Ravouxs believed he was a Spanish political exile. Adeline's story, that on first seeing one of Vincent's paintings, Martinez had exclaimed "What pig did that?", also sounds like a later bar-room invention.

Despite the problem of language, and Vincent's lack of interest in Hirschig's work, at least he had the company of fellow artists, which was what he had always craved. In many ways Auvers ought to have been an ideal environment, with its quaint thatched houses and narrow climbing streets providing a wealth of subject-matter within a short walk of the inn, which in its turn provided a stable base and regular nourishment. If his sufferings were to recur then there was Gachet, who might not be as accessible or as concerned as Rey or Peyron, but who was near to hand in an emergency.

From what can be pieced together about the order of his work in Auvers, Vincent seems to have followed his practice in St Rémy of starting close to his lodgings and only gradually moving farther out into the countryside. Thus his first paintings are of the narrow streets of the town with their old thatched cottages as well as the newer villas for the better-off, which he said he also liked. Only later did he climb up out of the village to the wide surrounding plain, where he could paint the spacious wheatfields or the Château d'Auvers in its grounds or, if he wished, look back to take in the panorama to the south with its view across the Oise.

More than any other period, the work done in Auvers resists a simple thumbnail description. As he offered few insights into his thinking at that time, much is speculation though some facts can be established. He began painting on canvases shaped as a double-square, twice as broad as they were long, ideal for panoramic landscapes. This has the effect of enveloping the spectator and inviting him or her 'into' the scene portrayed and was probably a direct result of his intense reaction to Puvis de Chavannes' painting which had been based on his own broad mural in Rouen. Vincent used this new format to make paintings of trees, roots and wheat-sheaves which he depicted so close-to they became even more impacted than the early paintings in St Rémy like the *Irises*. Nothing can be seen through or beyond them, leaving the spectator with a feeling of claustrophobia. Similarly, one notable feature of the village scenes and the wide fields is the way paths and roads appear to lead nowhere. Finally, in none of the paintings known to have been done in Auvers does the sun appear. One might have imagined that the burning, searing sun of Provence would have become somewhat diminished in the North, but that it should have been completely excluded is surely strange.

In more general terms, the Auvers paintings seem comparatively sober, with a less violent use of colour contrasts than the southern works. Much of this is due to his 'northern' palette, though it is hard to resist the thought that we are witnessing someone deliberately reining himself in after a wild, dangerous gallop which had ended in a fall. After the terrifying energy of the Arles canvases, there is an inevitable sense of regression, which has led some to speculate that his powers were failing, that like a singer whose voice has been pushed too far, the notes are no longer there.

It is, however, far more likely that he was going through a major realignment in his thinking, which had not yet found full expression in his work. The last time this had happened was in Paris and, as then, it is possible to discern different influences at work in the Auvers paintings, evidence that he was struggling to find a new direction. Strongest of all remained the influence of Millet and Vincent's return in imagination to the days in Nuenen, when he had seen himself as part of the tradition of the painters of peasants.

He wrote to his sister Willemina about a painting of the church in

Auvers, done some time around the end of his second week: *once again it is nearly the same thing as the studies I did in Nuenen of the old tower and the cemetery, only it is probable that now the colour is more expressive, more sumptuous.*

It was to be his last tribute to Father Millet. Memories of the *Church at Gréville* were evoked in the way the exaggerated bulk of the building dwarfed the woman in peasant costume walking away to the left. Interpretations of his intentions in this powerful painting can lead to the wilder shores of fantasy. The art-historian Marc Edo Tralbaut pointed out that Vincent had chosen to paint the apse of the church and had thus created a building with no visible entrance, a sign, according to Tralbaut, of his strained relationship with organised religion. This is more reasonable than Tralbaut's parallel assertion that the woman walking away to the left is a symbolic figure representing Eugénie, Kee, Sien and Margot returning to the past, while the empty road climbing away to the right is the path Vincent must take in the future. In reality that right-hand path led up to the village graveyard. This does seem rather fanciful, for at the time when he was working on the church he had entered a period of relative calm when he enjoyed some of the most peaceful and least troubled days of his recent life.

That Sunday Theo and Jo accepted Dr Gachet's invitation to visit, bringing baby Vincent with them, and they all passed one of the most carefree and happy days imaginable. Vincent delighted in showing his namesake all the animals in Gachet's garden – at one point he had twelve cats, five dogs, a goat, a pair of peacocks and a tortoise. After the inevitable lunch they all went on a long walk. It was the start of three weeks of uninterrupted peace, during which time Vincent's only concerns were to find a suitable room in which to store the paintings which languished at Tanguy's and also to have his remaining possessions sent up from Arles. Other than that, it was a pleasant round of painting excursions only hindered by interminable lunches at Dr Gachet's.

If he wanted models, there was no problem with the local people, for even the Ravouxs were unaware of his mental state and the fact that he had just spent a year in an asylum. He painted Adeline Ravoux – by her recollection, in total silence, puffing on his pipe the while – and Gachet's daughter Marguerite, in the garden of their house and also seated at the piano. He planned to paint her as she played the harmonium, a method used to soothe her father's melancholia – he was especially fond of 'Luther's Hymn' – but that portrait was never done.

He did, however, paint the child of Levert the local carpenter who made canvas stretchers for him, and two versions of a peasant woman in a large straw hat in the wheatfields, but at no point did he paint himself and with the exception of the two stunning portraits of Dr Gachet, it was landscape that dominated his work during the two months' stay. And in some of these landscapes the other, newer influence is just visible. In *Women Walking along in the Fields* the pale colours, of green grass, violet dresses, blue earth and background, seem to be taken directly from *Inter Artes et Naturam* and in a letter to Willemina Vincent gives a wonderful description of Puvis's painting and the extent to which it had redirected his own thinking:

> *The figures of the persons are dressed in bright colours, and one cannot tell whether they are costumes of today or on the other hand clothes of antiquity.*
>
> *On one side two women, dressed in simple long robes, are talking together, and on the other side men with the air of artists; in the middle of the picture a woman with her child on her arm is picking a flower off an apple-tree in bloom. One figure is forget-me-not blue, another bright citron yellow, another of a delicate pink colour, another white, another violet. Underneath their feet a meadow dotted with little white and yellow flowers. A blue distance with a white town and a river. All humanity, all nature simplified, but as they might be if they are not like that.*
>
> *This description does not tell you anything – but when one sees this picture, when one looks at it for a long time, one gets the feeling of being present at a rebirth, total but benevolent, of all the things one should have believed in, should have wished for – a strange and happy meeting of very distant antiquities and crude modernity.*

Was such a meeting possible in his own art? Was this, rather than a return to his earlier committed days, the new route he should take? After the enormous physical and spiritual efforts during his time in Arles, was another great outpouring possible? Perhaps all he needed was time, a period of experiment similar to the one he had undergone in Paris before the next great creative explosion could begin. For a moment it must have seemed possible. He was calm and comfortably set up, the attacks had not returned and there was no special reason why this new and even tenor should be disturbed.

Gauguin wrote to him about his various plans; he had met a

Dr Charlopin, a name close enough to charlatan to have led him to think twice, who had sold a patent at the current World's Fair in Paris and who, when his money came through, was apparently willing to buy sufficient of Gauguin's work to enable him to leave for Madagascar. In the meantime he was off to Brittany. Dr Peyron wrote to say his canvases had been despatched and they duly arrived in Auvers.

Even when Dr Gachet sent an invitation card with a Japanese figure on it, inviting Vincent to the double birthday of Marguerite and Paul on Sunday June 22nd, so curious a reminder of his own double birthday with the original Vincent Willem, does not appear to have in any way disturbed those placid days. It was a letter from Theo, dated June 30th, that first began to trouble him:

> We have gone through a period of the greatest anxiety; our dear little boy has been very ill, but fortunately the doctor, who was uneasy himself, told Jo, "You are not going to lose the child because of this."

Despite the reassurance, any hint that Vincent Willem, another Vincent Willem, might die was obviously devastating for the elder brother. One can only assume that Theo had imagined Vincent was well enough to support his own misery for once. The letter, unusually long, went on to unveil Theo's doubts and fears. Was the apartment big enough? Should they move? Should he indeed continue at Boussod et Valadon? Should they come to Auvers after all that summer or go straight to Holland?

It was, in retrospect, an unwise assumption that Vincent was in any sense cured. The following Sunday Vincent travelled to Paris to see the situation for himself, but this time their day together was in utter contrast to their previous country outing. Theo and Jo were exhausted, and while the child had recovered from an infection, apparently from the cow's milk he had been given, there was an atmosphere of the sick-room about the apartment. Theo's sole topic of conversation seems to have been his increasing desire to leave Boussod et Valadon and set up on his own, ever a subject to unnerve his brother. This charged atmosphere can hardly have been helped by a constant and unsettling stream of visitors, among them Albert Aurier and Toulouse-Lautrec, who stayed for lunch and tried to cheer them up by telling jokes about an undertaker's man he'd met on the stairs. Even that failed to improve matters and in the end Vincent decided not to wait for Guillaumin who was expected later in the day but to hurry back to Auvers.

A few days later, on July 9th, Jo wrote a letter to try to reassure him that all was now well. In his reply he tries to put a brave face on it but cannot hide how distressed he had been:

> *Back here, I still felt very sad and continued to feel the storm which threatens you weighing on me too. What was to be done – you see, I generally try to be fairly cheerful, but my life is also threatened at the very root, and my steps are also wavering.*

Then on July 15th, Vincent received a letter from Theo which shattered the calm of the previous weeks. In truth it was nothing he might not have expected: Theo and Jo had simply decided that they would take the child to visit his grandparents in Holland. It is impossible to explain why this upset Vincent to the extent it did. That he should be disappointed they were not coming to see him was only natural, but he clearly took their decision as an act of outright betrayal. If Theo had not been travelling, Vincent's silence would probably have alerted him to the fact that something was wrong. As it was, he and Jo were on the move for about five days until Theo left her and the baby with her parents in Amsterdam while he returned to Paris. It was only then that he began to worry. On July 22nd, he wrote to Vincent enclosing fifty francs, hoping no doubt to receive an encouraging response from his brother.

It was too late. Something had happened to Vincent that had put him beyond his brother's help. If he had had another attack similar to those he had suffered in Arles and St Rémy no one knew, for he was effectively unsupervised by then. All the reports of these lost days were written up much later and are frequently contradictory or self-justifying. The Ravouxs' tale was set out in an interview given by the daughter Adeline in mid-life when she was more concerned to elevate her father's role in the affair than to set down the truth. Likewise Paul Gachet saw it as his duty to protect the honour of his father. Ironically, the one fact which does emerge from Paul's memoir is the less than honourable one that the doctor had advance warning that something was wrong and in effect did nothing about it. According to Dr Gachet's story Vincent had come to his house as usual and had been looking at his collection of pictures, when he suddenly noticed that the painting of a nude by Guillaumin had never been framed. All at once Vincent was propelled into an uncontrollable rage, demanding to know why and insisting the error be rectified. In order to calm him, Levert, the ever-loyal carpenter, was sent for, and measurements taken. Somewhat mollified Vincent left, but when he next returned Levert had not yet finished the commission and, seeing the work still unframed, Vincent went into a violent frenzy and began ranting in Dutch. Dr Gachet, as had Gauguin and Dr Rey before him, fixed Vincent with a commanding glare and ordered him to desist. As before, Vincent scuttled away. When he recalled the incident, much later, Gachet suddenly remembered that at the height of his frenzy Vincent had plunged his hand into one of his pockets – had he, Dr Gachet wondered, been reaching for a gun with the intention of shooting him?

As with Gauguin, the story redounds against the teller. One can only wonder how a man, thought to be an expert on the aberrant behaviour of creative people, could have allowed Vincent to run off and not have tried to restrain him or at least to follow him to discover what would happen next.

No one at the auberge, neither the Ravouxs nor Tom, noticed anything was wrong. Vincent was still going out on his painting trips and coming back with finished canvases so there was no reason to suspect anything, especially as they had been kept in the dark about his mental state. As before there was a wide gulf between the reality of his life and his work, or perhaps it would be truer to say that while working the anguish of his mind was suppressed for a time.

When Vincent received Theo's letter with the fifty francs he began to draft a reply but must have decided that the tone was wrong, too despairing, too full of complaint. He folded the paper, put it in his pocket and wrote another, very close in some of its wording but altogether more positive, mainly about the work he was doing, and sent that instead.

The letter contained four sketches of the paintings he had been making. The garden of Daubigny's house, a scene with some thatched cottages and two views of the wheat fields. He had evidently been working on the two wheat fields for some time, because he mentioned them in his letter to Jo written before she left for Holland. The finished paintings are so strikingly different it might seem for once that there is a direct corollary between the mood they present and his own mental state. As one of the paintings is calm and serene while the other is tortured and violent, the assumption has always been that the first, the peaceful scene, was painted before Theo announced he was going to Holland, whereupon Vincent painted the second tortured version. According to this theory, the first painting would be *Wheat Fields under Clouded Sky*, two horizontal bands of green and yellow earth and white and blue sky which create an elevating sensation of infinity. He described it in what was to be his last letter to his mother and sister. He was, he said:

> *quite absorbed in the immense plain with wheat fields against the hills, boundless as a sea, delicate yellow, delicate soft green, the delicate violet of a dug-up and weeded piece of soil, checkered at regular intervals under a sky of delicate blue, white, pink, violet tones. I am in a mood of almost too much calmness, in the mood to paint this.*

But then came the letter from Theo and thus the second painting: *Crows over the Wheat Field*. Here the scene is pressed closer in on the spectator, who is confronted with three diverging paths, those to left and right falling out of the sides of the picture space, while the third leads nowhere, stopping dead at the heart of a writhing sea of ripe wheat over which an ominous flock of black crows wheels towards the trapped onlooker. The painting recalls the Van der Maaten engraving, as if the funeral procession has already passed out of sight. And the recollection of all those works in which dark birds menace the peace of the scene seem to confirm this picture as the last cry of the haunted artist living out his anguish in paint. Here surely is Vincent, the angst-ridden father of the modern movement, of Fauvism, Expressionism, Abstract Expressionism, progenitor of any art in which the tortured personality of the artist is the paramount feature of his work.

Perhaps it is hardly surprising that many of those who have written about Vincent should have seized on that picture as the key to his life's work. To them everything points to it being the last painting he ever made. The more fanciful have even suggested he was working on it when the final tragedy occurred. There is certainly a terrible symmetry to the theory, for most of the people he knew in Auvers were agreed that he had somehow got hold of a small revolver in order to scare away the crows which bothered him while he was working. Adeline Ravoux claimed that her father had lent it to him, but there was also another claimant to that peculiar honour, a René Secrétan, who in old-age insisted that the gun had been his. Once more it must be emphasised that Secrétan's anecdotes about Vincent show many signs of having been embellished over years of retelling.

René and his elder brother Gaston were the somewhat spoiled

children of a wealthy pharmacist who, when they were not studying at the fashionable Lycée Condorcet in Paris, were allowed to go on hunting trips, shooting and fishing, in the countryside around Auvers. According to René's somewhat boastful account, they could take whatever friends and young ladies they liked along with them. The nineteen-year-old Gaston was interested in art and seems to have formed a friendship with the outlandish-looking Vincent, whom they sometimes encountered painting by the Oise. Sadly for posterity, it was not Gaston who committed his memories to paper but the altogether more philistine René. He describes the practical jokes he and his other disagreeable playmates inflicted on the artist. He recalled Vincent's embarrassment if the boys and girls were kissing and he further claimed that he and Gaston had once spied on Vincent in the woods when he was masturbating. Embroidered though they certainly were, the tales say much about what Vincent often had to suffer from stupid people, though Gaston does seem to have wanted to help and, according to René, brought Vincent the bottoms of their father's cigar boxes for him to paint on. More important to our understanding of the tragedy which followed was René's contention that Vincent had 'lifted' the revolver from one of their hunting bags, though as he only discovered this after the tragedy had taken place, he was unable to say when the theft had occurred and thus could not give any clue as to how long Vincent had been planning some sort of violent act.

Had he, as Gachet subsequently believed, been wandering around with the revolver in his pocket for several days? Was that why he plunged his hand into his pocket during the incident over the unframed painting? It may be that throughout those empty days, when he believed himself abandoned and utterly alone, he had had the gun ever-ready should despair finally overtake him.

What happened at the last varies between the different accounts but the broad outline is reasonably clear.

On July 27th 1890, having eaten his lunch more quickly than usual, Vincent left the auberge to resume painting somewhere above the town. Having walked the kilometre and a half to the Château d'Auvers, he leant his easel against a haystack, went down into the path that ran through a gulley alongside the château wall, where he took out a revolver, placed it to his chest and pulled the trigger. At this point the Hollywood version has the black crows fly up in menacing panic while the wounded artist staggers and falls. Who knows what actually happened? And who can say why that particular day? As the letters and paintings over the previous ten days reveal, his reactions were not clearcut and may indeed have already passed from panic to resignation. It is often true that people do not kill themselves when they are at the deepest point of depression but at a point when they are coming out of the worst of a crisis and are once more able to take positive action, if 'positive' is the appropriate word. But did he truly intend to commit suicide?

As before, he had chosen a Sunday as the day of self-mutilation.

According to Adeline Ravoux's account, having pulled the trigger, he fainted. When he came to, he crawled about on all fours trying to find the weapon but failed. She claimed that they too could not find it the next day. There was a wound in his chest, he was badly hurt but could walk. He got to his feet and started to make his way back to town.

The Ravouxs were slightly perturbed that he had not returned for dinner but their day had been hard and they were enjoying their usual Sunday rest on the veranda when they saw him coming towards the auberge, slightly hunched as he walked. As he went into the café he brushed aside their enquiries with a few broken phrases, crossed to the billiard room and staggered to the stairs. In one version Madame Ravoux was said to have seen the blood and to have immediately gone after him; in another it was Adeline's father who assumed this role. Whichever it was, one of the Ravouxs eventually went to see what was wrong and found him curled up on the bed. Someone was sent to fetch the local practitioner Dr Mazery, who lived close by in one of Daubigny's former houses. At Vincent's insistence they also sent for Dr Gachet who arrived with his son Paul, who in his version, described how they had grabbed an emergency bag along with some electric leads lest one of the doctor's more *outré* cures might prove effective. When they arrived Mazery had already undressed Vincent but willingly went through his examination again. They could see the point of entry of the bullet and were relieved that there was so little loss of blood, but in those days before radiology they could only trace the passage of the object by gauging the victim's reactions to an external examination.

Having done this the two doctors dressed the wound then went into a neighbouring room to confer. Thirty years later, Paul reported his father's findings: he had seen that "... level with the edge of the left ribs, a little in front of the axillary line, the wound formed a little circle of dark red, almost black, surrounded by a purple halo, and bled with a thin stream of blood. The shot had been fired too low and too far out. The heart had not been hurt, nor, it seemed, had any other vital organ. The bullet must have gone through the left pleural cavity and had come to rest in the posterior mediastinum, in the neighbourhood of the large blood vessels, the spinal column, and the diaphragm. At all events, Vincent showed none of the symptoms of a serious chest wound, there was no hematopsy, no suffocation, and no appreciable shock."

In layman's terms the bullet had passed from just below his chest to somewhere near the base of his spine and, while no vital organs had been damaged, it could not be safely reached by the surgical techniques then available. A quarter of a century later, during the First World War, doctors still thought it better to leave shrapnel inside the wounded than to attempt removal by surgery. This indeed was the conclusion reached by the two men in the dark narrow room above the auberge. These two doctors were, however, probably the least suitable for Vincent's particular case that it is possible to imagine: Mazery was a typical country generalist whose only known speciality had been childbirth and post-natal care, while Gachet's views have already been well enough rehearsed to make clear that he was hardly the man to recommend surgery. It is hard to avoid speculating that the diagnosis might have been told to Paul later in an attempt to excuse what eventually happened. Apparently neither man considered trying to get Vincent to hospital. Mazery was happy to leave the patient in the hands of his friend and there are some indications that Gachet actually decided to do nothing because he felt that Vincent should be allowed to die if he so wished. But is that what Vincent truly wanted? While there are certainly cases where suicide seems the sad but merciful end to a life which had nowhere further to go, Vincent may have been on the point of extending his art in new and exciting ways. There was much that he could still have done and no reason to assume that his attacks were either permanent or necessarily worsening. It is possible to argue that he was improving, for while he had certainly been depressed in his early days in Auvers he does not appear to have had anything resembling the violent seizures which plagued him in Provence. His bungled performance with the revolver might have been a desperate gesture but not necessarily the final act. Yet when the two doctors agreed to do nothing and went their separate ways, Vincent's fate was sealed.

As Mazery left, Gachet went back into the bedroom to see if Vincent needed anything. He seemed perfectly calm and, when he asked if he might smoke, Gachet filled and lit his pipe for him. But when the doctor then asked for Theo's home address, the gallery being closed on Sundays, Vincent vehemently refused to give it. There was nothing to be done except leave him to rest. At this point everyone claims to have sat up with him, though all agreed he said nothing and just lay back constantly puffing on his pipe. The next morning Gachet dispatched Tom Hirschig with a letter for Theo at the gallery. While Theo was hurrying to the station, two policemen in Auvers, alerted by the buzzing gossip, arrived at the café to look into the matter. They went up to the room but having reassured themselves that it was not a question of murder went off to make their reports.

Theo's arrival about midday must have revived Vincent for his brother thought he looked better than expected. The two brothers were now alone, exchanging the occasional comment in Dutch, as if they were children again, or simply passing the hours in silence. Vincent asked after Jo and the baby, and Theo wrote a note to her in Holland which ended with the cheerful comment that Vincent had always deceived his doctors before. But as the day wore on into the evening it became clear such hopes were misplaced. Infection had set in and there was a period of near suffocation as he struggled for breath. When he realised his brother was dying, Theo got on the bed beside him and cradled his head in his arm.

I wish I could pass away like this, Vincent said.

Half an hour later his last wish was granted. He died at half past one in the morning of Tuesday July 29th, 1890, aged 37.

Ravoux pulled down the blinds of the auberge as if in family mourning, though he kept the restaurant open; Dr Gachet came round and made a drawing of Vincent on his deathbed; then both men went with Theo to the town hall to register the death in the presence of Monsieur Caffin, the mayor. The carpenter Levert was asked to make a coffin and he offered to lend a pair of trestles for it to rest on. The funeral was to be at 2.30 p.m. the following day. Theo sent instructions to Pontoise to have funeral invitations printed immediately but no sooner was this in hand than the local Catholic priest Abbé Teissier refused to let them use the parish hearse because Vincent was a suicide. Much time had then to be spent arranging for another hearse to be sent from the other commune across the river. Since the priest had made it clear that a church service was out of the question, it was decided Vincent would be buried without religious ceremony in the small graveyard above the town, on the edge of the broad wheat fields. Theo, Ravoux and Hirschig spent the rest of the day preparing the downstairs room he had used as a studio so that it resembled both a chapel of rest and a memorial exhibition. In the centre of the room Vincent lay in an open coffin resting on Levert's trestles. At the foot of the coffin they placed his palette and brushes with the easel and folding stool he had taken out on his painting trips. Theo hung as many paintings as could fit on to the walls, while Hirschig went out to collect greenery which they festooned around them.

Early the next morning, Wednesday July 30th, friends started to arrive by train from Paris. First came Andries Bonger with Père Tanguy and Lucien Pissarro; later Emile Bernard and Charles Laval. As they waited by the coffin Dr Gachet arrived with a bunch of sunflowers. More mourners came with yellow dahlias and other yellow blooms. Soon the room was vibrant with Vincent's glorious colour. When Bernard returned to Paris he described their day in a letter to Albert Aurier:

> At three o'clock the body was raised; his friends carried it to the hearse. Several people present wept – Theodorus van Gogh, who adored his brother, who had always supported him in his struggle for art and independence, not ceasing to sob pitifully. Outside, the sun was terribly hot. We climbed the hill of Auvers talking of him, of the bold forward thrust he gave to art, of the great projects that always preoccupied him, of the good he had always done to each of us. We arrived at the cemetery, a small new cemetery dotted with new tombstones. It is on the height dominating the harvest fields under the wide blue sky that he would have loved still – perhaps. Then he was lowered into the grave. Who would not have cried at that moment . . . the day was so much made for him that one could imagine that he was still alive. Dr Gachet (who is a great art lover and possesses one of the best Impressionist collections of today, an artist himself) wanted to say a few words to epitomise Vincent's life, but he too wept so much that he could only stammer a very confused farewell . . . the most beautiful. He retraced Vincent's efforts, indicated their sublime goal, spoke of the immense sympathy that he had for him

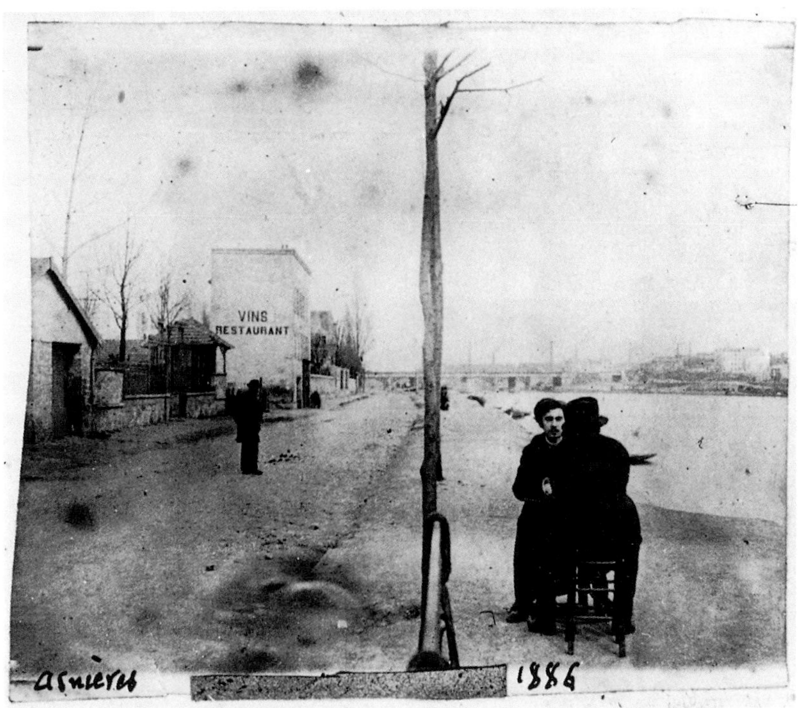

The last known photograph of Vincent, unhappily back view, seated with Emile Bernard on the banks of the Seine at Asnières in 1886. The bridges they both painted can be glimpsed in the distance.

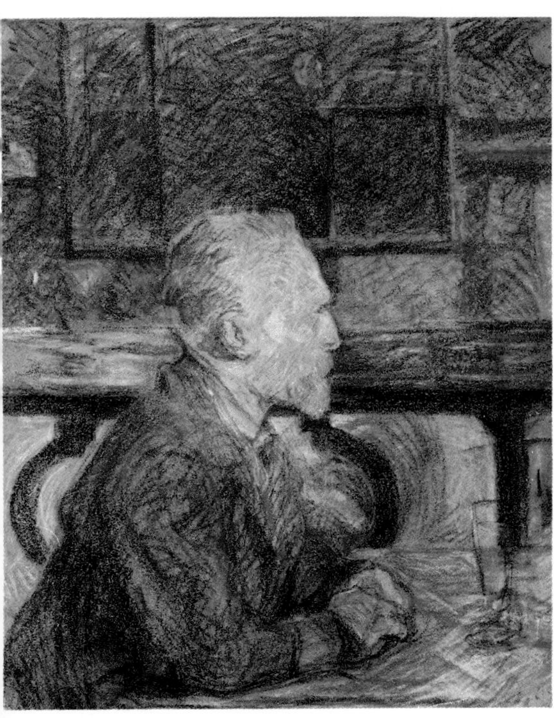

Toulouse-Lautrec's portrait of Vincent in the Tambourin Café, seated before a glass of absinthe.

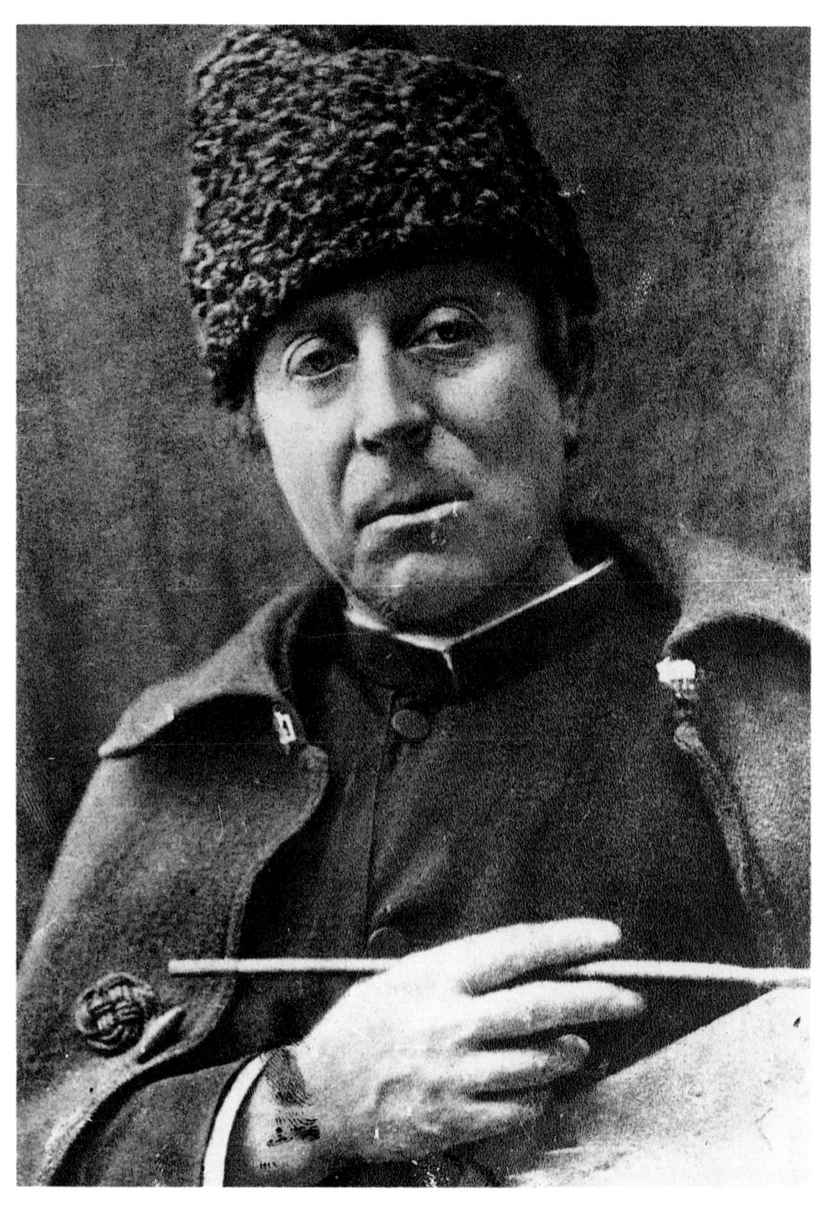

Paul Gauguin

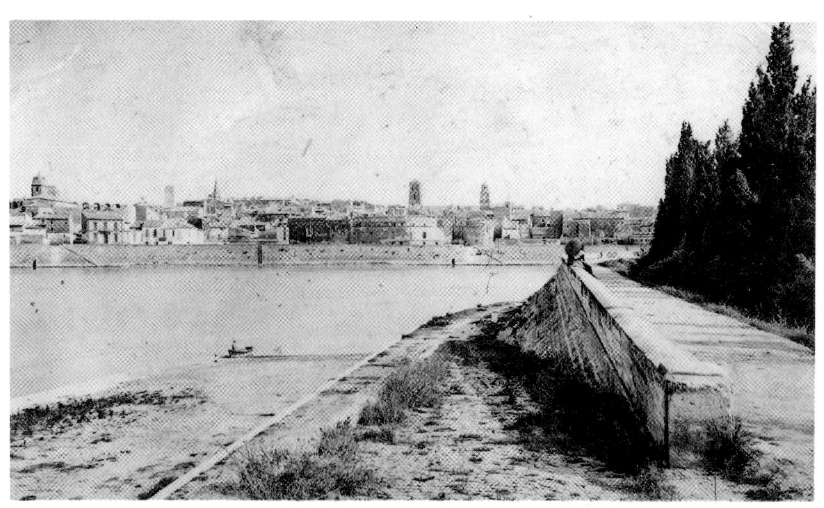

A view of Arles, c. 1880, from across the Rhône, a scene reminiscent of one of Vincent's starry-night pictures.

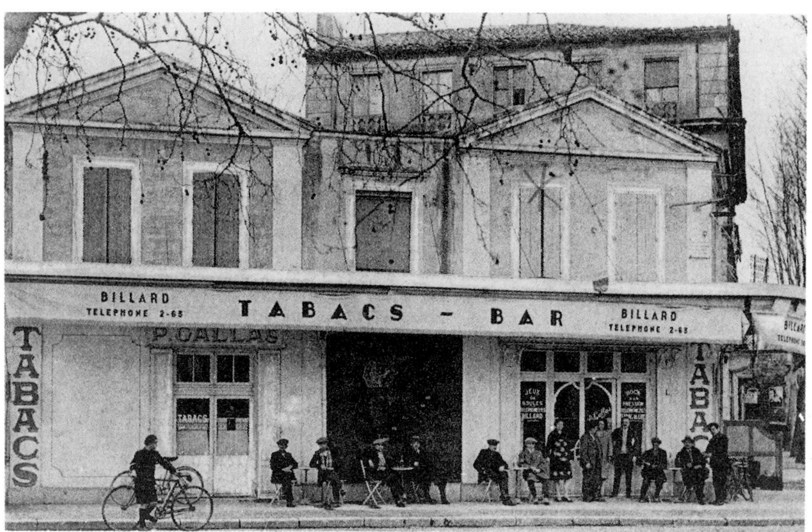

A later photograph of the yellow house where Vincent and Paul Gauguin lived in the winter of 1888.

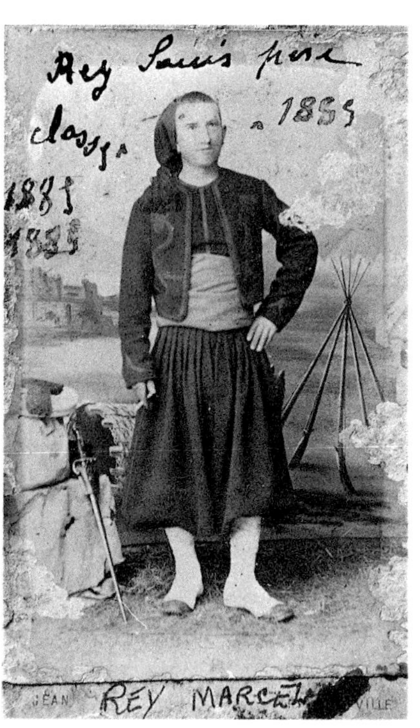

A Zouave infantryman of the 1880s.

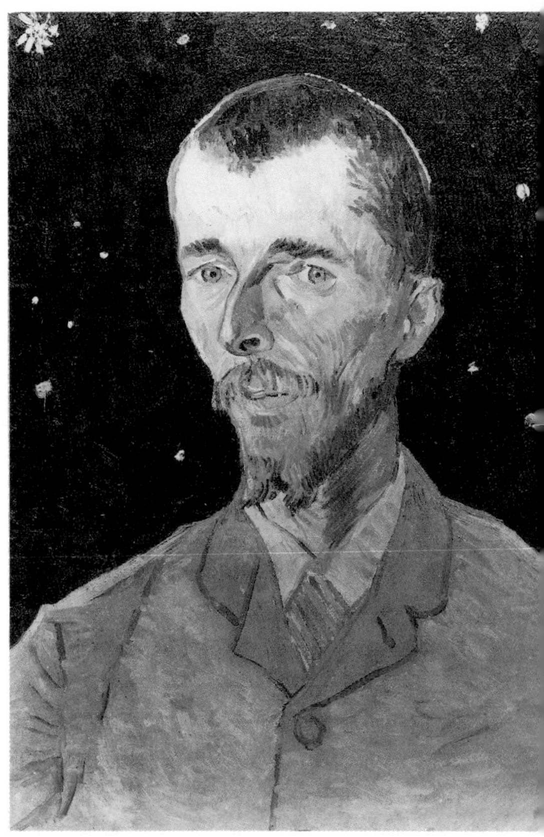

Vincent's portrait of the Belgian poet and painter Eugène Boch.

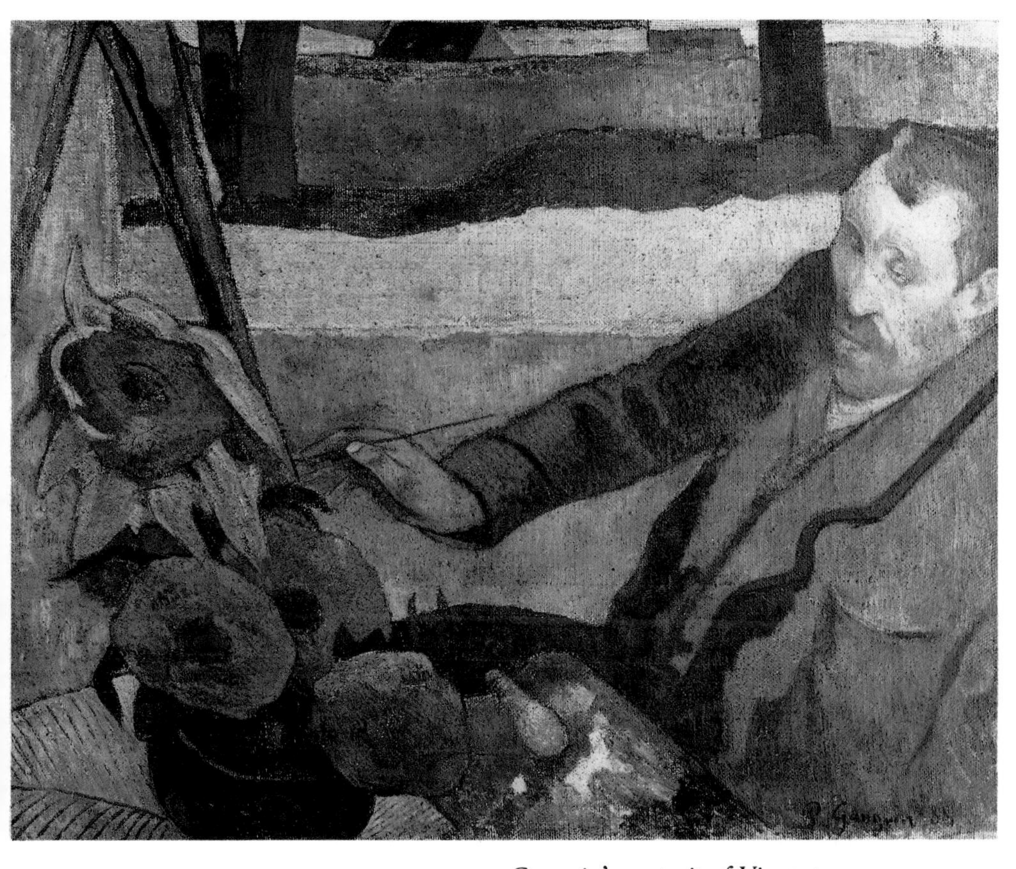

Gauguin's portrait of Vincent painting a bowl of sunflowers, of which Vincent said *It is certainly I, but it's I gone mad.*

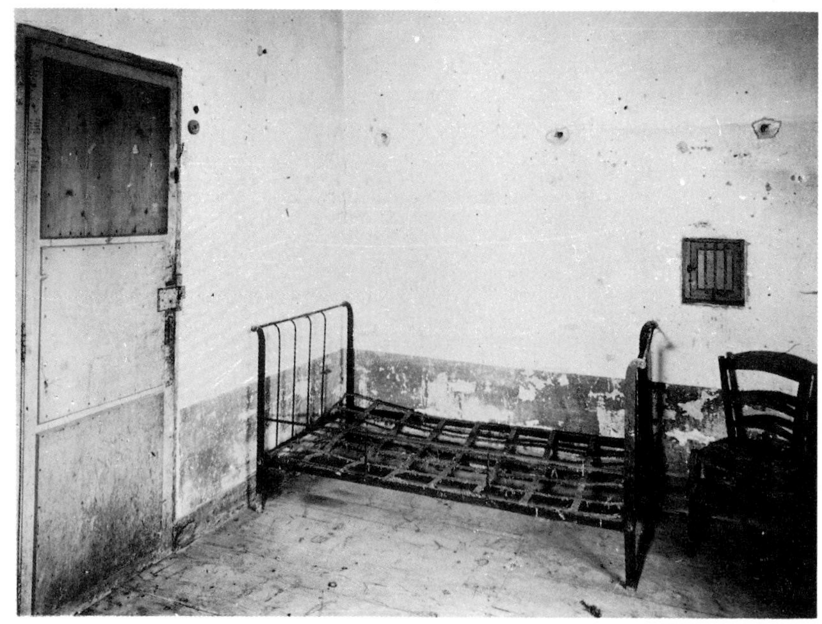

The ‘special bed’ in the isolation room in the hospital in Arles where Vincent was confined.

Part of the course of treatment Vincent underwent in the asylum in Saint-Rémy was a form of hydrotherapy in which he lay for hours in one of these baths.

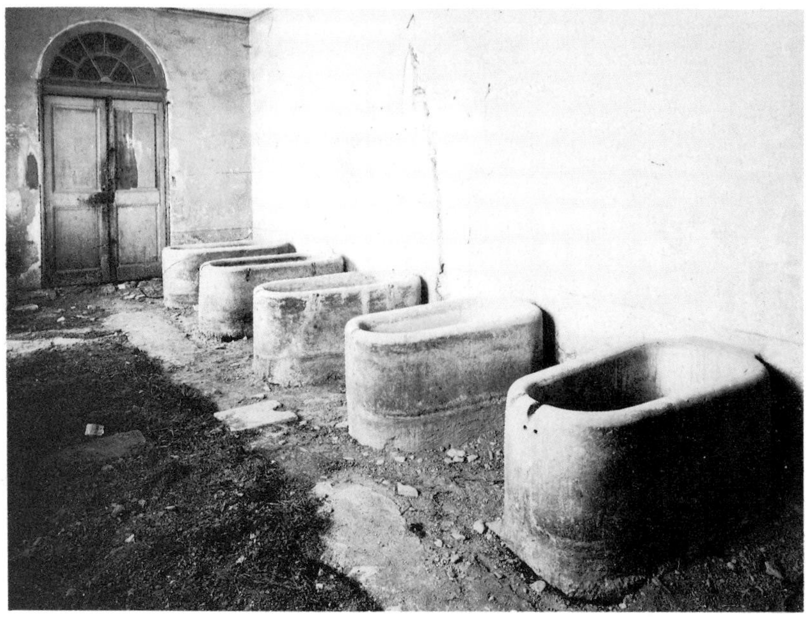

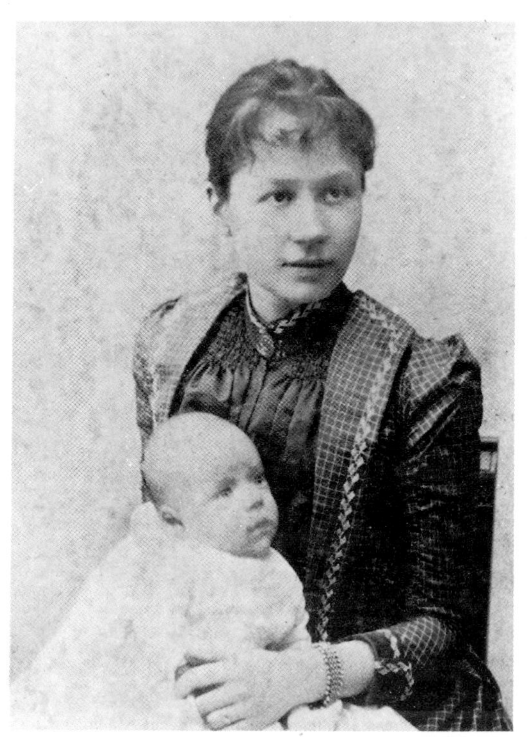

Theo's wife Jo and their baby Vincent Willem. Jo more than anyone would ensure that Vincent's work survived.

The Ravoux family sitting on the veranda of their café in Auvers-sur-Oise from where they first saw the wounded Vincent.

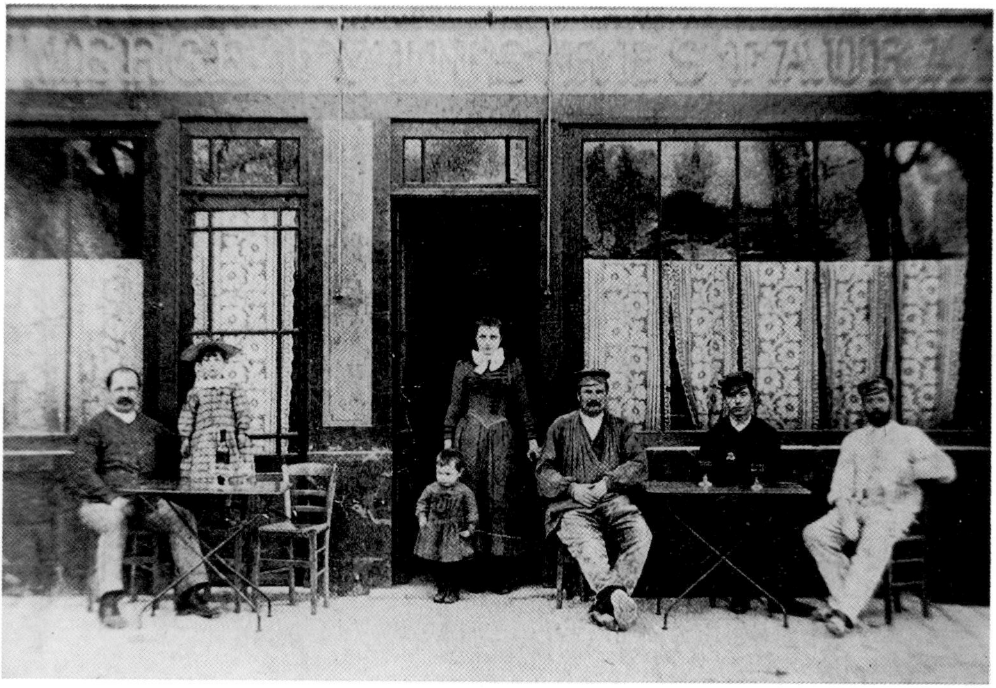

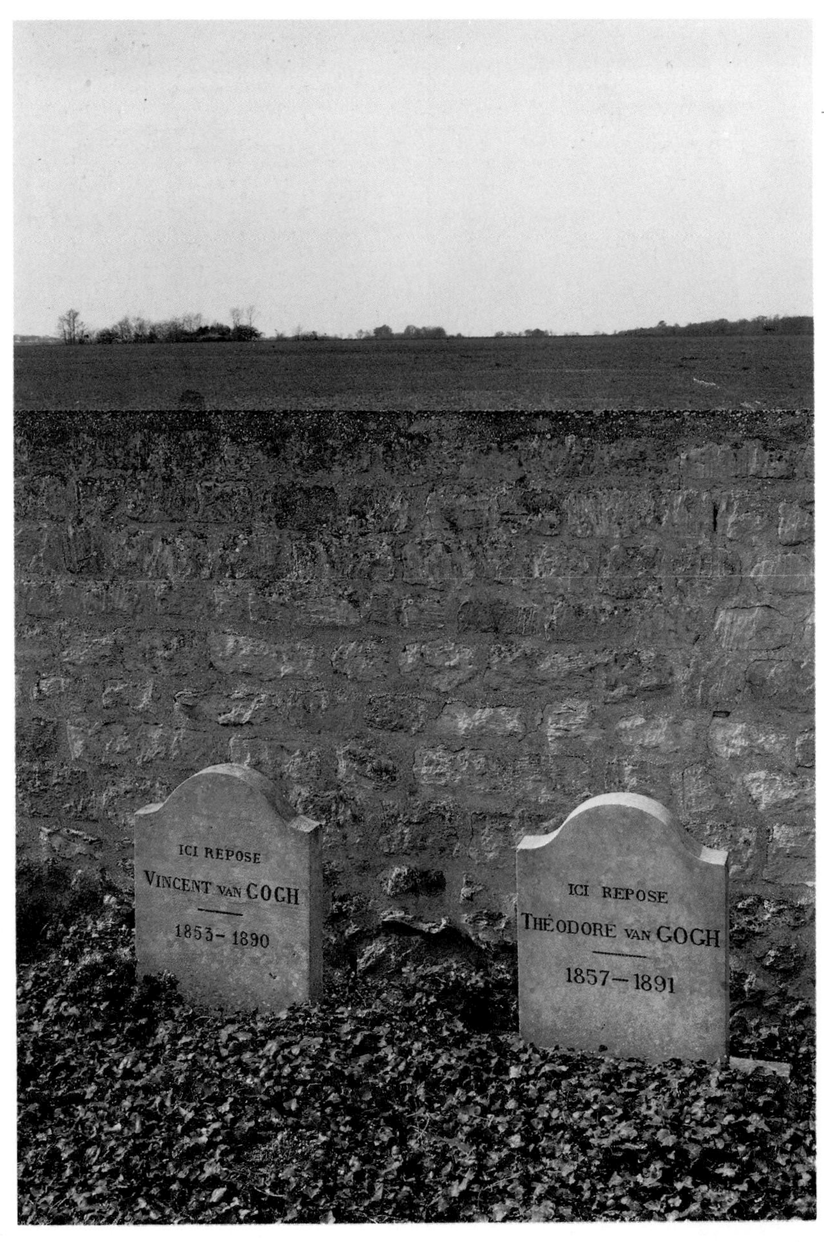
ICI REPOSE
VINCENT VAN GOGH
1853 - 1890
ICI REPOSE
THÉODORE VAN GOGH
1857 - 1891

> (whom he knew for only a short time). "He was," said Gachet, "an honest man and a great artist; he had only two aims: humanity and art. It was art he cherished above everything, which will make his name live." Then we returned. Theodorus van Gogh was broken with grief; each one of us was very moved; some withdrew to the country, others went back to the station. Laval and I returned to Ravoux's, and we talked of him.

Back in the memorial room at the inn, Theo offered the remaining friends a souvenir from among the collected paintings. This provoked the only sour memory of the day from Adeline Ravoux. She recalled that her father had asked only for her portrait and a painting of the town hall on Bastille day which Vincent had already promised him; by contrast, the Gachets, father and son, grabbed as many as they could.

When at last everyone had gone and Theo was alone once more, he was almost overwhelmed with grief. Then, while he was arranging Vincent's possessions, he came across the folded paper in his brother's jacket. As he read it, Theo could only conclude that it was a final message written just before Vincent had gone out and shot himself. With its confused swings between resignation and despair it certainly read like a suicide note. In one way it was full of love and understanding for Theo, proof that at the very end Vincent had wanted to show how much he admired the way his younger brother had preserved his integrity in the midst of all the commercial pressures at the gallery. But more than that, it acknowledged Theo's share in the creation of the paintings which, as Vincent expressed it *will retain their calm even in this catastrophe*. But it was the end of the note that pointed in the direction of death, for Vincent had clearly descended into a mood of abject despair:

> *Well, my own work, I am risking my life for it and my reason has half foundered because of it – that's all right – but you are not among the dealers in men as far as I know, and you can still choose your side, I think, acting with humanity, but* que veux-tu?

That it should all have ended so miserably was unbearable. Theo left for Paris to await Jo's return. He wrote to his mother to tell her of all that had passed since Vincent's death and his anguished message lays bare his pain:

> One cannot write how grieved one is nor find any solace. It is a grief that will last and which I shall never forget as long as I live; the only thing one might say is that he himself had found the rest he so much longed for ... Life was such a burden to him; but now, as often happens, everybody is full of praise for his talents ... Oh, Mother! He was so my own, own brother.

Although Theo was clearly unwell he forced himself to travel to Holland to see the family. His main concern was to ensure that Vincent's work would be protected and as the others had no interest in the paintings he easily persuaded Anna and her husband Jo van Houten, along with Elisabeth and Willemina, to sign a letter surrendering Vincent's entire estate to him.

When he returned to Paris he was, by his own admission, as thin as a cadaver. As he had done the previous summer, he suffered from a cough he could not shake off. He had to leave Andries and Jo to return to Auvers to begin the process of making an inventory of the estate, but before he did so, he tried to persuade his old rival Durand-Ruel to put on a memorial exhibition. When he eventually refused, Theo turned to the young Emile Bernard who agreed to organise something. Theo's other hope was that Albert Aurier would write an appreciation. He was willing, but as he was working on his first novel it would have to wait; two years later, when he was ready to begin, he suddenly contracted typhoid fever and died and the project along with him.

Theo's one obsession was to see that Vincent's wishes were carried out. He telegraphed Gauguin in Brittany: "Departure for tropics assured, money follows – Theo, Director." But there was no money, it was all a figment of his increasingly fevered mind. Those nearest to him ascribed such behaviour to profound grief, but in fact there was a serious physical cause: he was suffering from a complicated kidney infection which rapidly induced a feverish delirium. By October, Jo and Andries became seriously alarmed as his bouts of irritation grew into an uncontrollable rage which, on occasions, led to violence. Andries wanted to consult Dr Gachet, but after a sudden crisis at the gallery Theo took the matter in his own hands and entered the Maison Dubois, a specialist clinic in the Faubourg Saint-Denis, not far from Gachet's surgery. Gachet only just managed to see Theo before he transferred himself to the better known Maison de Santé du Dr Blanche. This famous sanatorium, founded by Emile Blanche, the early expert in mental health, was now run by his son Antoine-Emile and a colleague Dr Meuriot. Their response was similar to that given to Vincent. The two doctors recommended absolute calm and advised Theo voluntarily to enter the asylum in Passy where Dr Blanche the elder had been a leading consultant. As with Dr Gachet, the Blanches, father and son, were thought to combine advanced ideas on psychiatric treatment with a knowledge of the arts; another son was the painter Jacques-Emile Blanche, who had been one of Theo's clients, and their patients were the fashionable and the famous, much as old Gruby's had been.

Word of Theo's confinement soon spread throughout the narrow circle of avant-garde artists. Camille Pissarro relayed the disturbing news to his son Lucien:

> It appears that Theo van Gogh was ill before his madness; he had uremia. For a week he was unable to urinate; added to that were the worries, the sadness, and a violent argument with his employers concerning a Decamps painting. As a result of all this, in a moment of exasperation, he thanked the Boussods and suddenly went mad. He wanted to rent Le Tambourin [Segatori's café where Vincent had organised the exhibition of Japanese prints] in order to form an association of artists. Finally he became violent. He, who so loved his wife and child, wanted to kill them. In brief, they had to put him in Dr Blanche's sanatorium.

Boussod et Valadon lost no time in replacing him, much to the consternation of the artists whom he had so selflessly supported and who now found themselves friendless. Gauguin, still awaiting his promised money, decided he had been duped by Theo, though eventually he accepted the truth of what had happened. Nevertheless, he did his utmost to dissuade Bernard from organising Vincent's memorial exhibition on the grounds that it would harm them all by encouraging the notion that the new art was produced by madmen. Fortunately Bernard ignored him.

With calm and rest, Theo's infection retreated and the delirium abated but as with Vincent at St Rémy, it was clear that there was no 'cure' at Passy, so Jo took advantage of this remission to take him home to Holland. She decided to settle in Utrecht, the town where she had worked as a schoolteacher before their marriage, but they had no sooner arrived than he collapsed again. Once more the symptoms were largely those of mental disturbance and he was committed to a local asylum.

By early 1891 complications had set in. Theo already suffered from a weak heart, a condition that had plagued him since the days of Vincent's first arrival in Paris five years earlier. Now, he suffered the stroke which finally paralysed him. He passed into a coma and it was painfully obvious to Jo that the man she loved and to whom she had been married so briefly was about to be taken from her. For days he was effectively dead and it was only when a kindly doctor brought the local newspaper to his bed and read out a short paragraph on Vincent that there was any sign of life. At the mention of the name Theo stirred; the word Vincent was the only thing that could have penetrated his consciousness. It was the last sign of life. He died on January 25th, 1891, aged thirty-three, less than six months after the death of his beloved brother. Though his connections with the town were slight, Theo was buried in Utrecht. After the funeral Jo, along with baby Vincent Willem, travelled back to Paris where she hoped to begin the difficult process of gathering up the remnants of her shattered life.

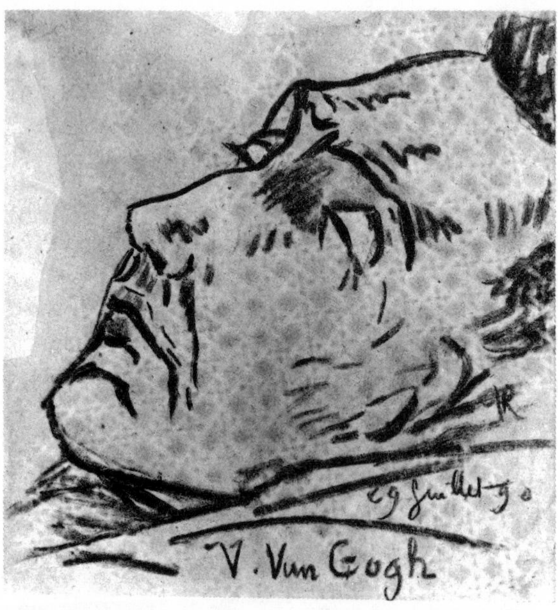

Dr Gachet's drawing of Vincent on his deathbed.

Epilogue

Two Gravestones

Today, when his paintings change hands for astronomical sums of money, to suggest that at the time of his death there was a possibility that Vincent van Gogh might have been completely forgotten, is to invite ridicule. There was, however, nothing inevitable about his success. When Theo died the works were scattered around Holland and France, many in the hands of people who had received them as gifts and had little or no appreciation of their artistic merits. Many indeed actively disliked them. The only substantial collection of paintings in the hands of a dealer were those stored by Père Tanguy in the attic of his shop and as the old man well knew, their commercial value was effectively nil.

It was left to Theo's widow Jo to perform the miracle of transforming the slender reputation of an obscure suicide who had exhibited a handful of works in a small number of avant-garde shows and who had effectively sold only one painting during his lifetime into that of the most famous artist of his day. No one encouraged her. Even her brother Andries advised her to get rid of the stacks of paintings and drawings, and the piles of letters which Theo had dutifully kept. She obstinately refused.

Her first move was to insist that the family confirm her son, Vincent Willem, as the sole heir to Theo's and thus to Vincent's estate. At Theo's death she was twenty-nine, Vincent Willem was a baby, not quite a year old. There were 550 paintings, several hundred drawings and a huge disordered stack of letters. Père Tanguy could not sell any of the paintings and her own first attempts to dispose of three via Durand-Ruel were no more successful and they were subsequently returned. No one wanted them.

Why did this young woman persist? She gave the answer herself in a letter written to a friend after she returned to Paris following Theo's funeral in Holland.

> The first evening that I spent again in our home, I turned to the bundle of letters because I knew I would meet him in them, and night after night I found solace there from my great misery. In those days I was not looking for Vincent but only for Theo, for every detail that concerned him . . .

Searching for the man to whom she had been married for a mere eighteen months, Jo van Gogh-Bonger slowly began to discover Vincent, a man she herself had known personally for only five days. It was an astonishing odyssey.

First there were practical matters to consider. As soon as it could be arranged she moved back to Holland where she and the baby settled in the village of Bussum, 15 kilometres from Amsterdam, at the Villa Helma where she took in boarders and did some translating for a literary weekly. *The Potato Eaters* hung over the fireplace, Gauguin's *Negress* above Theo's old sofa and every other wall was covered with Vincent's work. Gradually, as Vincent Willem grew up, he began to notice that the paintings came and went with increasing rapidity, evidence of the exhibitions being held as his Uncle Vincent's fame spread. It had been a slow start. Bernard's tiny memorial show in Paris in 1892, with a mere sixteen paintings, attracted scant attention and it was not until an exhibition at the Bernheim-Jeune galleries in 1901 brought the work to the attention of young artists such as Matisse, Derain and Vlaminck that Paris became fully aware of Van Gogh. A retrospective of his work at the Salon des Indépendants in 1905 extended his reputation in France but it was only when the Berlin dealer Paul Cassirer took an interest that there was significant movement in sales of the works. In the years leading up to the First World War it was Cassirer who did most to spread the word outside of France.

In 1901, Jo married Johan Cohen Gosschalk, a painter and writer on art. They moved to Amsterdam where he helped her organise one of the first major exhibitions, in 1905, at Amsterdam's Stedelijk Museum for which Gosschalk wrote the introduction to the catalogue. In 1910 they built a country house at Laren near Hilversum where the collection was then hung. Sadly, Gosschalk's health was as frail as Theo's and he died in 1912, leaving Jo, alone once more, to carry on her self-imposed task.

In that same year Roger Fry's major Post-Impressionist exhibition was held in London. With twenty-one Van Goghs, this did much to establish Vincent as one of the leading artists of what was now seen as a definable movement distinct from Impressionism. In the summer of 1912, the German Sonderbund exhibition in Cologne marked a climax with the inclusion of 108 Van Goghs, one third of which were now owned by German collectors, for by then sales of Vincent's canvases were under way. Initially the prices, where any sales at all took place, were derisory: after Tanguy's death in 1894, one painting was sold for thirty francs, possibly to the same Ambroise Vollard who had failed to meet Vincent at the Tambourin in 1887. Vollard was by then the first of the French dealer/collectors to jump on the slowly moving bandwagon, eventually rivalling Jo in the task of tracking down the works Vincent had abandoned in the various places where he had stayed.

Once more, people like the Roulins were brought into the story as Vollard's agents sought them out and bought up the portraits Vincent had given them. Old Roulin died in Marseilles in 1903 just late enough to hear the first whispers of his strange friend's growing fame.

For a time searching out lost paintings by Vincent became a hobby for the adventurous collector. Ravoux, who had by then left the inn at Auvers, thought he had been exceptionally clever when a passing American gave him forty francs for the two canvases, the *Town Hall on Bastille Day* and the portrait of his daughter Adeline. Others had lost or destroyed the gifts they had not treasured.

In 1910 Dr Rey was visited by a young painter called Charles Camion, who was doing his military service in Arles. As an 'intellectual' Camion was being victimised in the wake of the Dreyfus affair by his fellow soldiers and was glad to be able to get away from barracks from time to time and follow one of his artistic interests. He called on Rey to see if he knew of any paintings by Vincent. Slightly perturbed, the doctor asked him to return the next day and, after he had left, set about trying to discover what had happened to the portrait. It transpired that his parents had so disliked it they had stored it in the loft, but after a time it had been taken down and used to block up a hole in the chicken coop. Rey instantly retrieved it and did a hasty job of restoration before Camion's return the following day. As the doctor clearly had no time for it, Camion suggested he put him in touch with Vollard, and thus one of Vincent's finest portraits was sent to Paris in exchange for 150 francs. Vollard in turn sold it to Cassirer in Berlin, whence it passed to Druet back in Paris and thus to the Russian collector S. I. Shchukin. After the Revolution it entered the collection of the Pushkin Museum in Moscow and, today, remains in the possession of the Soviet Union.

As interest in Vincent increased, Jo herself accepted that sales from her own collection were necessary. Not only would this help her financially, but it would also ensure that Vincent's work would achieve wider circulation. Thus public collections in Britain were able to acquire Vincent's *Chair* and a version of the Sunflowers as early as the 1920s. In 1908 or 1909 a Dutch collector, Mrs Helene Kröller-Müller, started acquiring modern art by purchasing another version of the Sunflowers. She was to amass one of the largest single holdings of Vincent's work, especially of his drawings. Interest in his work was further advanced when the Fauves proclaimed Vincent one of their forerunners, as subsequently did the Expressionists and Abstract Expressionists. The new Museum of Modern Art in New York opened in 1929 with an exhibition of painters who were now seen as the four evangelists of the modern movement: Cézanne, Gauguin, Seurat and Van Gogh. Vincent's canonisation – by a church to which he had never belonged – was assured.

In the meantime Jo had been working on the letters. At first she delayed publication, arguing that Vincent's work should be better established in the public mind before details of his personal life were released. In 1914 the massive three-volume edition appeared in Amsterdam. The letters were published in the original languages in which Vincent had written them. The introduction was Jo's memoir of Vincent's life based mainly on her recollections of the things Theo had told her. This has remained the basis for all subsequent biographical writings. Recent scholarship has enabled historians to correct her dating of some of the letters and, though this has led to only slight adjustments to some aspects of Vincent's life, it has made considerable difference to the ordering of his work chronologically and thus to our understanding of his intentions. But no one would deny Jo the praise due to her for undertaking the seemingly impossible task of creating order out of over six hundred largely undated letters and notes. She withheld a few passages for reasons of family delicacy but these were quickly restored in a subsequent edition. Her memoir reflects the family's over-harsh opinion of Sien as a vicious drunkard, and those still alive at the time were protected by anonymity, thus Kee Vos was referred to as 'K', and Margot Begemann as 'Miss X'. Jo's only major editorial act was to cut out some of Vincent's religious ramblings, feeling that they would bore the reader. In order to present a fully balanced picture, these are to be restored in a new Dutch edition of the letters which will be published shortly.

The collected letters of Vincent van Gogh vie with Delacroix's Journal in offering the most profound insight into the creative process in the visual arts that we possess. Their publication completed the transformation of Vincent into the protean figure we know today. Yet no other artist is so accessible, almost every detail of his creative life and thought is known to us.

One result has been both the number and the range of books about him. These can, up to a point, be divided into the popular and the scholarly. The German art historian Meier-Gräfe, following the publication of the letters, was the first to write a best-selling popular life of the artist. Many followed, culminating in the American novelist Irving Stone's lightly fictionalised *Lust for Life*, first published in 1934. The book was the basis of the successful film of the same name released in 1956, starring Kirk Douglas as Vincent and Anthony Quinn as Gauguin. Such works did much to propagate an image of Vincent as an artistic super-hero, a martyr to his art, a man alone, not as other men, whose works spring from divine madness and who poured his colourful life directly on to his canvases. Predictably, scholars have despised such books for their often scant attention to historical detail, and for the fact that they wilfully ignore Vincent's own explanations of what he was trying to achieve and why.

It is not, however, as simple as that. It is arguable that the popularisers were only following the lead of the scholars, for it was they who settled on Vincent as a hero figure of modernism and depicted him as a warrior in the struggle against the Academies and Salons of the nineteenth century. They saw Vincent as a victim destroyed by an uncaring philistine artistic cabal which his successors ultimately brought low. Although Albert Aurier's article passed into temporary obscurity following his untimely death, it was his interpretation of Vincent as one of the 'Isolated Ones' that dominated academic thinking for many years. Such studies were often admirably scholarly, as was for instance Alfred

H. Barr's catalogue for the New York Museum of Modern Art's exhibition in 1935. But all too often the desire to justify Vincent's place in the struggle of the Modern Movement meant that writers had to play down, even to ignore his unwavering fidelity to the inspiration he derived from artists such as Jules Breton and Ernest Meissonier. It was likewise inevitable that some would ignore the uncomfortable fact that near the end of his life, far from looking forward to the wilder shores of the new, Vincent was returning to Father Millet as his touchstone of artistic greatness. An extreme example was a book by the art critic Philip James, who in 1950 dismissed the issue with these olympian words: "... his taste was often confused and even commonplace. He writes in loud and frequent praise of mediocre painters such as Breton, Lhermitte, Dupré and Meissonier."

Fortunately, there were other, more open-minded, authors eager to discover any detail about Vincent's life and work and who were not bound by the constraints of a theory which would lead them to exclude those facts that did not fit. First among these was the art historian Marc Edo Tralbaut, who virtually dedicated his life to Vincent and who went to extraordinary lengths to discover anyone who had any connection with him. For a time Tralbaut even published a private journal entitled *Van Goghiana* and his massive biography (1969), for many years the major work on the subject, is a wonderful hotchpotch of the essential and the trivial. Since then, the rare detail not unearthed by the remarkable Tralbaut has been tracked down by the type of passionate amateur whom Vincent's story continues to attract. It was a London postman, Paul Chalcroft, a man who spent all his free time making copies of Vincent's work, who in 1971 patiently uncovered the missing fragments of his life in Brixton, the most important being the name of Eugénie Loyer, whom the Van Gogh family had mistakenly thought was called Ursula, her mother's name.

In its day, Tralbaut's book was the definitive study of Vincent's life, but since its first publication twenty years ago, a number of details such as those established by Chalcroft have gradually accumulated both in learned journals and in popular publications, while at the same time there has been a considerable shift of emphasis in the way Vincent's work is assessed by the critics. Today's realisation that the Modern Movement is just another school of art and not the ultimate goal towards which the whole of art history was ineluctably moving has enabled art historians to look afresh at Vincent and to see what he was doing in terms other than those of struggle and conquest. This in turn has led to closer scrutiny of what Vincent himself said about his intentions. The result has been a series of major exhibitions covering in detail the various periods of his life – Van Gogh in Brabant, English Influences on Vincent van Gogh, Vincent van Gogh in Belgium, Van Gogh in Paris, Van Gogh in Arles, Van Gogh in St Rémy and Auvers – whose catalogues have brought together recent research, much of it arising out of the reordering of the relevant letters. These activities have been allied to a new assessment of Vincent's aims together with a redefinition of his place in nineteenth-century art, which itself has been the subject of considerable reappraisal. The material in this present book has been viewed in the light of these changes, especially the contributions to the various exhibition catalogues made by Ronald Pickvance and Bogomila Welsh-Ovcharov, which have transformed our view of Van Gogh. Professor Pickvance has done more than anyone to focus attention on the sources of inspiration which underpin Vincent's work, while Dr Welsh-Ovcharov succeeded in shedding light on the previously occluded area of Vincent's years in Paris, surely the most critical period of his development as an artist.

There has also been a parallel branch of Van Gogh studies which has concerned itself with his mental state. Over the last hundred years countless theories have been put forward to explain his illnesses and to relate them to his paintings. Some appear to have been dreamed up by people who were themselves of doubtful sanity and in sum they are so contradictory that the wise do well to ignore them. Fortunately, the one significant conclusion that can be reached from them is that whatever he was suffering from cannot be directly 'read' into his art, a fact which has been much emphasised in more recent scholarship. The image of Vincent as isolated Holy Fool, artist-sage or whatever, has finally been exposed as the nonsense it always was.

Possibly the most significant shift in this rethinking of Vincent's life came as a result of an inspired act of lateral thinking by the Dutch art-historian Dr Jan Hulsker. It was Hulsker who realised that the letter which Theo found in Vincent's jacket was not the last despairing cry of pain that he and everyone subsequently had assumed it to be. From the similarity of so much of the wording, Hulsker concluded that it was merely a draft which Vincent had rejected; the real letter had been sent on July 23rd, 1890 and Theo had already received it before he was summoned to Auvers by Dr Gachet.

The finished letter shows that Vincent was once more calm and composed:

> *As far as I'm concerned, I apply myself to my canvases with all my mind, I am trying to do as well as certain painters whom I have greatly loved and admired.*

Once the idea of some final act of anguished despair with a last 'suicide note' was undermined, a great deal else could be rethought. Why, for example, was it necessary to assume that the two wheat fields were his last paintings when there was no real evidence for such a conclusion? Indeed it is as reasonable to assume that it was one of the other four paintings he sketched in the posted letter which had preoccupied his final days. If one decides to accept that it was his painting of Daubigny's Garden which was the last work then our whole image of him is consequently transformed. He had intended to paint Daubigny's house and garden ever since his arrival in Auvers and had made a painted sketch from nature as early as June. He wished to do it in homage to the great man and he may even have thought of presenting it to his widow, who was still living in the house. Although the work has been retouched by lesser hands and the surface damaged, the final painting remains one of his most carefully composed and balanced works. In his last, posted, letter he described it as *one of my most purposeful canvases yet*, a far cry indeed from that last despairing howl so beloved of those who choose to see him as the archetype of the despairing, tragic genius.

The simple truth is that there is no one final painting. While Andries Bonger was helping Jo compile the inventory in Auvers he was told by Ravoux that a rather nondescript scene of a village street, where the thick blue brushstrokes of the sky are clearly incomplete, was the one Vincent had been working on last of all. In any case, on the day of the tragedy he had his easel and a canvas with him presumably because he was intending to paint somewhere near the château. In Vincent's own mind at least there was no last all-embracing painting.

Hulsker's was a happy discovery, for it has helped release us from a narrow view of Vincent's life. Someone as varied in his thinking and as wide-ranging in his interests could never be so easily pinned down. No matter what he suffered, despair was never the dominant element in his thoughts and the fact of his suicide does not alter that. As he said in one of his earliest letters to Theo, written in the dark days in the Borinage:

> *... I always think that the best way to know God is to love many things. Love a friend, a wife, something – whatever you like – you will be on the way to knowing more about Him; that is what I say to myself. But one must love with a lofty and serious intimate sympathy, with strength, with intelligence; and one must always try to know deeper, better and more.*

The Van Gogh family's troubles did not end with the deaths of the two brothers. A few years later their closest sister Willemina had to be interned in an asylum where she remained until she died in 1941, at the age of 79, the last of Pastor Theodorus' and Anna Carbentus' children to survive. The cause of her illness is not known though it must surely have had the same background of inherited depression and epilepsy as Vincent's malady. Whatever the cause, the unhappy Willemina withdrew totally from the world and for the greater part of her long life never uttered a word. Their mother was to lose her other son during her own lifetime: the youngest, Cor, died in Pretoria in 1900, seven months after the start of the Anglo-Boer war. Although he was listed among those killed in action in the Boer forces, there was an unconfirmed rumour that he had committed suicide. Anna Carbentus van Gogh died in 1907. Besides Willemina, there remained two other daughters – the eldest Anna, who had been estranged from Vincent since their father's death, and Elisabeth. Elisabeth had literary ambitions but her *Personal Recollections of Vincent van Gogh* published in 1910, is disappointing, only her reminiscences of their childhood in Zundert having much interest. Anna died in 1930 and Elisabeth in 1936.

In the end this summary of Vincent's 'apotheosis' must return to 'Jo' who began the whole process of publicising his life and work. In 1915, the year following the publication of the letters, her son Vincent Willem married Josina Wibaut. He had finished his training as an engineer and after a short period in France, he and his wife left for America, where Jo joined them in 1916. Living in New York, she embarked on the onerous task of translating Vincent's letters into English. In 1919 she returned to Holland as did her son and daughter-in-law a year later. It was at this point that the fact the family letters had specified Vincent Willem, and not herself, as sole beneficiary of the estate, becomes crucial to the story. The thirty-year-old Vincent Willem decided to assume control of his inheritance. It was a decision which engendered considerable friction with his mother, for he decided categorically to hold on to all the remaining pictures. His mother's policy of selectively selling off pieces so that Vincent's work could be shared by the world's major collections was abruptly terminated. While Vincent Willem was always ready to lend work to exhibitions, the vast bulk of the paintings were stacked unseen in an unheated spare room at Laren. To Jo this was intolerable. Only about twenty works could be hung in the house and even Vincent Willem's wife wrote to her sister: "Often, too, I feel rather sorry about the paintings. That is the only problem in my life with Vincent – our difference of opinion on owning the pictures."

Time was to justify Vincent Willem's inflexible approach. So many Van Goghs were already in private hands or in national museums that it began to make sense to keep so large a body of work together. Vincent himself had always dreamed that his works would not be seen in isolation and although the exact combinations of pictures he had planned was now impossible to achieve, it was clearly right to try to have a broad selection of paintings in one place. If Jo's policy of selling off the works had continued, the whole *oeuvre* might have been dispersed in twos and threes around the world.

Jo died in 1925. She was two-thirds of the way through the English translation of the letters. Despite the frustrations of the last years she must have known that she had largely succeeded in her self-appointed role as her brother-in-law's champion. Her own brother Andries had been proved utterly wrong in his suggestion that she should get rid of the work after Theo's death.

For his own part, Andries had gone on to become a major patron of the Symbolist artist Odilon Redon. After his wife Anne's death he had married again in 1934 and passed the remainder of his life in dilettante cultural pursuits similar to Dr Gachet's; he became a member of the Society of the Friends of Delacroix and followed with interest new research into Shakespeare. He too had moved back to Holland shortly after Theo's death, but would always make the journey to Paris if there was a major Impressionist exhibition to be seen. For a time he had been friendly with Emile Bernard, but the young man's interest in Catholicism gradually turned into a religious mysticism which alienated his friends and he and Andries saw less and less of each other.

Bernard settled in Egypt for ten years where he was joined by his sister Madeleine and Charles Laval. In 1894 Laval died there of tuberculosis, Madeleine the year after. Bernard's creative life drifted away, though he was to outlive them all, dying in Paris in 1941, a rarity among Vincent's close friends for never having quarrelled with him.

Vincent's conviction that he and his fellow artists were being forced to suffer too greatly in the cause of their art was confirmed by the subsequent lives of many of his friends. Seurat died prematurely of an infection in 1891, while heavy drinking carried off Toulouse-Lautrec in 1901 aged only thirty-seven. Happily, the good-hearted Signac was seventy-two when he died in 1935 after a rather jolly life with much travel to the sort of seaside places he loved. Gauguin, however, fully justified Vincent's theory. After one failed suicide he died, probably by his own hand, in the Marquesas Islands in 1903 whereupon his reputation experienced a similar surge to Vincent's. Others were less fortunate. Van Rappard died only two years after Vincent, to the end still nervously doubting his own abilities and unhappy with the results. Posterity has tended to take him at his own valuation, and such fame as he has rests mainly on his acquaintance with his friend.

Some minor characters have disappeared almost without trace. Adrien-Jean Madiol, the painter Vincent briefly knew in Brussels, also died shortly after him. His one painting that was preserved for posterity in the Museum at Courtrai in Belgium was destroyed during an air raid in the Second World War.

It was a bombing raid on London that obliterated the main surviving connection between Vincent and the English friend of his Paris days, Harry Gladwell. After serving his apprenticeship at Goupil's, Harry joined the family art-dealing business in London and following his father's death in 1879 became the senior partner in what was then known as Gladwell Brothers with branches in Regent Street, Kingsway and Gracechurch Street in the City. After Harry's death in 1927 at the age of seventy, his son Algernon took over, moving the business to Cheapside where he was eventually bought out by his manager Herbert Fuller who then transferred the business to its present site in Queen Victoria Street near to the Mansion House. Fuller also acquired a box containing the letters that Vincent had sent to Harry. Unfortunately they were never examined or copied and were incinerated when the gallery was bombed during the last war. One of Harry's surviving granddaughters has inherited his Bible, the last souvenir of those evenings in Montmartre when the two young men read aloud the scriptures and talked of God long into the night.

News of other members of the passing cast of Vincent's story has surfaced from time to time, in a more or less haphazard fashion, usually thanks to the whim of a journalist looking for the 'secrets' of a life which has assumed mythic proportions in the popular mind. One such, Pierre Weiller, was looking for a new apartment in Paris in the 1930s and had climbed the stairs to meet his putative landlady, a Madame Milliet. The door was opened by her husband, a man of distinguished appearance, very virile, whose face with its redoubtable moustaches and pointed beard had the elegant air of the 1880s. The writer had of course 'discovered' Vincent's Zouave officer, by then a retired Lieutenant-Colonel. Milliet had seen active service in Tunisia, Algeria, Morocco and during the First World War but peace-time service in a provincial barracks had not pleased him and he had retired. He was happy to answer any questions about Vincent, but was no more impressed by his one-time friend's talent than he had been before and had lost both Vincent's and Gauguin's gifts over the years. Milliet died during the dark days of the German occupation of Paris.

Throughout the 1930s Andries Bonger had been distressed by the rise of National Socialism, especially in his native Holland. It was perhaps fortunate that he died before he could suffer the spectacle of the invasion of his beloved France, his second home.

Not unexpectedly, the saddest of all these figures was Sien Hoornik, with whom Vincent had lived in The Hague. After years of drifting about Holland she eventually settled in Rotterdam where, in 1901, she took Vincent's advice and made a marriage of convenience to one Arnoldus van Wijk. He was fifty-one years old, but could at least give her son Willem, by then aged nineteen, a legitimate name. Sien, however, was still incapable of happiness and three years later, on November 12th, 1904, she carried out the threat she had once made to Vincent and drowned herself. Her son was to lead a somewhat unhappy life. Looked after by one of Sien's brothers, he took a job with the Dutch State Water Works. In the early 1970s a British journalist working in Amsterdam, Kenneth Wilkie, set out to prove that Vincent had descendants. He was told that Willem, by then dead, had been a collaborator during the Nazi occupation and jailed for a time after the war. But there was a son, Willy van Wijk, who was confidently identified by Wilkie as Vincent's true grandson, a discovery dismissed by every known expert on the simple grounds that his grandmother was already pregnant when she met Vincent.

Wilkie had more success with the descendants of Eugénie Loyer, the strong-minded young woman whose rejection of Vincent's proposal had set in train the events that ultimately led to his career and his suicide. Following clues offered in the discoveries of the local postman Paul Chalcroft, the man who tracked down the Loyers' address and clarified the confusion over Eugénie's name, Wilkie went on to find that she had indeed married the other lodger Samuel Plowman and that they had had a son Frank who had died in 1966. By dint of journalistic leg-work, Wilkie then tracked down a surviving descendant, Frank's married daughter Kathleen Maynard who now lives in Devon. Wilkie travelled down to see her and was shown a box with some photographs of Eugénie and other family mementoes. He asked if he could examine the contents himself and when he got to the bottom of the cardboard container discovered a little drawing, stained with tea or coffee and frayed at the edges. It was Vincent's sketch of the Loyers' house in Brixton, scene of some of the happiest and the saddest days of his youth. He had obviously given it to Eugénie as a present, a sign of his unspoken love.

After Jo's death, her son Vincent Willem van Gogh carried on the family tradition of opening his house to scholars who wished to view the collection. He willingly arranged loans for the continuing international exhibitions and amended where necessary his mother's editorial work on the letters. Not that things always ran smoothly. Vincent Willem's occasionally haughty manner seems to have alienated some people, the most prominent among them being Mrs Kröller-Müller, who had by then amassed the second largest collection of Vincent's work. She consequently refused to show them in conjunction with the Van Gogh family's collection. On a different level, there was the huge and unwelcome publicity surrounding the discovery in the late 1920s that many of the Van Goghs by then in circulation were fakes produced by a German dealer called Wacker. The 'Wacker Scandal' took on a more serious dimension when it was realised that the leading Van Gogh scholar J. B. de la Faille had admitted many Wacker forgeries into his vast *Catalogue Raisonné* of Vincent's *oeuvre*. He was obliged to issue a subsequent catalogue, *Les Faux van Gogh*, in a belated attempt to put matters right.

Throughout all this Vincent Willem continued to sit on his collection like a broody hen despite the efforts of various interested parties to prise the eggs from under him. In 1930 both he and Mrs Kröller-Müller were persuaded to forget their differences and combine their Van Gogh collections in a major loan exhibition at Amsterdam's Stedelijk Museum. Vincent Willem was then persuaded to agree that, apart from the best loved paintings hung in the family home in Laren, the bulk of the collection should remain on permanent loan at the Museum. In 1938 the Kröller-Müller works became a national collection and were housed in a specially designed museum in the stunningly beautiful Hoge Veluwe National Park near Otterlo. This left only the Van Gogh family collection as the major group of Vincent's paintings still in private hands. The sudden collapse of Holland during the Second World War inevitably halted any further moves to change the situation. On the eve of the German invasion, the loan works in the Stedelijk were hidden in an underground bunker in the coastal dunes near Castricum. A small group of paintings was stranded in the Dutch East Indies and a further group 'retained' by the Museum of Santa Barbara in California which the Dutch Government in Exile was able to exhibit across America in an attempt to arouse sympathy for the occupied nation.

In 1941 a fire at the house in Laren was speedily extinguished though Vincent's *Self-portrait in front of the Easel* was slightly damaged, which may have advanced the process of convincing Vincent Willem to make a more permanent provision for his much-loved pictures. After the Liberation, it was obvious that the family could no longer expect to retain such an asset. Although Vincent Willem was by profession a humble engineer who lived modestly without any sign of ostentation, his ownership of so many Van Goghs made him effectively the richest man in Holland. Such theoretical wealth could only mean that at his death the inheritance tax would be crippling and would oblige his children to do the very thing he dreaded most – sell off the collection. At the prompting of the Dutch state, the solution he eventually agreed to was complex but allowed for his various whims to be indulged. A Vincent van Gogh Foundation was set up, largely controlled by the family; the Dutch State then gave the Foundation sufficient funds to purchase the collection on condition that it was housed in a Museum to be built by the city of Amsterdam. Thus the family sold their entire collection – Vincent's paintings and drawings as well as the works by others which Theo had amassed – for approximately six million dollars, a huge sum, but by then far short of the actual market value. Vincent Willem devoted himself unstintingly to the realisation of the museum being built on Amsterdam's Museumplein within sight of the Rijksmuseum, where Vincent had stood for a day, entranced before Rembrandt's *The Jewish Bride*. The Rijksmuseum Vincent van Gogh was opened in 1973 and today houses the largest single collection of Vincent's paintings, as well as documentation on his life and temporary exhibitions of his and his contemporaries' work.

Vincent Willem died in 1978, outlived only by Marcelline Roulin, whom Vincent had painted as a baby proudly held up by her mother in Arles. She of course had no memory of Vincent but had always taken pride in seeing the portraits of her father, mother and brothers as well as herself reproduced in magazines. She had visited Arles while *Lust for Life* was being filmed in 1955 and had been astonished to see an actor, full beard and all, playing the part of her father. She died aged 93, on February 22nd, 1980, the last of Vincent's 'models' to have survived.

Vincent Willem had three sons, Theo, Johan, Floor and a daughter Mathilde. Theo was executed by the Germans for his role in the Dutch Resistance. Johan is presently Chairman of the board of the Van Gogh Foundation which includes Mathilde, Floor's son Willem and a representative of the Dutch state. None of the family has so far shown any inclination to become a painter and the only descendant to show any sign of their illustrious forebear's character is Johan's son Theo who makes controversial feature films but who is perhaps better known in his native land for his intemperate attacks on the critics whom he clearly despises.

The family still retains residual control over a number of letters and papers, some of which are still unavailable to scholars. Principal amongst these are Jo's diaries, which are permanently embargoed and which even the curators of the Van Gogh Museum, where the papers are stored, have not been allowed to read. It is thought unlikely that they contain anything which could radically alter our knowledge of Vincent's life. The family's past secretiveness was probably a result of Vincent Willem's rather eccentric attempt in later life, to maintain that they had never parted with any of his uncle's works. As Jo's diaries presumably contain references to such transactions it will be necessary to wait until his children decide to override this lingering ban and open up their grandmother's remaining papers. That day cannot be far off as they recently released all documents concerning Jo's transactions with the German art dealer Paul Cassirer which were subsequently published by the Foundation.

Despite his unhappy life, Vincent was in the end extraordinarily fortunate. Not only had Theo stood by him selflessly but his brother's widow had also devoted herself to establishing his reputation and was succeeded by her son whom Vincent had dandled on his knee a mere two or three times. In his own stubborn way it was Vincent Willem who had completed the task of ensuring that a major proportion of his uncle's work remained intact and easily accessible to the widest possible public. And it is this very public which makes Vincent's story a happy not a despairing one. Who could deny that in those crowds of every conceivable nationality queueing to see his work, he has finally achieved what he most dearly desired – to make art for ordinary people. The academics and the writers of popular life-stories, the makers of feature films and television documentaries, the erudite cataloguers of exhibitions and the printers of postcards and calendars have all helped to make Vincent the widest known and best loved artist of the modern era. His yellow chair, that simple object, is the most widely reproduced work of secular art. It is obvious that the members of the public who stand for hours to get into any exhibition of his work are drawn from a wider cross-section of society than normally go to art galleries. Compared to this vast endorsement of Vincent's achievement, the head-shaking over the phenomenal sums paid at auctions for his work seems a trifle irrelevant. What matter if $49,000,000 changes hands for one of his Irises as long as the canvas is not locked away in a bank vault, as happened to one of the Sunflowers for a number of years. We can only note with a wry smile that the portrait of Adeline Ravoux which her father had thought he had so cunningly sold for a few francs was bought at auction in 1988 for $13,750,000, a figure which apparently disappointed both press and public who had been expecting a record-breaking $15,000,000. It can be argued that the fuss, the scandal even, which surrounds such events can only widen public interest even further and help bring to his exhibitions those who might otherwise never have thought to go. The sour comments of certain critics who are horrified at the fact that such people misunderstand the work and are merely drawn to see the pictures by the popular myths about the artist's life sound like nothing more than an élite's anger at being deprived of its secret cult.

The Vincent van Gogh Museum in Amsterdam remains the first port of call for anyone wishing to understand the broad range of Vincent's work. It can readily be combined with a visit to the Rijksmuseum Kröller-Müller about an hour and a half's drive from Amsterdam in the direction of Arnhem. This museum houses not only a major selection of the paintings, including one of the early versions of *The Potato Eaters*, but also one of the largest collections of Vincent's drawings, though for reasons of conservation these can only be selectively exhibited on a temporary basis. Outside Holland the other major collection of Vincent's work was that amassed by Dr Gachet. After his death in January 1909, it passed to his son Paul who dedicated his life to preserving his father's memory in much the way Jo had done with Vincent's. Paul made the house in Auvers a shrine to a remarkably diverse intellect. In 1949, he began the series of donations from his father's collection to the Louvre, which culminated in 1954 with the gift of his last six paintings by Vincent, by then worth a fortune. Like Vincent Willem, Paul had lived modestly despite his theoretically stupendous wealth. Initially hung in the Jeu de Paume, the Gachet collection was transferred to the new Museum of the Nineteenth Century in the restored Gare d'Orsay when it opened in 1986. This extraordinary ensemble of all branches of the arts of the period at last allowed Vincent's work to be seen in the context in which it was conceived, as part of its own time and not as some isolated explosion into Modernism. By the resurrection from almost total obscurity of artists such as Breton, whose work had been consigned to their cellars by 'progressive' museum directors, Vincent was at last made part of the Musée Imaginaire he had always carried in his heart. The fury of some of the Modernists, unable to see that they themselves had become as hidebound as the academicians of the past, was proof enough that the conception realised in the Musée d'Orsay was correct; room was found even for one of Cormon's vast shaggy canvases. It is appropriate to remember that Vincent seldom dismissed any artist and wherever possible celebrated the good in what he saw.

For those with a taste for the sites where Vincent lived and worked, much still stands, though his habit of gravitating to the parts of cities in the process of transformation means that some of his temporary homes have been submerged by development. However, the church in Zundert can still be seen and beside it the original Vincent Willem's sad tombstone. Vincent's secondary school in Tilburg, that curious doll-like castle, is now the local town hall. The village of Nuenen maintains a small visitor's room in which details on the whereabouts of the church, the presbytery, the windmill, the de Groots' cottage and any other associated places can be found. Nuenen is one of the rare places that still retains something of the pastoral atmosphere which Vincent enjoyed. As to the cities: the Loyers' house in Hackford Road, Brixton, London, still stands, as does the Reverend Slade-Jones' house and church in Twickenham. The apartment block in the Rue Lepic, Paris, is still there and Montmartre, despite mass tourism, continues to evoke haunting memories of the artistic life of *fin de siècle* France. Naturally, it is to Provence that the true pilgrim must go and though none of Vincent's work remains to be seen there, much is as he knew it. The city of Arles has gone to great lengths to capitalise on the memory of the man its citizens once so viciously rejected and, though the local authorities foolishly failed to rebuild the Yellow House after it was bombed in the War, in 1989 they reopened the beautifully restored Hôtel-Dieu as a cultural centre and library. Some things, however, do not change and that same year saw the appearance of a Mme Jeanne Calment who, at 114, claimed to be the oldest person in France. According to the journalists who interviewed her, she clearly remembered Vincent coming into her family's shop to buy canvas. "He was horrible," she insisted, "always rude and upsetting people. I remember the night he chopped his ear off, like a slice of pâté. It was the last straw." So much for the good people of Arles.

Les Saintes-Maries-de-la-Mer is utterly spoiled but it is still possible to see the unchanged exterior of the hospital at St Rémy. But the most touching place of all is far from the sunlit south, in a part of Europe few would think of visiting, the abandoned coal-fields of the Borinage. The Denis house in Wasmes is still there in a bleak brick-built street, as is the Salon du Bébé where Vincent attempted to preach. The mines are closed down now and the area an economic backwater, though you can walk along the muddy lane which leads to the abandoned Marcasse pit and peer through the iron gates at the imposing ruins of a place that was responsible for so much human suffering. The Decrucqs' tiny house at Cuesmes has been restored as a rather pathetic museum. An atmosphere of grey abandon hangs over the Borinage, rusting pit-head towers and sickening monuments to death abound, yet the abandoned slag-heaps sprout odd tufts of greenery which give them a faintly Japanese look and on All Saints Day the mass of yellow chrysanthemums laid in the graveyards makes one think of Vincent and his golden vision.

Finally and inevitably, there is the little town of Auvers, a short train journey from Paris. It is still a place of great beauty, almost as Vincent knew it. As in Nuenen the local authorities maintain a centre that will direct the visitor to the Ravouxs' café, the Town Hall, Dr Gachet's house, the church and the path which climbs to the open plateau where wheat still grows and, yes, where black crows still wheel in the sky. Inside the square walled graveyard a sign directs the visitor to the spot, though this is not the original burial ground. When its fifteen-year lease expired in 1905, Dr Gachet endowed a new plot near the northern wall where he and Paul supervised the exhumation and reburial of Vincent's remains. In 1914, the year of the publication of Vincent's letters, Jo decided that Theo should be moved from Utrecht and buried beside the brother he had loved so dearly. By then Dr Gachet was dead, but Paul was present at the ceremony. Jo took a sprig of ivy from the Gachets' garden and planted it in the newly turned earth. A hundred years on it has flourished. Today, two identical headstones rise from a single green blanket of the plant that Vincent had always loved best.

Acknowledgements

My first thanks must go to my publisher John Curtis whose idea this was, closely followed by my friend and agent Andrew Best, who not only made the necessary contractual arrangements but went far beyond the call of duty in editing the first draft, a task ably continued by Alex MacCormick and Claire Trocmé. My thanks are also due to Jean Autret who spotted a number of errors while translating the book into French and to Julia Brown who tracked down even the most obscure pictures. Carolyn Doyle had the difficult task of typing the book not once but also the far more onerous one of doing it a second time for the final version – in both cases faultlessly. My appreciation is due to the staff of the Musée d'Orsay's library and documentation centre who ensure that it is 'user friendly' and where the photocopying machine is a tool of research and not a form of administrative torture – as for the National Art Library at the Victoria and Albert Museum . . . only the painful memory of the national art archives in Brussels stays my hand.

No one could have been more welcoming than Mr Han van Crimpen, Curator of the Rijksmuseum Vincent van Gogh in Amsterdam who, despite considerable pressure from his own publishing commitments, took the time to meet me and give me the benefit of his advice. Many friends have also given help with specialised information, notably my neighbour Dr David Watt who attempted to guide me through the more complex medical matters raised in the book. Likewise the Rev James Bentley who proposed a number of explanations for Vincent's choices of biblical quotations. I am very grateful to Sir Terence and Lady Conran who offered me their house in Provence while I was working on chapters nine and ten.

In the end the most fulsome expression of gratitude must go to the subject of the book himself. When I was a schoolboy in the fifties I was taken on a class outing to a major travelling exhibition of Van Gogh's work which was then at the Laing Art Gallery, Newcastle-on-Tyne. It was the first time that art meant anything real to me – an experience akin to the one most people enjoy on a first visit to the theatre, the hairs bristling on the back of the neck; a never quite to be repeated exaltation. In researching this book I have been able to rediscover something of that excitement. I am especially grateful for the exhibition that was held in the restored Hôtel-Dieu in Arles early in 1989 where I saw in the flesh the truly stunning portrait of Dr Rey and also came to see just how extraordinarily wonderful Vincent's drawings are. In a very real sense, this book has been an inadequate attempt to repay an enormous debt.

David Sweetman
Pittefaux – London
February 1990

Bibliography

Most of the information for this book was found in the standard sources listed below. The basic outline of Vincent's life was drawn from the information in the *Collected Letters* and Johanna van Gogh-Bonger's introduction to them. This information has been updated by the catalogues of the various exhibitions on specialist periods in his career which have been held over the past decade. These have taken account of the recent redating of many of the letters which has altered the chronology of Vincent's work at several key points in his life. I have where possible endeavoured to find out more about those characters previously thought to be peripheral to his story in order to give them the prominence he would have granted them. Much of my research was directed towards re-creating the cultural ambience of the late nineteenth century – its cities, ateliers, cafés and cabarets – the better to understand Vincent in the context of his own world as he would have seen it himself.

I have tried as hard as I could to avoid the words 'maybe' and 'perhaps' with which the thesis writer cloaks any uncertainties in his subject's doings. For example, Vincent *may* have met Gauguin during his first year in Paris, though he only mentions their having met in the following year. As he was so overwhelmed by his new friend it seems to me unlikely that he would have failed to register an earlier confrontation and with this in mind I have settled on 1887 as the year of their first encounter.

In other instances I have simply assumed that certain facts were the case when logic dictated that they were so – I assume he would have travelled from Brabant to The Hague by carriage to Breda then train to the coast as this was the most obvious method at the time.

Each book is listed once only, though a book which first appears under a particular chapter may have been consulted in succeeding chapters. The major, general works on Van Gogh that are still available have been marked with an asterisk.

General

*Gogh, Vincent van, *The Complete Letters of Vincent van Gogh*, Thames and Hudson, London 1958

*Hammacher, A. M. and R., *Van Gogh, a documentary biography*, Thames and Hudson, London 1982

McQuillan, Melissa, *Van Gogh*, Thames and Hudson, London 1989

Pool, Phoebe, *Impressionism*, Thames and Hudson, London 1967

*Rewald, John, *Post-Impressionism. From Van Gogh to Gauguin*, 3rd ed., The Museum of Modern Art, New York 1978

Studies in Post-Impressionism, Thames and Hudson, London 1986

Rosenblum, Robert, and Janson, H. W., *Art of the 19th Century – Painting and Sculpture*, Thames and Hudson, London 1984

Tralbaut, M. E., *Van Goghiana*, privately printed, P. Peré, Antwerp 1963–1975, 10 issues

Vincent van Gogh, Macmillan, London 1969

Treble, Rosemary, *Vincent, the paintings of Van Gogh*, Hamlyn, London 1989

Uitert, E. van, and Hoyle, M. (eds), *The Rijksmuseum Vincent van Gogh*, Meulenhoff/Landshoff, Amsterdam 1987

Vincent, Bulletin of the Rijksmuseum Vincent van Gogh, 4 vols, Amsterdam 1970–76

Zurcher, Bernard, *Vincent van Gogh, Art, Life and Letters*, Rizzoli, New York 1985

1. Funeral Procession through the Cornfields

Quesne-van Gogh, E. H. du, *Personal Recollections of Vincent van Gogh*, trans. K. S. Dreier, London 1913

**Van Gogh in Brabant*, exhib. cat. Noordbrabants Museum, 's-Hertogenbosch 1978–88, Wanders, Zwolle 1987

2. A Blank Canvas   3. Breakdown   4. Pray, my Soul

Broos, Ben, *Meesterwerken in het Mauritshuis*, Staatsuitgeverij, The Hague 1987

Brussels Salon 1872, Catalogue Explicatif, Imprimerie Adolphe Mertens, Brussels 1872

De Haagse School, exhib. cat. Haags Gemeentemuseum 1983

Forster, Dr Fr., *Illustrierter Wiener Fremdenführer*, Beck'sche Universitäts Buchhandlung, Vienna 1973

Gruyter, Dr Jos. de, *De Haagse School*, Lemniscaat, Rotterdam 1968

Marius, *Dutch Painters of the 19th Century*, 1st pub. Holland 1903, Eng. trans. 1908, re-edition Antique Collectors' Club (ed. G. Norman) 1973

Jean-François Millet, exhib. cat. Arts Council of Great Britain 1976

Osborne, Roy, *Lights and Pigments*, John Murray, London 1980
Paris Salon 1873, Imprimerie Nationale, Paris 1873
Pickvance, Ronald, *English Influences on Vincent van Gogh*, exhib. cat. Univ. of Nottingham, Arts Council of Great Britain 1974
Thomson, Dr Croel, 'The Brothers Maris', *The Studio*, special summer number, London 1907
Tilborgh, Louis van (ed.), *Van Gogh and Millet*, Rijksmuseum Vincent van Gogh, Amsterdam 1989
Wilkie, Kenneth, *The Van Gogh Assignment*, Paddington Press, London 1978

5. Under a Sulphur Sun

Dejollier, René, *Charbonnages en Wallonie 1345–1984*, Editions Erasme, Namur 1988
Duez, Georges, *Vincent van Gogh au Borinage*, Fédération du Tourisme du Hainaut, Mons 1986
Piérard, Jean, *Mon Pays, le Borinage*, Fédération du Tourisme du Hainaut, Mons 1978
Van Gogh en Belgique, exhib. cat. Musée des Beaux-Arts de Mons 1980

6. Theo

Ackerman, Gerald M., *Jean-Léon Gérôme*, Sotheby's Publications, London 1986
Adler, Kathleen, *Camille Pissarro*, B. T. Batsford, London 1978
L'Art belge, exhib. cat. Brussels, Société Royale des Beaux-Arts 1905
L'Art en Belgique 1880–1950, exhib. cat. Brussels, Palais des Beaux-Arts 1978
Belgian Art 1880–1914, exhib. cat. Brooklyn Institute of Art and Science 1980
Emile Bernard, exhib. cat. London, Kaplan Gallery 1964
Besson, Georges, *Paul Signac 1863–1935*, Les Editions Braun, Paris 1951
André Bonger en Zijn Kunstenaarsvrienden: Redon, Bernard, van Gogh, exhib. cat. Amsterdam, Rijksmuseum 1972
Boyer, Patricia Eckert (ed.), *The Nabis and the Parisian Avant-Garde*, Rutgers University Press, New Brunswick and London 1988
Brettell, Richard, et al, *The Art of Paul Gauguin*, National Gallery of Art, Washington 1988
Delevoy, Robert L., *Symbolists and Symbolism*, Skira, Rizzoli, New York 1978
Flippo, William G., *Lexicon of the Belgian Romantic Painters*, International Art Press, Antwerp 1981
Goncourt, Edmond and Jules de, *Paris and the Arts, 1851–1896, extracts from the Goncourt Journal*, ed. and trans. George J. Becker and Edith Philips, Cornell University Press, Ithaca 1971
Kunstler, Charles, *Pissarro*, Cassell, London 1988

Le Livre des expositions universelles 1851–1989, Union Centrale des Arts Décoratifs, Paris 1983
Milner, John, *The Studios of Paris*, Yale University Press, New Haven 1988
Opdebeek, Lodewijk, 'A.J. Madiol', *Vlaamsch en Vrij*, 4 Feb. 1894
Pissarro, Camille, *Correspondance de Camille Pissarro*, Presses Universitaires de France, Paris 1981
Rewald, John, 'Theo van Gogh, Goupil, and the Impressionists', *Gazette des Beaux-Arts* Jan. and Feb. 1973
Sheon A., *Monticelli*, exhib. cat. Pittsburg, Carnegie Institute Museum of Art 1978–79
'Monticelli and Van Gogh', *Apollo* June 1967
Shikes, Ralph E., and Harper, Paula, *Pissarro, his life and work*, Quartet Books, London 1980
Thompson, Belinda, *Gauguin*, Thames and Hudson, London 1987
Weber, Eugen, *France, Fin de Siècle*, Harvard University Press, Cambridge Ma. 1986

7. *The Potato Eaters*

Gelder, J. G. van, *Vincent van Gogh, The Potato Eaters*, Percy Lund Humphries, London 1948
Wolk, Johannes van der, *The Seven Sketchbooks of Vincent van Gogh*, trans. Claudia Swan, Thames and Hudson, London 1987

8. *Dark Green, with Black, with Fiery Red*

Castleman, Riva, and Wittrock, Wolfgang (eds), *Henri de Toulouse-Lautrec*, The Museum of Modern Art, New York 1985
Cate, Phillip Dennis, and Welsh-Ovcharov, Bogomila, *Emile Bernard – Bordellos and Prostitutes in Turn-of-the-Century French Art*, The Jane Voorhees Zimmerli Art Museum, Rutgers, New Brunswick 1988
Conrad, III, Barnaby, *Absinthe, History in a Bottle*, Chronicle Books, San Francisco 1988
'Fernand Cormon', *L'Académie du Japon moderne et les Peintres français*, exhib. cat. Tokyo, Ishibashi Foundation 1983
'Nécrologie: Mort de Fernand Cormon', *Le Temps* 22 March 1924
Figures de Corot, exhib. cat. Paris, Musée du Louvre 1962
Dubosc, Charles, *Soixante ans dans les ateliers des artistes*, Calmann-Lévy, Paris 1900
Dufura, Jacques, *Winds from the East – a Study in the Art of Manet, Degas, Monet and Whistler, 1856–86*, Almqvist and Wiksell International, Stockholm 1981
Galbally, Ann, *The Art of John Peter Russell*, Sun Books, Melbourne 1977

Gauguin, Paul, *Letters to his Wife and Friends*, ed. Maurice Malingue, trans. Henry J. Stenning, The Saturn Press, London 1946

45 Lettres à Vincent, Theo et Jo van Gogh, ed. Douglas Cooper, Rijksmuseum Vincent van Gogh, Amsterdam 1983

**Van Gogh à Paris*, exhib. cat. Musée d'Orsay, Ministère de la Culture et de la Communication, Paris 1988

Gray, Christopher, *Armand Guillaumin*, The Pequot Press, Connecticut 1972

Hartrick, A. S., *A Painter's Pilgrimage through Fifty Years*, Cambridge 1939

A. S. Hartrick, exhib. cat. London, Arts Council of Great Britain 1951

Honeyman, T. J., 'Van Gogh – A Link with Glasgow', *The Scottish Art Review*, vol. II no. 2, 1948

Julian, Philippe, *Montmartre*, Phaidon, Oxford 1977

Lejeune, Philippe (ed.), *Extraits du Journal de Fernand Cormon (1917–1918)*, Edition de la Fondation Taylor, n.d.

Musée d'Orsay, Guide, Ministère de la Culture et de la Communication, Paris 1986

Pichon, Yann le, *Gauguin: Life. Art. Inspiration*, trans. I. Mark Paris, Harry N. Abrams, New York 1987

Roskill, M., *Van Gogh, Gauguin and the Impressionist Circle*, London–New York 1970

Taillandier, Yvon, *Corot*, The Uffici Press, Milan 1967

Vollard, Ambroise, *Recollections of a Picture Dealer*, trans. Violet M. Macdonald, Dover Publications, New York 1978

Welsh-Ovcharov, B., *Vincent van Gogh and the Birth of Cloisonism*, Art Gallery of Ontario 1981

Vincent van Gogh – His Paris Period 1886–1888, Utrecht–The Hague 1976

9. The Yellow House

Chefs-d'Oeuvre de la Peinture, Musée Fabre, Montpellier 1988

Clébert, Jean-Paul, and Richard, Pierre, *La Provence de van Gogh*, Edisud, Aix-en-Provence 1981

Doiteau, V., and Leroy, E., 'La Folie de Van Gogh', *Aesculape* 1928

'Vincent van Gogh et le drame de l'oreille coupée', *Aesculape* July 1932

Gauguin, Paul, *Paul Gauguin's Intimate Journals*, trans. Van Wyck Brooks, pref. Emile Gauguin, Liveright, New York 1921

Van Gogh et Arles, exhib. cat. Hôpital Van Gogh, Arles 1989

Leroy, E., 'Le Séjour de Vincent van Gogh à l'asile de Saint-Rémy-de-Provence', *Aesculape* May, June, July 1926

Michon, Pierre, *Vie de Joseph Roulin*, Editions Verdier, Lagrasse 1988

*Pickvance, Ronald, *Van Gogh in Arles*, The Metropolitan Museum of Art, Harry N. Abrams, New York 1984

Priou, Jean-Noël, 'Van Gogh et la Famille Roulin', *Revue des PTT de France* May–June 1955
'Le Facteur de Vincent', *Références de la Poste*, Paris, No. 19, Automne 1987
Weiller, P., 'Nous avons retrouvé le Zouave de van Gogh', *Lettres Françaises* March 24–31 1955

10. Accompanied like a Dangerous Beast

Aurier, G.-A., 'Les Isolés – Vincent van Gogh', *Mercure de France* January 1890
Les Cahiers de van Gogh, Geneva 1957, nos 1 and 2 only
Défossez, Marie-Paule, *Auvers or the Painters' Eye*, Valhermeil, Paris 1986
Demory, Evelyne, *Auvers en 1900*, Valhermeil, Paris 1985
Doiteau, V., 'Deux "copains" de van Gogh inconnus, les frères Gaston et René Secrétan – Vincent tel qu'ils l'ont vu', *Aesculape* March 1957
Le Groupe des XX et son Temps, exhib. cat. Brussels, Musées Royaux des Beaux-Arts 1962
*Pickvance, Ronald, *Van Gogh in Saint-Rémy and Auvers*, The Metropolitan Museum of Art, Harry N. Abrams, New York 1986
Wattenmaker, Richard J., *Puvis de Chavannes and the Modern Tradition*, exhib. cat. Art Gallery of Ontario (revised edition) 1976

Epilogue Two Gravestones

Feilchenfeldt, Walter, *Vincent van Gogh and Paul Cassirer, Berlin*, Cahier, Rijksmuseum Vincent van Gogh 1988
Stone, I., *Lust for Life*, New York–Toronto 1934, London 1935. Film released 1956
Vincent, Guide to the Rijksmuseum Vincent van Gogh, Amsterdam n.d.
Vincent van Gogh, cat. of the Rijksmuseum Kröller-Müller, Otterlo 1983

List of illustrations

All illustrations come from the Vincent van Gogh Foundation/National Museum Vincent van Gogh, Amsterdam unless otherwise stated. Photographic sources appear in brackets. Dimensions are in centimetres, height before width.

Colour plates

Between pages 120 and 121

I Vincent van Gogh: *Self-portrait*, 1888. 60.5 x 49.4
Fogg Art Museum, Harvard University, Collection of Maurice Wertheim, Class of 1906

II Claude Monet: *Impression: Sunrise, 1872*, 48 × 63
Musée Marmottan, Paris (The Bridgeman Art Library)

III Vincent van Gogh: *The Potato Eaters*, 1885. 82 x 114

IV Georges Seurat: *Sunday Afternoon on the Island of La Grande Jatte*, 1884–6, 206 × 306
Art Institute of Chicago (The Bridgeman Art Library)

V Vincent van Gogh: *Père Tanguy*, 1887. 65 x 51
Private Collection (The Bridgeman Art Library)

VI Paul Gauguin: *Vision after the Sermon, Jacob Wrestling with the Angel*, 1888. 73 x 92
National Gallery of Scotland, Edinburgh

VII Vincent van Gogh: *Woman in the Café du Tambourin (Agostina Segatori)*, 1887. 55.5 x 46.5

VIII Vincent van Gogh: *Vase with Twelve Sunflowers*, 1888. 91 x 71
Bayerische Staatsgemäldesammlungen, Munich (The Bridgeman Art Library)

Between pages 280 and 281

IX Vincent van Gogh: *Langlois Bridge with Women Washing*, 1888. 54 x 65
State Museum Kröller-Müller, Otterlo

X Vincent van Gogh: *The Postman Roulin*, 1889. 65 x 54
State Museum Kröller-Müller, Otterlo

XI Vincent van Gogh: *The Café Terrace on the Place du Forum, Arles*, 1888. 81 x 65.5
State Museum Kröller-Müller, Otterlo

XII–XIII Vincent van Gogh: *The Bedroom at Arles*, 1888. 72 x 90

XIV Vincent van Gogh: *Portrait of Doctor Félix Rey*, 1889. 64 x 53
Hermitage, Leningrad (The Bridgeman Art Library)

XV Vincent van Gogh: *Road with Cypresses and Star*, 1890. 92 x 73
State Museum Kröller-Müller, Otterlo

XVI *Above:* Vincent van Gogh: *Wheat Field with Crows*, 1890. 50.5 x 100.5
Below: Vincent van Gogh: *Daubigny's Garden*, 1890. 53 x 104
Hiroshima Museum of Art

Black-and-white plates

Between pages 56 and 57

1 *Above:* Vincent van Gogh's birthplace, Zundert, Holland. Photograph. *Below:* Jacob Jan van der Maaten: *Funeral Procession through the Cornfields*. Lithograph. Rijksmuseum-Stichting, Amsterdam

2 *From top, left to right:* Vincent's Father. Vincent's Mother. Elisabeth van Gogh. Theo van Gogh. Anna van Gogh. Cornelis van Gogh. Willemina van Gogh. Photographs

3 *Above:* Vincent van Gogh at 13. Photograph. *Below:* Vincent van Gogh at 18. Photograph

4 *Left:* Uncle Vincent and Aunt Cornelia. Photograph. *Right:* Goupil's Art Gallery, The Hague. Photograph

5 *Above:* Laveille (after Millet): *Work in the Fields*. Engraving. *Below:* Jules Breton: *Blessing the Cornfields in Artois*, 1857. Château de Compiègne (Lauros-Giraudon)

6 *Above:* Vincent van Gogh: *Hackford Road, London.* Drawing. *Below:* Eugénie Loyer. Photograph

7 *Above:* Luke Fildes: *The Empty Chair, Gad's Hill*, 1870, Engraving. The Mansell Collection, London. *Below:* G. H. Boughton: *The Landing of the Pilgrim Fathers*, 1869. Sheffield City Art Gallery

8 *Above:* Uncle Jan in dress uniform. Photograph. *Below left:* Pastor Stricker. Photograph. *Below right:* Mendes da Costa. Photograph. Netherlands Museum of Literature, Gravenhage

Between pages 184 and 185

9 *Above:* Attrib. Philippe de Champaigne: *Woman in Mourning*. Musée du Louvre, Paris (Giraudon). *Below:* Kee Vos-Stricker and her son. Photograph

10 *Above:* Marcasse, pit number 8. Photograph by A. I. van Gogh. *Centre:* The Denis house. Photograph by A. I. van Gogh. *Below:* Vincent van Gogh: *The Miner's Return*, 1880. Drawing. State Museum Kröller-Müller, Otterlo

11 *Above:* Paul Cézanne and Camille Pissarro. Photograph. Roger-Viollet, Paris. *Below:* Henri Rivière: *The Théâtre d'ombres at the Chat Noir*, c.1888. Pen, ink and gouache. Jane Voorhees Zimmerli Art Museum, Rutgers. Mindy and Ramon Tublitz Purchase Fund

12 *Above:* Andries Bonger. Photograph. *Below:* Anton van Rappard. Photograph. *Right:* Anton Mauve. Photograph

13 *Above:* Vincent van Gogh: *Sien with a cigar*, 1882. Drawing. State Museum Kröller-Müller, Otterlo. *Below:* Margot Begemann. Photograph

14 *Above:* The church at Nuenen. Photograph. *Below:* Vincent van Gogh: *The Weaver*, 1884. Drawing

15 *Above left:* Hiroshige: *Bridge in the Rain*. Print. *Above right:* 54 rue Lepic, Paris. Photograph. *Below:* Vincent van Gogh: *Vegetable gardens at Montmartre*, 1886. Drawing

16 *Above:* Corman's studio. Photograph. Private Collection. *Below:* Moulin Rouge, Montmartre, 1900. Photograph. Roger-Viollet, Paris

Between pages 344 and 345

17 *Above:* Vincent van Gogh and Emile Bernard at Asnières, 1886. Photograph. *Below:* Henri de Toulouse-Lautrec: *Portrait of Vincent van Gogh*, 1887. Drawing

18 Paul Gauguin. Photograph. Roger-Viollet, Paris

19 *Above:* Arles, c.1880. Photograph. The Hulton-Deutsch Collection, London. *Below:* The Yellow House, Arles. Photograph

20 *Left:* Rey Marcel, a Zouave, c.1885. Photograph. Roger-Viollet, Paris. *Right:* Vincent van Gogh: *The Painter Eugène Boch*, 1888. Jeu de Paume, Paris (Bulloz)

21 Paul Gauguin: *Vincent van Gogh Painting Sunflowers*, 1888

22 *Above:* The special bed in the hospital in Arles. Photograph. *Below:* The baths at the asylum, St Rémy. Photograph

23 *Above:* Johanna van Gogh and her baby. Photograph. *Below:* Ravoux's Inn at Auvers-sur-Oise, 1890. Photograph

24 The graves of Vincent and Theo van Gogh. Photograph

Illustrations in the text

Page

viii Map

8–9 Family tree

14 Vincent van Gogh: *Dog*, 1862. Drawing. State Museum Kröller-Müller, Otterlo

35 *The Commune or Death – Women of Montmartre*, *Graphic* June 16th 1871. The Illustrated London News Picture Library, London

54 Vincent van Gogh: *Horse and carriage*. 1874. Drawing, from sketchbook for Betsy Tersteeg

76 Vincent van Gogh: *Ramsgate*, 1876. Drawing
110 Meyer de Haan: Portrait of Theo van Gogh, 1889
125 *Opening of the Paris Exhibition, 1878, Marshal Mac-Mahon at the entrance to the British section, Illustrated London News*, May 11th 1878.
The Illustrated London News Picture Library, London
232 Vincent van Gogh: *Reclining nude*, 1887. Drawing
329 Vincent van Gogh: *Dr Gachet*, 1890. Engraving.
348 Paul Gachet: *Vincent van Gogh on his death bed*, July 1890. Drawing.
Musée Auvers-sur-Oise (Giraudon)

Endpapers: Vincent van Gogh: Letter to John Russell, June 1888. Ink on paper. Justin K. Thannhauser Collection. The Solomon R. Guggenheim Museum, New York (Photo: David Heald, photograph © 1990 The Solomon R. Guggenheim Foundation)

Picture Research by Julia Brown

Index

Abadie, Paul, 215
absinthe, 228–30, 330
abstractions, 211–12
à Kempis, Thomas: *The Imitation of Christ*, 71–2, 80, 89–90
Amsterdam: VG visits galleries in, 40, 43, 87; VG studies in, 88–90, 94; Rijkmuseum, 40, 194; Trippenhuis, 40; Stedelijk Museum, 362; Rijksmuseum Vincent van Gogh, 363, 365
Anquetin, Louis, 233, 238, 242, 244, 260
Antwerp, 194, 196–9; Academy, 199–204, 220
Arles: VG moves to, 248–9; described, 250–2; VG's life and painting in, 252–5, 257–62, 277–83; brothels, 254, 283; closed community, 261–2; Gauguin in, 282–9; Hôtel-Dieu restored, 366
Art Moderne, L' (journal), 316
Asnières (France), 235–6, 241, 245
Aurier, Albert, 316–17, 323, 336, 344, 353; death, 346
Auvers-sur-Oise: VG in, 320, 324–33; paintings from, 333–5, 339; Van Gogh centre, 367

Baijens, Jan, 173, 178, 180–1
Barbizon (France): artists' colony and school, 18–19, 29, 31, 36, 61–2, 80
Bargue, Charles, 113, 118, 137–9, 144, 190, 202, 327
Barr, Alfred H., 353
Beardsley, Aubrey, 323
Begemann, Jacobus, 166, 176
Begemann, Louis, 177
Begemann, Margot: relations with VG, 169–70, 172, 176–7; takes poison, 177; commissions work from VG, 178; in VG's published letters, 353
Belgian Salon, 40
Belgium: secedes (1830), 13; VG visits, 40–1; *see also* Borinage; Brussels
Bemmel, Sophie van (Aunt Fie) *see* Carbentus, Sophie
Bernard, Emile: at Cormon's atelier, 222, 225; in Brittany, 225, 238, 245; and Gauguin, 226–7, 241; Tanguy helps, 226; at Lautrec's, 233; visits Bing's, 238; VG's association with, 241–2, 245; technique, 241–2; exhibits at Petits Boulevards show, 244; and VG's departure for Paris, 249; VG invites to Arles, 258, 273, 279; rejoins Gauguin, 273–5; Cloisonism, 274; Breton paintings, 274; military service, 282; letters from Gauguin in Arles, 285, 289; and Gauguin's return to Brittany, 306; VG criticises work, 312–13; and VG's memory paintings, 321; at VG's funeral, 344; and VG's estate, 347; organises VG memorial exhibition, 346–7, 350; settles in Egypt, 358–9; death, 359; *Christ at the Garden of Olives*, 312–13
Bernard, Madeleine, 273–5, 277, 282; death, 359
Bethnal Green (London): Museum, 56–7
Bible, Holy, 37, 57, 63–5, 69, 71
Bing, Samuel, 237–8, 270
Bismarck, Prince Otto von, 34
Blanche, Antoine-Emile, 347
Blanche, Emile, 346
Blanche, Jacques-Emile, 347
Blussé & Van Braam (Dordrecht booksellers), 85–6
Boch, Anna, 269, 315, 328
Boch, Eugène, 119, 269, 310, 315; VG portrait of, 278, 281
Bokma, Master, 96

Bonger, Andries (Theo's brother-in-law): friendship with Theo, 129, 191–3; visits VG, 192–3; and effect of VG on Theo, 218; relations with VG, 219, 324; and Theo's ill-health, 229; and VG's medical treatment, 246; marries Anne, 275; and VG's return to Paris from St Rémy, 324; at VG's funeral, 344, 346; and Theo's illness, 346; and VG's reputation, 349, 358; compiles VG inventory, 356; as patron of Redon, 358; remarriage and later career, 358; death, 360
Bonger, Anne (*née* van der Linden), 219, 275, 358
Bonger, Johanna Gezina *see* Gogh, Johanna Gezina van
Bonte, Pastor M., 101, 105, 108, 119
Borinage region (Belgium): VG's missionary work in, 95–105, 112–14, 117, 188; VG's drawings of, 105–6, 109–11, 113, 139; firedamp explosions, 106–7; strikes and political agitation, 107–8, 204; VG leaves, 118–19; Boch in, 269, 278; present dereliction, 366–7
Bosboom, Joseph, 26
Boudin, Eugène-Louis, 60
Boughton, George Henry: *The Landing of the Pilgrim Fathers*, 80, 82; *Puritans Going to Church*, 47
Bouguereau, Adolphe William, 270
Boussod et Valadon (company), 59, 64, 347; *see also* Goupil's
Boussod, Etienne, 59
Boussod, Léon: controls Goupil's, 44; supervises VG, 58, 63, 65, 68, 70–1; and Breton's visit, 67; relations with Theo, 126, 133, 170, 260, 275
Braat (of Blussé & Van Braam), 85–7
Braat, Frans, 85
Bracquemond, Félix, 198, 238
Breton, Jules: influence on VG, 30–1, 44–5, 354; Goupil's sell, 63; VG sees on visit to Goupil's, 67; VG plans to visit, 114–16; reputation, 365; *Blessing the Cornfields in Artois*, 30, 44; *Evening*, 45; *The Recall of the Gleaners*, 44–5, 118
Brittany, 226–7; *see also* Pont-Aven
Brixton *see* London
Bruant, Aristide, 228
Bruegel, Pieter, 98
Brussels: VG visits, 40, 42; mission school, 95–6, 109, 111; VG moves to, 118–19, 123; VG studies art in, 135–43; Les XX exhibitions, 310–11, 314–17
Bruyas, Alfred, 289, 326
Bunyan, John: *Pilgrim's Progress*, 80, 82
Bussum (Netherlands), 350

Cabanel, Alexandre, 275
Caffin, A., 343
Caillebotte, Gustave, 235
Calment, Jeanne, 366
Camargue *see* Saintes-Maries-de-la-Mer, Les
Camion, Charles, 351
Carbentus, Anna Cornelia *see* Gogh, Anna Cornelia van
Carbentus, Arie, 24
Carbentus, Jet *see* Mauve, Jet
Carbentus, Sophie (*née* van Bemmel; Aunt Fie), 24, 38–9
Carbentus, Willemina Catherina *see* Stricker, Willemina Catherina
Cassagne, Armand: *ABCD du Dessin*, 266
Cassirer, Paul, 350, 352, 364
Cézanne, Paul, 60, 130–1, 226, 310, 315, 325–7
Chalcroft, Paul, 354, 361
Chalet, Restaurant du (Paris; 'Grand Bouillon'), 244
Charlopin, Dr, 335
Chat Noir café (Paris), 129, 133–5, 212
Chat Noir, Le (magazine), 186
Chavannes, Pierre Puvis de *see* Puvis de Chavannes, Pierre
Chevreul, Eugène, 61, 185–6, 211–13, 220
Chrispeels, J., 109–11
Clichy, 235
Cloisonism, 134, 274
colour theory, 185–6, 194, 211–13, 242
Constable, John, 63
Cormon, Fernand (*born* Piestre): VG plans to study with, 179, 204, 209, 218; atelier, 220–5; death, 222; Boch attends atelier, 269; and Puvis de Chavannes, 323; canvas in Musée d'Orsay, 365; *The Flight of Cain*, 221; *Return from the Bear Hunt*, 221
Corot, Camille, 68, 130, 231, 325
Courbet, Gustave, 62, 200, 324–6
Courrières (Artois, France), 115–17, 175
Couture, Thomas, 323; *The Romans of the Decadence*, 44–5
Cuesmes (Belgium), 112, 117, 367
Cuvier, Baron Georges, 221

Daubigny, Charles, 324–5, 338, 356
Daudet, Alphonse, 251
Daumier, Honoré, 231, 289, 325; *The Drinkers*, 312
Decrucq, M. & Mme, 112–14, 118, 367
Degas, Edgar: exhibited, 60; Uncle Cent and, 62; in Paris, 64; as established

Impressionist, 217, 234; on Guillaumin, 243; Gauguin respects, 274, 289; admires Gauguin's work, 286
Delacroix, Eugène: use of colour, 61, 185–6, 194, 211, 222; technique, 202, 207; VG praises, 319; Journal, 353; *Femmes d'Alger*, 289; *Portrait of the Mulatto girl Aline*, 276, 289
Delarebeyrette, Joseph, 135, 207–8
Delon, Dr Albert, 298
Denis, Esther, 102, 105, 366
Denis, Jean-Baptiste, 101–2, 105, 366
Derain, André, 350
Dickens, Charles, 37, 153, 158; *Christmas Stories*, 318; *Hard Times*, 112
Divisionists, 235–6, 241, 313
Dordrecht (Netherlands), 85
Doré, Gustave, 46; *Prisoner's Round*, 318
Douglas, Kirk, 353
Drenthe (Netherlands), 159–65, 168
Druet, Etienne (Paris dealer), 352
Dubosc, Charles, 230
Dujardin, Edouard, 274
Dumas, Alexandre, the younger, 191
Dupré, Jules, 354
Durand-Ruel, Paul, 62, 73, 132–3, 190–1, 205, 346, 349
Dürer, Albrecht: *Death and the Knight*, 98
Dutch Club (Paris), 128–9

Eiffel, Gustave, 216, 245
Eindhoven (Netherlands), 173–4, 178, 196
Eliot, George, 37, 153; *Adam Bede*, 55; *Felix Holt*, 71; *Scenes of Clerical Life*, 71
Epiphanie, Sister, 304
Escalier, Patience, 272, 278
Etoile Bleue, L' (newspaper), 230
Etten (Netherlands), 70, 73, 84, 94, 112, 117, 145, 148, 287, 318

Faille, J. B. de la, 362
Fauré, Gabriel, 315
Fels, F. J. A., 19–20
Fénéon, Félix, 213
Fenger, W. N., 20
Ferry, Jules, 172
Fildes, S. L.: *The Empty Chair* (engraving), 153
Flaubert, Gustave: *La Tentation de Saint-Antoine*, 134
Franck, César, 315
Franco-Prussian War, 1870, 34–5
Frank, Rev., 112
Fry, Roger, 351
Fuller, Herbert, 359

Gachet, Marguerite, 325, 336; VG paints, 334
Gachet, Dr Paul: and Pissarro, 131, 320; takes in VG, 320–1, 324–33, 336; background, 325–6; practises art, 325, 329–30; VG's portraits of, 329–30, 335; medical practices, 331; invites Theo and family, 334; and VG's attack, 337–8; and VG's revolver, 338, 340; attends VG after shooting, 341–3; drawing of VG on deathbed, 343, 348; at VG's funeral, 344; acquires VG paintings, 345, 365; and Theo's illness, 346; collection donated, 365; house, 367
Gachet, Paul (son), 325, 336, 337, 341–2, 345, 365, 367
Gauguin, Emile (Paul's son), 284
Gauguin, Mette Sophie (*née* Gad; Paul's wife), 132, 245, 256–7
Gauguin, Paul: VG attacks with razor, 1, 290, 306; and Pissarro, 130–2, 247; exhibits, 210, 247; Bernard meets, 226–7; ceramics, 227, 247; travels, 238–9, 245–6; arguments, 240, 248, 256; at Signac's home, 241; meets VG on return to Paris, 244–7; leaves for Pont-Aven, 248, 256–7; invited to Arles, 249, 257, 264, 270, 273, 275–6, 279–82; writes to VG requesting help from Theo, 256; loneliness, 256–7; attitude to money, 270, 284–5; Bernard rejoins in Brittany, 273–5; Breton paintings, 274; correspondence with VG, 275, 336; Theo supports, 275–6; exchanges self-portraits with VG, 280; visits VG at Arles, 282–9; scorn for VG's methods, 285; sales, 286, 314; drinking, 286; portrait of VG, 289; VG throws glass at, 289; and VG's severing of ear, 291, 295; leaves Arles, 291; Pissarro helps, 310; in Pontoise, 325; and Charlopin, 335; Theo promises money to, 346–7; death and reputation, 359; *Avant et Après* (memoirs), 283; *Negress*, 350; *The Vision after the Sermon*, 282
Gautier, Armand, 325
Gauzi, François, 225
Gérôme, Jean-Léon: marriage, 29; style, 29, 127, 133, 138; and Albert Goupil, 59; success, 126; and Van Rappard, 126, 141; and Theo, 127–8; and Bargue, 137; opposes Manet memorial exhibition, 126, 171–2; drawing course, 202; Paris studio, 220; survival, 221; Segatori poses for, 231; sales, 275; and Puvis de Chavannes, 323
Gérôme, Marie (*née* Goupil), 29, 59
Gestel, Dimmen, 180, 186–7
Ginneken, Dr Cornelis van, 8

Ginoux, Joseph, 263, 266, 282, 314, 321
Ginoux, Marie, 263, 266, 271, 317–18, 321; portraits of, 285, 318–19, 330–1
Giverny, 239
Gladwell, Algernon, 359
Gladwell, Harry, 69, 71–3, 77, 79, 359
Gloanec, Marie-Jeanne, 256, 274, 282
Gogh, Anna van (VG's sister) *see* Houten, Anna van
Gogh, Anna Cornelia van (*née* Carbentus; VG's mother): marriage and children, 8–11; character and appearance, 10–11; home life, 14–15; at Helvoirt, 39; at Etten, 112; and VG's behaviour, 148; breaks leg, 169; VG cares for, 169–70, 172–3; and husband's death, 184; leaves Nuenen, 194; VG's 70th birthday self-portrait for, 311; reads Aurier's article on VG, 317; and VG's death, 345–6; death, 357
Gogh, Cornelia van (*née* Carbentus; VG's aunt), 10, 17–19
Gogh, Cornelis van (VG's brother; Cor), 11, 22, 39, 163, 311; death, 357
Gogh, Cornelis Marinus van (Uncle Cor), 10, 40, 89, 154, 156, 184
Gogh, Elisabeth van (VG's sister): born, 11; on VG's childhood, 12; describes VG, 22; education, 39, 143; and VG's departure for England, 73; and VG's estate, 346; death, 357; *Personal Recollections of Vincent van Gogh*, 357
Gogh, Florentius Marinus van (Theo's grandson; Floor), 363
Gogh, Hendrik Vincent (Uncle Hein), 10, 19, 40, 42, 53, 73; death, 93
Gogh, Johan van (Theo's grandson), 363
Gogh, Johanna Gezina van (*née* Bonger; Theo's wife; *later* Gosschalk; Jo): Andries Bonger and, 193; Theo courts, 219, 240, 297; pregnancy and child, 307, 310, 317; meets VG, 321–2, 328; appearance, 322; visits VG at Auvers, 334; and son's illness, 336–7; visit to Holland, 337; and VG's death, 343, 345, 355; and Theo's illness and death, 346, 348–9; champions VG's life and work, 349–51, 357, 364; second marriage and widowhood, 350; sells VG paintings, 352, 358; publishes VG's letters, 352–3, 358; in USA, 357; friction with son over VG inheritance, 358; death, 358; diaries, 363; reinters VG, 367
Gogh, Rear Admiral Johannes van (Uncle Jan), 10, 40, 87–8, 264
Gogh, Josina van (*née* Wibaut; Vincent Willem's wife), 357
Gogh, Mathilda Johanna van (Theo's granddaughter), 363
Gogh, Theo van (Theo's grandson), 363
Gogh, Theodorus van (VG's father; Dorus): marriage and children, 8, 11; as pastor, 9–10, 13, 88; character and appearance, 8–11, 95; relations with VG, 15–16, 37, 39, 70, 73, 84, 93, 95, 117, 148–9, 167, 170, 172, 181–3; and VG's education, 16–17; relations with brother Cent, 18; and VG's career in art, 23; at Helvoirt, 39; and VG's religious fervour and ambitions, 60, 84, 87, 93–5, 97; teaches Latin to VG, 93; and VG's instability, 95; visits VG in Borinage, 102; collapse, 140; visits VG in Brussels, 141–2; VG visits, 143–4; confrontation with VG, 148–9; visits VG in hospital, 155; and VG's relations with Sien, 156; at Nuenen, 163, 166–8, 170, 182; resigns from ill-health, 172; death, 184, 189
Gogh, Theodorus van (VG's brother; Theo): born, 11; close relations with VG, 11–13, 16, 41, 84, 118, 128; schooling, 22, 39; career in Goupil's, 26, 41, 54, 94, 108, 124–6, 129, 165; character and appearance, 41, 128–9; collects prints, 43; and VG's resignation from Goupil's, 70, 73; and VG's preaching, 81, 83; and VG's melancholia, 92; and VG in Borinage, 98, 100, 105, 107–8; 1889 portrait of, 110; visits VG in Borinage, 112–13; temporary rupture in relations with VG, 112–13; and VG's commitment to art, 116–18; money gifts to VG, 117–18, 142; and VG in Brussels, 123–4; expertise and knowledge of art world, 123–6, 128; meets Mac-Mahon, 124–5; supports and encourages VG as artist, 128, 138, 161, 237, 276, 364; life in Paris, 128–9, 219; mistress ('S'), 129, 140, 158, 205, 219; and Bonger, 129, 191–3; friendship with Pissarro, 130, 176, 190; supports Impressionists and new art, 130, 132–3, 135, 170–2, 190–1, 205, 275–6; allowance to VG, 138, 159, 199, 276; and Van Rappard's move to Brussels, 139–40; visits parents, 143; and Kee's refusal of VG, 146–7; and VG's relations with Sien, 155–6, 160–1, 170; and VG's use of colour, 158, 313; differences with Goupil's, 165, 169–70; VG makes demands on, 172, 181; visits VG in Nuenen, 176; and VG's proposals for local portraits, 179; at father's funeral, 184; and VG's *Potato Eaters*, 184, 186, 190, 192; sends Zola's *Germinal* to VG, 188; uncertainty over VG's genius, 205; and VG's presence in Paris, 204–9, 216,

218–20, 229, 236–7, 247; and sales of VG's work, 205–6; and Signac, 212; poor health, 218–19, 229, 263, 321–2, 347; courts Johanna, 219, 240, 297; visits Giverny, 239; and VG's departure for Arles, 249, 275; and VG's life in Arles, 253; and request for help from Gauguin, 256; and VG's suggestions for selling art, 258; and VG's orchard paintings, 259–61; and VG in Camargue, 265; difficulty in selling new art, 270; settles VG's debts, 270; supports Gauguin, 275–6, 286, 346–7; inheritance from Uncle Cent, 276; and Gauguin's visit to Arles, 280–1, 287, 289; and VG's severing of ear, 294–6; letter from Signac on VG, 301; marriage, 301, 322; supports VG in asylum, 305, 314; and VG's mental collapse, 308; moves, 310; and growing recognition of VG, 310–11, 317; birth of son, 317; and Gachet, 320–1; and VG's release from hospital, 321–3; and VG in Auvers, 328; visits Gachet, 334; and son's illness, 336; desire to leave Boussod et Valadon, 336; announces visit to Holland, 337–8, 339; and VG's attack, 338; visits dying VG, 343; at VG's funeral, 344–6; reads VG's final letter, 345, 355; and VG's estate, 346; delirium, death and burial, 346–9, 367

LETTERS FROM VG: 42–3, 47, 48, 66–7, 69, 72, 75, 83, 87, 92, 94, 100, 107–8, 113, 117–18, 123, 138, 140, 147–8, 153, 155–6, 159, 170, 179, 207, 240, 258–9, 265, 277, 287–8, 313, 320, 328, 338, 345, 355

Gogh, Vincent van (VG's grandfather), 8–10

Gogh, Vincent Willem van (the painter): name, 7, 9–10, 182; born, 8–9; childhood, 11–16; close relations with brother Theo, 11–13, 16, 41, 84, 118, 128; social sense, 13; relations with father, 15, 37, 39, 70, 73, 93, 117, 167, 170, 181–3; education, 16–17, 20–1; reading, 16, 37–8, 50, 55, 71, 80, 91, 108, 112, 117, 153, 158, 185, 318; leaves Tilburg school, 21–3; apprenticed to Uncle Cent, 23, 26–31, 38; life in The Hague, 24–6, 38; print collecting, 31, 35, 43, 66, 73, 105–6, 153; early artistic influences on, 29–33, 36; *aide-mémoire* sketches, 32; sympathy for poor, 37, 56, 78, 98, 104–5; studies Bible, 37, 57–8, 63–5, 69–71; appearance, 39, 41, 86, 88, 111, 128, 174–5, 181, 203, 244, 247, 331; early travels and visits to galleries, 40–1, 43–4; begins correspondence with Theo, 42–3; works in Brussels, 42; in London, 42–3, 45–9, 55–8, 63; works in Paris, 58, 64–70; learns English, 47, 96; unrequited love for Eugénie Loyer, 48–57, 114; nervous breakdown in London, 53–5; drawings for Betsy Tersteeg, 54–5, 146; and Impressionists, 62–3, 216–18; resigns from Goupil's, 70–1; teaching posts in England, 73–8; religious work with Slade-Jones, 78–81; and the simple life, 80–1; preaching, 81–3, 99, 109; religious mania, 83–4; returns to family, 84; works in Dordrecht booksellers, 84–7; instability and eccentricities, 85–6, 90, 96, 101; studies in Amsterdam for entrance to church, 87–90, 93–4; and Kee Vos, 89, 92, 97, 146–7, 151; generosity, 92; attends Brussels mission school, 96–7; violent behaviour, 97, 100; work in Borinage, 97–107, 112–14; self-mortification, 101–2; goes down coalmines, 102–4, 113; and socialism, 104; sketches mining life, 105–6, 109–11, 113, 139; dismissed from missionary work, 109; visits Pietersen, 109–12; starts serious drawing, 112–14, 118; walks to visit Breton, 115–16; commitment to art, 116–18, 161; leaves Borinage for Brussels, 118–19, 135–7; art studies in Brussels, 137–44; allowance from Theo, 138, 159, 199, 276; relations with Van Rappard, 139–43, 145–6, 159–60, 167; visits parents, 143; finds woman in The Hague, 147–8; confrontation with father, 148–9; relations with prostitutes, 149, 196, 254; developing technique, 149–50, 157–8, 161, 164, 168–9, 182, 235, 255; moves to The Hague, 149–50, 154; relations with Sien, 151, 153, 155–60; venereal disease, 155, 203, 246; leaves Sien, 161–3; life in Drenthe, 162–5; use and ideas of colour, 164, 175, 186, 194, 202, 217–18, 224, 235–6, 239, 242, 255, 268, 278, 280, 313; stays with family at Nuenen, 166–9; Drenthe paintings dispersed and burned, 168; cares for mother, 169–70, 172–3; and Margot Begemann, 169–70, 172, 176–8; music lessons, 174; paints local weavers, 175; designs panels for Hermans, 178; peasant portraits, 179–80, 183–4, 190; frugality, 180, 182; teaches Kerssemakers, 181–2; and father's death, 184–5, 189; still-life studies, 184–5, 193; lithographs, 186–7; ostracised by Nuenen Catholics, 193; confidence of posthumous fame, 195; in Antwerp, 196–203; influenced by Japanese art, 198–9, 237–9, 246, 248, 255,

Gogh, Vincent Willem van – *cont.*
268–9; attends Antwerp Academy, 199–204; figure-drawing, 202; tooth trouble, 203, 262; life in Paris, 204–48; attends Cormon's atelier, 220–5, 233; drinks absinthe, 229–30, 246; Lautrec portrait of, 229–30; paintings of boots, 229; nudes, 231–2; and Segatori, 232–3, 240; and Signac, 234–5; and Bernard, 241–2, 245, 247; and Guillaumin, 242–4; meets Gauguin, 244–7; ill health and treatment, 246, 262; self-portraits in Paris, 247–8; leaves Paris for Arles, 248–9; life and painting in Arles, 252–5, 257–64, 277–9; drinking and diet, 253, 262, 328; proposes artists' colony ('Studio of the South'), 258–9, 261–2, 277, 312; tree and orchard paintings, 258–61; uses reed pens, 261; wins Arles court case, 263; failed religious paintings, 270; sunflower paintings, 273, 277, 288, 307; wears candles in hat, 278; prepares for Gauguin's arrival in Arles, 279–82; exchanges self-portraits with Gauguin, 280–1; and Gauguin's stay in Arles, 282–9; memory paintings, 286–8; Gauguin portrait of, 288; throws glass at Gauguin, 289; razor attack on Gauguin, 290, 306; cuts off ear, 290–5; in hospital, 295–6, 301–2; self-portrait on release, 297; increasing derangement, 298–9; committed to asylum, 299–300; suicide attempts, 301, 308–9, 314; in St Rémy asylum, 302–6, 317–18; diagnosis, 305–6; kicks attendant, 307; suffers attacks, 308, 314, 317–19; self-portrait in St Rémy, 308–9, 330, 362; growing recognition, 310–11, 317; copies own works, 311; self-portrait for mother's 70th birthday, 311–12; paintings from prints, 312, 318; exhibited at 1890 Les XX show, 315; leaves St Rémy, 321–4; with Gachet in Auvers, 321, 324–33; painting sold, 328; Auvers paintings, 333–5, 339; suffers attack in Auvers, 337–9; has revolver, 339–40; shoots self, 341–3; death and funeral, 343–4; Gachet's deathbed drawing of, 343, 348; estate, 346–7; 1892 memorial exhibition, 346–7; posthumous reputation and success, 349–51, 364; letters published, 352–3, 358; studies and books on, 353–7; exhibitions and catalogues, 355; on loving, 357; fakes of works, 361–2; Amsterdam permanent loan collection, 362; Museum, 363; reinterred, 365

WORKS
At Eternity's Gate, 318
Bedroom, 312
Chair, 352
Crows over the Wheat Field, 339
Fishing Boats at Les Saintes-Maries, 300
Flowers and Sunflowers, 208
Gauguin's Chair, 288
Girl in White in the Woods, 158
Irises, 310, 333
Madame Roulin (*Woman Rocking*), 300, 313
Memories of the North (drawings), 320–1
Night Café, 285, 300
The Parisian Novels, 242
The Potato Eaters: sketches and painting, 184, 186–90, 192–3; lithograph, 186–7, 205; Jo hangs, 350; early version, 365
The Road with Cypresses and Star, 321
Self-portrait in front of the Easel, 362
Starlit Night, 300
Starry Night over the Rhône, 310
Sunflowers (series), 314, 352
Sunrise on the Plain, 165
Town Hall on Bastille Day, 351
Van Gogh's Chair, 288
Weaver Seen from the Front, 175
Wheat Fields under Clouded Sky, 339
Woman Reading a Novel, 313
Women Walking along the Fields, 335

Gogh, Vincent Willem van (VG's still-born brother), 7–8, 366

Gogh, Vincent Willem van (Uncle Cent): as VG's godfather, 9, 17–18, 20, 22–3, 68; career as art dealer, 10, 18–21, 25–7, 62–3, 126; relations with VG's father, 18; ill-health, 20, 53, 73; VG works with, 22, 41; retires, 63; in Paris, 68; aids VG on return from England, 84–5; severs relations with VG, 87; VG attempts to visit, 145; and VG's persistence with Kee Vos, 146; and brother Theodorus's death, 184; inheritance for Theo, 276

Gogh, Vincent Willem van (VG's nephew; Theo's son): born, 317; VG sees, 322, 328; visits Auvers, 334; illness, 336; taken on visit to Holland, 337; as VG's sole heir, 349, 357–8; and sale of VG's work, 350; marriage and emigration to USA, 357; preserves VG's collection, 358, 361, 364; sets up Foundation and Museum, 362–3; death, 363

Gogh, Willemina van (VG's sister; Wil): born, 11; schooling, 39; models for VG, 144; Van Rappard gives sketches to, 145; letter from Theo on living with VG, 236; and VG's memory paintings of Etten, 287; VG portrait of, 312; letter from VG in asylum, 314; reads Aurier's article on VG, 317; and VG with Gachet, 329; and VG's Auvers paintings, 333; letter from VG on

Puvis's painting, 335; and VG's estate, 346; mental illness and death, 357
Goncourt, Edmond & Jules de, 158, 330
Gorlitz, P. C., 86–7
Gosschalk, Johan Cohen, 350
Gosschalk, Johanna Gezina *see* Gogh, Johanna Gezina van
Goupil's (company), 22; VG works in The Hague branch, 25–7, 29–32, 41; Theo's career in, 26, 41, 54, 94, 108, 123–6, 129; Paris branch, 44, 58–60; VG at London branch, 43, 46–7, 58; VG loses interest in, 66; VG quits, 70–3, 84; at 1878 Paris World Fair, 125; Theo's differences with, 165, 169–70; *see also* Boussod et Valadon
Goupil, Adolphe, 19, 44, 58, 63, 137
Goupil, Albert, 58–9, 124, 127
Goupil, Marie, 29, 59
'Grand Bouillon' *see* Chalet, Restaurant du
Graphic (journal), 56–7, 144, 153
Groot, Cornelia de, 180, 183, 187–8
Groot, Sien de, 183, 193
Groux, Charles de: *Saying Grace*, 183
Groux, Henry de, 315
Gruby, Dr David, 191, 246, 263
Guilbert, Yvette, 228
Guillaumin, Armand, 60, 209, 218, 234, 242–4, 327, 336–7
Guyotin (art dealer), 170

Haan, Meyer de, 110
Haegen, M. van der (pedlar), 98
Hagborg, August (*born* Hagborgs), 231
Hageman, Victor, 201–2
Hague, The: VG in, 24–7, 38, 149–50, 154; school of painters, 25–7, 31–2, 44, 61–2; VG leaves, 43–4
Hals, Frans, 194
Hannick, Marinus, 19
Hartmann, Frederic, 178
Hartrick, Archibald Standish, 223–7
Hartsuiker, Albertus, 162
Haussmann, Baron Georges Eugène, 216–17
Havelaar, Just, 205
Havermaet, Piet van, 201
Helvoirt (Netherlands), 39, 42, 52, 63
Henry, Charles: *A Scientific Aesthetic*, 211
Hermans, Antoon, 173–4, 178, 180
Hiroshige Utagawa, 239
Hirschig, Anton (Tom), 332, 338, 343–4
Hoge Veluwe National Park, Otterlo *see* Rijksmuseum Kröller-Müller, Otterlo
Hokusai Katsushika, 198, 238
Hoorn, Rev. Keller van, 87
Hoorn, Piet van, 174
Hoornik, Christine Clasina Maria (Sien; *later* van Wijk): lives with VG, 151, 153, 155–60, 290; VG paints, 153, 155–7, 179; mother, 158–9; VG leaves, 161–2; works as washerwoman, 170; Jo's attitude to, 353; marriage and suicide, 360
Hoornik, Maria Willemina (daughter of above), 151
Hoornik, Willem *see* Wijk, Willem van
Houghton, Boyd: *The Commune or Death*, 35
Houten, Anna van (*née* van Gogh; VG's sister), 11, 39, 54–6, 143, 184, 187; death, 357
Houten, Jo van, 346
Houten, Sara van (VG's niece), 143
Hugo, Victor, 107, 158, 280; *La Légende des Siècles*, 222; *Les Misérables*, 117
Hulsker, Jan, 355–6
Huysmans, C. C., 19–20

Illustrated London News, 56–7, 153
Impressionist Exhibitions: 1st (1874), 60–1, 131; 2nd (1876), 63; 4th (1879), 130, 132–3; 8th (1886), 209–10
Impressionists: exhibit, 61–3, 65, 73, 172, 209–10; Gérôme and, 127; Pissarro and, 130–2; group disperses, 171; VG misunderstands, 176, 192, 199, 234; VG meets, 217–18; Tanguy and, 226; and Japan, 239; exclusiveness, 240
Ingres, Jean-Auguste-Dominique, 202, 213, 289
Isleworth, 77–9
Israëls, Jozef, 31–3, 36, 43, 63, 104–5, 150, 176, 186

James, Henry, 251
James, Philip, 354
Japan: influence of art from, 198–9, 237–9, 241–2, 246, 248, 255, 268–9
Jernberg, August, 40
Jones, Reverend *see* Slade-Jones, Rev. Thomas
Jong, Rev. N. de, 96
Jullian (librarian), 299

Kahn, Gustave, 267
Kant, Robert, 222
Kauffmann, Piet, 145
Kee *see* Vos, Cornelia Adriana
Kempis, Thomas à *see* à Kempis, Thomas
Kerssemakers, Anton, 181–2, 187, 194–5
Knoedler, Michel, 59
Knoedler, Roland, 165
Koning, Hans, 244, 275
Kröller-Müller, Helene, 352, 361

Kuyten, Leonardus, 174

Lamartine, Alphonse de, 251
Laren (Netherlands), 362
Lautrec, Henri de Toulouse- *see* Toulouse-Lautrec, Henri Marie Raymond de
Laval, Charles, 239, 244–5, 273, 279, 282, 344–5, 359
Léger, Fernand, 127
Levert (Auvers carpenter), 335, 337, 343
Leys, Baron Hendrik, 197, 201–2
Lhermitte, Léon, 183, 186, 190, 354
Lister, Joseph, Baron, 331
Livens (Levens), Horace, 201–2, 218
London: VG in, 42–3, 45–9, 55–8, 63, 78; social conditions, 56–7, 78
Longfellow, Henry Wadsworth, 91
Loti, Pierre: *Madame Chrysanthème*, 270
Loyer, Eugénie (*later* Plowman): VG's attachment to, 48–9, 51–7, 71, 114, 354; marriage to Plowman, 361; house, 366
Loyer, Jean-Baptiste (Eugénie's father), 48
Loyer, Ursula (Eugénie's mother), 48–9, 55, 82, 354
Luijtelaar, Fr Thomas van, 173, 193
Lust for Life (film), 353, 363
Luxembourg, Palais du (Paris), 44–5, 207
Lytton, Bulwer: *Kenelm Chillingly*, 72

Maaten, Jacob van der, 15, 25, 31, 38, 66, 89–91, 184, 189, 339
MacKnight, Dodge, 259–60, 269, 278
Mac-Mahon, Comte Marie-Edmé-Patrice-Maurice de, Duke of Magenta, 35, 124, 143
Macquoid, Percy: *Reflections* (engraving), 158
Madiol, Adrien-Jean, 140–1, 359
Manet, Edouard, 126, 131, 171–2, 176, 198, 324, 331
Manet, Eugène, 209–10
Maris, Jacob, 36, 63, 105
Maris, Thijs, 36, 98
Maris, Willem, 36
Marseilles, 248, 250
Martinez de Valdivielse, 332
Martinique, 245, 247, 256, 285
Marisse, Henri, 350
Mauritshuis (The Hague), 25, 28, 50
Maus, Octave, 310
Mauve, Anton: friendship with VG, 33, 44, 149; courts Jet, 33, 38, 50, 52; extremes of feelings and behaviour, 34, 151–2; paintings, 63, 105, 142; teaches and advises VG on art, 145, 147–54, 157, 168, 201, 258, 283; in remote Holland, 161; use of colour, 164; death, 257–8
Mauve, Jet (*née* Carbentus), 33, 38, 50, 52
Maynard, Kathleen, 361
Mazery, Dr Jean, 327, 341–2
Meier-Gräfe, Julius, 353
Meissonier, Ernest, 270, 317, 323, 354
Mendel, Samuel, 63
Mendes da Costa, Dr M. B., 88–90, 92–3
Mercure de France, Le (journal), 316–17
Meuriot, Dr, 347
Michelangelo Buonarroti, 190
Michelet, Jules: *L'Amour*, 50–2, 69, 72, 82, 156
Millais, John Everett: *Chill October*, 63, 189; *The Huguenot*, 47
Millet, Jean-François: influence, 29–30, 32–3, 36–7, 42, 80, 105, 118, 139, 144, 165, 178, 224, 233, 236, 317, 333–4, 354; death, 67–8; VG reveres, 62, 68, 116, 190, 319; VG buys prints of, 73; and Pissarro, 132, 218; decorates Hartmann salon, 178; biography of, 178, 188; 1887 exhibition, 239; *The Angelus*, 30; *Church at Gréville*, 189, 334; *Field Work*, 30, 312; *The Gleaners*, 29–30; *The Sower*, 144
Milliet, Paul-Eugène, 266–8, 273, 279–81, 285–6, 360
Mistral, Frédéric, 304
Moderniste, Le (journal), 316
Monet, Camille, 237
Monet, Claude: Impressionism, 60–2, 130, 133, 210, 234–5; and Pissarro, 130, 132; Theo sells, 190; collects japonaiserie, 237; and Giverny, 239; Sunflowers, 285
Monticelli, Adolphe, 135, 208–9, 248, 252, 264, 326
Montmajour monastery, 255, 260, 264, 266
Montmartre, 65, 68, 72, 214–17, 225, 241, 366
Montpellier, 276, 289, 326
Moody, Dwight Lyman and Sankey, Ira David, 57
Morisot, Berthe, 60
Morris, William, 80
Mourier-Petersen, Christian, 259–61, 263, 275
'Mousmé, La' (model), 270
Musée d'Orsay, Paris, 365
Museum of Modern Art, New York: opens (1929), 352; 1935 exhibition, 353

Nabis, Les (movement), 134
Nadar (Félix Tournachon), 60, 62
Napoleon III, Emperor of the French, 34, 131, 251
Neuvière (hospital bursar), 301

Nuenen (Netherlands): VG's parents in, 163, 165–6; VG in, 166–9, 172–4, 177–82, 193–4; tower, 165, 182, 189, 255; Theo visits, 191–2; VG's memories of, 333–4; visitor's room, 366

Obach, Charles, 46–7, 56, 58
Ornano, Superintendent d', 293–4, 298–300
Orsay, Musée d' *see* Musée d'Orsay
Otterlo *see* Rijksmuseum Kröller-Müller, Otterlo

Paris: Commune and siege (1871), 34–5, 44; Goupil's in, 44; VG visits, 44–5; VG works in, 58–60, 64–9; 1878 World Fair (Palais du Trocadéro), 124–5; Theo in, 124, 128–9; VG stays in, 204–48; development and planning, 215–16, 217; 1889 Universal Exhibition (Trocadéro), 216
Passy, 347
Petit, Georges, 133
'Petits Boulevards' artists, 242, 244, 247, 258
Peyron, Dr Théophile: superintends St Rémy asylum, 303–5; diagnosis of VG, 305, 314; treatment, 306; and VG's attacks, 308, 314, 317, 319; and VG's departure for Auvers, 321; sends VG's canvases to Auvers, 336; and VG's self-portrait, 362
Picasso, Pablo, 323
Pickvance, Ronald, 355
Picou, Henry, 41
Pietersen, Rev., 96–7, 109, 111–12
Pissarro, Camille: and Impressionism, 60, 130–3, 209, 240; friendship with Theo, 130, 176; sales, 170–1, 190, 206, 314; and Seurat, 209–10, 212–14; VG meets, 217–18, 247; influence on Gauguin, 227, 245; leaves for country, 243; supports 'Petits Boulevards' exhibition, 244; VG requests asylum with, 309–10, 320; in Pontoise, 325; and Gachet, 329; and Theo's illness, 347
Pissarro, Julie (Camille's wife), 171, 214, 320
Pissarro, Lucien (Camille's son): and father's rebuke to Eugène Manet, 209; influenced by Seurat, 214, 216; VG meets, 217; VG dedicates still-life to, 218, 232; and VG in Paris, 247; exhibits, 315; at VG's funeral, 344; and Theo's illness, 347
Plowman, Frank (Samuel's son), 361
Plowman, Samuel, 49, 52, 56; marries Eugénie Loyer, 361
Poe, Edgar Allan, 289
Pointillism, 235, 242, 316
Pont-Aven (Brittany), 226–7, 238, 241, 245, 248, 256–7, 264, 273–4
Portier, Alphonse, 205–6, 214, 216, 242
Post-Impressionism, 133, 240–1
Post-Impressionist exhibition, London, 1912, 351
Poulet, Jean-François, 307
Poynter, Sir Edward John: *Fight between More of More Hall and the Dragon of Wantley*, 47
Proust, Antonin, 171
Provily, Jan, 17
Provily, Piet, 17
Pulchri Studios (The Hague), 38, 150, 153
Puvis de Chavannes, Pierre, 323–4, 333; *Inter Artes et Naturam*, 323–4, 335

Quinn, Anthony, 353

Rachel (prostitute), 254, 292–4, 297
Ramsgate, 73–7
Raphael (Sanzio da Urbino), 289
Rappard, Anton van: VG meets, 128; with VG in Brussels, 139–42; works in countryside, 143, 145–6; visits VG, 154, 159–60; in Drenthe, 161; in Utrecht, 167; technique, 175; sketches, 175; and Impressionism, 176; advises VG on painting studies, 179; criticises VG's *Potato Eaters*, 188–9; seeks reconciliation with VG, 192–3; death, 359
Ravoux, Adeline, 331–2, 337, 339, 341, 345; VG portrait of, 334, 351, 364
Ravoux, Arthur-Gustave: VG stays with in Auvers, 327, 331–2, 334; and VG's revolver, 339; and VG's suicide, 341, 344; acquires VG paintings, 345; sells painting, 351; and VG's final painting, 356
Ravoux, Germaine, 332, 341
Redon, Odilon, 315, 358
Reid, Alexander, 208
Rembrandt van Rijn, 40, 90, 92, 117, 164; *Bible Reading*, 66; *The House of the Carpenter*, 96; *The Jewish Bride*, 194, 363; *Susanna Bathing*, 50
Renoir, Auguste: Impressionism, 60, 62, 133, 210, 234; and Pissarro, 130–2, 209; Theo sells, 190, 275
Renoir, Edmond, 60
Rey, Dr Félix, 293–6, 300–2, 305, 325, 351
Ridley, Mathew White: *The Miner*, 106
Rijkens, P., 85–6
Rijksmueum Kröller-Müller, Otterlo (Hoge Veluwe National Park), 362, 365

Rivet, Dr Louis, 246, 275
Rivière, Henri, 133–5, 212, 237
Robert, Alphonse, 292–3
Rochedieu, Rev. Emile, 108–9, 111
Rodin, Auguste, 323
Roelofs, William, 138–9, 159, 161
Roos family, 24
Rooy, Francis van, 180, 183
Roulin, Armand, 271–2, 295
Roulin, Augustine, 271, 295; VG portraits of, 290, 297–8, 307
Roulin, Camille, 271–2, 295
Roulin, Joseph: friendship with VG, 266, 278, 297, 315; life, 271–2; VG portraits of, 271–2, 288; Gauguin paints, 285; and Gauguin's drinking, 286; and VG's severing of ear, 293, 295–6; post in Marseilles, 297; VG sends paintings to, 315; death, 351
Roulin, Marcelline, 272, 297; death, 363
Rousseau (hospital pharmacist), 301
Rousseau, Théodore, 289
Rubens, Peter Paul, 194, 196–8, 202; *The Adoration of the Kings*, 197; *The Assumption of the Holy Virgin*, 196–7; *Isabella Brandt*, 50; *The Merchant Jan Michielsen* (triptych), 197
Ruskin, John, 80
Russell, John Peter, 223–4, 237, 248, 256, 259
Rysselberghe, Theo van, 315

'S' (Theo's mistress), 129, 140, 158, 205, 219
St Rémy-de-Provence, 302–5, 317–18, 330
Saintes-Maries-de-la-Mer, Les (Camargue, France), 209, 248, 264–5, 366
Salis, Rodolphe, 129
Salles, Rev. Frédéric, 295–300, 302–3, 315
Salon Carré ('Salle' Carré), Paris, 206–7
Salon des Indépendants, 171, 209, 227, 260, 310, 319; 1905 VG retrospective, 350
Salon des Refusés, 60
Salon du Champ-de-Mars, 323
Salvation Army, 57
Santa Barbara, California, 362
Schafrat, Johannes, 173–4, 187, 193–4
Scheveningen (Netherlands), 24, 32–3
Schmidt (Goupil's manager, Brussels), 123, 127, 138–9
Scholte, Hendrick, 163–4, 166, 168
Scholte, Zowina-Clasina, 164, 168
Schopenhauer, Arthur, 134
Schuffenecker, Emile, 256, 276, 289
Schuffenecker, Louise, 256
Schuitemaker (peasant), 144
Secrétan, Gaston, 340
Secrétan, René, 339–40
Sedan, Battle of (1870), 34
Segatori, Agostina, 230–3, 238, 240–1, 248, 347
Sensier, Alfred, 178, 188
Serret, Charles Emmanuel, 190
Seurat, Georges: influence, 171, 209–10, 214, 216, 233–4, 236, 243; scientific theories, 211–14; secretiveness, 212; methods, 213; on Gauguin, 227; jealousies, 240–1; attends 'Petits Boulevards' exhibition, 244; death, 359; *Bathing at Asnières*, 171; *Les Poseuses*, 234; *Sunday Afternoon on the Island of the Grande Jatte*, 210–14, 227, 234–5
Shchukin, S. I., 352
Siberdt, Eugeen, 200–1, 203
Sien *see* Hoornik, Christine Clasina Maria
Signac, Paul: and Seurat, 171, 209, 212–14, 227, 235; VG and, 234–5; leaves for South, 239; hospitality to Gauguin, 241; technique, 241–2; visits VG in Arles, 300–1, 308; exhibits, 315; death, 359; *Quai de Clichy*, 235
Sisley, Alfred, 60, 190, 270
Slade-Jones, Rev. Thomas, 78–82, 85, 95–6; house, 366
Slade-Jones, Mrs Thomas, 78–9
Sonderbund exhibition, Cologne, 1912, 351
Sophie, Queen of the Netherlands, 25, 39
Spencer, Herbert, 134
Spurgeon, Charles Haddon, 57
Stockum, family Van, 37
Stokes, William, 75–7
Stone, Irving: *Lust for Life* (fiction), 353
Stowe, Harriet Beecher: *Uncle Tom's Cabin*, 108, 318
Stricker, Cornelia Adriana *see* Vos, Cornelia Adriana
Stricker, Johannes Paulus (Uncle Stricker), 88, 93, 146–8, 184
Stricker, Willemina Catherina (*née* Carbentus), 88
'Studio of the South' (proposed), 258–9
Sutter, David, 211
Symbolism, 134, 324
synthetist style, 286

Tambourin, Le (Paris cabaret-restaurant), 230, 232–3, 238, 240–1, 347
Tanguy, Julien François ('Père'): character and appearance, 225–6; encourages VG, 226; friendship with VG, 233–4; VG portraits of, 242; and VG's debt, 270;

stores VG's work, 310, 316, 323, 328, 334, 349; shows VG's work, 314; at VG's funeral, 344; death, 351
Tasset & Lhote (Paris art suppliers), 260
Teissier, Abbé, 343
Teixeira de Mattos, Joseph, 88
Tersteeg, Betsy, 27, 54–5, 146, 150, 320
Tersteeg, Hermanus Gijsbertus: manages Hague branch of Goupil's, 27–8, 40, 43, 150; literary interests, 37; VG's relations with, 44, 118, 145, 156; in London, 64; and VG's art work, 150, 152; and VG's behaviour, 152; VG proposes as agent, 258; agrees to take art from Theo, 260; opposition to new art, 270
Tersteeg, Johan, 150
Tilburg (Netherlands), 20–2, 366
Toulouse-Lautrec, Henri Marie Raymond de: at Cormon's atelier, 222–4; relations with VG, 227–9, 233; portrait of VG, 229–30; takes absinthe, 230; describes Provence, 248–9; VG invites to Arles, 258; exhibits, 315; visits Theo, 336; death, 359
Trabuc, Charles Elzéard ('the Major'), 304, 307, 310–11
Tralbaut, Marc Edo, 334, 354
Trocadéro, Palais du *see* Paris
Turner, J. M. W., 63
Twickenham, 78–9

Urpar, Dr, 293

Valadon, René, 44, 63, 126, 133, 170, 260, 275; *see also* Boussod et Valadon
Valadon, Suzanne, 233
Valkes, Willem, 24, 38
van Gogh *see* Gogh (and similarly for other Dutch names)
Vandersanden (Eindhoven church organist), 174
Velasquez, Diego, 194
Vénissac, Madame (of Arles), 163
Verlat, Charles, 199–202
Vienna International exhibition, 1873, 43
Vierge, Daniel, 107
Vincent van Gogh Foundation, 362–3
Vinck, Frans, 202
Vingt, Les (Les XX; group), 310, 315–16
Virginie, Madame (brothel-keeper), 254, 277, 292
Vlaminck, Maurice de, 350
Vollard, Ambroise, 232, 351–2
Vos, Christoffel, 89, 96
Vos, Cornelia Adriana (*née* Stricker; Kee): VG's relations with, 89, 92, 97; refuses VG, 146–7, 151; in VG's memory painting, 287; anonymity in VG's published letters, 353
Vos, Johannes, 89, 97, 146

Wacker, Otto, 361
Wagner, Richard, 211
Wakker, Willem van de, 180
Wasmes (Belgium), 99, 366
Weiller, Pierre, 360
Weissenbruch, Jan, 41, 44, 152
Welsh-Ovcharov, Bogomila, 355
Wenkebach, Willem, 192–3
Whistler, James McNeill, 47, 198, 211
Wibaut, Josina *see* Gogh, Josina van
Wijk, Arnoldus van, 360
Wijk, Sien van *see* Hoornik, Christine Clasina Maria
Wijk, Willem van (Sien's son), 155–7, 290, 360
Wijk, Willy van, 361
Wilkie, Kenneth, 360–1

XX, Les (group) *see* Vingt, Les

Yellow House (Arles), 264, 268, 273, 281, 284, 286, 289–90, 296, 298–300, 302, 312, 366

Zola, Emile, 127, 134, 158, 181, 214; *Germinal*, 100, 103, 188; *La Joie de Vivre*, 185; *L'Oeuvre*, 199, 209
Zouaves: at Arles, 252–3, 266, 268, 285
Zundert (Netherlands), 10, 12–13, 366
Zuyderland, Adrianus Jacobus, 158

I heard Rodin had a beautiful head at the Salon.
I have been to the seaside for a week and very likely am going thither again soon. — Flat shore ~~[illegible]~~ sands — fine figures there like Cimabue — straight stylish.
Am working at a Sower.

The great field all violet. the sky & sun very yellow. it is a hard subject to treat.
Please remember me very kindly to Mrs Russell — and in thought I heartily shake hands.

Yours very truly
Vincent